D0854084

Managing capital flows and exchange rates
Perspectives from the Pacific Basin

The essays in this volume examine the theoretical and policy issues associated with international capital flows and exchange rates for emerging markets in the Pacific Basin region. Emerging market countries in both East Asia and Latin America offer a wide variety of examples for the comparative study of the implications of international capital flow surges and appropriate policy responses. The essays address four broad issues. First, they investigate the determinants of international capital flows, particularly the relative role of domestic and external factors in driving capital flows. Second, they inquire how predictable and contagious capital flow reversals and exchange rate crises are. Third, they explore what the domestic economic effects of capital inflows on emerging economies have been and, fourth, seek to suggest what are the appropriate responses by policy makers to capital inflow surges.

Reuven Glick is Vice-President in charge of the International Studies Section of the Research Department at the Federal Reserve Bank of San Francisco and Director of the Bank's Center for Pacific Basin Monetary and Economic Studies. Dr. Glick was formerly a professor of economics and international business in the Graduate School of Business of New York University and a consultant to the World Bank on international debt issues.

Dr. Glick is the author of many articles in the areas of international macroeconomic policy, international debt problems, and Pacific Basin financial market development. His articles have appeared in *Journal of Monetary Economics, International Economic Review, Journal of International Economics, Journal of Money, Banking, and Credit, Journal of International Money and Finance,* and *Economic Inquiry*. In addition, Dr. Glick coedited (with Michael Hutchison) *Exchange Rate Policy and Interdependence: Perspectives from the Pacific Basin* (Cambridge University Press, 1994).

Managing capital flows and exchange rates

Perspectives from the Pacific Basin

Edited by

REUVEN GLICK

CAMBRIDGE
UNIVERSITY PRESS

PUBLISHED BY THE PRESS SYNDICATE OF THE UNIVERSITY OF CAMBRIDGE
The Pitt Building, Trumpington Street, Cambridge CB2 1RP, United Kingdom

CAMBRIDGE UNIVERSITY PRESS
The Edinburgh Building, Cambridge CB2 2RU, UK http://www.cup.cam.ac.uk
40 West 20th Street, New York, NY 10011-4211, USA http://www.cup.org
10 Stamford Road, Oakleigh, Melbourne 3166, Australia

© Federal Reserve Bank of San Francisco 1998

First published 1998

Printed in the United States of America

Typeset in Times Roman 10/12pt, in Quark Xpress™ [BTS]

Library of Congress Cataloging-in-Publication Data
Managing capital flows and exchange rates: perspectives from the Pacific
basin / edited by Reuven Glick.
   p. cm.
   Essays originally prepared for a conference sponsored by the Center for
Pacific Basin Monetary and Economic Studies at the Federal Reserve Bank of
San Francisco, held Sept. 26–27, 1996.
   Includes bibliographical references.
   ISBN 0-521-62323-5 (hardcover)
   1. Foreign exchange – Government policy – Pacific Area – Congresses.
2. Monetary policy – Pacific Area – Congresses.   3. Capital movements –
Pacific Area – Congresses.   I. Glick, Reuven.   II. Center for Pacific Basin
Monetary and Economic Studies.
HG3997.55.E93   1998
332.4′56–DC21   97-30367
                                                    CIP

A catalog record for this book is available from the British Library

ISBN 0 521 62323 5 hardback

Contents

Contributors

Pierre-Richard Agénor
International Monetary Fund
and Georgetown University,
Washington, D.C.

Henning Bohn
University of California,
Santa Barbara

Kevin Cowan
Ministry of Finance,
Santiago, Chile

José De Gregorio
Universidad de Chile,
Santiago, Chile

Theo S. Eicher
University of Washington,
Seattle

Jeffrey A. Frankel
University of California,
Berkeley

Peter M. Garber
Brown University,
Providence, R.I.

Reuven Glick
Federal Reserve Bank of
San Francisco

Linda S. Goldberg
Federal Reserve Bank of
New York

Alexander W. Hoffmaister
International Monetary Fund,
Washington, D.C.

Steven B. Kamin
Board of Governors of the
Federal Reserve System,
Washington, D.C.

Michael Klein
Tufts University,
Medford, Mass.

Kenneth Kletzer
University of California,
Santa Cruz

Subir Lall
International Monetary Fund,
Washington, D.C.

Ronald I. McKinnon
Stanford University,
Stanford, Calif.

Richard A. Meese
University of California,
Berkeley

Huw Pill
Harvard University,
Cambridge, Mass.

Carmen M. Reinhart
University of Maryland,
College Park

Helmut Reisen
OECD Development Centre,
Paris

Andrew K. Rose
University of California,
Berkeley

Sergio L. Schmukler
University of California,
Berkeley

R. Todd Smith
International Monetary Fund,
Washington, D.C.

Mark M. Spiegel
Federal Reserve Bank of
   San Francisco

Linda L. Tesar
University of Michigan,
Ann Arbor

Stephen J. Turnovsky
University of Washington,
Seattle

Holger Wolf
New York University,
New York

Paul R. Wood
Board of Governors of
   the Federal Reserve System,
Washington, D.C.

Preface

The greater integration of developing countries with international capital markets in the last decade has made it easier to mobilize foreign funds for economic development. However, growing links between financial markets have also made these countries more vulnerable both to bad luck and bad policy. Any cessation and reversal of capital inflows is potentially more rapid and harmful.

The Mexican peso crisis of 1994–95 highlighted the point that large increases in capital inflows to developing countries can create problems as well as benefits. In the immediate aftermath of the peso crisis, many people asked, Who would be the next "Mexico" among developing countries? At the time Asian countries appeared to be less vulnerable to concerns about capital flow volatility and appropriate exchange rate levels. The Asian currency crisis that began during the summer of 1997 proved that Asian countries were vulnerable after all.

The essays in this volume provide a comprehensive analysis of the theoretical and policy issues associated with international capital flows as well as the responses of policy makers in recipient emerging markets. These essays were originally prepared for a conference titled "Managing Capital Flows and Exchange Rates: Lessons from the Pacific Basin" sponsored by the Center for Pacific Basin Monetary and Economic Studies at the Federal Reserve Bank of San Francisco on September 26–27, 1996. The conference brought together academics, central bankers, and other policy makers and researchers to review and compare the experiences of emerging market countries, particularly in East Asia and Latin America. All of the contributed essays were written after the occurrence of the peso crisis, but generally without the beneficial hindsight of the Asian currency crisis.

The theme of the conference was conceived with two purposes in mind. First, there was (and still is) a great need to enhance knowledge on

ix

the workings of emerging-market economies, both in Asia, which has been the fastest-growing region in the world economy during the past thirty years, and Latin America, whose history provides both positive and negative lessons about fostering economic development. Second, rapid economic and financial market changes in emerging countries have had considerable impact on the conduct of economic policy in these economies. The comparative study of various national experiences can yield insights into the interactions between policy and market changes.

The September 1996 conference was the fourth in a series sponsored by the Federal Reserve Bank of San Francisco on Pacific Basin monetary issues as part of its Pacific Basin program. Since 1974 the program has promoted cooperation among central banks in the Pacific Basin and sponsored research on major monetary and economic policy issues in the region. The research agenda has been supported through the contributions of the bank's own research staff as well as through international conferences. This work has been published in the bank's *Economic Review*, academic journals, and conference volumes. Previously published conference volumes include *Financial Policy and Reform in Pacific Basin Countries* (Lexington Books, 1986), and *Monetary Policy in Pacific Basin Countries* (Kluwer Press, 1988), both edited by Hang-Sheng Cheng, and *Exchange Rate Policy and Interdependence: Perspectives from the Pacific Basin*, edited by Reuven Glick and Michael Hutchison (Cambridge University Press, 1994).

The Center for Pacific Basin Monetary and Economic Studies was established by the bank in 1990 to open the program to greater participation by visiting scholars. The program was also augmented by the creation of a formal network of researchers in other central banks, universities, research institutes, and international organizations who share the bank's recognition of the importance of Pacific Basin economic issues.

This book is the joint product of many people. Besides the authors of the chapters, special thanks are due to Scott Parris of Cambridge University Press for his support in arranging publication of this volume; Brian MacDonald, for his work as production and copy editor; and Karen Santos Rosa, for her key role in organizing the conference and handling correspondence with the authors.

Finally, any opinions expressed in this volume are those of the respective authors and do not necessarily reflect the views of the organizations with which they are associated. Nor do they reflect the views of the Federal Reserve Bank of San Francisco or of the Board of Governors of the Federal Reserve System.

CHAPTER 1

Overview

Reuven Glick

1.1   Introduction

Capital inflows to developing countries have many beneficial effects. For capital-poor developing countries, capital flows can finance investment and foster economic growth. They may also bring with them growth-enhancing managerial expertise and technology. In addition, capital inflows can enable countries to smooth out their consumption over time and avoid costly economic adjustments in response to temporary adverse shocks to income.

Foreign capital inflows have also been problematic for policy makers in developing countries. Capital inflows can push up monetary aggregates and create inflation pressures. Allowing the exchange rate to appreciate in response to the higher demand for a country's currency created by the capital inflows can adversely affect international competitiveness and net exports. The buildup of international debt through ongoing current account deficits can undermine international creditworthiness. Capital inflows may exacerbate domestic financial distortions and fuel consumption booms, financial market bubbles, and banking crises. Concerns about capital flow reversals can compound worries about macroeconomic and financial market stability. The Mexican peso crisis of 1994–95 as well as the Asian currency crisis of 1997 provide recent examples of the vulnerability of developing capital-importing countries to abrupt reversals in capital flows.

Concerns about the implications of international capital flows for developing countries have grown with the sharply increased volume of these flows since the late 1980s. Net capital inflows for developing countries as a whole, as measured by the capital account surplus (including balance-of-payments errors and omissions) increased from $18 billion in 1988 to $164 billion in 1993. After the U.S. interest rate rise and Mexico

1

peso crisis in 1994, capital inflows to developing countries leveled off or declined, especially portfolio flows to various Latin America countries; however, inflows rebounded in the latter half of 1995 and amounted to almost $250 billion in 1995 (IMF, *World Economic Outlook*, October 1996, table A33).

Most of the increase occurred in private rather than official capital inflows. Net private capital inflows – which include foreign direct investment, portfolio equity, bond issues, loans, and other net liabilities – rose from $33 billion in 1988 to $154 billion in 1993 and $167 billion in 1995 (World Bank, *World Debt Tables*, volume 1, 1996, tables 1.1 and 1.2). The composition of these private inflows differs from that in the late 1970s and early 1980s, when syndicated bank lending was the main channel through which developing countries received funds from abroad. Now foreign direct investment and portfolio equity capital account for roughly 70 percent of total private flows.

The bulk of net private capital flows – almost 80 percent – has gone to East Asia and Latin America. Capital flows to East Asia averaged about $8 billion per year in the period 1986–89, and rose to $63 billion in 1993 and $98 billion in 1995. In Latin America, capital inflows averaged only $5 billion a year in the second half of the 1980s, then rose to $59 billion in 1993, before subsiding to $34 billion in 1995.

Within East Asia and Latin America, the distribution of private capital flows among countries has been highly concentrated. In East Asia, roughly half of the capital flows since 1990 was directed to China; the other major recipients were Malaysia, Thailand, and Indonesia. In Latin America, about 40 percent of the total capital flows over the period 1990–95 went to Mexico; most of the remainder went to Argentina, Brazil, and Chile.

From the perspective of most developing-country recipients, the magnitude of capital inflows has been quite large. Figures 1.1 and 1.2 plot annual data on net capital inflows and current account deficits for selected East Asian and Latin America economies, scaled by gross domestic product (GDP). (Net capital flows are defined to include balance-of-payments errors and omissions; the current account includes private and official transfers as well as net exports of goods and services.)[1]

Capital inflows rose significantly in Thailand in 1988, in Malaysia in 1989, and in Indonesia and the Philippines in 1990. At their peak in the early 1990s, capital inflows as a percentage of GDP were above 20

[1] Balance-of-payments data are from International Monetary Fund, *International Financial Statistics*. All figures are expressed as a percentage of gross domestic product, converted into U.S. dollars at the average annual exchange rate.

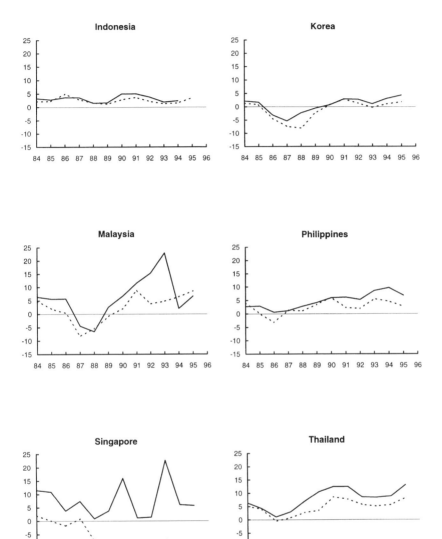

Figure 1.1. Net capital inflow (solid line) and current account deficit (dashed line): East Asia (percentage of GDP).

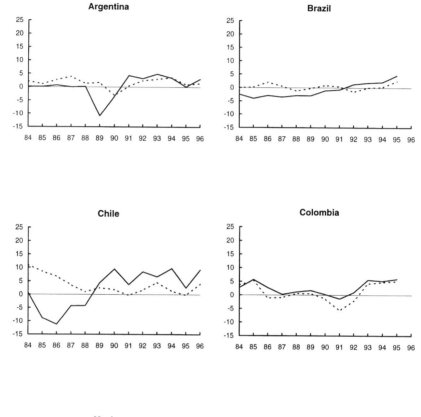

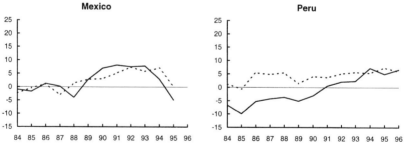

Figure 1.2. Net capital inflow (solid line) and current account deficit (dashed line): Latin America (percentage of GDP).

percent for Malaysia, 13 percent for Thailand, 10 percent for the Philippines, and almost 5 percent for Indonesia. In contrast, Korea experienced significant net capital outflows in the period 1986–89, peaking at 6 percent of GDP in 1987, followed by net inflows beginning in 1990. Taiwan (not shown) experienced large capital inflows in 1986 and 1989, amounting to almost 10 percent of GDP in 1987; since 1988, it has had only net capital outflows.

In Latin America, capital inflows surged first in Mexico in the late 1980s, followed by Chile in 1990, and Argentina, Brazil, and Colombia in the early 1990s. As a percentage of GDP, capital inflows peaked at more than 8 percent in Mexico in 1993, almost 10 percent for Chile in 1994, and almost 5 percent for Argentina in 1993.

Accompanying these capital inflows have been pressures on exchange rates, which individual countries have sought to resist to varying degrees. Although the stated exchange rate regimes of East Asian economies have varied widely, ranging from unilateral pegs to the U.S. dollar (Hong Kong since 1983), to fixed or adjustable pegs to a currency basket (Malaysia, Singapore; Korea until 1990; Indonesia, 1986 to 1997; Thailand, 1984 to 1997), to managed floats (Taiwan until 1989, Korea since 1990), for most of the past decade policy makers in almost all of these economies have tended to limit adjustment of their currencies against the U.S. dollar.

This is illustrated by Figure 1.3, which shows indices of monthly average nominal bilateral exchange rates for several Asian currencies against the U.S. dollar over the period 1985 through August 1997. (The indices are constructed so that an increase implies an appreciation of the local currency against the dollar.) The figure shows that, with the exceptions of the Singapore dollar and the Indonesian rupiah, the trends in regional exchange rates appear to be flat or dampened, in the sense that they have tended to return to their previous levels against the U.S. dollar or settled at new plateaus. In the early to mid-1990s, there is evidence of greater exchange rate flexibility in some countries in the region, such as Malaysia and the Philippines. During the summer of 1997 the baht depreciated roughly 25 percent after the currency was floated on July 2. The currencies of other countries in the region came under attack and also depreciated, though by lesser degrees. The Philippines permitted the peso to float downward in early July, Malaysia let the ringgit depreciate somewhat, and Indonesia, after first widening the bands of its crawling peg, let the rupiah float in mid-August.

As shown in Figure 1.4, most Latin American countries experienced significant nominal currency devaluations in the 1980s, following the 1982 debt crisis and other economic mishaps. (Note the different vertical

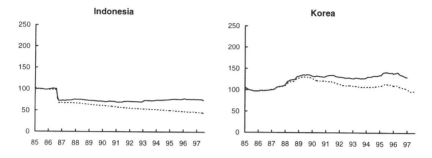

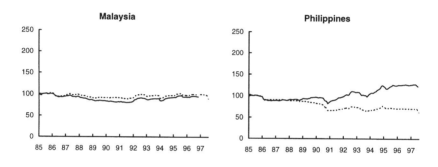

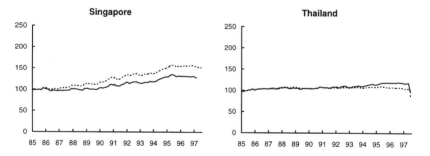

Figure 1.3. Real (solid line) and nominal (dashed line) bilateral exchange rate indices (US$/local currency): East Asia (1985 = 100). *Note*: An increase denotes an appreciation against the dollar.

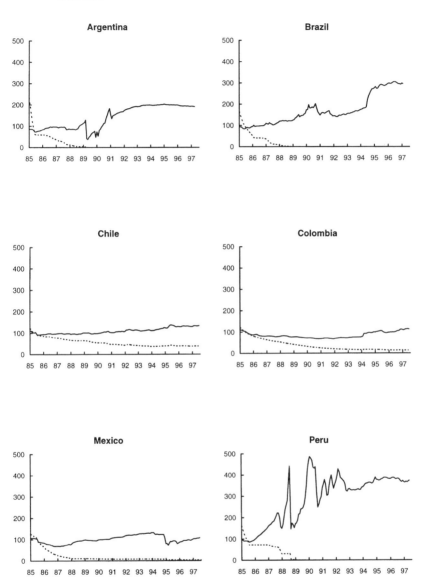

Figure 1.4. Real (solid line) and nominal (dashed line) bilateral exchange rate indices (US$/local currency): Latin America (1985 = 100). *Note*: An increase denotes an appreciation against the dollar.

scale used relative to that for Asian countries.) In the late 1980s a number of Latin American countries subsequently adopted exchange rate–based inflation stabilization programs, relying on the exchange rate as a nominal anchor. Mexico's Pacto stabilization plan involved initially fixing the peso against the dollar in October 1988, followed by a (gradual) preannounced depreciation within a band. (The peso was floated in the aftermath of the December 1994 crisis.) Argentina's Convertibility Plan fixed its exchange rate to the dollar in April 1991. Brazil's Real Plan set a ceiling on the exchange rate relative to the dollar beginning in July 1994. Chile adopted a crawling peg regime in the mid-1980s, as did Colombia in 1994.

Figures 1.3 and 1.4 also illustrate the behavior of the real exchange rate for the selected set of Asian and Latin America countries. (The real exchange rate is constructed using consumer price indices; an increase indicates a real appreciation of the local currency against the dollar.) The figures reveal that in most Latin America countries the real exchange rate appreciated significantly as inflows surged, in contrast to Asia where in many countries real appreciation was avoided. Specifically, in Latin America, Argentina, Brazil, and Mexico (prior to the December 1994 peso crisis) recorded strong real appreciations, while only Chile managed to avoid a significant real appreciation. In Asia (prior to the summer 1997 currency crisis), only Singapore and the Philippines experienced real appreciation, though to a lesser extent than observed in Latin America. Malaysia, Taiwan, and, to a greater extent, Korea and Indonesia managed to avoid significant real appreciation.

1.2   Plan of the book

The essays in this volume provide a comprehensive analysis of the theoretical and policy issues associated with international capital flows and exchange rates as well as the responses of policy makers in recipient emerging markets in Asia and Latin America. They address four broad issues.

First, what are the determinants of international capital flows and exchange rates? The relative role of domestic and external factors in driving capital flows is key to determining the appropriate policy responses. To the extent that domestic factors, particularly domestic economic policy, "pulled" capital into developing countries, a reversal of flows can be avoided by maintaining sound domestic economic policy to sustain the flows. In contrast, if capital is "pushed" by external conditions, the possibility of a capital flow reversal always exists when international financial conditions change. Four essays in the volume look at this issue. Bohn and Tesar examine bilateral U.S. international equity flows to Asia and assess the extent to which U.S. investors allocated their funds abroad in response to the pull of expected returns in foreign markets, or the push of changes in U.S. interest rates. Goldberg and Klein analyze the role of exchange rate changes for the pattern of direct investment flows and trade among the United States, Japan, Latin America, and Southeast Asia. Agénor and Hoffmaister analyze the endogenous responses of capital flows and exchange rates to underlying changes in domestic and foreign macroeconomic variables. Eicher and Turnovsky utilize a stochastic growth model to estimate the effects of changes in risk on international capital flows as well as other variables.

Second, what are the determinants of capital flow reversals and exchange rate crises? How well can such crises be predicted? Meese and Rose study how well speculative attacks in developing countries can be predicted by various macroeconomic indicators; they also estimate the probability of currency crashes. Garber and Lall discuss how derivative products may have contributed to Mexico's 1994 exchange rate crisis by creating undetected off-balance-sheet foreign exchange liabilities. Two other essays in this section discuss the extent to which financial market shocks in one country cause contagion or spillover effects for other countries and regions. Frankel and Schmukler discuss evidence from closed-end emerging-market equity funds indicating that Latin American financial markers were more vulnerable and were hit more directly than East Asian financial markets by the Mexican financial market shock of December 1994. Wolf studies stock return comovements of emerging markets over longer horizons and finds evidence suggesting that shocks to one market may spread to others.

Third, what are the effects of international capital flows, particularly on financial markets? Three essays address this question from different perspectives. Reisen discusses the causes and sustainability of capital inflows and associated current account deficits. He attributes capital flows to incentives to reallocate global capital in response to differential investment returns. McKinnon and Pill discuss how financial liberalization and the opening of capital accounts can lead to excessive borrowing to finance speculative or risky investments. Kamin and Wood examine evidence on how capital flows affect money demand, interest rates, and aggregate demand in Mexico as well as in other Latin America and East Asian countries.

Fourth, what are the appropriate responses by policy makers to capital inflow surges? Should they sterilize the impact of these inflows on monetary aggregates, impose capital controls, or allow the exchange rate to change? What are the relative costs of particular policies? Three essays address these questions. Kletzer and Spiegel evaluate the costs of sterilization of the effects of inflows on monetary aggregates, a common element of the policy mix adopted by most countries, as they seek to avoid altering exchange rates and monetary policy. Policy makers in many countries in Asia, Eastern Europe, and Latin America have resorted to controls on capital inflows, in addition to altering fiscal, monetary, and exchange rate policies in response to surges in capital inflows in the early 1990s. The essay by Reinhart and Smith examines whether controls are effective in reducing inflows or altering their composition and, even if effective, whether they are desirable. The essay by Cowan and De Gregorio examines Chile's recent experience with exchange rate management and capital controls implemented to deal with capital inflows.

The next section presents an analytical discussion of the individual essays and related literature, arranged according to the framework of issues discussed previously.

1.3   Determinants of capital flows and exchange rates

The question of why capital began flowing to East Asian and Latin American emerging markets in the late 1980s and early 1990s has attracted much attention. Policy decisions about how to deal with large capital inflows requires an understanding about what is driving such inflows. One view attributes the capital inflows to developing countries to external factors in industrial countries. In particular, lower short-term interest rates in the United States due to a business cycle downturn and expansionary monetary policy in the early 1990s "pushed" capital flows to emerging markets where ex ante returns were higher. U.S. short-term interest rates declined steadily from 1989, reaching in late 1992 the lowest levels since the early 1960s. Business cycle recessions in the early 1990s, first in the United States and later in Japan and many countries in Europe, made profit opportunities in developing countries appear relatively more attractive.

Another view argues that capital was "pulled" into developing countries by domestic factors, such as economic and structural reforms undertaken by these countries. The reforms attracting capital included improving macroeconomic performance through lower inflation and reductions in public sector deficits. Other reforms included reducing governmental controls over economic activity, privatizing state-owned firms, lowering tariffs and quantitative import barriers, and removing international capital controls. Effective inflation stabilization programs, improved fundamentals, and structural reforms reduced macroeconomic risks and encouraged incoming foreign investment.

Several researchers have sought to quantify the importance of external and foreign factors in attracting capital inflows to developing countries. Calvo, Leiderman, and Reinhart (1993), Fernández-Arias (1996), Fernández-Arias and Montiel (1996), and Frankel and Okongwu (1996) all conclude that external factors were a major cause, perhaps the major cause, of the capital inflows. Others, such as Schadler, Carkovic, Bennett, and Kahn (1993) argue that developments in foreign interest rates and growth, while important, are not the dominant causes of recent capital inflows because the timing of changes in these external factors does not coincide precisely with the surges in capital inflows. Moreover, Chuhan, Claessens, and Mamingi (1995) and Hernandez and Rudolph (1995) conclude that domestic factors, such as economic reforms and policies leading to improved macroeconomic performance and investment climates, were at least as important as external factors in attracting capital inflows to Latin America. Domestic factors help explain important differences across countries in the orders of magnitude of capital inflows received. For example, Malaysia and Thailand implemented reform programs prior to other countries in Asia. Argentina, Chile, and Mexico, with important domestic reforms, attracted much more capital than other countries in Latin America. But domestic reforms alone cannot explain why capital flows occurred in countries that did not undertake reforms at all, or why they occurred in some countries well after the implementation of reforms. In the early 1990s capital appeared to flow to many emerging market countries without any track records, rather than just to countries with established reputations of market reforms and sound economic policy. Clearly both external and domestic factors appear to have been important.

Bohn and Tesar (Chapter 2) examine the factors that have driven U.S. portfolio investment in foreign markets, focusing on equity flows to Asian financial markets (Japan, Hong Kong, Singapore, Malaysia, India, Indonesia, Korea, Pakistan, Philippines, Thailand, Taiwan, and China). They provide some basic statistics describing U.S. equity flows to foreign capital markets over the 1986–95 period. During this period, U.S. holdings of Asian equities increased more than twentyfold, rising from 16 percent to almost 30 percent of all U.S. foreign equity holdings, with most of the increase occurring since 1990. Over the same period, the share of Latin America, particularly Mexico, in U.S. foreign equity holdings rose from roughly 2 percent to over 9 percent. In spite of these trends, foreign equities still represent only about 8 percent of total U.S. domestic and foreign equity holdings – the standard home bias finding.

The bulk of portfolio equity investment in Asia has been directed to

Japan and Hong Kong, though holdings in Singapore, Malaysia, Korea, and Indonesia have increased dramatically in recent years. Significant differences in the timing of increased investment across countries lead Bohn and Tesar to conjecture that local rather than global factors were more important in explaining the pattern of capital flows over time. Bohn and Tesar apply a mean–variance portfolio model to test formally for the factors driving U.S. equity investment in foreign markets. Mean–variance portfolio analysis suggests that investors will increase their foreign portfolio holdings, and therefore make equity purchases, in markets where relatively high excess returns are expected. (As instruments for expected returns, they use lagged values of U.S. stock market returns and interest rates as well as lagged values of local asset returns.) Bilateral country regressions on monthly transaction data over the period 1986–95 support the hypothesis that excess returns drive portfolio allocation in the two largest Asian markets, Japan and Hong Kong. They find further support for this "return-chasing" hypothesis in the smaller Asian markets when the remaining countries are combined in a panel. There is also a significant time trend in U.S. net foreign purchases over time, reflecting the gradual erosion of home bias in the U.S. investment portfolio. Lagged net purchases of equity in a particular market are a significant determinant of current net purchases as well, indicating some lagged adjustment in portfolio allocations over time that is not explained by the simple expected-return model employed.

Bohn and Tesar conclude that global variables are not a significant determinant of U.S. equity investment (after controlling for the information content of these factors for forecasting excess returns and including a time trend and lagged adjustment term). They do find some evidence of cross-market linkages in U.S. equity purchases: after the October 1987 U.S. stock market crash, U.S. investors sold Japanese equities, and after the December 1994 peso crisis, U.S. investors were net sellers of Asian equity, though surprisingly not of Mexican equity. Thus the increase in U.S. investment in foreign equity markets has largely been due to local "pull" factors, such as high domestic returns, rather than global "push" factors, such as low U.S. interest rates.

Another factor affecting international investment flows, particularly direct investment, has been currency realignments. After the yen appreciated by over 50 percent against the U.S. dollar between 1985 and 1988, Japanese investment in Asia shifted in the late 1980s toward lower-cost, more labor-intensive locations in Southeast Asia, such as Malaysia and Thailand. The appreciation of the yen also boosted the international competitiveness and current account surpluses of the newly industrialized economies (NIEs), including Korea, Taiwan, and Singapore. Subsequent appreciation of the currencies of the NIEs influenced the flow of capital within the region as well. These currency realignments have also affected international trade flows.

The essay by Goldberg and Klein (Chapter 3) analyzes the effect of bilateral real exchange rate movements on U.S. and Japanese foreign direct investment and trade with a set of seven Southeast Asian and Latin American countries over the years 1978–93 – Argentina, Brazil, Chile, Indonesia, Malaysia, the Philippines, and Thailand. In recent years, both U.S. and Japanese foreign direct investment in Asia and Latin America have increased. Japanese investment has dominated in Asia, amounting to roughly two times as much as U.S. flows into the region. U.S. direct investment dominates in Latin America by an even greater margin. The United States represents about 20 percent of the total trade (exports plus imports) of the countries in both East Asia and Latin America. Japan accounts for close to 25 percent of East Asian trade activity, but less than 10 percent in Latin America.

The authors find that a depreciation in the domestic real exchange rate relative to the yen increases direct investment from Japan to Asia. This is consistent with the view that a real depreciation raises direct investment by lowering the cost of domestic labor and other inputs relative to that of foreign inputs and with claims about the potential hollowing out of the Japanese industrial sector as a result of a stronger yen. A depreciation in the real exchange rate relative to the yen also "crowds out" direct investment from the United States to Asia. However, no relationship is found between the real exchange rate and direct investment into Latin America.

The essay also examines the direct effect of foreign direct investment on trade flows, while holding constant the role of the real exchange rate. An interesting result is that Japanese direct investment significantly increases Southeast Asian imports from both Japan and the United States (consisting largely of production inputs), while U.S. direct investment reduces Asian imports. This implies that Japanese foreign direct investment complements Japanese trade, whereas U.S. foreign direct investment substitutes for U.S. trade with the region. Direct investment flows have no significant impact on imports into Latin America countries.

The essay identifies a "springboard relationship" between direct investment from the United States or Japan and exports from recipient nations. Specifically, exports from Latin America to the United States and Japan are significantly increased by direct investment from Japan. This in part reflects the fact that relatively low tariff levels in Latin

America encouraged Japan to locate production there for export to the United States. (Japanese investment in Mexico, in particular, appears associated with efforts to produce for export into the United States, free of tariffs under the North America Free Trade Agreement.) Analogously, U.S. direct investment significantly enhances exports from East Asian countries to Japan.

A more complete analysis of capital flows and the exchange rate necessarily requires recognition of the simultaneous determination of these variables (together with other asset prices and quantities). The essay by Agénor and Hoffmaister (Chapter 4) formally takes account of the endogeneity of capital flows and the real exchange rate and relates their movements to underlying changes in domestic and foreign macroeconomic variables. They formulate a dynamic optimizing model of a small open economy in which whether the real exchange rate appreciates or depreciates in response to an inflow of capital depends on initial conditions and on the source of the underlying shocks giving rise to the capital inflow.

They discuss two types of experiments: an increase in the world (risk-free) interest rate and the effects of an increase in government spending on home goods. The first experiment is relevant to the view that the cyclical decline in U.S. interest rates explains the capital flow surge to developing countries in the early 1990s. The most relevant case for examining the recent experience of developing countries in Asia and Latin America is to assume the economy is initially a net international debtor and that capital inflows are precipitated by a fall in foreign interest rates. In this case the model predicts that the real exchange rate should initially appreciate. For a debtor country, a fall in foreign interest rates will induce income and substitution effects, which result in a consumption boom and a wider current account deficit: declining interest rates reduce the present value of debt and create a positive income effect on consumption. With borrowing cheaper, the substitution effect also raises consumption. The increase in consumption leads to a real appreciation. (In the long run, however, the real exchange rate must depreciate in order to eliminate the current account deficit.)

The second experiment considers the effects of a tax-financed increase in government spending. Such an increase also leads to an initial appreciation of the real exchange rate, as long as the net demand for home goods rises. To the extent the spending increase (temporarily) raises the domestic interest rate, capital inflows occur as well.

Agénor and Hoffmaister quantitatively examine the relation between capital inflows and the real exchange rate in Korea, Mexico, the Philippines, and Thailand over the period from the early 1980s through 1994.

To summarize the dynamic interactions between capital flows, the real exchange rate, and their underlying determinants, the authors estimate a (near) vector-autoregressive system consisting of capital flows, the cyclical (i.e., detrended) real exchange rate, money base velocity, the (uncovered) interest rate differential between domestic and foreign assets, the change in the world interest rate, and government spending. (The last two variables are treated as block exogenous.) As the authors point out, the framework developed captures only short-run links among capital flows, the real exchange rate, and domestic and foreign shocks. It does not, for example, capture the possibility of long-run (trend) effects of capital flows on the real exchange rate through supply-side effects on capital accumulation and productivity changes. In addition, some of the results are sensitive to the detrending method employed.

Agénor and Hoffmaister find that a decline in world interest rates leads to a capital inflow in all of the Asian countries (though the effect for Thailand is rather small), but to a "perverse" initial capital outflow followed by an inflow in Mexico. It also leads to an initial real exchange rate appreciation in the Philippines and Thailand, a depreciation in Korea, but no significant effect in Mexico. The lack of any effect on the cyclical exchange rate in Mexico does not rule out the possibility that interest rate changes affect the long-run exchange rate trend. A positive innovation in government spending has significant effects only in Korea, leading to a (small) real appreciation and a reduction in capital inflows. This result may be explained either by the possibility that Korean residents have a stronger desire to sustain consumption over time or that they perceive domestic government spending changes as less persistent than residents in other countries. In either case, private consumption would tend to fall less in response to the government spending increase, thereby requiring a real appreciation to maintain home good equilibrium.

Other factors not explicitly considered by Agénor and Hoffmaister must be taken into account to explain why the real exchange rate in fact generally appreciated more for Latin American currencies than for Asian currencies as capital inflows increased. For the Asian countries, investment as a share of GDP increased considerably more during the capital inflows period than in most Latin America countries. If investment is biased more toward imported capital goods rather than domestic goods, other things equal, this works in the direction of generating smaller real exchange rate appreciations in Asia (Calvo, Leiderman, and Reinhart, 1996). The existence of a large, labor-intensive manufacturing export sector in East Asian countries may have made it easier to shift labor to the nontradables sector and also enabled these countries to accommodate capital inflows without much real exchange rate variation

(Sachs, Tornell, and Velasco, 1996b). Differences in fiscal spending be-havior may not have been significant enough to explain differences in the magnitude of real exchange rate appreciation. Several Latin America countries, notably Chile and Mexico, as well as Asian countries adopted major fiscal adjustment programs, at the time of capital inflows.[2] The real exchange rate appreciation of some Latin America countries also may be attributed to their adoption of exchange rate–based inflation stabiliza-tion programs during the inflow period, relying on the exchange rate as a nominal anchor. Although they sought to limit nominal exchange rate movements, the real exchange rate tended to appreciate nonetheless, as domestic price inflation continued to exceed foreign inflation, either because of inertia or imperfect credibility of the program itself.[3]

Risk plays an important role in international capital movements and allocation of the world capital stock. Eicher and Turnovsky (Chapter 5) argue that because small open developing countries are very prone to external and internal shocks they provide the appropriate case studies for applying open-economy models incorporating risk. The authors em-ploy a stochastic (continuous-time) growth model to analyze quantita-tively the effects of risk on key macroeconomic variables, such as real financial rates of return, portfolio shares, economic growth, and ex-change rate. Risk is measured in terms of the variances and covariances of exogenous shocks to domestic monetary and fiscal policies, foreign inflation, and productivity.

The authors use the model to compare and contrast the economic performances of Mexico and Indonesia during the period 1973–95. In terms of their economic structures and government policies, these two economies have many similarities. For example, both are oil exporters, and both undertook ambitious programs of financial and trade liberaliza-tion in the late 1980s. However, their growth, inflation, and exchange rate experiences have been quite different. Indonesia has grown more rapidly and steadily than Mexico. Also, Indonesia's inflation rate has

---

[2] For example, Thailand's fiscal balance as a percent of GDP changed from a deficit of 3.3 percent in 1986 to a surplus of 2.0 percent in 1988; Malaysia's fiscal deficit fell from 10.3 percent to 2.1 percent of GDP over the same period. Indonesia's fiscal deficit changed from 4.5 percent of GDP in 1986 to a surplus of 1.4 percent in 1990. See Bercuson and Koenig (1993, p. 12).

[3] Inertial inflation can be attributed to overlapping contracts or backward-looking expec-tations (Dornbusch and Werner, 1994). If the stabilization program is not perceived as fully credible, agents may increase their current domestic spending and appreciate the real exchange rate because they expect the interest rate, i.e., the effective price of current consumption, to be lower at the onset of the program than in the future when the program might fail.

been much lower, and its real exchange rate appreciated much less than Mexico's during the period of rapid capital inflows in 1990–94.

After calibrating the model to Indonesia and Mexico, the authors examine whether differences in the variance–covariance structure of exogenous shocks can explain cross-country differences in financial rates of return, portfolio composition, and growth rates. Because of probable changes in the underlying stochastic economic structure, the sample period is divided into three subperiods, 1973–81, 1982–88, and 1989–95. These three periods roughly correspond to periods of initial steady growth, oil shock and debt crisis (for Mexico), and economic recovery. They conclude that their model can explain the behavior of nominal asset prices, such as interest rates and exchange rates, reasonably well. However, the model misses badly when it comes to explaining portfolio shares and output growth rates. The poor fit to observed portfolio holdings is not surprising, and can be interpreted as a version of the "equity premium puzzle": the apparent inability to explain the high excess returns to holding equities.

More disappointing is the model's inability to account for differences in output growth rates. In general, the model greatly overpredicts Mexico's growth rate, and greatly underpredicts Indonesia's. The authors conjecture that incorporating productive government expenditure would resolve these discrepancies (since Indonesia's government spends more than Mexico's). An alternative explanation about why the growth rates are so far off stems from the model's property that high inflation raises growth (because of an induced portfolio shift toward higher yielding capital). Since Mexico's inflation rate was so much higher than Indonesia's, this tends to produce a higher predicted growth rate for Mexico. It is possible that accounting for some of the adverse effects of inflation on growth would help resolve this problem.

1.4   Exchange rate crises and contagion

Exchange rate crises are characterized by sudden, large outflows of foreign exchange reserves that trigger devaluations. What causes such events? Are currency and financial crises the inevitable punishment of a country's misdeeds, or are they simply random shocks perpetrated upon innocent economies by volatile speculators?

A fundamental proposition of open economic macroeconomics is that the viability of a fixed exchange rate regime and an open capital account requires maintaining long-run consistency between monetary, fiscal, and exchange rate policies. Ongoing monetization of fiscal deficits or bailout of an insolvent domestic banking system by the central bank, for example, breaks the balance between money demand and money supply required to maintain an exchange rate target. Excessive expansion of domestic credit leads to a gradual loss of foreign exchange reserves and, once the central bank becomes incapable of defending parity any longer, to abandonment of the fixed exchange rate. With rational expectations, exchange rate crises can be the equilibrium outcome of market anticipation of the central bank's inability to maintain an exchange rate peg because of the fundamental inconsistency between monetary, fiscal, and exchange rate policies.[4]

Another view is that speculative currency attacks are motivated not just by bad policy decisions, but also by self-fulfilling market expectations. This possibility arises when governments are viewed as optimizing agents, making choices between competing objectives that are subject to constraints depending on market participants' expectations. The resulting endogeneity of macroeconomic policies creates the possibility of multiple equilibria and self-fulfilling speculative attacks in the sense that speculators may or may not initiate an attack based on their beliefs about the willingness of policy makers to resist the pressure on the exchange rate.[5]

For example, if unemployment is high and the economy is weak, there is greater likelihood that the government will shift to more expansionary policies and abandon its exchange rate commitment with any further adverse output shock. A weak banking system can also compromise the central bank's ability to defend a currency peg in the face of adverse shocks that require a sharp, upward adjustment in interest rates, such as a sudden reversal of capital inflows. Concern for any of these internal objectives competes with the commitment to maintain a peg and creates a situation that can lead to abandonment of a peg in event of a speculative attack. Whether a crisis occurs depends on market expectations. In this situation, a crisis can be provoked by bad luck and/or bad news that leads market participants to revise their views about the government's ability to maintain an exchange rate peg.

It has proved somewhat difficult to distinguish empirically between these two theories of currency crises. For example, there is a widespread view that the European Monetary System (EMS) crisis of 1992 largely reflects self-fulling expectations (e.g., Eichengreen, Rose, and Wyplosz, 1995). In this view, in most EMS member countries whose currencies came under speculative attack, fundamentals did not appear inconsistent

---

[4] The seminal work in this area is Krugman (1979). Garber and Svensson (1995) provide an excellent survey of the literature.

[5] See Obstfeld (1986).

with pegged exchange rates: reserves were adequate; budget deficits, monetary growth, and inflation rates were low; and interest differentials between EMS members and Germany – a measure of credibility that financial markets monitored – did not predict the crisis. Others, such as Bordo and Schwartz (1996), reject this interpretation of the data and maintain that the EMS crisis as well as other historical crises that they examine occurred because of inconsistency between the fundamentals underlying domestic policy objectives and a pegged exchange rate.

A growing number of researchers have examined events before and after the devaluation of the Mexican peso in December 1994 to reveal lessons about the nature of exchange rate crises. Was Mexico's experience a "sudden death" caused by an unforeseen speculative panic by international investors, or was it a "death foretold" by evident disequilibria phenomena such as an overvalued real exchange rate and an unsustainable current account? Sachs, Tornell, and Velasco (1996a, 1996c) argue that Mexico's crisis was not foretold by the country's fundamentals. Market interest rates preceding the crisis of December 1994 did not appear to indicate an expected devaluation of the peso.[6] Mexico's fiscal policy was conservative, and the country's debt–GNP ratio was low by world standards. Rather they attribute the crisis to a speculative attack that was largely unexpected and represented a self-fulfilling panic that spread to other countries.

In contrast, Calvo and Mendoza (1996) argue that Mexico's "fall from grace" was foretold by its policy response to a downward shift in money demand following upward U.S. interest rate movements and Mexican political developments in 1994. To avoid raising domestic interest rates and harming a fragile domestic banking system while also limiting depreciation of the peso, Mexican authorities sought to sterilize the foreign exchange losses following the money demand shift by raising domestic credit. This policy stance was unsustainable and spawned the crisis.

Similar questions have also arisen about the predictability of the 1997 Asian financial crisis that began in Thailand. In Thailand's case, current account deficits (as high as 8 percent of GDP for much of the 1990s) raised concerns about the continued ability to finance them though capital inflows. Because Thailand pegged its exchange rate and allowed its inflation rate to creep up, the baht also experienced real appreciation, though not to the same extent as Mexico's peso did prior to its collapse. The appreciation of the baht, while tied to the U.S. dollar, especially

---

[6] The interest rate differential between dollar-denominated tesobonos and U.S. Treasury bills was relatively constant before the crisis, indicating no increase in the market risk premium for holding Mexican assets.

against the yen, hurt the competitiveness of Thailand's exports. The bursting of a real-estate market bubble, the fragility of Thailand's financial system, and the volume of foreign-currency denominated debt made it difficult for the government to maintain both high interest rates and a currency peg in the face of speculative capital outflows. Eventually the baht was floated and depreciated.

Meese and Rose (Chapter 6) attempt to identify plausible determinants of currency crises and ascertain whether knowledge of economic fundamentals can help policy makers predict currency crises in developing as well as industrial countries. They define a currency "crash" as a 25 percent depreciation in the level of the nominal exchange rate and at least a 10 percent increase in the rate of depreciation from the previous period. Employing an annual panel data set for 105 developing countries over the period 1971–92, the authors identify 135 currency crashes and 1,708 periods of tranquillity. The authors then seek to identify the determinants of currency crises using a nonstructural empirical analysis involving probit regressions, that is, without relying on a particular theory of speculative attacks. They find that high foreign interest rates, a high external debt burden, a *decrease* in bank claims, loose monetary policy, tight fiscal policy, and domestic recessions are all associated with currency crashes. They find no evidence that low levels of foreign currency reserves or high ratios of broad money to reserves are consistently associated with crashes. Nor is there any evidence that the degree of overvaluation relative to purchasing power parity or the size of the current account are associated with currency crashes.

They find differences in the determinants of currency crashes across regions. Asian countries, unlike Latin American and African countries, appear to be unaffected by world interest rates, or by any of the determinants of currency crashes used in the analysis. Much of the effects of foreign direct investment, domestic credit, and domestic recession seem to stem from the Latin America countries.

To determine whether knowledge of macroeconomic fundamentals can help policy makers predict currency crises, the authors use quarterly time series data from eight countries in the European Monetary System to calibrate two structural models of speculative currency attack. In these models, fundamentals are used to quantify the probability of a change in the currency regime.

In one model, the fundamental value of the exchange rate (determined by deviations between domestic and foreign reserves, domestic credit, real GDP, and short-term interest rates, as well as the deviation of the exchange rate from its purchasing power parity level) is used in an error–correction framework that takes into account the position of the spot rate in the parity band to determine the predicted value of the currency in the next quarter. The model has marginal in-sample predictive ability. However, out-of-sample performance is poor, and certain episodes when a crash was estimated to have high probability and no realignment occurred do not correspond to episodes generally thought to be unsuccessful speculative attacks.

The other structural model employed is a Markov regime-switching model with time-varying regime probabilities. In this setup, the probability of no-realignment conditional on whether a realignment occurred or did not occur in the preceding period is a (logistic) function of a linear combination of fundamental variables, including the interest rate differential (with respect to Germany), real incomes, money supplies, and deviations from purchasing power parity. The predictive ability of this model is also poor. The authors cannot reject the hypothesis that the transition probabilities are constant, independent of macroeconomic fundamentals.

The authors interpret these poor predictive results as suggesting that models of speculative attacks that emphasize only the importance of fundamentals are overly simplistic. It appears necessary to incorporate into the analysis nonstandard macroeconomic fundamentals, expectations variables, and political variables.

While Meese and Rose focused on macroeconomic fundamentals, Peter Garber and Subir Lall's essay (Chapter 7) studies the role that financial derivatives, such as forwards, options, and swaps, play in exacerbating an exchange rate crisis. The focus is on the Mexican exchange rate crisis of December 1994, but since these products are increasingly used by banks in Asia, the lessons learned from Mexico can be applied in Asia as well.

Their main argument is that offshore derivatives markets enable domestic banks to circumvent prudential and antispeculative regulations (e.g., on short-selling and margin positions). In particular, they discuss how Mexican banks, operating through their New York financial subsidiaries, were able in effect to take large net short positions in dollars. This looked good when Mexican interest rates exceeded U.S. rates, but when the peso was devalued it rapidly produced a liquidity crisis in the Mexican banking system. The extent of the overall short dollar position of Mexican banks was a surprise to Mexican authorities.

Overall, the policy implication is that the growth in derivatives should be regarded as a two-edged sword, which can be beneficial if used properly for risk management, but at the same time can be quite harmful if not. The appropriate policy response is not simply to ban these markets; doing so just drives them offshore, outside the regulatory purview of domestic authorities. Instead, authorities should create a regulatory environment that brings the markets onshore, and then invest in adequate supervisory infrastructure. This approach would allow countries to monitor the growth and proliferation of derivatives while allowing market participants to use them for risk management purposes. Another key implication of their analysis is that on-balance-sheet measures of assets and liabilities may not present an accurate picture of true financial conditions.

Spillover, or "contagion," effects from one country to other countries and regions attracted renewed attention in the aftermath of the Mexican crisis of December 1994. In Latin America, Argentina and Brazil came under the most severe pressure immediately after the crisis. The Argentine market fell 14 percent in dollar terms from December 19 to December 27, and the Brazilian market fell 17 percent over the same period. The Asian experience followed a different course. Initially, those countries that had attracted sizable capital inflows in recent years (e.g, Malaysia, Thailand, Indonesia, and the Philippines) were relatively unaffected by events in Latin America. During mid-January 1995, however, the exchange rate in most of those countries (as well as Hong Kong) came under increased speculative pressure; equity markets posted large losses. In January, stock market declines ranged from 7 percent in Malaysia to 13 percent in the Philippines. Domestic currency values came under similar pressures. Most central banks responded by intervening and raising interest rates in an effort to defend their currencies. As in Latin America, not all countries experienced the same degree or persistence of pressures. But, in most cases the speculative attack lasted for only a few days, though in the Philippines the pressures persisted well into March. What explains why some emerging markets experienced more of a "tequila hangover" effect than others? How much of a role did differences in fundamentals play here?

The Thai financial crisis also had a contagion effect, mainly but not exclusively in Asia. Following the depreciation of the baht on July 2, 1997, the currencies of Malaysia, Indonesia, and the Philippines, among others, also depreciated, though not by the same extent as the baht. Stock markets around the region also declined. Further analysis is necessary to discern how much of these developments is attributable to the desire by Thailand's neighbors to maintain their international competitiveness against the baht and how much to their exhibiting some of the same problematic economic symptoms as Thailand.

Frankel and Schmukler (Chapter 8) quantitatively assess the contagion effects of the Mexican peso crisis. They make use of weekly data on net asset values (NAVs) of local stocks and the prices of closed-end country funds for Asian and Latin American countries that are traded in New York. These data permit study of how the negative shock in Mexican equities was transmitted to the NAVs and country fund prices for other countries in Asia and Latin America.

Frankel and Schmukler exploit the fact that although country fund prices and the NAVs of the underlying stocks move together in the long run, in the short run a change in NAV need not be immediately transmitted to the fund price. This means that a change in equity prices in one country can have a more immediate effect on equity prices in other countries, as measured by their NAVs, than on its own country fund price. As a result, it is possible to test the channel through which contagion takes place: whether a shock in Mexican NAVs and fund prices is directly transmitted to other countries by affecting the NAVs of other countries' stocks, other country fund prices, or both.

Using cross-country correlation measures and time series techniques (Granger-causality tests), Frankel and Schmukler find that the Mexican peso shock produced spillover effects that are less strong in Asia than in Latin America. The shocks seemed to affect Latin American NAVs directly, while transmission to Asian NAVs "passed through" the New York investor fund community, rather than directly from equity prices in Latin America to equity prices in Asia. The data also show that comovements among the NAVs of different countries are stronger within regional markets – East Asia, Latin America, and New York – than between them.

The authors make some effort to ascertain the extent to which the decline in country fund prices can be attributed to economic fundamentals, based on simple bivariate cross-fund regressions. They conclude that countries with weaker external positions, as measured by high debt–export and current account deficit–GNP ratios, or low foreign reserve–GNP ratios experienced more severe negative spillover effects. This explains why the Philippines and Indonesia appeared more vulnerable to contagion effects, despite their location in East Asia, because of their relatively high debt–export ratios. Asian countries with relatively low debt–export ratios, such as Malaysia, Korea, and Taiwan, were less affected. Similarly, Chile was relatively less vulnerable to contagion effects than other Latin American countries because of its low debt–export ratio. Price falls of country funds also appeared to be negatively related to low export–GNP ratios; that is, more open economies appear to suffer less contagion. This can be interpreted as international investors viewing open economies as more reliable, because the cost of a policy reversal or default is greater to them.

These results may be compared with those of a study by Sachs, Tornell, and Velasco (1996b) which relates the degree of contagion to similar fundamentals. They construct a financial crisis index as a weighted average of devaluation and loss of international reserves after the Mexican financial shock. The factors that they identify as determining a country's vulnerability to financial crisis include an appreciated real exchange rate, a weak banking system, and low foreign exchange reserve levels. They find that this set of fundamentals goes far in explaining the degree of contagion in multivariate cross-country regressions. Countries, such as Malaysia, Indonesia, and Chile, with plentiful foreign exchanges reserves relative to their short-term liabilities, a stronger banking system, and an exchange rate that was not overvalued suffered only very short-lived downturns in capital inflows. In contrast, countries such as Mexico, Argentina, and the Philippines, with weaker fundamentals and scant reserves, were more vulnerable to reversals. They also conclude that the magnitude of current account deficits, the volume of capital inflows, and fiscal policy stances during this period do not explain why some countries were more affected than others in the aftermath of the December 1994 peso devaluation For example, large current account deficits, which have been blamed for Mexico's problems, were present in Malaysia and Thailand, which were relatively unaffected by events in Mexico. Brazil, which experienced considerable turbulence, had a modest current account deficit at the time of the crisis. This finding differs somewhat from that of Frankel and Schmukler who attribute some explanatory power to the current account deficit. Perhaps country fund prices are more sensitive to this fundamental than are exchange rates and foreign reserve holdings.

Holger Wolf's essay (Chapter 9) takes a longer-term view in assessing the linkages among the financial markets of emerging countries. Wolf uses U.S. dollar–denominated equity return data for twenty-four emerging countries that span roughly the mid-1980s to April 1995. He finds that monthly stock market returns in emerging countries are not highly correlated. The average (unconditional) correlation for country pairs is only .06. This finding suggests very little evidence for contagion.

Still, Wolf points out that the unconditional correlation of equity market indices is a poor (albeit popular) measure of contagion. Stock index returns are partly determined by sectoral composition. For example, in two markets where the oil sector is dominant equity prices may rise simultaneously in response to an oil price shock. The resulting high correlation would have little to do with contagion, at least as the term is conventionally defined. In addition, compositional differences in market indices may hide existing comovements. To the degree that returns differ across sectors and sectoral composition differs across markets, Wolf argues that it is necessary to correct market indices for compositional effects to obtain meaningful measures of country movements. He also argues that contagion is better measured after controlling for the comovements of fundamentals, such as macroeconomic performance, economic structure, and risk factors.

Based on return data disaggregated into 21 industry sectors for a smaller sample of 15 countries, Wolf finds that differences in sectoral composition indeed account for some of the low unconditional correlations of equity returns. After controlling for sectoral composition effects, the average correlation of returns rises for 88 out of the 105 country pairs he examines. However, the (absolute) average correlation of country returns (after controlling for sectoral composition) still remains small at 0.22. Still, the finding suggests that a good part of the benefit from international diversification documented in the literature might reflect gains from sectoral diversification rather than gains from country diversification.

To ascertain further the scope for contagion effects, Wolf examines whether cross-country return correlations are attributable to cross-country similarities in economic fundamentals. Wolf ranks countries according to fundamentals reflecting macroeconomic performance (growth in GDP and exports, the ratios of investment and exports to GDP, inflation, and inflation variability), economic structure (GDP per capita, total GDP, share of manufacturing exports in total exports), and exposure to risk (ratios of debt to GDP, of foreign currency reserves to imports or to debt, the fiscal and current account deficits as a fraction of GDP, and the variability of the terms of trade). If similarity along these dimensions reflects exposure to the same type of shocks, one would expect countries with similar fundamentals to exhibit above-average correlations. To the extent that this is so, the scope for contagion effects is lessened. Wolf also tests whether location and equity market development (as measured by barriers to entry and exit, withholding taxes, indicators of market size, liquidity and market depth, and proxies for information quality) influence the pattern of correlations, both of which could be consistent with contagion effects.

Wolf finds some weak support for an above-average return comovement for countries with better macroeconomic performance, that is, countries with high output and export growth, high investment and export ratios, and low inflation. However, differences in correlations are also significantly influenced by the development stage and geographic location of equity markets. In particular, markets in Asia exhibit significant above-average correlation with each other. This finding is consistent with, though not proof of, the existence of moderate geographically concentrated contagion effects. Wolf's results, of course, do not exclude the possibility of more pronounced correlation spikes of the sort identified by Frankel and Schmukler for shorter horizons, such as the period after the Mexican crisis.

1.5   Effects of capital inflows

Helmut Reisen's essay (Chapter 10) provides an overview of the determinants and effects of international private capital flows. He begins with a review of the arguments for the beneficial effects of foreign capital inflows from the perspective of neoclassical and new growth models as well as the intertemporal current account approach. The neoclassical view is that capital flows internationally in response to marginal capital productivity differentials and a country benefits when the domestic investment of foreign capital inflows raises the country's capital–labor ratio. However, the resulting rise in growth is only temporary as long as production technology remains unchanged by the capital inflow. Endogenous growth models suggest that capital flows can foster a permanent increase in long-term growth rate, by increasing the capital stock and improving a country's technology. The intertemporal approach emphasizes the consumption-smoothing benefits of capital flows by allowing a country to absorb adverse domestic output shocks by temporarily borrowing abroad.

A cursory examination of some empirical evidence on the economic benefits of capital inflows indicates an increase in the capital–labor ratio following capital inflow surges, and hence at least a temporary boost to income growth, for Thailand, Malaysia, and Chile, and less so for Indonesia and Argentina; for other countries the ratio remained relatively unchanged (Philippines, Peru) or fell (Mexico). Of course, it is premature to determine whether there has been any permanent increase in long-term growth. Reisen does not find any econometric evidence that the intertemporal approach can explain the presently high current account deficits for the countries in his analysis.

Reisen also formulates a measure of the long-run sustainability of capital inflows that depends on the desired debt–GDP ratio, desired foreign exchange reserves, import growth, and the potential growth rate. After calibrating this sustainability measure, Reisen concludes that the current account deficits for 1994 were well above their steady state for Mexico, Argentina, and the Philippines; nearer, though still somewhat above, the steady state for Malaysia and Thailand; and roughly in the steady state for Chile, Indonesia, and Peru.

Some, such as Calvo, question the usefulness of "sustainable" current account measures. They argue that balance-of-payments crises are more likely to stem from financial and other structural vulnerabilities, rather than flow disequilibria captured by current account deficits. According to this view, a "stock" measure of vulnerability, such as the ratio of the base or broad money supply to available foreign exchange reserves, provides a better measure of a country's exposure to the possibility that foreign investors will switch out of domestic assets and precipitate a crisis. For, if at the time of a sudden capital flow reversal and crisis the central bank is not willing to let the exchange rate depreciate, it must be prepared to cover all of its liquid liabilities with reserves. These reserves must cover not only direct liabilities, such as the monetary base, but also liquid liabilities of commercial banks as well as other contingent claims on the central bank, such as tesobonos, the short-term dollar-indexed debt issued by the Mexican Treasury.

The last section of Reisen's essay argues that the appropriate policy response to a current account deficit requires looking beyond its "sustainable" level to its source. Reisen addresses the merits of the so-called Lawson doctrine (espoused by former U.K. Chancellor of the Exchequer Nigel Lawson in the late 1980s) that maintains that current account deficits should only be of concern when they arise from fiscal budget deficits, rather than from private saving and investment decisions, since the latter reflect optimal market decision making. He dismisses this view by arguing that it ignores (1) Ricardian equivalence considerations that suggest that private decision making (at least in part) reflects a response to government behavior; (2) that private sector liabilities are often explicit or implicit contingent government liabilities, created through deposit insurance; (3) that private market distortions may arise from speculative bubbles, imperfect information, and failure by firms and consumers to internalize marginal social costs of borrowing; and (4) the hysteresis effects of overvalued exchange rates on competitiveness.

Empirical evidence is presented to show that private consumption booms, banking crises, and real appreciation have played roles in the capital inflow and current account deficit experiences of several Latin American countries (e.g., Argentina, Mexico, Peru). The Mexican experience clearly shows a country's vulnerability to crisis, even when capital inflows are largely private sector oriented. In contrast, Reisen points out that most Asian countries have been characterized by relatively greater investment of capital inflows and less real appreciation. Ideally, a first-best policy involves curbing the underlying causes of excessive private consumption, appreciation, and banking failures, for example, by better monitoring consumer debt, introducing greater nominal exchange rate flexibility, and/or improving bank regulation and supervision. Capital inflow controls may be still warranted, he suggests, as a second-best solution to reduce the risks of excessive foreign borrowing. Reisen also suggests that foreign direct investment should be encouraged over other forms of capital inflows. Foreign direct investment, he argues, is less subject to reversals, more likely to convey positive growth externalities, and more likely to be associated with physical investment. Hence, foreign direct investment is less likely than other capital flows to stimulate excessive private consumption and a real appreciation problem.

Reisen's view accords with the conventional wisdom on this subject, that direct investment inflows are much less volatile than other types of capital inflows, particularly portfolio investment (e.g., Corbo and Hernández, 1996). Hence, countries should be careful not to rely too heavily on capital inflows composed mainly of portfolio investments to finance their current account, as these flows could reverse themselves quickly. (The weakness of Thailand's situation has been partially attributed to the fact that incoming direct investment accounted for only about 10 percent of total capital inflows in recent years.) However, Claessens, Dooley, and Warner (1995) show, based on comparisons of the statistical time-series properties of various categories of capital flows, that foreign direct investment and other forms of long-term flows were as volatile and prone to reversal as short-term portfolio flows. These results have tended to qualify views that foreign direct investment should be regarded as more desirable than portfolio flows, although the consensus on the desirability of foreign direct investment and the dangers of portfolio inflows has not entirely been overturned.

Some researchers have asked whether countries undertaking major structural economic reform and macroeconomic stabilization programs are prone to engaging in excessive foreign borrowing that inevitably results in recession and financial crisis. In particular, exchange rate–based inflation stabilization plans, such as that of Argentina and Chile in the late 1970s and Mexico in the late 1980s, have been accused of sowing the seeds of their own destruction: in the early stages of the plan, credible domestic reforms foster optimism, capital inflows, and a boom in consumption. The consumption boom is usually financed by a sharp rise in bank credit, as banks borrow abroad excessively. This is especially likely to occur if, prior to the reforms, consumption lending had been more tightly rationed than investment lending, so that in response to a loosening of constraints, consumption spending rebounds to its unconstrained level. If domestic inflation adjusts down gradually to international levels, the pegging of the nominal exchange rate results in a cumulative real exchange rate appreciation and a deterioration of the current account. Financed by ongoing capital inflows from the rest of the world, the current account continues to widen to levels that, at some point, are perceived by the markets to be unsustainable. This perverse dynamic has made many countries vulnerable to speculative currency attacks and capital outflow reversals. The recent Mexican and Asian experiences provide examples of the problems of pegging the exchange rate for too long a period.

The essay by McKinnon and Pill (Chapter 11) develops a microeconomic model of overborrowing that arises from excessive risk taking by banks. This risk taking is exacerbated when banks intermediate capital inflows. In this model, bank lending serves a dual role for the nonbank private sector by providing resources for investment and by offering a signal about overall macroeconomic performance. However, (implicit or explicit) deposit insurance for banks, which protects them from the consequences of failure, leads them to lend excessively and monitor inadequately the macroeconomic risks affecting their borrowers' ability to repay. This distorts the signal to the private sector implicit in the volume of bank lending: rises in bank lending can be viewed as indicating a positive macroeconomic outcome and not excessive lending. Consequently, economic reform programs are likely to be characterized by overly optimistic expectations about the success of the reform that prompt capital inflows and excessive borrowing by the domestic private sector. Even when the extent of the moral hazard problem becomes apparent to private borrowers, the individual incentives they face may perversely encourage them to greater and more speculative borrowing, rather than to less borrowing. At the macroeconomic level, this results in growing financial fragility and macroeconomic instability that can lead ultimately to collapse.

The authors informally examine empirical evidence concerning the composition of credit expansion in Mexico, Indonesia, Korea, Malaysia, and Thailand. They find some symptoms of overborrowing in all countries, including large current account deficits financed by foreign borrowing and some bank fragility, particularly in Mexico and Indonesia. However, only in Mexico, and to a lesser extent, in Indonesia, is there evidence that borrowing has been overly concentrated in problem sectors, such as consumer credit, real estate, and construction. They also discuss the (ultimately unsuccessful) efforts by East Asian country policy makers to mitigate the problem of overborrowing by such regulatory polices as specific limits on commercial borrowing abroad and ceilings on domestic lending in areas such as consumer and real-estate credit. For example, Malaysia restricted consumer credit through limits on credit cards and credit for the purchase of automobiles. Thailand set limits on bank lending, particularly on loans for "non-productive activities," such as consumer and luxury real estate loans; it also reduced demand for foreign borrowing by instituting a 10 percent withholding tax on interest paid on foreign deposits. These results are consistent with other studies finding that domestic financial liberalization undertaken in countries without enhanced prudential supervision and regulation during the 1980s and 1990s was typically followed by a rapid expansion of domestic lending, often leading to financial sector difficulties (e.g., Sachs, Velasco, and Tornell, 1996b; Kaminsky and Reinhart, 1996). Nevertheless, East Asian countries did experience a Mexican-style financial crisis in 1997, a result McKinnon and Pill attribute to overinvestment in poor-quality projects rather than to overconsumption.

The essay contains a number of policy implications. It suggests that the strength and efficiency of financial institutions, including financial regulators, are important determinants of macroeconomic performance and of solutions to the overborrowing problem. It also implies that monetary authorities should seek to identify different phases of the overborrowing cycle by monitoring the composition of bank credit expansion, as well as its aggregate level. Another implication is that as long as capital inflows potentially exacerbate the market failure of the domestic banking system, limited capital controls may be an acceptable policy option. Alternatively, policy makers may adopt "negative" directed-credit programs, which would control excessive or speculative borrowing by limiting bank lending to problem sectors.

Kamin and Wood (Chapter 12) look closely at Mexico's experience with capital inflows, particularly the magnitude of their effect on domestic interest rates and aggregate demand. Mexico's macroeconomic performance over the period 1990–94 was characterized by rapid money growth, sharp (nominal and real) interest rate declines, rapid growth in bank lending, and a strong increase in private consumption, and ultimately, a financial crisis. While these developments are consistent with the purported effects of capital inflows, it is not clear if in fact they can be attributed solely to the inflows. These developments are also consistent with an exogenous expansion in domestic monetary policy.

The authors examine the impact of capital inflows on the supply of broad money (M2) by estimating the demand for M2 as well as a monetary reaction function that relates the domestic interest rate targeted by policy makers to inflation, output, and capital inflow levels. The essay carefully addresses simultaneity problems that commonly arise in this type of study. They find that both reserve changes and the capital account inflows lead to lower interest rates and increased money demand, but the capital account effect appears to affect interest rates primarily through its effect on reserve changes. Using simulation analysis, they find that capital inflows measurably reduced interest rates and raised (M2) money growth in the 1990s, but even without capital inflows, (real) money would have increased substantially. The authors argue that easing by Mexico's central bank would have independently led to the expansion of monetary aggregates, taking exception to those who attribute the monetary expansion solely to capital inflows.

The essay also examines the extent to which Mexican capital inflows may have been associated with greater consumption and/or investment rates. In addition, the authors examine whether capital inflows that enter in the form of foreign direct investment, which are less likely to be intermediated in the domestic banking system, may increase consumption less than portfolio investment. They find that capital inflows affect consumption positively, but the effect of the composition of these inflows is unclear. They find no effect of capital inflows on investment.

Lastly, the essay makes some cursory investigations concerning whether their results for Mexico apply to other nations in Latin America (including Argentina, Brazil, Chile, and Colombia) as well as in the Pacific Basin (Indonesia, Korea, Malaysia, the Philippines, and Thailand). In contrast to Mexico, the authors do not find any influence of capital inflows on interest rates in their cross-country sample. They also find that capital inflows have a greater impact on investment than on consumption, which contrasts with their results for Mexico.

1.6   Policy responses to capital inflows

Many emerging countries have been concerned with the effects of nominal exchange rate changes on their international competitiveness. Others have sought to combat inflation by using the exchange rate as a nominal anchor, and they have been reluctant to let it change – even appreciate – in response to capital inflows.

To the extent that capital inflows work to appreciate a currency's value, efforts by policy makers to maintain an exchange rate peg imply that the central bank must intervene by purchasing the foreign exchange brought in by the capital inflows. Such purchases increase the monetary base, generating inflationary pressure.[7] To the extent that capital inflows

---

[7] The extent of the inflationary pressure depends on the underlying cause of the capital inflows. If capital inflows primarily reflect an increase in the domestic demand for money, they will not have an inflationary impact. In contrast, if capital inflows reflect a fall in

are intermediated through the domestic banking system, increases in the monetary base may also lead to an expansion of bank deposits and corresponding expansion of bank loans. If bank supervision and regulation are not fully effective, the expansion of bank balance sheets associated with capital may worsen the fragility of the banking system.

How can authorities limit the impact of capital inflows on domestic monetary control and the financial system without changing the exchange rate? One way is by "sterilizing" the expansionary effects of foreign exchange intervention on the money supply by simultaneously contracting central bank credit. In developed financial markets, the contraction of domestic credit is typically accomplished through the open-market sale of treasury securities. In countries where financial markets are less developed, or ongoing budget surpluses preclude the issue of government bonds (e.g., Singapore), marketable treasury securities are often not available so other measures may be used, including increasing reserve requirements on bank deposits, curtailing borrowing from the central bank, and shifting government deposits from commercial banks to the central bank.

Sterilized intervention has been a common response by policy makers in many emerging-market countries to inflows of capital (Calvo, Leiderman, and Reinhart, 1994; Glick and Moreno, 1995; Folkerts-Landau and Ito, 1995). Mexico, for instance, sterilized inflows by selling government debt, including (peso-denominated) cetes and (peso-denominated, but dollar-indexed) tesobonos. In many countries (Chile, Colombia, Indonesia, Korea, and the Philippines) the central bank issued its own debt to conduct open-market operations. In some countries, such as Malaysia, open-market operations were initially conducted by selling public sector debt and then subsequently by selling central bank debt, as the central bank depleted its own holdings of government debt. Malaysia as well as Colombia also raised reserve requirements as an instrument of sterilization. Several countries (Indonesia, Malaysia, and Thailand) sterilized the effects of capital inflows by shifting deposits of the public sector or of pension funds from the banking system to the central bank. During 1991, the Mexican government also placed the proceeds of privatizations in the central bank to assist sterilization efforts.

Sterilization has several limitations, however. By limiting money growth, it tends to prop up domestic interest rates, which may encourage

<hr>

international interest rates or an increase in the domestic productivity of capital, the accumulation of foreign exchange reserves will lead, in the absence of sterilization, to an expansion of the monetary base that will tend to increase inflation.

more capital inflows. Moreover, by raising domestic interest rates, sterilization may serve merely to attract more capital inflows.[8] In addition, sterilization can have costly effects on the government's fiscal position. If capital inflows are attracted by high domestic returns, sterilization typically means that the monetary authorities are buying low-yielding foreign assets and selling high-yielding domestic assets. The interest differential can create a significant financing burden, often referred to as quasi-fiscal costs. (If the differential is soley attributable to a default risk premium on domestic assets, quasi-fiscal costs are zero.) Furthermore, if sterilization is achieved by increasing reserve requirements, the costs of commercial banking rise, thereby promoting disintermediation over time as new financial institutions and instruments arise to bypass controls. These costs of sterilization may be excessive if capital flows are very persistent.

The essay by Kletzer and Spiegel (Chapter 13) examines monetary and exchange rate management in a model that explicitly incorporates costs of sterilization. The authors develop a sticky-price model with imperfect asset substitutability in which a central bank engages in sterilization to lessen the influence of capital inflows on its policy targets. The quasi-fiscal costs of sterilization reflect the loss experienced by the central bank by holding foreign securities whose nominal yield is less than that paid on the domestic bonds issued to absorb the increase in domestic credit associated with capital inflows. The model demonstrates that if the sterilization process involves costs for the central bank, it will rationally choose to limit the extent of its sterilization activity.

The authors suggest that the true quasi-fiscal costs of sterilization to the central bank may not be as large as the deviation from interest rate parity. In particular, if the spread between the yield on domestic and foreign securities reflects a true default risk premium, then estimates of sterilization costs based on the deviation of interest rate parity will be biased upward by the degree of sovereign risk associated with the country. The authors therefore characterize their estimates of quasi-fiscal costs as "upper-bound" estimates. They generate these upper-bound estimates for six developing country nations that experienced large capital inflows – Korea, Singapore, Taiwan, Indonesia, Philippines, and Mexico. Their results indicate that even these upper-bound estimates of

---

[8] Even if sterilization is effective in limiting domestic monetary expansion, it may not insulate the economy from the effects of capital inflows, if capital inflows are triggered by an increase in domestic monetary demand that raises domestic interest rates, or if domestic interest-bearing assets are imperfect substitutes, and the inflows lead to a shift in composition of assets that is not offset by sterilization.

sterilization costs are usually quite small. However, they can become nontrivially large during brief periods of capital inflow surges.

The authors then conduct time-series and case studies to examine whether central bank behavior responded to these quasi-fiscal costs over the course of their sample. They estimate central bank reaction functions within a simultaneous equation framework that incorporates the feedback from the capital account response to domestic monetary policy. They find that although all of the countries aggressively sought to sterilize capital inflows, domestic monetary efforts were still offset to some extent by the capital inflows. Thus, sterilization was only partial. In addition, they find only limited evidence that the central banks of the nations in the sample responded to sterilization costs. In particular, while some measure of quasi-fiscal costs enters into the reaction function estimates for the Philippines, Taiwan, and Mexico, the authors find no evidence of a central bank response to quasi-fiscal costs for Korea, Indonesia, and Singapore.

When capital inflows are long lasting and sterilized intervention becomes too costly, a country may try other measures to limit the impact of capital inflows. One possibility is to adopt measures that make it more difficult or costly for foreigners to acquire domestic assets, such as ceilings on foreign borrowing by the domestic financial sector, prohibitions on the acquisition by foreigners of domestic securities, and taxes or reserve requirements on foreign deposits. Policy makers in many countries in East Asia, Eastern Europe, and Latin America have resorted to controls on capital inflows in addition to altering fiscal, monetary, and exchange rate policies in response to surges in capital inflows in the early 1990s. Are controls effective in reducing inflows, and, even if they are effective, are they desirable?

The case for the desirability of controls on capital inflows usually presumes high costs or constraints that limit the use of alternative policy responses to capital inflows, such as nominal exchange rate appreciation, sterilization, and fiscal restraint. Economic theory of the "second best" suggests that if there is an existing distortion in the real economic or financial system that causes borrowed resources to be misallocated and cannot be removed, then introducing an offsetting distortion may improve welfare. For example, if capital inflows finance speculative investments in real estate and the host country government typically bails out such large failed investments, then a ceiling or tax on capital inflows could be justified as second best, even though a preferable policy would be to eliminate bailouts and allow capital inflows. Another second-best case may arise when intertemporal relative prices are distorted in such a way as to encourage excessive borrowing, that is, when the real cost of foreign funds is perceived by private agents to be lower than the true value perceived by policy makers either because agents do not perceive government polices as credible or because they are affected by bubble or bandwagon effects. A second-best option is to impose capital controls. However, markets often find ways to circumvent capital controls, so their true effectiveness is an open question.

Reinhart and Smith (Chapter 14) examine the experiences of Brazil, Chile, Colombia, the Czech Republic, Malaysia, and Thailand through 1995 to draw tentative conclusions on the effectiveness of capital controls. Most capital control measures were temporary and targeted at short-term inflows. (This differs from a Tobin-type transactions tax, which is symmetrically applied to both outflows and inflows.) In theory, the introduction of such capital controls can be interpreted as a tax on domestic assets that allows the authorities to temporarily keep domestic interest rates above world levels. By (temporarily) raising the effective price of consuming today rather than in the future, controls (in theory) reduce current consumption, depreciate the real exchange rate, and reduce the current account deficit.

They then examine whether these policies were effective in reducing the volume of capital flows, influencing their composition, or achieving other macroeconomic goals, such as curbing a consumption boom, slowing monetary growth, and limiting pressures on the real exchange rate. They find evidence of a decline in the volume of capital inflows (in Chile, Malaysia, and the Czech Republic), a lengthening of the maturity composition of capital flows (in Chile, Colombia, and Malaysia), a slowing in reserve accumulation (in all countries except Brazil), and deceleration of monetary growth. There is little evidence of any real changes in consumption, the real exchange rate, or the current account following the imposition of controls.

They conclude in light of the recent experiences of countries that have imposed controls on capital inflows that these policies have been effective in the short run in either reducing the volume of inflows or affecting (rechanneling) their composition. The stance of monetary policy, in particular whether intervention is sterilized, during and after the introduction of the measures appears to have played a key role in influencing whether the outcome was "successful" or not. It is, of course, difficult to fully disentangle the effects of monetary policy and the controls themselves.

Most evidence indicates that controls or taxes can slow inflows in the short term, but that this effect dissipates as market participants find ways to evade the controls. Typically this requires host countries to restrict the opportunities for evasion by progressively widening the scope of the controls. For example, Chile broadened the coverage of its higher reserve requirements three times after it was introduced in June 1991. Moreover, in the long-run foreign investors may demand a compensating risk premium on the host country's debt and security obligations. In raising the cost of capital, they may distort capital allocation decisions, and impede the development of the domestic financial sector. These long-term costs must be weighed against any gains offered by controls.

Chile has a reputation in Latin America as a model economic reformer; it is sometimes referred to as the Asian "Tiger" of Latin America. After the 1982 debt crisis, Chile abandoned the fixed exchange rate regime in effect since 1979 and devalued 70 percent. Subsequently, a crawling peg regime with an exchange rate band was adopted, with the central parity of the peso devalued mechanically by the difference between domestic and foreign inflation. Following sound macroeconomic policies for over a decade, including maintaining a competitive exchange rate, raising domestic saving through tighter fiscal policy, and pension reform, as well as structural improvements, provided a good basis for Chile to respond to the challenge of the capital inflows of 1990s.

Cowan and De Gregorio (Chapter 15) review Chile's experience in managing capital inflows. Net capital flows changed from outflows in the mid to late 1980s to inflows of almost 10 percent of GDP in 1990. At the onset of the surge in inflows in the early 1990s, Chilean policy makers reacted by treating the inflows as temporary, resisting a nominal exchange rate appreciation, and mostly sterilizing the foreign exchange intervention. As the inflows persisted, sterilization efforts were reduced, and a combination of capital inflow restrictions and greater exchange rate flexibility was implemented. They attribute Chile's success not to any single instrument, but to its implementation of a comprehensive policy package.

As Cowan and De Gregorio describe, the capital flow restrictions took the form of reserve requirements applied to foreign currency liabilities for a one-year period, regardless of the maturity of the liability. By imposing a relatively higher cost on short-term inflows, this measure worked to tilt the composition of capital inflows toward longer maturities. While the capital controls only slowed the long-term pressures for appreciation, they permitted Chilean policy makers to maintain the domestic interest rate above international levels and to continue their efforts at reducing inflation.[9] At the same time, Chile allowed

---

[9] Soto and Valdés-Prieto (1996) provide an alternative view. They argue that Chile's capital controls were an ineffective tool of macroeconomic policy.

greater exchange rate flexibility through several discrete revaluations of the central parity rate as well as widening of the band. In 1995, a drift appreciation of 2 percent was incorporated into the purchasing power parity adjustment underlying the crawling peg.

In their empirical analysis, Cowan and De Gregorio examine how the changes in the parity rate and band width affected the volatility of the exchange rate and the credibility of Chile's crawling peg exchange rate regime. They find that greater variability in the central parity did not clearly lead to any increase in (nominal) exchange rate volatility. This confirms the results of target zone models that show that there is no monotonic relationship between the band width and variability of the exchange rate (e.g., Bertola and Cabellero, 1992), because, although variability within the band may rise as the band widens, expectations of realignment may decrease. In addition, they find that the variability of Chile's real exchange rate declined. They also use a drift adjustment method to contrast measures of expected realignments and hence of the credibility of the exchange rate regime. They find evidence that credibility diminished as the peso moved closer to the edges of the band.

Malaysia's experience provides a similar example of the use of multiple instruments employed in response to a massive volume of capital inflows. Capital inflows rose steadily from 3 percent of GDP in 1989 to over 20 percent in 1993. Well over half the net capital inflows were direct investment initially; later, other forms of capital (including foreign borrowing through the banking sector) became increasingly important.

Malaysia initially responded to capital inflows by intervening heavily in foreign exchange markets and limiting exchange rate fluctuations, which led to large increases in official reserve assets (amounting to over 11 percent of GDP in 1992). It also sterilized this intervention by reducing domestic credit in order to curb the upward pressure on monetary aggregates. The relative development of financial markets influenced the way that sterilization policies were implemented. Because open-market operations were limited by the absence of marketable government securities in the portfolios of the monetary authorities, transfers of government and Employee Provident Fund deposits to the central bank were arranged to sterilize the monetary effects of large net capital inflows. (The Employee Provident Fund, the government retirement program, is Malaysia's largest saver and holds 20 percent of total domestic financial assets.) Malaysia initially limited exchange rate fluctuations in spite of massive capital inflows. The value of the Malaysian ringgit was comparatively stable between 1989 and 1991, but as the capital flows continued, greater variability was allowed, and the ringgit appreciated 7 percent against the dollar in 1992.[10]

Continued surges in capital inflows prompted Malaysia's central bank to discourage such inflows in early 1994 by temporarily limiting banks' holdings of foreign funds, raising the cost of holding foreign deposits, imposing ceilings on the net external liabilities of domestic banks, and prohibiting the sale of short-term financial instruments to foreigners. These capital controls were later removed.

The withdrawal of capital from emerging-market economies following the Mexican devaluation and float in December 1994 had little lasting effect on Malaysia at the time. However, the depreciation of the baht during the summer of 1997 did put significant downward pressure on the ringgit. Policy makers responded in part by implementing controls on capital outflows and on stock market transactions, including restricting equity short sales, but these measures did little to curb foreign currency speculation and the ringgit depreciated further.

The Chilean and Malaysian experiences suggest that sound fundamentals were very important in explaining the ability of these countries to deal with capital inflows through the mid-1990s. Moreover, the willingness to allow greater exchange rate flexibility also appears to have been key. Thus, the policy response to large and volatile capital flows may require the use of multiple instruments, involving the coordination of monetary, fiscal, and exchange rate policies as well as policies that seek to discourage capital inflows or change their composition. At the onset of the surge of inflows, these countries reacted by treating the inflows as temporary, resisting a nominal exchange rate appreciation, and sterilizing foreign exchange intervention. As the inflows persisted, sterilization was reduced, and the domestic currency was allowed to appreciate. Measures to curb inflows were also implemented, though these controls were permanent in Chile's case and temporary in Malaysia's case.

A key element in the appropriate policy response is distinguishing between short-term and longer-term capital inflow episodes. For temporary inflows, sterilization may be feasible and desirable. For more permanent capital inflows having a longer-lasting impact on the real exchange rate, other policies may be more appropriate. For example, capital inflows associated with long-lasting increases in domestic productivity naturally lead to a trend appreciation in the real exchange rate, as has been the case for Japan for much of the post–World War II period. In

---

[10] Among other Asian countries, the Philippines also allowed greater variability of the exchange rate after 1992; Indonesia widened its intervention band twice in 1994.

this case, to the extent that nontradable goods represent a large share of government expenditures, cutting government spending may reduce the relative price of nontradables, effectively lessening the appreciation of the real exchange rate. However, the effectiveness of fiscal policy may be lessened by its short-run inflexibility. In the absence of any policy measures offsetting aggregate demand pressures on the real exchange rate, policy makers have no other option than to allow the real exchange rate to appreciate, either by domestic price inflation or nominal currency appreciation. To the extent that policy makers prefer limiting domestic price inflation, the requisite real appreciation requires letting the nominal exchange rate appreciate. The 1997 "surprise" reversal of international capital flows to emerging markets, particularly in Asia, highlights that further research on these issues is clearly warranted.

References

Bercuson, Kenneth, and Linda Koenig (1993). "The Recent Surge in Capital Inflows to Asia: Cause and Macroeconomic Effects," SEACEN Occasional Paper No. 15. Kuala Lumpur: Southeast Asian Central Banks.

Bertola, G., and R. Caballero (1992). "Target Zones and Realignments," *American Economic Review* 3: 520–36.

Bordo, Michael, and Anna Schwartz (1996). "Why Clashes between Internal and External Stability Goals End in Currency Crises, 1797–1994," *Open Economies Review* 7 (suppl. 1): 437–68.

Calvo, Guillermo, and Enrique Mendoza (1996). "Mexico's Balance-of-Payments Crisis: A Chronicle of a Death Foretold," *Journal of International Economics* 41 (November): 235–64.

Calvo, Guillermo, Leonardo Leiderman, and Carmen Reinhart (1993). "Capital Inflows and Real Exchange Rate Appreciation in Latin America: The Role of External Factors," *IMF Staff Papers* 40 (1): 108–51.

(1994). "The Capital Inflows Problem: Concepts and Issues," *Contemporary Economic Policy* 12 (July): 54–66.

(1996). "Inflows of Capital to Developing Countries in the 1990s: Causes and Effects," *Journal of Economic Perspectives* 10 (2): 123–39.

Chuhan, Punam, Stijn Claessens, and Nlandu Mamingi (1995). "Equity and Bond Flows to Latin America and Asia: The Role of Global and Country Factors," World Bank Policy Research Working Paper No. 1160. Washington, D.C.

Claessens, Stijn, Michael Dooley, and Andrew Warner (1995). "Portfolio Capital Flows: Hot or Cold?" *World Bank Economic Review* 9 (1): 153–74.

Corbo, Vittorio, and Leonardo Hernández (1996). "Macroeconomic Adjustment to Capital Inflows: Lessons from Recent Latin American and East Asian Experience," *World Bank Research Observer* 11 (February): 61–85.

Dornbush, Rudiger, and Alejandro Werner (1994). "Mexico: Stabilization, Reform, and No Growth," *Brookings Papers on Economic Activity*, no. 1: 253–97.

Eichengreen, Barry, Andrew Rose, and Charles Wyplosz (1995). "Exchange Market Mayhem: The Antecedents and Aftermath of Speculative Attacks," *Economic Policy* 21 (October): 249–312.

Fernández-Arias, Eduardo (1996). "The New Wave of Capital Inflows: Push or Pull?" *Journal of Development Economics* 48 (March): 389–418.

Fernández-Arias, Eduardo, and Peter J. Montiel (1996). "The Surge in Capital Inflows to Developing Countries: An Analytical Overview," *World Bank Economic Review* 10 (March): 51–77.

Folkerts-Landau, David, and Takatoshi Ito (1995). *International Capital Markets: Developments, Prospects, and Policy Issues.* Washington, D.C.: International Monetary Fund.

Frankel, Jeffrey, and Chudozie Okongwu (1996). "Liberalized Portfolio Capital Inflows in Emerging Markets: Sterilization, Expectations, and the Incompleteness of Interest Rate Convergence," *International Journal of Finance and Economics* 1 (January): 1–24.

Garber, Peter, and Lars Svensson (1995). "The Operation and Collapse of Fixed Exchange Rates." In Gene Grossman and Kenneth Rogoff, eds., *Handbook of International Economics*, vol. 3, pp. 1865–1911. Amsterdam: Elsevier.

Glick, Reuven, and Ramon Moreno (1995). "Capital Flows and Monetary Policy in East Asia." In *Monetary and Exchange Rate Management with International Capital Mobility: Experiences of Countries and Regions along the Pacific Rim*, Hong Kong Monetary Authority, pp. 14–48. Previously issued as Center for Pacific Basin Monetary and Economic Studies Working Paper No. PB94-08. Federal Reserve Bank of San Francisco.

Hernandez, Leonardo, and Heinz Rudolph (1995). "Sustainability of Private Capital Flows to Developing Countries: Is a Generalized Reversal Likely?" World Bank Policy Research Working Paper No. 1518. Washington, D.C.

Kaminsky, Graciela, and Carmen Reinhart (1996). "The Twin Crises: The Causes of Banking and the Balance of Payments Problems," International Finance Discussion Paper No. 544. Washington, D.C.: Board of Governors of the Federal Reserve System.

Krugman, Paul (1979). "A Model of Balance-of-Payments Crises," *Journal of Money, Credit, and Banking* 11: 311–25.

Obstfeld, Maurice (1986). "Rational and Self-fulfilling Balance of Payments Crises," *American Economic Review* 76: 72–81.

Sachs, Jeffrey, Aaron Tornell, and Andrés Velasco (1996a). "The Collapse of the Mexican Peso: What Have We Learned?" *Economic Policy* 22: 13–56.

(1996b). "Financial Crises in Emerging Markets: The Lessons from 1995," *Brookings Papers on Economic Activity*, no. 1: 147–215.

(1996c). "The Mexican Peso Crisis: Sudden Death or Death Foretold?" *Journal of International Economics* 41 (November): 265–83.

Schadler, Susan, Maria Carkovic, Adam Bennett, and Robert Kahn (1993). "Recent Experiences with Surges in Capital Inflows," IMF Occasional Paper No. 108. Washington, D.C.

Soto, M., and S. Valdés-Prieto (1996). "New Selective Capital Controls in Chile: Are They Effective?" Paper presented at the Conference on Capital Flows, Universidad Católica de Chile, July 30–31, Santiago.

PART I
DETERMINANTS OF CAPITAL FLOWS AND EXCHANGE RATES

CHAPTER 2

U.S. portfolio investment in Asian capital markets

Henning Bohn and Linda L. Tesar

2.1   Introduction

During the 1990s, U.S. purchases of Asian securities increased more than tenfold. By the end of 1995, U.S. investment in Asian equity and bond markets accounted for over 20 percent of the U.S. foreign portfolio. In this chapter we examine the factors that drive U.S. portfolio investment in foreign markets, focusing on flows to Asian equity markets.

We begin in section 2.2 by presenting some basic facts about the direction and volume of U.S. portfolio investment in foreign markets over the 1981–95 period. Although U.S. equity investment in Asia has increased dramatically over time, we find that there is considerable cross-country variation in the timing of U.S. investment and the volume of flows. Our data suggest that, relative to market shares, U.S. investors tend to underweight Japanese equity in their total foreign portfolio, and overweight Hong Kong equity. Lower-bound estimates of U.S. bond holdings indicate that U.S. investors hold only a small fraction of their international bond portfolio in Asian markets.

In section 2.3 we use our monthly transactions data to test for the factors driving U.S. equity investment in foreign markets. Mean–variance portfolio analysis suggests that investors will increase their portfolio holdings, and therefore make equity purchases, in markets where returns are expected to be high. Bilateral country regressions support this hypothesis in the two largest Asian markets, Japan and Hong Kong. When the remaining countries are combined in a panel, we find further support for the "return-chasing" hypothesis in the smaller Asian markets. We also find that lagged net purchases of equity in a particular market are a significant determinant of current net purchases, indicating that there is some lagged adjustment in portfolio allocations over time that is not explained by the simple expected-returns model.

43

Our results shed new light on the debate over whether the increase in U.S. investment in foreign equity markets has largely been due to global "push" factors, such as low U.S. interest rates, or local "pull" factors, such as high local returns. We find that global variables are not a significant determinant of U.S. equity investment after controlling for the information content of these factors for forecasting excess returns. We also find that there is a significant time trend in U.S. net purchases over time, reflecting the gradual erosion of home bias in the U.S. investment portfolio. We find little evidence of an October 1987 effect or a December 1994 peso crisis effect on U.S. purchases of foreign equity. This suggests that a "contagion" of shocks across equity markets is not apparent in U.S. transactions data except to the extent that such shocks affect local stock returns (see, e.g., Frankel and Schmukler, Chapter 8, and Wolf, Chapter 9, in this volume).

2.2   U.S. net purchases and holdings of Asian securities

In this section we provide some basic statistics describing U.S. transactions in Asian capital markets and the accumulation of U.S. holdings of Asian securities over the 1981–95 period. Our basic data source is monthly U.S. Treasury data on securities transactions between U.S. and foreign residents.[1] The data distinguish between stocks and bonds and between foreign and U.S. securities. Following Bohn and Tesar (1996a, 1996b), we assume that all transactions between U.S. residents and residents of a foreign country involve securities issued in that country. Given current trading practices, this assumption seems reasonable for equity transactions but it may be less plausible for bond transactions. Foreign equities are still largely traded in their respective home markets (perhaps with some qualifications in the cases of London and Hong Kong). In contrast, much of the volume of international bond trading takes place in the Euromarkets, mainly in London, which make the foregoing identifying assumption more problematic. Despite these problems we maintain that the transactions data – with full disclosure of their limitations – provide information about U.S. investment in foreign markets that is unobtainable from other sources.

2.2.1   U.S. holdings of foreign equity

Table 2.1 shows average monthly net purchases in twelve Asian markets from 1986 to 1995. The countries are Japan, Hong Kong, Singapore,

---

[1] Quarterly figures are published in the U.S. Treasury *Quarterly Bulletin*. We obtained the unpublished monthly data from the U.S. Treasury Department. For a detailed description of the data, see Tesar and Werner (1994).

Table 2.1. *U.S. net purchases in foreign equity markets (in millions of dollars)*

Country	1986	1987	1988	1989	1990	1991	1992	1993	1994	1995
Japan	-116.5	-540.8	62.3	81.9	51.5	1,160.2	370.3	516.6	1,226.2	1,622.6
Hong Kong	32.3	-57.8	26.4	-21.7	46.7	89.0	236.0	532.4	200.3	181.2
Singapore	-2.9	-2.7	-2.5	33.8	43.8	-13.8	42.3	112.7	0.8	71.2
Malaysia	0.6	7.7	1.9	2.3	11.3	-2.2	19.6	91.9	2.2	-12.1
India	0.2	0.0	0.0	0.1	-0.1	0.2	0.0	8.9	35.2	28.6
Indonesia	-0.2	0.0	0.0	-0.2	2.2	7.6	14.6	25.2	80.6	57.2
Korea	1.2	-0.8	-2.6	3.2	-2.5	0.0	38.8	104.4	140.0	136.4
Pakistan	0.0	0.0	0.0	0.0	0.0	-0.1	1.0	4.2	2.1	0.8
Philippines	-1.3	-2.5	2.0	0.8	1.8	2.2	18.2	10.2	38.3	40.9
Thailand	1.2	2.5	11.1	-0.2	3.5	7.5	10.1	4.0	16.0	-0.8
Taiwan	0.8	-1.8	-1.6	-1.0	-0.2	3.1	1.2	6.7	-9.2	12.9
China	9.2	-0.2	0.2	0.0	0.1	0.0	-0.3	8.9	49.0	13.3
Asia total	-75.2	-596.4	97.2	99.1	157.9	1,253.8	751.8	1,426.1	1,781.3	2,152.2
Excluding Japan	41.2	-55.7	34.9	17.2	106.4	93.5	381.5	909.5	555.2	529.7
Excluding Japan & Hong Kong	8.9	2.2	8.5	38.8	59.8	4.5	145.5	377.1	354.8	348.5
Latin total	8.8	31.5	-9.8	4.8	188.0	221.8	416.3	995.5	337.8	156.8
Mexico	0.3	1.6	0.8	0.8	88.5	173.2	230.4	427.9	100.4	13.2
Europe total	126.8	290.8	146.9	853.9	366.4	1,225.2	1,505.4	2,216.8	1,453.1	1,789.2
Foreign total	154.3	-90.1	163.2	1,088.5	768.4	2,664.0	2,688.2	5,224.2	4,005.9	4,226.7

Notes: Net purchases are gross purchases over the month less gross sales. The reported figures are monthly net purchases averaged over the year.
Source: U.S. Treasury Department, *Quarterly Bulletin* and unpublished data.

Table 2.2. *Summary of U.S. equity positions in Asia, December 1995 (in percent)*

Country	World market (including U.S.)		Foreign markets (excluding U.S.)		U.S. holding as share of local mkt. cap. (5)
	Holdings share (1)	Mkt. cap. share (2)	Holdings share (3)	Mkt. cap. share (4)	
Japan	1.38	25.17	17.02	41.20	2.11
Hong Kong	0.51	1.90	6.32	3.10	10.40
Singapore	0.11	0.98	1.35	1.61	4.29
Malaysia	0.05	1.02	0.56	1.66	1.72
India	0.01	0.42	0.15	0.69	1.12
Indonesia	0.05	0.27	0.61	0.45	6.94
Korea	0.11	0.90	1.34	1.47	4.66
Pakistan	0.00	0.05	0.02	0.08	1.22
Philippines	0.07	0.23	0.81	0.38	10.95
Thailand	0.03	0.69	0.34	1.13	1.56
Taiwan	0.01	0.82	0.07	1.34	0.26
China	0.04		0.43		

	(1)	(2)	(3)	(4)	(5)
Asia total	2.36	31.62	29.02	51.76	2.87
Excluding Japan	0.98	6.45	12.00	10.56	5.81
Excluding Japan & Hong Kong	0.46	4.56	5.68	7.46	3.90
Latin total	0.76	1.77	9.35	2.90	16.50
Mexico	0.22	0.47	2.72	0.77	17.95
Europe total	4.12	26.37	50.64	43.17	6.00
Foreign total	8.13	61.09	100.00	100.00	5.11
U.S. total	91.87	38.91			90.74

Source: Figures in columns (1), (3), and (5) are based on authors' calculations of U.S. holdings of foreign equity. Market capitalization (mkt. cap.) data are from the *Financial Times* and the International Finance Corporation.

Malaysia, India, Indonesia, Korea, Pakistan, Philippines, Thailand, Taiwan, and China. We define net purchases as gross purchases over the month less gross sales. Here and in the following tables we also display results for Latin America and Europe for comparison. Three observations emerge from Table 2.1. First, the volume of U.S. net purchases dramatically increased during the 1990s in most Asian countries and in Mexico. By the end of the sample, net purchases of Asian stock exceeded net purchases in Europe. Second, the surge in net purchases did not occur simultaneously in all markets. Third, while U.S. investors were often net sellers of foreign equity at the beginning of the sample, they were overwhelmingly net purchasers by the end of the sample. This reversal in net purchases is consistent with the general trend toward international diversification of investment portfolios in the 1990s.

We combine the net purchases data with local stock returns to estimate holding series using the perpetual inventory method. (Details of our computations are provided in the appendix.) Estimated end-of-year positions are shown in Table 2.2. Column 1 of Table 2.2 shows U.S. holdings in each market at end-1995 as a share of the total U.S. portfolio. The bulk of the portfolio is still held in U.S. stock, accounting for nearly 92 percent of the total portfolio. Of the remaining 8 percent, roughly 4 percent is allocated to Europe, 2.4 percent to Asia, less than 1 percent to Latin America, and most of the balance (not shown) to Canada. The second column provides market capitalizations in each country as a share of global equity market capitalization. While U.S. investors are "under" invested in all foreign markets relative to market weights, the underweighting is especially notable in Asian markets. Asian markets account for almost a third of the global total, while the U.S. portfolio weight in Asia is under 3 percent.

The third and fourth columns illustrate the relationship between U.S. holdings as a fraction of the total foreign portfolio, and market weights as a fraction of the global total excluding the United States. Again, the figures reveal the relative underweighting of holdings in Asian markets. However, the low Asian portfolio weight is largely due to the low holdings of Japanese equity at end-1995. U.S. holdings of Asian equity excluding Japan account for 12 percent of the U.S. foreign portfolio while the region's share of foreign market capitalization is 10.6 percent. By this standard, U.S. investors also "overweight" Latin American equity.

The last column shows U.S. holdings in each market as a fraction of local market capitalization. U.S. investors' holdings account for over 10 percent of the equity market value in Hong Kong and Philippines, and for 18 percent in Mexico. Thus, although the magnitude of foreign equity investment may appear to be "small" from the perspective of the U.S.

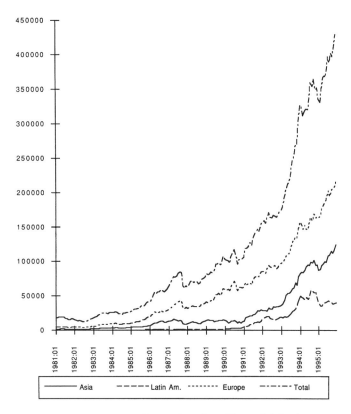

Figure 2.1. U.S. foreign equity holdings (in millions of dollars).

market, U.S. investors are significant shareholders in many foreign equity markets. The substantial variation in holdings across countries suggests that U.S. investors are not targeting market weights in allocating
their portfolio across foreign markets, contradicting the basic prediction
of the capital asset pricing model (see Bohn and Tesar, 1996b).

To get some sense of the evolution of the U.S. portfolio over time,
Figure 2.1 shows U.S. equity holdings in Asia, Europe, and Latin
America. Holdings in Europe have grown steadily since 1985 to approxi-
mately $220 billion at the end of 1995. The increase in U.S. holdings in
Asia began somewhat later, rising steadily since 1991. Holdings of Latin
American equity also picked up in 1991 but the expansion has been less
steady, primarily due to the volatility of Mexican equity returns.

Figure 2.2 shows the decomposition of the total foreign portfolio held
by U.S. investors in 1985, 1990, and 1995. Throughout the entire sample,

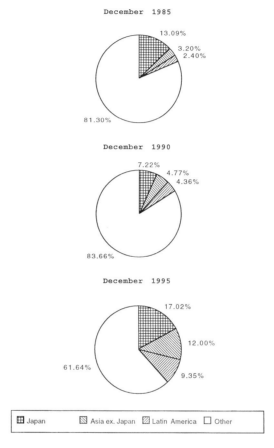

Figure 2.2. Composition of U.S. foreign equity holdings.

the majority of the portfolio is held in "other" equity markets, mostly Europe and Canada, though this share has declined from over 80 percent to 62 percent of the foreign portfolio. Japan's portfolio share has changed dramatically over the decade starting at 13 percent in 1985, dropping to 7.2 percent in 1990, and then increasing again to 17 percent by the end of the sample. The fraction of the portfolio allocated to Latin American and Asian markets excluding Japan has increased steadily over time.

Figure 2.3 shows the composition of the U.S. portfolio in Asia. The fraction of the portfolio allocated to Japan has declined steadily since 1981 from virtually 100 percent of the Asian portfolio to about 60 percent. This has been offset by proportionate increases in holdings in Hong Kong and the smaller Asian markets. The evolution of portfolio holdings

Figure 2.3. Composition of U.S. equity holdings in Asia (in percent of total U.S. equity holdings in Asia).

in four of the smaller markets (Singapore, Malaysia, Korea, and Indonesia) is shown in Figure 2.4. While U.S. holdings have increased dramatically in all four markets, there is considerable heterogeneity across the sample. Equity investment in Singapore, while generally high relative to the other three countries, expanded most dramatically during 1989 and 1990. In contrast, U.S. holdings in Korea reached a midsample peak in 1989, declined until 1992, and then increased through the end of the sample. The significant differences in the time series of holdings across countries are already an indication that local rather than global factors are important in explaining U.S. portfolio allocations over time.

2.2.2 Identifying market openings

In order to conduct the statistical analysis in section 2.3, we need to identify the period when foreign markets were open to U.S. investors.

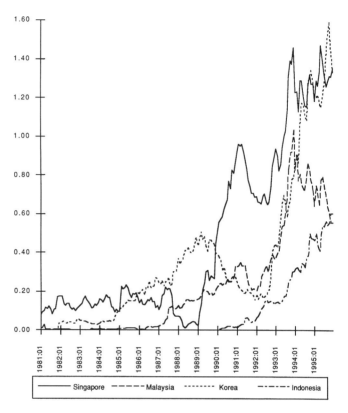

Figure 2.4. U.S. equity holdings in selected Asian countries (in percent of total U.S. foreign equity holdings).

One method of identifying market openings is to use information from official sources on capital market and trade restrictions. While this is the standard method used in the literature (see, e.g., Bekaert, 1995, and Buckberg, 1995), it has the disadvantage of assuming that all market restrictions are binding. As an alternative, our data set provides us with information on trading volume that may be more indicative of the actual restrictions faced by U.S. investors in each market. Therefore, we combine our trading data with regulatory information to choose market opening dates.

Table 2.3 lists each of the markets in our sample, a starting date for each country based on a threshold level of transactions, a starting date based on regulatory information, and our final choice of starting date for our statistical analysis. A country surpasses the transaction threshold if, after that date, there is at least one transaction of $1 million or more in

Table 2.3. *Market opening dates*

| Country | Starting dates based on | | |
	Threshold^a	Regulation	Start of base sample
Japan	1981:01	1981:01	1981:01
Hong Kong	1981:01	1981:01	1981:01
Singapore	1981:01	1981:01	1981:01
Malaysia	1986:05	1981:01	1987:01
India	1993:03	1992:11	1993:01
Indonesia	1989:08	1989:03	1990:01
Korea	1986:04	1992:01	1986:01
Pakistan	1992:01	1991:06	1992:01
Philippines	1986:02	1986:01	1986:01
Thailand	1986:06	1986:01	1986:01
Taiwan	1986:09	1987:01	1987:01
China	1991:11	1992:01	1992:01
Mexico	1981:01	1989:05	1981:01

^{a} Threshold = after this date there is at least one transaction of $1 million every quarter. Dates are given as year:month.

each quarter. In Japan, Hong Kong, and Singapore both criteria are satisfied for the entire sample period. In India, Indonesia, Pakistan, Philippines, Thailand, Taiwan, and China the two measures of openness either correspond exactly or are less than six months apart. When there is a slight discrepancy, we choose the beginning of the next calendar year after which both measures are satisfied. In Malaysia, we are unaware of significant capital controls after 1981. However, our transactions data suggest that U.S. investors did not actively trade in Malaysia until mid-1986. Therefore we select the beginning of 1987 as the opening date. In Korea and Mexico, the official opening dates are substantially later than the dates at which U.S. investors are active traders in the local market. Since the regulations apparently permitted foreign investors to transact, even if only in a limited way, we choose the threshold date as the beginning of the sample.[2]

[2] As a cross-check, we also examined average annual transactions (purchases plus sales) in each market. The dates at which there is a substantial burst in average transactions (in some cases a tenfold increase) coincides in most cases with our choice of starting dates. In the statistical analysis in this chapter we find that the results are not generally sensitive to the choice of starting date. In the few instances where the sample period matters, we note the differences in the text.

Table 2.4. *U.S. net purchases in foreign bond markets (in millions of dollars)*

Country	1986	1987	1988	1989	1990	1991	1992	1993	1994	1995
Japan	−504.6	74.2	−61.9	−229.7	198.8	−164.9	−3.9	−234.8	226.1	441.8
Hong Kong	−308.4	−180.9	−66.7	−63.2	−28.7	−344.2	−77.8	−157.6	−179.7	−50.7
Singapore	−52.8	−65.2	32.4	−4.8	−49.8	−36.2	43.5	5.8	−102.0	−72.5
Malaysia	−5.8	−17.2	3.0	−4.2	25.1	−11.2	−39.9	34.4	45.2	164.6
India	−4.8	−4.1	0.9	0.7	1.0	0.8	−0.6	1.2	−0.2	7.6
Indonesia	0.8	2.4	2.0	0.0	0.2	0.3	0.8	30.7	53.8	6.1
Korea	−0.1	−10.2	−62.8	−20.0	18.4	60.6	124.4	151.7	38.4	19.1
Pakistan	−0.1	0.0	0.0	0.0	0.1	0.1	2.1	−0.1	7.4	0.1
Philippines	−1.6	−8.6	−15.9	−15.4	−0.8	−3.2	−17.0	−4.8	3.0	31.5
Thailand	−1.6	−4.2	−9.7	0.4	−0.8	−7.3	25.8	−1.8	−14.2	26.8
Taiwan	−4.8	−11.2	−2.2	−3.2	−42.1	−194.6	−133.7	−206.5	−30.2	−49.8
China	14.9	11.8	−10.2	8.3	−14.1	−36.0	−33.7	18.3	−17.2	22.9

Asia total	−868.8	−213.3	−190.9	−330.9	107.4	−735.9	−109.9	−363.4	30.5	547.5
Excluding Japan	−364.2	−287.6	−129.0	−101.2	−91.4	−571.0	−106.0	−128.7	−195.6	105.7
Excluding Japan & Hong Kong	−55.8	−106.7	−62.3	−38.1	−62.8	−226.8	−28.2	28.9	−15.9	156.3
Latin total	−302.6	−102.5	−127.8	−136.8	549.8	−285.1	−54.7	−362.2	1,190.1	432.4
Mexico	−18.9	−19.8	7.6	−1.4	561.1	42.2	188.7	525.9	203.0	38.0
Europe total	1,374.9	717.0	506.9	618.6	325.5	1,645.9	1,107.1	6,189.2	−1,160.1	2,203.5
United Kingdom	1,139.1	766.1	514.7	718.8	40.2	1,332.0	1,403.8	4,786.2	−1,518.1	1,582.0
Canada	−16.8	143.0	350.8	205.1	614.2	614.9	603.1	878.6	419.0	674.9
Foreign total	307.2	662.3	619.4	457.4	1,829.1	1,235.8	1,300.4	6,698.1	768.7	3,910.7

Notes: Net purchases are gross purchases over the month less gross sales. The reported figures are monthly net purchases averaged over the year.

Source: U.S. Treasury Department, *Quarterly Bulletin* and unpublished data.

2.2.3   *U.S. holdings of foreign bonds*

As noted earlier, U.S. transactions data in foreign bond markets are more difficult to interpret than the data on equity transactions because much of the international bond trading takes place in Euromarkets. The problem becomes apparent in Table 2.4, which shows average monthly net bond purchases reported by the U.S. Treasury. In most years, reported net purchases of bonds in Europe and Canada exceed total foreign bond purchases, and coincide with large net *sales* of bonds in Asia. Taken literally the data would suggest that, starting from a realistic investment position in bonds at the beginning of the sample, U.S. investors took a substantial short position in Asian bond markets throughout most of the 1980s and 1990s. In our view, a more logical conclusion is that the reported net purchases of bonds *in* Asia do not represent the total purchases of *Asian* bonds.

Nonetheless, even the incomplete data show some interesting patterns that are worth reporting. Most notably, reported net bond purchases from most Asian countries reveal a recent turnaround from negative to positive values. If one assumes that prior holdings (adjusted for Euromarket purchases) were nonnegative, this implies that U.S. holdings of Asian bonds are now significantly positive.

We construct a simple lower-bound estimate of bond holdings, taking into account the indirect purchase of Asian and Latin American bonds on Euromarkets. (See the data appendix for a complete discussion of the computation of these estimates.) Figure 2.5 shows the estimated time-path of bond holdings since 1981. Latin American holdings show a jump in March 1990 associated with Mexican debt restructuring, and further rapid growth in 1993. The U.S. bond position in Asia quadrupled between mid-1992 and end-1995. Figure 2.6 illustrates the composition of the U.S. foreign portfolio in bonds at end-1995. Even after adjusting the figures for potential Euromarket purchases, U.S. bond holdings in the "other" markets, largely Europe and Canada, account for 80 percent of the portfolio. The remaining 20 percent is split between Latin America (13 percent), Japan (3 percent), and the smaller Asian markets (4 percent). Interestingly, U.S. bond holdings are tilted toward Latin American markets relative to the smaller Asian markets, whereas the reverse is true for equity holdings.

2.3   Statistical analysis of equity trading

We next use our data on U.S. transactions to identify the factors affecting U.S. portfolio investment in Asian markets. In particular, we test

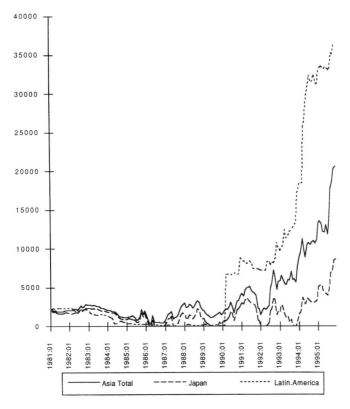

Figure 2.5. U.S. foreign bond holdings, lower-bound estimates (in millions of dollars).

whether observed U.S. net purchases in Asian markets are consistent with standard portfolio theory or whether additional factors, such as large swings in U.S. interest rates, play a significant role. Given the problems inherent in the bond data, our statistical analysis will focus on equity data.

To organize our analysis, we begin with the definition of net purchases in market k (NP_{kt}):

$$NP_{kt} = x_{kt}W_t - \left(1 + g_{kt}\right)\left(x_{kt}W_{t-1}\right) \tag{1}$$

where investment in market k at time t is the portfolio weight on market k, x_{kt}, multiplied by total wealth W_t. Net purchases reflect the change in the amount invested in market k taking into account capital gains (g_{kt}).

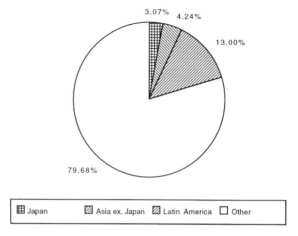

Figure 2.6. Composition of U.S. foreign bond holdings, December 1995.

Given the fact that wealth at time t is a function of the return on the total portfolio between $t - 1$ and t less consumption at t (i.e., $W_t = (1 + r_t^P)W_{t-1} - c_{t-1}$) net purchases can be approximated by:

$$NP_{kt} = \left(x_{kt} - x_{kt-1}\right)W_{t-1} + \left(d_t^P + g_t^P - g_{kt} - \chi_t\right)x_{kt-1}W_{t-1} \tag{2}$$

where d_t^P and g_t^P are dividends and capital gains on the investor's total portfolio and χ_t is consumption as a share of wealth. Equation (2) suggests that investors have two motivations for making net purchases. The first term is a "portfolio adjustment" term: investors will make net purchases in market k if they have revised the desired portfolio weight of market k. The second term we label the "portfolio rebalancing" effect, which reflects the investor's desire to spread his wealth across all securities and maintain fixed portfolio weights. In previous research (Bohn and Tesar, 1996a, 1996b) we test which of these effects best explains U.S. net purchases in the largest equity markets. We resoundingly reject the portfolio rebalancing motive as an important factor driving equity investment flows.[3] Therefore, in this chapter our empirical analysis will focus on the portfolio adjustment effect.

Standard portfolio theory provides a direct link between desired portfolio weights and risk and return (Cox, Ingersall, and Ross, 1985). Inves-

---

[3] The steady erosion of home bias in the U.S. investment portfolio itself contradicts the rebalancing hypothesis as a reasonable explanation of U.S. portfolio choice.

tors who trade off portfolio risk and return choose a vector of portfolio weights, $\bar{x}_t$, according to:

$$\bar{x}_t = \alpha \Sigma^{-1} \bar{\mu}_t + \xi_t \tag{3}$$

where α is the investor's coefficient of risk aversion, Σ is the covariance matrix of asset returns, and $\bar{\mu}_t$ is the vector of expected excess returns (returns in U.S. dollars less the U.S. safe interest rate). The last term, ξ_t, reflects hedge terms that could affect the optimal portfolio (see Bohn and Tesar, 1996b).

Substituting the solution for portfolio weights into (2) and dividing through by wealth yields our model of net purchases:

$$NPW_{kt} = e_k \left(\Sigma \right)^{-1} \left(\bar{\mu}_t - \bar{\mu}_{t-1} \right) \alpha + \varepsilon_{kt} \tag{4}$$

where NPW_{kt} is defined as net purchases scaled by lagged wealth (NP_{kt}/W_{t-1}), e_k is an indicator vector selecting market k, and the error term ε_{kt} captures all other determinants of net purchases, including the portfolio rebalancing effect. Note that because net purchases depend on the change in portfolio weights, any time-invariant hedge factor differences out and does not appear in equation (4). The effect of time variation in the hedge factor is included in the error term.

For an exact test of equation (4), one would need estimates of the time-varying components of the entire vector of stock returns. To simplify, we follow Bohn and Tesar (1996a) and focus on the relation between net purchases in each country and variations in expected excess returns in that country. That is, we estimate the regression equation

$$NPW_{kt} = \beta_0 + \beta_1 \mu_{kt} + \varepsilon_{kt} \tag{5}$$

where β_1 measures the marginal impact of variations in expected returns on net purchases. All other determinants of net purchases are subsumed in the error term.

In order to implement an empirical test of equation (5) we further need to form a forecast of excess returns. One method of obtaining forecasts of excess returns is to regress current excess returns, R_{kt}, on a vector of prediction variables, $\bar{q}_{kt}$, that are known at time $t - 1$:

$$R_{kt} = \gamma_0 + \gamma_1 \bar{q}_{kt-1} + \eta_{kt}. \tag{6}$$

Net purchases are then postulated to be positively related to the estimated vector of expected excess returns, $\hat{\mu}_{kt} = \hat{\gamma}_0 + \hat{\gamma}_1 \bar{q}_{kt-1}$. A potential problem with this approach is that unless we know the "true" model that investors use to estimate expected returns, an OLS regression of NPW_{kt}

on $\hat{\mu}_{kt}$ would suffer from measurement error bias. This problem can be avoided, however, if we instead regress NPW_{kt} on the *actual* return R_{kt}, using variables known at time $t - 1$ as instruments. Given (6), we use $\bar{q}_{kt-1}$ as the natural instrument set.[4] An open issue in this context is whether U.S. investors use information available at the end of period $t - 1$ when deciding to make net purchases, or if they exploit new information that accumulates during period t. We generally base our estimates on end-of-period $t - 1$ information, but we also examine instrumental variable regressions of net purchases on R_{kt+1}, with $\bar{q}_{kt}$ as instruments. We find that the results are similar but slightly weaker when forecasts are based on period t information.

Our set of instruments for forecasting returns include global as well as local variables. As global instruments we use the U.S. stock return lagged one month, one-month and two-month lags of the U.S. safe interest rate (the rate of return on the one-month Treasury bill from the Center for Research in Security Prices), the term structure of U.S. interest rates (measured as the difference between the yield on a long-term and one-month government bond), and the one-month lag of U.S. growth in industrial production. The list of local instruments varies somewhat across countries due to data availability. In all countries we include the return on the local stock market in U.S. dollars less the U.S. safe rate and the local dividend yield, both lagged one month. In Japan, Hong Kong, Singapore, Malaysia, India, Indonesia, Pakistan, Philippines, Thailand, and Mexico we also include the local interest rate and foreign currency return, again lagged one month.

2.3.1   Country regressions

We begin by examining the relationship between net purchases and returns on a country-by-country basis. Table 2.5 shows the results of a regression of net purchases scaled by total foreign holdings on our set of global and local instruments. We find that forecasted returns have significant explanatory power for explaining U.S. net purchases in Japan, Hong Kong, Singapore, and the regional aggregates for Asia, Asia excluding Japan, Europe, and total foreign purchases. The results are essentially unchanged when outliers are removed from the sample, suggesting that large swings in net purchases are not the observations driving the results.

---

[4] Surprisingly, we find that the bias is small. That is, our estimates from the regressions using the instrumental variable approach are remarkably similar to the estimates obtained from regressions of net purchases on forecasted excess returns.

Table 2.5. *Instrumental variable regression of net purchases on local excess returns*

$$NPW_{kt} = \beta_0 + \beta_1 R_{kt} + \varepsilon_{kt}$$

Country	Obs.	Full sample β_1	t-statistic	Excluding outliers β_1	t-statistic	Outliers
Japan	179	9.938	3.32**	10.494	3.42**	1
Hong Kong	179	0.637	2.40**	0.471	2.15**	2
Singapore	179	0.182	1.86*	0.139	1.79*	4
Malaysia	108	0.035	0.92	0.013	0.40	2
India	36	−0.004	−0.14	0.008	0.53	2
Indonesia	60	0.022	0.43	0.003	0.11	2
Korea	120	−0.177	−1.52	−0.158	−1.72*	2
Pakistan	48	0.003	0.47	0.006	1.36	2
Philippines	120	−0.027	−1.41	−0.014	−1.10	2
Thailand	120	0.000	0.00	0.004	0.10	2
Taiwan	108	−0.002	−0.16	0.003	0.24	1
Asia total	179	10.433	3.52**	10.433	3.52**	0
Excluding Japan	179	1.265	2.79**	1.398	3.38**	4
Europe total	179	10.354	2.55**	10.663	2.71**	1
Mexico	167	0.101	0.81	0.036	0.48	4
Foreign total	179	34.708	3.79**	34.920	3.83**	1

Notes: Excess returns are instrumented with the lagged vector of forecasting variables, q_{kt-1}. NPW_{kt} is defined as net purchases scaled by total foreign holdings. Outliers are defined as months in which the error term exceeds three times its standard deviation. The set of instruments excludes foreign exchange returns and the foreign interest rate in Hong Kong, Korea, Thailand, Taiwan, total Europe, and total foreign due to data availability. * = significance at the 10% level, and ** = at the 5% level.

The single exception is Korea where the coefficient becomes significant when the outliers are removed but with the opposite sign. As a robustness check, we compared the results for different starting dates when the regulatory date differed from our threshold date. The results differ only in Malaysia where we find a significant return effect for the 1981–95 sample, but the coefficient becomes insignificantly different from zero when outliers are removed from the sample. We also examined the possibility that investors are concerned about currency-hedged excess returns when making portfolio allocation decisions. We find that the inclusion of hedge terms does not help explain net purchases and so do not report the results here.

A full test of the theory in (4) requires that net purchases be regressed on the *change* in forecasted returns – that is, a regression of NPW_{kt} on $\hat{\mu}_{kt}$ and $\hat{\mu}_{kt-1}$. As in Bohn and Tesar (1996b), we fail to find the predicted negative effects of $\hat{\mu}_{kt-1}$.[5] A separate finding, however, is potentially relevant in this context. Namely, the time series for NPW_{kt} show substantial autocorrelation. This suggests that U.S. investors may respond somewhat sluggishly to news about expected returns. Without debating the question of rationality – slow adjustment could be a sign of inefficiency or it could be a rational response to concerns about the market impact of U.S. transactions in markets with limited liquidity – we will simply examine the factual question of whether there is evidence for slow adjustment.

To examine this question, consider the following partial adjustment model. Let x_{kt}^* be the "target" portfolio share implied by theory in equation (3). If x_{kt-1} differs from x_{kt}^*, we assume that a fraction δ of the deviation from the target is covered by net purchases, that is,

$$x_{kt} = x_{kt-1} + \delta\left(x_{kt}^* - x_{kt-1}\right). \tag{7}$$

By substituting in for lagged portfolio shares, we obtain

$$x_{kt} - x_{kt-1} = \delta x_{kt}^* - \delta^2 \sum_{i\geq 0}^{\infty} \left(1-\delta\right)^i x_{kt-1-i}^*, \quad 0 < \delta \leq 1. \tag{8}$$

With partial adjustment, net purchases should depend positively on current expected returns as specified in equation (3) (through x_{kt}^*) and negatively on a long distributed lag of past expected returns. This offers one explanation for why the first lag of expected returns is insignificant. Next, we can rearrange (8) to obtain:

$$x_{kt} - x_{kt-1} = \delta\left(x_{kt}^* - x_{kt-1}^*\right) + \left(1-\delta\right)\left(x_{kt-1} - x_{kt-2}\right). \tag{9}$$

If we write the target portfolio share as a function of expected returns and again treat the rebalancing term as part of the error term, we obtain the regression equation:

---

[5] Since this merely confirms our earlier findings, the details are omitted. These regressions are also problematic, because the instrumental variables approach is not valid for lagged returns. Hence, the negative results are based on substituting $\hat{\mu}$ for $\bar{\mu}$.

Table 2.6. *Instrumental variable regression of net purchases on local excess returns and lagged net purchases*

$$NPW_{kt} = \beta_0 + \beta_1 R_{kt} + \beta_2 NPW_{kt-1} + \varepsilon_{kt}$$

Country	β_1	β_2
Japan	6.634**	0.52**
Hong Kong	0.499*	0.24**
Singapore	0.109	0.33**
Malaysia	0.023	0.53**
India	−0.000	−0.14
Indonesia	0.028	0.06
Korea	−0.135	0.43**
Pakistan	−0.001	0.43**
Philippines	−0.022	0.16*
Thailand	−0.004	0.36**
Taiwan	−0.005	0.19*
Asia total	7.307**	0.54
Europe total	6.488*	0.36**
Mexico	0.081	0.19**
Foreign total	18.400**	0.57**

Notes: * = significance at the 10% level, and ** = at the 5% level.

$$NPW_{kt} = \beta_0 + \beta_1 \bar{\mu}_{kt} + \beta_2 NPW_{kt-1} + \varepsilon_{kt}. \qquad (10)$$

As before, we use actual returns instrumented by $\bar{q}_{kt-1}$ to estimate the coefficients.[6]

Table 2.6 shows the coefficients from a regression of net purchases on our set of instruments for excess returns as well as lagged net purchases. Lagged net purchases enter as a significant, positive determinant of current net purchases in all countries except India and Indonesia, suggesting that there are lagged adjustments in the portfolio over time. The presence of lagged net purchases in the regression does not diminish

---

[6] An attempt to include the lagged expected return $\hat{\mu}_{kt-1}$ would be even more problematic than before, because the lagged net purchases may provide additional information about the "true" lagged expected return, $E_{t-2}R_{kt-1}$. Hence, estimates of $\hat{\mu}_{kt-1}$ based on $\bar{q}_{kt-2}$ would contain a measurement error that is likely to be correlated with NP_{kt-1}/W_{t-2}.

the role of equity returns in Japan, Hong Kong, or at the regional level.[7]

Finally, we use our country regressions to test for the impact of the U.S. stock market crash in October 1987 and the Mexican peso crisis in December 1994 on U.S. investment in foreign markets. We find that an October 1987 dummy is significant only in Japan. The coefficient is strongly negative, indicating that U.S. investors sold Japanese equities during the crash. Interestingly, during the month of the peso crisis and the month following the crisis (December 1994 and January 1995) U.S. investors were net purchasers of Mexican equity. We also find that U.S. investors were net sellers of Asian equity in the month following the crisis although the time dummy is not significant.

In general, evidence from the largest Asian countries supports the theoretical model linking net purchases and expected equity returns. We also find that lagged net purchases are a significant determinant of current net purchases, possibly reflecting slow dynamic adjustment in portfolio weights over time.

2.3.2   Panel regressions

One potential problem with the country regressions based on data from the small Asian countries is that there is considerable volatility in net purchases and equity returns. This results in large standard errors of our estimates, making it difficult to reject the null hypothesis of zero coefficients. To address this problem, we assemble panel data sets that simultaneously exploit information from several countries. We combine the seven Asian countries that have market-opening dates near or before 1986 – Japan, Hong Kong, Singapore, Malaysia, Korea, Philippines, and Thailand – to form one panel with 120 observations per country covering January 1986 to December 1995. Separately, we combine the ten Asian countries that have market-opening dates during or before 1991 – Japan, Hong Kong, Singapore, Malaysia, Korea, Philippines, Thailand, Indonesia, Pakistan, and Taiwan – to form a panel with 48 observations per country covering January 1991 to December 1995. Since we found significant coefficients for Japan and Hong Kong in Tables 2.5 and 2.6, we also examine both panels excluding Japan and Hong Kong, to make sure that the panel results are not dominated by these two countries. This results

---

[7] Given the large presence of U.S. investors in some local equity markets, we examined whether our regressions are picking up a reverse causation from U.S. net purchases to equity returns. We find no evidence of this effect and therefore do not report the results here.

in a total of four panels. We mainly focus on the panel from January 1986 to December 1995, excluding Japan and Hong Kong, which we refer to as panel 1, because this data set covers a reasonably long time period and it is not dominated by the two "large" countries. Throughout, we control for cross-country differences in the level of net purchases by including country-specific fixed effects.

We begin by regressing net purchases scaled by total foreign holdings on expected excess returns, as suggested by equation (5):

$$NPW_{kt} = \beta_1 \mu_{kt} + \alpha_k + \varepsilon_{kt} \tag{11}$$

where the α_k are country fixed effects. We again use the actual returns, R_{kt}, instrumented by the vector $\bar{q}_{kt-1}$ to estimate the regression coefficients. The results are shown in the first row of Table 2.7. In panel 1, we find a significantly positive slope coefficient β_1 at the 5 percent level. Recall that the country-by-country analysis did not yield a significantly positive coefficient for *any* of the countries in this group for the same period. Upon examination, we find that the residuals of this regression show a positive time trend. When time is explicitly included in the regression (row 2), the slope coefficient β_1 is even larger and more significant. As in the country-by-country analysis, we find a significant effect of lagged net purchases (row 3). Expected returns still remain significant, however, when lagged net purchases are included in the regression.

The estimates with current rather than lagged information are also significant, but somewhat weaker (row 4 of Table 2.7). Since heteroskedasticity might be an issue in combining different countries, we also compute the heteroskedasticity-consistent standard errors and implied t-values (see column 5); the conclusions remain unchanged.

The results with Japan and Hong Kong (panel 2) and the results for the shorter panel, with and without Japan and Hong Kong (panels 3 and 4, respectively), are similar. Hence, Table 2.7 reports only the statistically most appropriate equation from each of these panels, with time trend and lagged net purchases when significant. We find that expected returns and lagged net purchases are significant in all panels, and that time is significant in all of the panels with the exception of the short panel excluding Japan and Hong Kong.

2.3.3   Local versus global factors

Our approach helps to shed new light on the role of global versus country-specific factors in explaining international capital movements. Calvo, Leiderman, and Reinhart (1993, 1996) have argued that much of

Table 2.7. *Panel analysis: the role of expected returns*

$$NPW_{kt} = \beta_1 R_{kt} + \alpha_k + \text{(other regressors)} + \varepsilon_{kt}$$

Panel	Countries/observations	β_1^a	t-statistic Ordinary	t-statistic White	Other regressors Time^b	Other regressors NPW_{kt+1}
Panel 1	5/120	0.86	2.18	2.51		
Panel 1	5/120	1.49	3.49	3.24	2.153**	
Panel 1	5/120	1.03	2.68	2.66	1.393**	0.358**
Panel 1	5/120	0.89^c	2.31	2.41	1.365**	0.363**
Panel 2	7/120	7.25	2.45	1.84	8.498**	0.523**
Panel 3	8/48	1.28	2.34	2.44		0.288**
Panel 4	10/48	6.14	2.22	2.41	20.054**	0.439**

Notes: The table shows coefficients from an instrumental variables regression of net holdings on actual excess returns, using lagged variables as instruments. Columns 4 and 5 show the ordinary and heteroskedasticity-corrected (White) standard errors for the return coefficients. The table also lists the coefficients on time and lagged net purchases when they appear as significant regressors. ** = significance at the 5% level.

The panels include:

Panel 1: Singapore, Malaysia, Korea, Philippines, Thailand.
Panel 2: Panel 1, Japan, Hong Kong.
Panel 3: Panel 1, Indonesia, Pakistan, Taiwan.
Panel 4: Panel 1, Japan, Hong Kong, Indonesia, Pakistan, Taiwan.

^{a} All coefficients multiplied by 1,000.
^{b} All coefficients multiplied by 100,000.
^{c} Excess returns are instrumented by current rather than lagged variables (i.e., instruments for R_{kt+1} rather than R_{kt}).

the recent capital inflows to developing countries were triggered by external developments, for example, by movements in U.S. interest rates and other global factors. Chuhan, Claessens, and Mamingi (1995) examine the role of country-specific versus global determinants in a panel framework similar to ours, and there is substantial overlap between their "determinants" of U.S. equity investment abroad and our instruments for excess returns.

In our notation, the approach in Chuhan, Claessens, and Mamingi amounts to regressing net purchases on a set of predictor variables (q_{kt}), which includes local variables (q_k^L) as well as global variables (q^G):

$$NPW_{kt} = \theta_L q_{kt-1}^L + \theta_G q_{t-1}^G + \alpha_k + \varepsilon_{kt}. \tag{12}$$

If one interprets (q_k^L, q^G) as a set of predictors for excess returns, (12) can be viewed as a reduced-form combination of (6) and (11). A key difference is that such reduced-form regressions do not impose the restriction that the set of coefficients (θ_L, θ_G) is proportional to γ_1, the linear combination of (q_k^L, q^G) that best predicts excess returns. To test the restrictions implied by (11) – that is, to examine whether prediction equations of the type estimated by Chuhan, Claessens, and Mamingi can be interpreted as reduced-form excess return regressions – one may add a subset of (q_k^L, q^G) to (11). Because the role of global variables has received the most attention in the literature, we examine the regression

$$NPW_{kt} = \beta_1 R_{kt} + \beta_2 q_{t-1}^G + \alpha_k + \varepsilon_{kt}, \tag{13}$$

to be estimated by instrumental variables with q_{kt-1}^L as instruments for R_{kt}.[8] The hypothesis that the predictor variables in (12) can be interpreted as signals about R_{kt} then amounts to a testable null hypothesis H_0: $\beta_2 = 0$.

Table 2.8 presents the results for our main panel (Singapore, Malaysia, Korea, Philippines, Thailand, for 1986–95). Regression (1) includes as global variables the six U.S. variables previously used as instruments (lagged U.S. excess returns, lagged U.S. dividend yield, lagged and twice-lagged U.S. safe rate, the spread between U.S. long-term and short-term rates, and lagged growth in industrial production), but includes neither a time trend nor lagged net purchases. At first sight, the results appear to support the hypothesis that global factors have a separate effect apart from expected returns. The lagged U.S. interest rate and the lagged term

[8] In principle, if $q = (q_k^L, q^G)$ includes M variables, one might include up to $M - 1$ of them in (13). But since only the remaining variables are available as instruments for R_{kt}, identification would be tenuous if too many variables were added. Indeed, we will further reduce the number of regressors here.

Table 2.8. *Panel analysis: local versus global factors*
$$NPW_{kt} = \beta_1 R_{kt} + \beta_2 q^G_{kt} + \alpha_k + \varepsilon_{kt}$$

Regressor	(1)	(2)	(3)
Local			
$\bar{\mu}_{kt}$	0.067	2.162	1.017
	(0.141)	(1.111)	(1.930)*
Global			
Excess return on U.S.	0.094	−0.098	
equity, lag 1	(0.386)	(−0.227)	
U.S. dividend yield less	20.335	−116.100	
the U.S. safe rate, lag 1	(0.255)	(−0.627)	
U.S. safe rate, lag 1	19.748	−123.500	
	(0.249)	(−0.689)	
U.S. safe rate, lag 2	−75.712	58.700	−4.027
	(−2.549)**	(0.688)	(−0.217)
U.S. term structure, lag 1	−81.526	34.700	−13.600
	(−2.971)**	(0.440)	(−0.646)
Growth in U.S. industrial	0.039	6.50	
production	(0.020)	(0.262)	
Time		0.002	0.001
		(1.580)	(2.445)**
NPW_{kt-1}		0.357	0.357
		(4.840)**	(5.241)**
Chi-square test for global			
variables	$p = 0.00002$	$p = 0.947$	$p = 0.674$

Notes: All coefficients except for lagged *NPW* have been multiplied by 1,000. All three regressions are run using panel 1 countries as defined in Table 2.7. All regressions include country dummies. We use lagged variables as instruments for local excess returns. The U.S. term structure is defined as the long-term U.S. interest rate less the one-month rate. Heteroskedasticity-consistent *t*-values are shown in parentheses below the coefficients. * = significance at the 10% level, and ** = at the 5% level.

spread are highly significant while the instrumented expected return becomes insignificant. Upon inspection, however, this result turns out to be misleading. Both the U.S. safe rate and the term spread show a downward time trend over our sample period. In regression (2), we add a time trend and lagged net purchases, variables that we found to be significant before (see Table 2.7, lines 1–3). Now the global variables are individually and jointly insignificant.

The insignificant coefficients for the expected stock return in regressions (1) and (2) are largely due to the scarcity of instruments. Variations in expected returns are only identified by the two local instruments, which induces severe multicollinearity. To reduce this problem, regression (3) includes only the two most promising global variables, the safe rate and the term spread. These two were individually significant in regression (1); the other four global variables plus the two local ones are used as instruments. In this regression, the expected return is marginally significant, though still less precisely estimated than in Table 2.7, row 3. The two global regressors are clearly insignificant.

Overall, the data provide no convincing evidence that U.S. interest rates or any other global variables have an independent influence on net equity purchases. Our analysis also suggests that one has to be very careful about the specification of the econometric tests to avoid misleading inferences. Contrary to previous studies, we find that U.S. net purchases of foreign equity are best explained by expected local returns and a linear time trend, which we interpret as the gradual erosion of home bias, rather than by swings in U.S. interest rates.

2.4   Conclusion

U.S. portfolio investment accounts for a substantial share of the capital flowing into Asian economies. We find that the allocation of U.S. equity investment across Asian markets is primarily driven by high expectations of local returns. We also find that lagged net purchases of foreign equity help to explain current net purchases, suggesting that there is a sluggish dynamic component to portfolio adjustment. We do not find evidence of a significant role for global variables, such as swings in U.S. interest rates, in explaining the pattern of U.S. equity investment.

Data Appendix

Data sources

Quarterly figures on U.S. net purchases of foreign equities and bonds are published in the U.S. Treasury *Quarterly Bulletin*. We obtained the unpublished monthly data from the U.S. Treasury Department. For the countries covered by the *Financial Times* data base (Japan, Hong Kong, Singapore, Malaysia, Mexico), we use the equity returns in local currencies and U.S. dollars and the dividend yields from the *Financial Times* indices. The monthly market capitalization data for these countries are from Datastream International. For the other Asian countries – Korea,

Philippines, Pakistan, Thailand, India, Indonesia, Taiwan, and China – we use equity returns in local currencies and U.S. dollars, dividend yields, and market capitalizations from the International Finance Corporation (IFC) data base. The U.S. safe rate is the CRSP return on one-month Treasury bills. Foreign short-term interest rates are from the International Monetary Fund, *International Financial Statistics* (series 60b, 60bc, or 60c) or interbank rates quoted by Datastream, depending on availability. Foreign currency returns are the change in spot rates minus the interest rate differential between the United States and the respective foreign country; or, if otherwise unavailable, the difference between interbank spot and lagged forward rates as quoted by Datastream. The data for the U.S. and for aggregates such as Europe and foreign total are from Bohn and Tesar (1996b).

Computation of equity holdings

To compute equity holdings from our data on net purchases, we need to make several assumptions about the transactions data.

We assume that the capital gain on the portfolio held by U.S. investors is approximately equal to the capital gains on country stock market indices. For the countries in the *Financial Times* data base (Japan, Hong Kong, Singapore, Malaysia) we use the *Financial Times* index. For all other countries we use IFC indices.

For some countries, we do not have capital gains data for the initial years of our sample and in these cases we assume zero capital gains.

With the exception of Japan, we do not have official figures for initial U.S. equity holdings at the beginning of the sample. Given the low reported holdings for the entire Asian region, we started the sample in 1976 assuming zero holdings for all countries except Japan. As a consequence, the standard perpetual inventory method yields slightly negative values of estimated holdings in the early years of our sample in some countries. It seems implausible that U.S. investors in the aggregate would hold a short position in a foreign stock market. In our view it is more likely a consequence of our assumption of zero initial holdings. Therefore, we reset the perpetual inventory to zero whenever the standard method yields negative values. For countries other than Taiwan, this resetting results in only minor adjustments to the holdings data.

Two countries present special problems. In Taiwan, the perpetual inventory method in conjunction with the assumption that U.S. investors earn the market return implies large negative estimated holdings in early 1989 and again in early 1995. This is probably due to the large monthly volatility of equity returns in Taiwan and the lack of information about the timing of intramonth transactions. In China we do not have returns data and therefore compute estimated holdings using the capital gains series for Hong Kong as a proxy. We include China here only for illustrative purposes and drop it from the statistical analysis in section 2.3.

Computation of bond holdings

Our working hypothesis is that some of the U.S. purchases of foreign bonds bought in the United Kingdom represent Eurobonds issued by a variety of countries. This is consistent with casual evidence about the structure of world bond markets. The reported data are also suggestive: reported U.S. bond purchases from the United Kingdom account for the bulk of total reported purchases, while purely domestic issues in the United Kingdom amount only to a small fraction of the world bond market. We do not know the issuer and currency composition of U.S. bond purchases from the United Kingdom. But it seems reasonable to infer that if the Treasury reports U.S. bond sales to third countries without reporting prior purchases from the same country, then the unreported purchases were most likely executed on the Euromarket, that is, officially reported as net purchases in the United Kingdom. We then cumulate net bond purchases, correcting for the "indirect" initial purchases on the Eurobond market. In Japan, Malaysia, Indonesia, Pakistan, China, and Mexico, reported gross sales are smaller or not much larger than reported gross purchases. Hence, the indirect (Euro) purchases that must be imputed to maintain nonnegative holdings are only a small fraction of the reported purchases (all under 10 percent). For Singapore, India, Korea, and Thailand, the implied Euromarket purchases are around 10 percent; but they are much higher for Hong Kong, the Philippines, and Taiwan. For the latter three countries, the reported bond data are highly problematic.

References

Adler, M., and B. Dumas (1983). "International Portfolio Choice and Corporation Finance: A Synthesis," *Journal of Finance* 38: 925–84.

Bekaert, Geert (1995). "Market Integration and Investment Barriers in Emerging Equity Markets," *World Bank Economic Review* 9 (1): 75–107.

Bohn, H., and L. L. Tesar (1996a). "U.S. Equity Investment in Foreign Markets: Portfolio Rebalancing or Return Chasing?" *American Economic Review* 86 (2): 77–81.

1996b. "The U.S. Investment Portfolio and the ICAPM." Unpublished manuscript, University of California at Santa Barbara.

Buckberg, Elaine (1995). "Emerging Stock Markets and International Asset Pricing," *World Bank Economic Review* 9 (1): 51–74.

Calvo, G., L. Leiderman, and C. Reinhart (1993). "Capital Inflows and Real Exchange Rate Appreciation in Latin America: The Role of External Factors," *IMF Staff Papers* 40 (1): 108–51.

1996. "Inflows of Capital to Developing Countries in the 1990s: Causes and Effects," *Journal of Economic Perspectives* 10 (2): 123–39.

Chuhan, P., Stijn Claessens, and Nlandu Mamingi (1995). "Equity and Bond Flows to Latin America and Asia: The Role of Global and Country Factors," World Bank Policy Research Paper No. 1160. Washington, D.C.

Cox, John C., Jonathan E. Ingersall, Jr., and Stephen A. Ross (1985). "An Intertemporal Asset Pricing Model with Rational Expectations," *Econometrica* 53: 363–84.

Tesar, L. L., and I. M. Werner (1994). "International Securities Transactions and Portfolio Choice." In J. Frankel, ed., *The Internationalization of Equity Markets*, pp. 185–216. Chicago: University of Chicago Press.

CHAPTER 3

Foreign direct investment, trade, and real exchange rate linkages in developing countries

Linda S. Goldberg and Michael Klein

3.1 Introduction

Trade flows and foreign direct investment (FDI) are linked in a variety of ways. Direct investment may encourage export promotion, import substitution, or greater trade in intermediate inputs, especially between parent and affiliate producers. These trade implications of foreign direct investment may be observed with flows between the host and source country as well as with third-country markets. In addition to this direct linkage, there is an indirect linkage between trade flows and direct investment since each shares the common determinant of the real exchange rate. In this chapter we work toward disentangling the magnitude of the direct and indirect linkages between trade flows and direct investment in order to trace completely the effect of the real exchange rate on each of these activities. The data we examine are for trade and investment between a set of developing countries in Southeast Asia and Latin America with both Japan and the United States.

As with much other empirical research, we find that the real exchange rate significantly affects trade. For our sample of developing countries, import elasticities with respect to real exchange rates exceed export elasticities. We also find that for Southeast Asian countries exchange rates affect direct investment not only from Japan but also from the United States. FDI from Japan into Southeast Asia has been very sensi-

The views expressed in this paper are those of the individual authors and do not necessarily reflect the position of the Federal Reserve Bank of New York or the Federal Reserve System. Maurice Obstfeld, Kei-Mu Yi, and participants at the conference on Managing Capital Flows and Exchange Rates: Lessons from the Pacific Basin at the Federal Reserve Bank of San Francisco, September 1996, provided useful discussion. Keith Crockett of the Federal Reserve Bank of New York provided excellent research assistance.

tive to changes in the yen–dollar exchange rate: dollar depreciations lead to investment surges from Japan. Moreover, holding constant the effect of the real exchange rate, direct investment from Japan promotes trade between Asia and both Japan and the United States. Japanese direct investment expands both the export and import linkages of Southeast Asia. United States FDI plays a different role in the region: it substitutes for Southeast Asian imports from the United States. In contrast to our findings for Southeast Asia, FDIs into Latin America from the United States and Japan are not responsive to real exchange rate changes. Moreover, the trade-promoting effects of this FDI appear to be weak or insignificant with regard to Latin American trade with the United States and Japan.

The next section sets the stage for our detailed empirical analysis by profiling the sectoral composition of trade and FDI between the respective Southeast Asian and Latin American countries and the United States and Japan. Section 3.3 presents the main econometric methodology and linkage results of the paper. Section 3.4 presents conclusions and emphasizes that the practice of dollar pegging by Southeast Asian countries was important for the expansion of trade and FDI linkages of that region. Countries in this region are adversely effected when the yen weakens vis-à-vis the U.S. dollar.

Our work complements three recent strands of analysis of international trade and capital flows. First, we add a temporal dimension and an explicit role for exchange rates to the insights gained from the (methodologically distinct) gravity approach to modeling trade and investment. Therein, country endowment sets and distance parameters provide a measure of natural tendencies toward interindustry and intraindustry trade flows (see Frankel, 1993, on Japan, and Eaton and Tamura, 1994, on flows between Japan and the United States and various regions of the world). Second, our focus on the *implications* of exchange rate movements for trade and capital flows between countries provides a nice complement to studies of the *determinants* of real and nominal exchange rate movements in Southeast Asia (see Frankel and Wei, 1994). Third, our work complements a literature on capital flows to developing countries, which in recent years has tended to focus more on hot money and short-term capital flows than on foreign direct investment (e.g., see Calvo, Leiderman, and Reinhart, 1993; Kletzer and Spiegel, Chapter 13, this volume; and Bohn and Tesar, Chapter 2, this volume). Our emphasis on FDI is especially pertinent in light of some recent developing country efforts to redirect the composition of capital inflows away from short-term and toward longer-term equity holdings.

3.2   Bilateral trade and FDI patterns

There have been dramatic changes in FDI activity over the 1980s. Although the United States continued its role as a large capital exporter, it also became a destination for increasing amounts of foreign capital. Japan's role as a source country for long-term capital ratcheted upward, via both increased merger-and-acquisition activity in industrialized countries and by increased greenfield investments in developing countries. With expanded privatization programs underway, foreign direct investment also regained prominence in Latin America and surged in many emerging market economies.

The resulting recent empirical and theoretical research on FDI has been largely oriented toward explaining the merger-and-acquisition phenomenon in industrialized nations (e.g., see Klein and Rosengren, 1994, and the collection of essays in Froot, 1993).[1] While the Southeast Asian experience also has received some attention recently (as in the collection of essays in Ito and Krueger, 1996), there has been very little systematic examination of FDI activity *in developing countries* or the role of currency movements in this context.[2]

Existing empirical studies of FDI into developing countries either purely document directional patterns or compare observed flows with some globally based benchmarks that are estimated from country characteristics. An example of the first group of studies is Kohsaka's (1996) careful tracing of levels and composition of capital flows to Latin America and Asia.[3] Examples of the second class of studies include work using gravity models. Eaton and Tamura (1994, 1996), for instance, relate the bilateral trade and investment flows of the United States and Japan with various regions to transportation costs (distance between countries), market size (population), overhead investment costs (human capital), and per capita GNP. Frankel (1993) and Frankel and Wei (1993) also use gravity models to compare the regionalism in trade flows of the United States and Japan, among other countries. These studies argue

---

[1] Goldberg and Kolstad (1995) show that exchange rate risk influences both trade and international investment flows, which in part substitute for trade. The pattern of effects of exchange rate risk on these flows depends on the correlations between shocks to exchange rates and shocks to demand and costs in respective home and foreign markets.

[2] Goldberg (forthcoming) explores the effects of exchange rate movements on total investment in Latin American countries, but does not break out the effects on domestic versus foreign investors.

[3] Kohsaka (1996) also discusses possible root causes of changing inter- and intraregional capital flows, especially in Asia, but does not formally specify or test any hypotheses.

that regional tendencies east in trade and investment flows, even after accounting for country characteristics. The United States is relatively tightly linked with Latin America, while Japan has "unexplained" deep ties to the rest of Asia.

In contrast to these studies, our empirical work is not directly concerned with whether excessive bilateral or regional linkages are observed in United States and Japanese transactions with Latin America or Southeast Asia. Instead, by examining the (time series) interactions between trade, FDI, and exchange rates, we provide stylized facts on the rich channels through which particular exchange rate movements strengthen or weaken international linkages.[4]

3.2.1   Interregional patterns of trade

The Southeast Asian countries in our sample include Malaysia, the Philippines, Indonesia, and Thailand (sometimes described as the ASEAN4 nations). These countries are large net recipients of private direct investment and long term capital flows, in contrast to the newly industrialized countries of Asia (NICs, i.e., Hong Kong, Korea, Singapore, and Taiwan)[5] in which domestic savings now exceed domestic investment. The Latin American countries that we explore in detail are Chile, Brazil, and Argentina,[6] each of which is a net importer of long-term capital.

Perspective on the centrality of the United States and Japan for financial and real activities for these regions is suggested by trade and FDI data (Table 3.1). Data on partner shares in country trade, calculated as bilateral exports plus bilateral imports relative to total trade, show that the United States represents about 20 percent of the total (direct) export and import activities of the countries in both Latin America and Southeast Asia. The fraction of trade activity accounted for by Japan is very different across the two regions: Japan accounts for close to 25 percent of trade activities of Southeast Asian countries, but is a much smaller (although not trivial) partner in trade for Latin

---

[4] Our results can be compared with Frankel and Wei's (1994) correlations between bilateral exchange rate variability and bilateral trade flows. The latter results show that variability per se slows trade mildly in some regions.

[5] Sometimes these countries are called the ANIEs, i.e., the Asian newly industrialized economies. The sum of the NICs, Southeast Asia, and China is sometimes referred to as Pacific Asia.

[6] Mexico is excluded due to its particularly close ties to the United States. The Latin American countries selected are significant trade and investment partners of the United States and Japan.

Table 3.1. *Trade shares with Latin American and Southeast Asian countries, 1993 (in percent)*

	United States	Japan	Europe	China
Argentina	17.2	3.8	26.1	1.3
Brazil	21.2	6.5	26.2	1.5
Chile	21.4	12.3	23.5	2.0
Latin American group	21.5	7.2	27.4	1.7
Indonesia	13.1	26.8	16.5	3.4
Malaysia	18.7	20.1	13.1	2.5
Philippines	26.4	19.6	12.6	1.2
Thailand	16.1	24.3	15.7	1.6
Southeast Asian group	17.4	23.0	14.7	2.3

Notes: Trade share is calculated as the sum of bilateral exports plus bilateral imports relative to total exports plus imports of the developing country.
Source: IMF, *Direction of Trade Statistics Yearbook, 1995.*

America. European countries together dominate the United States in absolute terms as a trade partner of Latin American countries, and are a more moderate partner for the Southeast Asian countries. China does not account for a large part of trade transactions for any of the countries of our sample, although there clearly is potential for this relationship to expand.

The dollar and yen play key roles in these trade flows. Country currencies either are formally tied to the United States dollar or give the dollar a high weight in basket pegs. The weight of the dollar in the currency baskets is generally about five times higher than the weights that would be suggested purely by volumes of direct trade with the United States. The historic phenomenon of dollar invoicing of trade may be an important component of explaining the "bias" toward the dollar in currency baskets. One reason is that the majority of resource-intensive transactions are invoiced in dollars. A second reason is that the majority of trade between Southeast Asian and Japanese countries is invoiced in dollars (Tavlas and Ozeki, 1992). Additionally, the Chinese yuan is in practice closely valued against the dollar, and further reinforces the dominance of the dollar in the baskets of Southeast Asian countries (Frankel and Wei, 1994).

The United States and Japan are important source countries for foreign direct investment. Table 3.2 provides a one-year snapshot of FDI from the United States and Japan into the respective countries of Latin

Table 3.2. *FDI into Latin American and Southeast Asian countries, 1993 (in millions of US$)*

Destination/source	United States	Japan	Europe[a]	World total
Argentina	956	34	304	6,305
Brazil	565	419	198	1,292
Chile	214	3	130	841
Latin American group	1,735	456	632	8,438
Indonesia	559	813	57	2,004
Malaysia	330	800	587	5,006
Philippines	298	207	116	1,025
Thailand	46	578	245	1,726
Southeast Asian group	1,233	2,398	1,005	9,761

[a] Europe includes Belgium, France, Germany, Italy, Netherlands, Portugal, Spain, Sweden, and the United Kingdom.
Sources: United States FDI data from the Bureau of Economic Analysis (BEA) and also published in the *Survey of Current Business*. Japanese FDI data from the Japanese Ministry of Finance, *Monthly Finance Review*. European FDI data in source country currencies from *OECD Direct Investment Yearbook*. Conversion to U.S. dollar values done using IFS period average exchange rates. World total FDI data from IMF, *International Financial Statistics*.

America and Southeast Asia. The United States maintains a dominant position in FDI into Latin American countries. Japan maintains a dominant position in FDI into Southeast Asia. The apparent "regionalism" in investment by these sources is robust to adjustments for natural resource and factor endowments and distance (Eaton and Tamura, 1994).[7]

---

[7] Annual FDI flows are quite variable over time, so annual ratios are indicative of relative scales of activity but not representative of long-run patterns in country investment shares. For reference, we also report the amount of FDI from Europe and the total of all FDI into the country, calculated from the balance-of-payments statistics of the country and reported in the IMF's *International Financial Statistics*. We do not present the source country FDI series as a percentage of the IFS total: these series from different sources are not compatible numbers. Unlike the trade data, the data on FDI flows into developing countries are less reliable and more volatile series. The FDI series that we utilize for the United States are flow data computed by the Bureau of Economic Analysis and reported in the Department of Commerce's *Survey of Current Business*. The shortcomings of these series have been extensively discussed elsewhere and will not be reiterated here (see Dewenter, 1995). Despite the criticisms of the U.S. FDI series, we still may be on much stronger grounds with this data, compared with our data on Japanese outward FDI, reported in the *Monthly Finance Review* of the Japan Ministry of Finance. Matsuoka and Rose (1994) report that MOF data exclude FDI resulting from retained earnings, the

Europe is a significant investment presence in both regions, but still is smaller (in terms of flows) than the United States in the Latin American countries, and than both the United States and Japan in Southeast Asia. In recent years, the NICS also have been large-scale investors in Southeast Asia.

3.2.2 *Sectoral composition of trade with United States and Japan*

In this section we provide a sectoral decomposition of the trade between each country and the United States and Japan. In the next section we provide the sectoral decomposition of FDI inflows into the same group of developing countries from the respective source countries.

United States exports to the panel countries of Southeast Asia and Latin America have a very similar (two-digit SIC) sectoral decomposition. Machinery (electrical and nonelectrical) and transportation equipment comprise roughly 65 percent of U.S. sales in each country. Chemicals and allied products further account for between 15 and 25 percent of U.S. exports to Latin America and between 5 and 17 percent of U.S. exports to Southeast Asia.[8]

Japanese exports to the Latin American countries also are heavily concentrated (roughly 80 percent) in machinery (including office equipment, electrical apparatus and appliances, and other electronics) and transportation equipment. There is a different profile for Japanese exports to Southeast Asian countries. Electrical machinery and transportation equipment are important, but account for only about 35 percent of Southeast Asian purchases from Japan. The remaining significant export categories are the types of goods that are direct inputs into Southeast Asian production activities: iron and steel products, power-generating equipment, and industrial machinery and equipment.

The imports of the United States and Japan from the respective panel countries are much more diffuse and differentiated by source country. U.S. imports from Latin America are heavily concentrated in food, leather, and primary metal products. By contrast, U.S. imports from Southeast Asian countries are concentrated in electrical and nonelectrical machinery (especially with regards to Malaysia) and apparel and textile products.

Japanese imports from Latin America primarily consist of raw mate-

---

opening and expanding of branches, and the purchase of land. Also, the MOF data are calculated by summing up nominal dollar investments over time, without price index adjustments.

[8] Data for 1993 are from the United States Bureau of Census data base.

rials and foodstuffs. Argentine exports are 70 percent foodstuffs, with residual exports mainly composed of nonferrous metals. Brazil and Chilean exports to Japan are mainly crude materials, foodstuffs, and metal products (ferrous and nonferrous). Japanese imports from Southeast Asia differ substantially across countries. Indonesia sells to Japan fuels as well as cork and wood manufactures. Malaysia sells fuel and nonfuel crude materials, and some manufactured products. Both the Philippines and Thailand export some foodstuffs, nonfuel crude materials (together representing about 50 percent of sales), and manufactured products.

3.2.3   Sectoral composition of FDI with United States and Japan

The bulk of recent U.S. investments into Latin America (especially outside of the banking and finance sectors) have targeted Brazil, although Argentina also receives significant quantities of direct investment from the United States. Inflows to Brazil have been concentrated in various manufacturing industries, and especially in the transportation equipment sector, which represents an important part of Brazilian exports to the United States. Direct investment by the United States into Argentina is concentrated in foodstuffs and various manufacturing industries, also paralleling the composition of Argentina exports to the United States.

United States direct investment into Southeast Asia has been significantly smaller than its flows into Latin America. For example, in 1993 these flows into Southeast Asia were less than a quarter of the flows to the three Latin American countries. More than half of the U.S. FDI into Southeast Asia went to the Indonesian petroleum and products sector, which currently does not export significant amounts to the United States. The remaining funds largely went to electronics manufacturing in Malaysia, in line with the bulk of U.S. purchases from that country.

Compared with the U.S. data, Japanese direct investment data are less complete in coverage and less detailed in their decomposition. Data on Japanese direct investment into Latin America and Southeast Asia are available as annual cumulative stocks disaggregated by industry and by area (North America, Latin America, Asia, Middle and Near East, Europe, Africa, and Oceania).[9] Direct investment into Latin America has mainly gone into banking and insurance and the transportation components of nonmanufacturing industries. Flows into manufacturing have been concentrated in the iron and ferrous metal and transportation

---

[9] The flows are the difference between cumulative annual stocks.

equipment sectors. These investment patterns contrast significantly with those of the United States and with Japanese investment patterns into Southeast Asia.

Japanese FDI into Southeast Asia is three to four times larger than its FDI into Latin America (excluding banking and insurance). Moreover, Japanese FDI in Southeast Asia is dispersed among a range of manufacturing and nonmanufacturing industries. These industries are much broader than the Southeast Asian industries that account for the bulk of exports to Japan. In fact, the industries that received significant funds from Japan were those industries which most resembled the pattern of production in Japan in the 1980s.

The differences in the sectoral pattern of direct investment by Japan and the United States to the countries in our sample may be a source of differences in the linkages among direct investment, trade, and the real exchange rate. In the empirical results that follow, we are able to study differences in direct investment from Japan or the United States, although the lack of sufficient sectoral data precludes us from drawing any inferences on the possibility that the source of these differences arises from a different sectoral mix.

3.3   Econometric results: FDI, trade, and real exchange rates

This section presents our empirical findings on the linkages among foreign direct investment, trade flows, and the real exchange rate between the developing countries and the United States and Japan. First, we present regressions for a time series panel of direct investment into each of the developing countries from either Japan or the United States. Real FDI is expressed as a function of bilateral real exchange rates and the real incomes of the source and host countries. Further regressions explore the determinants of the developing country exports to the imports from either the United States or Japan. The regressions express real exports and real imports as functions of real income, bilateral real exchange rates, and real direct investment from both source countries.

Overall, the empirical results document the significance of regional linkages between the real exchange rate and direct investment, and between the real exchange rate and trade flows. These results also demonstrate that direct investment into these developing countries affects their trade flows with industrialized countries, even after holding constant the independent contribution to trade of the real exchange rate. There are significant differences between the strength of the linkages observed for the Latin American and for the Southeast Asian countries. Moreover, the source of FDI – that is, Japan or the United States – has a strong influence on resulting effects of FDI on current and future trade patterns of the developing countries.

The data set used in these regressions consists of a cross-section time series panel of annual observations. The countries in the panel are Argentina, Brazil, Chile, Indonesia, Malaysia, Thailand, and the Philippines. We provide regression results for the full panel and for the subsets of the Latin American countries and the Southeast Asian countries. The time series runs from 1978 to 1993 or 1994, depending upon the country. All real exchange rates (RER^{us}, RER^j) are bilateral rates measured as prices in the panel countries relative to prices in either the United States or Japan: an increase in the real exchange rate index represents a real appreciation of the currency of the country in the panel with respect to the dollar or the yen, respectively. All estimation is done using a fixed-effects model, which effectively has a dummy variable for all but one of the countries included in the regression. The variables enter the regressions in logarithmic form, so that estimated regression coefficients are interpreted as elasticities.

3.3.1   Direct investment regressions

There are several channels through which real exchange rates may affect direct investment. In the developing country context, the most important channel may be that a depreciation of the real exchange rate reduces the cost of domestic labor (and other productive inputs) relative to foreign production costs. The depreciation increases labor demand and employment, thereby raising the return on capital. Thus, greenfield foreign direct investment increases in response to a depreciation. This channel suggests that we should expect to find a negative coefficient on the real exchange rate in a direct investment regression (where an increase in the real exchange rate represents a real appreciation of the domestic currency).

Exchange rates may also affect direct investment through an imperfect capital markets channel, as discussed in Froot and Stein (1991). In this case, a real depreciation of the domestic currency raises the wealth of foreign investors relative to that of domestic investors and thereby increases FDI.[10] This channel also has the prediction that a real depreciation increases FDI.[11] The imperfect capital markets channel for real

[10] Klein and Rosengren (1994) and Dewenter (1995) provide empirical support for this channel in inward FDI to the United States.
[11] The imperfect capital market channel has the additional prediction that the ratio of domestic to foreign investors (and relative shares of different foreign investors) in

exchange rate effects may be more relevant in merger and acquisition bids than in the greenfield investments that prevail in many developing countries. The exception for developing and emerging markets pertains to privatization efforts.

In contrast to these arguments, other causal channels suggest a positive coefficient between real exchange rate appreciation and FDI. One causal channel may be associated with domestic efforts to mitigate some of the distributional and aggregate effects of a real appreciation. For example, an appreciation of the domestic currency may yield an increase in imports, which, in turn, increases pressures for the implementation of protectionist policies. In this case direct investment may take place in anticipation of future tariff barriers that are precipitated by adverse exchange rate movements. The plausibility of this potential effect of exchange rates on FDI is supported by the considerable evidence that exists regarding the countercyclical nature of trade barriers.

Foreign direct investment regressions over the full panel of seven countries are presented in Table 3.3. In Tables 3.4 and 3.5 we provide FDI regression results when the Latin American countries are not pooled with the Southeast Asian countries. The dependent variable in these regressions is the logarithm of the annual real dollar value of direct investment from either the United States or Japan. The independent variables in these regressions include the logarithms of national income in the source country, lagged national income in the source country, lagged national income in the host country, and lagged bilateral real exchange rates with respect to both the yen and the dollar. Real exchange rates and host country national income are lagged to avoid simultaneity. Contemporaneous source country national income is included since it is unlikely that simultaneity bias arises with respect to this variable. Some regressions include an interactive regional dummy "LA" on exchange rate terms: this dummy variable equals one for Latin America and is zero otherwise.

In Table 3.3, column 4, observe that when the developing country currencies depreciate with respect to the yen (i.e., when RER^j falls), there is a corresponding increase in direct investment from Japan. However, regressions that include the dummy variable for Latin America (column 6) show that the real exchange rate and FDI linkage is statistically significant only for Southeast Asia and not significant for Latin America. The results in Table 3.4 further confirm the lack of significant linkages between the real exchange rate and foreign direct investment in

financing domestic investment opportunities should fall when the domestic currency depreciates.

Table 3.3. *Determinants of FDI from the United States and Japan into developing country panel*

	United States as FDI source			Japan as FDI source		
RER^j_{t-1}	-0.127		1.782***	-2.01***	-0.916	-3.06***
	(0.573)		(0.630)	(0.740)	(0.767)	(0.930)
RER^{us}_{t-1}	0.174	2.026**	-0.117	2.326***		5.082***
	(0.576)	(0.798)	(0.971)	(0.731)		(1.479)
$LA*RER^j_{t-1}$			-2.78***		1.149	2.047**
			(0.675)		(0.751)	(1.025)
$LA*RER^{us}_{t-1}$		-2.082**	1.065			-3.783**
		(0.812)	(1.077)			(1.654)
GDP^j_{t-1}	1.845***	2.271***	2.671***	1.241*	0.853	1.124
	(0.507)	(0.514)	(0.485)	(0.717)	(0.821)	(0.778)
$GDP^{fdi\ source}_t$	-3.651*	-3.186	-3.946	10.012	9.143	11.736*
	(2.888)	(2.715)	(2.570)	(6.128)	(6.509)	(6.235)
$GDP^{fdi\ source}_{t-1}$	3.479	2.709	3.336	-9.075	-6.834	-10.400*
	(3.226)	(2.795)	(2.867)	(5.938)	(6.315)	(6.051)
Constant	-16.006	-12.65***	-19.70**	-9.702	-32.7***	-8.684
	(9.972)	(4.955)	(8.897)	(13.404)	(10.931)	(13.236)
F-tests:						
RER^j, RER^{us}	0.06			5.25***		
$RER^j + LA*RER^j$			2.76*		0.64	
$RER^{us} + LA*RER^{us}$		0.09	2.51			
RER^j, $LA*RER^j$			6.25***			
RER^{us}, $LA*RER^{us}$						4.13***
adj. R2	0.720	0.739	0.778	0.776	0.783	0.784
No. obs.	98	98	98	105	105	105

Notes: *, **, *** = statistical significance at the 10%, 5%, and 1% levels, respectively. Standard errors in parentheses.

Table 3.4. *Determinants of FDI from the United States and Japan into Latin American panel*

	United States as FDI source		Japan as FDI source	
RER^j_{t-1}		−0.246	0.300	−1.881
		(0.682)	(0.415)	(1.439)
RER^{us}_{t-1}	−0.091	0.140		2.148
	(0.165)	(0.663)		(1.360)
GDP^j_{t-1}	5.460***	5.425***	0.124	−0.707
	(0.870)	(0.885)	(1.850)	(1.889)
$GDP^{fdi\ source}_t$	−6.826*	−6.552*	15.264	11.338
	(3.492)	(3.617)	(13.003)	(12.994)
$GDP^{fdi\ source}_{t-1}$	5.466	4.876	−12.462	−10.024
	(3.626)	(4.019)	(12.447)	(12.306)
Constant	−40.821***	−36.968***	−34.359*	0.535
	(6.461)	(12.516)	(19.216)	(29.034)
F-tests:				
RER^j, RER^{us}		0.21		1.52
adj. R2	0.899	0.897	0.667	0.680
No. obs.	42	42	45	45

Notes: *, **, *** = statistical significance at the 10%, 5%, and 1% levels. Standard errors in parentheses.

the subsequent year for any of the Latin American countries in our sample.

The results in Table 3.3, column 6, indicate that a 1 percent depreciation with respect to the yen causes an increase in direct investment from Japan to the Southeast Asian countries of 3.1 percent. However, the effect is highly statistically significant only when one also controls for the exchange rate movements of the developing country currency relative to the U.S. dollar. The domestic currency depreciation therefore potentially raises the return to Japanese investment in Southeast Asia relative to investment in Japan. In Table 3.3, column 6, subtracting the coefficients on RER^j from RER^{us}, which yields the coefficient on a yen–dollar real exchange rate, the resulting net coefficient suggests that a 1 percent appreciation of the yen against the dollar raises FDI into these countries by 8.1 percent. This finding is consistent with more anecdotal claims about the potential hollowing out of Japanese industrial sectors with respect to a strong yen.

Table 3.5. *Determinants of FDI from the United States and Japan into Southeast Asia panel*

	United States as FDI source		Japan as FDI source	
RER^j_{t-1}		1.462**	−0.761	−2.615***
		(0.695)	(0.702)	(0.720)
RER^{us}_{t-1}	1.168	−0.138		4.948***
	(0.768)	(0.968)		(1.077)
GDP^i_{t-1}	1.915***	1.811***	0.857	1.498**
	(0.601)	(0.583)	(0.862)	(0.745)
$GDP^{fdi\ source}_t$	0.038	−1.548	5.165	11.066*
	(3.289)	(3.266)	(6.596)	(5.748)
$GDP^{fdi\ source}_{t-1}$	−1.655	1.776	−2.658	−9.601*
	(3.399)	(3.667)	(6.552)	(5.767)
Constant	0.535	−20.910	−33.632	−5.895
	(6.871)	(12.167)	(13.487)	(12.949)
F-tests:				
RER^j, RER^{us}		3.45*		11.36***
adj. R2	0.328	0.373	0.668	0.760
No. obs.	56	56	60	60

Notes: *, **, *** = statistical significance at the 10%, 5%, and 1% levels. Standard errors in parentheses.

The results in Table 3.3, column 3, also suggest that an appreciation with respect to the dollar is associated with an increase in direct investment from the United States to Southeast Asia, but this result is not robust to the inclusion of the bilateral yen real exchange rate in the regression. Table 3.5 confirms these significant linkages between Southeast Asian bilateral exchange rates and direct investment from both Japan and the United States. From Table 3.5, column 4, observe that a 1 percent depreciation with respect to the yen increases direct investment from Japan by 2.6 percent and decreases direct investment from the United States by 1.5 percent. Also, column 4 shows that a 1 percent appreciation of the yen against the dollar increases direct investment from Japan by 7.6 percent. Column 2 shows that this same appreciation of the yen against the dollar reduces U.S. investment in Southeast Asia by 1.6 percent.

The coefficients on the (third-party) bilateral exchange rates in these regressions should be interpreted as showing the effects of real exchange rates holding constant the bilateral exchange rate between the host country and the source country. Thus, these coefficients reflect the effect of a change in the yen–dollar exchange rate on FDI to the countries in the panel. For example, an increase in the dollar–ringgit exchange rate, holding constant the yen–ringgit exchange rate, represents an increase in the dollar–yen exchange rate. Therefore, a positive coefficient on the dollar–ringgit real exchange rate in a regression of direct investment from Japan that also includes the yen–ringgit real exchange rate reflects the fact that an appreciation of the yen relative to the dollar, all else equal, increases direct investment from Japan to Malaysia.

3.3.2   Trade regressions

In this section we examine the direct effect of real exchange rates on the relative prices of developing country (bilateral) exports and imports, and also explore the indirect real exchange rate linkage via foreign direct investment. Foreign direct investment may also increase imports of intermediate inputs purchased by the host country, if the direct investment supports or creates links in the chain of production of a multinational firm. Imports of final goods purchased by the host country may decline in the wake of direct investment if that investment supports or creates a domestic industry that displaces purchases of final goods from the source country. Exports may also increase in the wake of direct investment as the producers in the source country use the host country as a platform for selling to third-country markets.[12]

Tables 3.6, 3.7, and 3.8 present the results of regressions that link the logarithms of direct investment and real exchange rates to the country's real bilateral imports (in millions of constant U.S. dollars) from the United States and Japan. The tables present results for, respectively, the full developing country panel, the Latin American country panel, and the Southeast Asian panel. Analogous regressions for real bilateral exports to the United States and Japan are provided in Tables 3.9, 3.10, and 3.11. All regressions include the logarithms of both contemporaneous and lagged real exchange rates, national income in both countries and current and lagged foreign direct investment flows.[13] The real exchange

---

[12] Goldberg and Kolstad (1995) also show that FDI can replace exports when the FDI is induced by the volatility of exchange rates.

[13] The U.S. producer price index (PPI) is used to convert the trade data into constant dollars. The bilateral real exchange rate data are expressed as price in the panel country relative to the PPI in the United States or Japan. The specific price deflator varies across the panel countries due to data availability. The PPI is used for Chile; the wholesale price index (WPI) is used for Indonesia, Thailand, and the Philippines, and the consumer price index (CPI) is used for Malaysia, Argentina, and Brazil.

Table 3.6. *Imports from the United States or Japan into developing country panel*

	Imports from United States		Imports from Japan	
RER_t	0.234***	0.266***	0.064	0.060
	(0.066)	(0.074)	(0.101)	(0.101)
RER_{t-1}	0.341***	0.315***	0.254**	0.262**
	(0.067)	(0.072)	(0.105)	(0.105)
GDP_t^i	1.785***	1.567***	2.921***	2.805***
	(0.506)	(0.564)	(0.717)	(0.728)
GDP_{t-1}^i	−0.2216	−0.117	−1.230*	−1.239*
	(0.519)	(0.545)	(0.696)	(0.714)
$GDP_t^{import\ source}$	−2.068**	−1.752*	−4.091**	−3.495*
	(0.947)	(1.010)	(2.081)	(2.124)
$GDP_{t-1}^{import\ source}$	1.928**	1.648	3.548*	2.998
	(0.971)	(1.046)	(2.017)	(2.053)
FDI_t^{us}	0.27	0.037		0.070
	(0.076)	(0.080)		(0.055)
FDI_{t-1}^{us}	0.034	0.027		0.003
	(0.078)	(0.082)		(0.056)
FDI_t^{japan}		−0.001	0.089***	0.088***
		(0.024)	(0.033)	(0.034)
FDI_{t-1}^{japan}		0.028	0.069**	0.067*
		(0.027)	(0.035)	(0.035)
Constant	−4.297**	−3.629*	−2.938	−2.405
	(1.825)	(2.155)	(3.600)	(3.615)
F-tests:				
RER_t, RER_{t-1}	79.97***	62.99***	8.40***	8.57***
FDI_t^{us}, FDI_{t-1}^{us}	1.61	1.74		1.65
FDI_t^{japan}, FDI_{t-1}^{japan}		0.64	12.56***	11.75***
adj. R2	0.913	0.912	0.944	0.944
No. obs.	84	83	97	97

Notes: Bilateral real exchange rates defined relative to import source. *, **, *** = statistical significance at the 10%, 5%, and 1% levels. Standard errors in parentheses.

rate in a particular regression is the bilateral exchange rate relative to the trade partner.

For the full panel of countries, the real exchange rate appreciation has the expected positive effect on imports, and the sum of the current and lagged real exchange rates is significant in all four regressions of Table

Table 3.7. *Imports from the United States or Japan into Latin American panel*

	Imports from United States		Imports from Japan	
RER_t	0.272***	0.288***	0.137	0.125
	(0.086)	(0.102)	0.130	0.132
RER_{t-1}	0.353***	0.339***	0.327**	0.333**
	(0.088)	(0.098)	(0.139)	(0.148)
GDP_t^i	1.292	0.924	3.047***	2.308*
	(0.889)	(1.033)	(1.028)	(1.208)
GDP_{t-1}^i	−0.678	−0.093	0.447	0.674
	(0.875)	(1.000)	(1.051)	(1.318)
$GDP_t^{\text{import source}}$	−0.986	−0.344	0.564	−0.171
	(1.979)	(2.230)	(4.005)	(4.391)
$GDP_{t-1}^{\text{import source}}$	1.086	0.776	−1.545	−0.690
	(1.901)	(2.149)	(3.480)	(4.136)
FDI_t^{us}	0.049	0.064		0.196
	(0.118)	(0.123)		(0.164)
FDI_{t-1}^{us}	0.080	0.105		−0.135
	(0.108)	(0.117)		(0.167)
FDI_t^{japan}		−0.026	0.037	0.039
		(0.036)	(0.048)	(0.051)
FDI_{t-1}^{japan}		0.023	−0.001	0.002
		(0.041)	(0.050)	(0.053)
Constant	−4.359	−3.386	−16.172**	−12.754*
	(4.512)	(4.728)	(6.377)	(7.398)
F-tests:				
RER_t, RER_{t-1}	44.85***	39.42***	9.35***	8.41***
FDI_t^{us}, FDI_{t-1}^{us}	1.79	2.58		0.20
FDI_t^{japan}, FDI_{t-1}^{japan}		0.00	0.29	0.32
adj. R2	0.904	0.901	0.792	0.788
No. obs.	42	41	41	41

Notes: Bilateral real exchange rates defined relative to import source. *, **, *** = statistical significance at the 10%, 5%, and 1% levels. Standard errors in parentheses.

3.6. Direct investment from Japan has a positive and significant impact on imports from Japan, a result consistent with a situation where direct investment is supported by subsequent trade in intermediate inputs from the source country.

In Latin American countries (Table 3.7), however, neither imports

Table 3.8. *Imports from the United States or Japan into Southeast Asian panel*

	Imports from United States			Imports from Japan		
RER_t	1.012***	0.848**	0.742**	1.242***	0.523**	0.590***
	(0.386)	(0.368)	(0.355)	(0.239)	(0.215)	(0.222)
RER_{t-1}	0.112	0.004	0.068	−0.278	0.008	0.051
	(0.381)	(0.364)	(0.347)	(0.264)	(0.205)	(0.229)
GDP^i_t	2.678***	3.055***	2.009***	7.312***	5.021***	5.331***
	(0.645)	(0.625)	(0.760)	(0.926)	(0.903)	(0.920)
GDP^i_{t-1}	−0.985	−0.882	−0.056	−6.025***	−4.438***	−4.650***
	(0.658)	(0.617)	(0.731)	(0.942)	(0.880)	(0.389)
$GDP^{import\ source}_t$	−1.783*	−1.107	−0.895	−5.388***	−7.135***	−7.456***
	(0.940)	(0.939)	(0.906)	(1.826)	(1.408)	(1.414)
$GDP^{import\ source}_{t-1}$	1.364	0.310	−0.181	6.412***	7.592***	7.966***
	(0.998)	(1.033)	(1.006)	(1.831)	(1.391)	(1.405)
FDI^{us}_t	−0.095		−0.037			−0.064
	(0.177)		(0.175)			(0.041)

	(1)	(2)	(3)	(4)	(5)	(6)
FDI_{t-1}^{us}		-0.214	-0.265*			0.011
		(0.144)	(0.139)			(0.039)
FDI_t^{japan}			0.077*		0.082**	0.081**
			(0.041)		(0.039)	(0.039)
FDI_{t-1}^{japan}			0.024		0.179***	0.172**
			(0.035)		(0.037)	(0.038)
Constant	-0.390	-1.888	1.779	-18.412***	-5.220	-6.910*
	(2.179)	(2.133)	(2.584)	(3.822)	(3.636)	(3.791)
F-tests:						
RER_t, RER_{t-1}	12.01***	6.95***	6.78***	19.50***	8.82***	10.35***
FDI_t^{us}, FDI_{t-1}^{us}		5.43**	5.49**			0.84
FDI_t^{japan}, FDI_{t-1}^{japan}			5.04**		34.17***	31.70***
adj. R2	0.919	0.929	0.935	0.920	0.955	0.955
No. obs.	42	42	42	56	56	56

Notes: Bilateral real exchange rates defined relative to import source. *, **, *** = statistical significance at the 10%, 5%, and 1% levels. Standard errors in parentheses.

from the United States or Japan are responsive to FDI from either source. The significance of FDI for imports in the full panel of countries was driven by the Southeast Asian results. As indicated in Table 3.8, direct investment from both the United States and Japan significantly affects goods imported by Southeast Asian countries. From column 3 observe that a 10 percent increase in direct investment from the United States *reduces* Southeast Asian country imports from the United States by about 3 percent over time. From column 6 observe that a 10 percent increase in direct investment from Japan *increases* imports from Japan by about 2.5 percent over time. Japanese direct investment is also shown to significantly increase Southeast Asian imports from the United States. This set of results could imply that United States FDI substitutes for United States trade with the region, while Japanese FDI leads to more externally-oriented local production.

A confirmation that there are direct (relative price) and indirect (via FDI) effects of real exchange rates on Southeast Asian imports is provided by regressions that exclude the FDI terms. The resulting coefficients on real exchange rates in these regressions that exclude FDI are roughly 20 percent lower for imports from the United States and 50 percent higher for imports from Japan. These elasticity adjustments are consistent with the results concerning the effects of direct investment on trade and the results presented earlier on the effects of the real exchange rate on direct investment. An appreciation of a country's real exchange rate decreases FDI which, in turn, decreases Southeast Asian imports from Japan, and increases Southeast Asian imports from the United States.

Tables 3.9, 3.10, and 3.11 present results for regressions of exports from the countries in the full panel, Latin American panel, and Southeast Asian panel, respectively, to either the United States or Japan. For the full panel of countries (Table 3.9) the real exchange rate coefficients in Table 3.9 indicate a J-curve effect with positive (albeit insignificant) coefficients on contemporaneous exchange rates and negative (and significant, in the case of Japan) coefficients on lagged exchange rates. The results (in Table 3.9, columns 3 and 6) indicate a positive effect of Japanese foreign investment on exports to both the United States and Japan. There is also a significant effect of direct investment from the United States on panel country exports to Japan. This finding is consistent with a situation where Japanese and American multinational firms' exports to the United States or Japan are increased by direct investment in countries in the panel.

The decomposition of the full panel into the Latin American and Southeast Asian country components reveals which relationships were

Table 3.9. *Exports to the United States or Japan from full developing country panel*

	Exports to United States			Exports to Japan		
RER_t	0.057	0.058	−0.001	0.110	0.068	0.066
	(0.101)	(0.102)	(0.100)	(0.092)	(0.094)	(0.088)
RER_{t-1}	−0.031	−0.031	−0.079	−0.185*	−0.237**	−0.224**
	(0.103)	(0.104)	(0.098)	(0.101)	(0.098)	(0.091)
GDP^i_t	1.076	1.164	0.136	2.20***	1.431**	1.311**
	(0.724)	(0.745)	(0.710)	(0.674)	(0.669)	(0.633)
GDP^i_{t-1}	0.181	0.119	0.739	−0.973	−0.556	−0.759
	(0.729)	(0.751)	(0.685)	(0.686)	(0.650)	(0.620)
$GDP^{export\ destination}_t$	1.522	1.417	2.956**	−0.414	−2.294	−0.836
	(1.326)	(1.353)	(1.264)	(1.980)	(1.944)	(1.846)
$GDP^{export\ destination}_{t-1}$	−0.911	−0.808	−2.673**	0.379	2.009	0.695
	(1.360)	(1.384)	(1.298)	(1.926)	(1.885)	(1.784)
FDI^{us}_t		−0.035	−0.010			0.118**
		(0.058)	(0.052)			(0.048)
FDI^{us}_{t-1}		0.021	−0.015			0.073
		(0.058)	(0.052)			(0.049)
FDI^{japan}_t			0.13***		0.072**	0.064**
			(0.031)		(0.031)	(0.029)
FDI^{japan}_{t-1}			0.067*		0.081**	0.074**
			(0.034)		(0.032)	(0.030)
Constant	−9.34***	−9.54***	−4.088	−3.945	2.391	3.505
	(2.491)	(2.583)	(2.565)	(3.112)	(3.363)	(3.142)
F-tests:						
RER_t, RER_{t-1}	0.07	0.07	0.65	0.56	2.73*	2.75*
FDI^{us}_t, FDI^{us}_{t-1}		0.05	0.22			14.57***
FDI^{japan}_t, FDI^{japan}_{t-1}			21.34***		13.45***	12.45***
adj. R2	0.863	0.860	0.888	0.944	0.950	0.957
No. obs.	98	98	97	98	97	97

Notes: Bilateral real exchange rates defined relative to export destination. *, **, *** = statistical significance at the 10%, 5%, and 1% levels. Standard errors in parentheses.

driving the results of Table 3.9. Specifically, the evidence provided in Tables 3.10 and 3.11 is suggestive of which countries in the panel serve as significant platforms for exporting by multinationals to the United States or Japan. Exports from Latin America to the United States are significantly increased by direct investment from Japan (Table 3.10). However, U.S. FDI into Latin America does not appear to promote further Latin

Table 3.10. *Exports to the United States or Japan from Latin American country panel*

	Exports to United States			Exports to Japan		
RER$_t$	0.009	0.006	-0.028	0.064	0.060	0.038
	(0.065)	(0.066)	(0.068)	(0.072)	(0.082)	(0.074)
RER$_{t-1}$	-0.069	-0.074	-0.967	-0.158*	-0.196**	-0.126
	(0.066)	(0.068)	(0.065)	(0.083)	(0.087)	(0.082)
GDP$_t^i$	-0.257	0.090	-0.357	1.87***	1.714**	1.284*
	(0.564)	(0.686)	(0.686)	(0.625)	(0.644)	(0.674)
GDP$_{t-1}^i$	0.693	0.519	1.011	0.117	0.294	-0.654
	(0.594)	(0.675)	(0.665)	(0.656)	(0.658)	(0.735)
GDP$_t^{export\ destination}$	2.481*	2.063	3.369**	1.231	-0.038	1.781
	(1.329)	(1.526)	(1.481)	(2.214)	(2.506)	(2.449)
GDP$_{t-1}^{export\ destination}$	-1.309	-0.938	-2.513*	-1.018	-0.030	-1.261
	(1.349)	(1.467)	(1.428)	(2.322)	(2.403)	(2.307)
FDI$_t^{us}$		-0.091	-0.055			0.143
		(0.091)	(0.082)			(0.091)
FDI$_{t-1}^{us}$		0.064	-0.003			0.086
		(0.083)	(0.078)			(0.093)
FDI$_t^{japan}$			0.07***		0.041	0.019
			(0.024)		(0.030)	(0.028)
FDI$_{t-1}^{japan}$			0.036		0.033	0.012
			(0.027)		(0.031)	(0.030)
Constant	-6.71***	-7.993**	-6.609**	-15.4***	-12.06***	-6.359
	(2.318)	(3.481)	(3.141)	(3.615)	(3.991)	(4.126)
F-tests:						
RER$_t$, RER$_{t-1}$	0.75	0.90	3.56*	1.17	2.05	0.99
FDI$_t^{us}$, FDI$_{t-1}^{us}$		0.13	0.69			8.88***
FDI$_t^{japan}$, FDI$_{t-1}^{japan}$			9.48***		3.14*	0.58
adj. R2	0.966	0.965	0.973	0.942	0.944	0.954
No. obs.	42	42	41	42	41	41

Notes: Bilateral real exchange rates defined relative to export destination. *, **, *** = statistical significance at the 10%, 5%, and 1% levels. Standard errors in parentheses.

American sales to the United States. The trade-promoting effects of Japanese FDI also is observed in Southeast Asia. In Table 3.11 observe that Southeast Asian exports to the United States and to Japan are both significantly increased by direct investment from Japan. By contrast, for these countries there is no significant increase in exports to either the United States or Japan associated with increased direct investment by the United States.

3.4   Conclusion

The empirical results provided in this chapter document two types of linkages between Latin American and Southeast Asian countries with the United States and Japan: the link between the real exchange rate and direct investment; and the link between the real exchange rate and trade. We show that direct investment into these developing countries affects their trade flows with industrialized countries, even after holding constant the contribution of the real exchange rate. There are significant differences in the linkages shown by regressions for the Latin American and for the Southeast Asian countries vis-à-vis the United States and Japan. In general, real exchange rates have the most significant effect on trade and FDI patterns for Southeast Asia. In this region the effects of FDI on subsequent trade also are strongest. Moreover, the source of FDI – that is, Japan or the United States – influences the degree and direction of the trade effects of FDI.

Our results provide evidence of a number of statistically significant linkages. A real depreciation of the currencies of the Southeast Asian countries with respect to the yen both increases foreign direct investment to these countries from Japan and decreases foreign direct investment to these countries from the United States. Foreign direct investment from Japan to the Southeast Asian countries increases imports from Japan. These imports largely consist of inputs to production. Foreign direct investment from Japan to the Southeast Asian countries also is associated with an increase in exports from these countries to both the United States and Japan. These exports comprise both machinery and (for Japan) raw materials. We also show that foreign direct investment from Japan to Latin America is associated with an increase in the exports of these countries to the United States. These exports consist of machinery and transportation equipment, and some food, leather, primary metals, and raw materials.

For Southeast Asian countries the real exchange rates that we examine are closely related to their nominal exchange rates. The nominal exchange rate regime therefore presents a relevant context for interpretation of our results. Most Southeast Asian countries have pursued basket pegs. Frenkel and Wei (1994) showed that, with the exception of high yen weights observed in the baskets during 1985–86, the weight of the dollar in Southeast Asian currency baskets often was between 90 and 100 percent.[14] Thus, Southeast Asian (and Latin American) countries use the

---

[14] Frenkel and Wei (1994) estimate the weights on various currencies in practice in the basket pegs pursued by Asian countries. These computations are done by regressing

Table 3.11. *Exports to the United States or Japan from Southeast Asian country panel*

	Exports to United States			Exports to Japan		
RER_t	1.723***	1.741***	1.37***	0.91***	0.279	0.266
	(0.480)	(0.486)	(0.493)	(0.308)	(0.319)	(0.338)
RER_{t-1}	0.743	0.677	0.710	0.143	0.364	0.455
	(0.497)	(0.511)	(0.489)	(0.340)	(0.304)	(0.348)
GDP^i_t	3.416***	3.397***	1.612	5.26***	2.053	2.188
	(0.939)	(0.952)	(1.153)	(1.194)	(1.341)	(1.401)
GDP^i_{t-1}	-1.665*	-1.767*	-0.232	-3.56***	-0.952	-0.983
	(0.950)	(0.967)	(1.137)	(1.214)	(1.308)	(1.350)
$GDP^{\text{export destination}}_t$	2.675**	2.504	2.540*	0.887	-1.031	-1.106
	(1.282)	(1.309)	(1.273)	(2.355)	(2.091)	(2.154)
$GDP^{\text{export destination}}_{t-1}$	-1.979	-1.686	-2.079	-0.932	0.310	0.366
	(1.345)	(1.393)	(1.353)	(2.361)	(2.067)	(2.140)
FDI^{us}_t		0.011	0.016			-0.026
		(0.056)	(0.054)			(0.063)
FDI^{us}_{t-1}		0.051	0.038			-0.026
		(0.054)	(0.052)			(0.063)

FDI$_t^{japan}$			0.135**		0.167***	0.171***
			(0.056)		(2.898)	(0.059)
FDI$_{t-1}^{japan}$			0.002		0.106*	0.104*
			(0.051)		(0.056)	(0.057)
Constant	−5.472*	−5.561*	−2.072	−8.991*	4.580	3.735
	(2.758)	(2.792)	(3.050)	(4.927)	(5.401)	(5.774)
F-tests:						
RER$_t$, RER$_{t-1}$	66.17***	59.13***	34.97***	13.9***	5.86**	5.64**
FDI$_t^{us}$, FDI$_{t-1}^{us}$		0.68	0.55			0.36
FDI$_t^{japan}$, FDI$_{t-1}^{japan}$			4.61**		17.04***	16.18***
adj. R2	0.863	0.860	0.872	0.927	0.945	0.943
No. obs.	56	56	56	56	56	56

Notes: Bilateral real exchange rates defined relative to export destination. *, **, *** = statistical significance at the 10%, 5%, and 1% levels. Standard errors in parentheses.

United States dollar as the main benchmark against which their own currencies are valued. An open question concerns the role of the performance of countries not included in the sample in diverting trade or investment from the countries we study here. For example, the real exchange rates of Korea, Singapore, or Taiwan may have had an influence on investment in Indonesia, Malaysia, the Philippines, or Thailand.

The existence of the peg arrangements in which the dollar has a dominant role, in conjunction with our findings about the direction and strength of empirical linkages between exchange rates, trade, and FDI, provide support for a significant role of exchange rate movements in the rapid development of production and trade by manufacturing industries in Southeast Asia: the appreciation of the yen against the dollar since the mid-1980s was a crucial element in this expansion. Yen appreciation against the U.S. dollar since 1985 stimulated Japanese FDI into the dollar area of Southeast Asia (but not into Latin America). These investments furthered the trade linkages of Southeast Asian countries with respect to both Japan and the United States. By pegging to the dollar, Southeast Asian countries became extremely attractive targets for investment and trade when the yen appreciated. Analogously, yen depreciation against the dollar, under the dollar-denominated exchange rate regime of Southeast Asian countries, leaves these countries adversely exposed as a target for FDI and as a comparably attractive trade partner.

Data appendix: Sources and data range

Japan

External direct investment by industry and area from *Monthly Finance Review*, Japan Ministry of Finance, August issues, 1978–80 to 1994.

Aggregate export and import data from IMF, *Direction of Trade Statistics*, 1979–95.

Disaggregated 1- and 2-Digit Standard Industry and Trade Classification (SITC) bilateral exports and imports from United Nations Trade data base.

Exchange rates (real effective and bilateral U.S. dollar rate) from IMF, *International Financial Statistics*, 1979–95 (annual average).

Price indices from IMF, *International Financial Statistics*, 1979–95.

Gross domestic product and GDP deflator from IMF, *International Financial Statistics*, 1979–95.

respective foreign currency values against the domestic currency, with all exchange rates expressed relative to a "neutral" base, the Swiss franc.

United States

Direct investment by destination from Bureau of Economic Analysis (BEA), 1978–93.

Direct investment by industry and destination from U.S. Department of Commerce, *Survey of Current Business*, 1993.

Aggregate export and import data from IMF, *Direction of Trade Statistics*, 1979–95.

Disaggregated 1- and 2-Digit Standard Industrial Classification (SIC) bilateral exports and imports from Bureau of Census data base, 1983–95.

Exchange rates (real effective and bilateral U.S. dollar rate) from IMF, *International Financial Statistics*, 1979–95 (annual average).

Price indices from IMF, *International Financial Statistics*, 1979–95.

Gross domestic product and GDP deflator from IMF, *International Financial Statistics*, 1979–95.

Latin America: Argentina, Brazil, Chile

Exchange rates (real effective and bilateral U.S. dollar rate) from IMF, *International Financial Statistics*, 1979–95 (annual average).

Price indices from IMF, *International Financial Statistics*, 1979–95.

Gross domestic product and GDP deflator from IMF, *International Financial Statistics*, 1979–95.

Southeast Asia: Indonesia, Malaysia, Philippines, Thailand

Exchange rates (real effective and bilateral U.S. dollar rate) from IMF, *International Financial Statistics*, 1979–95 (annual average).

Price indices from IMF, *International Financial Statistics*, 1979–95.

Gross domestic product and GDP deflator from IMF, *International Financial Statistics*, 1979–95.

References

Calvo, G., L. Leiderman, and C. Reinhart (1993). "Capital Inflows to Latin America: The Role of External Factors," *IMF Staff Papers* 40 (1): 108–51.

Dewenter, K. (1995). "Do Exchange Rate Changes Drive Foreign Direct Investment?" *Journal of Business* 68 (3): 405–33.

Eaton, J., and A. Tamura (1994). "Bilateralism and Regionalism in Japanese and U.S. Trade Direct Foreign Investment Patterns," *Journal of the Japanese and International Economies* 8: 478–510.

(1996). "Japanese and U.S. Exports and Investment as Conduits of Growth." In T. Ito and A. Krueger, eds., *Financial Deregulation and Integration in East Asia*, pp. 51–72. Cambridge, Mass.: NBER; Chicago: University of Chicago Press.

Frankel, J. (1993). "Is Japan Creating a Yen Bloc in East Asia and the Pacific?" In J. Frankel and M. Kahler, eds., *Regionalism and Rivalry: Japan and the U.S. in Pacific Asia*, pp. 53–85. Chicago: University of Chicago Press; Cambridge, Mass.: NBER.

Frankel, J., and S. J. Wei (1993). "Trade Blocs and Currency Blocs," NBER Working Paper No. 4335, April. Cambridge, Mass.

——— (1994). "Yen Bloc or Dollar Bloc? East Asian Exchange Rate Policies." In T. Ito and A. Krueger, eds., *Macroeconomic Linkage*, pp. 295–329. Chicago: University of Chicago Press; Cambridge, Mass.: NBER.

Froot, K., ed. (1993). *Foreign Direct Investment.* Chicago: University of Chicago Press; Cambridge, Mass.: NBER.

Froot, K., and J. Stein (1991). "Exchange Rates and Foreign Direct Investment: An Imperfect Capital Markets Approach," *Quarterly Journal of Economics* 106 (4): 1191–1217.

Goldberg, L. (forthcoming). "Exchange Rates and Investment Response in Latin America." In B. J. Cohen, ed., *International Trade and Finance: New Frontiers for Research: Festschrift in Honor of Peter B. Kenen.* Cambridge: Cambridge University Press.

Goldberg, L., and C. Kolstad (1995). "Foreign Direct Investment, Exchange Rate Variability, and Demand Uncertainty," *International Economic Review* 36 (4): 855–73.

Ito, T., and A. Krueger, eds. (1996). *Financial Deregulation and Integration in East Asia.* Cambridge, Mass.: NBER; Chicago: University of Chicago Press.

Klein, M., and E. Rosengren (1994). "The Real Exchange Rate and Foreign Direct Investment in the United States: Relative Wealth vs. Relative Wage Effects," *Journal of International Economics* 36 (3–4): 373–89.

Kohsaka, A. (1996). "Interdependence through Capital Flows in Pacific Asia and the Role of Japan." In T. Ito and A. Krueger, eds., *Financial Deregulation and Integration in East Asia*, pp. 107–42. Cambridge, Mass.: NBER; Chicago: University of Chicago Press.

Matsuoka, M., and B. Rose (1994). *The DIR Guide to Japanese Economic Statistics.* New York: Oxford University Press.

Tavlas, G., and Y. Ozeki (1992). "The Internationalization of Currencies: An Appraisal of the Japanese Yen," IMF Occasional Paper No. 90, January. Washington, D.C.

CHAPTER 4

Capital inflows and the real exchange rate: Analytical framework and econometric evidence

Pierre-Richard Agénor and Alexander W. Hoffmaister

4.1 Introduction

The magnitude of the capital inflows recorded by developing countries in recent years has raised a variety of issues in the context of macroeconomic management. One of the main challenges faced by policy markers around the world has been how to limit the potentially adverse effects of these inflows on the real exchange rate and the current account. Figure 4.1 illustrates the behavior of the real exchange rate in a group of Asian and Latin American countries since the early 1990s. In most Latin American countries, the real exchange rate experienced a significant real appreciation since the beginning of the inflow episode; in Asia, such a phenomenon was less common. More specifically, while countries like Chile and Malaysia (and, to a greater extent, Korea and Indonesia) have managed to avoid a significant real appreciation, others like Argentina, Mexico (prior to the December 1994 peso crisis), Peru, and the Philippines have recorded a strong real appreciation. In Brazil, the real exchange rate also appreciated significantly between 1991 and end 1994, prior to the adoption of the Real stabilization plan.

As argued in several recent studies, two key factors determine the evolution of the real exchange rate in response to a surge in capital inflows. The first is the macroeconomic policy response. In several countries in Latin America (most notably, Argentina and Mexico and, more recently, Brazil), a fixed (or predetermined) exchange rate has played a key initial role in the authorities' strategy to reduce inflation. But as a

We would like to thank, without implication, Hamid Faruqee, James Gordon, Reuven Glick, Kenneth Kasa, Alfredo Leone, John McDermott, Jonathan Ostry, Carmen Reinhart, Peter Wickham, and participants at the conference for very helpful discussions and comments, and Brooks Calvo for research assistance. The views expressed in this chapter do not necessarily represent those of the International Monetary Fund.

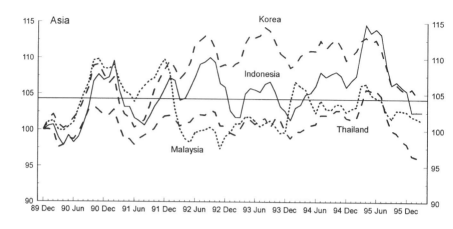

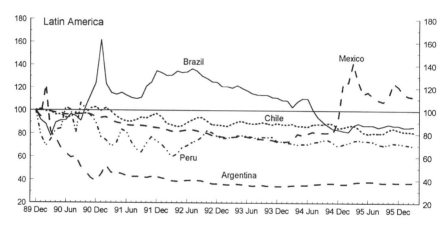

Figure 4.1. Real exchange rates in Asia and Latin America (December 1989 = 100). *Note*: An increase is a depreciation. *Source*: IMF, Information Notice System.

result of inertial factors, continued increases in prices of nontraded goods have often led to upward pressure on the real exchange rate.[1]

The second factor that determines the impact of capital inflows on the real exchange rate relates to the composition of these flows, and their effects on the composition of aggregate demand. As documented by

---

[1] Another important element in the policy response during the early phase of the capital inflows episode has been sterilization. But as emphasized by numerous authors – see, notably, Calvo, Leiderman, and Reinhart (1996), and Frankel and Okongwu (1996) – sterilization has been largely ineffective.

various researchers, a large proportion of capital inflows to Latin America in the past few years has taken the form of portfolio investment rather than foreign direct investment, in contrast with what occurred in some Asian countries. The fact that capital flows to Latin America were associated mostly with an increase in consumption (with a large component consisting of expenditure on nontradable goods), rather than investment, may explain the large real appreciation observed in some countries. Table 4.1 shows indeed that in Latin America private consumption (as a proportion of GDP) rose by more, and total investment by less, than in Asia since the early 1990s.[2]

The purpose of this chapter is to provide an analytical and quantitative framework for the study of the macroeconomic effects of capital inflows (and their determinants) on short-term fluctuations of the real exchange rate in a fixed (or predetermined) exchange rate regime. Section 4.2 presents the conceptual framework. Section 4.3 develops an econometric model (based on vector autoregression techniques) linking capital inflows, domestic and foreign interest rates, government spending, money base velocity, and the cyclical (or short-term) component of the real exchange rate. The analysis focuses on four countries: Korea, Mexico, the Philippines, and Thailand.[3] Generalized variance decompositions are used to assess the relative importance of various factors in explaining real exchange rate fluctuations, whereas the effects of shocks to world interest rates and government spending are assessed using generalized impulse response functions. The concluding section summarizes the main results of the chapter and discusses some implications of the analysis.

4.2   Analytical Framework

The link between capital movements and the real exchange rate has been addressed in a number of recent studies. A detailed analysis of the effects of various "pull" (domestic) and "push" (external) factors on these variables has been provided by Agénor (1996), in the context of a flexible

---

[2] For a more detailed discussion, see Calvo, Leiderman, and Reinhart (1996) and the recent study by Corbo and Hernández (1996), which compares the experiences of four Latin American countries (Argentina, Chile, Colombia, and Mexico) and five East Asian countries (Indonesia, Korea, Malaysia, the Philippines, and Thailand) with capital inflows.

[3] While the choice of countries was partly dictated by data availability, the selected group presents some interesting contrasts regarding the macroeconomic effects of inflows. See Corbo and Hernández (1996), Glick and Moreno (1995), and Koenig (1996). All these countries did not, however, pursue a fixed (or predetermined) exchange rate regime during the whole sample period – an issue to which we return.

Table 4.1. *Asia and Latin America: Macroeconomic indicators (annual averages; in percent of GDP, unless otherwise noted)*

	1983–89	1990–95	1994	1995
Asia[a]				
Real GDP[b]	6.3	6.5	7.0	7.4
Consumer price inflation[b]	6.7	8.0	7.6	7.6
Private consumption	62.4	58.4	58.2	58.8
Private saving[c]	22.9	22.0	22.2	22.6
Fiscal balance[d]	−4.2	−2.3	−2.0	−1.9
Current account balance	−0.7	−2.1	−1.7	−2.9
Real effective exchange rate[e]	−3.8	−1.0	1.6	−0.4
Net capital inflows	2.0	3.6	3.4	4.0
Change in reserves	−1.4	−1.6	−1.3	−0.7
Total saving	24.6	27.7	28.2	28.5
Total investment	25.0	29.8	29.9	31.3
Latin America[f]				
Real GDP[b]	2.1	2.6	4.9	0.8
Consumer price inflation[b]	180.5	230.8	263.6	40.8
Private consumption	64.1	67.3	67.5	65.8
Private saving	16.4	13.9	13.9	15.5
Fiscal balance[d]	−4.4	−0.1	0.1	−0.5
Current account balance	−0.6	−1.8	−2.8	−1.8
Real effective exchange rate[e]	−0.3	3.5	6.0	−1.2
Net capital inflows	0.7	3.3	2.3	3.6
Change in reserves	−0.2	−1.5	0.7	−2.3
Total saving	20.1	18.5	18.0	18.2
Total investment	20.0	20.5	21.1	20.0

[a] India, Indonesia, Korea, Malaysia, the Philippines, Taiwan, and Thailand.
[b] Annual percentage change. An increase is an appreciation.
[c] For Indonesia, private saving data for 1983–89 refer to 1988–89 only.
[d] Reflects only central government expenditures and revenues, implying the fiscal balance does not equal net public sector saving.
[e] An increase is an appreciation.
[f] Argentina, Brazil, Chile, Colombia, Mexico, Peru, and Venezuela.
Source: International Monetary Fund *World Economic Outlook* database.

price, two-sector optimizing model of a fixed exchange rate economy. A key feature of the model is the assumption that domestic private borrowers (lenders) face an upward- (downward-)sloping supply curve of funds on world capital markets, and internalize the effect of capital market imperfections in making their portfolio decisions. This leads to a setting in which capital is imperfectly mobile internationally – a feature of the model that appears to be well supported by the evidence for developing countries (Agénor and Montiel, 1996). By allowing domestic interest rates to be determined through the equilibrium condition of the money market instead of foreign interest rates (as implied by uncovered interest rate parity, under perfect capital mobility), feedback effects on capital inflows induced by changes in overall domestic macroeconomic conditions can be better analyzed.[4]

Formally, consider a small open economy in which perfect foresight prevails and four types of agents operate: households, producers, the government, and the central bank. The nominal exchange rate (defined as the home currency price of foreign currency) is devalued at the constant rate ε. The economy produces both traded and nontraded goods, using capital and homogeneous labor. The capital stock in each sector is fixed, and labor is perfectly mobile across sectors.

4.2.1 Households

Households supply labor inelastically and consume both traded and nontraded goods. Consumption decisions follow a two-step process: households first determine the optimal level of total consumption, and then allocate that amount between consumption of the two goods. If we assume that government expenditure does not yield direct utility, the representative household's discounted lifetime utility can be written as

$$\int_0^\infty \left\{ \ln m + \frac{c^{1-\eta}}{1-\eta} \right\} e^{-\rho t} dt, \quad \rho > 0 \tag{1}$$

where ρ denotes the rate of time preference (assumed constant), c total consumption expenditure, and m real money balances, measured in terms of the price of the consumption basket, P. The parameter η is positive and different from unity. The instantaneous utility function is assumed to be additively separable in consumption and real money balances. Households hold three categories of financial assets in their portfolios: domestic money (which bears no interest), domestic govern-

---

[4] The model does not require the rate of time preference to be equal at all times to the world interest rate, as is the case (to ensure a stationary level of consumption) in standard, infinite-horizon optimizing models of small open economies. This is particularly important when analyzing the effect of changes in the world interest rate, since the arbitrary assumption that such shifts are accompanied by an equal change in the rate of time preference is not required.

ment bonds (the real stock of which is b), and foreign bonds b^*. Real wealth of the representative household a can thus be defined as

$$a = m + b + b^*. \tag{2}$$

Both b and b^* are measured in terms of the price of the consumption basket. Specifically, $b^* \equiv EB^*/P$, where E is the nominal exchange rate and B^* represents foreign borrowing measured in foreign currency terms.

The flow budget constraint is given by[5]

$$\dot{a} = q + ib - c - \tau + \left(i^* - \theta\right)b^* + \varepsilon b^* - \pi a, \tag{3}$$

where q denotes net factor income (derived later), τ the real value of lump-sum taxes, i the domestic nominal interest rate, and π the domestic inflation rate. The term $-\pi a$ accounts for capital losses on total wealth resulting from inflation, and εb^* the capital gain resulting from the increase in the domestic currency value of foreign assets due to exchange rate depreciation. The rate of return on foreign bonds $i^* - \theta$ consists of an exogenous "base" (or risk-free) interest rate i^* and an endogenous discount θ, which captures risk factors and is positively related to the outstanding level of foreign assets held by the household.[6]

Specifically, we use the linear approximation $\theta \simeq \gamma b^*/2$, where $\gamma > 0$. In the first stage of the consumption decision process, households treat ε, π, q, i, i^*, and τ as given, internalize the effect of their portfolio decisions on θ, and maximize (1) subject to (2) and (3) by choosing a sequence $\{c, m, b, b^*\}_{t=0}^{\infty}$. Let $r = i - \pi$ denote the domestic (consumption-based) real rate of interest and $\sigma = 1/\eta$ the intertemporal elasticity of substitution. The optimality conditions are given by:

$$c^{\eta}/m = i, \quad \Rightarrow \quad m = c^{\eta}/i, \tag{4}$$

$$b^* = \left(i^* + \varepsilon - i\right)/\gamma, \tag{5}$$

$$\dot{c}/c = \sigma\left(r - \rho\right), \tag{6}$$

together with the transversality condition $\lim_{t \to \infty}(e^{-\rho t}a_t) = 0$. Equation (4) is the money demand function and is derived by equating the marginal rate of substitution between consumption and real money balances to the opportunity cost of holding money, the domestic nominal interest rate.

---

[5] Except as otherwise indicated, partial derivatives are denoted by corresponding subscripts, while the total derivative of a function of a single argument is denoted by a prime. A sign over a variable refers to the sign of the corresponding partial derivative. Also, by definition, $\dot{x} \equiv dx/dt$.

[6] See Agénor (1996, 1997) for a detailed discussion of this specification.

Equation (5) indicates that holdings of foreign bonds are positively related to the difference between the sum of the risk-free foreign interest rate and devaluation rate, and the domestic interest rate. Equation (6) shows that total consumption rises or falls depending on whether the domestic real interest rate exceeds or falls below the rate of time preference.

In the second stage of the consumption decision process, the representative household maximizes a Cobb-Douglas subutility function $v(c_N, c_T)$, where c_N denotes purchases of nontraded goods, and c_T expenditure on traded goods, subject to the budget constraint $P_N c_N + E c_T = Pc$, where $P_N(E)$ denotes the price of the home (traded) good.[7] The solution to this program yields the familiar result according to which the representative household sets the marginal rate of substitution between home and traded goods equal to their relative price $z \equiv E/P_N$, that is, the real exchange rate:

$$c_N/c_T = \delta z/(1-\delta), \tag{7}$$

where δ denotes the share of home goods consumption in total consumption expenditure, which is allocated according to

$$c_N = \delta z^{1-\delta} c, \quad c_T = (1-\delta) z^{-\delta} c. \tag{8}$$

The consumer price index P is thus:

$$P = P_N^\delta E^{1-\delta}, \quad 0 < \delta < 1 \tag{9}$$

so that

$$\pi = \varepsilon - \delta \dot{z}/z. \tag{10}$$

4.2.2 Supply side

Technology for the production of both traded and nontraded goods is characterized by decreasing returns to labor:

$$y_h = y_h(n_h), \quad y_h' > 0, y_h'' < 0, \tag{11}$$

where y_h denotes output of good h (with $h = N, T$), and n_h the quantity of labor employed in sector h. From the first-order conditions for profit maximization, the labor demand functions can be derived as

---

[7] The world price of the traded good is normalized to unity.

$$n_T^d = n_T^d(\bar{w}_T), \quad n_N^d = n_N^d(z\bar{w}_T), \tag{12}$$

where w_T is the product wage in the traded goods sector. Nominal wages are perfectly flexible. w_T is thus determined by the equilibrium condition of the labor market:

$$n_T^d(w_T) + n_N^d(zw_T) = n^s,$$

where n^s denotes the (exogenous) supply of labor. This equation implies that the equilibrium real wage (measured in terms of traded goods) is negatively related to the real exchange rate:

$$w_T = w_T(z). \quad w_T' < 0, \quad |w_T'| < 1. \tag{13}$$

Substituting this result in equations (12), and noting that $d(zw_T)/dz > 0$ yields the sectoral supply functions:

$$y_N^s = y_N^s(\bar{z}), \quad y_T^s = y_T^s(\overset{+}{z}). \tag{14}$$

4.2.3 *Government and the central bank*

The only function of the central bank is to ensure the costless conversion, at the official parity, of domestic money into foreign money, and vice versa. Since there is no credit, the real money stock is equal to

$$m = z^\delta R, \tag{15}$$

where R is the central bank's stock of net foreign assets, measured in foreign currency terms. Real profits of the central bank consist of interest on its holdings of foreign assets $i^* z^\delta R$, and capital gains on reserves $\varepsilon z^\delta R$, which are transferred to the government.

The government consumes only home goods, in quantity g_N. For simplicity, it is also assumed to compensate private agents for the loss in interest income incurred as a result of imperfections in world capital markets.[8] It balances its budget by levying lump-sum taxes on households. Setting the constant level of domestic bonds to zero, the budget constraint of the government is thus

$$\tau = z^{\delta-1}g_N + \theta b^* = (i^* + \varepsilon)z^\delta R. \tag{16}$$

---

[8] This assumption is, of course, somewhat artificial, since households are assumed to make their portfolio decisions without internalizing the fiscal policy rule. However, for the purpose at hand, it does simplify the algebra, without affecting the main implications of the analysis. Agénor (1997) provides a full treatment.

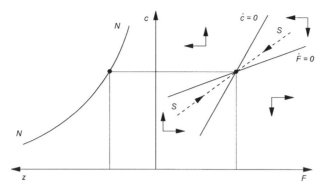

Figure 4.2. Steady-state equilibrium.

4.2.4 Market-clearing conditions

To close the model requires specifying the equilibrium conditions for the home goods market and the money market. The former condition is given by

$$y_N^s = \delta z^{1-\delta} c + g_N. \tag{17}$$

Using equation (4), the equilibrium condition of the money market can be solved for the market-clearing interest rate:

$$i = i\!\left(\overset{+}{c},\ \overset{-}{m}\right). \tag{18}$$

4.2.5 Dynamic structure and steady state

As described in detail by Agénor (1996), the dynamic structure of the model can be reduced to a first-order differential equation system involving two variables: private consumption c (which is a jump variable) and the economy's net stock of foreign assets $F = R + B^*$, which evolves gradually over time as a result of changes in the current account balance:

$$\dot{F} = i^* F + y_T^s - c_T. \tag{19}$$

The steady-state equilibrium of the model is depicted in Figure 4.2. The curve NN on the left-hand side of the figure shows the combinations of consumption and the real exchange rate that are consistent with equilibrium in the market for nontraded goods (equation (17)). On the right-hand side of the figure, the locus $[\dot{F} = 0]$ gives the combinations of c and F for which the current account is in balance (derived from equation (19)), whereas the locus $[\dot{c} = 0]$ depicts the combinations of c and F

for which consumption does not change over time. Saddlepath stability requires that the $[\dot{c} = 0]$ curve be steeper than $[\dot{F} = 0]$ curve. The saddlepath SS slopes downward, so that a current account deficit, for instance, must be accompanied by a higher level of private consumption and an appreciating exchange rate. The steady-state solution is obtained by setting $\dot{c} = \dot{F} = 0$. From equation (9), $\tilde{\pi} = \pi_N = \varepsilon$, where π_N is the nontraded goods inflation rate. From equation (6),

$$\tilde{r} = \tilde{i} - \varepsilon = \rho. \tag{20}$$

Substituting this result in (5) yields

$$\tilde{b}^* = \left(i^* - \rho\right)\big/\gamma, \tag{21}$$

and from (4) and (20):

$$\tilde{m} = m\big(\tilde{c},\ \rho + \varepsilon\big). \tag{22}$$

Finally, from equation (19),

$$\tilde{y}_T^s - \tilde{c}_T = i^* \tilde{F}.$$

Thus, the steady-state solution of the model is such that the current account must be in equilibrium, domestic inflation and the rate of inflation in the price of home goods are equal to the devaluation rate, and the real interest rate is equal to the rate of time preference – so that the domestic nominal interest rate is equal to the rate of time preference plus the devaluation rate. Real holdings of foreign bonds are proportional to the difference between the world interest rate and the rate of time preference, indicating that in the long run domestic private agents can be net creditors (debtors) only to the extent that their rate of time preference is lower (greater) than the foreign discount rate.

4.2.6   *Shocks, capital flows, and relative prices*

To illustrate the functioning of the model, consider a permanent, unanticipated increase in government spending on home goods g_N, financed by an increase in lump-sum taxes (equation (16)). This shock has no long-term effect on the domestic nominal interest rate, as implied by equation (20), and no effect on private holdings of foreign assets, as implied by equation (21). The associated increase in lump-sum taxes exerts a negative wealth effect, which leads private agents to reduce consumption. The "crowding out" effect is not complete, however, so that the real exchange rate must appreciate to maintain equilibrium of the market for nontraded goods. The fall in private spending is associated with a reduction in real money balances, since domestic interest rates do not change (equation (22)). But the shock has an ambiguous effect on the economy's stock of net foreign assets. The reason is that the appreciation of the real exchange rate has an adverse effect on output of traded goods. Since both production and consumption of traded goods fall, the net effect on the trade balance cannot be ascertained a priori; thus, whether the service account surplus (and thus the economy's stock of net foreign assets) must increase or not cannot be determined unambiguously.[9] The two panels in Figure 4.3 illustrate the two cases.

On impact, since the increase in lump-sum taxes associated with the rise in government spending represents a negative wealth effect, private consumption always falls. But the movement in the real exchange rate is now ambiguous and depends on the strength of consumption smoothing effects. If the degree of intertemporal substitution is low (so that private consumption changes by a relatively small amount, implying that net absorption of home goods rises), the real exchange rate will appreciate. Real money balances also fall on impact. But since both private consumption and money holdings fall, the domestic nominal interest rate (and thus the interest rate differential) may either rise or fall on impact; with a low degree of intertemporal substitution it tends to rise – as illustrated in both panels of Figure 4.3. The increase in the rate of return on domestic assets implies that holdings of foreign bonds must fall, so that the economy experiences capital inflows. Because of the monotonicity of the adjustment path toward the new long-run equilibrium, the stock of net foreign assets continuously rises or falls during the transition according to whether it rises or falls in the new steady state. During the transition, consumption rises (falls), and the real exchange rate appreciates (depreciates), if net foreign assets increase (decline).

Consider now the effects of a permanent reduction in the world risk-free interest rate, i^*, and suppose that the country is initially a net creditor ($\tilde{F} > 0$).[10] The long-run effects are a reduction in aggregate

[9] As shown by Agénor (1996) – and, in a related context, by Penati (1987) – the outcome depends, in particular, on the sensitivity of production in the traded goods sector to changes in relative prices.

[10] Many economists have attributed a large role to the cyclical reduction in interest rates in the United States in explaining the surge in capital inflows to developing countries in the early 1990s. See Calvo, Leiderman, and Reinhart (1996), Fernández-Arias (1996), Fernández-Arias and Montiel (1996), and Frankel and Okongwu (1996). Agénor (1996) discusses the effects of various other shocks in the foregoing model, in particular, a positive money demand shock, and an increase in productivity in the tradable sector.

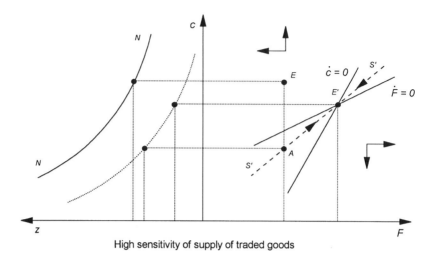

High sensitivity of supply of traded goods

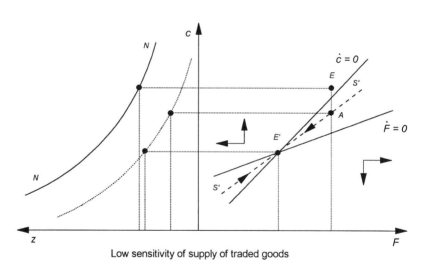

Low sensitivity of supply of traded goods

Figure 4.3. Increase in government spending on home goods.

consumption, a depreciation of the real exchange rate, and a reduction in total holdings of foreign assets. At the initial level of the real exchange rate, the reduction in the world interest rate lowers interest income. To maintain external balance, consumption must therefore fall. At the same time, the reduction in the rate of return on foreign assets reduces private demand for foreign bonds. Since consumption falls, real money balances – with the nominal interest rate remaining constant – must also fall. Thus, at the initial level of relative prices, the overall stock of foreign assets falls – compounding the initial negative effect on interest income and the current account. The reduction in consumption expenditure lowers demand for nontraded goods and leads to a depreciation of the real exchange rate, together with an increase in output of traded goods. The fall in consumption of traded goods and the expansion of output of tradables bring about the required improvement in the trade balance, which restores external equilibrium.

Since the steady-state stock of foreign assets falls, the transition (given the permanent nature of the shock and the monotonic nature of the adjustment path) must involve a sequence of current account deficits. However, on impact the real exchange rate may either appreciate or depreciate. The initial effect of a reduction in the rate of return on foreign assets is a fall in interest income for the economy as a whole (since overall holdings of foreign assets cannot change on impact), a reduction in the private demand for foreign bonds, and an increase in the demand for domestic currency holdings. This instantaneous portfolio shift takes place through an inflow of capital (a discrete reduction in private holdings of foreign bonds) and an offsetting movement in central bank holdings of foreign assets, which leads (under unsterilized intervention) to a discrete increase in the real money stock. However, whether domestic interest rates rise or fall to maintain equilibrium in the money market cannot be ascertained a priori, because the real exchange rate (and thus aggregate consumption) may appreciate or depreciate on impact.

Intuitively, the ambiguity emerges as a result of conflicting wealth and intertemporal effects on consumption. On the one hand, the expected future reduction in interest income (induced by the reduction in the world interest rate *and* the level of financial wealth) tends to reduce immediately (at the initial level of the real exchange rate) private expenditure and increase saving. On the other, a reduction in the world interest rate encourages agents to save less (and consume more) today, since the rate of return on foreign assets has fallen (intertemporal effect). Because the initial effect on aggregate consumption is ambiguous, the real exchange rate may either appreciate or depreciate on impact.

If the degree of intertemporal substitution is large, aggregate consumption will rise on impact, and the real exchange rate will appreciate. This is the case characterized in the upper panel in Figure 4.4. Because consumption of both home and traded goods increases, the trade balance (which, in the initial equilibrium, is characterized by a deficit equal in

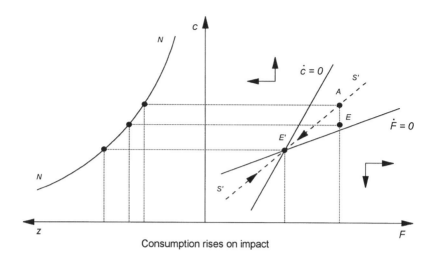

Consumption rises on impact

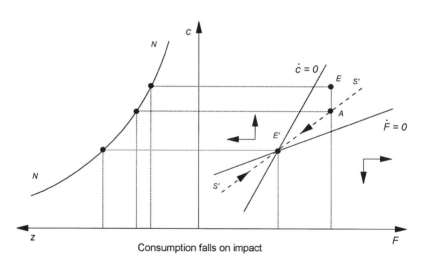

Consumption falls on impact

Figure 4.4. Reduction in the world interest rate (net creditor country).

absolute value to interest income on net foreign assets) tends to deteriorate. The real appreciation leads to a reduction in output of traded goods, which compounds the effect of the increase in consumption on the trade deficit. Since interest income received on the initial stock of assets always falls, the economy generates a current account deficit on impact. Real money balances unambiguously increase whereas private holdings of foreign bonds fall. The increase in the domestic money stock (induced by the discrete portfolio adjustment) tends to lower the domestic interest rate on impact, but the increase in consumption tends to raise it. The net effect is in general ambiguous. The increase in domestic interest rates, of course, reinforces the effect of a reduction in the world interest rate on the demand for foreign bonds, and further stimulates capital inflows.

The transition period is characterized by a continuous reduction in the stock of foreign assets (associated with current account deficits), a fall in consumption, and a depreciation of the real exchange rate. The fall in consumption and the expansion in output of traded goods (resulting from the real depreciation) tend to reverse over time the adverse effect of the initial appreciation on the trade balance. The trade deficit falls over time, eventually turning into a trade surplus. However, because interest payments continue to fall with the reduction in the stock of assets, improvements in the trade balance are not large enough to prevent the current account from remaining in deficit until the new steady state is reached. Because the devaluation rate does not change, the nominal interest rate must fall in order to return to its initial value and ensure equality between the real interest rate and the rate of time preference. And since the domestic interest rate falls, holdings of foreign assets by the private sector tend to increase during the transition, thereby leading to capital outflows and lower reserve accumulation by the central bank. The domestic money stock is thus falling during the transition.

If the degree of intertemporal substitution is sufficiently small, consumption will fall on impact and the real exchange rate will depreciate. This is the case characterized in the lower panel in Figure 4.4. Although the fall in consumption of traded goods and the expansion of output of these goods (resulting from the real depreciation) lead initially to an improvement in the trade balance, the reduction in interest income is large enough to generate a current account deficit. The net effect on the domestic interest rate is now unambiguously negative, since consumption falls. This tends to increase the demand for foreign bonds. Because both the world interest rate and the domestic interest rate fall, however, whether the net effect on real money balances and the demand for foreign bonds is positive or negative cannot be determined a priori. Thus, the economy may experience either capital inflows or capital outflows. If the reduction in the world interest rate is larger than the induced reduction in the domestic interest rate, holdings of foreign bonds will fall and the economy will experience capital inflows on impact. Real money balances in this case will rise. Despite the reduction in private expenditure on both categories of goods and the depreciation of the real exchange rate (which stimulates output of traded goods), the fall in interest income ensures that the current account remains in deficit. The domestic interest rate rises gradually toward its initial level, stimulating further capital inflows. With consumption falling and domestic interest rates increasing, real money balances tend to fall over time.

Consider now the case of a net debtor country ($\tilde{F} < 0$). The long-run effects of a permanent reduction in the world interest rate are again a reduction in consumption, a depreciation of the real exchange rate, and a reduction in total holdings of foreign assets – that is, an increase in foreign debt. The initial effect of the reduction in the cost of borrowing on world capital markets is an increase in private foreign indebtedness, which results in higher interest payments and a deterioration of the service account. To maintain external balance in the long run, the initial trade surplus (which is just equal, in absolute terms, to the initial deficit in the service account) must increase. Consumption must therefore fall. This leads to a depreciation of the real exchange rate, which in turn stimulates output of traded goods and further improves the trade balance. Because the nominal interest rate remains constant, real money balances – and thus official reserves – fall also. With foreign borrowing by private agents increasing, and net foreign assets held by the central bank falling, the economy's external debt unambiguously rises.

The impact effects of a permanent reduction in the world interest rate on private spending and relative prices, in contrast to the case where the economy is initially a net creditor, can be signed unambiguously. As illustrated in Figure 4.5, consumption increases, and the real exchange rate appreciates. This is because the wealth and intertemporal effects operate now in the same direction: the reduction in the world interest rate not only encourages agents to save less (and consume more) today, but it also lowers the debt burden and generates a positive wealth effect. Although the trade balance and the service account move in opposite directions (the former deteriorates, whereas the latter improves), the net effect is a current account deficit on impact; and if the degree of intertemporal substitution is sufficiently low, the domestic interest rate will rise on impact, and the economy will experience a capital inflow. Because of the permanent nature of the shock and the monotonic nature of the adjustment process, the current account remains in deficit throughout the transition period, with consumption falling toward its new, lower steady-state level, and the real exchange rate depreciating – with both effects contributing to a gradual reversal of the initial deterioration in the trade deficit. During the transition, with the domestic interest rate returning to its initial value, the economy experiences capital outflows.

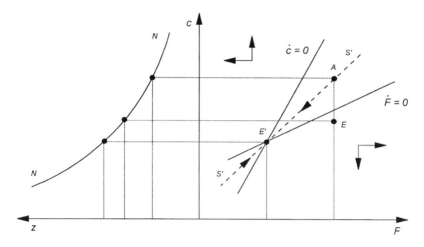

Figure 4.5. Reduction in the world interest rate (net debtor country).

4.3 Econometric analysis

As noted in the introduction, although the links between capital movements and the real exchange rate have been documented in several descriptive studies, there exist very few attempts to examine these links in a quantitative framework. This section presents an econometric analysis that may be useful in that regard. The analysis is based on a near-vector autoregression (near-VAR) model, which captures some of the key relationships emphasized in the analytical model described in the previous section.[11] We begin by presenting the methodology. We then examine variance decompositions and the dynamic response of the system to shocks.

4.3.1 Methodology

The specific variables that are included in our near-VAR model are a broad measure of capital inflows in proportion of aggregate output (denoted ky), changes in the uncovered interest rate differential ($idiff$), government expenditure as a proportion of aggregate output (gy), money base velocity ($veloc$), the change in the "world" interest rate (iw), and the temporary component of the real exchange rate (lzc), which is

---

[11] Some recent contributions to the analysis of the macroeconomic effects of capital inflows have used a VAR framework. See Abdel-Motaal (1995), and Morandé (1992). Hamilton (1994) provides a general discussion of VAR and near-VAR approaches.

denoted TCRER and whose derivation is explained later. The near-VAR approach allows us to treat the government spending–output ratio and changes in the world interest rate as block exogenous variables. The endogenous block consists therefore of capital flows, changes in the interest rate differential, TCRER, and velocity. Precise definitions of all variables are given in the appendix. In particular, the world interest rate is proxied by U.S. interest rates.

In line with the analytical model described in the previous section, where the *stock* demand for foreign assets is related to the *level* of the interest rate differential, we relate *changes* in the interest rate differential to capital *flows* in the empirical model.[12] Our empirical specification – whose statistical adequacy is established later – captures the key feature of our theoretical framework, namely, the view that capital movements respond not only to external factors (such as changes in world interest rates) but also to changes in domestic macroeconomic conditions, as captured by movements in domestic interest rates and fiscal policy. The addition of money base velocity plays the role of a "control" variable, which is meant to capture indirect effects of changes in the money supply on capital flows, through their effect on domestic interest rates.

The focus on the TCRER is motivated by two considerations. First, from a statistical point of view, the real exchange rate in the group of countries considered here is not stationary (as indicated by the unit root tests discussed later), while the other variables described earlier are stationary. Detrending the real exchange rate avoids mixing stationary and nonstationary variables in our econometric model. Moreover, the data for the countries in this study (as noted later) are available only for a time span of twelve years or less, whereas available statistical methods require much longer time series to provide reliable long-run inference. From an economic point of view, focusing on the TCRER is related to the assumption that, in line with the analytical framework described in the previous section, it is the stock of net foreign assets, rather than changes in this stock (capital flows), that affect the trend (or steady-state) value of the real exchange rate. The (stationary) temporary component can be interpreted as transitory deviations from the long-run path, resulting from short-term cyclical and speculative factors.[13]

---

[12] Our treatment of the link between interest rate differentials and the demand for foreign assets may ignore long-run information. In practice, however, given the short size of the sample and available techniques, we are skeptical that these data could be used to make informative long-run inferences.

[13] Note that the cyclical component does not necessarily represent "disequilibrium" movements but rather, as illustrated in the model here, transitional (equilibrium) adjustment

To decompose the real exchange rate into a nonstationary (trend) component and a stationary one, two commonly used techniques are implemented here. The first is the Beveridge-Nelson (BN) approach, the second the Hodrick-Prescott (HP) filter. To highlight the main features of these techniques, suppose that the observed variable x_t has no seasonal component and can be expressed as the sum of a trend x_t^* component and a cyclical component, x_t^c:

$$x_t = x_t^* + x_t^c. \tag{23}$$

At period t, the econometrician can observe x_t but cannot measure either x_t^* or x_t^c. The BN approach is motivated by the observation that many macroeconomic time series are well captured by ARIMA processes. Specifically, suppose that the series x_t follows an ARIMA($p, 1, q$) process. Beveridge and Nelson (1981) showed that any such process can be represented in terms of a stochastic trend plus stationary component, where the former is a random walk (possibly with drift) and the latter is an ARIMA($p, 0, q$) or, more compactly, ARMA(p, q) process.[14]

Formally, the model for $\{x_t\}_{t=0}^T$, where T is the sample size, can be written as

$$\Psi(L)(1 - L)x_t = \mu + \Theta(L)\varepsilon_t, \tag{24}$$

where L is the lag operator, $\Psi(L) = \Sigma_{h=0}^p \phi_h L^h$, $\Theta(L) = \Sigma_{h=0}^q \theta_h L^h$, μ is a constant term, and ε_t is an i.i.d. error. Inverting $\Psi(L)$ gives $(1 - L)x_t = \gamma + B(L)\varepsilon_t$, where $\gamma = (\Sigma_{h=0}^p \phi_h)^{-1}\mu$, and $B(L) = \Psi(L)^{-1}\Theta(L)$. Recursively substituting for x_t and assuming that $x_0 = \varepsilon_\tau = 0$ (for $\tau \leq 0$) yields

$$x_t = \gamma t + B(L)\sum_{\tau=1}^t \varepsilon_\tau,$$

which can be rewritten as (Blackburn and Ravn, 1991):

$$x_t = \gamma t + b\sum_{\tau=1}^t \varepsilon_\tau + G(L)\varepsilon_\tau, \tag{25}$$

where $b = \Sigma_{h=0}^\infty b_h$, $G(L) = \Sigma_{k=0}^\infty g_k L^k$, and $g_k = -\Sigma_{h=k+1}^\infty b_h$. The trend and cyclical components are given respectively by $x_t^* = \gamma t + b\Sigma_{\tau=1}^t \varepsilon_\tau$ and

---

to shocks to fundamentals. For an analysis (in an error–correction framework) of the effects of fundamentals on the real exchange rate, see Chinn (1996), Faruqee (1995), and Montiel (1996). The last-named study emphasizes the role of productivity differentials as well as relative stocks of foreign assets.

[14] See also Cuddington and Winters (1987) and Miller (1988). The BN technique has been used by, among others, Baxter (1994) in modeling real exchange rates.

$x_t^c = G(L)\varepsilon_t$. Thus, the trend component follows a random walk with drift. The equivalent representation is therefore

$$x_t^* - x_{t-1}^* = \gamma + b\varepsilon_t, \quad x_t^c = G(L)\varepsilon_t.$$

The second technique used here to define the cyclical component of the real exchange rate is the HP filter.[15] The technique consists essentially in specifying an adjustment rule whereby the trend component of the series x_t moves continuously and adjusts gradually. Formally, the unobserved component x_t^* is extracted by solving the following minimization problem:

$$\underset{x_t^*}{Min}\left[\sum_{t=1}^{T}\left(x_t - x_t^* \right)^2 + \lambda\sum_{t=2}^{T-1}\left[\left(x_{t+1}^* - x_t^* \right) - \left(x_t^* - x_{t-1}^* \right) \right]^2 \right]. \quad (26)$$

Thus, the objective is to select the trend component that minimizes the sum of the squared deviations from the observed series, subject to the constraint that changes in x_t^* vary gradually over time. The Lagrange multiplier λ is a positive number that penalizes changes in the trend component. The larger the value of λ, the smoother is the resulting trend series.[16] By manipulating the first-order condition of the minimization problem (see King and Rebelo, 1993), a time domain representation of the HP filter can be developed in which the trend component x_t^* is represented by a two-sided symmetric moving-average expression of the observed series:

$$x_t^* = \sum_{h=-\infty}^{\infty}\alpha_{|h|}x_{t+h}, \quad (27)$$

where the parameters $\alpha_{|h|}$ depend on the value of the Lagrange multiplier λ.

Both of the foregoing decomposition techniques have their limitations. The difficulty with the BN approach results precisely from its flexibility: in practice, identifying the polynomials $\Psi(L)$ and $\Theta(L)$ requires considerable judgment, and choosing among alternative

---

[15] For a discussion of the properties of the HP filter and a comparison with other detrending methods, see Blackburn and Ravn (1991), King and Rebelo (1993), and Cogley and Nason (1995).

[16] In general, the choice of the value of λ depends on the degree of the assumed stickiness in the series under consideration. Here, we follow the usual practice of setting λ to 1,600 with quarterly time series. However, it should be noted that this choice is somewhat arbitrary; a more appropriate procedure would be to choose a value of λ using a data-dependent method.

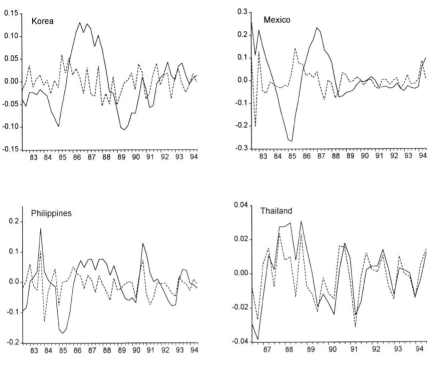

Figure 4.6. Temporary component of the real exchange rate. — = Hodrick-Prescott filter, - - - - = Beveridge-Nelson filter.

parameterizations can be arbitrary. The HP filter has also been the subject of criticism (see Stadler, 1994, pp. 1768–69). In particular, it has been argued that it removes potentially valuable information from time series (King and Rebelo, 1993), and that it may impart spurious cyclical patterns to the data (Cogley and Nason, 1995). Nevertheless, using both procedures here provides a way of testing the sensitivity and robustness of the econometric results to be described.

4.3.2   *Unit root tests and ARMA models*

Figure 4.6 shows the TCRERs derived by using both the BN and HP techniques. An ARMA process for the first differences of (the logarithm of) the real exchange rate was selected on the basis of conventional criteria, starting from an ARMA(2,2) to economize on degrees of free-dom. The models selected were an ARMA(0,1) for Korea, ARMA(2,0) for Mexico, ARMA(2,2) for the Philippines, and ARMA(1,1) for Thailand. As shown in the figure the two series for Thailand are fairly similar throughout the sample period. For the other countries these series show similar movements of the TCRER during the 1990s. In the early part of the sample, however, these series show different movements of the TCRER. For example, the HP filter suggests that the TCRER depreciated from 1985 through 1987 for these other countries, whereas the BN filter suggests the reverse. Note further that the HP filter seems to identify a fairly regular cyclical movement for Korea and Mexico.

Prior to estimating the near-VAR model, each set of series was tested for stationarity. Augmented Dickey-Fuller (ADF) and Phillips-Perron (PP) unit root tests were employed (see Dickey and Rosanna, 1994). The results of these tests – based on a unit-root null versus a trend-stationary alternative – are reported in Appendix Table 4.A1. In general, both test statistics give similar results, although in a few cases differences exist and the significance level is not always large. In almost all cases, the results support the assumption that the "world" interest rate (proxied by the U.S. Treasury bill rate) is differenced stationary, whereas all the other variables are stationary in levels. Note that for Korea, there appears to be only weak evidence of stationarity of the TCRER obtained by the HP filter; this feature of the data is accounted for in the estimation of the near-VAR, as indicated later.

4.3.3   *Variance decompositions*

The near-VAR model (with seasonal dummies in each equation) was estimated using the two different measures of the TCRER discussed previously over the period from the first quarter of 1982 through the third quarter of 1994 for Korea, Mexico, and the Philippines, and from the third quarter of 1986 through the third quarter of 1994 for Thailand.[17] For consistency across countries and to conserve degrees of freedom, estimation for each country was performed with two lags.[18] The near-VAR model for Mexico includes a dummy variable (equal to one from the 1988 fourth quarter onward) to account for the stabilization program implemented in the late 1980s; this dummy is statistically significant. We

---

[17] Related to the weak evidence of stationarity of the TCRER obtained with the HP filter for Korea indicated previously, the near-VAR model estimated for that country proved unstable. To deal with this problem, a deterministic time trend was added to the model for Korea.

[18] Standard lag length tests (using Akaike's Information Criterion) suggested that for Korea, Mexico, and the Philippines two lags were appropriate, whereas for Thailand one lag was sufficient. However, for consistency, we used a uniform lag length.

also tried adding a dummy variable for NAFTA (one from the 1993 fourth quarter onward) but this variable was not statistically significant.

The statistical adequacy of the near-VAR models used in this study was tested with a multivariate generalization of the Granger causality test. This generalization is essentially a multivariate likelihood ratio test and the resulting test statistic is distributed as χ^2 with degrees of freedom equal to the number of regressors excluded in the null hypothesis. Specifically, we test the null hypothesis that iw and gy are jointly block exogenous against the alternative hypothesis that $i\omega$ and gy are part of the "endogenous" VAR system. The resulting χ^2 with 20 degrees of freedom (five variables with two lags each excluded from two equations) did not reject the null hypothesis at conventional levels of significance in any of the countries considered in this study.

The estimated models were used to perform "generalized" VAR analysis, as proposed by Koop, Pesaran, and Potter (1996). An attractive feature of this approach is that it does not suffer from the "compositional effect" inherent in standard VAR analysis. As is well known, variance decompositions and impulse response functions derived from standard VAR analysis depend on the ordering of the variables used to obtain the orthogonal shocks.[19] This dependence reflects the fact that changing the ordering changes the implicit linear combination of the VAR innovations used to obtain the orthogonal shock, that is, changing the ordering changes the "composition" of the orthogonal shock.

Generalized VAR analysis is based on rethinking what is to be "recovered" from the estimated VAR (or near-VAR) model. Specifically, consider impulse responses. Typically a VAR is subjected to an orthogonal shock, and the impulse responses trace out the dynamic response of the model to that shock. Note that implicitly these impulse responses compare the evolution of the model following the shock to a baseline model not subject to the shock. Generalized impulse responses (GIR) build upon this idea and propose to look instead at a "typical" historical shock. GIR compares the "average" dynamic responses of the model given a "typical" historical shock and the history of the model, compared with the "average" baseline model not subject to the shock, given the history of the model. Specifically, GIR compares the conditional expectation of a variable in the model given an arbitrary current shock v_t and history ω_t, to the conditional expectation of that variable given history:

---

[19] Analysts conducting so-called atheoretical empirical investigations frequently note that their results are robust to the ordering used. However, robustness to different orderings does not guarantee that standard VAR analysis has succeeded in recovering economically meaningful shocks. For a detailed discussion of this issue, see Cooley and LeRoy (1985) and Keating (1996).

$$GIR(x_{t+k}, \upsilon_t, \omega_t) = E\left[X_{t+k}\middle|v_t, w_t\right] - E\left[X_{t+k}\middle|\omega_t\right].$$

For example, consider an economy where the real exchange depends only on fiscal policy and world interest rates. Suppose further that in this economy the data show that when a negative world interest rate shock is observed, the authorities respond with a contractionary fiscal shock. The GIR of the real exchange rate to a world interest rate shock in this economy would trace out, on average, the evolution of the real exchange rate to a typical world interest rate shock – given the historically observed fiscal shocks. It should be clear that since the GIR captures the historically observed information regarding shocks in the data, it does not pretend to recover the responses to a "pure" world interest rate shock.

Likewise, the generalized variance decompositions (GVD) measure does not pretend to measure the percentage of the variance attributed to "pure" shocks. Specifically, in our example, the percentage of the variance of the real exchange rate attributed to the typical world interest rate would also capture the historically observed information regarding shocks in the data. Note that, to the extent that historical shocks are in fact correlated, the GVD will typically not add up to 100 percent.

Table 4.2 presents the GVD of the TCRER at four-quarter intervals (up to sixteen quarters). At short forecasting horizons, the importance of composite shocks to the TCRER dominate movements of TCRER. Note, however, that composite shocks associated with *idiff* play a fairly substantive secondary role in Korea and Thailand at the four-quarter horizon, explaining somewhere in the order of 20 and 40 percent respectively. The evidence for Mexico and the Philippines on this issue is less clear and depends on the filter used to measure the TCRER. In particular, the evidence from the BN filter in both countries suggests that shocks associated with *idiff* play a substantive role in explaining movements of TCRER at the four-quarter horizon – 30 and 50 percent respectively in Mexico and the Philippines – but the evidence from the HP filter does not find this secondary role. With the notable exception of Korea,[20] at this forecasting horizon composite shocks associated with *gy* also appear to explain movements in the TCRER, but the magnitude of this effect is

---

[20] This contrasts with recent evidence on the importance of "pure fiscal" shocks in explaining real exchange rate movements in Korea. See Hoffmaister and Roldós (1996) for details. For Korea, the lack of importance of composite "fiscal" shocks in our findings could be associated with the fact that the large fiscal adjustments that occurred during the 1980s coincided with contractionary monetary shocks, as noted by Corbo and Nam (1992). Thus, the composite shock associated with *gy* would tend to reflect offsetting effects of fiscal and monetary policies.

Table 4.2. *Generalized variance decomposition of TCRER*

Quarters	HP filter						BN filter					
	iw	*idiff*	*lzc*	*ky*	*gy*	*veloc*	*iw*	*idiff*	*lzc*	*ky*	*gy*	*veloc*
Korea												
1	0.2	24.0	100.0	1.1	0.9	0.5	0.4	18.7	100.0	0.1	0.1	0.0
4	10.9	29.0	69.0	9.6	2.4	6.4	8.5	12.4	62.8	19.1	5.3	3.9
8	14.9	22.7	46.4	10.7	3.5	18.0	8.4	12.0	60.7	20.3	5.5	5.1
12	11.5	17.5	36.7	8.3	9.3	22.0	8.4	12.0	60.5	20.4	5.5	5.2
16	10.4	15.0	31.5	7.6	13.4	22.9	8.4	12.0	60.4	20.4	5.5	5.3
Mexico												
1	0.0	17.4	100.0	11.2	1.9	0.0	0.0	2.3	100.0	7.8	2.8	0.3
4	5.0	5.9	50.3	27.3	4.5	0.6	12.1	28.8	49.0	11.3	20.3	7.3
8	9.8	4.2	46.8	24.6	8.4	0.6	11.7	29.5	47.0	10.9	21.8	7.2
12	11.2	4.0	45.5	23.8	8.9	0.8	11.5	30.0	46.5	10.9	22.2	7.3
16	11.6	3.9	45.2	23.5	9.2	0.8	11.5	30.0	46.4	10.8	22.2	7.3
Philippines												
1	4.3	5.0	100.0	0.4	3.0	6.5	5.3	0.1	100.0	0.9	8.6	3.8
4	6.0	17.5	32.0	3.0	30.6	2.8	12.2	50.1	34.4	0.5	10.2	12.9
8	9.7	13.4	20.1	2.3	42.8	5.0	14.6	48.4	32.7	1.4	9.8	13.0
12	10.9	13.7	20.4	2.4	41.2	6.0	14.6	48.3	32.6	1.4	9.9	13.0
16	11.1	13.7	20.5	2.4	40.8	6.3	14.6	48.3	32.6	1.4	9.9	13.1
Thailand												
1	5.5	25.9	100.0	1.8	9.3	1.5	8.9	15.6	100.0	3.6	22.2	8.1
4	22.7	32.3	19.4	16.5	11.6	31.0	21.9	53.7	28.6	5.1	15.6	26.3
8	21.6	32.1	16.6	21.0	13.6	27.6	21.8	52.0	27.7	6.9	15.9	26.0
12	21.9	32.0	16.3	21.0	14.0	27.2	21.9	52.0	27.7	6.9	15.9	26.0
16	21.9	32.0	16.3	21.0	14.0	27.2	21.9	52.0	27.7	6.9	15.9	26.0

Notes: Based on the estimated near-VAR models discussed in the text. The percentage of the variance attributed to the historical shocks associated with each variable does not necessarily add up to 100.

filter dependent. Although in Thailand the effect of composite shocks associated with *gy* explain a fairly stable share of the movements of the TCRER (15 and 10 percent respectively with the BN and HP filters), this is not the case in Mexico or in the Philippines. In Mexico, these composite shocks explain about 20 percent of the movements of the TCRER when measured with the BN filter but only about 5 percent when measured with the HP filter. In the Philippines, filter dependence is also evident: when the BN filter is used 10 percent of the movements of TCRER are explained by shocks associated with *gy* and 30 percent when the HP filter is used.

At sixteen quarters, the bulk of the movements of the TCRER are no longer associated with "own" composite shocks and suggest that the other composite shocks in the model play a role in explaining TCRER. Composite shocks associated with *iw* explain roughly about 10 percent of the movements of TCRER in Korea, Mexico, and the Philippines at this forecasting horizon, and in Thailand they appear to explain about 20 percent. Composite shocks associated with *idiff* explain about 15 and 40 percent of the movements of the TCRER in Korea and Thailand respectively, whereas these shocks explain somewhat less in Mexico and the Philippines when the HP filter is used to calculate the TCRER and explain more when the BN filter is used. Composite shocks associated with *ky* appear to explain about 10 percent of the movements of the TCRER in Korea, Mexico, and Thailand – with some filter dependence evident – but a negligible amount in the Philippines. Composite shocks associated with *gy* appear to explain between 10 and 15 percent of the movements of the TCRER in all countries (except in Korea and the Philippines where the BN filter suggests a small percentage). And finally, composite shocks associated with *veloc* explain about 15 percent of the movements of TCRER in Thailand, about 10 percent in Philippines, about 5 to 20 percent for Korea, and a smaller amount for Mexico.

Table 4.3 presents the GVD of *ky* at four-quarter intervals (up to sixteen quarters). Perhaps the most striking feature is the high degree of autonomy exhibited by these capital flows, that even after sixteen quarters the "own" composite shock still explains somewhere between 60 and 70 percent in all countries. Composite shocks associated with *iw*, *gy*, and *veloc* explain a much smaller amount of the movements in the TCRER at sixteen quarters, each accounting for roughly 10 percent.

4.3.4   *Dynamic response to shocks*

As discussed above, the transitional dynamics induced by a temporary change in any variable in the near-VAR model can be traced using GIRs.

Table 4.3. *Generalized variance decomposition of ky*

Quarters	HP filter						BN filter					
	iw	idiff	lzc	ky	gy	veloc	iw	idiff	lzc	ky	gy	veloc
Korea												
1	0.4	6.0	1.1	100.0	17.8	2.2	0.0	2.0	0.1	100.0	20.6	0.6
4	2.5	7.5	6.5	84.4	15.8	5.6	3.6	3.0	3.4	85.2	18.8	3.0
8	3.1	7.2	6.2	74.9	15.2	12.0	3.7	2.8	3.7	78.4	17.8	8.6
12	2.9	6.5	6.4	64.7	16.7	15.5	3.9	2.6	3.6	74.3	16.2	11.9
16	3.3	6.3	7.0	57.0	18.2	17.0	4.0	2.4	3.5	72.1	15.1	13.6
Mexico												
1	6.6	3.8	11.2	100.0	0.6	2.4	6.8	1.9	7.8	100.0	0.2	1.6
4	11.0	6.4	8.4	73.2	9.8	7.3	11.8	6.7	5.3	70.6	12.8	3.0
8	13.7	6.2	9.3	69.9	10.5	7.0	22.4	7.1	4.9	61.8	15.9	2.6
12	13.9	6.2	9.5	69.1	10.8	6.9	22.4	7.1	4.9	61.5	16.3	2.6
16	13.9	6.2	9.6	68.9	10.8	6.9	22.4	7.1	4.9	61.4	16.4	2.6
Philippines												
1	3.1	5.5	0.4	100.0	0.4	3.6	3.4	4.1	0.9	100.0	0.4	4.2
4	2.9	4.7	2.4	83.6	5.4	11.5	3.4	3.6	2.0	85.7	4.9	9.3
8	6.1	8.1	4.0	72.3	7.9	16.5	5.3	8.0	2.2	75.4	7.9	14.6
12	6.2	8.2	5.4	69.0	10.1	17.2	5.3	9.0	2.3	72.1	9.5	16.6
16	6.3	8.3	5.7	68.2	10.4	17.6	5.3	9.5	2.3	70.5	10.2	17.7
Thailand												
1	0.7	6.4	1.8	100.0	0.8	0.7	2.1	1.4	3.6	100.0	1.3	8.1
4	3.5	13.7	3.7	63.2	13.9	6.1	12.6	15.1	16.1	61.0	13.6	7.8
8	5.1	13.8	3.7	60.5	16.3	6.2	13.0	15.0	16.2	58.3	14.6	9.0
12	5.1	13.9	3.7	60.4	16.3	6.3	13.1	15.0	16.1	58.1	14.8	9.0
16	5.1	13.9	3.7	60.3	16.3	6.3	13.2	15.0	16.1	58.1	14.8	9.0

Notes: Based on the estimated near-VAR models discussed in the text. The percentage of the variance attributed to the historical shocks associated with each variable does not necessarily add up to 100.

Here we examine shocks to government spending and the world interest rate.[21] We view these two experiments as particularly useful (in light of the discussion provided in section 4.2) to assess the effect of "pull" (internal) and "push" (external) factors.

4.3.4.1 World interest rate shock: GIRs and their one-standard error bands for the TCRER and capital inflows associated with a one-standard deviation reduction in the world interest rate iw are illustrated in Figures 4.7 and 4.8, for both measures of the TCRER.[22] Since the world interest rate variable enters in first-differenced form, this shock is tantamount to a permanent shock to the level of the variable, and matches closely the experiment performed in the first part of the chapter. To save space, movements in the other variables of the system are not shown, although the behavior of the (change in) interest rate differentials is described here.

Consider first the behavior of capital inflows. The results obtained with the HP filter (Figure 4.7) suggest that a significant increase in capital inflows occurs on impact in the case of Korea and one quarter after the shock in the case of the Philippines; in the latter case, an increase in inflows also occurs in the fifth and sixth periods.[23] In both countries, the movement in inflows reflects a significant increase in (the change in) the interest rate differential between domestic and foreign assets, which improves the attractiveness of domestic assets. The results obtained with the BN decomposition (Figure 4.8) also suggest that capital inflows in Korea and the Philippines increase significantly on impact and in the first quarter after the shock – with no discernible effect in the subsequent periods in the case of Korea, despite a significant increase in the interest rate differential in the third quarter after the shock. They also indicate a significant increase in the interest rate differential in the Philippines after

[21] As noted earlier, these shocks correspond to "historically correct" composite shocks and should not be viewed as "pure structural" shocks. For example, the GIR function for a iw shock shows the evolution of the variables in the model to the typical historical iw shock that reflects the historical correlation of shocks to that variable with shocks to other variables in the model.

[22] In all figures the dotted lines for the GIRs show one standard error bands in each direction and are based on 1,000 Monte Carlo replications. In each replication we sample the near-VAR coefficients and the covariance matrix from their posterior distribution. From these replications we calculate the square root of the mean squared deviation from the impulse response in each direction. By construction these bands contain the impulse response function but are not necessarily symmetric. See Kloek and Van Dijk (1978) for details of the posterior distributions.

[23] Throughout this discussion a "significant" change means that the interval defined by the error bands does not contain the value zero.

two quarters, with capital inflows increasing significantly and showing some persistence.

For Thailand, the results with the HP filter indicate that capital inflows do not appear to be very responsive to the interest rate shock, although a slightly significant effect can be detected in the second quarter after the shock – mirroring a significant improvement in the interest rate differential at that period. The results obtained with the BN decomposition show a more significant effect in the second quarter (which again mirrors the movement in the interest rate differential) and a slight recovery in the third quarter. The response of capital movements in Mexico is somewhat counterintuitive: with both filtering methods, there is a significant reduction in capital inflows on impact (despite the fact that the interest rate differential shows no significant movement during that period). Results obtained with the BN filter indicate another fall between the third and sixth quarters. Those obtained with the HP filter, however, suggest a slightly positive effect in the first quarter after the shock.

Consider now the movements in the TCRER. In Korea and Mexico, both filtering methods indicate that there is no significant effect on the TCRER on impact. After one quarter, however, there is a slight real appreciation (which does not persist) in Mexico, whereas in Korea, two quarters after the shock, the TCRER depreciates, with the effect showing some persistence (notably with the HP filter) until the sixth quarter. The TCRER subsequently appreciates with the HP filter, but a comparison with the results obtained with the BN filter suggests that this effect is not robust. In both Thailand and the Philippines, the GIRs show a slight depreciation of the TCRER, followed by a statistically more significant appreciation in the first and second quarters after the shock. The response of the TCRER in both countries is more short-lived with the BN filter. For the Philippines, and in line with the drop in capital inflows noted earlier, the TCRER depreciates after the fourth quarter – a movement that displays some persistence over time.

4.3.4.2 Government spending shock: Figures 4.9 and 4.10 illustrate the GIRs and their one standard error bands for the TCRER and capital inflows associated with a one standard deviation change in the government spending–output ratio gy.[24] Results obtained with both the HP and BN filters show very similar results for Korea, namely a significant

---

[24] Note that here, in contrast to the previous experiment, we are looking at a temporary rather than permanent shock; thus, a comparison of the empirical results and the theoretical predictions described earlier should focus on the short-term (impact) effects of the shock.

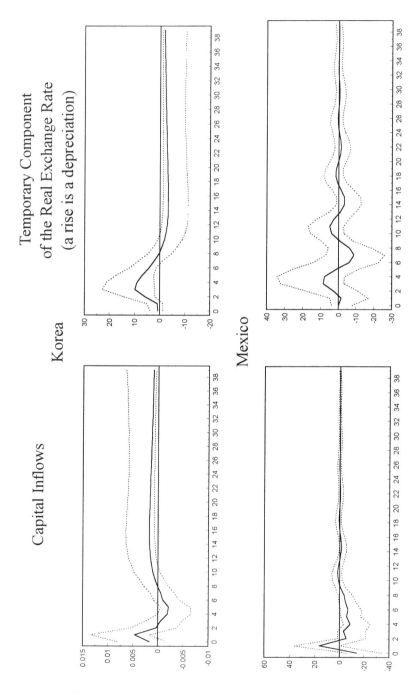

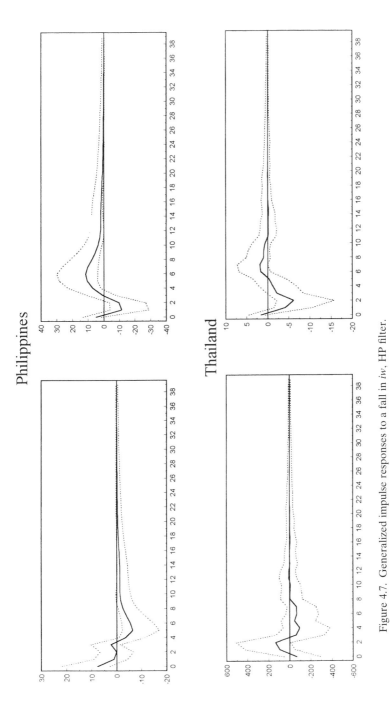

Figure 4.7. Generalized impulse responses to a fall in iw, HP filter.

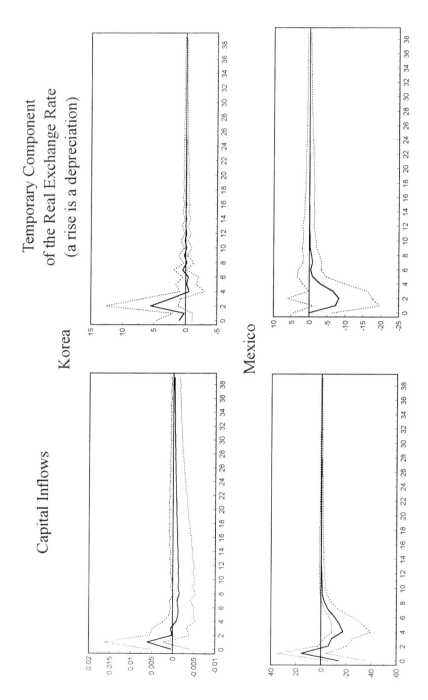

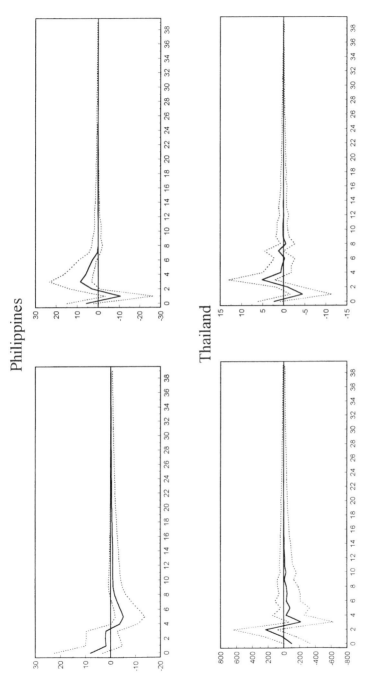

Philippines

Thailand

Figure 4.8. Generalized impulse responses to a fall in iw, BN filter.

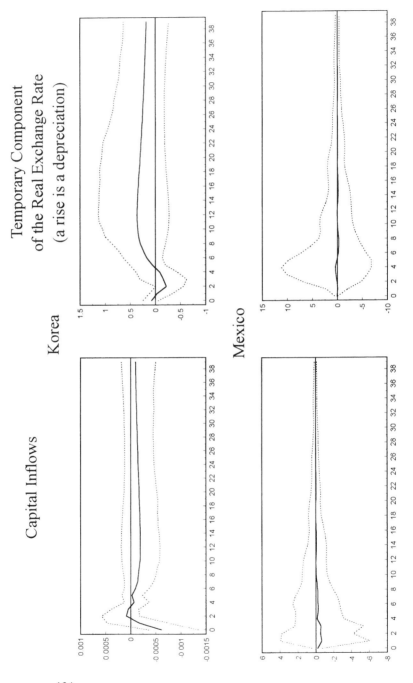

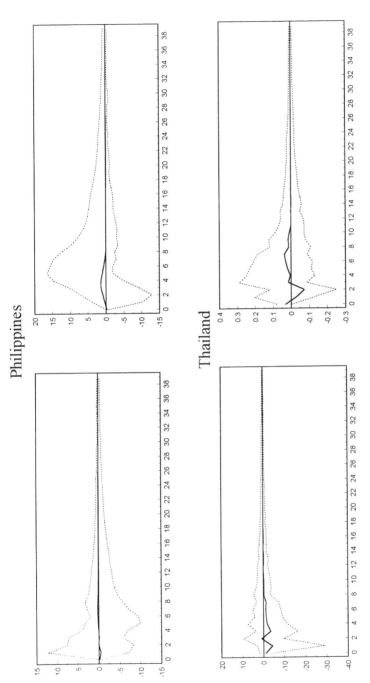

Figure 4.9. Generalized impulse responses to a rise in *gy*, HP filter.

135

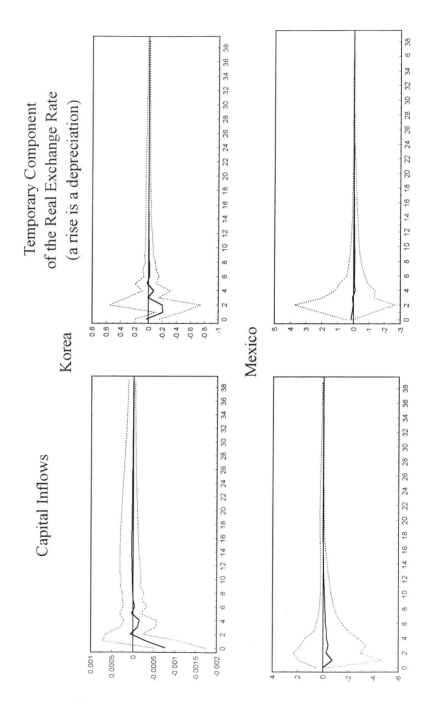

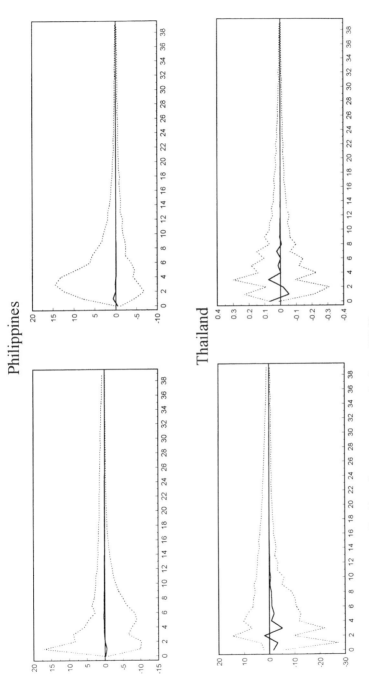

Figure 4.10. Generalized impulse responses to a rise in *gy*, BN filter.

reduction in capital inflows (which mirrors again a reduction in the interest rate differential) when the shock takes place, with little persistence over time. For all the other countries, the predictions obtained with the two filters are again consistent: there appears to be no statistically significant effect of an innovation in the government spending–output ratio on capital movements.

The response in the TCRER is statistically significant only in the case of Korea and Thailand, when looking at the results obtained with the BN filter. In Korea, the TCRER appreciates slightly after one quarter, whereas it depreciates slightly in Thailand. In both cases, the effect is short-lived.

To summarize, therefore, the GIRs suggest that a negative innovation in the (change in) world interest rate leads to a capital inflow in all Asian countries and an initial outflow followed by an inflow in the case of Mexico, with little persistence over time; a significant appreciation of the TCRER is observed (with a one-quarter lag) in the Philippines and Thailand, with some degree of persistence in both countries, whereas no discernible effect can be detected in the case of Mexico. In Korea, the TCRER depreciates significantly in the second quarter after the shock. A positive innovation in the government spending–output ratio has significant effects only in the case of Korea, leading to a reduction in capital inflows and a slight appreciation of the TCRER. Both effects are short-lived. With both types of shocks, movements in capital flows appear to be closely related to changes in the rate of return differential between domestic and foreign assets.

How do these quantitative results fare in light of the predictions of the analytical model described in the first part of the chapter? At the outset, it should be noted that the empirical model does not capture all the complexities involved in the theoretical model, and that by its very nature, a VAR-type methodology does not allow us to identify structural relationships and transmission mechanisms. Nevertheless, it is clear that the response of capital inflows and the real exchange rate in some of the Asian countries to changes in world interest rates is broadly consistent with the predictions of the model, as described in the net debtor case. The pattern of capital inflows in Mexico (an initial reduction followed by an increase) is somewhat more difficult to rationalize. It should be kept in mind, however, that our econometric model aims only at explaining short-term, *cyclical* movements in the real exchange rate; it cannot be excluded that capital inflows (or, more precisely, movements in the economy's stock of net foreign assets) induced by changes in world interest rates may have a significant effect on the *trend component* of the real exchange rate. Our approach, by design, does not account for some of the longer-run factors (such as productivity differentials) that might prove relevant to evaluate the existence of this type of effects.

Regarding the effects of the government spending–output ratio, both the existence (as in the case of Korea) and the absence (as is the case for the other countries) of a significant effect on capital inflows and the real exchange rate are consistent with the prediction of the analytical framework. As noted earlier, although private consumption is likely to fall on impact, thereby partly offsetting the increase in public expenditure on total absorption, the degree to which consumption falls determines the ultimate impact on the real exchange rate. One way of looking at the empirical results obtained here is therefore to view private spending as falling relatively little in Korea (thereby requiring a real appreciation to maintain equilibrium of the market for home goods), and falling by a more or less equal amount in the case of the other countries. The interpretation would thus be that private agents in Korea have a lower degree of intertemporal substitution (a stronger desire for consumption smoothing) than in the other countries considered here. Alternatively, it is possible that in Korea the increases in gy were viewed mostly as temporary, whereas in the other countries these shocks were mostly viewed as having more persistence. In this case, the GIR for Korea following a gy shock would reflect the perception that gy would not remain high and thus consumption would not tend to fall as much as otherwise. Of course, a direct test of these propositions, using a more structural approach than the one developed here, would be desirable in order to corroborate these assertions.

Four other factors, which are not captured in the analytical model presented earlier, may prove relevant in assessing the differences in the response of the TCRER to domestic and external shocks in the countries analyzed here: the composition of capital flows, the degree of sterilization, the intensity of capital controls, and the degree of flexibility in exchange rate policy.

1　As noted in the introduction, to the extent that capital inflows take the form of long-term flows, their short-term impact on the real exchange rate is likely to be more limited. However, in all the countries considered (particularly Korea and Thailand), the share of foreign direct investment in total flows remained fairly small during the period under study.

2　The existence of capital controls, to the extent that they are binding, would affect the link between capital flows and interest rate differentials – and thus the effect of the former variable on short-term fluctuations in the real exchange rate. In countries such as Korea, for instance, the capital account was relatively closed in the early 1980s, and liberalization proceeded only at a gradual pace in the past fifteen years. Introducing in the quantitative model an index of the intensity of capital controls might improve the performance of the model – at least in the case of Korea.

3   As also noted in the introduction, and as documented by Corbo and Hernández (1996), these policies have differed quite markedly among Asian and Latin American countries – including those considered in this study. The use of money base velocity as a "control" variable helps to capture, albeit imperfectly, some of the effects of sterilization policy on money supply and (indirectly) domestic interest rates. The use of a more direct measure of the stance of intervention policy may be an important issue for future research.

4   Finally, the lack of evidence on the links between changes in the world interest rate, government spending, and the TCRER may reflect the fact that countries have allowed the nominal exchange rate to depreciate, in order to alleviate pressures on nontradable prices and the real exchange rate induced by capital inflows. Mexico, in particular, has followed at times a relatively flexible policy during the period under consideration.[25] Accounting for endogenous policy responses of this type would also enhance our understanding of the links between capital movements and changes in relative prices.

4.4   Summary and conclusions

The purpose of this chapter has been to examine the links between capital inflows and the real exchange rate in a fixed (or predetermined) exchange rate regime. The first part presented a brief analytical discussion of these linkages. Two types of experiments were discussed: an increase in government spending on home goods, and a reduction in world interest rates. This latter experiment is particularly interesting, since many economists have attributed a large role to the cyclical reduction in interest rates in the

[25]   A dual exchange rate system was in force in Mexico between 1982 and November 1991, with a crawling peg operated for the official exchange rate during December 1982 and February 1988. The official exchange rate was kept fixed between February 1988 and January 1989, and a preannounced crawl was implemented during January 1989 to November 1991. The dual rate regime was then abolished and a preannounced crawling peg was put in place until December 1994.

United States in explaining the surge in capital inflows to developing countries in the early 1990s.[26] The analysis suggests that a permanent reduction in the world interest rate leads to a steady-state reduction in the economy's net stock of foreign assets and a real depreciation, regardless of whether the country considered is a net creditor or a net debtor in the initial steady state. On impact, however, whereas the real exchange rate always appreciates in the net debtor case, in the net creditor case it may either appreciate or depreciate – depending on the relative strength of wealth and intertemporal substitution effects.

The second part estimated a near-VAR model linking capital inflows, changes in ex post interest rate differentials, the government spending–output ratio, money base velocity, and the temporary component of the real exchange rate (TCRER). Because there is no obvious criterion for discriminating among alternative techniques for decomposing a time series between a trend and a temporary component, two alternative methods were used: the Hodrick-Prescott filter and the Beveridge-Nelson decomposition.

The near-VAR model was estimated for Korea, Mexico, the Philippines, and Thailand. Variance decompositions, based on a generalized approach proposed by Koop, Pesaran, and Potter (1996), suggest that only a small percentage of the movements of the temporary component of the real exchange rate is associated with "historically correct" shocks to capital flows. Regarding the importance of historical shocks to the government spending ratio, the variance decompositions suggest that they also play a small role in these movements in Mexico, the Philippines, and Thailand, but somewhat surprisingly not in Korea.

Generalized impulse response functions – based also on the Koop-Pesaran-Potter technique – indicate that a negative innovation in the (change in) world interest rates leads to a capital inflow in all Asian countries and to a "perverse" capital outflow in Mexico, with little persistence over time; a significant appreciation of the TCRER is observed (with a one-quarter lag) in the Philippines and Thailand, with some degree of persistence in both countries, whereas no discernible effect can be detected in the case of Mexico. In Korea, the TCRER depreciates significantly in the second quarter after the shock. A positive innovation in the government spending–output ratio has significant effects only in the case of Korea, leading to a reduction in capital inflows and a slight appreciation of the TCRER. Although both effects are statistically

[26] See Calvo, Leiderman, and Reinhart (1996), Fernández-Arias (1996), Fernández-Arias and Montiel (1996), and Frankel and Okongwu (1996).

significant (in the sense defined earlier), they are small and short-lived. With both types of shocks, movements in capital flows seem to mirror closely changes in interest rate differentials between domestic and foreign assets.

It is worth emphasizing that the econometric framework developed here aims only at capturing the short-run links between capital inflows, movements in the real exchange rate, and domestic and foreign shocks. It is also possible that, in addition to short-term (demand-type) effects, capital flows may also affect the long-run (trend component) of the real exchange rate – via their supply-side effects on, for instance, capital accumulation and productivity changes across sectors. These potential effects are also worth studying. Nevertheless, our results do suggest that the view according to which real appreciation follows systematically from capital inflows should be taken with care. Capital flows respond endogenously to perceived changes in relative rates of return between domestic and foreign assets; in turn, domestic rates of return are influenced by macroeconomic equilibrium conditions and the overall policy stance. In particular, policy inconsistencies (such as the combination of an expansionary fiscal policy with a relatively tight monetary policy) tend to generate equilibrium changes in asset prices and yields, which affect capital movements and may put upward pressure on the relative price of nontraded goods through wealth and income effects. The methodology described here, by taking into account the endogenous nature of capital flows, provides a useful framework for exploring their short-term macroeconomic effects.

Appendix: Data and unit root tests

The data used to estimate the VAR model are quarterly values for the period from the third quarter of 1982 to the third quarter of 1994 for Korea, Mexico, and the Philippines, and from the third quarter of 1986 to the third quarter of 1994 for Thailand. All data were obtained from the IMF's *International Financial Statistics (IFS)*, except the index of industrial output for Thailand, which was obtained from unpublished IMF material. z is (the inverse of) the IMF's real effective exchange rate, used to calculate the temporary component of the real exchange rate. ky is a broad measure of capital inflows measured in proportion of output, y. Capital inflows are calculated as the sum of net direct investment in the domestic country (*IFS* line 78*bed* minus line 78*bdd*), the net increase in portfolio liabilities (*IFS* line 78*bgd* minus line 78*bfd*), net increase in other investment liabilities (*IFS* line 78*bid* minus line 78*bhd*), and net errors and omissions (*IFS* line 78*cad*). y is GDP at current prices for

Appendix Table 4.A1. *Order of integration: Unit root test statistics*

Country	Variable	k	ADF test Test statistic	PP test
Korea	*ky*	0	−4.557***	−4.848***
	idiff	0	−2.914	−3.208*
	lzc:HP	3	−2.731	−3.267*
	lzc:BN	0	−7.052***	−7.006***
	gy	2	−5.317***	−9.703***
	veloc	1	−2.270	−3.991**
Mexico	*ky*	0	−6.813***	−6.815***
	idiff	1	−5.403***	−7.818***
	lzc:HP	4	−4.827***	−2.697
	lzc:BN	0	−7.845***	−7.857***
	gy	0	−7.378***	−7.443***
	veloc	4	−1.746	−2.048
Philippines	*ky*	0	−5.878***	−5.835***
	idiff	0	−4.941***	−5.076***
	lzc:HP	4	−4.401***	−3.080
	lzc:BN	0	−6.405***	−8.585***
	gy	0	−4.839***	−4.931***
	veloc	0	−3.878**	−3.421*
Thailand	*ky*	0	−4.183***	−4.121***
	idiff	0	−5.211***	−5.263***
	lzc:HP	4	−3.703**	−2.823
	lzc:BN	1	−4.917***	−5.536***
	gy	1	−4.206**	−3.544**
	veloc	3	−0.633	−8.942***
U.S. Treasury-bill rate	level	3	−2.923	−3.054
	iw	1	−5.321***	−4.941***

Notes: Variables are as defined in the text. Estimation period begins in the third quarter of 1982 and ends in the third quarter of 1994, except for Thailand, for which estimation begins in the third quarter of 1986. k denotes the number of lags in the ADF test. *,**, and *** denote rejection of the null hypothesis of a unit root at the 10%, 5%, and 1% significance levels. Critical values are from MacKinnon (1991).

Korea, Mexico, and the Philippines; for Thailand, an index of nominal output was derived by multiplying the industrial output index by the consumer price level. $idiff$ is the change in the quarterly interest rate differential, calculated as $(1 + i/100)^{1/4} - (1 + i*/100)^{1/4} E_{+1}/E$, where i and $i*$ are the domestic and foreign interest rates (at annual rates), and E the average nominal exchange rate. i is the interest rate on three-month treasury bills for Mexico and the Philippines, and the interbank interest rate for Korea and Thailand. $i*$ is either the three-month U.S. Treasury bills rate (used for Mexico and the Philippines) or the federal funds rate (for Korea and Thailand).[27] E is the period average spot exchange rate of one U.S. dollar at time t to E units of domestic currency. We thus use the ex post (i.e., realized) domestic currency rate of return on foreign assets. iw is the change in $(1 + i*/100)^{1/4}$. gy is the ratio of government expenditure at current prices to nominal GDP. Government spending is measured as the sum of expenditure plus lending minus repayment (IFS lines 82 and 83).

References

Abdel-Motaal, Karim (1995). "Capital Flows to the Middle East in the 1990s: Quantifying the Role of Internal and External Factors." Unpublished manuscript, Harvard University, Department of Economics, Cambridge, Mass.

Agénor, Pierre-Richard (1996). "The Surge in Capital Flows: Analysis of 'Pull' and 'Push' Factors." Unpublished manuscript, International Monetary Fund, Research Department, Washington D.C. Forthcoming in *International Journal of Finance and Economics*.

(1997). *Capital-Market Imperfections and the Macroeconomic Dynamics of Small Indebted Economics*, Princeton Study in International Finance No. 82. Princeton, N.J.: Princeton University Press.

Agénor, Pierre-Richard, and Peter J. Montiel (1996). *Development Macroeconomics*. Princeton, N.J.: Princeton University Press.

Baxter, Marianne (1994). "Real Exchange Rates and Real Interest Differentials: Have We Missed the Business-Cycle Relationship?" *Journal of Monetary Economics* 33: 5–37.

Beveridge, S., and Charles Nelson (1981). "A New Approach to Decomposition of Economic Time Series into Permanent and Transitory Components with Particular Attention to the Measurement of the Business Cycle," *Journal of Monetary Economics* 7: 151–74.

Blackburn, Keith, and Morten O. Ravn (1991). "Univariate Detrending of Macroeconomic Time Series," Working Paper No. 22. Aarhus University, Denmark.

---

[27] The results obtained by Chinn and Frankel (1995) suggest that it may be more appropriate to use Japanese interest rates, rather than U.S. interest rates, to measure the foreign rate of interest for some Asian countries.

Calvo, Guillermo A., Leonardo Leiderman, and Carmen M. Reinhart (1996). "Inflows of Capital to Developing Countries in the 1990s: Causes and Effects," *Journal of Economic Perspectives* 10: 123–39.

Chinn, Menzie D. (1996). "Sectoral Productivity, Government Spending and Real Exchange Rates: Empirical Evidence for OECD Countries." Unpublished manuscript, University of California at Santa Cruz, Department of Economics.

Chinn, Menzie D., and Jeffrey A. Frankel (1995). "Who Drives Real Interest Rates in the Pacific Rim: The United States or Japan?" *Journal of International Money and Finance* 14: 801–21.

Cogley, Timothy, and James M. Nason (1995). "Effects of the Hodrick-Prescott Filter on Trend and Difference Stationary Time Series: Implications for Business Cycle Research," *Journal of Economic Dynamics and Control* 19: 253–78.

Cooley Thomas F., and Stephen F. LeRoy (1985). "Atheoretical Macroeconometrics: A Critique," *Journal of Monetary Economics* 16: 283–308.

Corbo, Vittorio, and Leonardo Hernández (1996). "Macroeconomic Adjustment to Capital Inflows: Lessons from Recent Latin American and East Asian Experience," *World Bank Research Observer* 11: 61–85.

Corbo, Vittorio, and Sang-Woo Nam (1992). "Recent Evolution of the Macroeconomy." In Vittorio Corbo and Sang-Mok Suh, eds., *Structural Adjustment in a Newly Industrialized Country: The Korean Experience*, pp. 35–67. Baltimore: Johns Hopkins University Press.

Cuddington, John, and L. Alan Winters (1987). "The Beveridge-Nelson Decomposition of Economic Time Series," *Journal of Monetary Economics* 19: 125–27.

Dickey, David A., and Robert J. Rossana (1994). "Cointegrated Time Series: A Guide to Estimation and Hypothesis Testing," *Oxford Bulletin of Economics and Statistics* 56: 325–53.

Faruqee, Hamid (1995). "Long-Run Determinants of the Real Exchange Rate: A Stock-Flow Perspective," *IMF Staff Papers* 42 (1): 80–107.

Fernández-Arias, Eduardo (1996). "The New Wave of Capital Inflows: Push or Pull?" *Journal of Development Economics* 48: 389–418.

Fernández-Arias, Eduardo, and Peter J. Montiel (1996). "The Surge in Capital Inflows to Developing Countries: An Analytical Overview," *World Bank Economic Review* 10: 51–77.

Frankel, Jeffrey A., and Chudozie Okongwu (1996). "Liberalized Portfolio Capital Inflows in Emerging Markets: Sterilization, Expectations, and the Incompleteness of Interest Rate Convergence," *International Journal of Finance and Economics* 1: 1–24.

Glick, Reuven, and Ramon Moreno (1995). "Capital Flows and Monetary Policy in East Asia." In *Monetary and Exchange Rate Management with International Capital Mobility: Experiences of Countries and Regions along the Pacific Rim*, Hong Kong Monetary Authority, pp. 14–48. Previously issued as Center for Pacific Basin Monetary and Economic Studies Working Paper No. PB94-08. Federal Reserve Bank of San Francisco.

Hamilton, James D. (1994). *Time Series Analysis*. Princeton, N.J.: Princeton University Press.

Hoffmaister, Alexander W., and Jorge E. Roldós (1996). "The Sources of Macroeconomic Fluctuations in Developing Countries: Brazil and Korea."

Unpublished manuscript, International Monetary Fund, Research Department, Washington D.C.

Keating, John W. (1996). "Structural Information in Recursive VAR Orderings," *Journal of Economic Dynamics and Control* 20: 1557–80.

King, Robert G., and Sergio Rebelo (1993). "Low Frequency Filtering and Real Business Cycles," *Journal of Economic Dynamics and Control* 17: 207–31.

Kloek, Tuen, and Herman K. Van Dijk (1978). "Bayesian Estimates of Equation System Parameters: An Application of Integration by Monte Carlo," *Econometrica* 46: 1–20.

Koenig, Linda M. (1996). "Capital Inflows and Policy Responses in the ASEAN Region," IMF Working Paper No. 96/25. Washington, D.C.

Koop, Gary, M. Hashem Pesaran, and Simon N. Potter (1996). "Impulse Response Analysis in Nonlinear Multivariate Models," *Journal of Econometrics* 74: 119–47.

MacKinnon, James (1991). "Critical Values for Cointegration Tests." In Robert Engle and Clive W. Granger, eds., *Long-Run Economic Relationships: Readings in Cointegration*, pp. 267–76. Oxford: Oxford University Press.

Miller, Stephen M. (1988). "The Beveridge-Nelson Decomposition of Economic Time Series: Another Economical Computational Method," *Journal of Monetary Economics* 21: 141–42.

Montiel, Peter J. (1996). "Exchange Rate Policy and Macroeconomic Management in ASEAN Countries." Unpublished manuscript, Williams College, Department of Economics, Williamstown, Mass.

Morandé, Felipe G. (1992). "Dynamics of Real Asset Prices, the Real Exchange Rate, and Foreign Capital Inflows: Chile, 1976–1989," *Journal of Development Economics* 39: 111–39.

Penati, Alessandro (1987). "Government Spending and the Real Exchange Rate," *Journal of International Economics* 22: 237–56.

Stadler, George W. (1994). "Real Business Cycles," *Journal of Economic Literature* 27: 1750–83.

CHAPTER 5

Risk and financial development: A comparative case study of Mexico and Indonesia

Theo S. Eicher and Stephen J. Turnovsky

5.1   Introduction

Risk plays an important role in the allocation of the world capital stock and in the growth performance of individual economies. During recent years several economists have developed intertemporal stochastic models directed at investigating these issues. Early models by Solnik (1974), Stulz (1981, 1986, 1987), and Adler and Dumas (1983) focus on the implications of risk for international portfolio allocation. More recently, authors such as Grinols and Turnovsky (1994), Turnovsky and Grinols (1996), Turnovsky (1993), and Obstfeld (1994) have analyzed the implications of risk for economic growth and welfare. The framework adopted by these authors describes risk in terms of Brownian motion processes and generates an equilibrium in which the means and variances of relevant variables are jointly determined. This mean–variance equilibrium has formed the basis for important empirical work pertaining to interest parity relationships, and the determination of foreign exchange risk premia; see Frankel (1986), Lewis (1988), and Engel and Rodrigues (1993).

The prototype model adopted by these authors describes a highly developed, small open economy. However, risk is likely to be a more pervasive and influential phenomenon for the economies for less developed countries (LDCs). These countries are typically exceedingly vulnerable to external stochastic influences, such as terms-of-trade shocks and oil shocks. Also, by their very nature, LDCs' internal economic conditions are inherently volatile, because of shallow capital and financial markets, and excessive amounts of government regulations, as

We thank Charles Engel and the conference discussant Ken Kasa for helpful comments on an earlier draft, Paul Gruenwald for assistance with data, and Quan Ha for research assistance.

well as being subject to greater domestic political instability. Thus, one might argue that stochastic general equilibrium models may indeed be more relevant to the analysis of LDCs.

But despite this there has been little formal assessment of risk on the performance of such economies. One issue that has attracted the attention of development economists is that of the effect of export instability on growth. The empirical analyses of Kenen and Voidodas (1972), Voidodas (1974), Yotopoulos and Nugent (1976), and Ozler and Harrigan (1988) have resulted in a multitude of seemingly conflicting correlations between measures of export instability and growth. Brock (1991) and Turnovsky (1995, chap. 15) have employed a simple stochastic growth model to provide a conciliation between these diverse findings in terms of the sources of the underlying stochastic disturbances.

In this chapter we use the insights of the stochastic general equilibrium growth model to help understand the effects of risk on the real, risk-adjusted return to capital, capital flows, exchange rate policy, and economic growth in two Pacific Basin economies, Mexico and Indonesia, over the period 1973–95. Two important factors render the Mexican and Indonesian economies as interesting case studies to use as empirical applications of stochastic general equilibrium models. First, both countries are dynamically and rapidly developing, despite their exposure to (identical) severe world price shocks that affected their major export commodity (crude oil). Second, while the structures of these economies are quite similar, their economic experiences over the past twenty-five years have been markedly different.[1] While the 1970s were periods of solid growth in both economies, thereafter their experiences diverged. Through the 1980s, Mexico experienced hyperinflation and a debt crisis, whereas Indonesia continued as a model of economic development. In fact, it is a challenging task to subject the stochastic model to the varied experiences of the two countries and examine which parts of the model improve our insights into the performance of these economies.

Our analysis is based on a nominal model of exchange rate determination under stochastic conditions developed in Grinols and Turnovsky (1994) and, on its extension, Turnovsky and Grinols (1996). This model derives the equilibrium nominal exchange rate and growth rate in an intertemporal optimization framework of a small open economy subject to stochastic shocks of both domestic and foreign origin. The sources introduced include a domestic monetary shock, domestic fiscal and productivity shocks, and a foreign price shock. The model allows us to analyze in detail the effects of risk (as measured by vari-

---

[1] Not only the economic, but also the political structure of the countries is quite similar.

ances) on key macroeconomic variables such as the (1) rate of inflation, (2) nominal exchange rate, (3) portfolio allocation, (4) real returns and risk premia, (4) rate of growth, and (5) implied and optimal rates of exchange depreciation.

The method we adopt draws upon the calibration methods adopted by real business cycle theorists and others, though at a less formal level (see, e.g., Cooley, 1995). In some cases, in particular with respect to data relating to real rates of return, it is possible to calibrate the model against the data with reasonable precision. But for other aspects, in recognition of the limitations of such a small stochastic model, our focus is in using the insights it offers to help understand the qualitative empirical experiences of these countries. The model is used to examine four specific sets of issues: (1) real financial rates of return and real risk premia, (2) composition and stability of portfolio shares over time, (3) growth, and (4) implications for the rate of exchange rate depreciation.

The critical innovations introduced in this stochastic general equilibrium framework are the variances of those variables whose stochastic shocks influence key equilibrium relationships. These variances need to be constructed and this is done by considering the sum of squared residuals of these variables about their respective means. To do this requires a fairly long time period and we estimate the variance using annual data over the twenty-three year period 1973–95 (inclusive). The basic model assumes stationarity of the underlying stochastic structure, an assumption that is at best dubious for these two economies over this recent period. Accordingly, we also break down the overall twenty-three year period into three subperiods, 1973–81, 1982–88, and 1989–95, estimating the variances over each. These three periods roughly correspond to (1) periods of initial steady growth, (2) oil shocks and debt crisis (Mexico), and (3) recovery. This enables us to consider and compare the behavior of the two economies over various subperiods associated with different degrees of risk.

Our results suggest that LDCs do indeed provide appropriate applications for models that incorporate risk. Overall, the model does better in explaining nominal behavior than it does real growth. For example, we find that once real interest rates are amended to incorporate price shocks explicitly, the additional variance component, although unimportant for the United States, becomes a reasonably significant component of the rate of return in Indonesia, and is crucial in the case of Mexico. Both risk-adjusted real returns show clear patterns that reflect the variations in uncertainty in the two economies. The application of the model to exchange rate policy suggests that over the long run it tracks the actual rates of exchange depreciation of both Mexico and Indonesia reasonably well, particularly the latter. We examine the implied and optimal rates of exchange rate depreciation, and the model suggests that Mexico and Indonesia did not devalue sufficiently during times of macroeconomic instability. The models also suggest a path of more gradual devaluation should have been followed, in stark contrast to both countries' sporadic and dramatic devaluations during terms-of-trade crises.

The calibration of the portfolio shares is more problematic. As with other stochastic models, we run into issues related to the equity premium puzzle. In his numerical calibrations of a similar stochastic growth model, Obstfeld (1994) found that in order to obtain plausible portfolio shares he needed to assume a coefficient of relative risk aversion of at least six, and indeed other researchers have suggested values in excess of eighteen as being plausible; see Kandel and Stambaugh (1991). We find that in some periods the variances are simply too small relative to the differences in the real rates of return, making the portfolio share very sensitive to assumptions one chooses to make about the degree of risk aversion. In interpreting our results here it is probably better to focus on the patterns of shares across the time periods, rather than their absolute levels. With this caveat, we suggest that the stochastic model accounts quite well for changing portfolio distributions that reflect capital flow fluctuations into Mexico and Indonesia. For Mexico, the implied variation in portfolio shares clearly indicates (1) the positive effects of the Brady plan in terms of the resumption of private capital inflows, (2) the large volume of foreign borrowing by both the Mexican private and public sector, (3) the resumption of foreign financing, and (4) the deterioration of the current account. The Indonesian portfolio share instead reflects the country's easy and stable access to the world financial market. Again we find that the model captures the effects of financial and macroeconomic instability quite well.

Our calibrations for the growth rate suggest that investors were not properly compensated for the added risk in Mexico, because the high variance is also associated with high risk and in a free market this would cause domestic investors to reduce their holdings of domestic capital in their portfolios. Alternatively, with the restrictions on capital movements, investors are not free to adjust their portfolios in ways predicted by the theory and consequently we get this overstatement of the growth rate. In comparing the implied growth rate and the respective depreciation for Mexico and Indonesia, we find evidence for Rodrik's (1996) assertion that the positive correlation between government size and openness is driven by the fact that larger governments can better insure and smooth external shocks.

The remainder of the chapter is set out as follows. Following this introduction we provide some background on Mexico and Indonesia. Section 5.3 then summarizes the important aspects of the stochastic general equilibrium models we shall employ for our analysis. Section 5.4 applies the model to the recent experiences of Mexico and Indonesia, while section 5.5 draws some conclusions.

5.2   Background on Mexican and Indonesian economic conditions

After discovering oil in the early 1970s, Mexico and Indonesia shared similar growth paths with 6.3 and 7.2 percent annual growth rates, respectively, between 1970 and 1980.[2] The average annual growth rates of the 1980s (1980–93) show, however, a wide disparity with Mexico's 1.6 percent annual growth being only a fraction of Indonesia's 5.8 percent. This marked bifurcation of the growth paths in the early 1980s occurred despite the fact that the countries' comparable development strategies were rocked by identical exogenous shocks. Mexico banked its initial phase of development on skyrocketing oil revenues in the 1970s, as also did Indonesia. In the early 1980s, however, oil prices declined sharply and tight fiscal policies in the United States and Britain increased world interest rates abruptly. Around 1986, both countries faced a second dramatic oil shock (due to a depreciating dollar), which was also accompanied by a major earthquake in Mexico. Both countries pegged their real exchange rate to the dollar, by allowing some gradual nominal depreciation accompanied by large, intermittent discrete devaluations.

Table 5.1 summarizes the mean annual inflation rates and the mean per capita growth rates of output and consumption for the two countries over the full period 1973–95, as well as the three subperiods, 1973–81, 1982–88, and 1989–95. These are annual averages and the standard deviations reflect the fluctuations in these averages over the various periods. These figures conveniently summarize the divergent growth paths followed by the two economies. Overall, Mexico is seen to be a higher-inflation, lower-growth, and higher-variability economy (as measured by the coefficient of variation). Whereas Indonesia reduced its inflation rate steadily since the 1973–81 period, in Mexico the period 1982–88 was one of hyperinflation, with inflation gradually declining more recently. Indonesia sustained positive growth throughout, whereas in Mexico the period of hyperinflation was also one of steady decline in output and

[2] The data in this chapter are based on *International Financial Statistics*; the brief and selected survey of the Mexican events is based on Dornbusch and Werner (1994), Gould (1995), and Aspe (1993). The brief review of events in Indonesia is drawn from Bhattacharya and Pangestu (1992).

Table 5.1. *Background statistics (in percent)*

Year	Inflation Mean	Inflation St. dev.	Output Growth[a] Mean	Output Growth[a] St. dev.	Consumption Growth[a] Mean	Consumption Growth[a] St. dev.
Mexico						
1973–81	18.1	6.2	5.0	3.2	3.7	12.6
1982–88	88.0	29.0	–4.6	5.8	–3.6	5.1
1989–95	19.5	9.7	2.2	2.9	2.5	3.5
1973–95	39.3	35.9	1.2	5.8	1.1	5.3
Indonesia						
1973–81	18.3	10.0	9.2	6.5	5.7	6.9
1982–88	8.5	2.3	2.6	4.9	2.9	3.0
1989–95	8.4	1.2	4.9	7.0	4.3	10.5
1973–95	12.5	8.4	5.9	6.6	4.4	7.1

[a] Real per capita growth.

consumption. Finally, although recently prices have become quite stable in Indonesia, the growth rates of output and consumption, while greater than those of Mexico, are also more variable.

5.2.1 *Mexico*

Until the mid-1970s, Mexico was a low-inflation country. During that period Mexico pursued inward-looking policies, increased government spending, and price controls. The 1973 oil price rise brought expansionary fiscal and monetary policies. A balance-of-payments crisis developed and Mexico devalued the peso by 60 percent in 1976, the year of huge oil discoveries. Instead of structural adjustment after the oil discoveries, the Portillo government implemented a massive fiscal expansion largely financed by external borrowing, leading to the debt crisis with the fall of oil prices in the early 1980s.

In response to this first oil price decline, a widening current account deficit, and tripling external debt (49 percent of GDP), the Mexican government devalued the peso by 260 percent, announced the suspension of debt service, nationalized the banking system, and imposed strict capital controls. With the aid of an IMF-sponsored reform package, the Mexican government embarked on a sequence of tentative public sector reforms. Despite the fact that Mexico averaged net transfers of 5 percent of GDP per annum between 1982 and 1988, official institutional lending (largely by the World Bank) was the only source of foreign capital during that time period. Inflation and money growth did not slow, however, because the initial reduction in the fiscal deficit, and renewed fiscal expansion in 1984, were financed by inflation tax.

During the period 1985–86, Mexico was hit hard by the second negative oil shock in conjunction with the sharp depreciation of the dollar, shortly after a major earthquake in Mexico City. The economy degenerated into hyperinflation, until the government announced a credible program to cut inflation through tight monetary policy and wage and price controls in November 1987 (Pacto 1987). The Pacto between unions, business, and government would see fifteen subsequent extensions and amendments, well into the 1990s. While inflation was soon brought under control, large sums of capital did not start to flow back into the country until the Brady Plan was announced in 1989. Private lending subsequently increased faster and in larger amounts than expected. Capital flows were further aided by a banking reform, financial deregulation, and a booming stock market that rose by 125, 25, and 50 percent in 1991, 1992, and 1993, respectively.

An increase in the tax base and greater public savings did not offset, however, the sharp decline in private savings between 1989 and 1992. Consumer credit increased 50 percent per annum and commercial bank credit to enterprises increased by 25 percent. With massive capital inflows the current account deteriorated from a $3.5 billion surplus in 1987 to a $24 billion deficit in 1992. The bonanza of the post-Brady years was also accompanied by an increasing overvaluation of the Mexican peso. Shortly before the peso collapse in December 1994, Dornbusch and Werner (1994) argued (somewhat clairvoyantly) for at least a 20 percent devaluation, largely to reverse a period of negligible growth and significant demand shifts toward foreign goods.

5.2.2 *Indonesia*

During the oil boom of the 1970s the financial system of Indonesia was still in the early stages of development. There was a gradual increase in regulatory government control in order to prevent looming "Dutch disease" problems associated with the adverse effects of real exchange rate appreciation on nonoil exports. Distortions and rent seeking were rampant, as was the expansion of government enterprises.

In Indonesia, the external shocks in the form of declining oil prices constituted an average of 3 and 15 percent of GDP in 1982 and 1986, respectively.[3] Both shocks were followed by drastic adjustments. The rupiah was devalued 28 percent in March 1983, and public expenditures were curtailed significantly. The reduction of the inflation rate below 5 percent was achieved at the cost of negative growth in 1982 and declining investment until the mid-1980s. Just when the economy had recovered to a solid 5 percent growth and continued low inflation, the second oil shock brought about a 34 percent deterioration in the terms of trade. The government immediately devalued the rupiah by 31 percent and cut fiscal investment by 25 percent. The fiscal deficit was reduced from 4.1 to 1.3 percent of GDP by 1990.

While the first adjustment period was characterized by increased fiscal control and regulation, the second oil shock brought a period of wide-spread economic liberalization. Another devaluation proceeded wide-spread trade and financial liberalizations in 1988 and 1989, respectively. These reforms were the impetus for increased economic activity, with growth and inflation stable at around 7 percent. The liberalizations also introduced uncertainty into the macroeconomic landscape, which mani-fested itself in roller-coaster stock market performances and bankrupt-cies of large financial institutions. However, with a low foreign debt ratio of about 30 percent of GDP, private investment and lending remained strong. The introduction of private financial institutions and fully liberal-ized interest rates generated some instability in the money multiplier and resulted in strong money growth, a surge in external borrowing, and a surging current account deficit between 1990 and 1992.

5.3   A stochastic general equilibrium model

This section briefly illustrates the analytical structure underlying our numerical analysis. It is based on the stochastic general equilibrium representative agent model developed by Grinols and Turnovsky (1994) and Turnovsky and Grinols (1996), where details are provided. Here we merely highlight the main equilibrium relationships that we shall consider.

5.3.1   Prices and asset returns

At each instant of time, the agent chooses his rate of consumption and allocates his portfolio of wealth among four assets: domestic money, M; domestic bonds, B, which are assumed to be nontraded; foreign bonds,

---

[3] In addition to declining oil prices, Indonesia suffered from declining tin, palm oil, and rubber prices.

B^*; and equity claims on capital, both of which are internationally traded.

The three prices in the model are P, the domestic price of the traded good; Q, the foreign price of the traded good; and E, the exchange rate, measured in terms of units of domestic currency per unit of foreign currency. These prices evolve according to:

$$\frac{dP}{P} = pdt + du_p \tag{1a}$$

$$\frac{dQ}{Q} = qdt + du_q \tag{1b}$$

$$\frac{dE}{E} = edt + du_e \tag{1c}$$

where pdt, qdt, and edt are the rates of change of P, Q, and E over the instant dt. The terms du_p, du_q, and du_e are temporally independent, normally distributed random variables with zero means and variances $\sigma_p^2 dt$, $\sigma_q^2 dt$, and $\sigma_e^2 dt$. With free trade, price movements must be tied to one another by the purchasing power parity (PPP) relationship

$$P = QE \tag{2}$$

which through stochastic differentiation implies

$$p = q + e + \sigma_{qe} \tag{3a}$$

$$du_p = du_q + du_e \tag{3b}$$

where $\sigma_{qe} dt$ is the instantaneous covariance between du_q and du_e. While the foreign price level Q is always assumed to be exogenous to the small open economy, the determination of P and E depends upon the policy of the monetary authority.

Domestic and foreign bonds are assumed to be short bonds, paying deterministic nominal interest rates of i and i^*, respectively. Given the stochastic structure of the economy, the real rates of return to domestic consumers on money, the domestic bond, and the foreign bond are respectively

$$dR_M = r_M dt - du_p; \quad r_M \equiv -p + \sigma_p^2 \tag{4a}$$

$$dR_B = r_B dt - du_p; \quad r_B \equiv i - p + \sigma_p^2 \tag{4b}$$

$$dR_F = r_F dt - du_q; \quad r_F \equiv i^* - q + \sigma_q^2. \tag{4c}$$

The understanding of how the variance contributes to the return is crucial to the understanding of the modeling of risk in a Brownian motion stochastic framework. The real rates differ from the well-known deterministic quantities by two terms, the stochastic component and the variance. Consider the rate of return on money, which can be defined as $dR_M = d(1/P)/(1/P)$. If we take the second-order differential, this expression yields $dR_M \approx -dP/P + (dP/P)^2$, where the second term equals $\sigma_p^2 dt$. Due to the convexity of $1/P$ in P, the variance of the stochastic component in P contributes positively to the expected rate of return. The intuition is analogous to standard portfolio frontier analysis, where higher risk requires higher return to render the investor indifferent between assets of various risks.

An immediate, but important, consequence of considering the rates of return in a stochastic context is that the variance of the price level is introduced as a component of the real rate of return. As will become evident in our numerical analysis, this additional term is unimportant for the United States. In a macroeconomic environment where prices are relatively stable, the variance component is negligible compared to the usual measure $(i - p)$ and can safely be ignored. In contrast, in both Mexico and Indonesia, periods of rapidly changing prices were associated with large variances in prices, to such a significant extent that the variance is comparable in magnitude with the conventional rate of return and indeed dominates it in some cases.

The flow of output, dY, is produced from capital, dK, by means of the stochastic constant returns (A-K) technology

$$dY = \alpha K dt + \alpha K dy \tag{5}$$

where α is the (constant) marginal product of capital and dy is a temporally independent, normally distributed, stochastic process with zero mean and variance $\sigma_y^2 dt$. In the absence of adjustment costs, the real return on equity (capital) is

$$dR_K = r_K dt + du_k \equiv \alpha dt + \alpha dy. \tag{4d}$$

Equation (4d) establishes a relation between the real rate of return on equity and the marginal physical product of capital that depends solely on the magnitudes of α and dy.

5.3.2   *Consumer optimization*

The representative agent is assumed to select portfolio of assets and a rate of consumption to maximize expected lifetime utility. Utility depends upon consumption $C(t)$ and real money balances $M(t)/P(t)$, as represented by the isoelastic utility function

$$E \int_0^\infty \frac{1}{\gamma} \left(C(t)^\theta \left(\frac{M(t)}{P(t)} \right)^{1-\theta} \right)^\gamma e^{-\rho t} dt, \quad -\infty < \gamma < 1; \quad 0 \le \theta \le 1 \qquad (6a)$$

subject to the wealth constraint:

$$W = \frac{M}{P} + \frac{B}{P} + \frac{EB^*}{P} + K \qquad (6b)$$

where W denotes real wealth, and the stochastic wealth accumulation equation:

$$dW = W \left[n_1 dR_M + n_2 dR_B + n_3 dR_K + n_4 dR_F \right] - C(t) dt - dT \qquad (6c)$$

where portfolio shares are: $n_1 \equiv (M/P)/W$ = share of portfolio held in money; $n_2 \equiv (QB/P)/W$ = share of portfolio held in government bonds; $n_3 \equiv K/W$ = share of portfolio held in equity (capital); $n_4 \equiv (EB^*/P)/W$ = share of portfolio held in foreign bonds; dT = taxes paid. Note that we permit n_4 to be negative, interpreting that as a net debtor.

Taxes are endogenously determined to satisfy the government constraint, specified in equation (9a), and therefore include a stochastic component reflecting the changing need for taxes. Because in a growing economy taxes and other real variables grow with the size of the economy, measured here by real wealth, we relate total taxes to wealth according to

$$dT = \tau W dt + W dv \qquad (7)$$

where dv is a temporally independent, normally distributed random variable with zero mean and variance $\sigma_v^2 dt$. The parameters τ and dv must be set so as to ensure that the government's budget constraint is met.

The first order optimality conditions to this problem can be written in the form:

Consumption: $$\frac{C}{W} = \frac{\theta}{1 - \gamma\theta} \left[\rho - \beta\gamma - \frac{1}{2} \gamma(\gamma - 1)\sigma_w^2 \right] \qquad (8a)$$

Money holdings: $$n_1 = \left(\frac{1-\theta}{\theta} \right) \frac{C/W}{i} \qquad (8b)$$

Equities and bonds: $$(r_K - r_B) dt = (1 - \gamma) \text{cov} \left[dw, \, du_k + du_p \right] \qquad (8c)$$

$$(r_F - r_B) dt = (1 - \gamma) \text{cov} \left[dw, \, -du_q + du_p \right] \qquad (8d)$$

where

$$dw \equiv -\left(n_1 + n_2\right)du_p + n_3 du_k + n_4 du_q - dv$$

denotes the stochastic component of dW/W, and

$$\beta \equiv n_1 r_M + n_2 r_B + n_3 r_K + n_4 r_F - \tau$$

$$\sigma_w^2 \equiv \frac{E(dw)^2}{dt} = \left(n + n_2\right)^2 \sigma_p^2 + n_3^2 \alpha^2 \sigma_y^2 + n_4^2 \sigma_q^2 + \sigma_v^2$$

$$- 2\left(n_1 + n_2\right)n_3 \alpha \sigma_{py} - 2\left(n_1 + n_2\right)n_4 \sigma_{pq} + 2\left(n_1 + n_2\right)\sigma_{pv}$$

$$+ 2n_3 n_4 \alpha \sigma_{yq} - 2n_3 \alpha \sigma_{yvK} - 2n_4 \sigma_{qv}.$$

These relationships will eventually be embedded into our stochastic general equilibrium. Of particular relevance will be (8c) and (8d) that describe the differential real rates of return on the assets in terms of their respective real risk differentials, as measured by the covariance with the overall market return.

5.3.3   Government policy

Government policy is described by the choice of government expenditures, the printing of money and bonds, and the collection of taxes, all of which must be specified subject to the government's flow budget constraint:

$$d\left(\frac{M}{P}\right) + d\left(\frac{B}{P}\right) = dG - dT + \frac{M}{P}dR_M + \frac{B}{P}dR_B \tag{9a}$$

where dG denotes the stochastic rate of real government expenditure.

Government expenditure policy is specified by the stochastic relationship

$$dG = g\alpha K dt + \alpha K dz \tag{9b}$$

where dz is an intertemporally independent, normally distributed random variable with zero mean and variance $\sigma_z^2 dt$.

Monetary growth is specified by the stochastic growth rule

$$\frac{dM}{M} = \mu dt + dx \tag{9c}$$

where μ is the mean monetary growth rate and dx is an intertemporally independently distributed, random variable with zero mean and variance $\sigma_x^2 dt$. This equation reflects how monetary policy is chosen and encompasses a potentially rich set of policies some of which are discussed by Turnovsky and Grinols (1996). To be concrete, we shall assume that the monetary authority sets the mean growth rate, μ, directly.

Debt policy is formulated in terms of maintaining a fixed ratio of domestic government (nontraded) bonds to money

$$\frac{B}{M} = \lambda \tag{9d}$$

where λ is a policy parameter set by the government. This specification can be thought of as being a stochastic version of a balanced-growth equilibrium assumption and has a well-established history in the monetary growth literature (see, e.g., Foley and Sidrauski 1971). In the present international context, the choice of λ also reflects sterilization policy. Given the policy specification (9b) – (9d), both the mean and the stochastic component of taxes dT must be set in order to meet the government budget constraint (9a).

5.3.4 Product market equilibrium and balance of payments

Net exports of the physical commodity are determined by the excess of production over domestic uses, $dY - dC - dK - dG$. Balance-of-payments equilibrium, in turn, requires the transfer of new foreign bonds (in excess of interest on earlier issues) to finance net exports of the domestic country. This is expressed in real terms by the relationship.

$$d\left(\frac{B^*}{Q}\right) = \left[dY - dC - dK - dG\right] + \left(\frac{B^*}{Q}\right) dR_F. \tag{10}$$

The solution can be characterized as one where risks and returns on assets are unchanging through time so that the same allocation of portfolio wealth is chosen at each instant of time.

In addition, there are some technical considerations such as the determination of initial price levels (through appropriate jumps) and certain feasibility conditions (such as intertemporal solvency conditions) to be met. These aspects are not discussed here.

5.3.5 Equilibrium growth, consumption, and portfolio shares

Sections 5.3.1–5.3.4 determine a macroeconomic equilibrium in which the deterministic and stochastic components of the relevant equilibrium variables are endogenously determined. The equilibrium determines both real and nominal quantities, and can be characterized as one where risks and returns on assets are unchanging through time so that the same allocation of portfolio wealth is chosen at each instant of time. With portfolio shares remaining constant over time, all real components of wealth must grow at the same stochastic rate. For our purposes, the equilibrium can be summarized by the following pair of equations that determine the share of capital in the traded portfolio of the consumer's portfolio, $\omega \equiv n_3/(n_3 + n_4)$, and the equilibrium growth rate, ψ:

$$\omega = \frac{\alpha - \left(i^* - q + \sigma_q^2\right)}{\left(1 - \gamma\right)\left(\alpha^2\sigma_y^2 + \sigma_q^2\right)} + \frac{\sigma_q^2}{\alpha^2\sigma_y^2 + \sigma_q^2} \tag{11a}$$

$$\psi = \omega\alpha\left(1 - g - c\right) + \left(1 - \omega\right)\left(i^* - q + \sigma_q^2\right) \tag{11b}$$

where $c \equiv C/Y = C/(\alpha K) = C/(\alpha n_3 W)$. Equation (11a) provides an explicit solution for the relative share of capital in the traded portfolio of the representative agent's portfolio. This equation is a standard expression in stochastic models, describing the net position in terms of the risk-adjusted differential real rate of return plus a hedging component. It is determined entirely by real quantities and is therefore *independent* of the domestic government's finance policy. Equation (11b) expresses the mean growth rate as a weighted average of the domestic source of growth and the growth attributable to interest earnings from abroad, the weights being the relative portfolio shares, ω, $(1 - \omega)$, respectively. The consumption–mean income ratio, c, depends on the C/W ratio and the portfolio share of domestic capital, n_3, both of which are endogenously determined, along with the remaining portfolio shares, particularly the share of money, n_1.

Having determined ω, the remainder of the equilibrium can be determined in terms of the domestic nominal rate, i, debt policy, λ, and other exogenous real parameters, such as the exogenous sources of risk in the form of output, monetary, and foreign price shocks, σ_y^2, σ_x^2, σ_q^2; preferences θ, ρ; technology, α; and the government share in output, g. An important consequence of the specification of debt policy by (9d) is that the equilibrium growth rate depends on the domestic nominal interest rate, i. This provides the avenue through which government policy is able to influence the real part of the equilibrium. The fact that the equilibrium real growth rate depends on the monetary growth rate (inflation) through the interest rate is a dynamic manifestation of the familiar Mundell-Tobin effect. It means that the superneutrality of money associated with the traditional Sidrauski (1967) model does not apply in the present context, even though it has been shown to extend to other stochastic growth models in which the residual financing of the government budget is through lump-sum taxation or equivalently debt issuance.

5.3.6   *Nominal quantities*

Once government finance policy is specified, the equilibrium solutions for (1) the rate of inflation, p; (2) the rate of exchange depreciation, e; and (3) the domestic nominal rate of interest, i, can be attained from the following three relationships:

$$p = q + e - \omega \sigma_q^2 \tag{12a}$$

$$p = \mu - \psi(i, \lambda) + \sigma_w^2 \tag{12b}$$

$$i = \alpha + p - \sigma_x^2 - (1 - \gamma)\alpha^2 \omega \sigma_y^2 - \gamma \sigma_w^2. \tag{12c}$$

Equation (12a) is just the PPP equation (3a); equation (12b) describes the adjustment in inflation necessary to maintain portfolio balance along the equilibrium growth path; equation (12c) is obtained by evaluating the consumer optimality condition (8c). These equations are expressed in terms of the variances of exogenous variables. Target values for p, e, or i depend on the choice of monetary instrument. In general, this can be accomplished in a multiplicity of ways:

Financial growth rate: The monetary authorities can attain the target rate of interest, $\bar{i}$ say, by directly setting the common growth rate of its financial assets in accordance with

$$\mu = \bar{i} + \psi(\bar{i}, \lambda) - \alpha + \sigma_x^2 + (1 - \gamma)\alpha^2 \omega \sigma_y^2 - (1 - \gamma)\sigma_w^2. \tag{13a}$$

Exchange rate depreciation: Alternatively, the monetary authorities can target the rate of exchange depreciation and allow their financial liabilities to adjust appropriately. In this case the implied rate of exchange depreciation can be expressed by the risk-adjusted nominal interest differential:

$$e = \bar{i} - i^* + \gamma\left[\sigma_w^2 - (1 - \omega)\sigma_q^2\right] + \sigma_x^2. \tag{13b}$$

It is important to note that under certainty these policies are equivalent in all respects.

5.3.7   *Optimal exchange rate policy*

An important issue is to determine the extent to which the exchange rate policy followed by Mexico and Indonesia was close to being optimal. This issue can be conveniently addressed by determining the optimal rate of exchange depreciation, $\hat{e}$, where the welfare criterion we consider is the welfare of the representative agent, as specified by the intertemporal utility function (6a), evaluated along the equilibrium balanced-growth path.

The issues involved can be seen most clearly in the case of the logarithmic utility function when the optimized welfare criterion can be expressed as:

$$
X\left(K_0 + \frac{B_0^*}{Q_0}\right) = \frac{\theta}{\rho}\ln(\theta\rho) + \frac{1-\theta}{\rho}\ln n_1 + \frac{\psi}{\rho^2} + \frac{1}{\rho}\ln\left(\frac{\omega}{n_3}\right)
$$
$$
+ \frac{1}{\rho}\ln\left(K_0 + \frac{B_0^*}{Q_0}\right) - \frac{1}{2\rho^2}\sigma_w^2.
$$
(14)

Apart from exogenous constants, and the initial stock of traded assets, intertemporal welfare depends upon four elements. The first is the utility from holding real money balances: $((1 - \theta)/\rho)\ln n_1$. The second term, ψ/ρ^2, is the utility resulting from the growth of wealth, insofar as this increases future consumption possibilities. The third, represented by the term $(1/\rho)\ln(\omega/n_3)$, results from wealth effects due to initial jumps in the exchange rate. The final term, $-(1/2\rho^2)\sigma_w^2$, represents the welfare losses due to the exogenous sources of real risk to the economy.

Government financial policy, however conducted, affects welfare only through the first three channels, doing so through its impact on the nominal interest rate i. Turnovsky and Grinols (1996) show that for the logarithmic utility function, the optimal interest rate target is determined by the quadratic equation in i

$$
i^2 - \rho(1+\lambda)(1-\theta)i - \rho^2(1+\lambda)^2\theta(1-\theta) = 0
$$
(15)

whose positive root,

$$
\hat{i} = \frac{\rho(1+\lambda)(1-\theta)}{2}\left[1 + \sqrt{1 + \frac{4\theta}{1-\theta}}\right]
$$
(15′)

is the optimal domestic nominal interest rate. Interestingly enough, the optimal nominal interest rate is independent of the stochastic characteristics of the economy. This is a consequence of the logarithmic utility function; for the more general constant elasticity utility function, $\hat{i}$ does indeed depend upon the variances impinging on the economy. The optimal rate of exchange depreciation is then obtained by combining (15′) with (13b).

5.4   Application to the Mexico and Indonesian experiences

5.4.1   *Inflation, risk, and rates of return*

The natural starting point for the analysis of risk in the two economies is a summary of the returns on domestic securities and foreign (proxied by U.S.) securities as given in equations (4a)–(4c). The two key components of these asset returns are the variances of the inflation rates in the domestic and foreign economies. Data on these are not available and need to be constructed. For all three economies, the United States (the foreign economy), Mexico, and Indonesia, these have been constructed using the following procedure. Annual data on the consumer price index (CPI) and six-month Treasury bills have been taken for the twenty-three-year period 1973–95. In order to give some idea of behavior and structural changes over different periods, these have been broken down into the three periods, 1973–81, 1982–88, and 1989–95, which coincide nicely with external and internal shocks in the respective economies. For each period, the mean is the true sample mean and the variance is derived from the variance of the actual observations about the sample mean.[4] Although these figures are reported in percentages, in calculating them we have computed them in absolute terms and only at the end converted them to percentage terms for convenience (see Frankel, 1988). Notice that in all three economies the risk, as measured by the coefficient of variation, over the entire period exceeds that of all subperiods. This is because it includes changes between 1981 and 1982, and 1988 and 1989, which were periods of relatively large variations, but which, being end-points, are excluded from any subperiod.

Table 5.2 summarizes the relevant characteristics of inflation, risk, and rates of return for the three economies. Table 5.2a presents the results for the United States. Inflation drops from over 8 percent in the latter 1970s to an average of around 3.5 percent from 1982 on. The variance of the inflation rate, while higher in the earlier period of higher inflation, is small throughout. Over the entire period the variance adds only about ten basis points to the nominal interest rate and only one basis point during recent years. Hence any adjustments for risk in determining the real returns on money and bonds in the United States are modest.

Table 5.2b presents the corresponding figures for Mexico. Starting with a mean inflation rate of about 26 percent at the onset of its balance-

---

[4] It is basically analytically identical to take the variance of the deviations from the linear trend.

Table 5.2. *Risk and rates of return (in percent)*

Year	Inflation mean	Inflation st. dev.	Nominal interest	Real return on money	Risk-adjusted return on bonds	Conventional return on bonds	Real risk premia
a. United States[a] (foreign economy)	q	σ_q	i^*	$-q + \sigma_q^2$	$i^* - q + \sigma_q^2$	$i^* - q$	
1973–81	8.330	3.000	8.434	−8.240	0.194	0.104	
1982–88	3.560	1.095	7.839	−3.548	4.291	4.279	
1989–95	3.492	1.265	5.297	−3.476	1.821	1.805	
1973–95	5.528	3.178	7.159	−5.427	1.732	1.631	
b. Mexico[b]	p	σ_p	i	$-p + \sigma_p^2$	$i - p + \sigma_p^2$	$i - p$	$r_B - r_F$
1973–81	18.067	6.217	14.391	−17.701	−3.3	−3.676	−3.5
1982–88	88.028	29.048	67.790	−79.6	−11.8	−20.238	−16.1
1989–95	19.507	9.747	27.460	−18.557	8.903	7.953	7.082
1973–95	39.309	35.886	33.904	−26.431	7.473	−5.405	5.741
c. Indonesia[c]	p	σ_p	i	$-p + \sigma_p^2$	$i - p + \sigma_p^2$	$i - p$	$r_B - r_F$
1973–81	18.270	9.995	9.600	−17.3	−7.77	−8.670	−7.865
1982–88	8.514	2.324	13.700	−8.5	5.2	5.186	0.949
1989–95	8.401	1.225	19.201	−8.386	10.815	10.800	8.994
1973–95	12.548	8.361	13.596	−11.849	1.747	1.048	0.015

[a] For the United States, the nominal interest rate is based on the six-month Treasury bill.

[b] For Mexico, nominal interest is based on the six-month treasury bill rate, except 1972–75 which are deposit rates from Buffie (1990).

[c] For Indonesia, nominal interest is based on six-month time deposits, except 1994–95, which are lending rates; information for 1994 is from the National Trade Databank, and for 1994 and 1995 from the *Economic & Business Review Indonesia*, July 10, 1996.

of-payments and debt crisis, the inflation rate soared to an average 66 percent after oil prices declined sharply in the early 1980s and the fiscal deficit exploded. Without any serious policy adjustment, the inflation rate never settled and the collapse of the oil price in 1986 caused yet another surge in the inflation rate, which reached nearly 100 percent in 1986–87 and averaged 88 percent for the period 1982–88. After a series of reforms, most notably the Pacto and the Brady Plan, inflation dropped dramatically to under 10 percent by 1990–92, and averaged under 20 percent for our third subperiod.

But the mean inflation rate is only one factor influencing the real return. In contrast to the United States, the variance, or the measured risk in Mexico, is a significant component of the real return. Although over the initial period of relatively stable prices it adds only around thirty-six basis points to the rate of return, during the period of hyperinflation in 1982–88 it adds around 8.5 percentage points, while during the recent period of renewed growth its adds 1 percent. Over the entire period, which also includes the variances of the "break years," 1981–82 and 1988–89, it adds nearly 13 percent to the real rate of return. Indeed, these results for Mexico highlight nicely how, in a high-risk environment, the inflation variance becomes an important component of the real rate of return, and how its neglect may give misleading implications for the rate of return. For example, the conventional measure of the real interest rate, $(i\text{-}p)$, reported in Table 5.2b suggests a negative real rate of return on bonds over the entire period 1973–95, whereas the high variance of the inflation rate during that period implies that the real return was actually quite large and positive. The final column of Table 5.2b provides estimates of the real risk premium and suggests over the entire period it averaged around 5.7 percent. The negative risk premium of 16.1 percent during the period of instability, 1982–88, does not seem plausible. It is a reflection of the hyperinflation during that period and the failure of the nominal interest rate risk sufficiently to compensate for it. At the same time, the variance of the price level does help pull the risk premium up in the right direction.

The reason for this difficulty lies in the financial markets. Given the economic conditions, one would expect the interest rate to adjust. But being government controlled, the interest rate was unable to respond as necessary. We do not view this as necessarily being a weakness of the model, but rather a reflection of extreme government intervention that a model based on free markets cannot reasonably be expected to capture.

Table 5.2c presents analogous measures for Indonesia. Despite a bout of inflation as oil prices collapsed in the early 1980s, there was immediate

Table 5.3. *Portfolio shares (ω) for different*
degrees of risk aversion (expressed as a fraction)

	Risk aversion $(1 - \gamma)$		
Year	1	3.3	10
Mexico			
1973–81	−7.311	−2.193	−0.731
1982–88	−1.904	−0.571	−0.190
1989–95	7.331	2.199	0.733
1973–95	0.442	0.133	0.044
Indonesia			
1973–81	−7.222	−2.167	−0.722
1982–88	14.379	4.314	1.438
1989–95	290.129	87.039	29.013
1973–95	0.019	0.006	0.002

adjustment and the mean inflation rate remains moderate over the entire period, being only a few percentage points higher than in the United States. Except during the initial period, when inflation was rapidly declining, the price variance is much smaller than that of Mexico, and somewhat larger than that in the United States. In relative terms it is not too different from that in the United States when taken over the entire period. Over time, it moves from being less stable than that in the United States to more stable over the recent period 1989–95.[5]

As in the United States, risk associated with Indonesian price shocks has become a minor component of the real return on domestic bonds, being reduced from almost 1 percentage point in the 1970s to just 1.5 basis points in the 1990s, though over the entire period it averages around 70 basis points. The risk premium on average is much lower than that of Mexico, presumably being a reflection of Indonesia's more successful management of foreign debt and inflation. The negative risk premium in the 1970s is a reflection of the high domestic inflation of that period, coupled with the absence of a developed domestic financial market.

[5] At first sight, a somewhat counterintuitive aspect of these results is that a high mean rate of inflation does not necessarily mean a high variance. Also periods of rapidly diminishing inflation are associated with high variance.

5.4.2 Share of domestic capital in traded portfolios and implications for capital inflows

The formal model focuses on portfolio shares. Within this framework, international capital flows are reflected in the change in the portfolio share associated with traded bonds. For debtor countries like Mexico and Indonesia, the fraction of traded bonds held in their respective portfolios, n_4, is negative. The key measure in the model is given by $\omega = n_3/(n_3 + n_4)$, the share of capital in the traded portfolio. If we assume $n_3 > 0$, debtor economies will thus be associated with values of $\omega > 1$, when $0 > n_4 > -n_3$, or $\omega < 0$, when $n_4 < -n_3 < 0$.

Under the assumption of freely adjusted capital, the formal model expresses the mean return to capital as α and its variance as $\alpha^2 \sigma_y^2$. This measure poses two problems for the calibration of the model. The first is one of scale. The fact that the basic model is a stochastic constant returns to scale model means that the choice of α reflects population size and this is compounded in the variance measure. The second difficulty arises from imperfections of the domestic capital market in developing countries.

Initial attempts to estimate ω using various postulated values for α yielded unsatisfactory results.[6] Hence, given the imperfections in the domestic capital markets, we decided to proxy the returns to capital with the returns to domestic bonds. This involves replacing α in (11a) by $i - p + \sigma_p^2$, thus leading to:

$$\omega' = \frac{\left(i - p + \sigma_p^2\right) - \left(i^* - q + \sigma_q^2\right)}{\left(1 - \gamma\right)\left(\sigma_p^2 + \sigma_q^2\right)} + \frac{\sigma_q^2}{\sigma_p^2 + \sigma_q^2} \tag{11a'}$$

Estimates of ω' for Mexico and Indonesia using this measure are provided in Table 5.3. As in Obstfeld (1994), for example, the estimates for portfolio shares are crucially sensitive to the assumed degree of risk aversion, and so results are reported for three values: the logarithmic utility function ($\gamma = 0$), an intermediate degree of risk aversion, $(1 - \gamma) = 3.3$, and for a high degree of relative risk aversion, $(1 - \gamma) = 10$. In both countries a higher degree of risk aversion decreases the fraction of the domestic asset in the portfolio. This is plausible, since capital in both Mexico and Indonesia is much riskier than investing abroad.

The instability of the estimates of ω' makes them difficult to interpret. The large swings in ω' across the subperiods, associated with vastly

---

[6] Another approach would be to use data on stock returns for Mexico and Indonesia, but unfortunately we were able to locate such data for only the past few years of our sample.

different characteristics make the mean value estimated over the entire period of dubious behavioral significance. But the fact that generally we find $\omega < 0$ or $\omega > 1$ is consistent with the two countries being debtor economies.

In the case of Mexico, taking the case $(1 - \gamma) = 3.3$ as being perhaps the most plausible, one detects a clear pattern in ω' over time that can be interpreted as being broadly consistent with historical experience. The large negative value of ω' in the 1970s is consistent with a large portfolio share of domestic capital, n_3, reflecting the growth of that period, accompanied by an even larger portfolio share of foreign capital, n_4, as huge external debt was accumulated during that period, reaching 49% of GDP in 1982 (see Dornbusch and Werner, 1994). The marked drop in ω' (in absolute magnitude) over the period of the debt crisis is consistent with reduced holdings of capital, associated with the negative growth of that period, plus the reduction in capital inflows resulting from the country's loss of access to foreign capital markets. Finally, the switch in ω' to being positive over the period 1989–95 is consistent with recovery and more responsible foreign borrowing following the announcement and implementation of the Brady plan. The value $\omega' \approx 2$ nicely reflects the positive effects of the Brady plan in terms of the resumption of private capital inflows, the large volume of foreign borrowing by both the Mexican private and public sector, the resumption of foreign financing, and the deterioration of the current account to a massive $24 billion deficit in 1982. Thus, the model does quite well in accounting for the changing share of domestic and foreign assets in Mexico portfolio holdings.

The estimates of ω' for Indonesia reflect the country's easier access to the world market. Throughout the sample period, Indonesia has a higher share of domestic capital in the portfolio than does Mexico. This is not surprising since Indonesia experienced sudden and drastic reforms after each terms-of-trade shock, such as credit, hiring and wage freezes, and small variations in the money supply. Interestingly enough, the model again picks up the period of financial and macroeconomic instability. A surge in foreign borrowing can be detected beginning in 1989 when financial liberalization led to both a dramatic expansion of the financial sector and foreign capital inflows. The values of ω' for the 1989–95 period are obviously implausible. The difficulty is a technical one, attributable to a combination of low U.S. real returns, coupled with high real interest rates in Indonesia, and low variances in both U.S. and, more particularly, Indonesian inflation rates over that period. This makes it impossible to reconcile the rates of return with the variances and plausible portfolio shares. More variance must be introduced into the Indonesian rate of return to explain the risk premium for that period.

5.4.3 *Economic growth*

The basic expression for economic growth in (11b) is expressed in terms of the weighted average of domestic and foreign sources of growth, the weights being the relative importance of capital and foreign bonds in the domestic investor's portfolio. The equation is not specific to the Grinols-Turnovsky model, but just like many of our previous equilibrium relationships, is characteristic of growth relationships generic to stochastic models (see e.g., Obstfeld, 1994). For purposes of computing portfolio shares, we had proxied α by r_B, the return on domestic bonds. We have computed growth rates using this same approximation in (11b). Table 5.4 reports these growth rates corresponding to the three values of the risk aversion parameter, γ.

The predictions for the growth rate are disappointing, although there are some positive aspects. Turning first to Mexico, we see that the forecast growth rate over the entire period is around 1.73 percent which overstates the average growth rates of consumption and output by around 0.6 percentage points. This estimate is independent of the portfolio share, ω. This is because the domestic sources of growth, as measured by $(1 - c - g)r_B$, happen to be approximately equal to the foreign return, r_F. It is also clear from the table that a value of $(1 - \gamma)$ somewhere between 1 and 3.3 will track the two growth rates over the period 1973–81. In addition, the estimated growth rate of around 1.8 percent for the recent period is quite close to the actual growth rate of around 2.3–2.5 percent. However, the model completely fails to predict the contraction of the period 1982–88, instead estimating strong positive growth for that period! The problem is that the rate of return is a positive function of the variance of inflation. Given the high variances in the period 1982–88, the model predicts a high risk premium and thus high average growth rates. It suggests that investors were not properly compensated for the added risk in Mexico, since the high variance is also associated with high risk. In a free market this would cause domestic investors to reduce holdings of domestic capital in their portfolios. Alternatively, with restrictions on capital movements, investors are not free to adjust their portfolios in ways predicted by theory and, consequently, we get this overstatement of the growth rate. Both effects seem to seriously skew our implied results.

Since the expression for ψ in (11b) is derived from the current-account balance relationship (10), α more appropriately refers to the output–capital ratio, Y/K, or some such measure of productivity of capital, rather than a rate of return. For Mexico these data are available from the *International Financial Statistics* (*IFS*) but perform no better. We

Table 5.4. *Consumption shares (c), government shares (g) (as fractions), and output growth rates (ψ) (in percent)*

Year	g	c	1-c-g	Risk aversion (1 – γ)			Actual growth	
				1 ψ	3.3 ψ	10 ψ	Consumption	Output
Mexico								
1973–81	0.101	0.674	0.225	7.0	2.2	0.9	3.730	4.993
1982–88	0.091	0.648	0.261	18.3	8.5	5.7	-3.648	-4.552
1989–95	0.096	0.703	0.201	1.590	1.752	1.798	2.532	2.224
1973–95	0.097	0.670	0.233	1.736	1.733	1.732	1.056	1.201
Indonesia								
1973–81	0.103	0.654	0.243	15.1	4.7	-1.7	5.711	9.198
1982–88	0.103	0.595	0.301	-34.8	-7.4	0.40	2.950	2.629
1989–95	0.090	0.544	0.365	619.734	187.195	63.612	4.298	4.905
1973–95	0.100	0.607	0.292	1.709	1.725	1.730	4.441	5.892

have employed the real return to capital as defined by the World Bank (the rate of growth of GDP as a percentage of the average investment rate) but this does not result in any improvement in the forecast growth rates.

Interestingly enough, the model also predicts a growth rate of around 1.72 percent for Indonesia over the entire period 1973–95, and again this is independent of the degree of risk aversion. This is because the estimate of the average portfolio share is $\omega' \approx 0$, so that the growth rate is effectively determined entirely by the foreign component. Although data on the rate of return on capital cannot be constructed from *IFS* data, the numbers using the return on bonds as a proxy are more plausible for Indonesia. This is likely so because conditions were more stable in Indonesia, so that bond and capital returns moved relatively closer in tandem. The results capture the qualitative pattern of Indonesian growth, namely positive growth, followed by a reduction, and then an improvement. However, in all cases the magnitudes of the changes are seriously overstated, with declines being predicted for 1982–88. The absurd growth rate for the more recent period is a direct consequence of the unrealistically high estimated values of ω, which is completely out of line with the risk and return characteristics of domestic and foreign assets.

Overall, the model *overpredicts* the growth rates of Mexico and *underpredicts* the growth rates of Indonesia. One reason why this may be so is due to the role of government expenditures. One striking difference between Mexico and Indonesia is in the fraction of output devoted to government expenditure. While it averaged around 9 percent for Mexico, it is around three times that for Indonesia. One limitation of the model is that it treats government expenditure purely as a drain on output, so that other things being equal, a country with a smaller fraction of government expenditure will have a lower growth rate. This does not capture the productive use to which government expenditure was put in improving productivity and thereby enhancing the growth rate. Maybe even more importantly, Rodrik (1996) has recently found a statistically robust positive association between a country's degree of openness and the size of its government. He provides strong evidence that this surprising correlation is due to the fact that government expenditures function to insure against or mitigate and smooth the effects of external shocks. In our context this is an important insight, since both countries opened up to the world market and the greater degree of insulation possible through government expenditures may have given Indonesia an important edge when it came to reducing macroeconomic instability.

5.4.4   *Exchange rate depreciation*

Finally we examine the implications of this stochastic model for exchange rate policy. Recalling (13b), the implied rate of exchange depreciation, corresponding to any arbitrarily set target value $\bar{i}$ of the nominal interest rate, is:

$$e = \bar{i} - i* + \gamma\left[\sigma_w^2 - (1-\omega)\sigma_q^2\right] + \sigma_x^2. \tag{13b}$$

The optimal rate of exchange depreciation, $\hat{e}$, is then given by:

$$\hat{e} = \hat{i} - i* + \gamma\left[\sigma_w^2 - (1-\omega)\sigma_q^2\right] + \sigma_x^2, \tag{13b$'$}$$

where $\hat{i}$ denotes the optimal nominal interest rate target. In the case of the logarithmic utility function, $\hat{i}$ is determined by (15$'$). For numerical purposes we shall assume values of $\theta = 0.8$, $\rho = 0.045$, $\lambda = 5$. This implies an optimal nominal interest rate of around 14 percent, which we have arbitrarily applied to both countries. In addition, given the arbitrariness of these parameters, we shall assume that $\hat{i} = 14$ percent for all assumed values of the risk aversion parameter. It is interesting to note that even for the logarithmic utility function, uncertainty still affects the optimal rate of exchange depreciation. In contrast to the real returns that are functions of variances of the prices, or the capital shares that are functions of the variances of the domestic productivity and foreign price shocks, the optimal rate of exchange depreciation depends on the variance of the monetary growth rate. The calculation of that variance, necessary to compute the optimal exchange rate policy, was done in exactly the same way as the estimation of the variance of the inflation rate.

The results for the two countries are set out in Table 5.5 and show a striking contrast. The first pair of columns in the two parts of the table report the means and standard deviations of the monetary growth rates in the two economies. After 1991, the mean and standard deviation of the Mexican monetary growth rate is high relative to that of Indonesia, which reflects their differential adjustment policies after being struck by identical external shocks. The next two pairs of columns of the table report: (1) the implied rate of exchange depreciation, that is, the rate of exchange depreciation predicted by the model corresponding to (13b), and (2) the optimal rate of exchange depreciation, corresponding to the optimal, rather than the actual, nominal interest rate, as computed by (13b$'$). These are compared with the actual rates of exchange depreciation followed in the economies, as reported in the final column. In all cases these are averages of the annual rates of depreciation over the various subperiods, as well as over the entire sample period, and thus

Table 5.5. *Actual, implied, and optimal exchange rate depreciation (in percent)*

Year	Money growth		Optimal depreciation: Risk aversion $(1 - \gamma)$			Implied depreciation: Risk aversion $(1 - \gamma)$			Actual depreciation
	Mean	St. dev. (σ_x)	1	3.3	10	1	3.3	10	
Mexico									
1973–81	28.418	5.7	5.9	3.3	−7.0	6.3	3.7	−6.7	23.115
1982–88	66.196	24.9	12.4	11.9	10.1	66.1	65.6	63.9	40.276
1989–95	37.383	43.778	27.868	27.586	26.810	41.328	41.046	40.270	15.907
1973–95	42.644	31.169	16.556	16.179	14.941	36.460	36.083	34.845	27.634
Indonesia									
1973–81	34.027	8.3	6.3	5.9	4.4	1.9	1.5	1.0	5.959
1982–88	12.146	3.9	6.3	6.1	5.4	6.0	5.8	5.1	16.456
1989–95	19.668[a]	15.794[a]	11.197	6.239	−2.759	16.398	11.440	2.442	4.201
1973–95	23.497	13.271	8.602	7.781	4.910	8.198	7.377	4.506	8.619

[a] 1989–92 only.

represent a smoothing of the discrete changes that took place within each period. Note that the optimal exchange rate depreciation depends crucially on the optimal steady-state interest rate, which is little more than a guess, taken in conjunction with (15′). Hence, the *level* of the results for the optimal exchange rate depreciation should be regarded with caution. This is particularly so since it reflects long-run steady-state behavior, and Mexico, in particular, was surely a long way from its steady state during the 1980s.

The differences between the two countries could hardly be more dramatic. Mexico underwent two large devaluations of around 260 and 180 percent in 1982 and 1986, respectively. The actual rate of exchange depreciation averaged out to over 27 percent at annual rates over the twenty-three-year period, though there were large variations over the various subperiods. The rate of depreciation implied by the model suggests an annual average depreciation rate of around 36 percent during the period. Of this, about 9 percentage points are due to the variance in the monetary growth rate over the period. Interestingly enough, it appears that the actual depreciation rate over the entire period closely matched the interest parity relationship, $e = i - i*$, with the Mexican authorities neglecting the role of risk. Indeed, the role of risk is particularly important during the more recent period of the 1990s when the variance of the monetary growth rate accounts for around 19 percentage points of the implied depreciation rate. Over that period as well they appear to be operating under a simple interest parity relationship.

Thus the comparison of the implied depreciation rate with the actual depreciation suggests that Mexico did not devalue sufficiently during the 1980s and early 1990s. Indeed, the view that the Mexican peso was grossly overvalued during that period has been expressed by Dornbusch and Werner (1994) and our analysis suggests that the neglect of risk may be an important factor. If this is ignored, a comparison of $\hat{i}$ with $i*$ suggests that the peso was approximately in equilibrium during that period, which is clearly (and in retrospect) counterfactual. The interesting thing about comparing the pattern describing the optimal depreciation rates with the actual is that it suggests that Mexico should have depreciated at a generally increasing rate during the 1980s and early 1990s. But this should be viewed with some caution, given that the optimal nominal interest rate has been assumed to be 14 percent throughout.

The second panel in Table 5.5 presents the optimal, implied, and actual rates of exchange depreciation for the case of Indonesia. The striking feature of these results is how remarkably close both the optimal and implied rates of exchange depreciation are to the actual rate of exchange depreciation over the full period, suggesting that from a long-run standpoint Indonesia was following close to an optimal monetary policy. With a more stable monetary policy, the variance of the monetary growth rate contributes more modestly to the implied and optimal rates of depreciation (around 1.75 percentage points over the entire horizon). While the model performs quite well in the 1970s it seriously underpredicts the rates of depreciation of the 1982–88 period. Closer examination of the data and circumstances indicates, however, that the model is sensitive enough to pick up the extreme degree of financial repression during that period, due to a nationalized banking system, restricted capital flows, and a government-imposed interest rate of 6 percent. The implied and optimal rates of depreciation are severely affected by the Indonesian interest rate, which was clearly divorced from economic fundamentals. This distortion is picked up by the model to generate the implausibly low depreciation during this period.

However, the pattern of implied and predicted depreciation improves relative to the historical experience as financial liberalization is implemented. After financial liberalization, the implied rate of depreciation reflects Indonesia's relatively stable monetary growth rate over the 1980s, and suggests that its monetary and exchange rate policy was not far from the implied depreciation rate. Again the optimal rate reflects the pattern of the implied rate, but the level is too low.

By the early 1990s we find the same pattern in Indonesia as in Mexico. Massive deregulation and the ensuing investment boom introduced financial instability that led to increased risk and money growth. As in the case of Mexico, Indonesia did not devalue the rupiah to the extent that the implied risk-adjusted interest rate suggests. Compared with that of Mexico, Indonesia's relatively more stable macroeconomic environment generated an annual implied rate of depreciation (10.6 percent) that is close to the actual (9 percent).[7] As in the Mexican case, the model predicts that this depreciation should have been managed in a much more gradual manner than the Indonesian authorities instituted.

5.5   Conclusion

This chapter employs a stochastic general equilibrium growth model to see what insights it offers into the effect of uncertainty on the real, risk-adjusted return to capital, capital flows, exchange rate policy, and

---

[7] Here we compare annual rates of depreciation between 1984–91, because of the severe degree of financial repression in the early 1980s. If we compare 1980–91, the implied and actual rates are 5.2% and 10.1%, respectively.

economic growth in two LDCs, Mexico and Indonesia. Both countries in particular, and LDCs in general, are vulnerable to exogenous world price shocks, such as oil shocks, and are subject to relatively greater domestic instability of both an economic and political nature. Thus one might reasonably expect that stochastic general equilibrium models may be highly relevant to the analysis of macroeconomic policy in LDCs.

Our results suggest that the stochastic monetary growth model does offer useful insights into the experiences of Mexico and Indonesia since the early 1970s. For example, we find that once real interest rates are amended to incorporate price shocks explicitly, the additional variance component becomes a crucial component of the rate of return during periods of high and variable prices. Although this is not significant for the United States, with its relatively stable prices, it is generally important for Mexico as well as for Indonesia during the 1970s. After accounting for the variance of inflation, our analysis suggests that the average real rate of return on bonds in Mexico since 1973 was around +7.5 percent rather than −5.4 percent, when this element is ignored. In addition, the Mexican inflation variance shows a clear pattern that reflects the tremendous variation in the degree of risk in the economy, and picks up nicely both the hyperinflation and the debt crisis (1982–90). Although the variance of inflation is smaller in Indonesia than in Mexico, it is larger as a percentage of the mean in Indonesia than in Mexico, and also larger in terms of absolute size in Indonesia than in the United States. Interestingly enough, the inclusion of risk allows us to highlight that not only inflationary but also *disinflationary* episodes can be characterized by high degrees of uncertainty.

With respect to portfolio shares, we find that the model is consistent with the changing composition of domestic and foreign assets held in Mexico. The implied variation in the portfolio shares over time clearly indicates (1) the positive effects of the Brady plan in terms of the return of private capital inflows, (2) the large volume of foreign borrowing by both the Mexican private and public sector, (3) the return of foreign financing, and (4) the deterioration of the current account. The Indonesian portfolio share instead reflects the country's easy and stable access to the world financial market. Throughout the sample period, Indonesia has a higher share of domestic capital in its portfolio than does Mexico. Again we find that the model captures the effects of financial and macroeconomic instability.

While our overall estimates of the growth rate are not particularly successful, it is not too bad over certain subperiods. However, it completely misses the 1982–88 contractionary period in Mexico. Our calibrations suggest that investors were not properly compensated for the added risk in Mexico over that period, since the high variance is also associated with high risk and in a free market this should cause domestic investors to reduce holdings of domestic capital in their portfolios. Alternatively, with restrictions on capital movements, investors are not free to adjust their portfolios in ways predicted by the theory, and consequently we get this overstatement of the growth rate. In comparing the implied growth rates for Mexico and Indonesia, we find evidence for Rodrik's (1996) assertion that the positive correlation between government size and openness is driven by the fact that larger governments can better insure and smooth external shocks.

Finally, we examined the implied and optimal rates of exchange rate depreciation within the stochastic model and find that the model does well explaining the pattern of both the Mexican and Indonesian exchange rate fluctuations. Our calibrations show that the level of the optimal depreciation is slightly below what one would expect, but that depends on the optimal or assumed stationary growth interest rate. Most importantly, both the implied and the optimal depreciations suggest that Mexico did not devalue sufficiently in the early 1990s. For Indonesia, with its relatively stable monetary growth rate over the 1980s we find that exchange rate policy was not far from the implied or optimal rate of depreciation. Nevertheless, the model again suggests that the rupiah was not sufficiently devalued during the time of macroeconomic instability in Indonesia.

Overall, we find that the model does quite well in helping us understand the nominal part of the system, such as inflation, rates of return, and exchange rate behavior. But it is less successful when it comes to explaining growth and the real part of the economy. There are two main reasons for this. First, the production side of the model is crude, being the simplest A-K technology. In developing countries factors such as infrastructure, technology, education, and human capital are critical determinants of growth performance, and, although risk may be an important part of the story, these other factors need to be taken into account if we are to have any hope of explaining growth performance. Second, both countries were subject to episodes during which real variables were set artificially by the government: financial repression in Indonesia, and the nationalization of the banks in Mexico. In such cases it is not necessarily the case that the model is off, but rather that it is incapable of accounting for such extreme policy interventions.

References

Adler, M., and B. Dumas (1983). "International Portfolio Choice and Corporation Finance: A Synthesis," *Journal of Finance* 38: 925–84.

Aspe, P. (1993). *Economic Transformation the Mexican Way*. Cambridge, Mass.: MIT Press.

Bhattacharya, A., and M. Pangestu (1992). "Indonesia: Development Transformation since 1965 and the Role of Public Policy." Paper presented at the World Bank East-West Center, Honolulu, Hawaii.

Brock, P. L. (1991). "Export Instability and the Economic Performance of Developing Countries," *Journal of Economic Dynamics and Control* 15: 129–47.

Buffie, E. F. (1990). "Economic Policy and Foreign Debt in Mexico." In J. Sachs, ed., *Developing Country Debt and Economic Performance*, vol. 2, pp. 393–551. Chicago: University of Chicago Press.

Cooley, T. F., ed. (1995). *Frontiers of Business Cycle Research*. Princeton N.J.: Princeton University Press.

Dornbusch, R., and A. Werner (1994). "Mexico: Stabilization, Reform, and No Growth," *Brookings Papers on Economic Activity*, no. 1: 253–91.

Engel, C. M., and A. P. Rodrigues (1993). "Tests of Mean-Variance Efficiency of International Equity Markets," *Oxford Economic Papers* 45: 400–19.

Foley, D. K., and M. Sidrauski (1971). *Monetary and Fiscal Policy in a Growing Economy*. New York: Macmillan.

Frankel, J. A. (1986). "The Implications of Mean–Variance Optimization of Four Questions in International Macroeconomics," *Journal of International Money and Finance* 5(March suppl.): 53–75.

(1988). "Recent Estimates of Time-Variation in the Conditional Variance and in the Exchange Rate Risk Premium," *Journal of International Money and Finance* 7: 115–25.

Gould, D. M. (1995). "Mexico's Crisis: Looking Back to Assess the Future," *Federal Reserve Bank of Dallas Economic Review*, no. 2: 2–12.

Grinols, E. L., and S. J. Turnovsky (1994). "Exchange Rate Determination and Asset Prices in a Stochastic Small Open Economy," *Journal of International Economics* 36: 75–98.

Kandel, S., and R. F. Stambaugh (1991). "Asset Returns and Intertemporal Preferences," *Journal of Monetary Economics* 27: 39–71.

Kenen, P. B., and C. S. Voidodas (1972). "Export Instability and Economic Growth," *Kyklos* 25: 791–804.

Lewis, K. K. (1988). "Inflation Risk and Asset Market Disturbances: The Mean–Variance Model Revisited," *Journal of International Money and Finance* 7: 273–88.

Obstfeld, M. (1994). "Risk-taking, Global Diversification, and Growth," *American Economic Review* 84: 1310–30.

Ozler, S., and J. Harrigan (1988). "Export Instability and Growth," Working Paper No. 486, University of California at Los Angeles, Department of Economics.

Rodrik, D. (1996). "Why Do More Open Economies Have Bigger Governments?" NBER Working Paper No. 5537, April. Cambridge, Mass.

Sidrauski, M. (1967). "Rational Choice and Patterns of Growth in a Monetary Economy," *American Economic Review* 57: 534–44.

Solnik, B. H. (1974). "An Equilibrium Model of the International Capital Market," *Journal of Economic Theory* 8: 500–24.

Stulz, R. (1981). "A Model of International Asset Pricing," *Journal of Financial Economics* 9: 383–406.

(1986). "The Demand for Foreign Bonds," *Journal of International Economics* 15: 235–58.

(1987). "An Equilibrium Model of Exchange Rate Determination and Asset Pricing with Nontraded Goods and Imperfect Information," *Journal of Political Economy* 95:1024–40.

Turnovsky, S. J. (1993). "Macroeconomic Policies, Growth, and Welfare in a Stochastic Economy," *International Economic Review* 35: 953–81.

(1995). *Methods of Macroeconomic Dynamics*. Cambridge, Mass.: MIT Press.

Turnovsky, S. J., and E. L. Grinols, (1996). "Optimal Government Finance Policy and Exchange Rate Management in a Stochastically Growing Economy," *Journal of International Money and Finance* 15: 687–716.

Voidodas, C. S. (1974). "The Effect of Foreign Exchange Instability on Growth," *Review of Economics and Statistics* 56: 410–12.

Yotopoulos, P. A., and J. B. Nugent (1976). *"Economics of Development: Empirical Investigations*. New York: Harper and Row.

PART II
EXCHANGE RATE CRISES AND CONTAGION

CHAPTER 6

Exchange rate instability: Determinants and predictability

Richard A. Meese and Andrew K. Rose

6.1   Introduction

Exchange rates have been unstable in the late 1990s. The tight and stable links between the members of the European Monetary System (EMS) that characterized the first few years of the decade were destroyed by a series of speculative attacks in the fall of 1992 and the summer of 1993. But exchange rate instability is not limited to the currencies of industrialized countries, as shown clearly by the attack on the Mexican peso of December 1994 and the "tequila hangover," which affected many developing countries afterward. In this chapter, we provide evidence on the determinants and predictability of such cases of exchange rate instability.

The chapter is divided into two parts. In the first, we use an annual panel of 105 developing countries over the time period 1971 through 1992 to search for a set of plausible stylized facts associated with currency *crashes* (which are close to, but not identical with currency *crises*). The methodology is nonstructural; currency crashes are linked to domestic and foreign macroeconomic variables using probit regressions. In section 6.2 we define currency crashes, explain the variables of interest, and present our data set, methodology, and results.

Missing observations and poor quality data preclude the analysis of structural models of currency crashes for the majority of developing countries, so in the second part of the chapter we focus attention on developed countries where macroeconomics fundamentals are available at a quarterly frequency. Also, given the geographic heterogeneity in the results of our exploratory data analysis of developing countries, we focus on particular country experiences with a quasi-fixed exchange rate

We thank Peter Garber and Reuven Glick for helpful comments on an earlier draft.

regime. In particular, we examine seven countries in the EMS over the period 1979 through 1992.

We employ a nontraditional approach to calibrate our exchange rate models for currencies in quasi-fixed exchange rate regimes. Over a decade of empirical research on models of exchange rate determination has taught us that it is difficult to forecast the future magnitude of major bilateral exchange rate changes, although fundamental information does help explain the direction of exchange rate change over longer predictive horizons.[1] In keeping with this research finding, we do not attempt to forecast the level of quasi-fixed exchange rates, but rather we use fundamental information to generate probability statements as to the likelihood of a speculative currency attack.

Both of the models we consider are calibrated by choosing parameter values to maximize the probability of correctly identifying currency crashes using EMS data. To avoid sample selection bias in assessing models of currency crises, we examine four possible outcomes: no change in the actual central parity in a given quarter versus a prediction of either a realignment or no realignment, and a change in a central parity versus a prediction of either a currency realignment or no realignment.

In section 6.3 we set forth our structural models of currency crises, explain the data, and report results for both in- and out-of-sample experiments. Section 6.4 concludes the chapter.

6.2   Currency crashes

6.2.1   *Definition*

In this part of the chapter, we analyze a number of different possible *determinants* of currency crashes, using a large panel of data. We begin by pooling our data (but investigate the homogeneity assumption directly).

We begin by defining a *currency crash* as a nominal depreciation of the currency of at least 25 percent that is also at least a 10 percent increase in the rate of depreciation. We use the change in the natural logarithm of the nominal bilateral dollar exchange rate (multiplied by 100). So as to preclude using the same economic observation twice, we exclude currency crashes that are close together, with a two-year "exclusion window" around crashes. Thus, independent crashes have to be

---

[1] See Taylor (1995) for a survey, and Mark (1995) and Chinn and Meese (1995) for evidence on longer-run predictability of currency movements.

separated by at least two years of data. This procedure also allows us to handle high-inflation countries. In doing so, we follow Frankel and Rose (1996) quite closely; they provide further discussion of the concept.

Eichengreen, Rose, and Wyplosz (1994) define a currency *crisis* as an attack on a currency. Crises are measured by unusual swings in reserves, interest rates, or exchange rates (or combinations thereof). Because the first two responses are defense mechanisms used by central banks to ward off speculative attacks, currency crises need not be successful attacks in the sense that the exchange rate need not change in the course of an attack (think of the unsuccessful attack on the French franc in September 1992). Unlike currency *crises*, currency *crashes* do not include unsuccessful speculative attacks. We concentrate on *crashes* rather than *crises* for a few reasons. Reserve data are notoriously imperfect even for industrialized countries; and many developing countries do not have market-determined interest rates (at least for long spans of time). In addition, defense mechanisms for developing countries are more difficult to quantify than for developed countries, because they include not only (sterilized and nonsterilized) monetary policy, but also actual and threatened capital controls. Further, international organizations, such as the International Monetary Fund and the World Bank, sometimes provide rescue packages in response to currency crashes. For all these reasons, we restrict our focus to identifiable large changes in exchange rates.

Our definition results in 135 identified currency crashes and 1,708 noncrash periods of tranquillity (i.e., periods not within two years of a crash), which we use as the control sample for probit analysis. The actual countries and years of crashes are tabulated in Appendix Table 6.A1.

6.2.2 *Variables of interest*

We are interested in a wide variety of candidate explanatory factors for currency crashes. These include: (1) a *foreign* variable, the external interest rate; (2) proxies for the *vulnerability* of the country to a crash, including measures of the size of the domestic bank sector and of international reserves; (3) the *level* and *composition* of external debt; (4) domestic *monetary and fiscal policy*; (5) international indicators of *competitiveness*, such as the real exchange rate and the current account; and (6) domestic *growth*.

The measure of the foreign interest rate we use is a weighted average of six northern short-term (money market) interest rates (those for the United States, Germany, Japan, France, the United Kingdom, and Switzerland, where the weights are proportional to the proportion of the country's external debt denominated in the relevant currency).

We use four proxies for the country's *external vulnerability*. Sachs, Tornell, and Velasco (1996) suggest that countries that have experienced rapidly growing ratios of bank loans to GNP are vulnerable to attack since regulators are likely to be overwhelmed by lending booms. Of course, high or growing ratios of bank loans could also represent a windfall of promising investment opportunities (triggered, e.g., by exogenous developments in the terms of trade), so there is no *empirical* presumption that an increase in bank loans need be associated with an *increase* in the probability of a crash. We explore their hypothesis by examining both the *level* and the *growth rate* of the ratio of banks' claims on the private sector to GNP (later we broaden this definition). Another measure of vulnerability, much focused on recently by Calvo and others, is the ratio of M2 to reserves, and we also use this variable. Finally, we include the ratio of reserves to imports, a variable that has been used as a measure of reserve adequacy informally since at least the debt crisis of the early 1980s.

We measure the *burden* of the external debt by including the ratio of the debt to GNP. But we also include seven ratios that characterize different aspects of the debt's *composition*. These include the parts held by commercial banks, the fraction that is concessional, the part that is variable rather than fixed rate, the fraction that is short-term, the ratio of foreign direct investment to debt, the fraction issued to the public sector, and the fraction held by multilateral institutions (such as the World Bank).

We include two broad measures of macroeconomic stabilization policy. *Fiscal* policy is measured by including the ratio of the government's budget surplus (+) or deficit (−) to GNP. Our proxy for *monetary* policy is the growth rate of domestic credit.

We include both the ratio of the current account to GNP and the real exchange rate as indicators of *external competitiveness*. The latter variable is simply the deviation from purchasing-power parity (PPP) vis-à-vis the United States (the foreign monetary "anchor"country of relevance for most developing countries during the sample), and calculate it as the country-specific average bilateral real exchange rate over the period in question.

Finally, we include the growth rate of real GNP.

6.2.3   *The data set and methodology*

The data set (which overlaps extensively with that used by Frankel and Rose, 1996) was mostly extracted from the 1994 World Bank's *World Data* CD-ROM. Exact definitions of the variables are tabulated in

Appendix Table 6.A2. It consists of annual observations from 1971 through 1992 for 105 countries.[2] The sample was selected, with respect to choice of both country and time, to maximize data availability. However, numerous observations are missing for individual variables. We have checked the data using both simple descriptive statistics and graphical techniques. We have also used exchange rates and interest rates from the IMF's *International Financial Statistics* CD-ROM.

We use a multivariate model where all the variables are employed simultaneously. Throughout, we pool all the available data across both countries and time periods, and estimate the unbalanced panel probit models using maximum likelihood. (An intercept is included in all regressions but is not recorded.) Since the estimated model is nonstructural, our interpretations are necessarily guarded and shed only indirect light on causality.

Because probit coefficients are not easily interpretable, we report the effects of one-unit changes in regressors on the probability of crash (expressed in percentage points), evaluated at the mean of the data. We also tabulate the associated z-statistics, which test the null hypothesis of no effect. Diagnostic statistics follow at the bottom of the table, including joint hypothesis tests for the significance of all slope effects, and the significance of a variety of other hypotheses. The latter tests are chi-squared Wald tests, with degrees of freedom indicated in parentheses.

6.2.4   Results

Table 6.1 contains our most important results; we begin our analysis there.

As expected, increases in northern interest rates are associated with

---

[2] The countries include Algeria, Argentina, Bangladesh, Barbados, Belize, Benin, Bhutan, Bolivia, Botswana, Brazil, Burkina Faso, Burundi, Cameroon, Cape Verde, Central African Republic, Chad, Chile, China, Colombia, Comoros, Congo, Costa Rica, Cote d'Ivoire, Djibouti, Dominican Republic, Ecuador, Arab Republic of Egypt, El Salvador, Equatorial Guinea, Ethiopia, Fiji, Gabon, Gambia, Ghana, Grenada, Guatemala, Guinea, Guinea-Bissau, Guyana, Haiti, Honduras, Hungary, India, Indonesia, Islamic Republic of Iran, Jamaica, Jordan, Kenya, Republic of Korea, Lao People's Democratic Republic, Lebanon, Lesotho, Liberia, Madagascar, Malawi, Malaysia, Maldives, Mali, Malta, Mauritania, Mauritius, Mexico, Morocco, Myanmar, Nepal, Nicaragua, Niger, Nigeria, Oman, Pakistan, Panama, Papua New Guinea, Paraguay, Peru, Philippines, Portugal, Romania, Rwanda, St. Vincent and the Grenadines, Sao Tome and Principe, Senegal, Seychelles, Sierra Leone, Solomon Islands, Somalia, Sri Lanka, Sudan, Swaziland, Syrian Arab Republic, Tanzania, Thailand, Togo, Trinidad and Tobago, Tunisia, Turkey, Uganda, Uruguay, Vanuatu, Venezuela, Western Samoa, Republic of Yemen, Federal Republic of Yugoslavia, Zaire, Zambia, and Zimbabwe.

Table 6.1. *Benchmark probit estimates*

	$\delta F(x/\delta x)$	$\|z\|$
Foreign interest rate	**1.1**	**4.2**
Bank claims/GNP	**−25.**	**3.9**
Change in BC/GNP	−24.	1.2
M2/reserves	.02	1.0
Reserves/imports	−.00	1.4
Debt/GNP	**.05**	**2.5**
Commercial bank/debt	.03	.2
Concessional/debt	−.09	1.5
Variable rate/debt	.10	.7
Short term/debt	.12	1.0
FDI/debt	**−.33**	**2.7**
Public sector/debt	**.21**	**2.4**
Multilateral/debt	−.02	.2
Government budget/GNP	**.31**	**2.3**
Domestic credit growth	**.11**	**3.9**
Current account/GNP	.08	.8
Overvaluation	.03	1.1
GNP growth rate	**−.35**	**2.9**
Sample Size	825	
Pseudo-R2	.23	
H_0: All slopes = 0; $\chi^2(18)$	**121**	
H_0: Vulnerability = 0; $\chi^2(4)$	**25**	
H_0: Characteristics = 0; $\chi^2(7)$	**24**	
H_0: Macro policy = 0; $\chi^2(2)$	**18**	
H_0: External = 0; $\chi^2(2)$	2	

Notes: Probit slope derivatives multiplied by 100, to convert into percentages. Absolute values of z-statistics tabulated for hypothesis of no effect. Model estimated with a constant, by maximum likelihood. Figures in boldface are significant at the 5% level.

currency crises by an amount that is both economically and statistically significant. A one point increase in the foreign interest rate is associated with a 1 percentage point increase in the probability of a crash.

The four measures of external vulnerability fare less well. Both the level and the growth rate of bank claims (BC) to GNP are *negatively* associated with the probability of a crash, though only the first effect is significant at conventional levels of statistical confidence. This may be a result of the much broader sample coverage (in terms of both countries and time) of this chapter compared with the work of Sachs, Tornell, and Velasco. But the negative correlations are also sensible, if one interprets them as representing the effects of an increased supply of investment projects (resulting from, e.g., exogenous changes in the terms of trade) rather than from a burst in unregulated lending. Neither of the reserve adequacy measures is statistically or economically significant. However, a joint test of all four slopes labeled "vulnerability" is quite statistically significant.

The burden of the external debt enters sensibly and significantly, an increase in the debt–GNP ratio raising the probability of a crash. However, only a few of the characteristics of the debt are individually significantly associated with crashes (though both a decrease in the fraction of foreign direct investment (FDI) and an increase in the share of public sector debt are sensibly associated with an increase in crash likelihood). This probably reflects the collinear nature of the composition variables; the seven variables are highly significant in a joint test of the significance of the slopes (labeled "characteristics").

Looser monetary policy (as proxied by faster credit growth) is associated with an increase in the probability of a crash, as seems sensible. However, tighter fiscal policy is also linked to an increase in crash probability (possibly because of the short-run recessionary effects engendered, or because crashes trigger austerity measures). Hence, it is unsurprising that the two effects are jointly significant (the test is labeled "macro policy").

Neither the degree of overvaluation nor the size of the current account is associated strongly with a crash, either individually or jointly ("external"). The former result is almost surely the result of the crash (Frankel and Rose, 1996) because we are investigating crashes in the nominal exchange rate, which almost always coincide with crashes in the real exchange rate.[3] The second result is now considered standard. Finally, countries tend to be in recessions around the time of currency crashes, though the interpretation of this result is unclear (since crashes may be either the result of a recession, or the cause of a downturn, or both).

To sum up, we find many reasonable results in our benchmark regressions. High northern interest rates, a high external debt load, a *decrease*

---

[3] Indeed, our model can be viewed as an attempt to explain nominal overvaluation using a wide-ranging set of fundamentals. These fundamentals are almost as likely to explain real overvaluation.

in bank claims, loose monetary policy, tight fiscal policy, and recessions are all associated with currency crashes. The negative results are also interesting. We find no evidence that low levels of reserves or high ratios of broad money to reserves are consistently associated with crashes. We also find little evidence that current account deficits are strongly linked to currency crashes.

Table 6.2 provides three different sensitivity analyses. The first substitutes a broader measure of banking claims for the more narrow measure. We include the claims of the banking sector on both state and local governments and nonfinancial public enterprises to claims on the private sector of the economy. However, the results are not significantly affected; the negative and significant effect of the *level* of bank claims to GNP remains. Next, we trim outliers of the M2–reserve ratio, setting values of this ratio that are more than 2.5 standard deviations from the mean to missing values. We do this because a run on reserves can lower the denominator of this ratio close to zero (or negative!), potentially distorting the scale of the variable. However, this perturbation appears to have essentially no effect on the results. Finally, we eliminate the majority of the external debt characteristics; again, the results are not substantially altered.

Table 6.3 contains two more substantive perturbations. First, we use an alternative definition of the regressand. Instead of defining crashes using a 25 percent depreciation threshold, which is also a 10 percent increase in the rate of depreciation within a two-year window, we use a 20 percent threshold which is also a 5 percent increase in the rate of depreciation without any window. Second, we substitute moving averages of the contemporaneous and two lagged values of the regressors (divided by three) in place of the contemporaneous regressor values. However, the results appear to be quite robust to both perturbations.[4]

Finally, Table 6.4 estimates our default specification (of Table 6.1) for Asian, Latin American, and African countries. Here, we do find much more dramatic differences. First, Asian countries, unlike Latin and African countries, appear to be unaffected by world interest rates. Indeed, there are essentially no significant individual (or joint) effects of *any* of the determinants on the probability of Asian crashes (even though 5 percent of the sample observations were crashes). Next, much of the significant effects of both the bank–GNP ratio and of the debt burden

---

[4] We have also investigated a number of sensitivity analyses which are not tabulated. For instance, exclusion of the many participants in the African Financial Cooperation (CFA) franc zone does not alter our results substantively. We have also searched for nonlinear effects and interactions between slopes and regional dummies without finding economically substantive differences.

Table 6.2. *Sensitivity analysis*

	Broad banking $\delta F(x/\delta x)$	$|z|$	Trimmed M2/reserves $\delta F(x/\delta x)$	$|z|$	Excluded debt $\delta F(x/\delta x)$	$|z|$
Foreign interest rate	**1.1**	**4.2**	**1.0**	**4.2**	**1.1**	**4.3**
Bank claims/GNP	**−23.**	**3.8**	**−22.**	**3.6**	**−.17**	**2.7**
Change in BC/GNP	−27.	1.4	−24.	−1.2	−.39	1.8
M2/reserves	.02	1.4	.02	.5	.01	.8
Reserves/imports	−.00	1.2	−.00	1.4	−.00	1.2
Debt/GNP	**.06**	**2.7**	**.06**	**2.7**	**.08**	**4.0**
Commercial bank/debt	.04	.3	.00	.0		
Concessional/debt	−.09	1.6	−.08	1.5		
Variable rate/debt	.08	.6	.13	1.0		
Short term/debt	.14	1.1	.09	.7		
FDI/debt	**.33**	**2.7**	**−.31**	**2.7**	**−.32**	**2.6**
Public sector/debt	**.22**	**2.5**	**.17**	**2.1**		
Multilateral/debt	−.02	.2	−.01	.2		
Government budget/GNP	.25	1.8	**.34**	**2.5**	**.35**	**2.4**
Domestic credit growth	**.11**	**4.0**	**.10**	**3.8**	**.14**	**5.1**
Current account/GNP	.08	.8	.09	.9	**.23**	**2.3**
Overvaluation	.04	1.3	.03	.8	.02	.5
GNP growth rate	**−.36**	**2.9**	**−.36**	**3.0**	**−.42**	**3.2**
Sample size	825		811		825	
Pseudo-R2	.24		.24		.20	
H_0: Slopes = 0; $\chi^2(18)$	**122**		**119**		**103**	
H_0: Vulnerability = 0; $\chi^2(4)$	**25**		**21**		**18**	
H_0: Characteristics = 0; $\chi^2(7)$	**23**		**22**			
H_0: Macro policy = 0; $\chi^2(2)$	**18**		**18**		**29**	
H_0: External = 0; $\chi^2(2)$	2		1		5	

Notes: Probit slope derivatives multiplied by 100, to convert into percentages. Absolute values of z-statistics tabulated for hypothesis of no effect. Model estimated with a constant, by maximum likelihood. Figures in boldface are significant at 5% level.

evidently stem from African data. On the other hand, much of the FDI, domestic credit, and output effects seem to stem from Latin America. Thus, we find significant heterogeneity in the sample when one looks across country groupings (although Frankel and Rose found little when splitting the sample over *time*).

Table 6.3. *Further sensitivity analysis*

	Alternate crash definition		Moving average regressors	
	$\delta F(x/\delta x)$	$|z|$	$\delta F(x/\delta x)$	$|z|$
Foreign interest rate	**.95**	**3.1**	**1.21**	**3.7**
Bank claims/GNP	**−21.**	**3.0**	**−24.**	**3.8**
Change in BC/GNP	−29.	1.3	−34.	1.0
M2/reserves	.00	.2	.04	1.8
Reserves/imports	−.00	.7	**−.01**	**2.5**
Debt/GNP	**.08**	**3.9**	−.05	1.7
Commercial bank/debt	.13	.9	.11	.7
Concessional/debt	**−.15**	**2.2**	−.07	1.1
Variable rate/debt	−.05	.3	.12	.8
Short term/debt	.13	1.0	**.33**	**2.5**
FDI/debt	**−.48**	**3.0**	**−.90**	**3.4**
Public sector/debt	.19	1.9	**.33**	**3.6**
Multilateral/debt	.14	1.8	−.09	1.3
Government budget/GNP	**.38**	**2.5**	.33	1.9
Domestic credit growth	**.14**	**4.9**	**.07**	**2.3**
Current account/GNP	.08	.7	−.11	.9
Overvaluation	**.08**	**2.0**	.04	1.0
GNP growth rate	**−.68**	**4.8**	**−.48**	**2.4**
Sample size	1,101		646	
Pseudo-R2	.19		.27	
H_0: Slopes = 0; $\chi^2(18)$	**153**		**117**	
H_0: Vulnerability = 0; $\chi^2(4)$	**15**		**31**	
H_0: Characteristics = 0; $\chi^2(7)$	**20**		**40**	
H_0: Macro policy = 0; $\chi^2(2)$	**26**		8	
H_0: External = 0; $\chi^2(2)$	5		2	

Notes: Probit slope derivatives multiplied by 100, to convert into percentages. Absolute values of z-statistics tabulated for hypothesis of no effect. Model estimated with a constant, by maximum likelihood. Figures in boldface are significant at 5% level.

6.3   Can the probability of a currency crash be predicted?

The results of the previous section suggest that models of currency crashes ought to focus on a particular geographic area. In addition, the methodology of section 6.2 examined currency movements over a one-

Table 6.4. *Regional estimates*

	Asia		Latin America		Africa	
	$\delta F(x/\delta x)$	$|z|$	$\delta F(x/\delta x)$	$|z|$	$\delta F(x/\delta x)$	$|z|$
Foreign interest rate	−.28	.9	**1.2**	**2.1**	**1.6**	**5.6**
Bank claims/GNP	−14.	1.7	−7.4	.7	**−38.**	**4.2**
Change in BC/GNP	−30.	1.2	17.7	.6	−6.5	.2
M2/reserves	−.02	.2	.28	1.7	.01	.7
Reserves/imports	−.01	1.1	.00	.7	−.01	1.0
Debt/GNP	−.04	.8	.02	.4	**.04**	**2.0**
Commercial bank/debt	−.09	.6	.21	1.1	−.28	1.6
Concessional/debt	−.06	1.1	−.14	.7	−.09	1.3
Variable rate/debt	.11	.7	.10	.5	.22	1.3
Short term/debt	.17	1.4	−.42	1.7	.17	1.2
FDI/debt	−.10	.7	**−.87**	**2.1**	**−.27**	**2.4**
Public sector/debt	.10	1.0	**.36**	**2.4**	.07	.7
Multilateral/debt	−.07	.9	−.02	.1	.02	.3
Government budget/GNP	−.12	.6	.68	1.9	.15	1.0
Domestic credit growth	−.00	.1	**.13**	**3.0**	.04	1.3
Current account/GNP	−.02	.1	.33	1.0	.01	.2
Overvaluation	.03	1.0	−.04	.4	.01	.3
GNP growth rate	−.15	1.1	**−.89**	**3.2**	−.13	1.1
Sample size	222		217		355	
Pseudo-R2	.28		.42		.33	
H_0: Slopes = 0; $\chi^2(18)$	23		**76**		771	
H_0: Vulnerability = 0; $\chi^2(4)$	6		4		**22**	
H_0: Characteristics = 0; $\chi^2(7)$	6		**18**		12	
H_0: Macro policy = 0; $\chi^2(2)$	0		**11**		2	
H_0: External = 0; $\chi^2(2)$	1		1		0	

Notes: Probit slope derivatives multiplied by 100, to convert into percentages. Absolute values of z-statistics tabulated for hypothesis of no effect. Model estimated with a constant, by maximum likelihood. Figures in boldface are significant at 5% level.

year window. Our finding that macroeconomic fundamentals help explain currency crash episodes over a one-year interval is of limited use to policy makers who need to respond more quickly to potential crises. Thus in this section we concentrate on a single geographic area (Europe), use higher frequency data (quarterly), and examine the predictability of currency crash probabilities using macroeconomic fundamentals that were available to policy makers one quarter before the currency crash occurred.

We concentrate on the predictability of crash probabilities, and not on the predictability of currency movements themselves for two reasons. First, current generation exchange rate models have had only limited success explaining currency movements at horizons inside of one year, and, second, few researchers have attempted to use macroeconomic fundamentals to explain the conditional probability of an exchange rate crash. A notable exception is the recent work by Bekaert and Gray (1996), who formulate a model of exchange rate behavior in a target zone, and estimate the model using weekly data for the franc–deutschemark rate in the European Monetary System. Here we consider a larger set of EMS currencies, a broader set of macroeconomic fundamentals, and a much different approach to the selection of model parameters.

"First-generation" speculative attack models pioneered by Krugman (1979) and Flood and Garber (1984a) suggest that deteriorating fundamentals are associated with currency crises. In contrast, "second-generation" models of speculative attack (such as those of Flood and Garber, 1984b, and Obstfeld, 1986, 1994, 1996) admit the possibility that currency pegs may be attacked even though macroeconomic fundamentals are sound enough for the peg to have survived in the absence of a speculative run, because speculators believe that the authorities would change policy in the event of a successful attack. Technically, the two models are observationally equivalent. In a world with uncertain fundamentals, it is not possible to uniquely identify the self-fulfilling element in a currency crisis. More importantly, an attack triggered by a fully expected change in fundamentals would appear to the econometrician to be a self-fulfilling attack (since no actual change in fundamentals need appear *before* the attack). On the other hand, the changes in actual macroeconomic fundamentals that one would expect if second-generation models explained the data well do not actually seem to coincide very closely with attacks. Differences between these episodes provide another rationale for examining countries individually, when trying to assess currency attack probabilities.

6.3.1   *Two models of currency crises*

Our first model relies on the following definition of the equilibrium or fundamental value of the exchange rate. The fundamental exchange rate

s_t^f is derivative to a Girton and Roper (1977) model of exchange market pressure and deviations from PPP:

$$s_t^f = a_1\left(r_t - r_t^*\right) + a_2\left(d_t - d_t^*\right) + a_3\left(y_t - y_t^*\right) - a_4\left(i_t - i_t^*\right) - a_5 u_t \quad (1)$$

where r_t is the ratio of reserves to the monetary base; d_t is the ratio of domestic credit to the monetary base; y_t is real GDP; i_t is the short-term interest rate; and u_t is the deviation of the exchange rate from its PPP level. An asterisk denotes a foreign variable; all variables except interest rates are in logs; all model parameters are expected to be positive; and a_3 and a_4 can be interpreted as the income elasticity and interest rate semielasticity of money demand.[5]

While the exploratory data analysis of section 6.2 considered additional explanatory variables as indicators of currency crash episodes, in this section we consider only those variables consistent with the traditional monetary approach to exchange rate determination. A decade of empirical research on monetary models, however, has highlighted the difficulty in using this set of fundamentals to predict currency movements short term. Thus we use the fundamental exchange rate in an error correction term so that our structural model only imposes constraints on the long-run comovements of the exchange rate and monetary fundamentals. In addition, our goal is to predict currency crash probabilities, not the actual level of the exchange rate.

Toward this end we define the predicted value of the currency in quarter t, using information from quarter $t - 1$ as:

$$s_{t|t-1} = s_{t-1} + a_6 B_{t-1} - a_7\left(s_{t-1} - s_{t-1}^f\right). \quad (2)$$

In equation (2) B_t is a variable measuring the spot rate position in the parity band, and a_7 is the error correction parameter. Variables like B_t are common in the empirical target zone literature; see, for example, Bekaert and Gray (1996) or Engel and Hakkio (1996). We define B_t as:

$$B_t = \frac{s_t - s_t^L}{s_t^U - s_t^L} - .5 \quad (3)$$

where the L and U superscripts on s_t stand for the lower and upper bounds of the target zone, respectively. The band variable B_t lies in the closed interval $[-.5, .5]$, and is equal to zero when s_t is equal to the midpoint of the band.

Now let σ_t denote the conditional variance of the quarterly, logarith-

[5] In equation (1) we attempt to mitigate measurement problems in reserves by employing a backward looking four-quarter moving average of this variable.

mic exchange return.[6] The exchange rate is converted to a probability statement p_t about the regime by using the logistic transformation of the standardized expected change in the exchange rate:

$$x_t = \frac{s_{t|t-1} - s_{t-1}}{\sigma_{t-1}}; \quad p_t = \frac{e^{x_t}}{1 + e^{x_t}}. \tag{4}$$

No currency regime change is forecast whenever $a_8 < p_t < a_9$, where the lower and upper bounds are additional parameters to be estimated.

All parameters are chosen by restricted grid search to maximize the probability of correctly predicting the currency regime next quarter, as explained later. However, changes in central parity occur infrequently in our data set, and since policy makers assign more implicit weight to these events, we equally weight the probability of correctly predicting no change in regime and the probability of correctly predicting a currency realignment.

In order to understand our criterion function, define the dummy variable $d(1, t) = 1$ if no realignment occurred and none was predicted, and zero otherwise; $d(2, t) = 1$ if no realignment occurred and one was predicted, and zero otherwise; $d(3, t) = 1$ if a realignment occurred and none was predicted, and zero otherwise; and $d(4, t) = 1$ if a realignment occurred and one was predicted, and zero otherwise. Let N denote the total number of quarterly observations for any particular country, and let the sum over the N observations for each $d(i, t)$ equal N_1, N_2, N_3, and $(N - N_1 - N_2 - N_3)$, respectively. We choose parameter estimates to maximize the criterion function:

$$d = \sum_{t=1}^{N} \frac{\left(N - N_1 - N_2\right)d\left(1,t\right) + \left(N_1 + N_2\right)d\left(4,t\right)}{2\left(N - N_1 - N_2\right)\left(N_1 + N_2\right)}. \tag{5}$$

The function lies in the interval [0, 1], and has a value of .5 for the naive prediction that there will never be any currency realignment. Note also, that realignment and no-realignment episodes are equally weighted regardless of their frequency in the sample.

When maximizing expression (5), we restrict the parameter search so that only economically meaningful parameter values are considered for a_1 through a_7. The range of values considered for the two money demand parameters, a_1 and a_2; the income elasticity, a_3; and the coefficient on PPP deviations, a_5, is [0.0, 1.0]. The interest rate semielasticity a_4 range is [0.0, 10.0]; the error correction parameter a_7 range is [0.0, 0.4]; and the band-

---

[6] We do not jointly estimate the conditional variance of the exchange return but, instead, use a moving average of squared exchange rate changes up to period t-1.

width parameter a_6 range is $[-1.0, 1.0]$. The lower and upper bounds on the logistic probability limits, a_8 and a_9, range from $[.005, .5]$ and $[.5, .995]$, respectively.

The money demand parameters are consistent with both theoretical priors, and with long-run elasticities estimated by Stock and Watson (1993) using U.S. data, and by Boughton (1991) using a subset of OECD countries. Estimated adjustment speeds to PPP and error correction parameters in exchange rate models invariably indicate slow responses of actual to fundamental values. Thus the majority of grid values we consider for a_5 and a_7 are consistent with slow adjustment speeds. We do however, consider the two extremes of no adjustment and instantaneous adjustment as possible outcomes of the search. We arbitrarily truncate the lower and upper probabilities, a_8 and a_9, at levels consistent with a five standard deviation event.

All parameters in the exchange rate equations (1) and (2) are allowed to attain a zero value. Hence we allow the data to tell us the fundamental variables are irrelevant for the analysis, just like a conventional estimation setting when t-ratios are low. Also, since d is an average, we can generate an estimate of its variance, $S(d)^2$, using conventional methods.[7] The test statistic for testing the null hypothesis of no predictive ability for currency regimes is thus:

$$z = \frac{d - 1/2}{\sqrt{S(d)^2}}. \tag{6}$$

Under suitable regularity conditions, the z-statistic (6) is asymptotically distributed as a standard normal variate. However, in our case d is the maximal value achieved during a parameter grid search. To correct for the upward bias in the statistic, we provide simulated marginal significance values for d using pseudodata that are calibrated to mimic our experiments for EMS countries.[8]

In Table 6.5 we report the results of our analysis. The first five columns correspond to the country and values of $d(i, t)$, $i = 1, \ldots, 4$,

---

[7] To do this we sum the autocovariances of the elements inside the summation in expression (5), and weight them using a Fejer kernel – i.e., the weighting scheme proposed by Newey and West (1987).

[8] In particular, we use draws from a uniform random number generator to assign values to the dummy variables $d(i, 1)$, $i = 1, \ldots, 4$. The probabilities that the four dummy variables are equal to one are set equal to .4, .4, .1, and .1 respectively. Then the statistic d is calculated by taking the maximum over 100 trials, each with $N = 60$ observations. The process is then simulated 10,000 times to generate critical values. The median value of d for this simulation is .63.

Table 6.5. *In-sample predictive statistics and coefficient estimates for structural model: Equations (1) and (2)*

	Predictive statistics							Coefficient estimates								
Country	d(1, t)	d(2, t)	d(3, t)	d(4, t)	d	z	Simulated significance level	Range	r	d	y	i	B	ecm	Lower prob. bound	PPP
United Kingdom	5	2	0	1	.86	1.81	.01	4/90–3/92	1.0	0.0	1.0	0.0	0.5	.2	.01	.95
France	32	21	1	5	.72	4.65	.21	2/79–4/93	0.0	1.0	1.0	0.0	0.0	.4	.4	.8
Italy	41	3	6	4	.67	3.79	.33	2/79–3/92	0.0	1.0	0.5	5.0	0.0	.3	.3	1.0
Belgium	29	11	2	5	.72	3.84	.21	2/79–4/90	0.0	1.0	1.0	5.0	0.0	.3	.3	.8
Denmark	41	12	1	5	.80	5.57	.04	2/79–4/93	0.5	1.0	0.0	10.0	0.0	.2	.2	.8
Holland	54	3	1	1	.72	4.39	.21	2/79–4/93	0.5	0.0	0.0	0.0	0.0	.3	.3	.95
Ireland	42	6	2	5	.79	5.75	.05	2/79–4/92	1.0	0.5	1.0	10.0	0.0	.2	.025	.8

Notes: All money demand variables defined as differentials (i.e., domestic minus German). Exchange rates are expressed relative to the deutschemark. Since all currencies depreciated with respect to the deutschemark over the sample, only the lower probability bound on exchange rate changes is relevant. ecm denotes error correction term.

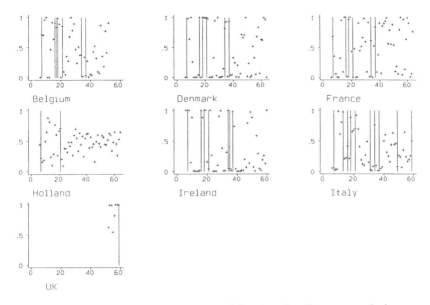

Figure 6.1. Regime collapse probabilities. Actual realignments marked.

respectively. The d-statistic (equation 5) is tabulated in column six; the z-statistic (equation 6) in column seven; and the simulated marginal significance level of d is reported in column eight. Column nine contains the sample range for each country. Simulated critical values indicate that the models have marginal in-sample predictive ability. The second panel of Table 6.5 contains the values of the parameters that maximize (5) for each of our seven EMS countries. There is considerable uniformity in the values of the parameters chosen by our grid search.

Next we consider the out-of-sample performance of the model. We do this by sequentially optimizing (5), and then forecasting the regime one quarter ahead. We implement this rolling optimization procedure using the last two-thirds of each data set. The results are dismal. In no case is the value of d greater than one half.

All the evaluation metrics presented thus far have a "knife edge" quality in that they do not account for model predictions of a currency crash that are near (but not exactly in) the quarter of the crises. To further assess the usefulness of the structural model given by equations (1) and (2), we plot seven crash probabilities in Figure 6.1 (one for each country), along with a spike for realignment dates. The graphical analysis suggests that the U.K., Dutch, and Irish models generated high probabilities of a crash in and around quarters when the attack actually succeeded, and generated much lower crash probabilities during nonrealignment periods. Unfortunately, many of the high-probability episodes (when no realignment occurred) do not necessarily line up with periods generally thought to be unsuccessful speculative attacks. Last, the probability model is much less useful for the other four countries.

Given the disappointing predictive results for our first monetary model, we try one more technique to forecast currency crises. Our second model has a simpler structure than the first, while retaining the feature that fundamental information enters only through the determination of currency regime probabilities. The model is an example of a Markov regime-switching model pioneered by Hamilton (1989). Recent extensions of the model by Filardo (1994) and Diebold, Lee, and Weinbach (1994) allow for time-varying regime probabilities as in equation (4). Here we assume the process for the spot rate s_t follows

$$s_t = \beta_{R(t)} + s_{t-1}^C + \gamma\left(s_{t-1} - s_{t-1}^C\right) + \varepsilon_t \tag{7}$$

where s_t^C is the central parity, and the $R(t)$ subscript on the intercept $\beta_{R(t)}$ denotes the regime or state in period t.

The model is motivated by the empirical exchange rate literature, which suggests that the quarterly spot rate is well approximated by a random walk (i.e., gamma near one). In this model, one can interpret the expected central parity in period t to be the sum of $\beta_{R(t)}$ and s_{t-1}^C. We also allow for heteroskedasticity in the disturbance term of (7), as both Bekaert and Gray (1996) and Engel and Hakkio (1996) report evidence of time-varying volatility in their empirical models of exchange rates within a target zone.

Equation (7) is driven by a Markov process with time-varying probabilities. Define $p(z_t)$ as the probability of no realignment (state 1) given that the previous quarter was also a regime of no realignment (state 1), and $q(z_t)$ as the probability of no realignment this period (state 1) given that one occurred last period (state 2). Each probability is calculated as a logistic function of a linear combination of fundamental variables z_t, as in the second part of equation (4). Variables included are differential (domestic minus German) interest rates, real incomes, money supplies, deviations from PPP, and a constant term. In order to conserve degrees of freedom we have combined reserves and domestic credit into a single money supply variable for this exercise.

We allow separate coefficients in the logistic functions for both probabilities p and q, so these equations have a total of ten parameters. Equation (7) has two constant terms, two disturbance variances, and a single parameter γ, so the model has a total of fifteen parameters. The short time series of EMS observations for the United Kingdom precludes estimation of our model for this country.

The country models are estimated by maximum likelihood (assuming normally distributed errors) subject to two conditions. First, we again consider only a grid search over economically meaningful parameter estimates (the same set of parameter values we used for the first structural model). Second, in order to economize on computer time, we maximize the "complete data" likelihood function, assuming the two states of the model are known. They correspond to the actual dates of currency realignments.[9]

We first test the null hypothesis that the transition probabilities are constant and independent of macroeconomic fundamentals, using a likelihood ratio test. We are unable to reject that null for any country, as marginal significance levels are never less than 25 percent. In addition to the formal statistical test, it is the case that unconstrained estimates of regime probabilities p and q show little variation over time. Point estimates of the parameters in the logistic functions for p and q are quite similar to those reported in Table 6.5 for our previous model.

Values of the five parameters in (7) do not vary much by country. In all cases the regime 1 constant term is near zero, while the regime 2 intercept is always negative. Again, we obtain this result because the sample contains only currency depreciations relative to the deutschemark. Disturbance variance estimates increase by a factor of two on average, for the regime of a currency realignment. Estimates of γ range from .5 to .75 across our six EMS countries. These values are smaller than we expected, given that quarterly exchange rate changes (for a single regime model) are well approximated by a random walk. For the model with fixed transitional probabilities, the estimated probabilities p and q correspond to their sample analogues, given our assumption of known regimes. The similarity of parameter estimates across EMS countries suggests that pooling the data might provide a more powerful test that fundamentals drive conditional regime probabilities. Note, however, that our results are consistent with Bekaert and Gray (1996) who also find that macroeconomic fundamentals do not explain realignment probabilities in their target zone model for the franc–deutschemark rate, or with Rose and Svensson (1993) who conclude that the September 1992 EMS crisis was a surprise to market participants.

---

[9] Clearly this is a weakness of the analysis, since a more general treatment of currency crashes would define regime 2 as any period of exchange rate pressure, not just one in which a change in central parity occurred. See Hsieh (1994) and Martinez Peria (1996) for more detailed studies on the use of regime-switching models using EMS data.

6.4   Conclusion

Both of our attempts to quantify the probability of a currency crash using quarterly macroeconomic fundamentals fail miserably. The standard set of macroeconomic variables is known to have little explanatory power for the level or change in bilateral exchange rates. The same can be said for models that use these fundamentals to quantify the probability of currency regimes. Our results are based on an analysis that explicitly chooses parameter estimates to maximize the predictability of currency realignments. We interpret the dismal results as evidence that first-generation currency crisis models are overly simplistic. Although our results do not necessarily validate new crisis models of currency attacks, they do suggest that political variables, expectations variables, or non-standard macroeconomic fundamentals are missing from the analysis.

Our nonstructural data analysis on annual data for developing countries yields more insights into the determinants of currency crashes. We find that high northern interest rates, a high external debt load, a decrease in bank claims, loose monetary policy, and domestic recessions are all associated with currency crashes. However, when the data are split into geographic regions (Africa, Asia, and Latin America), heterogeneity in the results makes it difficult to draw strong policy conclusions.

Appendix Table 6.A1. *Currency crashes*

Argentina 1981	Argentina 1984	Argentina 1987
Burundi 1984	Benin 1981	Burkina Faso 1981
Bangladesh 1975	Bolivia 1973	Bolivia 1982
Brazil 1979	Brazil 1983	Brazil 1987
Brazil 1992	Bhutan 1991	Botswana 1985
Central African Rep. 1981	Chile 1973	Chile 1982
Chile 1985	Cote d'Ivoire 1981	Cameroon 1981
Congo 1981	Comoros 1981	Costa Rica 1981
Costa Rica 1991	Dominican Republic 1985	Dominican Republic 1990
Algeria 1991	Ecuador 1983	Ecuador 1986
Egypt 1979	Egypt 1990	Ethiopia 1992
Gabon 1981	Ghana 1978	Ghana 1983
Guinea 1986	Gambia 1984	Guinea-Bissau 1984
Guinea-Bissau 1987	Guinea-Bissau 1991	Equatorial Guinea 1981
Guatemala 1986	Guatemala 1990	Guyana 1987
Guyana 1991	Honduras 1990	Indonesia 1979
Indonesia 1983	India 1991	Jamaica 1978
Jamaica 1984	Jamaica 1991	Jordan 1989
Laos 1976	Laos 1980	Laos 1985
Laos 1988	Lebanon 1984	Lebanon 1987

Appendix Table 6.A1. *(cont.)*

Lebanon 1990	Sri Lanka 1978	Lesotho 1984
Morocco 1981	Madagascar 1981	Madagascar 1987
Maldives 1975	Maldives 1987	Mexico 1977
Mexico 1982	Mexico 1986	Mali 1981
Myanmar 1975	Malawi 1992	Niger 1981
Nigeria 1986	Nigeria 1989	Nigeria 1992
Nicaragua 1979	Nicaragua 1985	Nicaragua 1988
Peru 1976	Peru 1981	Peru 1985
Peru 1988	Philippines 1983	Paraguay 1984
Paraguay 1987	Romania 1973	Romania 1990
Rwanda 1991	Sudan 1982	Sudan 1985
Sudan 1988	Sudan 1991	Senegal 1981
Sierra Leone 1983	Sierra Leone 1989	El Salvador 1986
El Salvador 1990	Somalia 1982	Somalia 1985
Somalia 1988	Sao Tome & Principe 1987	Sao Tome & Principe 1991
Swaziland 1984	Syrian Arab Republic 1988	Chad 1981
Togo 1981	Trinidad & Tobago 1986	Turkey 1978
Turkey 1984	Turkey 1988	Turkey 1991
Tanzania 1984	Tanzania 1992	Uganda 1981
Uganda 1984	Uruguay 1975	Uruguay 1983
Uruguay 1990	Venezuela 1984	Venezuela 1987
Vanuatu 1981	Zaire 1976	Zaire 1979
Zaire 1983	Zaire 1987	Zaire 1991
Zambia 1983	Zambia 1989	Zambia 1992
Zimbabwe 1983	Zimbabwe 1991	

Appendix Table 6.A2. *Variable definitions and World Data mnemonics*

Commercial bank debt	DT DOD DCBK CD
Concessional debt	DT DOD ALLC CD
Variable rate debt	DT DOD VTOT CD
Public sector debt	DT DOD PUBC CD
Total debt	DT DOD DECT CD
Short-term/total debt	DT DOD DSTC ZS
Multilateral/total debt	DT DOD MLAT ZS
Foreign direct investment	BN KLT DINV CD
Portfolio investment	BN KLT PORT CD
Debt/annual exports	DT DOD DECT BX
Debt/GNP	DT DOD DECT GN
Interest payments/GNP	DT INT DECT GN
Reserves/monthly imports	FI RES TOTL BM
Exchange rate	PA NUS ATLS
M1	FM LBL MONY CN

Appendix Table 6.A2. *(cont.)*

M2-M1 [quasi-money]	FM LBL QMNY CN WB
Private claims	FM AST PRVT CN
S&L government claims	FM AST LGOV CN
Nonfinancial public enterprise claims	FM AST PENT CN
International reserves	FI RES TOTL CD WB
Current account/GNP	BN CAB XOTR ZS
Government fiscal balance	GV BAL OVRL CN
Gross national product	NY GNP MKTP CN
Domestic credit	FM AST DOMS CN
GNP per capita	NY GNP MKTP KD 87
Net long-term capital flow	BN KLT XRSL CD
Net short-term capital flow	BN KST XRSL CD
Average interest rate	DT INR DPPG
Average private interest rate	DT INR PRVT
Lending rate	FR INR LEND
Debt denominated in dollars	DT COM USDL ZS
Debt denominated in deutschemarks	DT COM DMAK ZS
Debt denominated in yen	DT COM JYEN ZS
Debt denominated in French francs	DT COM FFRC ZS
Debt denominated in pound sterling	DT COM UKPS ZS
Debt denominated in Swiss francs	DT COM SWFR ZS

References

Bekaert, Geert, and Stephen F. Gray (1996). "Target Zones and Exchange Rates: An Empirical Investigation," NBER Working Paper No. 5445. Cambridge, Mass.

Boughton, James (1991). "Long Run Money Demand in Large Industrial Countries," *IMF Staff Papers* 38 (1): 1–32.

Chinn, Menzie, and Richard Meese (1995). "Banking on Currency Forecasts: How Predictable Is Change in Money?" *Journal of International Economics* 38: 161–78.

Diebold, Francis X., Jon-Haeng Lee, and Gretchen C. Weinbach (1994). "Regime Switching with Time-varying Transition Probabilities." In C. Hargreaves, ed., *Non-Stationary Time Series Analysis*, pp. 283–302. Oxford: Oxford University Press.

Eichengreen, Barry, Andrew K. Rose, and Charles Wyplosz, (1994). "Speculative Attacks on Pegged Exchange Rates: An Empirical Exploration with Special Reference to the European Monetary System," CEPR Discussion Paper No. 1960. Centre for Economic Policy Research, London.

Engel, Charles, and Craig S. Hakkio (1996). "The Distribution of Exchange Rates in the EMS," *International Journal of Finance and Economics* 1: 55–67.

Filardo, Andrew J. (1994). "Business Cycle Phases and Their Transitional Dynamics," *Journal of Business and Economic Statistics* 12: 299–308.

Flood, Robert, and Peter Garber (1984a). "Collapsing Exchange-Rate Regimes: Some Linear Examples," *Journal of International Economics* 17: 1–13.

(1984b). "Gold Monetization and Gold Discipline," *Journal of Political Economy* 92: 90–107.

Frankel, Jeffrey, and Andrew K. Rose (1996). "Currency Crashes in Emerging Markets: An Empirical Treatment," International Finance Discussion Paper No. 534. Washington, D.C.: Board of Governors of the Federal Reserve System.

Girton, Lance, and Don Roper (1977). "A Monetary Model of Exchange Market Pressure Applied to Post-war Canadian Experience," *American Economic Review* 67: 537–48.

Hamilton, James D. (1989). "A New Approach to the Economic Analysis of Nonstationary Time Series and the Business Cycle," *Econometrica* 57: 357–84.

Hsieh, Chan-Tai (1994). "Identifying Speculative Attacks in the European Monetary System." Unpublished manuscript, University of California at Berkeley.

Krugman, Paul (1979). "A Model of Balance-of-Payments Crises," *Journal of Money, Credit, and Banking* 11: 311–25.

(1996). "Are Currency Crises Self-Fulfilling?" *NBER Macroeconomics Annual*, pp. 345–78. Cambridge, Mass.

Mark, Nelson C. (1995). "Exchange Rates and Fundamentals: Evidence on Long-Horizon Predictability," *American Economic Review* 85: 201–18.

Martinez Peria, Maria S. (1996). "A Regime Switching Approach to the Study of Speculative Attacks and Devaluations: A Focus on the EMS Crisis." Unpublished manuscript, University of California at Berkeley.

Newey, Whitney N., and Kenneth D. West (1987). "A Simple, Positive Semi-definite, Heteroskedasticity and Autocorrelation Consistent Covariance Matrix," *Econometrica* 55: 703–8.

Obstfeld, Maurice (1986). "Rational and Self-Fulfilling Balance of Payments Crises," *American Economic Review* 76: 72–81.

(1994). "The Logic of Currency Crises," *Banque de France Cahiers Economiques et Monetaires* 43: 189–213.

(1996). "Discussion of 'Are Currency Crises Self-Fulfilling?'" *NBER Macroeconomics Annual*, pp. 393–403. Cambridge, Mass.

Rose, Andrew, and Lars E. O. Svensson (1993). "European Exchange Rate Credibility before the Fall," *European Economic Review* 38: 185–216.

Sachs, Jeffrey, Aaron Tornell, and Andrés Velasco (1996). "Financial Crises in Emerging Markets: The Lessons from 1995," NBER Working Paper No. 5576. Cambridge, Mass.

Stock, James, and Mark Watson (1993). "A Simple Estimator of Cointegrating Vectors in Higher Order Integrated Systems," *Econometrica* 61: 783–820.

Taylor, Mark P. (1995). "The Economics of Exchange Rates," *Journal of Economic Literature* 33: 13–47.

CHAPTER 7

Derivative products in exchange rate crises

Peter M. Garber and Subir Lall

7.1   Introduction

This chapter describes the role played by derivative products in the Mexican exchange rate crisis triggered by the devaluation of the Mexican peso in December 1994. In the speculative attacks on Mexico's exchange rate system, derivative products affected the dynamics of the exchange rate during the crisis and added to the turbulence in the exchange rate in the months after the peso's collapse. It is well known that speculators use forward and options contracts to short a currency prior to and during a speculative attack. Moreover, a wide array of other kinds of products, even those in which the ultimate speculator takes a long position in the currency, can play a major role in the dynamics of a currency crisis. This chapter, however, will concentrate on the role of derivatives that are not traditionally regarded as currency contracts in exchange crises.

The use of derivatives in the Mexican crisis provides a key example of the impact of these products on market behavior – there was large-scale use of offshore structured notes on peso products, tesobono and cetes swaps, and equity swaps prior to the crisis. The structured notes were used by onshore financial institutions to take highly leveraged positions in peso products and short dollar positions to take advantage of high peso interest rates. Similarly, the swaps allowed leveraged positions in securities financed by short dollar positions that permitted domestic institutions to circumvent regulations against holding securities on margin. Margin calls on these products on Mexican customers after the initial devaluation generated the final collapse of the peso and other asset values and exacerbated the turbulence in the exchange markets in January and February 1995, as Mexicans scrambled to get dollars to cover the margin calls. Indeed, efforts by Mexican banks to cover the short dollar positions implied by their derivative positions led to large-scale selling of the peso immediately prior to the December 1994 floating of the peso. Most of these products existed as means of avoiding Mexican onshore prudential and antispeculative regulations. Their offshore incarnations in such volumes came as a surprise to Mexican authorities and caused them to underestimate the short dollar position of the overall Mexican financial system.

Such products exist for financial systems in other emerging markets, particularly in Latin America and East Asia. The lesson for other emerging market countries is that a measured and controlled introduction of derivative products onshore is bound to be circumvented by offshore products, barring a stringent supervisory system (see Garber, 1996).

7.1.1   *Extent of the derivative markets*

The credit that fuels the onset of a balance-of-payments crisis may be derived from several sources. It may arise from the possession of assets in a weak currency country, which can be used to collateralize bank credit to gain funds for delivery in settlement of spot exchange transactions. Alternatively, holders of assets can attempt to sell them outright in secondary markets and sell the proceeds in spot exchange markets. In such cases, the dealers in the markets must have access to credit from the weak currency banking system. The banking system then assumes both a foreign exchange position that it must pass on to a central bank and a creditor position in the weak currency that it would like to balance. Ultimately, the credit for an attack on a weak currency must come from the attacked central bank itself, because it is the only player in a crisis willing to relieve the banks of these positions.[1]

The advent and growth of derivative products has not changed the basic connection between the availability of weak currency credit and the virulence of speculative attack. Derivatives are simply means of gaining credit – for both inflows and outflows – though perhaps more rapidly and in more diverse ways than were previously available. They also simultaneously provide means of leveraging an attack and funding pure speculators who overlay those who are trying to cover long asset positions.

The recent Bank for International Settlements (BIS) survey (1996) indicated that the notional value of over-the-counter (OTC) derivative products outstanding was $47 trillion in March 1995, and of this about 55

---

[1] For example, Mexico supplied credit for the attack on its reserves by sterilizing the effect of the reserve outflow on its monetary base. See Folkerts-Landau, Ito, et al. (1995).

percent comprised cross-border transactions.[2] Most of this amount consisted of simple interest rate products such as swaps, and most cross-border transactions occurred between industrial countries.[3] For other derivative products, there are, nevertheless, large notional values outstanding in absolute terms – equity-based products and structured notes and options, which may be quite complex – and these are also used to an ever expanding extent in key emerging-market countries.[4]

Specifically, of the $47.5 trillion in OTC notional values, 61 percent was in interest rate instruments, and 37 percent was in foreign exchange instruments, including outright forwards and swaps. Equity contracts amounted to 1.25 percent and commodity-related instruments were 0.75 percent of the overall notional value. Exchange-traded contracts outstanding, net of double counting, amounted to $8 trillion, almost all of which were interest rate contracts. Gross market values were $2.2 trillion of OTC contracts.

Of the interest rate products, 50 percent was cross-border, while 56 percent of foreign exchange products was cross-border.[5] For equity products, cross-border position data are not reported by the BIS. The market or replacement value of outstanding derivatives is about 4.6 percent of the notional value. For comparison, the total stock of international securities in OECD countries was $26.3 trillion, and international banking assets excluding securities holdings were $8.3 trillion in March 1995.[6]

---

[2] The global nature of the markets is underlined by the large amount of business contracts with counterparties located abroad. See BIS (1996), p. 24.

[3] Thus, the problem of inferring market risk from balance-of-payment data applies especially with regard to the positions of industrial countries. Academic investigations of the lack of cross-border portfolio diversification based on capital account data are fatally compromised by this gap in the data.

[4] In East Asian financial centers, of course, large scale OTC trading in East Asian currency derivatives occurs in baht, ringgit, and rupiah. Domestic banks are often the main offshore investors in these markets, taking positions against their local currencies to hedge their exposure. Popular products with Asian counterparts in the financial centers are warrants, structured notes with embedded equity, with Hong Kong or U.S. banks being the main dealers supplying local banks and corporations. The business is driven by regulations in other countries, such as Korea, Taiwan, and India. Koreans, for example, use synthetics to circumvent withholding taxes. Deals may be booked anywhere, such as in the Caymans or British Virgin Islands, so it is not easy to assess the risk exposures of intermediaries. Foreign firms are queried in the financial centers on their OTC activity only if it is regarded as imprudent rather than merely a means of circumventing regulations.

[5] See BIS (1996), p. 23, table D3.

[6] Notional amounts do not reflect payment obligations. They do reflect the price exposure in the underlying markets and they are useful for comparison with the underlying amounts outstanding. See BIS (1996), p. 24.

Derivatives have well-known benefits for banks and the financial system in that they provide ready means of redistributing various risks from those who may initially bear them to those who want to bear them. They separate credit from currency risk and allow a restructuring of maturity and interest rate risk inherent in various financial contracts. On the other hand, such contracts are relatively difficult for regulators and senior management of banks to understand. Banks have the ability to adjust rapidly their positions so that the extent of market risks in a given bank are not generally well known to regulators. This allows banks to make their positions and risk taking relatively opaque. In systems with well-functioning risk-management techniques and profitable, well-capitalized banks, such difficulties are not necessarily a problem because banks have an incentive to control their risks and position taking. In other systems, however, the risks that banks may take in the market may exacerbate losses to capital in potential devaluations and indeed may provide an additional reason for either speculators or hedgers to attack a currency because of the enhanced fiscal pressure that governments will experience in resolving troubled banks.

More importantly, however, derivatives in offshore markets exist as a major means of circumventing domestic regulation aimed either at enforcing prudential behavior on protected financial institutions or at reducing the magnitude of speculation. The extent of this circumvention is unknown to regulators, and the revelation of the size of the short position of the domestic financial system in foreign exchange at the time of an exchange crisis therefore arrives as an unpleasant surprise.

The chapter proceeds as follows. Section 7.2 briefly introduces a few concepts regarding the use of derivatives in currency and financial markets – namely, the use of currency-based forward and options markets in the midst of a speculative attack and the effects of dynamic hedging. Derivative markets tend to dry up completely or at least spreads widen dramatically in crises, and this illiquidity is reflected in high implicit volatilities in various contracts. We will describe the effect of the availability of derivative products on the dynamics of an exchange crisis – notably, the nature of the derivative products that are used to gain credit in an attack, the implications of various trading strategies on the evolution of an attack, and the effects that the strategies have on the ability to defend against an attack. Ultimately, all derivative products discussed are used to assume exchange rate positions, and a description of the main foreign exchange channels is a basis for understanding the whole spectrum of instruments.

In section 7.3, we will consider the uses of derivative products in the 1994–95 Mexican crisis. Mexico was not a country that permitted a widespread or rapid domestic evolution of derivative products, particularly in currency markets. The domestic ability to use forward and futures contracts was limited by regulation, but there were listed stock warrants in existence onshore. Various instruments for taking positions in volume against the peso, however, did exist, notably in the form of the tesobonos, which effectively provided a means of engaging in a forward sale of the peso to the Mexican government itself. Offshore, of course, any kind of instrument could be traded; and several types – equity swaps, tesobono swaps, structured notes, and cetes swaps – played an important role in driving the currency turbulence in the months after the December 1994 devaluation of the peso.

We will examine in some detail the functioning of the tesobono market and how its operations could move the exchange rate established in the weekly *fixings*. We will also examine the working of the coberturas market, the market in forward contracts permitted internally between licensed intermediaries and domestic end-users. We will, however, dwell mainly on the offshore OTC products that emerged in 1993 and 1994 because of their effects on the postcollapse exchange market dynamics.

Section 7.4 presents some policy implications.

7.2   Theoretical behavior of currency-based derivatives in a crisis

The theoretical literature on speculative attacks and balance-of-payments crises has taken two directions. Krugman (1979) and Flood and Garber (1984a) analyzed the dynamics of a speculative attack that results from an inconsistent policy mix, such as budget deficits financed by money creation and a fixed exchange rate system, which leads to the drawing down of foreign exchange reserves and an eventual attack on the remaining reserves. The proximate cause of the collapse of the fixed exchange rate was a one-time attack on the foreign exchange reserves of the country, rendering the country unable to defend the fixed exchange rate parity. Key results in this literature were the determination of the timing and magnitude of this attack.

In the second round of research on exchange rate crises, self-fulfilling attacks – crises that arose without obvious *current* policy inconsistency – were central. An attack justified itself by generating shifts in postattack monetary, fiscal, or exchange rate policies. In such models, the attitude of speculators was crucial to whether an attack occurred. If speculators as a group decided not to attack the exchange rate regime, it could continue; and their collective decision would prove to have been justified. If speculators decided to attack, the fixed exchange rate system would collapse into an inflationist regime, and their attack would also prove to have been justified. Such multiple equilibria attacks were studied in Flood and Garber (1984b) and Obstfeld (1986b) and have recently been extended in Obstfeld (1994).[7]

Notwithstanding its extensive development, the speculative attack literature has evolved entirely in the context of macroeconomic modeling and in an assumed environment in which securities and exchange markets are always liquid. The only discontinuity in the models is in the foreign exchange holdings of central banks and not in exchange rates.[8] This constant liquidity is a feature that contradicts the universal loss of liquidity that emerges in the several days in which a speculative attack explodes and in the extreme volatility that can last for several months in the aftermath of an attack. Although the general macroeconomic principles of speculative attacks are still relevant, the existing literature has limitations in analyzing financial market developments during the attack and in its aftermath.

To gain an understanding of the source of the volatility associated with a foreign exchange crisis, we must turn to the details of the underlying capital markets and particularly of the derivatives markets. Unfortunately, there is no general model of the sequence of instruments that are brought to bear against a currency, so we must be somewhat taxonomic in our examination, but we will concentrate on two standard methods – short selling of a currency through forward contracts and through put options and dynamic hedging – along with the normal end game of borrowing from the central bank and selling on the spot market.

In the run-up to an attack on a fixed exchange rate, short positions are taken by speculators who intend to profit from an expected devaluation of the currency. The underlying principle is that of acquiring cheap credit in the currency under attack and profiting from the fall in value of the domestic currency after accounting for the cost of acquiring credit. Attacks that use forward contracts are the cheapest way of attacking a currency because they are off–balance sheet items that do not require the use of costly bank reserves and they attract reduced capital requirements.

---

[7] See Eichengreen and Wyplosz (1993) for a recent application of this view to the European exchange rate mechanism (ERM) crisis. The literature on speculative attacks has been extended in many different directions such as through the introduction of capital controls (Wyplosz, 1986) and borrowing facilities (Obstfeld, 1986a). See Garber and Svensson (1995) for a review of the speculative attack literature.

[8] In discrete time speculative attack models with uncertainty, there can be a discontinuity in the exchange rate, but there is never any disruption or illiquidity in markets.

7.2.1   *Attacks using forward contracts*

In the most typical form of a speculative attack on a weak currency, speculators and hedgers acquire forward contracts with banks to deliver the weak currency in return for the strong currency at some date in the future, by which time the currency is expected to have collapsed. Because this creates an unbalanced currency position, banks will try to offset this position by writing offsetting forward contracts with other agents to deliver the weak currency or by creating a synthetic contract that mimics the outright forward contract. A synthetic forward contract can be created by using a spot currency transaction linked with a foreign exchange swap.

Given market sentiments during an exchange rate crisis, the only agent with whom banks can contract the offsetting position is the central bank. The central bank is forced to intervene to preserve the exchange rate and usually to place a ceiling on money market interest rates, and it does so by either selling offsetting forward contracts or by lending domestic currency through the discount window and buying it back at the foreign exchange window.

Banks, as dealers in the foreign exchange market, post a bid–ask spread in the forward market that reflects their cost of holding inventories and their perception of the central bank's ability and willingness to relieve them of their unbalanced positions. Banks also control the amount of forward contracts they supply to speculators, which determines the supply of liquidity to speculators during an attack.[9] In addition to such forward contracts, international banks supply a wide variety of structured notes that allow other market participants, notably domestic banks, to take off-balance-sheet positions in currencies and provide credit either in the weak or the strong currency. In our description of methods used to attack the Mexican peso in section 7.3, we will elaborate on the nature of such notes.

7.2.2   *Speculation using foreign exchange options*

Options are also actively used for hedging and speculation in the foreign exchange market. A typical put option confers on the owner the right but not the obligation to deliver the weak currency at a preagreed exchange

---

[9] The literature on the behavior of currency forwards at the time of a crisis is still in its infancy. The theoretical behavior of forward-based markets as described in the text is derived in Lall (1994). Also see Garber and Lall (1996).

rate to the writer of the option. Therefore, a speculator betting on devaluation will acquire a put option in the weak currency. The bank that sells the option either writes an offsetting option or recreates the offsetting security synthetically by acquiring positions in the two currencies and balancing the portfolio as required by the usual option-pricing formulas.

A dynamic hedging strategy used by banks to offset put options written by them may create the perverse effect of causing a sell-off of the weak currency as interest rates rise, instead of purchases that a central bank imposing a squeeze hopes to induce.[10] The net effect of the interest rate increase depends on the size of the buying of weak currency caused by the squeeze relative to the dynamic hedging activity.

7.3 The behavior of the Mexican derivatives markets in the exchange crisis

The current view of the proximate sources of the Mexican exchange crisis is that the selling of the peso in November and December 1994 arose primarily from "domestic addresses" – equities and government securities held by "foreign addresses" did not change in sufficient magnitude to match the bulk of the decline in Mexican foreign exchange reserves.[11] It is conceivable that domestic or domestically based entities were better informed of the prospects in the immediate future and chose to protect the value of their peso-denominated assets and Mexican equities. The subsequent exchange market turbulence from January through March 1995 was attributed to speculation about the rescue package and the Mexican policy reform package, although the form of the speculation was unspecified. In this section, we will argue that the magnitude of the outstanding derivative products in Mexican underlying securities, their method of booking, and their management played a key role in the collapse itself and in the exchange market volatility during the postcollapse float. Their existence also makes problematic the use of the designations of "foreign" and "domestic" addresses for categorizing particular security holders as the impetus for peso sell-offs. In this section, we describe the various products extant at the time of the crisis and the methods used by international banks to control credit and market risk in their positions.

---

[10] See Garber and Spencer (1995) for the details of how the interest rate defense can trigger sales of the weak currency.
[11] See, e.g., Folkerts-Landau, Ito, et al. (1995), pp. 7–8.

7.3.1   Tesobonos

The tesobono is a short-term discount security whose payoff is indexed to the peso–dollar exchange rate. In 1994, pressure on Mexican exchange reserves led to a restructuring of public finance through a program to supplant substantial amounts of peso-denominated cetes with tesobono instruments. As an indexed instrument, the tesobono itself is a derivative product; and it provided the markets a means of shorting the peso forward, effectively with the Mexican government itself as the counterparty through its policy of stabilizing the exchange rate. It also was heavily used as an underlying instrument in tesobono swaps. The mechanics of operations in both the tesobono and the tesobono swaps were intimately connected to the turbulence in the foreign exchange markets that followed the December 1994 devaluation.

Both the purchase on primary issue and the payoff on tesobonos were settled in pesos. Until they were made payable directly in dollars after the delivery of funds through the rescue packages of the International Monetary Fund (IMF) and U.S. Treasury, tesobonos were bought at a reference index called a *fix* in a primary market operated by the Banco de Mexico. They were also redeemed in accordance with the fix at maturity. Until the end of February 1995, the fix was the average exchange rate as of 11:00 A.M. that the Banco de Mexico calculates daily from the peso–dollar exchange rate quotations of the six largest participants in the exchange market.[12] The two extremes were dropped and the arithmetic average of the remaining rates was computed.

For primary issue, bids on tesobonos were submitted at 9:30 A.M. on Tuesday mornings. The bids were in interest rates and quantities in dollar equivalents. Peso settlement for successful bidders occurred two days later on Thursday. Because the fix at which the tesobonos would be sold were not known until 11:00 A.M., the bidder did not know how many pesos were required to purchase the dollar amount of tesobonos submitted in the bid. The potential buyer might take the risk of exchanging dollars into pesos after 11:00 A.M. to settle a successful bid. More likely, the buyer would purchase for a few basis points a guarantee from a Mexican bank that he could both obtain the required pesos at the fix current at the inception of the tesobonos and convert the pesos into dollars at the fix current at maturity.

---

[12] Banamex was the largest participant with about a 30% market share of the exchange market. Bancomer and Serfin each had about 10% of the market. There are five key market makers – Banamex, Bancomer, Serfin, Citibank, and Nafinsa, the government development bank.

To cover their assumed risk from these guarantees, the Mexican banks executed the implied foreign exchange transactions at 11:00 A.M., the fix time. Prior to the 1994 devaluation, fluctuations in the exchange rate were small enough that the potential for significant exchange rate movement was minimal between the fix time and a moment afterward when tesobono holders either purchased or sold their pesos. By January and February 1995, however, exchange rate fluctuations and reduced liquidity in the exchange market were significant enough that the expiration dates of the tesobonos had become a node of exchange rate instability.[13]

To generate the appropriate liquidity, the banks informed the market about the quantity of dollar sales or purchases that would fall onto the exchange markets due to tesobono operations. In particular, at maturity, the banks would announce some days in advance the peso sales they expected to make to cover their risk from the guarantees. The goal was that the market should organize liquidity deep enough to handle large anticipated transactions at 11:00 A.M. on expiration day.[14] Of course, this information moved the value of the fix and determined both the amount of pesos that the Mexican government would receive on primary issue and pay out at maturity.[15] Ideally, enough liquidity would appear by fix time that there would be no jump in the exchange rate in the minute before and after the fix, so the banks would have been approximately covered. In preparation for the Tuesday exchange market demands for tesobono-related transactions, institutions started accumulating dollar positions on Friday and Monday. This tended to generate a weekly seasonal in the two months after the devaluation until the Mexican

[13] As is typical in an exchange crisis, the bid–ask spread on dollars went from a normal 25–50 basis points to 500 basis points during the crisis. Exchange rates fluctuated by up to 10 percent on some days in the aftermath of the crisis.

[14] There was, of course, some speculation about how many of the tesobonos would roll over rather than result in a net sale of pesos. For instance, Mexican bank holdings of tesobonos usually were rolled over. By offering the guarantee, banks knew in advance approximately the size of the exchange outflow that would arise from tesobono redemptions.

[15] Under the old rules, six banks were polled for their ask price for dollars for a minimum commitment of $100,000 as of 11:00 A.M. Under a new procedure, there are now eight participants in the "fix"; and bid prices are for minimum commitments of $5 million. The highest and lowest bid rates are eliminated and the remaining six are averaged. Also, the eight banks that are polled are selected randomly, where the probability of being polled depends on market share. This procedural change was implemented because of the fear that the market was being manipulated – banks that had guaranteed to tesobono-holding clients the conversion of their pesos at the fix had an interest in reporting an artificially depreciated exchange rate at the fix to assure that the peso would appreciate immediately afterward.

government guaranteed the exchange rate at the fix. The exchange rate depreciated until reaching a low at the fix, and it appreciated until the next Friday or Monday; the effect of this speculation was to smooth out the movements in the exchange rate in the presence of foreseeable ebbs and flows of selling pressure.

7.3.2   Coberturas

Coberturas are the instruments traded in the short-term peso forward market that has been operating in Mexico and whose settlement is exclusively in pesos. Although it was in theory the only formal forward-based market for pesos until the reintroduction of peso futures at the Chicago Mercantile Exchange, there has also been a peso forward market in New York where gains are paid in dollars. The forward market in pesos is arbitraged over the books of the large New York securities houses that are active in this market. Prior to the peso crisis, this arbitrage allowed the existence of a true peso–dollar forward market with settlement in both currencies. The nature of the arbitrage that allowed for the creation of such a forward market is explained after the description of the coberturas market that follows.

The maturity of cobertura contracts is freely negotiable between the parties up to a period of one year, and the premium on the contract is also determined freely by the counterparties. The Banco de Mexico authorizes the institutions that may intermediate in the cobertura market, based on their creditworthiness and subject to their meeting other technical requirements. Each cobertura is supposed to be between an end user and an intermediary. Regulation required that financial intermediaries deal only with nonfinancial end users, but this regulation was quickly circumvented through the establishment of nonfinancial subsidiaries by financial intermediaries whose sole business was to participate as position-taking end users in the coberturas market.

Two types of complementary contracts were undertaken in this market: the purchase of foreign exchange cover and the sale of foreign exchange cover. In the purchase of foreign exchange cover, the buyer pays the intermediary a "hedge price," which is a premium in local currency. In the event of a peso depreciation, the contract confers on the buyer the right to receive from the intermediary an amount in pesos equivalent to the change in value of the notional principal due to the exchange rate depreciation. Specifically, he receives in pesos on the maturity date the product of the percentage of depreciation and the quantity of dollars hedged. In the event of an appreciation, the buyer must pay the counterparty the difference in value of the principal between the contractual and the settlement date. A buyer could then be completely hedged against a depreciation of the peso–dollar exchange rate.

In a sale of foreign exchange cover, the seller receives a premium from the counterparty. The counterparty can demand collateral equivalent to the premium, depending upon the perceived creditworthiness of the seller. Under this contract, in the event of a depreciation, the seller is obligated to pay the intermediary completely for the change in the value of the notional principal. Conversely, in the event of an appreciation, the seller is paid the amount hedged times the rate of appreciation. The seller is thus hedged against peso appreciation in such a contract.

For purposes of both contracts, the calculation of the appreciation or depreciation rate is made by taking the difference between the equilibrium exchange rate published in the *Diario Oficial* on the bank working day prior to the day the contract is entered into and the equilibrium exchange rate published on the bank working day prior to the maturity date.

The particular form that the cobertura has taken was itself a regulatory compromise between the political unpopularity of speculation that used peso forward markets as its vehicle and the recognition that a forward market of some sort was vital to provide a means of hedging against peso currency risk. The solution to this dilemma was to create a disguised forward contract that started out in the money and that was called a "cobertura" to remove connotations of speculation, although corporates could contract coberturas even if they had no currency exposure to cover. In other words, any corporate entity could become a buyer or a seller of coberturas. The limitation imposed on financial institutions to deal only with final, nonfinancial users was quickly circumvented, as mentioned earlier, through the establishment of nonfinancial subsidiaries whose only business was to engage in the coberturas market. Hence, everyone was an end user and there was no practical limitation on the use of this market to speculate – that is, to take uncovered positions.

The coberturas market also created the opportunity for arbitrage that enabled a complete forward market with settlement in both currencies between large New York houses. Arbitrage would occur, for example, if the coberturas market valued the peso more on a given date than the New York forward market. A New York house would buy the peso forward in New York and sell in the coberturas market. On expiry, if the peso had risen, the arbitrager would receive settlement of dollars on the New York contract and deliver pesos on the cobertura. Effectively, this created a true forward contract, thereby circumventing Mexican regulations. Positions could be taken against the peso through this "true" forward market although regulations did not allow for the existence of a market that settled in both currencies, which was believed necessary for speculation by foreigners.

A new regular forward market is emerging in Mexico that is expected to displace the coberturas market completely. Currently, there are four or five authorized participants in this forward market. Entry into this market is tightly regulated by the Banco de Mexico, depending primarily on a demonstration of a sophisticated risk-control system.

7.3.3   Tesobono swaps

Tesobono swaps were a second important group of offshore derivative operations, and they provided a means of leveraging the tesobono. These operations permitted a circumvention of the regulations of the Comision Nacional de Valores that forbid holding financial assets on margin in Mexico. Industry sources in Mexico report that about $16 billion of tesobonos were involved in tesobono swaps at the time of the devaluation.[16]

The leverage involved in a tesobono swap can be most readily examined by considering first a nearly equivalent tesobono repurchase agreement. As an example, consider a New York investment firm that is willing to lend dollars for one year against tesobono collateral. The firm will engage in a repurchase agreement with a Mexican bank to buy tesobonos at their current value and to resell them in a year at the original price plus a dollar interest rate.[17] Suppose the dollar rate is equal to the London interbank offer rate (LIBOR) plus 100 basis points, with the interest rate to be settled and repriced quarterly. In 1994, the typical tesobono repo had a maturity of one year and required between 10 and 20 percent margin, which produces a leverage between 10 to 1 and 5 to 1. The Mexican counterparty would, for example, buy $500 worth of tesobonos in Mexico and sell them to the New York firm for $400 for later repurchase at $400 plus interest. The tesobonos would be delivered to the New York firm through its custodial account, usually with Citibank, Mexico.[18] The gain to the Mexican bank is that it pays LIBOR

---

[16] About $29 billion of tesobonos were outstanding at the end of December 1994. About $16.1 billion of outstanding tesobonos on December 19, 1994, were held by "foreign addresses."

[17] In the swap form of the deal, of course, only net amounts were due in each settlement period.

[18] The tesobonos would then be held in the "foreign address" category, although their ultimate holder had a domestic Mexican address.

plus 100 to finance tesobonos that may pay the equivalent of LIBOR plus 300. The gain to the U.S. lender is that it gets to place dollar funds at LIBOR plus 100.[19]

When the peso crisis arrived, the market value in dollars of tesobonos suddenly fell. This resulted both indirectly from rumors that capital controls might be imposed and through the failed auction of January 1995 in which the government accepted an unfavorable yield. The fall in market value reduced the value of the collateral and triggered margin calls to deliver dollars or close out the positions.

Suppose, for example, that the typical tesobono fell by 15 percent in dollar value, to the extent that they could be valued at all. For the tesobono repo in the foregoing example, collateral is now insufficient to the extent of $75, and a margin call to deliver this amount in cash is sent to the Mexican bank. The Mexican bank must now either go to the exchange market at the depreciated peso exchange rate to acquire the $75 or close out the position. To close the position requires the delivery of $400 in cash.

A tesobono swap places both parties in the same risk position as a repurchase. Suppose the New York firm swaps tesobono yield for LIBOR plus 100 basis points against a $500 notional principal and requires $100 as collateral from its Mexican counterparty. The payoffs to the two counterparties are identical to those of the repurchase. To hedge, the New York firm will purchase $500 in tesobonos directly from the market, so once again the tesobonos will be held by "foreign addresses," although Mexican domestic residents will bear the tesobono risk.[20]

---

[19] Why the New York firms did not just directly hold tesobonos for a higher gain is a subject of dispute among market participants in Mexico. Some market participants argue that the New York firms did not want to carry directly the credit risk of the tesobonos but still wanted to make dollar loans at premium prices. Others claimed that they were worried about their ability to sell pesos realized from the tesobonos at the exchange rate "fix" used to determine the peso settlement. Finally, since many institutions were already direct tesobono holders, they may have reached position limits, and this was just another way of earning a premium dollar yield through the tesobono market.

[20] The tesobonos associated with these swaps are held by foreign addresses. If the swap position is suddenly closed, domestic addresses will buy back the tesobonos at some predetermined price through a termination option that might require payment of a penalty of 10 or 20 basis points. Then the data should indicate a sudden shift in ownership from foreign to domestic addresses. Payment of margin will show up as an exchange market disturbance of a smaller magnitude, but it will not show up as a shift in the ownership categories.

By regulation, securities held by foreign addresses are segregated into special accounts at Indeval, the securities depository. Data on securities held by foreign or domestic addresses are published monthly by the Comision Nacional de Valores, but they are available on a daily basis. Daily data are considered misleading: they consist of informa-

Again, if tesobono prices jumped downward because of suddenly increased default risk, the New York counterparty would send out a margin call.

The scramble for dollars to cover such margin calls and position close-outs was associated with the currency turmoil of January and February 1995. If the $16 billion figure for tesobono swaps and repos is accurate, the margin calls associated with a 15 percent price decline would have triggered a sale of pesos to acquire $2.4 billion in a thin exchange market.[21]

The attack that undid the peso came the day after the initial devaluation on December 20, 1994. Immediately after the initial devaluation, the large suppliers of the derivative products to the Mexican banks calculated that the devaluation would further deteriorate the loan portfolios of these banks. This is the reason that the devaluation came as a surprise – the New York investment firms had thought that the Mexican authorities knew about the derivative positions of their banks and therefore would not exacerbate the problem with a devaluation. On recalculating their counterparty risk resulting from the devaluation, the suppliers of the derivative products, including tesobono swaps immediately precipitated margin calls. The $5 billion expended by the Banco de Mexico on December 21, 1994, was the result, as Mexican banks sold pesos to meet margin calls.

7.3.4   Cetes swaps

Cetes swaps and repos also were undertaken in large volumes with offshore counterparties.[22] These deals were similar to the tesobono swaps and repos except that the collateral was cetes. These operations were regarded as more aggressive than the tesobono swaps because of the much greater currency risk. In return, however, there was a much greater spread between cetes and LIBOR interest rates. The typical deal might require a payment of LIBOR plus 500 basis points to the dollar lender, while cetes might yield 25 percent with an anticipated depreciation of 4 percent, for a spread to the Mexican bank entering the deal of 10 percent, based on LIBOR of 6 percent. Margin requirements were

tion on actual transfers of securities provided by securities houses responsible for the receipt of the securities. Transfers reported to Indeval may lag by two or three days the crediting of a foreign address with the securities on the security house's books. Over the course of a month, these lags will be mostly eliminated, but they create short-term inaccuracies.

[21] Of course, tesobono values did not fall uniformly because of the different maturities.

[22] These were undertaken for ajustabonos and pagares as well as for cetes.

higher for cetes swaps than for tesobono swaps because of the currency risk, so the devaluation and surge in cetes interest rates triggered large margin calls.

7.3.5 Brady bond swaps

In addition to the swaps in short-term Mexican paper, there was a large volume of Brady bond swaps, which provided a means to Mexican banks of leveraging Brady bond positions. This allowed Mexican banks to reap a return both on the rising dollar yield curve and Mexico country risk. These were typically three-month contracts booked as repos with interest rates on the dollar legs set at LIBOR plus 100 basis points.

7.3.6 Structured notes

Structured notes are investment vehicles with coupon payments and principal repayments that are driven by formulas that can vastly leverage the initial capital invested. Nevertheless, in value accounting systems they can be booked as normal investments and in the currency denominated in the prospectus. More than simply magnifying the usual market risks associated with investment positions, structured notes provide an easy method for circumventing prudential regulations on currency positions or interest rate mismatches.

During 1994, Mexican financial institutions took large positions in structured notes with investment houses in New York. Booked as claims with dollar principal and dollar payoffs, these notes in fact were currency bets that allowed the banks to leverage their investment into a short dollar and long peso position to take advantage of the positive interest rate spreads between peso and dollar money markets.[23] Because Mexican regulators did not know about the nature of these notes, under Mexican accounting rules they were booked as a balanced dollar position and not counted against the regulatory net currency position limit of a maximum of 15 percent of capital. When the devaluation occurred, Mexican banks had much larger net short dollar positions than regulators had realized.

Structured notes existed in many forms. For example, a Mexican bank might buy a note with a one-year maturity from a New York investment

---

[23] In Malaysia, these instruments, known as "principal adjusted coupon notes," serve the same purpose of providing leverage in acquiring domestic currency positions through foreign exchange financing.

house for \$1.[24] The coupon on the note and the principal on the note are payable in dollars. Suppose that the coupon is 85 percent. The principal repayment, however, depends negatively on the peso value of the dollar – it will be $[1 + 5 \times (s_0 - s_1)/s_1]$, where s_0 is the initial peso value of the dollar and s_1 is the value at maturity. If the peso has depreciated by 50 percent at maturity, from say three to six pesos per dollar, the principal repayment will be –\$1.50. The overall payout is then –\$0.65. Note that this is the payoff structure of a position that is short \$3 at a market dollar interest rate of 5 percent per year and long twelve pesos at a market peso interest rate of 25 percent per year. Effectively, the initial \$1 investment has been leveraged fourfold.

As a safety feature for the bank, however, such structured notes placed a cap on the potential losses to the investor. For example, in no case could the principal redemption plus coupon payment be less than zero. This meant that the structured note included an option for the bank to sell the implied short dollar–long peso position to the New York investment house for \$0. Alternatively stated, the New York investment house was short a put option on a long peso–short dollar asset. Normally, this would be far out of the money and therefore require little delta-hedging. A large enough movement in the exchange rate, however, would require the New York firm to establish suddenly an appropriate delta hedge.[25]

Mexican banks face Banco de Mexico regulations that restrict foreign exchange net positions to a maximum of 15 percent of capital. According to the regulatory definitions of what constituted foreign exchange – an asset or liability whose principal and coupon were denominated in a foreign currency – the \$1 that was originally paid to acquire the structured note would enter the books as a long \$1 position, even though its payoff was equivalent to a short \$3 position. In addition, some banks could count it against their liquidity ratio because its short maturity allowed it to be classified as a liquid deposit.

If the bank had borrowed the initial \$1 used to purchase the note, it would have posted a balanced foreign exchange position on net for regulatory purposes. When the exchange rate was devalued in December

---

[24] Most major New York financial engineering firms sold such products – e.g., Bankers Trust, Merrill Lynch, Bear-Stearns, Donaldson, Lufkin, and Morgan Stanley.

[25] Overall, the investment house would have a position from the note equivalent to being short twelve pesos worth of cetes, long \$3 worth of Treasury bills, and short a put option on the short dollar–long peso position. To hedge the note, it could buy the peso by investing in cetes and short the dollars by borrowing them to buy cetes. The evaporation of the hedged position with the exercise of the put would leave the firm with only the loss on the hedge. Thus, a large enough exchange rate movement would cause losses for both the Mexican bank and the New York firm.

1994, however, the asset value fell to zero, leaving the bank with an unbalanced dollar liability. In scrambling to cover this imbalance, the Mexican banks had to sell pesos, contributing to the postdevaluation December attack on the Banco de Mexico.

After losing the principal and coupon on the note, there were no further loss implications for the Mexican bank. The New York investment house, however, now had only the long peso–short dollar position used to hedge the original note. At this point, the foreign banks started taking losses.[26]

This type of structured note was a financial engineering device to circumvent prudential regulation.[27] Only the principal is booked, in accordance with value accounting principles. The structured note payoff formula component is not booked – it is an off-balance-sheet item. That is the accounting trick – one can alter the nature of the booking through a complicated payoff formula.

Accounting regulations for the determination of foreign exchange positions in Mexico have recently been changed to be consistent with a risk accounting principle.[28] In the past, the long position in dollars was,

---

[26] In preparation for the suddenly likely exercise by the Mexican bank of its put option, the New York investment house would normally have wanted to delta hedge by shorting the peso, but it was difficult to take a short position in the peso during the crisis. Market participants argue that a close substitute was then to short "Mexico like" currencies, such as those of Argentina, Brazil, or Venezuela. Shorting other currencies that would behave similarly to the peso would provide a cover, though there would still be basis risk. Such short selling to cover structured notes on the Mexican peso provides some linkage for the transfer of pressure on the Mexican peso to the other currencies.

[27] The use of structured notes to circumvent regulation is general. For example, regulations in Malaysia have barred foreign banks from lending in ringgit. Foreign banks, however, have created a structure that is dollar-denominated to avoid this regulation. Like the structured note in the Mexican case, however, the interest payment is structured as a coupon rate multiplied by the "adjusted principal" – the principal multiplied by the ratio between the current spot exchange rate and the future realized spot rate. This formula translates the note into a ringgit loan.

The Bank of Thailand permits forwards and simple swaps among banks, although it discourages strongly leveraged positions that might appear in structured notes. There are structured notes linked to the return on the stock exchange of Thailand (SET) index. Domestic banks are end users of OTC derivative products, so the Bank of Thailand requires banks to report offshore derivatives positions. Although there is a prohibition onshore of short selling and transactions are taxed, there apparently is not yet a significant amount of offshore transactions aimed at circumventing these regulations, since Thai companies are not yet very active offshore. Nevertheless, in one general type of deal done to avoid withholding taxes, a company may borrow yen and swap to baht – there is no withholding tax on swaps.

[28] Principles of risk accounting are not generally accepted or understood. Where risks are being taken by a bank is still not well defined. Risk accounting is currently a subject of

through value accounting principles, defined as a dollar asset without taking into account the sensitivity of the asset to the payoff characteristics. The new definition of foreign exchange positions leans on a risk accounting principle: the position is classified as unbalanced if it generates potential gains or losses from the movement of the exchange rate.[29]

7.3.7   *Equity swaps and repurchase agreements*

The market in equity swaps also existed to circumvent Mexican financial market regulations: the regulation that prohibited buying securities on margin and the regulation that limited the possibility of short selling.[30] Market participants characterized the market in offshore equity swaps as very large.

The benefits to market participants of the existence of this market are obvious. Speculators can leverage and gain larger positions, and hedgers of long positions held either directly or implicitly in the form of option deltas could short stock to cover their positions.[31] The market arose

discussion among regulators in industrial countries, and they are coming down on the side of self-regulation because they feel they are unable to determine the risk posture of a derivative book in a timely manner.

[29] The Comision Nacional Bancaria determines the accounting standard, and it still works on a value accounting standard. The Banco de Mexico, however, can impose an accounting standard for reporting of foreign exchange positions. The difference between these standards arises because the comision must account in book value terms to keep track of bank operations.

[30] Offshore equity swap markets also exist for Malaysia and Thailand, among others, also in order to avoid curbs on short selling and leveraging.

[31] With equity swaps, it was possible for the offshore counterparty to establish a short equity position. For example, if a New York house had sold a put on Mexican equity, it would cover by shorting the shares. For the Mexican warrant issuer, which generally sold call options, the market provided the opportunity to go long in the shares and short in dollars. For such issuers, participation in the equity swap market was associated with their warrant programs. For instance, the issue of a $10 million notional amount in a single call option on Mexican shares might be hedged with an equity swap of $5 million worth of shares. Only casas de bolsa can issue domestic equity warrants, and they were required to hedge their positions closely, either with the purchase of a similar option or through delta hedging. Indeed, only for the purpose of delta hedging a warrant position is an equity swap permissible for them. Of course, through their offshore subsidiaries, they can undertake any transactions that the market will bear. There was, however, a lack of liquidity in the equity swap market because the maturity of the swap was three or six months; and this precluded their use for continuous delta-hedging. They could be used, however, to establish the initial delta hedge, with adjustment to the hedge made through shorting in other ways.

to complete the liquidity of the rising domestic equity and warrant markets.

Technically, stock swaps might be swaps or repurchase agreements. The repurchase agreement aspect is perhaps easier to analyze, though swaps predominated. The transaction involves selling shares currently at a given price and repurchasing them for a fixed price in one year, for example. The interest rate payable to the purchaser of the stock, typically LIBOR plus 200 basis points, is settled and repriced quarterly. The initial purchase price might be $100 for $125 worth of shares, so there is a 20 percent margin.[32]

The offshore firm that initially purchases the shares has the right to dispose of the shares if it wishes. If it sells the shares on receipt, it has effectively used the repurchase to short Mexican shares, thereby circumventing the domestic constraints on short selling. If the initial seller of shares in the repurchase is an offshore subsidiary of a Mexican bank, the Mexican bank has circumvented the regulation against a Mexican bank's lending equity for short selling.

At maturity, the offshore lender may or may not resell actual shares to the borrower of funds. Many transactions were for physical delivery, but others might have allowed for cash settlement only. In many cases, individuals, especially those who were borrowing against controlling blocks of shares, wanted the stock back.[33]

With the collapse of the peso and the stock market, the margin in the equity repos was more than wiped out, triggering margin calls from New York in the form of cash or Treasury bills. The response varied by client: some institutions claim that the margin calls triggered enormous sell orders in the stock market to acquire sufficient cash to close out positions, whereas others report that their clients invariably delivered new funds rather than have positions closed. In either case, the Mexican institutions and individuals engaged in these repos had to sell pesos to get margin or close out their positions, adding to the turmoil of the exchange and stock markets.

---

[32] The dollar purchase price would be delivered to the initial seller of the shares – the funds would be used to purchase $100 worth of shares. Thus, the initial seller of shares is actually long shares and has a 5 to 1 leverage of initial capital. The shares are delivered into accounts of the offshore financial institution that is lending funds; typically, these would be at Citibank, Mexico acting as custodian. In turn, Citibank would have stock accounts in Indeval.

[33] As a result, the disposition of voting rights was an important issue in these swaps. The offshore buyer might guarantee that the voting rights would be ceded to the seller for all shares that remained in the possession of the offshore buyer, but it did not necessarily guarantee that it would be holding all the shares at any given moment.

Again an equity swap establishes leveraged positions equivalent to a repurchase agreement. Suppose that a New York firm agrees to swap the total return on a Mexican stock for LIBOR plus 200 basis points on a notional amount of $125 and requires $25 in collateral from its Mexican counterparty. To hedge its short equity position, the New York firm directly buys $125 in the Mexican equity, thereby appearing as a foreign investor in Mexican shares. The risks borne by the two counterparties are the same as in the foregoing repurchase example – the Mexican counterparty is taking a long position in Mexican shares and a short position in short-term dollar loans, while the New York counterparty has only a long position in short-term dollar loans.

It is a general view among market participants and bank regulators that prohibiting the holding of financial assets on margin in Mexico was a mistake. The effect was merely to drive such activity offshore rather than to limit it, and this made the magnitude and nature of the leveraging of positions opaque to the authorities.

7.3.8   *Ajustabono-backed securities*

Ajustabonos are inflation-indexed Mexican government securities that had long been held by Mexican banks. In addition to paying a relatively fixed real interest return, ajustabonos could be counted as foreign exchange assets in determining regulatory foreign exchange positions, so Mexican banks funded their ajustabono positions with dollar borrowings. When real interest rates rose in 1992, Mexican banks found that their ajustabono positions were frozen because they did not want to realize the capital losses on their investment portfolios. The solution was to contract financial structures with New York banks and investment houses through which the ajustabonos could be used as collateral.

For example, a U.S. and a Mexican securities firm associated with a bank would jointly organize a company in the Caymans or in Bermuda, which would agree to purchase ajustabonos at face value, with the funding provided from the sale of two series of securities, one senior and one junior, both denominated in dollars. Suppose that the deal involved a Mexican bank's selling $120 million par value worth of ajustabonos to the company. The Mexican partner might put up $20 million and receive $20 million par value of the junior securities, which it would sell to the bank. Denominated in dollars, the junior notes could be counted as a foreign exchange asset in determining regulatory positions. The U.S. firm would invest $100 million and receive $100 million par value of the senior securities. The senior securities would be designed to pay a relatively secure dollar yield, which could be paid if the exchange rate did not depreciate excessively, and would be sold for LIBOR plus. The payoff on the junior securities was like that of a structured note – if the exchange rate did not depreciate, it would pay a high yield and make good the losses on the ajustabonos. If the exchange rate depreciated, the yield or principal of the junior note would decline according to a predetermined formula.

When the banking authorities became aware that the return on the junior notes was correlated with the peso, they required that 100 percent of the notes be covered with foreign exchange. Market sources estimate that $2 billion of the junior notes were outstanding in 1994. The banks began to cover their positions in September 1994, which contributed significantly to the drain on official reserves in the period prior to the devaluation.

7.3.9 *Listed equity warrants*

The Mexican market in equity warrants started in 1992 as a first, tightly controlled step in introducing traded domestic options. The Comision Nacional de Valores determined that the first options traded in Mexico should be listed on the Mercado de Valores under strict surveillance. Gradually, as market infrastructure, risk control systems, and human capital suitable to the markets developed, it was intended that onshore markets for additional instruments would be permitted. The market now consists of warrants for about twenty-five individual shares and the market index, each of which may have emissions from several casas de bolsa and with varying maturities, strike prices, and types of warrant.

To avoid a concentration of risk taking in the financial institutions through this instrument, the issuers of warrants in Mexico had to hedge either through the acquisition of a similar warrant offshore or through delta hedging that would mimic the warrant. Thus, the issuer of the warrant would be covered theoretically against market price movements, both in the equity market and in the exchange market. The establishment of the hedge was carefully monitored and managed by the Mercado de Valores.

The market value of outstanding warrant issues was about $430 million at the end of August 1995. The firms Accival, Serfin, and Atlantico dominate trading and position taking in warrants. Accival has the largest volume share in the cash market in equities as well as in the market in individual stock and index warrants, with a share fluctuating between 60 and 70 percent.[34] Mexican warrants have peso strike prices, while off-

---

[34] Accival undertakes its warrant operation through a joint venture with Swiss Bank, which has been in effect since 1994. Accival and Swiss Bank jointly manage their warrant book

shore warrants on Mexican issues generally have dollar strike prices. A typical operation involved a Mexican brokerage's selling a warrant in Mexico and buying an OTC option offshore to cover. The currency risk was hedged in the cobertura market, and the differential in premiums would provide the profit.

Generally, end users in the onshore warrants market were unhedged, and the speculation involved an optimistic view of the equity market – most warrants are calls. As a result, most losses from the collapse of stock prices in this market were incurred by individual clients, so speculation did not greatly exacerbate the capital losses in the financial institutions. Because the market consisted primarily of call options, defaults did not occur.

Options trading was a profitable business through 1994 for the large Mexican banks. In December 1994, however, with the collapse of the stock market and the evaporation of liquidity in the markets, positions were frozen and it was no longer possible to continue to hedge them dynamically. Issuers in Mexico are short volatility – they are sellers of warrants and cannot usually cover their position perfectly with another option. To hedge their positions, they must by regulation use a dynamic hedging strategy, which, in combination with the short warrant position, is regarded as taking a position in volatility. If volatility increases, they lose because the value of their short warrant position increases while the value of their hedge does not. As a result, issuers took some loss for the year, but the end-of-year loss was mostly offset by their profits from options trading during the year.

7.4   Policy issues and implications

Financial derivatives allow positions to be taken by speculators and hedgers that affect both the dynamics of an exchange rate attack and the impact on the domestic banking system of a successful attack. In this

and share the profits. Swiss Bank issues warrants in Europe. Accival issues warrants in Mexico, and the position is jointly hedged. Dollar funding is provided by Swiss Bank, as well as technology training and systems support. Stock positions in warrant trades are covered through Accival's position-taking in spot equity markets. The typical financial transaction for Accival and Swiss Bank would be as follows. Suppose that Accival sells call warrants on equity with strikes in pesos, a position equivalent to being short stock and long currency. To cover, Accival would have to be long stock and short pesos in a synthetic operation. The funding for the short currency positions, however, was provided by Swiss Bank in dollars. To cover the position in the warrant contract, however, it was necessary for Accival to be short pesos. In order to cover the exchange risk, Accival hedged with coberturas – that is, it could effectively buy the value equivalent of the dollar forward and sell pesos to create a short peso position on net.

sense, notwithstanding their usefulness as hedging instruments, they can greatly complicate the management of a fixed exchange rate system, as well as exacerbating weaknesses in the domestic banking system.

This has to be contrasted with the benefits that such instruments provide in managing risks for market participants, as well as imposing discipline on errant monetary authorities. However, the punishment for an errant central bank becomes more swift and automatic than in the base case where positions against weak currencies are taken by means of acquiring and selling bank deposits. The potential fallout of an attack can be greater and, in some cases, more ruinous for the banking system. Certainly, the net positions of domestic players vis-à-vis foreign creditors can come as a much greater surprise than in the past.

The policy implication that emerges from this is that the growth of derivatives should be seen as a two-edged sword that can be very beneficial if used properly but can be harmful if not. Banning such instruments outright is not at all effective unless combined with other stringent measures such as the imposition of capital controls, which entails high economic and efficiency costs and goes against the grain of liberalization of financial markets and capital flows. Not only would the banning of derivatives cause inefficiencies, but it would drive the market offshore where regulation can be successfully circumvented. Therefore, the instruments will still be there, but they will be outside the regulatory purview of the authorities.

The solution to this is for countries to create a regulatory environment that brings the markets onshore, and to invest in sophisticated regulatory and supervisory infrastructure. Such an approach would allow countries to monitor the growth and proliferation of derivatives while allowing market participants to use them for risk management purposes. It would also allow them to change the regulations that govern derivatives use to adapt to the improving state of the domestic financial markets and banking system, and their improving ability to bear risk.

7.5   Conclusion

In this chapter, we have examined the nature of the derivatives used in an attack on a country's foreign reserves. These derivatives can include simple forward contracts, swap contracts, and options contracts in the currencies themselves, and interest rate contracts or equity contracts. The effect of the existence of these instruments in large amounts on the dynamics of a currency crisis is only now being addressed by researchers.

Although regulations have contained their onshore use in many emerging market countries, such instruments are proliferating offshore in international financial centers to provide a method to circumvent domestic prudential or antispeculative regulations. Specifically, prior to the December 1994 attack on the peso, Mexican regulations effectively precluded domestic short selling because banks could not lend any Mexican securities; similarly, purchase of securities on margin was banned. Also, regulation eliminated currency futures and forwards because of a ban on using peso-based settlement banks. Regulation also precluded banks from taking unbalanced foreign exchange positions greater than 15 percent of capital.

These regulations could be avoided through the use of offshore derivative products. For example, widespread use of offshore equity, cetes, and tesobono swaps emerged to circumvent the regulation against margin purchases. In this way, Mexican banks and other financial institutions through New York subsidiaries would, after depositing a 25 percent dollar margin, effectively borrow dollars from New York houses, purchase Mexican securities, deposit the securities with the lender as collateral, and gain from the spread over dollar LIBOR. Similarly, Mexican banks could sell equity outright to their New York subsidiaries, which could then sell short.

Position regulations on foreign exchange were circumvented through the use of structured notes sold to Mexican banks by New York houses. A Mexican bank could borrow dollars in New York and purchase a dollar denominated deposit from the lender. The payoff on the deposit would be in dollars, thereby allowing the Mexican bank to remain balanced in foreign exchange for regulatory purposes. The payoff on the deposit, however, was tied to the peso–dollar exchange rate in a manner that provided multiple leverage to the Mexican bank. If the peso weakened dramatically, the value of the deposit would be wiped out. Thus, the Mexican bank effectively took an unbalanced foreign exchange position.

Such products were outstanding in large amounts; and they exacerbated the crisis, in the months after the devaluation and especially at the time of the devaluation, because of the margin calls associated with declining collateral values. They existed in amounts and positions apparently opaque to financial market supervisors.

It is evident from the Mexican episode that prudential regulations can be easily undermined by use of offshore products and through complicated corporate structures impenetrable to regulators. The mere imposition of regulations is not sufficient to prevent the behavior that domestic authorities are trying to avoid – that requires a large investment in the supervisory apparatus, the domestic powers, and the offshore reach of the supervisors, along with a political consensus that supervision will not be undermined.

Policy approaches to dealing with the proliferation of derivatives instruments are two-pronged: (1) bring markets onshore and invest in sophisticated regulation and supervision systems, and (2) foster international cooperation between industrialized and developing countries to bring offshore markets also within the umbrella of supervision.

References

Bank for International Settlements (1996). *Central Bank Survey of Foreign Exchange and Derivatives Market Activity, 1995*. Basle.

Eichengreen, Barry, and Charles Wyplosz (1993). "The Unstable EMS," *Brookings Papers on Economic Activity*, no. 1: 51–124.

Flood, Robert, and Peter Garber (1984a). "Collapsing Exchange-Rate Regimes: Some Linear Examples," *Journal of International Economics* 17 (1): 1–13.

——— (1984b). "Gold Monetization and Gold Discipline," *Journal of Political Economy* 92 (1): 90–107.

Folkerts-Landau, David, Takatoshi Ito, et al. (1995). *International Capital Markets: Developments, Propects, and Policy Issues*. Washington, D.C.: International Monetary Fund.

Garber, Peter (1996). "Managing Risks to Financial Markets from Volatile Capital Flows: The Role of Prudential Regulation," *International Journal of Finance and Economics* 1 (3): 183–96.

Garber, Peter, and Subir Lall (1996). "The Role and Operation of Derivative Markets in Foreign Exchange Crises," February. Unpublished manuscript, Brown University, Providence, R.I.

Garber, Peter, and Michael Spencer (1995). "Foreign Exchange Hedging with Synthetic Options and the Interest Rate Defense of a Fixed Exchange Rate Regime," *IMF Staff Papers* 42 (3): 490–516.

Garber, Peter, and Lars Svensson (1995). "The Operation and Collapse of Fixed Exchange Rates." In Gene Grossman and Kenneth Rogoff, eds., *Handbook of International Economics*, vol. 3, pp. 1865–1911. Amsterdam: Elsevier.

Krugman, Paul (1979). "A Model of Balance-of-Payments Crises," *Journal of Money, Credit, and Banking* 11: 311–25.

Lall, Subir (1994). "Bank Behavior in an Exchange Rate Crisis." In *Essays in Banking, Liquidity and Speculative Attacks on Fixed Exchange Rate Regimes*, pp. 55–87. Ph.D. dissertation, Brown University.

Obstfeld, Maurice (1986a). "Speculative Attacks and the External Constraint in a Maximizing Model of the Balance of Payments," *Canadian Journal of Economics* 19: 1–22.

——— (1986b). "Rational and Self-fulfilling Balance of Payments Crises," *American Economic Review* 76: 72–81.

——— (1994). "The Logic of Currency Crises," *Banque de France Cahiers Economiques et Monetaires* 43: 189–214.

Wyplosz, Charles (1986). "Capital Controls and Balance-of-Payments Crises," *Journal of International Money and Finance* 5: 167–79.

CHAPTER 8

Crisis, contagion, and country funds: Effects on East Asia and Latin America

Jeffrey A. Frankel and Sergio L. Schmukler

8.1   Introduction

Among the debates that gained – or regained – interest after the Mexican crisis of December 1994 has been one concerning "contagion." Although contagion effects have been much discussed, relatively little research has studied this phenomenon directly. In the present chapter we study spillover effects using data on closed-end country funds. We look at contagion from Mexico City to the international investor community in New York City, and from there to various local markets in Asia and Latin America. We study spillover effects not only between regions but also within them.

Country funds provide a useful tool to study contagion or spillover effects, because two values are available for each fund. Country funds trade in New York City, while their underlying assets trade in the equity markets of each respective country at their net asset value (NAV).[1] Even though the country fund is a different way of holding the underlying assets, the fund price is not typically equal to its NAV. In consequence, we are able to compare the investor demand for basically the same assets in two different parts of the world. This enables us to look separately at how changes in Mexican asset prices affect other country fund prices and NAVs.

The authors would like to thank Neil Ericsson, Reuven Glick, Steve Kamin, Graciela Kaminsky, Richard Lyons, Carmen Reinhart, and Paul Wood for helpful comments. We also thank Don Cassidy, of Lipper Analytical Services, and Thierry Wizman for the country fund data. Sergio Schmukler would like to acknowledge support from the Consejo Nacional de Investigaciones Científicas y Técnicas, República Argentina.
[1] In addition to locally traded assets, some country funds hold American Depository Receipts (ADRs).

One of the present authors used the message of country fund prices in 1994 to warn about the possibility of a coming repeat of the international debt crisis of 1982, originating again in Latin America. We take the liberty of quoting at length:

> An interesting possible hypothesis regarding recent capital inflows is that foreign residents are more optimistic about domestic assets than are domestic residents. A widely-held interpretation of the massive capital flight from Latin America that took place in 1982 and the years immediately preceding it is that residents of these countries correctly perceived dangers ahead, at a time when foreign banks were foolish enough to be still lending eagerly.... Nevertheless, anyone who is concerned about a possible replay of 1982 – as are Calvo, Leiderman, and Reinhart (1993) – wants to be vigilant to any future signs that the locals are again losing confidence. Unfortunately, capital flight can only be estimated with a lag of a quarter or two (and, even then, very imperfectly).
>
> Another place where it might be useful to look are the prices of country-funds that invest in the stock markets of a number of Latin American and Asian countries.... Fluctuations in the premium of the U.S. price of the fund over the net asset value could be a measure of fluctuations in the difference in expectations of U.S. versus local investors.
>
> For most of these funds this premium has been higher (or the discount has been lower) during the period 1990–1992 than during the preceding three years, suggesting bullish sentiment on the part of foreign investors.... Mexico and Brazil ... show a clearly higher level of relative U.S. investor confidence in the three years from 1990 ... Taiwan and Thailand ... show a clearly *lower* level of U.S. investor confidence, again as compared to the end of the 1980s. If our interpretation of the data is correct, that they represent the confidence of U.S. investors relative to local investors, [the results] suggest a possible replay of the period leading up to 1982: booms based relatively firmly on the ground in the case of East Asia, but based excessively on the enthusiasm of U.S. investors in the case of Latin America.[2]

In Frankel and Schmukler (1996a), we study how the three Mexican funds each turned from discounts to premia at the time of the December 1994 Mexican devaluation. We interpret this change as an indication of Mexican investors reacting first to the Mexican devaluation, given that they seemed to have better information about Mexico. In this chapter, we extend that work, by looking at how the Mexican crisis had spillover effects on other markets. In particular, we study how markets in Latin

---

[2] Frankel (1995), pp. 180–87. The same warning was made in Frankel (1994a), p. 17; (1994b), p. 254.

America and Asia were hit by the crisis. In addition, country funds allow us to see the reaction of the New York community of investors that buy emerging-market securities. This may shed light on the nature of international contagion.

Among the questions that we are able to address in this chapter are the following. Is there contagion from shocks such as the Mexican crisis? Is there evidence that financial markets are more closely linked within regions than in a global perspective? Are countries hit in different ways within each region? Does a shock in Mexican equities go through local markets to Wall Street or the other way around? Does Chile behave more like an Asian country and the Philippines more like a Latin American country (and, if so, why)? Do fundamentals seem to be correlated with the extent of contagion?

The chapter is organized as follows. Section 8.2 summarizes the contagion literature that appeared after the Mexican crisis, and distinguishes between different types of contagion. It also presents some known facts about country funds, summarizing the findings of Frankel and Schmukler (1996a, 1997). Section 8.3 displays some descriptive statistics, documenting the correlation across countries generally observed. Section 8.4, the heart of the chapter, contains Granger-causality tests of contagion. It first focuses on how country fund prices and net asset values are linked. Then, it studies through what channel a change in Mexican equities affects fund prices and NAVs in other regions, using a different methodology from previous contagion papers. Section 8.5 explores differences in patterns across countries, and relates the magnitude of spillovers to balance-of-payments fundamentals. Section 8.6 presents conclusions.

8.2   Contagion of different types

8.2.1   *Previous contagion studies*

The Mexican crisis of December 1994 has generated concerns that are specific to this crisis as well as other issues that had been raised previously, but are now being reexamined in light of the new evidence. Among them, the issue of contagion, in this episode dubbed the "tequila effect," has particularly regained attention.

A subset of the contagion papers approaches the issue as part of more comprehensive models of international financial linkages. Burki and Edwards (1995) and Folkerts-Landau et al. (1995) describe how different countries, particularly those in Latin America and Asia, were hit after the Mexican collapse. Goldfajn and Valdés (1995) provide theoretical support for how shocks are propagated to other countries, focusing on the role of financial intermediation.

Calvo and Reinhart (1995) address the issue directly by looking at weekly returns on equities and Brady bonds, for Asian and Latin American emerging markets. They find evidence of higher comovement after the Mexican crisis than before. They also find differential regional patterns, suggesting regional rather than global contagion. Valdés (1996) uses secondary market debt prices and country credit ratings to show contagion in Latin America. He demonstrates that fundamentals are unable to explain cross-country comovement of creditworthiness. On the other hand, Wolf (Chapter 9, this volume) fails to find strong evidence of contagion after controlling for sectoral composition – using data on total returns of individual stocks published by the International Finance Corporation. However, he finds a higher correlation among Asian markets, even when he controls for market fundamentals, consistent with contagion.

Several of the contagion studies mentioned earlier are either purely descriptive or use simple correlation coefficients to draw conclusions about transmission effect. Some also control for fundamentals, and look at the correlation matrix of the residuals. Comparing correlations calculated with different subsamples is one way to study links among variables. Principal component analysis has also been used. A finding of high correlation has often been claimed as evidence of contagion. However, there exist two very different interpretations of this finding, since there is no universally accepted definition of the term.

On the one hand, high cross-country correlation coefficients may be due to similar fundamentals or to common external shocks – as one would expect in a very wide variety of models. We can call these high correlations "fundamentals contagion." Bordo, Mizrach, and Schwartz (1995), for example, find high correlation among stock prices in emerging markets over the period 1984 to 1995, and yet are able to attribute most of it to fundamentals (either a correlation of in-country fundamentals, or a sharing of external fundamentals). They describe such contagion as "pseudo systemic risk."

At the other extreme, we would also find high cross-country correlations if self-fulfilling expectations make investors leave all emerging markets when a shock hits one of them. In this context, some use the term to refer to simultaneous speculative attacks or bubble-burstings that are unrelated to fundamentals. We can call this type of contagion "herding behavior contagion" or "true contagion."

An example of herding behavior modeling can be found in Calvo (1995). He shows that the tequila effect can be explained in a context of costly information and diversification opportunities. When investors have a set of investment alternatives they have less incentive to obtain costly information regarding individual countries. Investment in each particular country becomes more sensitive when investment opportunities increase. Investors are able to switch to other countries when they receive bad news about one nation. Therefore diversification leads to more ignorance and herding behavior on the part of international investors.

This tendency has been remarked upon in the past. It was said that Colombia suffered from a loss in banker confidence in the 1982 crisis along with the rest of Latin America, even though it had followed better policies than the other debtors. More recently, it has been said that many unlikely countries attracted capital inflows in 1991–93 because they were identified in investors' minds with other borrowers that had undertaken more serious reforms (Calvo, Leiderman, and Reinhart, 1993).

In between the two extreme types of contagion lie some institutional explanations for high correlations. For example, a fund that invests in Latin America markets or in all emerging markets may be led by capital losses on its Mexico holdings to sell other holdings (in order to keep its country shares in proper proportion), thereby depressing prices in other countries' stock markets. In the case of open-end funds, managers may be also forced to raise cash to meet redemptions whenever there is a price fall in one country.

We are particularly interested in the hypothesis that mutual fund managers or holders on Wall Street respond to an adverse shock in one emerging market by selling securities in other emerging markets, and that this is the specific mechanism whereby the shock is transmitted. If markets were perfectly efficient and integrated, there would be no discernible difference in the reactions of prices of country funds in New York versus the corresponding equity prices in emerging markets themselves. Standard models of correlation based on fundamentals assume perfect efficiency and integration, as do standard models of contagion based on speculative bubbles or currency crises. But the country funds do not behave in this way, as we shall see.

8.2.2   Country fund contagion

Country fund data are well suited to get at a particular aspect of what we mean by contagion. They offer an opportunity to test whether the transmission of a negative shock from one emerging market to another "passes through" the community of New York mutual funds on the way.

It also gives us the opportunity to study the effects on different regions as well as the effects on separate countries within each region. Contagion transmitted via New York may be the consequence of institutional practices, but it may also reflect herding behavior on the part of country fund managers or holders.

This chapter uses weekly data from several Asian and Latin American country funds to investigate spillover effects from one market to others. Closed-end country funds have been established as vehicles to hold equities from different foreign markets. They provide a way to invest in remote countries without having to buy equities directly in local markets. Each consists of a fixed number of shares, invested in stocks from a particular country. They are traded for a price in New York City. Their net asset value (NAV) is calculated by aggregating the values of the underlying assets at their individual prices in the domestic market and converting to U.S. dollars.

Closed-end country funds are known usually to trade on average at a discount,[3] a phenomenon called the discount puzzle. Because the price and the NAV ultimately represent the price of the same asset, one would expect them to be equal to each other, so that the discounts would be zero. However, since the shares cannot be redeemed, holding shares of a country fund is not equivalent to holding the basket of constituent stocks. In Frankel and Schmukler (1996a), we show that there is little possibility of direct or pure arbitrage. Nevertheless, one would still expect investors to react to large discounts (or premiums) by doing some kind of indirect arbitrage, which works to correct gradually over time unusually large gaps between the fund price and NAV.

Different hypotheses have been suggested to explain the gaps between country fund prices and NAVs. They necessarily rely on imperfect liquidity or frictions in the markets. Hardouvelis, La Porta, and Wizman (1994) suggest that discounts reflect international investors' sentiments. They test the idea expressed in De Long, Shleifer, Summers, and Waldmann (1990) and in Lee, Shleifer, and Thaler (1991) that noise traders interact with rational investors by driving prices away from fundamentals.

In Frankel and Schmukler (1996a) we propose that discounts may reflect expectations of international investors that differ from those of domestic investors. It is assumed that country funds are mostly held by foreign investors, while domestic investors mostly buy securities directly in the local stock markets. If foreign investors know that they are further

---

[3] Discounts are equal to $\log(\text{NAV}_t/\text{price}_t)$.

away from information, they are willing to pay on average a lower value for the same asset. This is an instance of asymmetric information studied in Frankel and Schmukler (1997).

Frankel and Schmukler (1996a) extend that argument by hypothesizing that movement in the discount reflects movement in the relative expectations of foreign investors. We test whether there is evidence of asymmetric information. We do find that before the Mexican crisis, local investors reacted as the front-runners of the crisis, as if they had a different information set. The evidence suggests that, while local investors lost confidence beforehand, the confidence of the international community collapsed only after the devaluation, and to a lesser degree.

We also find cointegrating relationships between fund prices and NAVs. Frankel and Schmukler (1997) find that although most fund prices and NAVs are nonstationary, they tend to be linked by a linear relationship in the long run. The cointegrating vectors are in general $(1, -1)$, as theory suggests. A change in the NAV is fully transmitted to its country fund price in the long run, even though in the short run the transmission is only partial, since the adjustment coefficients are relatively small.

If a change in NAV were transmitted to its price instantaneously, we would not be able to test for Granger-causality between a local market and the corresponding country fund in New York. We would only be able to test for Granger-causality among country funds. It would be impossible to distinguish between a country fund's NAV and price at all, since they would move together. In fact, however, a change in NAV takes time to be fully transmitted to its price. This means that it can have a more immediate effect on equity prices in other countries, as measured by their NAVs, than on its own fund price. In consequence, country funds enable us to test the channel through which contagion takes place: whether a shock in Mexican NAVs is directly transmitted to other countries by affecting the other country fund NAVs, prices, or both.

8.3   Correlation across countries: descriptive statistics

8.3.1   *Was there contagion?*

We begin by looking at how country funds behaved around the Mexican crisis. Figure 8.1 plots Latin American country fund NAVs and prices from mid-1994 until March 1996. The most dramatic box is the one that plots Mexican country funds around the week of the devaluation. Their NAVs and prices all turned down sharply just before the devaluation.

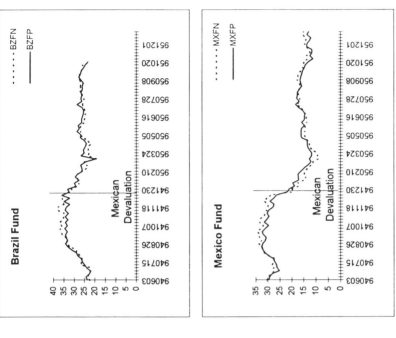

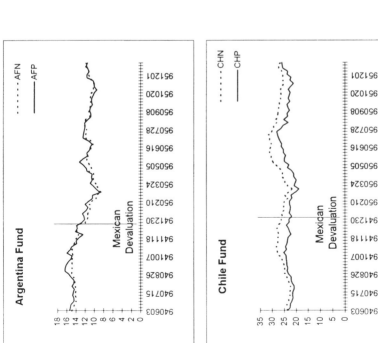

Figure 8.1. Latin American country fund NAVs and prices.

In the case of the other Latin American country funds, there was also a downturn of NAVs and prices after December 20, 1994. Although not plotted, the Latin American regional funds also fell at that time. (Their composition varies over time and a significant share of Mexican stocks might explain the fall.) The rest of the countries present less dramatic changes.

Most country funds had hit their lowest point by March 1995. Table 8.1 tabulates the percentage change in country fund prices relative to prices on December 2, 1994. It shows that most prices dropped by December 30 of that year. They continued falling by January 27, and reached their lowest prices by March 10. The percentage change was much more dramatic over the three-month period, particularly for the Latin American funds.

Emerging Asian country funds, plotted in Figure 8.2 (part A and part B), show comparable evidence, though the declines are smaller than in Latin America. Some funds, like the Korean ones, seemed initially to be unaffected by the devaluation. Other funds, including Latin American ones, display a downturn in the last quarter of 1994 (which may be due to increases in the U.S. interest rate). In summary, contagion was evident in most emerging markets by the end of January 1995, but was even more obvious by mid-March 1995. The largest decline in Asia occurred in the Philippines. The smallest decline in Latin America took place in Chile.

The Mexican crisis and its spillover effects on developing markets were also thought to cause pressures on currencies of industrial countries. The early 1995 decline in the U.S. dollar was partly attributed to this phenomenon. At that time, the Bank of Mexico used the U.S. swap facilities, and the Federal Reserve's Foreign Exchange Desk intervened to buy pesos for the account of the Bank of Mexico. The Canadian dollar also hit a nine-year low. In Europe, the Italian lira, the British pound, and the Spanish peseta declined against the stronger German deutschemark.

Several factors may explain the delay in contagion displayed in Table 8.1. The peso devaluation of December 20 was initially perceived as a Mexican balance-of-payments problem. It was after December that the fragile banking situation became evident.[4] In addition, the Mexican political situation turned more delicate by the end of February, when Raul Salinas, brother of the former president Carlos Salinas, was arrested in connection with Ruiz-Massieu assassination. The political conflict between Carlos Salinas and President Zedillo intensified by early March. Lastly, the announcement of an economic plan was postponed several

---

[4] In mid-March the Argentine financial sector was about to collapse due to large deposit withdrawals.

Table 8.1. *Percentage change in country fund prices, base date 12/2/94*

Country Fund	Symbol	By 12/30/94	By 1/27/95	By 3/10/95
Asia				
China Fund	CHN	−12.17	−13.04	−16.52
First Philippine Fund	FPF	−2.52	−19.50	−28.30
Greater China Fund	GCH	−16.38	−15.52	−16.38
India Fund	IFN	2.13	−6.38	−19.15
India Growth Fund	IGF	−15.08	−12.63	−21.79
Indonesia Fund	IF	−9.47	−18.43	−24.21
Jakarta Growth Fund	JGF	2.86	−18.10	−12.86
Jardine Fleming China Fund	JFC	−14.29	−16.22	−20.95
Jardine Fleming India Fund	JFI	−11.71	5.71	−24.32
Korea Equity Fund	KEF	−6.67	−18.67	−18.67
Korea Fund	KF	7.06	−8.24	−5.88
Korean Investment Fund	KIF	0.97	−2.91	−5.82
Malaysia Fund	MF	−10.32	−11.61	−18.06
Pakistan Investment Fund	PKF	−5.26	−18.42	−26.32
ROC Taiwan Fund	ROC	3.26	−4.35	−10.87
Singapore Fund	SGF	−6.30	−11.02	−14.96
Taiwan Equity Fund	TYW	2.15	−9.02	−15.05
Taiwan Fund	TWN	11.59	−14.29	−23.67
Templeton China World Fund	TCH	−16.33	−9.00	−21.43
Templeton Vietnam Oppty. Fund	TVF	−16.51	−13.76	−23.85
Thai Capital Fund	TC	0.00	2.41	−15.04
Thai Fund	TTF	−10.50	−9.68	−19.50
Latin America				
Argentina Fund	AF	−14.16	−19.47	−31.86
Brazil Equity	BZL	−5.00	−21.36	−43.57
Brazil Fund	BZF	−18.93	−15.71	−54.37
Chile Fund	CH	1.10	−1.64	−17.53
Emerging Mexico Fund	MEF	−30.14	−47.95	−57.53
Mexico Equity and Income Fund	MXE	−27.49	−35.67	−59.65
Mexico Fund	MXF	−27.31	−40.56	−56.63

times, which was interpreted as political inability to deal with the crisis. According to some views, MeXico's government did not present a sound macroeconomic plan until mid-March 1995. Then, Mexican financial markets started to recover.

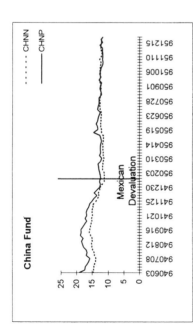

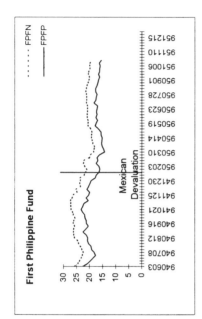

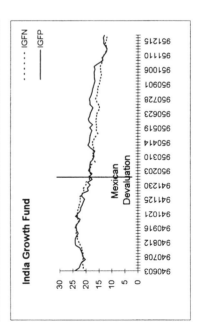

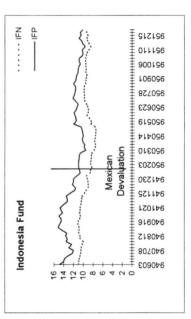

242

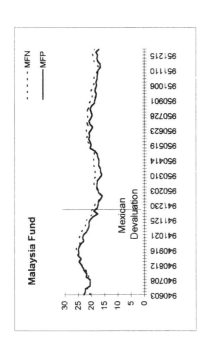

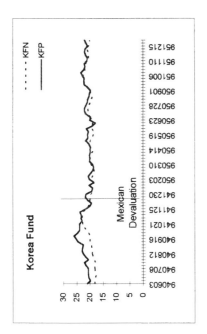

Figure 8.2. Part A: Asian country fund NAVs and prices.

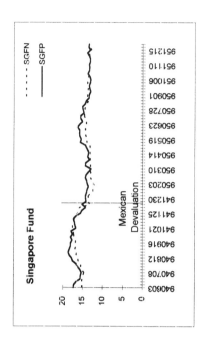

Pakistan Investment Fund

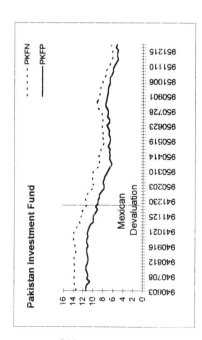

Singapore Fund

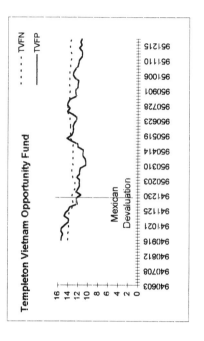

Taiwan Fund

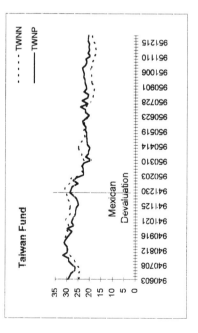

Templeton Vietnam Opportunity Fund

244

245

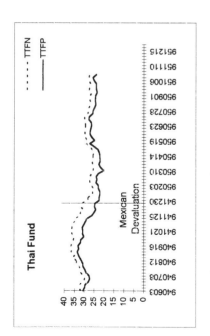

Figure 8.2. Part B: Asian country fund NAVs and prices.

Table 8.2. *Correlation of country fund prices and NAVs, Asia, 7/92–3/96*

Country fund	Symbol	CHNP	CHNN	FPFP	FPFN	GCHP	GCHN	IGFP	IGFN	IFP	IFN	JGFP	JGFN	JFCP	JFCN
China Fund	CHN	1.00	1.00	0.35	0.36	0.71	0.94	0.11	0.10	0.50	0.48	0.44	0.38	0.69	0.82
First Philippine Fund	FPF	0.35	0.36	1.00	1.00	0.32	0.28	0.13	0.07	0.37	0.34	0.34	0.29	0.31	0.23
Greater China Fund	GCH	0.71	0.94	0.32	0.28	1.00	1.00	0.10	0.08	0.42	0.50	0.36	0.39	0.74	0.85
India Growth Fund	IGF	0.11	0.10	0.13	0.07	0.10	0.08	1.00	1.00	0.17	0.05	0.15	0.03	0.02	0.08
Indonesia Fund	IF	0.50	0.48	0.37	0.34	0.42	0.50	0.17	0.05	1.00	1.00	0.60	0.79	0.47	0.43
Jakarta Growth Fund	JGF	0.44	0.38	0.34	0.29	0.36	0.39	0.15	0.03	0.60	0.79	1.00	1.00	0.40	0.36
Jardine Fleming China Fund	JFC	0.69	0.82	0.31	0.23	0.74	0.85	0.02	0.08	0.47	0.43	0.40	0.36	1.00	1.00
Korea Fund	KF	0.21	0.22	0.19	0.02	0.19	0.26	0.23	0.09	0.14	0.18	0.14	0.14	0.18	0.32
Korean Investment Fund	KIF	0.39	0.16	0.28	0.07	0.27	0.20	0.20	0.02	0.16	0.15	0.26	0.08	0.25	0.26
Malaysia Fund	MF	0.42	0.50	0.42	0.25	0.43	0.44	0.08	0.26	0.39	0.49	0.40	0.42	0.38	0.45
ROC Taiwan Fund	ROC	0.30	0.21	0.23	0.22	0.20	0.20	0.16	0.05	0.35	0.10	0.24	0.04	0.21	0.10
Singapore Fund	SGF	0.49	0.23	0.36	0.45	0.34	0.20	0.21	0.16	0.39	0.39	0.42	0.40	0.42	0.24
Taiwan Fund	TWN	0.13	0.23	0.21	0.21	0.12	0.21	0.17	-0.02	0.34	0.05	0.17	0.06	0.10	0.17
Thai Capital Fund	TC	0.53	0.55	0.42	0.31	0.46	0.52	0.11	0.17	0.38	0.47	0.45	0.36	0.45	0.51
Thai Fund	TTF	0.51	0.53	0.40	0.23	0.34	0.51	0.17	0.18	0.34	0.40	0.36	0.29	0.34	0.53

Table 8.2. *(cont.)*

Country fund	Symbol	KFP	KFN	KIFP	KIFN	MFP	MFN	ROCP	ROCN	SGFP	SGFN	TWNP	TWNN	TCP	TCN	TTFP	TTFN
China Fund	CHN	0.21	0.22	0.39	0.16	0.42	0.50	0.30	0.21	0.49	0.23	0.13	0.23	0.53	0.55	0.51	0.53
First Philippine Fund	FPF	0.19	0.02	0.28	0.07	0.42	0.25	0.23	0.22	0.36	0.45	0.21	0.21	0.42	0.31	0.40	0.23
Greater China Fund	GCH	0.19	0.26	0.27	0.20	0.43	0.44	0.20	0.20	0.34	0.20	0.12	0.21	0.46	0.52	0.34	0.51
India Growth Fund	IGF	0.23	0.09	0.20	0.02	0.08	0.26	0.16	0.05	0.21	0.16	0.17	-0.02	0.11	0.17	0.17	0.18
Indonesia Fund	IF	0.14	0.18	0.16	0.15	0.39	0.49	0.35	0.10	0.39	0.39	0.34	0.05	0.38	0.47	0.34	0.40
Jakarta Growth Fund	JGF	0.14	0.14	0.26	0.08	0.40	0.42	0.24	0.04	0.42	0.40	0.17	0.06	0.45	0.36	0.36	0.29
Jardine Fleming China Fund	JFC	0.18	0.32	0.25	0.26	0.38	0.45	0.21	0.10	0.42	0.24	0.10	0.17	0.45	0.51	0.34	0.53
Korea Fund	KF	1.00	1.00	0.58	0.83	0.23	0.16	0.07	0.02	0.18	0.07	0.12	0.05	0.17	0.17	0.34	0.26
Korean Investment Fund	KIF	0.58	0.83	1.00	1.00	0.28	0.04	0.08	-0.03	0.27	0.10	0.16	0.00	0.24	0.17	0.36	0.21
Malaysia Fund	MF	0.23	0.16	0.28	0.04	1.00	1.00	0.11	0.14	0.44	0.49	0.21	-0.02	0.49	0.49	0.37	0.46
ROC Taiwan Fund	ROC	0.07	0.02	0.08	-0.03	0.11	0.14	1.00	1.00	0.36	0.17	0.50	0.51	0.29	0.17	0.32	0.10
Singapore Fund	SGF	0.18	0.07	0.27	0.10	0.44	0.49	0.36	0.17	1.00	1.00	0.28	0.12	0.41	0.32	0.46	0.23
Taiwan Fund	TWN	0.12	0.05	0.16	0.00	0.21	-0.02	0.50	0.51	0.28	0.12	1.00	1.00	0.27	0.21	0.38	0.15
Thai Capital Fund	TC	0.17	0.17	0.24	0.17	0.49	0.49	0.29	0.17	0.41	0.32	0.27	0.21	1.00	1.00	0.70	0.91
Thai Fund	TTF	0.34	0.26	0.36	0.21	0.37	0.46	0.32	0.10	0.46	0.23	0.38	0.15	0.70	0.91	1.00	1.00

Notes: Country fund symbols in column headings with "P" suffixes denote price correlations; symbols with "N" suffixes denote NAV correlations. All variables are first-differenced logarithms.

8.3.2   *Are comovements higher within regional markets than across them?*

As a more systematic approach to the empirical analysis, we look at whether the shock in Mexico may have affected Latin American markets more strongly than Asian markets. We find that there is some degree of intraregional comovement. However, it is evident that investors did not treat each country fund equally. This section analyzes the extent of comovement.

Table 8.2 shows correlations of first-differenced Asian country fund prices and NAVs over the period-July 1992 to March 1996; Tables 8.3 and 8.4 do so for Latin America, and for the cross-correlations between the two regions.[5] All the variables have been first-differenced, since we found in our previous work that most NAVs and prices cannot reject nonstationarity.

Two main conclusions can be drawn from the pattern of correlations. First, Latin American NAVs show higher comovement among themselves than do prices of Latin American funds. (For 30 out of 42 country pairs the NAV correlation is higher than the fund price correlation, in terms of changes.) These relationships hold especially for Mexican country funds. Second, the cross-correlations among fund prices are larger than the cross-correlations among Asian and Latin American NAVs. (For 83 out of 105 country pairs the country fund price cross-correlation is higher than the NAV correlation.) In the case of Asia, it is more difficult to suggest an overall conclusion.

The correlation pattern supports the idea that the Mexican crisis may have impacted Latin America more directly, and to a greater extent, than Asia. It also suggests that the shock to Asia may have been transmitted via changes in country fund prices. More generally, the correlations suggest that fund prices and NAVs tend to be more connected to the market where they are traded than to the country where the underlying assets are located.

If markets were perfectly integrated, country fund NAVs and prices would move in the same way. But the fact that there is segmentation allows us to study the reaction of different kinds of investors to shocks. If cross-country correlations were as high for NAVs as they are for fund prices, then one would most naturally attribute the correlations to common fundamentals. However, fund prices in Asia and Latin America are more highly correlated across regions than NAVs. This suggests the

---

[5] We excluded the country funds that started trading after 1992, in order to avoid working with a reduced sample.

Table 8.3. *Correlation of country fund prices and NAVs, Latin America, 7/92–3/96*

Country fund	Symbol	AFP	AFN	BZFP	BZFN	BZLP	BZLN	CHP	CHN	MEFP	MEFN	MXEP	MXEN	MXFP	MXFN
Argentina Fund	AF	1.00	1.00	0.23	0.27	0.26	0.19	0.34	0.36	0.32	0.53	0.32	0.48	0.30	0.48
Brazil Equity Fund	BZL	0.23	0.27	1.00	1.00	0.83	0.82	0.28	0.14	0.16	0.33	0.27	0.28	0.30	0.39
Brazil Fund	BZF	0.26	0.19	0.83	0.82	1.00	1.00	0.31	0.06	0.20	0.23	0.25	0.18	0.26	0.33
Chile Fund	CH	0.34	0.36	0.28	0.14	0.31	0.06	1.00	1.00	0.20	0.34	0.28	0.34	0.30	0.26
Emerging Mexico Fund	MEF	0.32	0.53	0.16	0.33	0.20	0.23	0.20	0.34	1.00	1.00	0.53	0.88	0.75	0.86
Mexico Equity and Income Fund	MXE	0.32	0.48	0.27	0.28	0.25	0.18	0.28	0.34	0.53	0.88	1.00	1.00	0.62	0.71
Mexico Fund	MXF	0.30	0.48	0.30	0.39	0.26	0.33	0.30	0.26	0.75	0.86	0.62	0.71	1.00	1.00

Notes: Country fund symbols in column headings with "P" suffixes denote price correlations; symbols with "N" suffixes denote NAV correlations. All variables are first-differenced logarithms.

Table 8.4. *Correlation of country fund prices and NAVs, Asia–Latin America, 7/92–3/96*

Country Fund	Symbol	AFP	AFN	BZLP	BZFN	BZFP	BZLN	CHP	CHN	MEFP	MEFN	MXEP	MXEN	MXFP	MXFN
China Fund	CHN	0.14	0.26	0.17	0.12	0.14	0.12	0.28	0.18	0.19	0.33	0.18	0.24	0.26	0.30
First Philippine Fund	FPF	0.27	0.13	0.10	-0.04	0.16	0.05	0.27	0.05	0.23	0.14	0.20	0.11	0.22	0.20
Greater China Fund	GCH	0.13	0.20	0.17	0.07	0.10	0.13	0.10	0.24	0.17	0.22	0.06	0.13	0.24	0.17
India Growth Fund	IGF	0.03	-0.03	0.04	-0.01	0.09	0.07	0.19	0.01	0.22	-0.10	0.19	-0.07	0.18	-0.09
Indonesia Fund	IF	0.20	0.13	0.14	0.14	0.11	0.13	0.32	0.15	0.16	0.11	0.15	0.06	0.16	0.11
Jakarta Growth Fund	JGF	0.20	0.16	0.17	0.12	0.16	0.08	0.30	0.14	0.07	0.13	0.13	0.09	0.13	0.14
Jardine Fleming China Fund	JFC	0.24	0.15	0.23	0.03	0.18	0.09	0.26	0.15	0.22	0.18	0.18	0.08	0.28	0.13
Korea Fund	KF	0.11	0.16	0.13	0.10	0.08	0.07	0.14	0.25	0.15	0.15	0.25	0.12	0.15	0.10
Korean Investment Fund	KIF	0.17	0.13	0.21	0.06	0.25	0.05	0.20	0.15	0.14	0.04	0.19	0.00	0.15	0.03
Malaysia Fund	MF	0.20	0.25	0.20	0.03	0.14	0.00	0.20	0.11	0.25	0.22	0.27	0.24	0.27	0.21
ROC Taiwan Fund	ROC	0.11	0.11	0.19	-0.01	0.12	0.01	0.15	0.11	0.06	0.11	0.08	0.05	0.21	0.13
Singapore Fund	SGF	0.11	0.08	0.30	-0.08	0.27	-0.04	0.34	0.10	0.15	0.06	0.20	0.02	0.28	0.03
Taiwan Fund	TWN	0.19	0.02	0.18	0.03	0.17	0.09	0.22	0.04	0.00	0.04	0.16	-0.05	0.15	0.01
Thai Capital Fund	TC	0.18	0.08	0.26	0.08	0.21	0.03	0.25	0.08	0.11	0.10	0.15	0.04	0.22	0.05
Thai Fund	TTF	0.20	0.16	0.23	0.10	0.24	0.06	0.33	0.14	0.07	0.24	0.17	0.17	0.16	0.10

Notes: Country fund symbols in column headings with "P" suffixes denote price correlations; symbols with "N" suffixes denote NAV correlations. All variables are first-differenced logarithms.

possibility of overreaction on the part of New York investors. Joint changes in fund prices may reflect changes in U.S. investors' sentiments with respect to emerging markets, not related to fundamentals.

8.4 Granger-causality tests

8.4.1 *Do the Granger-causality results support the previous finding?*

As a second approach to studying the degree of regional comovement, we estimate all the possible combinations of Granger-causality tests. In other words, we look at how past changes in country fund NAVs and prices as well as discounts affect present changes of country fund NAVs and prices. We separately test whether each country fund Granger-causes each of the other country funds, with respect to both price and NAV. We work with an error–correction model specification, due to our previous finding of cointegration between country fund prices and NAVs. The models estimated are:

$$\Delta P^a_t = \varpi^{\mathrm{I}} + \alpha^{\mathrm{I}} disc^a_{t-1} + \sum_{i=1}^{L} \beta^{\mathrm{I}}_{1i}\Delta N^a_{t-i} + \sum_{i=1}^{L} \beta^{\mathrm{I}}_{2i}\Delta P^a_{t-i} + \gamma^{\mathrm{I}} disc^b_{t-1}$$

$$+ \sum_{i=1}^{L} \kappa^{\mathrm{I}}_{1i}\Delta N^b_{t-i} + \sum_{i=1}^{L} \kappa^{\mathrm{I}}_{2i}\Delta P^b_{t-i} + \tau^{\mathrm{I}} MXFdisc^a_{t-1}$$

$$+ \sum_{i=1}^{L} \theta^{\mathrm{I}}_{1i}\Delta MXFN_{t-i} + \sum_{i=1}^{L} \theta^{\mathrm{I}}_{2i}\Delta MXFP_{t-i} + \sum_{i=1}^{L} \omega^{\mathrm{I}}_i\Delta tbill_{t-i} + \upsilon_{1t},$$

$$\Delta N^a_t = \varpi^{\mathrm{II}} + \alpha^{\mathrm{II}} disc^a_{t-1} + \sum_{i=1}^{L} \beta^{\mathrm{II}}_{1i}\Delta N^a_{t-i} + \sum_{i=1}^{L} \beta^{\mathrm{II}}_{2i}\Delta P^a_{t-i} + \gamma^{\mathrm{II}} disc^b_{t-1}$$

$$+ \sum_{i=1}^{L} \kappa^{\mathrm{II}}_{1i}\Delta N^b_{t-i} + \sum_{i=1}^{L} \kappa^{\mathrm{II}}_{2i}\Delta P^b_{t-i} + \tau^{\mathrm{II}} MXFdisc^a_{t-1}$$

$$+ \sum_{i=1}^{L} \theta^{\mathrm{II}}_{1i}\Delta MXFN_{t-i} + \sum_{i=1}^{L} \theta^{\mathrm{II}}_{2i}\Delta MXFP_{t-i} + \sum_{i=1}^{L} \omega^{\mathrm{II}}_i\Delta tbill_{t-i} + \upsilon_{2t}.$$

We estimate each equation separately to see the effect of each country fund's NAV (denoted by N) and price (P) on other NAVs and prices. Country fund a is the endogenous variable while country fund b is the exogenous variable in the model. (The delta operator Δ denotes lagged first differences.) We control for changes in the U.S. interest rate (*tbill*), because Calvo, Leiderman, and Reinhart (1993) and others find it to be the principal external factor explaining capital inflow episodes in emerging markets in the early 1990s. We also control for changes in the NAV and price of the biggest Mexican fund (MXF).[6] Furthermore, due to the presence of cointegration we include lagged fund discounts (*disc*), as error–correction terms associated with restricted cointegrating vectors. Such restrictions on price and NAV appear plausible since, as reported previously, we have tested for cointegrating vectors and found them in general to be $(1, -1)$.[7]

The results are summarized in Tables 8.5 and 8.6. (Detailed results can be found in Frankel and Schmukler [1996b, appendix 2].) The tables tabulate Wald statistics that test the following joint hypotheses:

$$H_0:K_1^I = K_2^I = \gamma^I = 0$$

  $\Rightarrow$ country fund b does not Granger-cause
  country fund a price,

$$H_0:K_1^{II} = K_2^{II} = \gamma^{II} = 0$$

  $\Rightarrow$ country fund b does not Granger-cause
  country fund a NAV,

where Ks stand for the vector of k coefficients. We tried different lag specifications but only report the two-lag results.[8]

Tables 8.5 and 8.6 present the Granger-causality results for the largest country fund in each country of Asia and Latin America, respectively. These funds, listed along the left-hand margin of the tables, are taken to be representative. The first four columns of figures report the percentage of cases in which the prices and NAVs of each of these funds is Granger-caused ("explained by") or Granger-causes ("explains") all other Asian and Latin American funds (as indicated by a 10 percent significance level for the Wald statistics). The second and third sets of four columns report the percentage of cases of significant Granger-causality tests for other Asian and Latin America funds separately.

Tables 8.5 and 8.6 confirm the findings of the correlation results in Tables 8.2, 8.3, and 8.4. Latin American NAVs are more explained by Latin American funds than are Latin American fund prices. Latin American funds also explain changes in NAVs more than changes in fund prices. Within Asia, the evidence turns less conclusive. Some

---

[6] For instance, if we do not include the Mexico Fund we would artificially be giving explanatory power to the Argentina Fund NAV, which is very correlated with Mexican fund NAVs. It might also introduce omitted variable biases.

[7] Frankel and Schmukler (1997) test different specifications, including simultaneous estimation of the cointegrating vector. Those results lead us to impose the restrictions here.

[8] The results appear robust to various lag structures. We finally chose the two-lag specification since, following the general-to-specific methodology, we found that more lags were not statistically significant.

Table 8.5. *Significant Granger-causality test results, Asia, 1/4/85–3/8/96 (in percent)*

Country fund	Symbol	All funds				Asian funds				Latin American funds			
		Price is explained by	Explains price of	NAV is explained by	Explains NAV of	Price is explained by	Explains price of	NAV is explained by	Explains NAV of	Price is explained by	Explains price of	NAV is explained by	Explains NAV of
China Fund	CHN	17	21	28	14	19	29	33	19	14	0	14	0
First Philippine Fund	FPF	34	17	28	21	33	24	29	24	43	0	29	14
India Growth Fund	IGF	41	14	21	17	43	14	24	19	43	14	14	14
Indonesia Fund	IF	31	21	28	0	24	29	33	0	57	0	14	0
Korea Fund	KF	24	38	10	41	29	43	14	38	14	29	0	57
Malaysia Fund	MF	14	17	7	34	14	10	5	33	14	43	14	43
Pakistan Investment Fund	PKF	17	21	24	24	19	19	33	29	14	29	0	14
Singapore Fund	SGF	31	7	34	24	38	10	33	10	14	0	43	71
Taiwan Fund	TWN	28	14	31	10	29	14	33	5	29	14	29	29
Templeton Vietnam Oppty. Fund	TVF	14	14	21	14	14	10	19	19	14	29	29	0
Thai Fund	TTF	10	21	31	41	10	29	38	52	14	0	14	14
Average		24	18	24	22	25	21	27	23	25	14	18	23

Notes: Numbers indicate the percent of cases for which the Wald statistic was significant at 10%. Asia has a total of 22 country funds; Latin America has a total of 7 country funds. Beginning of sample range varies by country fund; see Table 8.A1.

Table 8.6. *Significant Granger-causality test results, Latin America, 1/4/85–3/8/96 (in percent)*

Country fund	Symbol	All funds				Asian funds				Latin American funds			
		Price is explained by	Explains price of	NAV is explained by	Explains NAV of	Price is explained by	Explains price of	NAV is explained by	Explains NAV of	Price is explained by	Explains price of	NAV is explained by	Explains NAV of
Argentina Fund	AF	7	10	14	14	5	14	9	18	17	0	33	0
Brazil Fund	BZF	17	34	28	10	14	45	27	14	33	0	33	0
Chile Fund	CH	14	7	7	7	14	5	5	5	17	17	17	17
Mexico Fund	MXF	3	69	17	24	5	73	18	9	0	67	17	83
Average		10	30	16	14	9	34	15	11	17	21	25	25

Notes: Numbers indicate the percent of cases for which the Wald statistic was significant at 10%. Asia has a total of 22 country funds; Latin America has a total of 7 country funds. Beginning of sample range varies by country fund; see Table 8.A1.

countries appear to be more connected through NAVs, whereas others are more related through country fund prices. Nevertheless, averaging the figures across countries suggests that Asian NAVs are explained to a greater extent by Asian country funds than are Asian fund prices. Asian funds also explain more changes in Asian NAVs than in Asian fund prices.

The link between the two regions clearly suggests that Latin American funds explain Asian country fund prices more than Asian fund prices explain Latin American fund prices. On average, Latin American funds explain prices of Asian funds 34 percent of the time, while the reverse causality, from Asian funds to Latin American prices, holds only 9 percent of the time. The prices of Asian funds are caused by Latin American funds more often than are NAVs.

We should remark that although the data in some cases go from 1985 to 1996, most country funds only started trading in the 1990s.[9] Therefore, these results may reflect largely the big shock of the 1994 Mexican crisis. This may explain why there seems to be Granger-causality from Latin America to Asia and not otherwise. Some years from now we will be able to test whether the relationships revealed here continue to hold.

8.4.2   Did contagion "pass through" New York?

In this section we test whether there is contagion specifically from Mexico and, if so, whether the transmission passes through New York. In order to do that, we put together part of the results from the previous Granger-causality estimations in Tables 8.7 and 8.8. We look at how changes in the biggest Mexican fund Granger-causes prices and NAVs of other Asian and Latin American funds. We only report the cases of the Mexico Fund (MXF) as an exogenous variable, since that fund seems to be the driving force among all Mexican funds. The other two Mexican funds, which are appreciably smaller in size, were found to be Granger-caused by changes in MXF.

The separate estimation of equations for fund prices and NAVs allows us to look at the channel through which contagion takes place. A shock in a Mexican NAV may affect both the other country fund price directly, as well as the other NAV. It may also affect the other NAV, and through it the other country fund price. Conversely, the channel may go through fund prices to NAVs.

We know that there is cointegration between each country fund NAV and price. Therefore, a permanent shock to NAVs (prices) will prompt

---

[9] The dates of initial public offerings (IPOs) are detailed in Appendix Table 8.A1.

Table 8.7. *Granger-causality of Asian funds by the Mexico Fund, 1/4/85–3/8/96*

Country fund	Symbol	H_0: Price is not Granger-caused	H_0: NAV is not Granger-caused
China Fund	CHN	18.98***	4.99
First Philippine Fund	FPF	19.03***	11.17**
Greater China Fund	GCH	5.79	8.15
India Fund	IFN	14.63**	2.88
India Growth Fund	IGF	11.67**	4.06
Indonesia Fund	IF	15.72***	9.16
Jakarta Growth Fund	JGF	12.26**	7.52
Jardine Fleming China Fund	JFC	6.92	4.92
Jardine Fleming India Fund	JFI	4.21	4.77
Korea Equity Fund	KEF	10.22*	2.68
Korea Fund	KF	23.14***	7.74
Korean Investment Fund	KIF	11.73**	5.63
Malaysia Fund	MF	10.87*	4.30
Pakistan Investment Fund	PKF	11.93**	3.05
ROC Taiwan Fund	ROC	5.85	4.04
Singapore Fund	SGF	21.66***	4.93
Taiwan Equity Fund	TYW	3.38	2.84
Taiwan Fund	TWN	17.43***	6.07
Templeton China World Fund	TCH	9.00	4.86
Templeton Vietnam Oppty. Fund	TVF	9.85*	11.38**
Thai Capital Fund	TC	17.60***	6.85
Thai Fund	TTF	20.38***	6.73
Percentage of null hypotheses rejected at			
10%		73	9
5%		59	9

Notes: Granger-causality tests reported as Wald statistics. * = significance at 10% level, ** = at 5% level, and *** = at 1% level. Beginning of sample range varies by country fund; see Table 8.A1.

prices (NAVs) to adjust gradually to the long-run relationship. The model specification allows us to estimate whether the long-run effect goes through the price–NAV cointegration, or whether both country fund prices and NAVs are affected directly from changes in the Mexico Fund. In other words, by controlling for past changes in the endogenous country fund NAV and price, we can test whether exogenous past

Table 8.8. *Granger-causality of Latin American funds by the Mexico Fund, 1/4/85–3/8/96*

Country fund	Symbol	H_0: Price is not Granger-caused	H_0: NAV is not Granger-caused
Argentina Fund	AF	7.95	11.26**
Brazil Equity Fund	BZL	14.34**	6.81
Brazil Fund	BZF	14.00**	13.07**
Chile Fund	CH	16.45***	13.24**
Emerging Mexico Fund	MEF	2.85	18.11***
Mexico Equity and Income Fund	MXE	25.83***	35.86***
Percentage of null hypotheses rejected at			
10%		67	83
5%		67	83

Notes: Granger-causality test results reported as Wald statistics. * = significance at 10% level, ** = at 5% level, and *** = at 1% level. Beginning of sample range varies by country fund; see Table 8.A1.

changes in MXF are statistically significant in explaining both current changes in country fund NAVs and prices, either one of them, or neither of them.

The hypothesis tests reported in Tables 8.7 and 8.8 show that, at a 10 percent significance level, Mexico Granger-causes 83 percent of Latin American NAVs and 67 percent of Latin American fund prices. At the same time, it Granger-causes 73 percent of Asian fund prices and 9 percent of Asian NAVs. Similar results are found for a 5 percent significance level. This evidence supports the view that Mexican shocks may have passed to Asia through New York, while they hit Latin American stock markets more directly.

This kind of direct contagion to Latin America and indirect spillover to Asia suggests that crises such as during December 1994 are somehow regional, at least in the short run. This was also supported by the correlation patterns and by Tables 8.5 and 8.6, which show how country fund NAVs and prices comove. Latin American funds appear more connected with the Mexican funds than are those of Asia. This is consistent with the argument of Calvo and Reinhart (1995) that the crisis was more regional than global. Nevertheless, there is transmission to Asia.

8.5   Why are some countries affected differently than others?

8.5.1   *Different patterns in different countries?*

Even though we have already found that fund NAVs and prices are correlated with other fund NAVs and prices, depending on the market in which they trade, this section asks whether individual countries react in different ways. A first glance at Table 8.1 points in that direction. By March 10, 1995, Brazilian and Argentine fund prices had suffered the biggest falls, while Chile was the least affected in Latin America. Table 8.6 also shows that Mexico is basically the only country that explains changes in NAVs and prices within Latin America country funds. The two biggest Latin American countries, Brazil and Mexico, are the only ones in the region that explain changes in Asian fund prices, and to a lesser degree Asian NAVs.

Although the entire region is affected by a shock like the Mexican crisis, each country is not hit in the same way. Chile, a country thought to have strong economic fundamentals, is much less influenced than those that are considered to be in economic situations similar to Mexico's, like Argentina. This conclusion is consistent with other findings. Burki and Edwards (1995) point out that Argentina, Brazil, and Venezuela were the countries that suffered the most severe consequences after the Mexican crisis, while Chile and Colombia showed a stronger position. The Folkerts-Landau et al. (1995) section on spillover effects points out that the Argentine and Brazilian stock markets were the most affected by the 1994 peso devaluation.

In Asia, the First Philippine Fund price decreased 28 percent, almost the same as Argentina's fall. Other countries present mixed evidence, depending on the country fund we look at. The sharpest declines were experienced in Indonesia, Pakistan, Taiwan, and Vietnam. Table 8.5 confirms this relationship more generally. It shows that the two countries whose country fund NAVs and prices are more often explained by Latin America than by Asia are the Philippines and Indonesia. At the other extreme, Korean funds were the least hit by the crisis, falling only around 6 percent after December 1994. Again, this finding holds more generally: the Korea Fund is the Asian fund whose price and NAV is least often explained by Latin America.

Tables 8.7 and 8.8 also help to understand how the Mexico Fund is related to other country funds. As pointed out in the previous section, Table 8.7 says that most Asian country funds are hit through changes in New York, rather than in Mexico City. The only countries that turn out not to be directly explained by the Mexico Fund are big countries like

China and India, as well as Taiwan. Note that these tests reflect average relationships over our sample period, whereas the Mexican crisis refers only to one specific point in time.

The price declines reported in Table 8.1 might also be due to external sources unrelated to Mexico. Nevertheless, there is some correspondence. The countries whose funds are hit both directly and indirectly are the Philippines and Vietnam. These are among the funds that experienced the greatest decline after December 1994. The Philippines has often in the literature been described as more closely related to Latin America than to Asia.

Table 8.8 shows that the NAV of Argentina, the country most associated with Mexico, is hit directly. The Argentina Fund price is affected through changes in the Argentine NAV–price relationship. This can be interpreted as Argentina's NAV being very sensitive and reacting very fast to changes in Mexican NAVs. The Mexico Fund is not statistically significant in explaining the Argentina Fund price because this effect is entirely captured by the Argentine NAV (which is included in the regression).

8.5.2 Is contagion related to fundamentals?

We have seen that countries appear to be affected in different ways by the crisis in Mexico. We now ask why. We take 1994 economic fundamentals as exogenous, and relate them to the different contagion measures that we have developed: the fall in fund prices from December 2, 1994, to March 10, 1995, and the results from the Granger-causality test.[10] We do not perform serious econometric analysis since we only have twenty-nine country funds. We would need more country funds to carry out a more comprehensive analysis. Furthermore, it is beyond the scope of this chapter to determine why spillover effects from the Mexican crisis were so widespread. Notwithstanding, we are able to get a first impression on why spillovers happened in the way described previously.

Figure 8.3 suggests that the fall in country fund prices after December 1994 was positively related to changes in the debt–export ratio and to the current account deficit–GNP ratio. Descriptive statistics for the fundamentals and simple regression results are reported in Tables 8.9 and 8.10. Countries with weaker external positions were the ones that suffered

---

[10] Data on economic fundamentals obtained from the World Bank *World Debt Tables* included GNP, exports of goods and services, current account balance, international reserves, and international debt stock. U.S. interest rate data were obtained from the International Finance Division data base, Board of Governors of the Federal Reserve System, Washington, D.C.

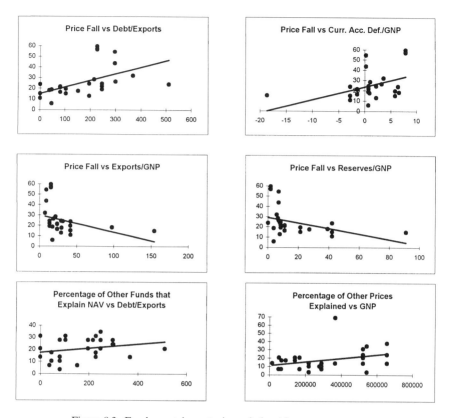

Figure 8.3. Fundamentals-contagion relationships.

higher negative spillover effects. Specifically, the countries with the most sensitive equity funds tend to be those with the highest debt–export ratios: in Asia they are Vietnam, Pakistan, India, the Philippines, and Indonesia. The least sensitive tend to have the lowest debt–export ratios: Taiwan, Malaysia, and Korea.

Price falls of country funds also appear to be negatively related to two other ratios: exports–GNP and reserves–GNP. The former relationship says that more open countries appear to suffer less contagion. This can be interpreted as investors viewing open economies as more reliable, because the cost of a policy reversal or default is higher. Reinforcing this interpretation is that the debt–export ratio is found significant in explaining the country fund price fall, while the debt–GNP ratio was not. Sachs (1985) made a very similar point. Given the size of their external debts,

Table 8.9. *Fundamentals ratios 1994 (in percent)*

	CADEF/EXP	CADEF/GNP	EXP/GNP	DEBT/EXP	DEBT/GNP	RES/GNP
Latin America						
Argentina	47.9	3.6	7.6	368.0	27.8	5.8
Brazil	2.4	0.2	9.3	298.2	27.9	7.1
Chile	3.0	0.9	30.0	151.8	45.5	27.4
Mexico	51.2	7.9	15.4	228.1	35.2	1.8
Asia						
China	-6.1	-1.5	24.0	80.4	19.3	11.1
India	5.2	0.7	13.8	247.5	34.2	8.4
Indonesia	7.5	2.2	29.3	195.8	57.4	7.9
Korea	3.9	0.7	17.7	46.9	15.3	3.9
Malaysia	6.7	6.6	97.9	37.7	36.9	39.2
Pakistan	17.3	3.3	18.8	300.4	56.6	7.1
Philippines	4.8	1.0	21.7	215.7	46.8	6.7
Singapore	-12.1	-18.7	154.3	NA	NA	91.0
Taiwan	-6.7	-2.8	42.0	0.4	0.2	42.1
Thailand	13.9	5.8	41.8	103.1	43.1	21.4
Vietnam	20.3	6.4	31.6	510.7	161.3	0.1

Notes: CADEF = current account deficit; EXP = exports of goods and services; DEBT = international debt stock; and RES = international reserves.

Table 8.10. *Determinants of country fund declines*

Dependent variable	Constant	Independent variable		Adjusted R-squared
Price fall	15.11	0.06	Debt/exports	0.23
	(3.58)	(3.02)		
Price fall	23.56	1.25	Curr. acc.	0.15
	(8.93)	(2.43)	deficit/GNP	
Price fall	29.98	−0.16	Exports/GNP	0.07
	(7.67)	(−1.76)		
Price fall	29.29	−0.27	International	0.09
	(8.44)	(−1.93)	reserves/GNP	
Percentage of other funds that explain the NAV	17.43 (6.59)	0.02 (1.36)	Debt/exports	0.03
Percentage of other fund prices explained	11.30 (2.64)	0.00002 (1.81)	GNP	0.08

Notes: Results reported for regression of price decline over period 12/2/94 to 3/10/95 on economic fundamentals, for 29 country funds. T-statistics in parentheses.

he argues that Latin American countries were hit more strongly mainly because of their weak export sectors.

In addition, we take the percentage of cases that each NAV is explained by other country funds in the sample-wide causality tests, and relate it to the debt–export ratio. We find that countries with higher proportional debt stocks tend to be more sensitive, in that their equity prices are explained by shocks in other countries. Finally, we find that countries with large GNPs are more likely to have spillover effects on other countries than are small economies. The bigger the country, the more changes in its country fund NAVs or prices explain other fund prices. This finding is consistent with Calvo and Reinhart (1995), who find one-way causality from large to small countries. They show that the capital account balances of small countries are affected by changes in larger countries in the region, but not conversely.

We have also studied the dynamics of contagion. We generated impulse-response functions and calculated variance decompositions. We analyzed how shocks in the Mexico Fund NAV and price are transmitted to other country fund prices. Shocks in Mexico appear to have more permanent and bigger effects in Latin America than in Asia. In the latter case, some country funds exhibit price overshooting soon after the shock. The long-run effect is less important for Asian than for Latin American country funds. The variance decomposition results are very sensitive to the ordering of equations. We do not report these results in order to save space, and because of their lack of robustness.

8.6   Conclusion

This chapter used a set of data on closed-end country funds to test contagion. It showed how shocks such as the Mexican devaluation crisis of December 1994 may have been transmitted to other emerging markets. It confirmed some previous suppositions on how Asia and Latin America were affected.

We first showed that both Asian and Latin American country fund prices suffered a significant drop after the Mexican crisis. We then illustrated that Latin American NAVs show high comovement among themselves, compared with the price correlations. We found similar results for country fund prices across regions (traded in New York), compared with NAVs across regions (traded in the local markets). These fund prices and NAVs seem to be not only related to the underlying assets, but also to the markets where they trade. The overall evidence for Asia is less conclusive. We estimated all possible combinations of three-variable country fund models in an error–correction form. These models allowed us to test for Granger-causality. The results from these estimations are consistent with the pattern of correlations.

We used bivariate error–correction models to test whether the biggest Mexican fund helps to predict changes in other fund NAVs and prices. We showed, using the Mexico Fund, that Mexican shocks may have been transmitted directly to Latin American NAVs. At the same time, the effect appears to pass through New York to Asia. Changes in the Mexico Fund affect Asian country fund prices, but not NAVs, once we control for lagged changes in NAVs and prices.

Finally, we studied whether the contagion is purely regional. We found that individual countries were affected differently. The Philippines, usually claimed to be similar to Latin America, was hit directly from Mexico. Argentina, the Latin American country thought to have similar economic fundamentals to Mexico, was also hit directly. Furthermore, when we relate the extent of the crisis with some measures of fundamentals, we find interesting results. Price falls in country funds after December 1994 are positively related to weak fundamental measures, while they are negatively related to strong fundamental ones.

Similarly, those NAVs that are seen to be especially sensitive throughout the sample tend to have large debt–exports ratios. This is consistent with the general finding of stronger vulnerability to contagion in Latin America than in Asia, as well as deviations of Chile and the Philippines (respectively) from the general finding. In addition, contagion appears to be more powerful when coming from large countries than small ones.

In this chapter, we tested whether there is evidence of contagion. However, we did not test if that contagion is due to herding behavior or fundamentals contagion. Investors may have sold other country funds because of generalized fears with respect to Latin America, or because they perceive the countries in the region as having similar fundamentals. Nevertheless, our finding that contagion often passes through the New York investor community suggests that institutional details play a role, contrary to the pure models of fully integrated efficient markets. At the same time, our finding that such variables as debt–export ratios help determine vulnerability suggests that economic fundamentals also play a role, contrary to the pure models of speculation and contagion as herd behavior.

Appendix Table 8.A1. *Closed-end country funds and their initial public offering (IPO) dates*

Country funds	Symbol	IPO Date
Argentina Fund	AF	10/11/91
Asia Pacific Fund	APB	2/24/87
Asia Tigers Fund	GRR	11/18/93
Brazil Equity Fund	BZL	4/3/92
Brazil Fund	BZF	3/31/88
Chile Fund	CH	9/26/89
China Fund	CHN	7/10/92
Emerging Mexico Fund	MEF	10/2/90
Emerging Tigers Fund	TGF	2/25/94
First Philippine Fund	FPF	11/8/89
Fidelity Adv. Emerging Asia Fund	FAE	3/18/94
Greater China Fund	GCH	7/15/92
India Fund	IFN	2/14/94
India Growth Fund	IGF	8/12/88
Indonesia Fund	IF	3/1/90
Jakarta Growth Fund	JGF	4/10/90
Jardine Fleming China Fund	JFC	7/16/92
Jardine Fleming India Fund	JFI	3/3/94

Appendix Table 8.A1. *(cont.)*

Country funds	Symbol	IPO Date
Korea Equity Fund	KEF	11/24/93
Korea Fund	KF	8/22/84
Korean Investment Fund	KIF	2/13/92
Latin America DLR Income Fund	LBF	7/24/92
Latin America Equity	LAQ	10/22/91
Latin America Discovery	LDF	6/16/92
Latin America Investment	LAM	7/25/90
Malaysia Fund	MF	5/8/87
Mexico Equity & Income	MXE	8/14/90
Mexican Fund	MXF	6/3/81
Pakistan Investment Fund	PKF	12/16/93
Roc Taiwan Fund	ROC	5/12/89
Singapore Fund	SGF	7/24/90
Schroder Asian Growth Fund	SHF	12/22/93
Scudder New Asia Fund	SAF	6/18/87
Taiwan Equity Fund	TYW	7/18/94
Taiwan Fund	TWN	12/16/83
Templeton China World Fund	TCH	9/9/93
Templeton Vietnam Oppty. Fund	TVF	9/15/94
Thai Capital Fund	TC	5/22/90
Thai Fund	TTF	2/17/88

References

Bordo, Michael D., Bruce Mizrach, and Anna J. Schwartz (1995). "Real versus Pseudo-International Systemic Risk: Some Lessons from History," NBER Working Paper No. 5371, December. Cambridge, Mass.

Burki, Shahid Javed, and Sebastian Edwards (1995). "Latin America after Mexico: Quickening the Pace," August. Unpublished manuscript, World Bank, Washington, D.C.

Calvo, Guillermo (1995). "Varieties of Capital Market Crises." Center for International Economics Working Paper No. 16, University of Maryland at College Park.

Calvo, Guillermo, Leonardo Leiderman, and Carmen Reinhart (1993). "Capital Inflows and Real Exchange Rate Appreciation in Latin America: The Role of External Factors," *IMF Staff Papers* 40 (1): 108–51.

Calvo, Sara, and Carmen Reinhart (1995). "Capital Flows to Latin America: Is There Evidence of Contagion Effects?" Unpublished manuscript, World Bank and International Monetary Fund, Washington, D.C.

De Long, J. Bradford, Andrei Shleifer, Lawrence H. Summers, and Robert Waldmann (1990). "Noise Trader Risk in Financial Markets," *Journal of Political Economy* 98 (4): 703–38.

Folkerts-Landau, David, Takatoshi Ito, et al. (1995). *International Capital Markets: Developments, Prospects, and Policy Issues.* Washington, D.C.: International Monetary Fund.

Frankel, Jeffrey A. (1994a). "Introduction." In *The Internationalization of Equity Markets*, pp. 1–20. Chicago: University of Chicago Press.

(1994b). "Sterilization of Money Inflows: Difficult (Calvo) or Easy (Reisen)?" In Roberto Steiner, ed., *Afluencia de Capitales y Estabilizacion en America Latina*, pp. 241–67. Bogota: Fedesarrollo.

(1995). "Recent Changes in the Financial Systems of Asian and Pacific Countries." In Kuniho Sawamoto, Zenta Nakajima, and Hiroo Taguchi, eds., *Financial Stability in a Changing Environment*, pp. 161–200. New York: St. Martin's Press.

Frankel, Jeffrey A., and Sergio L. Schmukler (1996a). "Country Fund Discounts and the Mexican Crisis of December 1994: Did Local Residents Turn Pessimistic before International Investors?" *Open Economies Review* 7 (suppl. 1): 511–34.

(1996b). "Crisis, Contagion, and Country Funds: Effects on East Asia and Latin America," Center for Pacific Basin Monetary and Economic Studies Working Paper No. PB96-04. Federal Reserve Bank of San Francisco.

(1997). "Country Funds and Asymmetric Information." Center for International Development and Economic Research Working Paper No. C97-087. University of California at Berkeley.

Goldfajn, Ilan, and Rodrigo O. Valdés (1995). "Balance of Payment Crises and Capital Flows: The Role of Liquidity." Unpublished manuscript, Massachusetts Institute of Technology, Cambridge, Mass.

Hardouvelis, Gikas A., Rafael La Porta, and Thierry A. Wizman (1994). "What Moves the Discount on Country Equity Funds?" NBER Working Paper No. 4571. In J. Frankel, ed., *The Internationalization of Equity Markets*, pp. 345–403. Chicago: University of Chicago Press.

Lee, Charles, M. C., Andrei Shleifer, and Richard Thaler (1991). "Investor Sentiment and the Closed-end Fund Puzzle," *Journal of Finance* 46 (1): 75–109.

Sachs, Jeffrey, D. (1985). "External Debt and Macroeconomic Performance in Latin America and East Asia," *Brookings Papers on Economic Activity*, no. 2: 523–73.

Valdés, Rodrigo (1996). "Emerging Markets Contagion: Evidence and Theory." Unpublished manuscript, Massachusetts Institute of Technology, Cambridge, Mass.

CHAPTER 9

Comovements among emerging
equity markets

Holger C. Wolf

9.1   Introduction

Investment in emerging equity markets, and notably in Southeast Asia,
has risen rapidly over the past decade (Frankel, 1993). Securitization and
privatization have boosted asset supplies, while the gradual removal of
restrictions on capital account transactions in emerging markets and
investment restrictions in mature markets, improvements in accounting,
prudential and regulatory systems, and, not least, stable macroeconomic
policies have raised demand. As a result, private-to-private flows increasingly replaced the previously dominant public-to-public flows: while
official flows increased slightly from $41 billion in 1988 to $54 billion in
1993, private flows dramatically accelerated from $33 to $159 billion over
the same period. As Bohn and Tesar (Chapter 2 in this volume) discuss,
markets in Asia have been particularly adept at tapping world capital
markets, accounting for almost two-thirds of new issues.

   Despite these strides toward greater integration, investment advice
for emerging markets continues to be habitually prefaced with the warning "caution, high risk." Part of this risk is fundamental, reflecting the
vagaries of the economic, social, and political development process. Yet
the casual reader of the business and financial press cannot avoid the
impression that the higher risk also reflects the volatile behavior of
investors themselves, a behavior apparently not always based on fundamentals in the recipient countries.

   According to this view, investment in emerging markets is largely
undertaken by novice investors and mutual fund managers with little
understanding of fundamentals: "Yet one can still find mutual-fund man-

I thank Maha Ibrahim for excellent research assistance and the International Finance
Corporation for kindly making the Emerging Market Data Base available. I am grateful to
Richard Lyons and to Reuven Glick for many valuable comments.

agers investing in the region whose knowledge of Latin America scarcely goes beyond steaks and sombreros."[1] These investors are ready to rush "lemming like"[2] into and out of markets at the slightest provocation, boosting volatility far beyond the levels justified by a detached view of fundamentals. This fickleness of mind is further aggravated by investors' apparent inability to differentiate among markets, leading them to lump fast growing economies with stellar fundamentals together with problem-plagued, would-be miracle economies into the single class of "emerging markets." Strong "contagion effects" between markets are the result: "[T]he governments of Argentina and Brazil, among others, have strenuously tried to show 'we are not like Mexico,' but turbulence has hit markets across the board as the herd instinct continues to take flows away from emerging countries."[3]

Whether such contagion effects are indeed present is of some concern. From the investor's point of view, the benefits of international diversification[4] shrink if returns to emerging stock markets are predominantly driven by common factors external to these markets themselves. From the policy maker's perspective, contagion effects imply sudden costly "irrational" capital flow reversals caused by factors outside their control, reducing the benefits of financial opening (Calvo, 1995a, 1995b).

The academic literature, in contrast to the business press, has not accorded "contagion" – defined as a comovement of asset markets not traceable to a common comovement of fundamentals – a major role in explaining comovements across emerging markets, at least over the longer term.[5] The relative lack of interest may partly reflect the difficulty of measuring contagion: by virtue of its definition as a comovement between markets that cannot be attributed to a comovement of fundamentals, any measure of contagion is only as good as the measure of fundamentals. Given the multitude of possible fundamental variables, any finding in favor of contagion is also consistent with an absence of contagion and a comovement of some unmeasured fundamental.

Is contagion in fact as prevalent as the recent business press suggests? As a first stab at the data, one might look at the comovement of actual returns, leaving aside for the moment the question whether the comovement reflects comovements of fundamentals. This measure does

---

[1] *Economist, Survey on Latin American Finance* 337 (December 9, 1995): 3.
[2] *Economist* 335 (May 13, 1995): 71–73.
[3] *The Banker* (February 1995): 23.
[4] Levy and Sarnat (1970), Solnick (1974), Lessard (1974, 1976), and Black and Litterman (1991), inter alia.
[5] Notable exceptions are Calvo (1995a) on the theoretical side, and Calvo and Reinhart (1995) and Frankel and Schmukler (Chapter 8 in this volume) on the empirical side.

not provide much support for contagion. During the three most recent three-year periods, dollar returns in the top twenty emerging markets differed dramatically, with a total range between the highest and lowest return of above 300 percent in every period, and a range of 100 percent even if the five top and the five bottom performers are excluded. Nor were monthly returns particularly highly correlated. Table 9.1 reports, for individual emerging markets, statistics on the correlations of monthly returns over the period 1988 to 1993 vis-à-vis a set of twenty other emerging markets. The results are in line with the general tone of the academic literature:[6] the mean correlation equals 0.13, for nine markets the correlation does not significantly differ from zero, and the maximum average correlation of any one equity market with all other equity markets amounts to just 0.25 for Malaysia. Markets in Asia exhibit the highest mean correlation, followed by markets in Latin America and in Europe and the Near East. On first sight, the unconditional correlation of stock market indices thus provides only limited evidence for contagion, at least over extended periods.

Although the unconditional correlation of market indices has been the preferred evidence in favor of contagion in the business press, it is in fact a quite poor measure, for two reasons. First, index returns are partly determined by sectoral composition and partly obscured by idiosyncratic noise. If two emerging markets are dominated by equities in a single sector (say, petroleum) and changes in global circumstances (say, a change in the oil price) cause a simultaneous rise in the price of equities in this sector in both countries, the aggregate indices will display high correlation, yet this correlation has little to do with "contagion" as the term is used.[7] The direction of this bias is ex ante ambiguous: just as sectoral similarity can misleadingly suggest market comovements, compositional differences can hide existing comovements. To the degree that returns differ across sectors and sectoral composition differs across markets, it thus becomes necessary to correct market indices for composition effects to obtain meaningful measures of comovements.

Is this caveat of empirical importance? Table 9.2 suggests it might be. The first column reports, for each country, a similarity index defined as the sum of the absolute differences between the fraction of total market capitalization in that country accounted for by each sector and the cross-country average fraction of market capitalization for that sector. A value of zero implies an equal distribution of sectors in the country as in the

---

[6] See Claessens, Dasgupta, and Glen (1993, 1995a, 1995b), Claessens (1995), and Errunza and Losq (1985).
[7] See Roll (1992).

Table 9.1. *Bilateral correlations of equity returns with other emerging markets, 1988–93*

	Mean	Min.	Max.
Asia	0.18		
China	0.21**	−0.43	0.70
India	0.14**	−0.26	0.58
Indonesia	0.23**	−0.26	0.53
Korea	0.05	−0.57	0.28
Malaysia	0.25**	−0.22	0.64
Pakistan	0.15**	−0.18	0.55
Philippines	0.23**	−0.18	0.70
Sri Lanka	0.14**	−0.45	0.55
Taiwan	0.20**	−0.15	0.65
Thailand	0.22**	−0.24	0.62
Latin America	0.11		
Argentina	0.06	−0.26	0.79
Brazil	0.04	−0.34	0.31
Chile	0.06	−0.32	0.46
Colombia	0.26**	−0.23	0.58
Mexico	0.15**	−0.21	0.51
Peru	0.21**	−0.26	0.79
Venezuela	−0.03	−0.45	0.46
Europe/Near East	0.04		
Hungary	0.07	−0.57	0.50
Jordan	−0.00	−0.43	0.41
Poland	0.05	−0.27	0.50
Turkey	0.02	−0.45	0.36

Note: **Denotes significance at 5% level.

universe of emerging stock markets; lower index numbers imply greater similarity. Malaysia is revealed to be the market most similar; Colombia and Nigeria are the markets least similar to the average. Overall, Asian markets display less sectoral divergence from the cross-country average than markets in other regions. Column three lists, for each country, the sector whose market capitalization-share deviates most from the cross-country average; that is, the sector which is least similar to the average. The following two columns present the country and world capitalization shares of that sector, illustrating the numerical significance of differences in market structure. The last column reports the average annual return

Sectoral stock composition by country

Country	Similarity index	Least similar sector	Share in country market (%)	Share in world market (%)	Sector	Sectoral stock return — Average annual return, 1984–93 (%)
Asia						
Malaysia	0.97	Diversified holding	15.8	5.6	Communications	51.3
Korea	0.73	Communications	2.0	13.8	Electricity/gas	27.4
Thailand	0.87	Banking	36.1	14.6	Rubber prod.	24.5
Taiwan	0.92	Communications	0.0	13.8	Food	24.3
Indonesia	0.94	Communications	0.0	13.8	Transp. equip.	23.2
Philippines	1.01	Food	25.5	4.2	Electric equip.	23.0
Pakistan	1.13	Chemicals	24.9	2.5	Banking	13.3
India	1.23	Chemicals	18.1	2.5	Insurance	9.3
Latin America					Cement/glass	31.6
Brazil	0.80	Electricity/gas	23.0	9.3	Paper	21.7
Mexico	1.09	Communications	33.3	13.8	Prim. metals	14.6
Chile	1.11	Electricity/gas	37.0	9.3	Agriculture	13.8
Venezuela	1.12	Electricity/gas	30.6	9.3	Textile prod.	12.9
Argentina	1.17	Communications	47.4	13.8	Petroleum	8.3
Colombia	1.31	Food	26.0	4.2	Fabric. metals	12.5
Europe/Near East					Brokerage	6.9
Jordan	1.21	Banking	57.1	14.6	Construction	22.4
Nigeria	1.60	Food	38.6	4.2		
Turkey	1.06	Petroleum refining	18.4	2.8		
Zimbabwe	1.11	Services	15.8	1.9		

Notes: Similarity index defined as the sum of absolute differences between fraction of total market capitalization accounted for by each sector and average cross-country fraction of market capitalization of that sector; lower number indicates greater similarity.

Source: Author's calculations based on International Finance Corporation data.

for each sector over the period 1984 to 1993, illustrating the wide range in annual returns from 6.9 for firms in the brokerage industry to 51 percent for the communications industry. Over the same period, the *annual* range of sectoral returns was above 100 percent and the coefficient of variation was above one in all but three years. There are thus substantial grounds to expect, ex ante, that composition effects may significantly influence aggregate stock index returns and thus correlations.

Even if composition effects were controlled for, the use of unconditional correlations remains problematic. Contagion, in the sense typically used, refers to comovements that cannot be attributed to changes in perceived fundamentals. In consequence, contagion is better measured by the correlation of returns controlling for fundamentals, than by unconditional correlations. For instance, though both the Hungarian and Taiwanese markets declined in the aftermath of the 1994–95 Mexican crisis, Hungary shared most of the problems leading to the crisis in Mexico – low savings, large current account deficits, low reserves – whereas Taiwan did not. The decline in the Taiwan market might thus on first sight be viewed as a contagion effect, but the decline in the Hungarian market, in the wake of reevaluations of the risk–return trade-off based on the new information revealed by the Mexican crisis, cannot.

In this chapter we reexamine the case for contagion effects taking account of these issues. We begin by constructing a measure of equity market comovements that controls for composition effects and idiosyncratic noise. We then ask whether *differences* in bilateral correlations can be related to country characteristics. Specifically, we ask whether countries with similar characteristics in terms of macroeconomic performance, development stage, and risk factors exhibit above-average correlations, and, conversely, whether country pairs with above-average correlations exhibit greater similarities along these dimensions.

It might be useful to also set out what we do *not* attempt to do. We do not aim to explain the *average* level of correlations across emerging markets. We do not consider shocks affecting the entire group of emerging markets. We do not examine issues of pricing efficiency in these markets (Bekaert and Harvey, 1995a, 1995b; Cashin and McDermott, 1995; Cashin, Kumar, and McDermott, 1995). Nor do we link the results formally to a particular model of asset pricing. Rather, the chapter attempts to answer two fairly basic questions. First, what is the extent of comovements of "market factors" across emerging stock markets? Second, are differences in bilateral comovements systematically linked to country characteristics?

Our results may be summarized briefly. First, we find that differences in sectoral composition have reduced the extent of stock market comovements. Controlling for sectoral composition, we find the conditional correlation of country returns exceeds substantially the unconditional correlation of market indices. The increase is quite widespread. Of the 105 country pairs we examine, for 88 the correlation of conditional country returns exceeds the correlation of market index returns. This finding suggests that a good part of the benefits from international diversification documented in the literature might reflect gains from sectoral and idiosyncratic diversification rather than from "market" diversification. However, while exceeding the correlation of index returns, the average correlation of country returns remains small at 0.22; furthermore, we find substantial cross-section variability in the correlations.

We next examine whether observed differences in correlations can be linked to differences in "fundamentals." Whereas we find weak support for an above-average comovement of countries with the best macroeconomic performance, overall the explanatory power of fundamentals – which are measured quite roughly and at low frequency – for the correlation pattern is less than convincing. Furthermore, we find that differences in correlations are significantly influenced by the degree of development of emerging stock markets and by their location, a finding consistent with, though not proof of, moderate contagion.

In the next section, we begin by presenting some stylized facts regarding the equity returns used in the chapter. We then turn to the decomposition of individual stock returns into country, sector, and idiosyncratic return components. Section 9.3 examines whether the market correlations thus obtained can be attributed to shared fundamentals, and section 9.4 concludes the chapter.

9.2 Data and stylized facts

The empirical evidence reported here is based on the U.S. dollar–denominated total return series on individual stocks contained in the Emerging Markets Data Base (EMDB) published by the International Finance Corporation (IFC). The data base covers twenty-four countries and twenty-one sectors, listed in Table 9.3. The longest sample span ranges from January 1976 to April of 1995. The first full year for which returns are available for each country is indicated in parentheses. While the full data set is used to estimate country effects, only the fifteen markets with complete data from 1988 are included in the sample used to examine contagion effects.

Table 9.3. *Data set: countries and sectors*

Countries[a]	Sectors
Argentina (1984)	Agriculture, forestry, fishing
Brazil (1988)	Mining
Chile (1976)	Construction
China (1993)	Food and tobacco
Colombia (1985)	Textile products
Hungary (1993)	Paper
Indonesia (1990)	Chemicals
India (1990)	Petroleum refining
Jordan (1979)	Rubber and plastics
Korea (1976)	Stone, clay, glass, concrete
Malaysia (1985)	Metals
Mexico (1976)	Industrial, commercial computer equipment
Nigeria (1985)	Transportation equipment
Pakistan (1985)	Misc. manufacturing
Peru (1993)	Transport
Philippines (1985)	Communications
Poland (1993)	Utilities
South Africa (1994)	Banking
Sri Lanka (1993)	Other finance, insurance, real estate
Taiwan (1985)	Services
Thailand (1976)	Miscellaneous, wholesale and retail trade
Turkey (1987)	
Venezuela (1985)	
Zimbabwe (1976)	

[a] Year in parentheses indicates first year data available.

The return to an equity at time t, r_t^{ij}, can be decomposed into a country component common to all stocks in country i, α_t^i; into a sector component common to all stocks (globally) in sector j, β_t^j; and into an idiosyncratic component, v_t^{ij}. The country effect then provides a measure of the market return controlling for sectoral effects:

$$r_t^{ij} = \alpha_t^i + \beta_t^j + v_t^{ij}. \tag{1}$$

Effects are defined via a reference country (India) and a reference sector (food),[8] and extracted via a fixed-effect regression for each set of

---

[8] Alternatives are use of a generalized inverse (Zervos, 1994) and referencing relative to the sample mean (Heston and Rouwenhorst, 1994).

Table 9.4. *Granger causality between equity markets*

Country		Causes	Is caused by
Argentina	(ARG)	TUR	BRA
Brazil	(BRA)	ARG	IND, JOR, MAL, MEX, PHI, THA
Colombia	(COL)	ZIM	THA
Indonesia	(IND)	BRA	PHI
Jordan	(JOR)	BRA	
Korea	(KOR)		TUR
Malaysia	(MAL)	BRA, MEX	
Mexico	(MEX)	BRA	MAL, PHI
Pakistan	(PAK)	THA, ZIM	
Philippines	(PHI)	BRA, IND, MEX	
Thailand	(THA)	BRA, COL, ZIM	PAK, VEN
Turkey	(TUR)	KOR, ZIM	ARG
Venezuela	(VEN)	THA	
Zimbabwe	(ZIM)		COL, PAK, THA, TUR

monthly returns. The number of observations gradually increases over time, ranging between 400 and 1,300 stocks.

Country and, to a lesser extent, sector effects together explain between a third and half of the variance of returns on individual stocks. The result is in line with earlier studies (Divecha, Drach, and Stefek, 1992; Zervos, 1994) finding country effects dominate sector effects, with total explanatory power in the 33–50 percent range. Comparing results for emerging and developed markets reveals the primacy of country over sectoral effects to be a common feature of both, though the dominance of market effects is more pronounced for the emerging markets.[9]

Comparing the correlations of the conditional country returns and the (unconditional) total returns reveals total returns to be less correlated (0.06 vs. 0.22), although they include global shocks affecting all sample countries, whereas the country returns by construction do not. The results suggest that a large part of what are often labeled benefits from

---

[9] See Beckers, Grinold, Rudd, and Stefek (1992), Lessard (1974, 1976), Adler and Dumas (1983), Solnik and De Freitas (1988), Grinold, Rudd, and Stefek (1989), Drummen and Zimmermann (1992), Roll (1992), and Heston and Rouwenhorst (1994) for a small sample of work on developed markets. The last work cited is closest in approach to this chapter in terms of isolating country effects.

international diversification may rather reflect sector and idiosyncratic diversification.[10]

Table 9.4 examines the presence of causality effects between markets, applying Granger-causality tests for the 1985–95 period to examine temporal linkages between the estimated country effects. The Philippines and Thailand are found to Granger-cause three other markets, out of fourteen markets in the sample.[11] Brazil and Zimbabwe, being Granger-caused respectively by six and four other markets, seem most sensitive to developments elsewhere. Overall, there is little evidence for global leaders, nor for the type of regional spillover effects from larger to smaller markets found for capital flows (Calvo and Reinhart, 1995), though the results do not exclude such causality patterns for shorter periods following specific events, such as the 1994–95 Mexico crisis.

9.3   Equity market correlations and fundamentals

The correlations of country effects provide measures of comovements free of composition and idiosyncratic elements and thus provide a promising basis for assessing the presence of significant contagion effects among subgroups of emerging markets. We now examine whether differences in correlations can be linked to differences in fundamentals. Specifically, we ask whether countries that are similar exhibit above-average correlations and, conversely, if countries with above-average correlations display above-average similarity. To the extent that either question can be answered positively, the scope for long-term contagion effects declines. A negative answer is less informative, as high correlations among "dissimilar" markets could be suggestive of "contagion" effects, but might also be a reflection of shortcomings in the necessarily rough way in which we measure similarity.

If the set of relevant fundamentals for country effects were known and available at monthly frequency, a comparison between the correlation patterns of country effects and fundamentals would answer the question directly. Alas, neither condition is fulfilled, and, given the short sample period, use of annual data, while feasible, would reduce the number of observations quite severely. Instead, we opt for an indirect, if weaker, test. We rank countries for a broad range of potential fundamentals drawn from the realm of macroeconomic performance, economic structure, and exposure to risk. To the degree that similarity along these

---

[10]   The results are not a reflection of measuring returns in a common currency, the dollar, inducing spurious "market" correlations reflecting common exchange rate movements. Exchange rates explain less than 5 percent of the variance of the country effect.

[11]   The sample was restricted to countries with data beginning in 1990 or before.

dimensions proxies for exposure to the same type of shocks, one would expect countries with similar fundamentals to exhibit above-average correlations, an empirically testable proposition.

The range of variables potentially relevant as macrofundamentals driving stock markets is quite substantial and itself the subject of a large literature.[12] We group fundamentals into three broad categories, aiming to capture, respectively, the notions of "performance," "structure," and "risk."[13]

The "performance" variable category aims to capture whether the economy as a whole is performing well according to traditional economic criteria. On the real side, this group includes the growth rates of aggregate GDP per capita and exports and the ratios of exports and investment to GDP, and on the nominal side, the average inflation rate and the coefficient of variation of the inflation rate. The "structure" variable category includes variables proxying for the development stage of the economy. It includes GDP per capita, total GDP, the share of exports in GDP, and the share of manufacturing exports in total exports. Finally, the "risk" variable category contains variables proxying for the susceptibility of the economy to economic shocks, including the ratios of debt and debt service to GDP, the ratio of reserves to imports, the ratio of reserves to debt, the fiscal and current account deficits as fractions of GDP, and the variability of the terms of trade.

We also consider whether stock market development influences correlation patterns, as would be consistent with contagion effects. The market development measures include restriction variables (barriers on entry and exit, withholding taxes), variables proxying for market size (market capitalization as a fraction of GDP, market capitalization in U.S. dollars, trading volume as a fraction of GDP), variables proxying for liquidity and market depth (trading volume as a fraction of capitalization, average company size, market concentration [share of capitalization accounted for by the ten largest firms], and the number of stocks), and a composite variable proxying for information quality, including information on publication of brokerage reports, accounting standards, investor protection standards, and financial disclosure standards.

The macrodata were taken from the World Bank *World Tables*, the restriction data are from various issues of the IFC *Yearbook* and from

---

[12] See, e.g., Ammer and Mei (1993), Bordo, Mizrach, and Schwartz (1995), Buckberg (1996), Claessens and Rhee (1993), Ferson and Harvey (1993, 1994), Harvey (1994, 1995), and Levine and Zervos (1994, 1995).

[13] For work relating these variables to stock market performance and capital flows, see Calvo and Reinhart (1995), Hernandez and Rudolph (1995), Mullin (1993), and Walter (1993) inter alia.

Demirguc-Kunt and Levine (1996). The data set used for this section includes only countries for which data from at least 1988 onward are available, leaving a sample of fifteen countries.[14] To achieve comparability, countries were sorted by each of the seventeen "fundamentals" and ten market development variables and given a rank of 1 to 15 for each variable.

The second column of Table 9.5 reports the coefficient obtained by regressing the 105 bilateral correlations on a constant and the absolute rank difference of the two countries, for each of the twenty-seven variables. If similarity increases the comovement of country returns, we would expect a *negative* coefficient. Overall, the results are quite poor. Among the performance, structure, and risk variables, only differences of the mean inflation rate are associated with a significant difference in the correlation of returns.

Column (2) reports whether the average bilateral correlation is greater in countries with better fundamentals. Specifically, the column reports the coefficient obtained by regressing the bilateral correlations on a constant and a dummy equal to 1 if both countries are in the top five in rankings of each variable. The results suggest that top performers – countries with high output and export growth, high investment and export ratios, and low inflation – tend to exhibit an above-average correlation. In contrast, countries with high per capita GDP *levels* and large economies exhibit below-average correlations, maybe suggesting beginning differentiation. Among the risk variables, no consistent pattern emerges; indeed, countries with the highest risk factors display below-average correlations. The latter finding in particular may, however, reflect the fairly long sample period.

In addition to these fundamentals, we also examine whether correlations differ by stock market development, reported in the bottom part of the table. The preponderance of the evidence suggests that more developed markets exhibit an above-average correlation, a finding consistent with, though not proof of, "contagion."

We next turn to a multivariate regression of correlations on the rank differences of the economic performance variables and the market development indicators as well as an Asia dummy to capture residual geographic effects. The high degree of multicollinearity, of course, sharply reduces the significance of individual variables. Our interest here lies in the explanatory power of the performance variables vis-à-vis the market development variables. In a regression excluding the Asia

---

[14] Argentina, Brazil, Chile, Colombia, Jordan, Korea, Malaysia, Mexico, Nigeria, Pakistan, the Philippines, Thailand, Turkey, Venezuela, and Zimbabwe. Taiwan had to be excluded because comparable macroeconomic data were not available. Except for Turkey and Brazil, data are available from 1985 onward.

Table 9.5. *Correlations, fundamentals, and market development*

Variable	Absolute rank difference (1)	Both countries in top five (2)
Performance variables		
Mean inflation	−0.017**	0.164**
CoV of inflation	−0.002	0.076
GDP growth	0.009	0.288**
GDP per capita growth	0.009	0.023
Export growth	−0.003	0.189**
Export/GDP	−0.009	0.194**
Investment/GDP	−0.001	0.206**
Structural variables		
GDP per capita	0.003	−0.182**
GDP	−0.000	−0.150**
Manuf. exports/Total exports	−0.001	0.084
Risk variables		
Debt/GDP	0.002	−0.032
Reserves/Imports	0.003	−0.132**
Debt service/Exports	−0.005	0.149**
Current account/GDP	0.001	0.127*
Reserves/Debt	0.007	−0.183**
Fiscal deficit	0.000	−0.028
Terms of trade volatility	0.006	−0.040
Stock market variables		
Total cap./GDP	−0.011**	0.039
Total capitalization	0.009	0.131*
Turnover/GDP	0.005	0.064
Company size	0.006	0.206**
Top 10 share	−0.006	0.309**
Trading volume/Cap.	0.004	−0.009
No. of stocks	−0.005	−0.117*
Entry/exit barriers	−0.001	−0.063
Information quality	0.000	0.024
Withholding taxes	−0.000	0.113*

Notes: Column (1) reports coefficient of regression of bilateral stock return correlations on the absolute rank difference for each variable. Column (2) reports coefficient of regression of correlations on dummy if both countries are ranked in top five of variable ranking. ** and * denote significance at 1% and 5% levels respectively. Variable rankings for current account deficit: largest deficit = 1, fiscal deficit: largest deficit = 1, entry/exit: least restrictive = 1, withholding taxes: lowest taxes = 1, information: best information = 1.

Table 9.6. *Similarity index of fundamentals and market development*

Most similar	Mean rank difference	Least similar	Mean rank difference
Brazil-Mexico	2.57	Mexico-Nigeria	7.39
Korea-Thailand	2.85	Korea-Zimbabwe	7.46
Colombia-Venezuela	3.25	Nigeria-Thailand	8.21
Malaysia-Thailand	3.39	Malaysia-Nigeria	8.53
Colombia-Turkey	3.42	Korea-Nigeria	8.64

Note: Similarity index is defined as sum of the absolute rank difference between countries in rankings of fundamentals; larger numbers indicate less similarity.

dummy variable, the orthogonal component of fundamentals explains 22.9 percent of the variance of correlations, the orthogonal component of the stock market variables contributes another 9.6 percent to the explained variance, with another 8.4 percent jointly attributable, for a total explained fraction of 40.9 percent. The Asia dummy enters both economically and statistically highly significantly, with a coefficient of 0.235 and a t-statistic above 5. Adding the Asian dummy to a regression already including the stock market development and fundamentals variables raises the explained fraction of the variance substantially, from 40.9 to 56.1 percent.

The regression results suggest that similarities in fundamentals go some way toward explaining correlation patterns. If we control for these variables, however, similarities in stock market development and geographical location also contribute substantially to the explanatory power. Both of these results are consistent with – though not proof of – contagion effects. Of course, the conclusions are conditional on the quality of our variables; it cannot be ruled out that the Asia effect captures other fundamentals not included in the regression.

We next construct a measure of overall similarity between any two countries, defined as the sum of the absolute rank differences between the countries over the twenty-seven variables. Table 9.6 reports the five most similar and least similar country pairs. Nigeria is seen to be the clear outlier, with an average rank difference of more than eight (out of a maximum of fourteen) vis-à-vis Thailand, Malaysia, and Korea. On the other end of the spectrum, Brazil and Mexico, Thailand and Korea, and Colombia and Venezuela are quite similar across the twenty-seven variables in the data set.

The 10 percent of country pairs with the greatest similarity over the entire set of variables displays an almost 50 percent above-average correlation, though the difference is marginally insignificant ($t = 1.52$). The correlation remains above average for the top 20 and top 30 percent of country pairs in terms of similarity, though the difference declines and is neither economically nor statistically significant. At the opposite end of the spectrum, the least similar countries do not display correlations significantly different from the sample mean.

9.4   Conclusion

For those that think of Latin America in terms of generals, jungles and sackfuls of worthless currency, it may be time to overhaul some myths. Things have changed. [S]oldiers have long since goose-stepped back to the barracks, their power usurped by squadrons of technocrats and battalions of economic miracle makers. (*Financial Times*, August 27–28, 1994)

Mexico's currency crisis has dimmed expectations for economies throughout Latin America. The crisis and the border war . . . between Peru and Ecuador have raised some fundamental questions in the minds of investors about the wisdom of investment in Latin America. [S]ome may well retire from the region for good. (*Financial Times*, February 20, 1995)

The history of investment in South America throughout the last century has been one of confidence followed by disillusionment, of borrowing cycles followed by widespread defaults. (Royal Institute of International Affairs, 1937)

Over the past decade, private capital flows to emerging markets have dramatically risen. The inflows have generally been cautiously greeted by governments aiming to enhance integration with international financial markets. Yet, in the 1990s just as in the 1980s, the transition from closed to integrated financial systems has not been without cost. In particular, policy makers have been concerned with the potentially disruptive consequences of capital flow reversals. To the degree that such reversals reflect domestic policies, adoption of stringent fiscal and monetary policies, possibly augmented with restrictions on some types of capital flows, could be used to mitigate the likelihood and extent of reversals. More recently, in particular in the wake of the Mexican crisis, the possibility of reversals more related to the fickleness of investor sentiment – referred to in the two quotations from the *Financial Times*, barely six months apart – than to changes in domestic fundamentals under the influence of policy makers has attracted increased attention. To the degree that such "contagion effects" – capital flow reversals unrelated to fundamentals – are indeed present, financial integration, even though desirable long term, may impose significant costs (Williamson, 1993; Gooptu, 1993).

The presence of contagion has been widely inferred from high correlations of aggregate indices, mostly over very short durations. We have argued in this chapter that such unconditional correlations do not, in fact, provide good indicators of contagion effects, for two reasons. First, aggregate returns were shown to be subject to very significant *composition effects*. Though theoretically ambiguous, in the data these composition effects led to an understatement of market comovements; controlling for composition effect thus raised the scope for contagion. Even after correction for composition effects, however, the unconditional correlation provides an unsatisfactory gauge of contagion effects, as it does not allow discrimination between comovements caused by comovements of fundamentals – which are not attributable to contagion – and "nonfundamental" comovements, which might.

In the second part of the chapter, we attempted to make some headway in determining whether comovements can be attributed to fundamentals. Our results here are decidedly mixed. We found weak evidence that the correlation of countries with better macroeconomic performance exceeds the average sample correlation. The force of this finding is however diminished by our failure to find evidence for the reverse link: country pairs with above-average correlations of market returns do not seem to be more similar to each other than the average of all country pairs. In addition, we found two pieces of evidence consistent with, though not proof of, contagion. First, even controlling for fundamentals, the characteristics of the stock market itself contribute significantly to explaining differences in bilateral return correlations. Second, even controlling for fundamentals, the geographic location of markets matters – specifically, markets in Asia exhibit a significantly above-average correlation with each other.

Overall, our results thus do not support the presence of strong contagion effects, but leave room for more modest, geographically concentrated contagion effects. In interpreting the results, a number of caveats must however be considered. First, we have focused here on the presence of contagion within a subgroup of emerging markets; our results do not logically exclude the presence of sizable shocks common to the set of all emerging markets, though the very low correlation of returns suggests that this is not a major concern. Second, we have focused on the long run; our results do not exclude the possibility of more pronounced shorter-term correlation spikes (Calvo and Reinhart, 1995; Frankel and Schmuckler, Chapter 8, in this volume), though, of course, the policy significance of contagion diminishes the shorter the duration of such spikes. Third, reflecting the lack of high-frequency data on fundamentals, we have been forced to rely on rough proxies of the *likelihood* of markets suffering similar shocks rather than of the shocks themselves.

References

Adler, Michael, and Bernard Dumas (1983). "International Portfolio Choice and Corporation Finance," *Journal of Finance* 38: 925–84.

Ammer, John, and Jianping Mei (1993). "Measuring International Economic Linkages with Stock Market Data," International Finance Discussion Paper No. 449. Washington, D.C.: Board of Governors of the Federal Reserve System.

Beckers, Stan, Richard Grinold, Andrew Rudd, and Dan Stefek (1992). "The Relative Importance of Common Factors across the European Equity Markets," *Journal of Banking and Finance* 16: 75–95.

Bekaert, Gert, and Campbell Harvey (1995a). "Time-Varying World Market Integration," *Journal of Finance* 50: 403–44.

(1995b). "Emerging Equity Market Volatility," NBER Working Paper No. 5307. Cambridge, Mass.

Black, Fischer, and Robert Litterman (1991). "Global Portfolio Optimization." Unpublished manuscript, Goldman Sachs, New York.

Bordo, Michael, Bruce Mizrach, and Anna Schwartz (1995). "Real versus Pseudo-International Systemic Risk: Some Lessons from History," NBER Working Paper No. 5371. Cambridge, Mass.

Buckberg, Elaine (1996). "Institutional Investors and Asset Pricing in Emerging Markets," IMF Working Paper No. 96/2. Washington, D.C.

Calvo, Guillermo (1995a). "Varieties of Capital Market Crises," Center for International Economics Working Paper No. 15. University of Maryland at College Park.

(1995b). "Managing Economic Reform under Capital Flow Mobility." Unpublished manuscript, University of Maryland at College Park, Department of Economics.

Calvo, Sara, and Carmen Reinhart (1995). "Capital Flows to Latin America." Unpublished manuscript, University of Maryland at College Park, Department of Economics.

Cashin, Paul, Manmohan Kumar, and John McDermott (1995). "International Integration of Equity Markets and Contagion Effects," IMF Working Paper No. 95/100. Washington, D.C.

Cashin, Paul, and John McDermott (1995). "Informational Efficiency in Developing Equity Markets," IMF Working Paper No. 95/58. Washington, D.C.

Claessens, Stijn (1995). "The Emergence of Equity Investment in Developing Countries: Overview," *World Bank Economic Review* 9 (3): 1–17.

Claessens, Stijn, Susmita Dasgupta, and Jack Glen (1993). "Stock Price Behavior in Emerging Stock Markets." In Stijn Claessens and Sudarshan Gooptu, eds., *Portfolio Investment in Developing Countries*; pp. 323–51. World Bank Discussion Paper No. 228. Washington, D.C.

(1995a). "Return Behavior in Emerging Stock Markets," *World Bank Economic Review* 9 (3): 131–51.

(1995b). "The Cross Section of Stock Returns: Evidence from Emerging Markets," World Bank Discussion Paper No. 1505. Washington, D.C.

Claessens, Stijn, and Moon-Whoan Rhee (1993). "The Effect of Equity Barriers on Foreign Investment in Developing Countries," NBER Working Paper No. 4579, December. Cambridge, Mass.

Demirguc-Kunt, Asli, and Ross Levine (1996). "Stock Market Development and Financial Intermediaries." *World Bank Economic Review* 10: 291–321.

Divecha, Arjun, Jaime Drach, and Dan Stefek (1992). "Emerging Markets: A Quantitative Perspective," *Journal of Portfolio Analysis* 19 (Fall): 41–50.

Drummen, Martin, and Heinz Zimmermann (1992). "The Structure of European Stock Returns," *Financial Analysts Journal* 48 (July–August): 15–26.

Errunza, Vihang, and Etienne Losq (1985). "The Behavior of Stock Prices on LDC Markets," *Journal of Banking and Finance* 9: 561–75.

Errunza, Vihang, Etienne Losq, and Prasad Padmanabhan (1985). "Tests of Integration, Mild Segmentation, and Segmentation Hypotheses," *Journal of Banking and Finance* 16: 949–72.

Ferson, Wayne, and Campbell Harvey (1993). "An Exploratory Investigation of the Fundamental Determinants of National Equity Market Returns," NBER Working Paper No. 4595, December. Cambridge, Mass.

(1994). "Sources of Risk and Expected Returns in Global Equity Markets," *Journal of Banking and Finance* 18: 775–803.

Frankel, Jeffrey (1993). "The Internationalization of Equity Markets," NBER Working Paper No. 4590, December. Cambridge, Mass.

Gooptu, Sudarshan (1993). "Portfolio Investment Flows to Emerging Markets." In Stijn Claessens and Sudarshan Goopto, eds., *Portfolio Investment in Developing Countries*. World Bank Discussion Paper No. 228. Washington, D.C.

Grinold, Richard, Andrew Rudd, and Dan Stefek (1989). "Global Factors: Fact or Fiction?" *Journal of Portfolio Management* 16 (Fall): 79–88.

Harvey, Campbell (1994). "Predictable Risk and Return in Emerging Markets," NBER Working Paper No. 4621. Cambridge, Mass.

(1995). "The Risk Exposure of Emerging Equity Markets," *World Bank Economic Review* 9 (1): 19–50.

Hernandez, Leonardo, and Heinz Rudolph (1995). "Sustainability of Private Capital Flows to Developing Countries." Unpublished manuscript, World Bank, Washington, D.C.

Heston, Steven, and Geert Rouwenhorst (1994). "Does Industrial Structure Explain the Benefits of International Diversification?" *Journal of Financial Economics* 36: 3–27.

International Finance Corporation (various years). *Emerging Stock Market Factbook*. Washington, D.C.

Lessard, Donald (1974). "World, National, and Industry Factors in Equity Returns," *Journal of Finance* 24: 379–91.

(1976). "World, Country, and Industry Relationships in Equity Returns," *Financial Analysts Journal* 32: 2–8.

Levine, Ross, and Sara Zervos (1994). "International Capital Flow Liberalization and Stock Market Development: A Cross-Country Event Study." Unpublished manuscript, World Bank, Washington, D.C.

(1995). "Policy, Stock Market Development, and Long-Run Growth." Unpublished manuscript, World Bank, Washington, D.C.

Levy, Haim, and Marshall Sarnat (1970). "International Diversification of Investment Portfolios," *American Economic Review* 50: 668–75.

Mullin, John (1993). "Emerging Equity Markets in the Global Economy," *Federal Reserve Bank of New York Quarterly Review* 18 (Summer): 54–83.

Roll, Richard (1992). "Industrial Structure and the Comparative Behavior of International Stock Indices," *Journal of Finance* 47: 3–41.

Solnik, Bruno (1974). "Why Not Diversify Internationally Rather Than Domestically?" *Financial Analysts Journal* 30: 91–135.

Solnik, Bruno, and A. De Freitas (1988). "International Factors of Stock Price Behavior." In S. Khoury and A. Ghosh, eds., *Recent Developments in International Banking and Finance*, vol. 2, pp. 259–76. Lexington, Mass.: Lexington Books.

Walter, Ingo (1993). "Emerging Equity Market," *ASEAN Economic Bulletin* 10 (1): 1–19.

Williamson, John (1993). "Issues Posed by Portfolio Investment in Developing Countries," In Stijn Claessens and Sudarshan Gooptu, eds., *Portfolio Investment in Developing Countries*, pp. 11–17. World Bank Discussion Paper No. 228. Washington, D.C.

World Bank (various years). *World Debt Tables*. Washington, D.C.

Zervos, Sara (1994). "Industry and Country Components in International Stock Returns." Unpublished manuscript, University of Rochester, Department of Economics, Rochester, N.Y.

PART III
EFFECTS OF CAPITAL INFLOWS

CHAPTER 10

Net capital inflows: How much to accept, how much to resist?

Helmut Reisen

10.1 Introduction

In January 1994, two central bank governors gave a strikingly contrasting answer to the question about whether to worry about large current account deficits. The governor of the Reserve Bank of India said in a public lecture (Bank for International Settlements *Review* No. 14, 1994): "The ease with which the [current account] deficit can be financed should not become the criterion for incurring debt. Taking several factors into account our country should move towards reaching a level of current account deficit which is no more than 1% of GDP." The governor of the Banco de Mexico, meanwhile, told the *Economist* that the current account deficit was not a problem because it was associated with the inflow of foreign funds, rather than expansionary fiscal or monetary policy. A year later, foreign and domestic investors forced Mexico to reduce the deficit on its current account from almost 8 percent of GDP in 1994 to near zero. Currently, countries such as Malaysia, Peru, and Thailand are running deficits as high or even higher than Mexico did before the latter's currency crisis emerged.

The current account deficits analyzed in this chapter share three important features. First, they are "private sector driven" in the (non-Ricardian) sense that they do not reflect government budget deficits. This chapter examines the experiences of four Asian and four Latin American countries that have not had public sector deficits during the 1990s, but have received sizable capital imports. With the public budget in balance and private capital internationally mobile to these

I thank Guillermo Larraín and Julia von Maltzan for valuable assistance as well as Guillermo Calvo and Reuven Glick for helpful comments.

289

countries, the current account is determined by private sector savings–investment decisions. Second, the current account deficits are "overfinanced" (except, of course, in the midst of currency crises), implying a positive overall balance of payments and rising levels of foreign exchange reserves. Third, these deficits are partly financed by cyclical capital flows, as has been generally the case for a large share of emerging-market inflows during the 1990s (see, e.g., Calvo, Leiderman, and Reinhart, 1996). Their cyclical determination makes these flows subject to reversal.

The abundance of private capital inflows confronts many Asian and Latin American authorities with a transfer problem. They must decide whether to accept or resist the capital inflow, or how much to accept or how much to resist. This chapter analyzes this decision by focusing on their costs and benefits. The chapter does not provide recommendations for how to resist capital inflows through such policies as macroeconomic restraint, sterilized intervention, or capital controls. Nor does it provide policy advice for preventing financial crises (see, e.g., Goldstein, 1996; Reisen, 1996).

The chapter is structured as follows. First, the benefits of foreign saving inflows (rather than of gross capital mobility per se) are reviewed. These benefits include enhancing growth through capital accumulation and consumption smoothing through risk sharing. Section 10.2 summarizes the implications of the neoclassical and new growth models as well as the intertemporal approach to the current account as to the magnitude of these benefits. Second, section 10.3 presents various long-term sustainability measures of debt-augmenting capital flows. Because large current account deficits will not be financed by foreigners forever, authorities need to know the required magnitude and time profile of the subsequent adjustment back to payments balance. Since a deficit that is unsustainable in the long run is not necessarily an "excessive" deficit in the short run, the size of the current account deficit does not give rise to normative judgments; what matters, rather, is the *source* of the deficit. Section 10.4 makes a case for resisting some or all foreign savings when unsustainable currency appreciation, excessive risk taking in the banking system, and a sharp drop in private savings coincide. Thus, the appropriate policy response is to strike a balance between the benefits of consumption smoothing and financing viable investment, on the one hand, and the economic costs of excessive private borrowing, on the other. A case can be made that foreign direct investment is less likely than other capital flows to stimulate excessive private consumption and a real appreciation problem.

10.2   The benefits of (net) capital inflows

This section summarizes the benefits of foreign borrowing, as suggested by different strands of the development and open economy macroeconomics literature. According to the "two-gap" structural development literature (Chenery and Bruno, 1962; McKinnon, 1964), growth is limited not only by a country's ability to save, but also by foreign savings with which to buy necessary imported inputs. However, since the current account deficits under attention in this chapter are assumed to be overfinanced by foreign capital inflows, an abundance of foreign exchange, rather than a scarcity, underlies the analysis. Discussion of the two-gap literature is therefore omitted. We can immediately move then from the structuralist approach to mainstream economic thinking concerning the benefits of capital inflows.

10.2.1   *Neoclassical considerations*

In the neoclassical general equilibrium framework, the benefits of capital inflows into (capital-)poor countries arise from divergences in the marginal productivity of capital across countries. If labor in advanced countries is equipped with better and more capital than labor in developing countries, capital can be used more productively by being relocated to the latter.

The simplest of neoclassical models, the two-country Kemp-MacDougall model (MacDougall, 1960), illustrates the basic insights about the benefit of capital inflows as well as their optimal size. The model assumes savings are a fixed proportion of per capita income in each country. The marginal product of capital is higher in the poor country than in the rich country in autarky, and diminishes in each country as the capital–labor ratio rises. With perfect capital mobility, the poor country benefits from capital inflows, until its marginal product of capital is equated to that of the rich country, and both in turn are equal to the world interest rate.

The size of the optimal net capital inflow rises with the difference between the autarkic marginal product of capital in the poor country and the world interest rate, and falls the faster its marginal capital productivity declines with a higher capital–labor ratio. The poor country's per capita income rises by an amount equal to the marginal output of capital times the amount of capital inflow minus the income payments on the capital stock located at home. (The rich country, of course, gains as well from its capital export, since the output loss due to capital relocation is more than compensated by interest and dividend payments from investment in the poor country.) In the new, long-run equilibrium, output grows at the same rate as in the closed economy.

The Kemp-MacDougall model crucially assumes that the capital inflow is invested, not consumed, and that the capital–labor ratio is raised by the inflow, until the steady-state capital ratio is reached. The inflow is not consumed, as long as the world interest rate exceeds the country's rate of time preference. The model implies a debt cycle scenario according to which trade and current account deficits first incurred as capital is imported give way to a trade surplus and later a current account surplus after output has expanded and payments on foreign borrowing have ceased. Concerns about debt stocks and the size of the financial and real transfer over the debt cycle are unwarranted because they adjust automatically. Foreign investors are assumed to bring in capital goods and take away part of the additional production through dividend payments, thereby resolving the transfer problem. The traditional neoclassical model thus seems more appropriate for characterizing foreign direct investment (FDI) inflows than other types of capital flows.

But mere capital accumulation does not guarantee that a country benefits from capital inflows. First, in the presence of sufficiently misguided policies, inflows can "immiserize." Second, an upward-sloping supply of capital implies that the cost of capital inflows rises at the margin. These circumstances explain how, even on standard neoclassical grounds, governments can be justified in resisting part of the capital inflows.

Models of "immiserizing" inflows have been developed by Bhagwati (1973), Johnson (1967), and Brecher and Diaz-Alejandro (1977). Tariff-induced inflows of capital magnify the welfare losses due to distorted consumption and production patterns by stimulating capital accumulation in protected sectors and by attracting foreign capital into these sectors, if foreign capital receives the full (untaxed) value of its marginal product. As Calvo (1996) suggests, drastic structural reform in most capital-importing countries has made the "immiserizing inflow" argument less relevant today. But these reforms do not guarantee that countries have moved to a Pareto optimum. The persistence of other distortions, arising, for example, from high marginal tax rates combined with full deductability of interest payments, may stimulate private credit booms; additional distortions may be reintroduced by policy makers through controls applied during a capital-outflow crisis.

There is also an "optimum tariff"–type case for taxing capital inflows. Harberger (1985) suggests levying an optimal tax on foreign borrowing, if the recipient country faces an upward-sloping supply of credit, to equate its tax-inclusive average cost to the higher marginal cost. A related argument can be made for capital-importing net debtor countries, if such a tax succeeds in improving their joint capital terms of trade by dampening the world interest rate.

Even in the absence of any distortions or externality costs, further evidence that the net benefits of capital inflows may be small in the standard neoclassical framework comes from growth accounting (Krugman, 1993). Adding human capital accumulation to the standard Solow growth mode, output growth can be written as

$$\dot{Y} = \alpha \dot{K} + \beta \dot{H} + \left(1 - \alpha - \beta\right)\dot{L} + \dot{\theta} \tag{1}$$

where dots represent growth rates of output Y, physical capital K, human capital H, and labor L, α and β are the physical and human capital shares in national income, and $\dot{\theta}$ is the growth rate of the Solow technology residual. Mankiw, Romer, and Weil (1992) have found that the three variables K, H, and L of an augmented Solow model explain almost 80 percent of the cross-country variation in income per capita of a Summers-Heston country sample of ninety-eight nonoil countries. Their estimates imply a physical capital share α of 0.31 and a human capital share β of 0.28. Assuming an average capital–output ratio of 2.5 and an average current account deficit of 4 percent of GDP (a stylized description of major capital importers), the Solow model predicts an increase in the growth rate of capital of 1.6 percent. The resulting increase in the short-run growth of output is only 0.50 percent.

10.2.2 Endogenous growth

Endogenous growth models, unlike neoclassical models that imply decreasing returns to capital, are characterized by the assumption of nondecreasing returns to the set of reproducible factors of production. Equation (1) gives rise to endogenous growth if $\alpha + \beta = 1$, so that

$$\dot{Y} = \alpha \dot{K} + \beta \dot{H}. \tag{2}$$

Equation (2) says that long-term growth can be explained entirely by growth in capital, without any appeal to an exogenous Solow technology residual. This implies external economies to capital accumulation: the elasticity of output with respect to capital greatly exceeds its share of GDP at market prices. Such externalities create a presumption that the benefits of capital inflows must be much higher than those implied by the standard neoclassical approach.[1] In the neoclassical growth model, countries benefiting from large inflows initially should experience large increases in capital accumulation, with their growth rates peaking on impact, then gradually slowing back to the steady-state rate. To change the growth rate of the capital recipient permanently though, the inflow must not only increase the economy's level of capital equipment and output, but it also must affect the economy's production function. In contrast with the Solow growth framework (where technological change is exogenously given), the new growth literature highlights the dependence of growth rates on the state of technology relative to the rest of the world.

Despite the optimistic predictions of the endogenous growth model for the benefits of inflows, however, Cohen (1993) finds for a sample of thirty-four developing debtor countries that benefited from renewed access to the world financial markets in the 1970s, capital accumulation was actually less than for other developing countries. This observation cannot be explained by endogenous factors, such as the initial output per capital level and the initial stock of capital. Rather, capital accumulation failed to increase because much of the capital inflow leaked into consumption.

For foreign direct investment flows, in contrast to debt-creating flows, the optimistic assessment of endogenous growth has been validated by Borensztein, De Gregorio, and Lee (1995). They find in a cross-country regression framework for sixty-nine developing countries over the period 1970–89 that for each percentage point of increase in the FDI–GDP ratio, the rate of growth of the host economy increases by 0.8 percentage points. The contribution of FDI to long-term growth results from two effects. First, FDI adds to capital accumulation, because it stimulates domestic investment, rather than crowding out domestic investment by competing in domestic product markets or financial markets. The complementarity of FDI and domestic investment is explained by their complementarity in production and by positive technology spillovers. Second, FDI stimulates growth through the embodied transfer of technology and efficiency, provided the host country has a minimum threshold stock of human capital with which to exploit these gains.

---

[1] However, if returns to capital are constant, then the rate of return on capital will not be decreasing in the capital–labor ratio. In this case there is no incentive in the endogenous growth model for capital to flow from rich to poor countries, because returns on capital need not be larger in poor countries (Krugman, 1993).

10.2.3 *The intertemporal approach to the current account*

In the models considered so far, the benefits of capital inflows derive from net capital inflows that are fully invested and raise the level or the growth rate of GDP. However, the benefits of capital flows not only come from directing world savings to the most productive investment opportunities, but also from allowing individuals to smooth consumption over different states of nature by borrowing or diversifying portfolios abroad. Developing countries are likely to benefit greatly from the international pooling of country-specific risks that would result in intertemporal smoothing of consumption levels.[2] First, poor countries tend to be more shock-prone than richer countries. Second, since their per capita income is low, any downside adjustment will hurt more than in countries with higher consumption levels.

In principle, the intertemporal approach to the current account can help answer the question of how much capital flows to accept by running current account deficits. International capital mobility opens the opportunity to trade off present levels of absorption against future absorption. If saving falls short of desired investment, foreigners have to finance the resulting current account deficit, leading to a rise in the country's net foreign liabilities. The intertemporal approach views the current account as the outcome of forward-looking dynamic saving and investment decisions (Obstfeld and Rogoff, 1994), which are driven by expectations of future productivity growth, interest rates, and other factors. This approach, in principle, is able to provide a benchmark for defining "excessive" current account deficits in the context of models that yield predictions about the equilibrium path of external imbalances (Milesi-Ferretti and Razin, 1996).

Table 10.1 collects predictions of the intertemporal approach about how the "equilibrium" (first-period) current account should respond to a fall in the world interest rate and a reform-induced productivity rise – two impulses that have figured prominently in the discussion on the determinants of recent capital flows to emerging markets. The results in the table imply:

---

[2] The benefits of portfolio diversification are particularly strong in the case of fully funded pensions. Industrial countries with aging populations can escape part of their demographic problems by investing in emerging markets, while poor countries can diversify away some of the idiosyncratic risks stemming from higher exposure to country-specific shocks by investing some of their pension assets in industrial countries (Reisen, 1994a, 1997).

Table 10.1. *Current account effects predicted by the intertemporal approach*

Shock	Temporary			Persistent		
	Saving	Investment	Current account	Saving	Investment	Current account
Fall in the world interest rate below permanent average rate						
Net debtor countries	+	0	+	NA	NA	NA
Net creditor countries	–	0	–			
Rise in productivity						
Country-specific	+	0	+	–	+	–
Global	+	0	+	+	+	0

Source: See Glick and Rogoff (1995), Obstfeld and Rogoff (1994), and Razin (1995).

1 Capital-importing countries, as net foreign debtors, should increase their saving in response to cyclical portfolio flows which are interest rate driven. The current account deficit should decline (or move into surplus) as people smooth consumption in the face of temporarily low interest payments. For net creditor countries, temporarily low interest rates should result in opposite current account effects. If a net debtor country widens its current account deficit in response to temporary interest rate reductions, the response may well destabilize rather than smooth the intertemporal consumption path.

2 Likewise, the intertemporal approach does not necessarily predict an increasing current account deficit when capital flows are attracted by country-specific productivity surges. The "equilibrium" response of the current account depends crucially on the expectation of whether the productivity surge is temporary or permanent. In both cases, the productivity surge raises output immediately, but only a persistent rise in productivity raises permanent income. The reason is that only a permanent productivity surge induces investment and a higher future capital stock. The rise in permanent income also causes consumption to rise more than output, resulting in a larger current account deficit as a result of lower saving and higher investment. In contrast, a transitory increase in productivity should result in an opposite current account effect (a lower deficit), since there is no effect on investment and agents save part of any transitory increase of income (in the permanent income model of consumption).

3 Productivity surges should not necessarily be interpreted as country-specific in origin, but can be part of a broader global shock. Since all countries cannot import their current accounts in response to a persistent productivity-enhancing shock common to all countries, world interest rates rise until global savings and investment are balanced. This should dampen consumption in net debtor countries sufficiently to offset the consumption effects arising from higher permanent income brought about by higher investment. In contrast, a global transitory productivity shock produces excess world saving and thereby exerts downward pressure on interest rates. A temporary drop in world interest rates results in lower current account deficits for net debtor countries, as analyzed previously.

It is noteworthy that – among the capital-flow determinants discussed here – the intertemporal approach predicts a widening of current account deficits (for net debtor countries) only if the country enjoys a permanent country-specific productivity boom.[3]

10.2.4   The evidence on benefits

How much economic benefit have our sample countries derived from inflows of foreign capital? Have current account deficits been excessive in view of the benefits (or costs, see subsequent discussion)? Let us consult some data to confront the theories surveyed so far. Recall that the standard neoclassical approach assumes that foreign savings are fully invested and that investment raises a country's capital–labor ratios. The country imports foreign savings in response to any difference between the efficiency and borrowing cost of investment. Table 10.2 shows that all of the sample countries should have benefited from foreign savings, given the strong differenential between their efficiency and cost measures. That difference is particularly strong for Thailand, Malaysia, and Chile; it is weaker for Mexico, Peru, and the Philippines, with Argentina and Indonesia in between. Strikingly, labor was only equipped with more capital in those countries where capital was most efficient (i.e., Argentina, Chile, Indonesia, Malaysia, and Thailand). By contrast, the capital–

---

[3] Individual country estimates for the period 1970–90, following the reduced-form regression in Glick and Rogoff (1995), do not find a significant impact of domestic productivity on changes in the current account. It should be noted, however, that Glick and Rogoff obtain a low level of explanatory power in their estimates of current account determinants. The R^2 in their individual country time series regressions ranges between 3 and 49 percent, indicating an incompletely specified model.

Table 10.2. *Efficiency, average borrowing cost, and capital–output ratios (in percent)*

Country	Efficiency[a] avg. 1987–94	Real interest cost[b] avg. 1988–94	First year of capital inflow	Capital–labor ratio, % change up to 1993
Argentina	18.9	3.5	1991	+8.0
Chile	24.4	3.8	1990	+21.2
Mexico	13.2	4.3	1989	−23.1
Peru	n.a.	3.2	1992	−1.0
Indonesia	20.4	3.0	1990	+18.1
Malaysia	22.7	2.9	1989	+24.0
Philippines	13.5	3.0	1992	+1.2
Thailand	27.8	3.3	1988	+40.6

[a] Efficiency is defined as the inverse of the ratio of the investment rate to the real GDP growth rate.
[b] Defined as average cost of new commitments in U.S. dollar terms minus U.S. CPI inflation rate.
Sources: J.P. Morgan, *Emerging Markets Economic Outlook*, September 1995; World Bank, *World Debt Tables, 1996*, vol. 2; and World Bank data files.

labor ratio fell strongly in Mexico during its inflow period, excluding any benefits arising from standard neoclassical considerations.

What happened to growth and income convergence since capital inflows began in these countries? Table 10.3 reports purchasing power parity (PPP)-adjusted GNP per capita output levels as well as potential growth rate estimates. Since GDP can be seen as the result of the transformation of factors of production into output, a theoretically appropriate way to estimate potential GDP is to combine estimates of the available volume of factor inputs with a numerically specified production function. However, even small estimation errors for the individual parameters of the production function (e.g., output elasticities, rate of technical progress, or degree of excess capacity) can lead to rather implausible estimates for potential output. Instead, a simpler approach, the peak-to-peak method is employed, which uses only actual GDP data.

This method is implemented for each country by first identifying the peaks of actual GDP across business cycles and connecting these data points by interpolation. The procedure is applied for two different observation periods, for 1960–95 (for Malaysia, 1970–95), and for the period since the year of "openness" reform as classified by Sachs and Warner (1995) until 1995. For Argentina and Peru, Sachs and Warner classify the

Table 10.3. *Income growth and convergence*

Country	PPP estimates of GNP per capita (U.S. = 100)		Potential GDP growth rate since openness reform[a]	Actual GDP growth rate since first year of inflow
	1990	1994		
Argentina	21.9	33.7	4.3	5.4
Chile	29.0	34.4	4.2	6.4
Mexico	28.0	27.2	1.8	1.7
Peru	12.7	13.9	7.8	5.9
Indonesia	11.0	13.9	6.1	7.1
Malaysia	27.6	32.6	6.5	8.9
Philippines	10.9	10.6	2.6	3.8
Thailand	21.6	26.9	7.2	9.7

[a] Calculated by peak-to-peak method; see text.
Sources: World Bank, *World Development Report*, 1992 and 1996; and J.P. Morgan, *World Financial Markets*, various issues.

year of opening as 1991, for the Philippines 1988, for Mexico 1986, and for Chile 1976; for other countries the observation periods coincide. Annual GDP data are used, except for Peru and the Philippines where good quarterly data are available and where the reform period is relatively short. The interpolated peak GDP series can be seen as an approximation of the highest attainable level of output at each point in time.

In a second step, the average ratio of actual GDP to the highest attainable GDP for each cycle is calculated, giving a measure of the "normal" degree of slack in each economy. This ratio is then used to scale the series of highest attainable GDP to derive estimates for potential GDP. The *annual* growth rate of potential GDP is then obtained by regressing the potential GDP series on a time trend. The results give generally plausible estimates, except possibly for Mexico and the Philippines, where potential growth for the period since openness reform is lower than for the full period. The results reported in Table 10.3 use the growth rates of potential GDP obtained for the period since reform.

Observe from Table 10.3 that, except for Mexico and the Philippines, PPP-adjusted per capita income converged in all of the recipient countries. Observe also that, with the noticeable exception of Mexico and

Peru, *actual* GDP growth rates since the inflows began exceed the estimates of *potential* growth rates since the sample countries have "opened up." However, it is still too early to arrive at any solid judgment on whether the recent capital inflows have raised efficiency and growth rates permanently.

How well then does the intertemporal approach explain actual current account balances in our eight sample countries?

Table 10.4 explores the issue in more detail by examining changes in saving and investment balances following each country's increase in capital inflows. As Table 10.4 shows, the observed shift in savings–investment balances for our eight sample countries often does not suit the theoretical predictions:

1   In Argentina and Peru private consumption rose strongly. Only a permanent rise in productivity, which should have raised investment rates as well, or a temporary drop of actual output below potential could have justified the observed rise in private consumption rates. But there was no rise in observed investment rates, while actual output rose strongly.

2   The Mexican story is slightly different, because output growth remained extremely low during the inflow period. There was some moderate rise in investment rates, but most of the switch in the current account balance was due to a private consumption boom. Such a boom could be partly justified by higher public savings, current income levels being below potential, or expectations of higher permanent income (as indicated by higher investment), but the size of the switch in private consumption is clearly excessive.

3   There was also a rise in private consumption, as a fraction of GDP, in Malaysia and the Philippines. In both countries the rise was offset by higher public savings and validated by higher investment rates (indicating expectations of higher permanent income levels).

4   Chile, Indonesia, and Thailand responded to capital inflows with falling private consumption rates, although their output growth initially rose (above potential), public savings rose (implying no Ricardian offset), and the strong rise in investment rates and productivity certainly warranted expectations of higher permanent income. Note finally that Indonesia and Chile reduced their external deficits as a result of strong increases in savings. Indonesia differs from Chile and Thailand, however, in one respect: productivity declined during the inflow period, suggesting a fu-

Table 10.4. *Changes in saving and investment balances*

| | Change[a] | | | | First year of capital inflows | Memo | |
| | | | | | | Year when current account deficit peaked | Peak current account deficit[b], % of GDP |
Country	Current account	Investment	Saving	Private consumption			
Argentina	−2.1	+0.4	−1.7	+4.2	1991	1994	3.5
Chile	+1.3	+4.3	+5.6	−0.2	1990	1993	2.1
Mexico	−5.3	+1.8	−3.5	+5.8	1989	1994	7.8
Peru	−2.5	−0.8	−3.4	+3.9	1992	1995	6.4
Indonesia	+1.1	+4.6	+5.7	−4.3	1990	1996	4.0
Malaysia	−8.2	+8.8	+0.6	+2.4	1989	1995	8.5
Philippines	−2.4	+3.5	+1.1	+3.6	1992	1994	4.5
Thailand	−5.4	+11.8	+6.4	−5.6	1988	1995	8.3

[a] Changes are calculated as the annual average level from first year of inflows until 1994 minus the annual average level from 1986 until the first year of capital inflows. All balances expressed as percent of GDP. Based on national account data; saving rates were derived as residual.

[b] Data for 1995 are estimates and for 1996 are forecasts.

Sources: IMF, *International Financial Statistics* for all countries except Mexico; IMF, *World Economic Outlook*, May 1995, for Mexico data; J.P. Morgan, *World Financial Markets*, second quarter 1996 for peak current account deficit data.

ture drop in the country's investment rate and worsening of its current account deficit.

The evidence suggests two lessons, one for theorists and one for practitioners. The insight for theory is that the intertemporal approach fails to predict the macroeconomic responses of most capital flow recipient countries. In the case of Chile, the existence of effective capital controls may provide part of the explanation for the failure of the intertemporal approach (which assumes full capital mobility). In the case of the other sample countries (for which full openness to capital flows can be assumed), "excessive" private consumption (Argentina, Mexico, Peru) and "excessive" savings (Thailand) responses must be explained by determinants not captured by the consumption-smoothing approach.

The insight for practitioners is that current account deficits were excessive in Mexico and are probably now so in Peru as well. Malaysia's and Thailand's deficits, although high, cannot be labeled as "excessive," however. In these countries capital inflows were used for investment that exploits high efficiency and rising total factor productivity. Moreover, foreign saving inflows have thus far been accompanied by rising national savings in these countries.

10.2.5   *Conclusions I*

This section has surveyed several strands of the economic literature for hypotheses regarding the benefits of *net* capital inflows. Perhaps surprisingly, in the current context of heavy portfolio flows and nonbinding foreign exchange constraints (which were emphasized earlier by the two-gap literature), the benefits of large net inflows are generally small.

Even if net capital inflows are fully invested rather than consumed, neoclassical growth models do not promise grandiose benefits. The resulting rise in the capital ratio only affects short-term growth, not a country's long-term growth rate, as long as capital flows do not affect the production function. But even such a modest benefit may not be realized, when capital flows are immiserizing due to distortions, or when the rising marginal costs of foreign borrowing are not taken into account by economic agents. Endogenous growth models promise more, but they do not promise large capital flows to capital-poor countries when marginal capital returns are nondecreasing. Moreover, the benefits are large only when capital flows carry externalities that improve a country's efficiency, externalities that can only be exploited when a certain level of human capital is already present in the country.

The intertemporal approach to the current account identifies circumstances that justify welfare-enhancing current account deficits. Among the determinants for recent capital flows to emerging markets, however, the approach predicts a large current account deficit only when a country-specific productivity surge raises permanent income. Permanent productivity increases and technological spillovers emphasized by the new growth literature are most likely embodied in foreign direct investment inflows to a largely undistorted economy.

10.3 Long-term sustainability of current account deficits

10.3.1 Debt dynamics

It is a common fallacy to confuse unsustainability with undesirability. Foreign savings need not necessarily be resisted because they finance a current account deficit that is unsustainably large. In particular, during reform episodes a deficit may occur because of a desired stock adjustment from financial assets into real assets in the case of an investment boom, because the expected profitability of real assets has improved. The corresponding deficit in the current account is inevitably temporary, yet desirable as well. This is a valuable lesson from the intertemporal approach.

But a large deficit will not be financed by foreigners forever. There will at some point inevitably have to be adjustment back to payments balance. It is thus not only important to know the *sources* of the current account deficit (see section 10.4), but also the *size* and the *time profile* of the balancing adjustment. That makes long-term sustainability of the current account deficit a benchmark of which authorities should be aware.

This section presents a conventional debt dynamics equation to derive a measure of intertemporal solvency, emphasizing the role of potential GDP growth, the real exchange rate, and the desired level of foreign exchange reserves.[4] The section builds on recent work by Milesi-Ferretti and Razin (1996) and Edwards, Steiner, and Losada (1995).

Let us first consider an economy in steady state, with liabilities as a fraction of the country's GDP that foreigners are willing to hold in equilibrium, denoted by d, which can be interpreted as an "equilibrium

---

[4] Interest payments on outstanding debt and the resource transfer (the noninterest current account) are ignored to keep the focus on the sustainable current account deficit. The loss of information is minor to the extent that average interest costs do not vary much across the sample countries.

portfolio share." Note that foreign direct investment is *not* typically governed by portfolio considerations; multinational companies seek to internalize agglomeration benefits by concentrating (rather than diversifying) their FDI flows; and, while markets do watch a country's foreign debt–GDP ratio, they are not as concerned about the level of FDI-related liabilities. Consequently, FDI flows are excluded from the subsequent discussion on long-term sustainability. In equilibrium – that is, with d held constant – the country accumulates net liabilities, equal to the current account deficit, CAD, plus the net accumulation of international reserves, FX, both as fractions of GDP, in proportion to its long-run GDP growth rate, γ:

$$CAD + \Delta FX = \gamma d. \tag{3}$$

Long-run GDP growth exerts two indirect effects on the steady-state current account that are consistent with a stable debt–GDP ratio. First, as the economy expands, the desired level of international reserves also grows. Edwards, Steiner, and Losada (1995) assume that in equilibrium the authorities set their desired reserve holdings in terms of the number of months of imports. The demand for international reserves may also depend on uncertainty created by variability in the balance of payments (Heller and Khan, 1978). Uncertainty in the balance of payments is ignored here, however. Denoting real annual import growth by η, the change in the desired reserve ratio can be written as

$$\Delta FX = \left[(1+\eta)/(1+\gamma)\right]FX - FX. \tag{4}$$

Incorporation (4) into (3) yields

$$\gamma d = CAD + \left[(\eta-\gamma)/(1+\gamma)\right]FX. \tag{5}$$

A second channel through which GDP growth indirectly affects debt dynamics is the Balassa-Samuelson effect, according to which *relative* output growth differences generate real exchange rate appreciation, driven by the evolution of productivity differentials between traded and nontraded goods in the domestic economy and in the rest of the world. Real exchange rate appreciation per unit of GDP growth, denoted by ε, reduces both debt and foreign exchange reserves as a fraction of GDP, so that equation (5) can be rearranged to give

$$CAD = (\gamma+\varepsilon)d - \left[(\eta+\varepsilon-\gamma)/(1+\gamma)\right]FX. \tag{6}$$

Equation (6) describes the steady-state current account deficit that can be sustained over the long run if the debt ratio remains constant and desired reserves rise in proportion to import growth.

Table 10.5 provides numerical estimates of equation (6) for four Latin American and four Asian countries. The memo variables d (external debt/GDP) and FX (international reserves/GDP) refer to 1995 estimates as given in J.P. Morgan, *World Financial Markets*. Figures for the potential growth rate parameter γ are calculated by the peak-to-peak method as described in section 10.2.4 and reported in Table 10.3. The parameters ε and η are estimated as described later.

Estimates of the real exchange rate appreciation effect of GDP growth relative to the U.S. rate are obtained from Larraín's (1996) analysis of the determinants of real exchange rates for a sample of twenty-eight Asian and Latin American countries over the period 1960–90. These estimates control for the effects of other determinants, namely government spending, degree of openness, and the terms of trade. The parameter ε is calculated by scaling these figures by the annual growth rate of potential GDP. Note that since the relationship between real exchange rates and relative GDP levels is nonlinear, a given estimate of the growth rate of potential GDP implies greater real equilibrium exchange rate appreciation at higher relative income levels; witness the difference between Malaysia and Indonesia, for example.

Estimates of the future annual real import growth rate, η, are extrapolated out of the reform period sample for each country. Argentina's annual import growth may seem implausibly high, but it must be recognized that Argentina is still a very closed economy in terms of the import ratio m and that the potential for natural trade through, for example, the Mercosur free-trade agreement is far from exhausted.

Table 10.5 displays the results of calibrating equation (6) for the long-run steady-state current account ratio for constant target debt and reserve levels relative to GDP. Since a high debt ratio can be sustained by a larger deficit in the current account than a smaller debt ratio, it is assumed for all sample countries that foreign investors are comfortable with tolerating a debt ratio of 50 percent, that is, $d^* = 50$. This is roughly equal to the level in Peru or Thailand, countries about which the financial press has expressed concern. The target level of foreign exchange reserves for all countries, FX^*, is assumed to be equal to half the import ratio (six months of imports). Note that because of their low potential growth rates, both Mexico and the Philippines must achieve a current account surplus in the steady state.

Table 10.6 compares the steady-state measure of the current account

Table 10.5. *Steady-state current account deficit (in percent of GDP)*

Country	CAD	=	$(\gamma + \varepsilon)d^*$	–	$[(\eta + \varepsilon - \gamma)/(1 + \gamma)]FX^*$	Memo	
						d	FX
Argentina	1.6		(0.043 + 0.007)50		[(0.318 + 0.007 − 0.043)/1.043]3.5	33	5.0
Chile	2.0		(0.042 + 0.006)50		[(0.069 + 0.006 − 0.042)/1.042]11.4	34	22.0
Mexico	−0.6		(0.018 + 0.000)50		[(0.126 + 0.000 − 0.018)/1.018]14.0	68	5.8
Peru	3.8		(0.078 + 0.009)50		[(0.152 + 0.009 − 0.078)/1.078]6.5	51	12.7
Indonesia	3.0		(0.061 + 0.004)50		[(0.073 + 0.004 − 0.061)/1.061]9.9	54	8.8
Malaysia	1.7		(0.065 + 0.014)50		[(0.111 + 0.014 − 0.065)/1.065]39.6	42	29.1
Philippines	−0.6		(0.026 + 0.001)50		[(0.112 + 0.001 − 0.026)/1.026]16.6	59	8.7
Thailand	2.8		(0.072 + 0.010)50		[(0.133 + 0.010 − 0.072)/1.072]19.7	48	19.2

Note: See text for explanation.

Table 10.6. *Current account balance measures, 1994 (in percent of GDP)*

	Actual	Cyclically adjusted[a]	Cyclically and FDI adjusted[b]	Steady state[c]
Argentina	−3.5	−3.0	−2.6	−1.6
Chile	−1.5	−1.5	+2.1	−2.0
Mexico	−7.8	−7.1	−4.9	+0.1
Peru	−4.5	−3.5	+1.2	−3.8
Indonesia	−1.6	−0.4	+0.9	−3.0
Malaysia	−5.9	±0.0	+6.5	−1.7
Philippines	−4.4	−4.3	−2.8	+0.6
Thailand	−5.9	−1.1	+2.0	−2.8

[a] The cyclically corrected deficit adjusts imports for the difference in actual and potential GDP.
[b] Adjusts cyclically corrected deficit by adding FDI/GDP inflows.
[c] From Table 10.5 with sign reversed.

balance with the actual balance and with cyclically-adjusted and FDI-adjusted balance measures, all for the year 1994 (the last year for which FDI data were available). Observe that the FDI and cyclically-adjusted current account deficit was higher than the steady-state deficit in Argentina, Mexico, and the Philippines. In contrast, the high deficits in countries such as Malaysia and Thailand appear to be sustainable.

10.3.2 Conclusions II

The section suggested measures against which to judge whether actual current account deficits are sustainable in the long run. Actual deficit numbers alone cannot provide information about long-term sustainability. Any judgment needs to consider debt–GDP levels (current versus that tolerated by investors), official foreign exchange reserves (current versus targeted), potential GDP growth rate, import growth, the Balassa-Samuelson effect, and the structure of capital inflows. Sustainability considerations do not make sense for FDI flows, as long as there is no widely held notion about the sustainability of net foreign liabilities associated with the stock of FDI invested in a country.

10.4   Problems with excessive current account deficits

This section discusses some problems with the notion of "excessive" current account deficits. The benefits of foreign saving inflows – consumption smoothing and income growth – will not materialize when current account deficits represent excessive current consumption or when foreign funds are misallocated. A balance-of-payments crisis will then be unavoidable. It is useful, however, to review some of the arguments for why excessive consumption and unsound investment surges are likely to occur even in the absence of public sector deficits and distortions.

10.4.1   *The Lawson doctrine*

Commenting on concerns about the United Kingdom's balance of payments in a speech to the International Monetary Fund, the U.K. Chancellor Nigel Lawson concluded in September 1988 (a year before a deep crisis with falling output and surging unemployment set in): "we are prisoners of the past, when U.K. current account deficits were almost invariably associated with large budget deficits, poor economic performance, low reserves and exiguous net overseas assets. The present position could not be more different." What came to be internationally known as the Lawson doctrine is a proposition that has been most eloquently expressed by W. Max Corden (1977; and, with some qualifications, 1994):

> The current account is the net result of savings and investment, private and public. Decentralized optimal decisions on private saving and investment will lead to a net balance – the current account – which will also be optimal. There is no reason to presume that governments or outside observers know better how much private agents should invest and save than these agents themselves, unless there are government-imposed distortions. It follows that an increase in a current account deficit that results from a shift in private sector behaviour should not be a matter of concern at all. On the other hand, the public budget balance is a matter of public policy concern and the focus should be on this. (Corden, 1994)

The fact, however, that large current account deficits primarily reflected a private sector saving–investment imbalance did not prevent private capital markets from attacking currencies in Chile (early 1980s), in the United Kingdom and the Nordic countries (late 1980s), and in Mexico and Argentina (mid-1990s). So what was wrong with the Lawson doctrine?

1   In a forward-looking rational-expectations framework, current account balances are always the result of private sector decisions, with or without public sector deficits. With Ricardian equivalence, a public budget deficit immediately stimulates private savings to pay for future taxes. People who subscribe to the Lawson doctrine are thus saying that they do not believe in Ricardian equivalence (i.e., they believe in optimal private sector decisions, but not in rational expectations). In fact, the Ricardian offset coefficient has been estimated to average 0.5 for developing countries (Edwards, 1995); other things equal, a deterioration in the current account equal to 5 percent of GDP thus requires the public sector deficit to worsen by 10 percent of GDP.

2   Current private sector liabilities are often contingent public sector liabilities. Foreign creditors may force governments to turn private sector debt into public sector obligations, as happened in Chile after 1982. Furthermore, private sector losses tend to be absorbed eventually by the public sector, either through foregone tax revenue or through costly resolutions of banking crises, in particular when financial institutions are deemed "too large to fail." Balance-of-payments and financial crises are often caused by common factors, such as domestic financial liberalization, implicit deposit insurance, or exchange rate–based stabilization plans (Kaminsky and Reinhart, 1996).

3   Observed and expected returns to saving and investment can be distorted by various market failures: (a) Private borrowers may not internalize the rising marginal social cost of their private borrowing that arises from the upward-sloping supply of foreign capital (Harberger, 1985). (b) Excessively optimistic expectations about permanent income levels after major changes in policy regime can lead to overborrowing, because financial market institutions fail as efficient information conduits between depositors and borrowers (McKinnon and Pill, 1995; Chapter 11 in this volume). Financial market bubbles may add to this boom mentality by discouraging private savings through wealth effects.

4   A worsening current account deficit may lead to an unsustainable appreciation in the real exchange rate. Such an appreciation can conflict with development strategies based on the expansion of exports and efficient import substitution, which rely on a reliable and competitive exchange rate. Overvalued exchange rates cause suboptimal investments, which are costly

Table 10.7. *Macroeconomic adjustment in selected countries (in percent)*

Country	Year	Current account/GDP	Real GDP growth	Real private consumption growth per capita	Real exchange rate appreciation
Chile	1980	−7.1	7.8	1.5	22.0
	1981	−14.5	5.6	2.4	8.4
	1982	−9.5	−14.1	−12.4	−20.6
	1983	−5.6	−0.7	−5.1	−20.4
Mexico	1993	−6.5	0.6	−2.1	5.8
	1994	−7.8	3.5	3.7	−3.7
	1995	−0.3	−6.9	−9.2	−28.1
Argentina	1993	−2.9	6.0	1.2	7.4
	1994	−3.5	7.4	3.7	1.7
	1995	−0.8	−4.4	−9.2	0.4

Sources: IMF, *International Financial Statistics*; J.P. Morgan, *World Financial Markets*; author's calculations.

to reverse; undermine active trade promotion, export diversification, and productivity growth; and breed capital flight. Large swings in real exchange rates, often a result of temporary capital flows, have been found to depress significantly machinery and equipment investment and thus long-run growth performance (Agosín, 1994).

5   Markets are concerned with country risk and a country's total debt ratio (as now also stressed by Corden, 1994). Therefore, the current account as a whole, and not just the sources of its change, is relevant. Once debt ratios and current account deficits exceed certain levels (see section 10.3), decentralized decision making can lead to excessive borrowing from a national point of view (again, due to the Harberger externality), particularly when increased borrowing is for consumption rather than for investment.

Table 10.7 displays three hard-landing episodes in Latin America where the required switch in the current account went along with sharp drops in real GDP, even sharper cuts in private per capita consumption, and often a strong depreciation in the real exchange rate. During these episodes, the benefits of consumption smoothing and growth enhancement through foreign savings did indeed ring hollow.

10.4.2   *Private spending booms*

As defined earlier, large current account deficits may represent "excessive" private consumption, as was suggested in section 10.2.4 for Argentina, Mexico, and Peru. The empirical link between consumption booms, surges in bank lending, and subsequent banking crises is well documented (Gavin and Hausmann, 1996). Therefore, payments deficits owing to private spending booms suggest great risks to the public sector – risks of tax revenue losses and costly bank crisis resolutions, as documented by Table 10.8.

While it seems obvious that such costs imposed on the public sector suggest governments should engage in measures to moderate private spending booms (such as restrictive fiscal policies or credit restrictions on private borrowers), it is less straightforward to conclude that resistance to large current account deficits should be included in such measures. Distortions should be corrected at the source; balance-of-payment and banking crises seem to originate in either domestic financial deregulation, implicit deposit insurance, or protracted exchange rate–based stabilization plans:

1 Since the 1980s, the link between banking crises and balance-of-payments crises has strengthened. Kaminsky and Reinhart (1996) identify seventy-one balance-of-payments crises and twenty-five banking crises during the period 1970–95. While they find only three banking crises associated with the twenty-five balance-of-payments crises during 1970–79, they find twenty-two banking crises for the forty-six payments crises over 1980–95. They find that financial liberalization (which occurred mostly since the 1980s) plays a significant role in creating a private lending boom and explaining the probability of a banking crisis. A banking crisis, in turn, helps to create a currency crisis. There is also clear evidence for OECD countries that rapid and extensive financial deregulation has tended to lower household savings by lessening liquidity constraints (Blundell-Wignall and Browne, 1991). While most of that drop in private savings could be interpreted as a temporary stock adjustment to a higher consumption path, there is evidence that household saving rates have remained low (Andersen and White, 1996).

2 Information asymmetries, reinforced by the lack of institutions

Table 10.8. *Episodes of systemic banking crises with large capital inflows*

Country	Scope of crisis	Cost of rescuing banks (% of GDP)
Argentina, 1980–82	16% of assets of commercial banks; 35% of total assets of finance companies	55.3
Chile, 1981–83	45% of total assets	41.2
Israel, 1977–83	Entire banking sector	30.0
Finland, 1991–93	Savings banks	8.2
Mexico, 1995–96	Commercial banks' past due to gross loan ratio reaches 9.3% in February 1995	12–15

Sources: Bank for International Settlements, *63rd Annual Report*, 1993; Caprio and Klingebiel (1996).

that monitor and supervise credit risk, produce moral hazard and adverse selection. Firms with a high risk–return profile have an incentive to borrow heavily, as their exposure is limited by bankruptcy laws. Consumers incur excessive debt when they feel that their debt is not comprehensively monitored. In principle, banks and other intermediaries may attempt to reduce credit risk through credit rationing. This limits the extent to which liberalization can ease liquidity constraints. But when the government insures deposits against adverse outcomes, it alters how the banking system views the risks associated with making loans – it introduces moral hazard. This results in higher bank lending, which in turn can underpin excessively optimistic expectations about the success of reform (McKinnon and Pill, 1995; Chapter 11 in this volume).[5]

3   Exchange rate–based stabilization plans have often been accompanied by a boom in bank lending, which in turn fuels a boom in

---

[5] In other words, bank lending supports excess credibility of liberalization and stabilization programs. For liberalization programs perceived as temporary (a hypothesis that does not seem apt to describe existing policy regimes in most capital-importing countries), it was a *lack* of credibility that was used to explain temporary spending booms as residents exploited a "window of opportunity" (Calvo, 1987).

consumption spending. Unlike with money-based stabilization, disinflation produces a rise in real-money balances, as a result of central bank intervention to peg the currency and of money demand rising as domestic wealth holders convert their assets back into domestic currency. As long as foreign exchange intervention is unsterilized the capital inflows are fully intermediated through the banking system. This allows a boom in credit to agents who have been rationed previously as a result of inflation and financial repression (Sachs, Tornell, and Velasco, 1996; Reisen, 1993). Subsequently, overvaluation due to inflation inertia causes a recession and a deterioration of bank assets as a result of nonperforming loans and lower asset prices.

Even though the source of these private spending booms is domestic, one must ask whether foreign saving inflows worsen the boom (Corden, 1994). In the absence of foreign capital inflows, the spending boom would manifest itself not in a current account deficit, but in higher interest rates. The critical question then is what kind of investment would be crowded out by the rise in domestic interest rates. With ineffective bank supervision (as a result, e.g., of too rapid financial deregulation), the average productivity of borrowing may decline as risk-averse investors withdraw from the pool of potential borrowers. The failure to finance productive investment would be the cost of the decision not to accept capital inflows, with the excess of the risk-adjusted domestic interest rate over the world interest rate as a measure of the distortion created by that decision. The result for the decision about whether to accept or resist inflows would be ambiguous.

In the McKinnon-Pill model the closed-economy financial market failure is reflected in higher financial yields, but its effect on aggregrate quantities – borrowing and consumption – is ambiguous, depending on offsetting income and substitution effects. Excessively optimistic expectations about future permanent income levels, resulting in both overconsumption and overinvestment, lead to excessive borrowing from the rest of the world. This distortion is reinforced by foreign savings. The McKinnon-Pill solution to the distortion is similar to a Pigou-Harberger tax (specifically, a reserve requirement on foreign deposits) that achieves the optimal balance of consumption smoothing and excessive borrowing.

The first-best solution to the boom distortion triggered by exchange rate–based stabilization is to announce, at the start of the stabilization plan, that the peg will be temporary, and will be followed by more nominal exchange rate flexibility. Although this is easier said than done, it does not do away with the immediate remonetization and real exchange rate appreciation that characterize the first phase of disinflation. Temporary support from selective controls on short-term capital controls may well be needed (Hausmann and Reisen, 1996).

10.4.3   *The real appreciation problem*

If the scope for sterilized intervention is limited,[6] and if foreign savings are partly spent on nontradables, a protracted current account deficit will be associated with a real appreciation of the exchange rate. But there is no mechanical link between the size of the deficit and the magnitude of the appreciation. To the extent that the shift in the current account balance represents higher investment, the increased resource transfer is likely to be spent on additional imports of capital goods and intermediate goods. In such a case, the real transfer will be "effected" largely through the transfer of purchasing power, with little effect on relative prices. But when the current account deficit largely represents a consumption boom, the transfer of purchasing power will not solve the real transfer problem by itself, since a large part of the additional purchasing power is likely to fall on nontradables. In such cases, a shift in relative prices – a real appreciation of the exchange rate in the recipient country – will be necessary.

This lesson from the interwar transfer debate is supported by Table 10.9. The table suggests that the real appreciation problem only appeared when capital inflows were mostly consumed rather than invested and saving fell, as for Argentina, Mexico, and Peru. Estimates of the "unwarranted" appreciation ("net appreciation") are derived from data in the United Nations Income Comparison Project, as reported in the World Bank's *World Development Report*. According to the Balassa-Samuelson effect, poor countries tend to be "cheap" in PPP terms, since services tend to be cheaper in these countries. In fact, there is a strong nonlinear correlation between PPP-adjusted per capita incomes relative to U.S. income and the deviation of the currency below PPP (Reisen, 1993). By 1990, neither Argentina nor Peru was a "cheap" country in PPP terms as determined by their relative per capita incomes. Since then, however, their currencies have strongly appreciated, as did the Mexican peso until 1994. Only a small part of that appreciation (in Mexico's case, none) is due to the "catch-up" effect associated with the property that relative growth (compared with the U.S. growth rate) leads to trend appreciation of the real exchange rate. The "unwarranted" appreciation

---

[6] On sterilized intervention in Asia and Latin America, see Reisen (1994b).

Table 10.9. *Saving and real exchange rate appreciation (in percent)*

Country	Change in domestic saving rate since inflows started[a]	Index of undervaluation[b]		Real appreciation[c]	Catch-up appreciation[d]	Net appreciation[e]
		1990	1994			
Argentina	−1.7	50	93	+43	8	+35
Chile	+5.6	31	40	+9	3	+6
Mexico	−3.5	32	60	+28	0	+28
Peru	−3.4	42	59	+17	1	+16
Indonesia	+5.7	24	24	±0	1	−1
Malaysia	+0.6	38	41	+3	7	−4
Philippines	+1.1	31	35	+4	0	+4
Thailand	+6.4	30	35	+5	5	+0

[a] From Table 10.4.
[b] Nominal income per capita at current exchange rates relative to PPP-adjusted income per capita, i.e., index of undervaluation relative to the dollar (100 = no undervaluation).
[c] Change in degree of undervaluation between 1990 and 1994; positive number indicates appreciation.
[d] Real exchange rate appreciation due to GDP growth relative to the U.S. rate, as derived from Larraín (1996).
[e] Residual (change minus catch-up appreciation).
Sources: World Bank, *World Development Report*, 1992 and 1996; Larraín (1996).

is likely to conflict with development strategies based on the expansion of exports and efficient import substitution, which center on a reliable and competitive exchange rate.

10.4.4   Is foreign direct investment special?

From 1970 to 1982, Singapore ran annual current account deficits equal to 12.1 percent of GDP on average; in the early 1970s, the deficit peaked at around 20 percent of GDP several times. Almost half of the corresponding net capital inflows consisted of foreign direct investment (FDI). Real GDP growth averaged more than 8.6 percent per year over the period, and the domestic saving rate doubled from 21 percent in 1970 to more than 40 percent in 1982, but a balance-of-payments crisis never developed. This anecdotal evidence in support of the view that FDI lessens the possibility of later balance-of-payments problems is supported by Frankel and Rose (1996) and Meese and Rose (Chapter 6 in this volume). Both studies find in a panel of annual data for over 100 developing countries from 1971 through 1992 that a high ratio of FDI to debt is associated with a low likelihood of a currency crash. This raises the question whether FDI is special with respect to its macroeconomic implications. There is a strong presumption that indeed it is:

1   Foreign direct investment is largely determined by noncyclical considerations, such as long-term profitability expectations. Consequently, it is less subject to sudden shifts in investor sentiment. While on an annual basis, large fluctuations of foreign direct investment *flows* are regularly observed, foreign direct investment *stocks* are largely illiquid and irreversible.[7] This observation is reinforced by Mexico's experience in 1995, when its capital account showed only a slightly reduced net inflow of foreign direct investment after the crisis in 1994.

2   The Harberger externality does not apply to foreign direct investment. Even if the supply schedule of FDI is upward-sloping, FDI is likely to produce positive external spillovers, improving the host country's production function (Borensztein, De

---

[7] Using quarterly balance-of-payments flow data for changes in *net* claims of FDI, portfolio equity and "long-term" and "short-term" flows, Claessens, Dooley, and Warner (1995) find that capital account labels do not provide any information about the volatility of flows. In particular, they argue that FDI and long-term flows are not more persistent than other types of flows. However, the primary policy concern here is with *reversals* of foreign investment, a concern not addressed by Claessens and coauthors, who base their analysis on quarterly time series properties of net, rather than gross, inflows.

Gregorio, and Lee, 1995). Moreover, returns to FDI are state-contingent and less affected by sovereign risk considerations than are other forms of foreign capital inflows. As a result, foreign direct investment is less subject to any upper limit of engagement, in contrast to debt flows.

3 To the extent that FDI is not induced by privatization (which represents, other things being equal, just a change in owner-ship), FDI inflows exert less upward pressure on the real exchange rate, minimizing the risk of adverse "Dutch disease" effects on exportables. Because FDI is likely to crowd in domestic investment, to the extent that it is "green plant" investment, it generates a corresponding movement in the demand for foreign exchange by stimulating imports. Moreover, by stimulating investment rather than consumption, FDI creates an ex ante home goods excess supply in the recipient country. Through both of these channels FDI tends to depreciate the real exchange rate to stimulate the demand for home goods (Artus, 1996). Table 10.10 shows that capital flows to East Asia, in contrast to flows to Latin America, were more in the form of "green plant" FDI, suggesting less upward pressure on real exchange rates in the region.

10.4.5 *Conclusions III*

The size of the current account deficit does not give rise to normative judgments; a deficit equal to 3 percent of GDP may be "excessive" in one country, while a deficit of 12 percent of GDP may be justified for another country. What distinguishes such deficits is not so much whether they are driven by public sector or private sector decisions, because there is some evidence for a Ricardian offset and because private debt is a contingent public sector liability. Rather what matters for governments is the source of the current account deficit. Foreign savings should be resisted to some extent when they are seen to finance excessive consumption or unproductive investment.

How much foreign savings should be resisted in such a case? The answer depends primarily on the nature of the source that ultimately gives rise to the spending boom and on the composition of the capital inflow. Private spending booms mostly originate in prior domestic deregulation, because of the interaction of implicit or explicit deposit insurance with an existing boom mentality, and/or a disinflation brought about by an exchange rate–based stabilization program. Resisting foreign savings thus is not necessarily a first-best policy response. If more

Table 10.10. *Foreign direct investment and privatization, 1990–94 (in billions of dollars)*

	Latin America	East Asia (excluding China)
Net private capital inflows	173.8	110.0
Raised through privatization	22.2	3.8
Net foreign direct investment inflows	71.3	47.2
Raised through privatization	13.0	2.0
"Traditional" foreign direct investment	58.3	45.2
% of net private capital inflows	33.5	41.1

Sources: World Bank, *World Debt Tables, 1996*; author's calculations.

nominal exchange rate flexibility, effective prudential regulation and bank supervision, and gradual domestic financial reform succeed in keeping private savings rates stable and productive investment financed, all the better. If, instead, an unsustainable currency appreciation, excessive risk taking in the banking system, and a sharp drop in private savings coincide, there is a case for resisting foreign capital inflows. The appropriate policy response then must balance the benefits of consumption smoothing and financing viable investment and the risks of excessive borrowing.

A case can be made that an open economy should accept all foreign direct investment, unless it creates new distortions as a result of new trade restrictions and as long as it can be absorbed by the existing stock of human capital. Foreign direct investment is less constrained by considerations of sovereign risk and portfolio limits on investment than other types of capital flows; and by crowding in domestic investment and having a limited initial impact on consumption (possibly unless privatization-induced), foreign direct investment is unlikely to generate a real appreciation problem.

References

Agosín, M. R. (1994). "Saving and Investment in Latin America," UN Conference on Trade and Development Discussion Paper No. 90. Geneva, Switzerland.
Andersen, P. S., and R. W. White, (1996). "The Macroeconomic Effects of

Financial Sector Reforms: An Overview of Industrial Countries." Unpublished manuscript, Bank for International Settlements, Basle.

Artus, P. (1996). "Le financement de la croissance par endettement extérieur," Working Paper No. 1996-05/T. Paris: Caisse des Dépôts et Consignations.

Bhagwati, J. N. (1973). "The Theory of Immiserizing Growth: Further Applications." In M. B. Connolly and A. K. Swoboda, eds., *International Trade and Money*, pp. 45–54. Toronto: Toronto University Press.

Blundell-Wignall, A., and F. Browne (1991). "Macroeconomic Consequences of Financial Liberalisation: A Summary Report," ESD Working Paper No. 98. Paris: Organisation for Economic Co-operation and Development.

Borensztein, E., J. De Gregorio, and J.-W. Lee (1995). "How Does Foreign Direct Investment Affect Economic Growth?" NBER Working Paper No. 5057. Cambridge, Mass.

Brecher, R. A., and C. F. Diaz-Alejandro (1977). "Tariffs, Foreign Capital, and Immiserizing Growth," *Journal of International Economics* 7 (4): 317–22.

Calvo, G. (1987). "On the Costs of Temporary Policy," *Journal of Development Economics* 27: 147–69.

(1996). "Varieties of Capital Market Crises," Center for International Economics Working Paper No. 15. University of Maryland at College Park.

Calvo, G., L. Leiderman, and C. Reinhart (1996). "Inflows of Capital to Developing Countries in the 1990s: Causes and Effects," *Journal of Economic Perspectives* 10 (2): 123–39.

Caprio, Jr., G., and D. Klingebiel (1997). "Bank Insolvency: Bad Luck, Bad Policy, or Bad Banking?" In M. Bruno and B. Pleskovic, eds., *Annual World Bank Conference on Development Economics, 1996*, pp. 79–104. Washington, D.C.: World Bank.

Chenery, H. B., and M. Bruno (1962). "Development Alternatives in an Open Economy: The Case of Israel," *Economic Journal* 57: 79–103.

Claessens, S., M. P. Dooley, and A. Warner (1995). "Portfolio Capital Flows: Hot or Cold?" *World Bank Economic Review* 9 (1): 153–74.

Cohen, D. (1993). "Convergence in the Closed and in the Open Economy." In A. Giovannini, ed., *Finance and Development: Issues and Experience*, pp. 99–114. Cambridge: Cambridge University Press.

Corden, W. M. (1977). *Inflation, Exchange Rates, and the International System.* Oxford: Oxford University Press.

(1994). *Economic Policy, Exchange Rates, and the International System.* Oxford: Clarendon Press.

Edwards, S. (1995). "Why Are Saving Rates So Different across Countries?: An International Comparative Analysis," NBER Working Paper No. 5097. Cambridge, Mass.

Edwards, S., R. Steiner, and F. Losada (1995). "Capital Inflows, the Real Exchange Rate, and the Mexican Crisis of 1994." Unpublished manuscript, World Bank, Washington, D.C.

Frankel, J., and A. K. Rose (1996). "Currency Crashes in Emerging Markets: Empirical Indicators," NBER Working Paper No. 5437. Cambridge, Mass.

Gavin, M., and Haúsmann, R. (1996). "The Roots of Banking Crises: The Macroeconomic Contex," Inter-American Development Bank Working Paper No. 318. Washington, D.C.

Glick, R., and K. Rogoff (1995). "Global versus Country-Specific Productivity

Shocks and the Current Account," *Journal of Monetary Economics* 35 (May): 159–92.

Goldstein, M. (1996). "Presumptive Indicators/Early Warning Signals of Vulnerability to Financial Crises in Emerging-Market Economies." Unpublished manuscript, Institute for International Economics, Washington, D.C.

Harberger, A. (1985). "Lessons for Debtor-Country Managers and Policymakers." In G. W. Smith and J. T. Cuddington, eds., *International Debt and the Developing Countries*, pp. 236–57. Washington, D.C.: World Bank.

Hausmann, R., and H. Reisen, eds. (1996). *Securing Stability and Growth in Latin America: Policy Issues and Prospects for Shock-Prone Economies.* Paris: Organisation for Economic Co-operation and Development.

Heller, H. R., and M. S. Khan (1978). "The Demand for International Reserves under Fixed and Floating Exchange Rate," *IMF Staff Papers* 25 (4): 623–49.

Johnson, H. (1967). "The Possibility of Income Losses from Increased Efficiency or Factor Accumulation in the Presence of Tariffs," *Economic Journal* 77: 151–4.

Kaminsky, G., and C. M. Reinhart (1996). "The Twin Crises: The Causes of Banking and Balance-of-Payments Problems," Center for International Economics Working Paper No. 17. University of Maryland at College Park.

Krugman, P. (1993). "International Finance and Economic Development." In A. Giovannini, ed., *Finance and Development: Issues and Experiences*, pp. 11–23. Cambridge: Cambridge University Press.

Larraín, G. (1996). "Productividad del Gasto Publico y Tipo de Cambio Real." In F. Morandé and R. Vergara, eds., *Análisis Empirico del Tipo de Cambio en Chile.* Santiago: Centro de Estudios Públicos and Georgetown University, Institute for Latin American Developing Economy Studies.

MacDougall, G. D. A. (1960). "The Benefits and Costs of Private Investment from Abroad: A Theoretical Approach," *Economic Record* 36: 13–35.

Mankiw, N. G., D. Romer, and D. N. Weil (1992). "A Contribution to the Empirics of Economic Growth," *Quarterly Journal of Economics* 107 (2): 407–37.

McKinnon, R. (1964). "Foreign Exchange Constraints in Economic Development and Efficient Aid Allocation," *Economic Journal* 74: 388–409.

McKinnon, R., and H. Pill (1995). "Credible Liberalizations and International Capital Flows: The Overborrowing Syndrome." Unpublished manuscript, Stanford University, Stanford, Calif.

Milesi-Ferretti, G. M., and A. Razin (1996). "Sustainability of Persistent Current Account Deficits," NBER Working Paper No. 5467. Cambridge, Mass.

Obstfeld, M., and K. Rogoff (1994). "The Intertemporal Approach to the Current Account," NBER Working Paper No. 4893. Cambridge, Mass.

Razin, A. (1995). "The Dynamic-Optimizing Approach to the Current Account: Theory and Evidence." In P. Kenen, ed., *Understanding Interdependence: The Macroeconomics of the Open Economy*, pp. 169–98. Princeton, N.J.: Princeton University Press.

Reisen, H. (1993). "Integration with Disinflation: Which Way?" In R. O'Brien, ed., *Finance and the International Economy*, Amex Bank Review Prize Essays, vol. 7, pp. 128–45. Oxford: Oxford University Press.

(1994a). "On the Wealth of Nations and Retirees." In R. O'Brien, ed., *Finance* and the *International Economy*, Amex Bank Review Prize Essays, vol. 8, pp. 86–107. Oxford: Oxford University Press.

(1994b). *Debt, Deficits, and Exchange Rates*. Brookfield, Vt.: Edward Elgar Publishing.

(1996). "Managing Volatile Capital Inflows: The Experience of the 1990s," *Asian Development Review* 14 (1): 1–25.

(1997). "Liberalizing Foreign Pension Fund Investment: Positive and Normative Aspects," *World Development* 25: 1173–82.

Sachs, J., and A. Warner (1995). "Economic Reform and the Process of Global Integration," *Brookings Papers on Economic Activity*, no. 1: 1–118.

Sachs, J., A. Tornell, and A. Velasco (1996). "Financial Crises in Emerging Markets: The Lessons from 1995," NBER Working Paper No. 5576. Cambridge, Mass.

CHAPTER 11

The overborrowing syndrome: Are East Asian economies different?

Ronald I. McKinnon and Huw Pill

11.1 Introduction

December 1994 marked a watershed in Mexican macroeconomic and development strategy. An apparently well-designed program of macroeconomic stabilization and structural economic reform collapsed into financial crisis – a crisis marking the culmination of a boom–bust cycle we have previously labeled the "overborrowing syndrome" (McKinnon, 1993; McKinnon and Pill, 1996). Mexico's experience is far from unique. Chile in the late 1970s enjoyed a similar boom after extensive economic liberalization, only to collapse into crisis in 1982. Even industrialized economies are not immune. Britain's consumption boom of the late 1980s was sparked by the Thatcher administration's economic reforms, but culminated in devaluation and deep recession in the early 1990s. Similar episodes occurred in Scandinavia and the Antipodes.

Since the Mexican crisis, the effort expended in assessing which country would be the "next Mexico" has been considerable. This chapter investigates how predictable was the 1997 Southeast Asian crisis. Were Malaysia, Thailand, and Indonesia overborrowing and susceptible to financial crisis? Or were conditions in these East Asian economies different? A cursory examination of the macroeconomic data justified concern. Table 11.1 summarizes the relevant data for the three Southeast Asian nations plus Korea. On the macroeconomic criteria suggested by Goldstein (1996), similarities to Mexico were striking. Malaysia, Thailand, and Indonesia all had large current account deficits, financed by borrowing from abroad. Credit-driven spending booms induced domestic demand greatly to exceed output, and maintained high levels of investment. These features are characteristic of overborrowed countries. Moreover, they replicated the Mexican experience prior to the December 1994 crisis.

Nevertheless, there are important differences between Mexico and the Southeast Asian economies. In the Asian nations, real appreciation of the currency had largely been avoided (see Table 11.1), whereas real appreciation in Mexico during 1990–94 is widely believed to have resulted in an overvaluation of more than 25 percent (Dornbusch and Werner, 1994). Asian investment has continued at high levels. Savings rates have remained extremely high by world standards, in contrast to the catastrophic fall of private saving seen in Mexico before the December 1994 crash. Without a recurring history of financial crisis, expropriation, and hyperinflation,[1] confidence in the integrity of the domestic financial system appeared stronger. With residents more willing to hold domestic financial assets, especially bank deposits, Asian financial systems are much deeper than those in Latin America (Rojas-Suárez and Weisbrod, 1995). This greater financial depth seemed, before the 1997 Asian crisis, to offer a potential financial buffer to real economic shocks.

Initially, we believed that solving the overborrowing problem was merely a matter of "getting the exchange rate right." If severe under- or overvaluation of the currency could be avoided, and anticipated exchange rate movements remained aligned with interest rate differentials, it seemed that a rapidly liberalizing economy could absorb capital efficiently. Overborrowing was a result of exchange rate mismanagement. These monetary and exchange rate issues have spawned a huge literature, which is conveniently systemized by Agénor and Montiel (1996). Of course, proper management of the monetary system and the foreign exchange rate during the reform process remains of the utmost importance. However, in this chapter, we argue that the *real* consequences of economic stabilization, liberalization, and reform also have central explanatory roles. To focus analysis at this deeper level, we largely abstract from the complications introduced by money and the foreign exchanges. Following Conley and Maloney (1995), we use a simple Fisherian framework, where borrowing and lending decisions are made in real, rather than nominal terms. Clearly, this is both an abstraction and a simplification. Appropriate management of the exchange rate *is* vital, and failures along this dimension may be an important explanation of the performance of Mexico relative to Southeast Asia. Nevertheless, we argue that real factors are central to explanations of the overborrowing syndrome and focus on the issues that they raise.

---

[1] Indonesia did suffer through a period of chronic inflation during the mid-1960s, a result of fiscal profligacy during the last years of the Sukarno regime. This episode is more distant than the Mexican inflations of the early and mid-1980s, and is probably differentiated from current developments by a marked political and economic regime shift, in contrast to Mexico.

Table 11.1. *Macroeconomic indicators in selected countries, 1990–95*

Country and indicator	Units	1990	1991	1992	1993	1994	1995
Indonesia							
Real growth	GDP, % per annum	9.0	8.9	7.2	7.3	7.5	7.6
Inflation rate	CPI, % per annum	9.9	10.0	5.0	10.2	9.6	9.0
Money supply growth	M2, % per annum	26.0	24.2	22.2	22.0	20.2	24.1
Current account deficit	% of GDP	2.8	3.1	1.9	1.3	1.6	4.0
Savings rate	% of GDP	36.7	35.9	38.2	35.3	35.3	36.0
Real effective exchange rate	% appreciation, per annum	-2.2	-2.2	-3.1	2.7	-1.3	-0.6
Malaysia							
Real growth	GDP, % per annum	9.7	8.7	7.8	8.3	9.2	9.3
Inflation rate	CPI, % per annum	3.1	4.4	4.7	3.6	3.7	3.4
Money supply growth	M2, % per annum	9.6	14.4	22.6	22.1	14.7	22.8
Current account deficit	% of GDP	2.1	9.0	3.2	4.5	5.9	8.9
Savings rate	% of GDP	33.4	32.1	35.5	35.4	37.6	37.2
Real effective exchange rate	% appreciation, per annum	-4.5	-2.9	6.5	-0.5	-3.2	1.5

Thailand

Real growth	GDP, % per annum	11.6	8.4	7.9	8.3	8.7	8.6
Inflation rate	CPI, % per annum	6.0	5.7	4.1	3.4	5.1	5.8
Money supply growth	M2, % per annum	21.1	19.8	15.6	18.4	12.9	17.4
Current account deficit	% of GDP	8.5	7.7	5.7	5.6	5.9	7.5
Savings rate	% of GDP	33.7	34.6	34.2	35.0	35.2	34.2
Real effective exchange rate	% appreciation, per annum	0.1	0.2	-1.4	0.8	-0.4	1.7

Korea

Real growth	GDP, % per annum	9.1	8.2	5.1	5.8	8.4	9.2
Inflation rate	CPI, % per annum	8.6	9.4	6.1	4.8	6.2	4.5
Money supply growth	M2, % per annum	17.2	21.9	14.9	16.6	18.7	15.0
Current account deficit	% of GDP	0.6	0.2	-0.1	-0.3	1.0	1.9
Savings rate	% of GDP	36.2	36.4	35.2	35.4	35.5	37.0

Sources: International Financial Statistics, Washington, D.C.: International Monetary Fund; *Asian Development Outlook*, New York: Oxford University Press for the Asian Development Bank; L. M. Koenig (1996), "Capital Inflows and Policy Responses in the ASEAN Region," IMF Working Paper No. 96/25, Washington, D.C.

We introduce a simple model of the overborrowing syndrome. It describes *economic transition:* an economy is transformed from a repressed state into one that is much more liberalized, within a space of only three or four years. This closely resembles Mexico in the early 1990s and Chile in the late 1970s. Our model has been successful in explaining the fall in saving in the Mexican and Chilean episodes. However, Malaysia, Indonesia, and Thailand have been on a high-growth, high-saving, and economically liberal path for more than a decade. The sudden transition from repressed to liberalized state, and the resulting surge of optimism or euphoria that drives behavior in our model, were less pronounced. Overconsumption, and its worrying implications for financial and macroeconomic stability, was less applicable to analysis of Southeast Asian countries. Nevertheless, they still were susceptible to overinvestment as described by our model.

Our previous analyses of overborrowing emphasized the role of the domestic financial system in controlling the pace and direction of credit expansion, financed by inflows of capital from overseas. While an expansion of credit can be beneficial for economic development, too rapid an expansion may result in excessive loosening of overall credit conditions (Gavin and Hausman, 1995). Moreover, experience of financial crises throughout the world has shown that certain types of lending – particularly real-estate finance, consumer credit, and loans to bank insiders or affiliates – have been more problematic than others. In countries where the banking system is sound and efficient, rapid credit expansion generated by capital inflows is less likely to create additional risk to financial and macroeconomic stability. Either banks are able to internalize the macroeconomic effects of credit growth on their borrowers' ability to pay, or they are forced to do so by the regulatory authority. In contrast, in countries where credit institutions are not well regulated and market failures exist in the financial system, capital inflows create opportunities for banks to expand lending for misguided or speculative purposes, exposing the economy to greater systemic financial risk and macroeconomic instability.

Kaminsky and Reinhart (1996) have shown that banking crises and currency crises are often closely linked, with the former, on average, preceding the latter. In retrospect, it is clear that the vulnerability of a weakened banking sector was an important constraint on the Mexican authorities' response to a deteriorating balance-of-payments situation in 1994. Information about the banking sector may therefore offer important signals about the likelihood of a wider macroeconomic crisis.

Drawing on the earlier descriptive work of Kindleberger (1989) and Galbraith (1990), we use our model to develop a simple chronology of the boom–bust, overborrowing cycle. It is then possible to evaluate how closely the Southeast Asian economies have followed this path and how close they were to its culmination in financial crisis. We assess whether the policy reactions of the relevant monetary authorities and governments were appropriate and timely.

11.2   A simple model of the overborrowing syndrome[2]

The economy consists of a large number (N) of atomistic, risk-neutral firm-households placed in a simple Fisherian two-period setting. These firm-households produce and consume a single, composite commodity good that is freely tradable with the rest of the world. Each household receives an endowment (m_1, m_2) of the good.[3] Households choose a consumption plan (c_1, c_2) to maximize utility $U(.)$, taking the real interest rate (r) and technology as given. Preferences described by this utility function are homothetic over consumption in the two periods.

Initially, firms are confined to a traditional production technique $F(.)$ that exhibits decreasing returns to scale over all levels of investment. Structural economic reform permits the introduction of modern technology $\alpha G(.)$, which has increasing returns over some range, but requires an initial fixed start-up investment, K. Production of the composite good using the modern technology can be undertaken by a number of different methods, which we label "sectors." The choice over sector is in the hands of the firm-household. In general, we assume that firm-households choose to invest across a broad portfolio of sectors unless they have identifiable incentives to concentrate production in one sector.

The success of the structural reform is uncertain ex ante. The productivity of the modern technology (α) is therefore a random variable. Initially, we focus on modeling this economywide real shock as a major potential increase in overall future productivity. The move from extensive tariff and quota protection to free trade, complemented by the general deregulation and privatization of domestic industry, is a leading example. The sweeping liberalizations in Chile after 1975 and in Mexico after 1989 both qualify as "real" macroeconomic shocks of the kind we are trying to model. Both generated enormous excitement and people expected that national output and household incomes would be much

---

[2] Following McKinnon (1973), Krugman (1979), and McKinnon and Pill (1996), the solution presented in this chapter is graphical. For a more formal, algebraic exposition, see Pill (1996).

[3] Here and throughout the chapter, subscript numerals 1 and 2 refer to period 1 and period 2 of the Fisherian model.

higher in the future. Yet how much aggregate output and income would actually increase was highly uncertain. The payoffs made during the liberalization depended on how well the macroeconomy responded to the newly liberalized regime. How can we best model this real-side shock and the related uncertainty it introduces and then relate both to what is going on in the financial sector?

Suppose that the macroeconomic productivity shock α is drawn from a probability distribution, $Q(\alpha)$. The realization of α occurs in two stages. At the beginning of the first period, a drawing is made from probability distribution $q_1(\hat{\alpha})$. The outcome of this drawing is known only to the banks – they have privileged knowledge about the state of the macroeconomy that is not directly available to the nonbank private sector. Only during the second period is the value of α itself realized. This is drawn from a distribution $q_2(\alpha \mid \hat{\alpha})$, with expected value $\hat{\alpha}$ in period one. The realization is common knowledge. In setting credit conditions – the price and availability of bank lending – banks offer an implicit signal to the nonbank private sector of their privileged information regarding the realization of $\hat{\alpha}$. Domestic firm-households, perhaps naively, rely on these implicit signals from the "expert" banking system to assess the success of macroeconomic reform.

Because of the technical indivisibility introduced by fixed start-up costs, only firms that have access to credit will be able to exploit the modern technology (McKinnon, 1973, chap. 2). Credit expansion will therefore affect the real economy through two interrelated channels. Easy credit conditions are a signal of successful structural reform and therefore should stimulate real economic activity indirectly, as expectations of permanent income are revised upward. Moreover, credit expansion enables firms to exploit the more productive modern technology, increasing real activity directly. A well-behaved financial system will ensure consistency between the signaling and direct effects. However, market failure in the banking system introduces the possibility that contradictions between these two channels may emerge. These contradictions form the basis of our explanation of the overborrowing syndrome.

Bank liabilities are central to the domestic payments system, a vital component of a modern economy. In consequence, they are generally believed to enjoy a central bank guarantee, even in the absence of an explicit deposit insurance scheme. This is an example of the time-consistency problem (Kydland and Prescott, 1977). However strongly the monetary authorities claim they will not bail out the financial system in the event of financial crisis, the claim is not credible. Should a crisis occur, the authorities will always choose to facilitate the bailout – if necessary, raising funds through the inflation tax rather than see the payments system destroyed.

Market failure in the financial system may arise from this, possibly implicit, guarantee of bank deposits.[4] It will introduce *moral hazard* into the banking system's behavior. Bank depositors are protected from the consequences of poor outcomes of the macroeconomic shock. Banks' loan decisions will be affected with, as we have seen, implications for the real economy (Cho, 1986). Where banking supervision is effective, regulators will ensure that banks do not exploit the potential for moral hazard and credit conditions will accurately reflect the privileged information about macroeconomic developments enjoyed by the banking sector. However, where regulators are unable to control the moral hazard problem, the signal implicit in credit conditions will be distorted in a direction that may lead to overborrowing and increase financial and macroeconomic instability.

In our simple framework, this process is formalized as follows. Prior to lending decisions being finalized at the start of period one, banks know the realization of $\hat{\alpha}$ – and thus the distribution $q_2(.)$ from which the final drawing of α will be taken. Deposit insurance protects banks from outcomes in the lower tail of this distribution – realizations of α worse than $\ddot{\alpha}$, the shock that causes general private sector default.[5] They will set credit conditions using a risk assessment based on the truncated distribution (with mean $\hat{\alpha}'$), rather than the true underlying distribution (with mean $\hat{\alpha}$). Clearly, $\hat{\alpha}'$ is unambiguously greater than $\hat{\alpha}$.

Having described the endowments, technology, preferences, and information conditions, we solve this model in three policy environments: the *financially repressed economy* (FRE), where usury laws and other restrictions on the financial system prevent the emergence of a private capital market; the *domestically liberalized economy* (DLE), where a competitive domestic financial system exists but is isolated from the international capital market; and the *internationally liberalized economy* (ILE), where the capital account of the balance of payments is open and the domestic financial system is fully integrated with a perfectly elastic

---

[4] Since this failure arises from the inability of the authorities to manage the moral hazard problem associated with their (albeit possibly implicit) intervention, it perhaps should be called "institutional failure" rather than market failure. We are grateful to Francisco Gil-Diaz of the Banco de Mexico for this point. Nevertheless, for consistency with our previous paper, we continue to use the label "market failure" here.

[5] In the event of widespread default by private debtors, the government will impose a tax (e.g., the inflation tax) on the unearned second-period income of domestic residents to pay off bank depositors. This process is described in section 11.2.4 and, more formally, in Pill (1996).

international capital market. In solving the model, we use three distinct solution concepts: a *first-best* (FB) solution, where the financial system is well behaved (in the sense described earlier, namely that credit conditions offer the correct implicit signals about macroeconomic developments); a *rational beliefs* (RB) equilibrium, where the nonbank private sector believes the implicit signals offered by credit conditions (despite the existence of market failure in the financial system) because of ex ante observational equivalence with the first-best equilibrium; and, a *pseudorational beliefs* (PRB) equilibrium, where the nonbank private sector is aware of financial market failure. This combination of environments and solution concepts results in a 3 × 3 matrix of outcomes (summarized in Table 11.2) that we will use to characterize the various stages of our chronology of the overborrowing cycle.

11.2.1   *The financially repressed economy*

No private capital market exists in the FRE. Consequently, firm-households cannot borrow. It is impossible to overcome the technological indivisibility in modern techniques. Production is confined to the traditional technology. Firm-households optimize at point A in Figure 11.1. Consumption equals production in each period. There is no financial saving. In the absence of any financial system, the distinctions among the three solution concepts – which revolve around the extent of financial market failure and perceptions of it – are not relevant. The FRE merely offers a useful benchmark case for comparison with the outcomes for more liberalized financial systems.

11.2.2   *The domestically liberalized economy*

In the DLE, a domestic private capital market emerges. Banks can raise deposits from those households that continue to exploit traditional technology. These deposits are lent to other firms, allowing them to overcome the technological indivisibility in the modern technique. Two conditions must be satisfied in equilibrium. First, because households are identical, each must achieve the same level of utility (Krugman, 1979). Their opportunity sets must be the same. Since firms are optimizing, the intertemporal budget constraint must be simultaneously tangent to both production possibility schedules, $f(.)$ and $\alpha g(.)$.[6] The real interest rate (r_{DLE}) is therefore determined solely by technological

---

[6] The lower case annotation for technology (f and g) represents the production possibility frontiers corresponding to the two production functions (F and G, respectively).

Table 11.2. Solutions to the simple two-period Fisherian model of overborrowing

		Financially repressed economy, FRE *Usury laws and other restrictions prevent the emergence of a domestic private capital market.*	Domestically liberalized economy, DLE *Domestic capital market operates; capital controls isolate the domestic financial system from international markets.*	Internationally liberalized economy, ILE *Capital controls are abolished and the domestic financial system is fully integrated into international capital markets.*
First best, FB	*Financial system is well behaved and signals implicit in credit conditions are correct.*	No financial saving occurs. Rate of return on real investments is low.	Borrowing occurs as modern technology is exploited. Real interest rates rise to a moderate, positive level. Welfare improves over FRE.	All residents borrow from abroad at world interest rate to invest in modern technology. Welfare higher than in DLE first-best equilibrium.
Rational beliefs equilibrium, RB	*Financial market failure corrupts signals implicit in credit conditions; NBPS not aware of problem.*	In the absence of a private capital market, RB equilibria cannot obtain.	Real interest rates rise to "excessive" levels. Borrowing may be greater or less than in FB equilibrium.	Excessive borrowing from abroad, while domestic real rates remain constrained to international levels. Overinvestment and overconsumption.
Pseudorational beliefs equilibrium, PRB	*NBPS aware of market failure; allowed for when making investment decisions.*	In the absence of a private capital market, PRB equilibria cannot obtain.	Borrowing grows above RB levels, despite higher real interest rate, as NBPS exploits moral hazard by investing in more speculative sectors.	Borrowing grows further, becoming yet more excessive relative to FB. Borrowing increasingly undertaken to finance speculative or procyclical activities.

Note: NBPS = nonbank private sector.

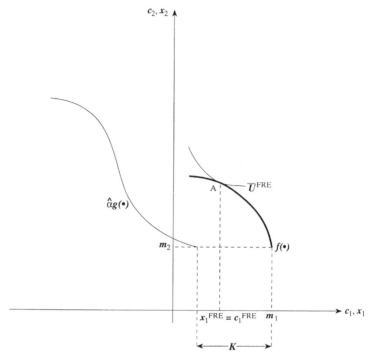

Figure 11.1. Equilibrium in the financially repressed economy (FRE).

factors.[7] Second, the capital market must clear. Optimizing firms will produce at the points of tangency in Figure 11.2: point A, generating cash flow x_1^M from the modern technology; and, point B, generating cash flow x_1^T from the traditional technology. All households consume c_1^{DLE} in the first period. Consequently, aggregate bank deposits by those firm-households that continue to use traditional techniques – $N_T(x_1^T - c_1^{DLE})$ – must equal aggregate borrowing by investors in modern technology – $N_M(c_1^{DLE} - x_1^M)$.[8]

Figure 11.2 represents the first-best (FB) equilibrium, where the financial system accurately reflects its privileged knowledge of $\hat{\alpha}$ when setting credit conditions. There is no financial market failure. Although welfare is unambiguously greater than in the FRE, total saving

---

[7] In a simple Fisherian two-period model, the slope of the intertemporal budget constraint is equal to $-(1 + r)$, where r is the real interest rate.

[8] N_T and N_M are the number of firm-households employing the traditional and modern production techniques respectively.

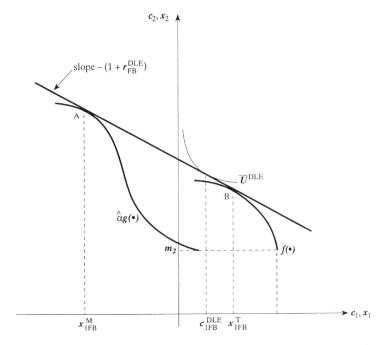

Figure 11.2. First-best solution in the domestically liberalized economy (DLE).

$(m_1 - c_{1FB}^{DLE})$ may be higher or lower, since income and substitution effects are offsetting.

In the rational beliefs (RB) equilibrium, banks exploit the potential for moral hazard implied by the implicit guarantee of bank deposits. Using the truncated distribution for the macroeconomic shock, they set credit conditions based on an expected value $\hat{\alpha}'$, which is unambiguously greater than $\hat{\alpha}$ (as shown in Figure 11.3). Nonbanks, perhaps naively, continue to believe the financial system is well behaved. Ex ante, they are unable to distinguish between outcomes due to financial market failure and those associated with a well-behaved financial system but a higher realization of the macroeconomic shock. The behavior of the nonbank private sector is consistent with rationality – and the forward-looking expectations and sustainability conditions that it implies in the intertemporal context – under the implicit economic model they believe, one in which the financial system is well behaved and the macroeconomic shock is favorable. Since this model cannot be refuted given available data, it is admissible and consistent with a wider and more plausible notion of rationality than that associated with conventional rational

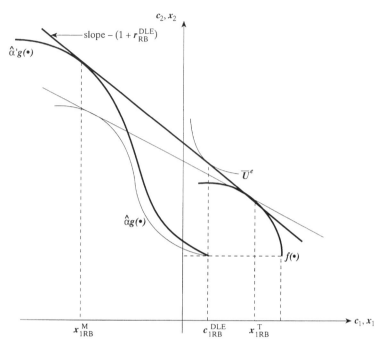

Figure 11.3. Rational beliefs equilibrium in the domestically liberalized economy (DLE).

expectations equilibria. This is the essence of the rational beliefs approach (Kurz, 1994, 1997).

The RB equilibrium has a higher real interest rate, $r_{RB}^{DLE} > r_{FB}^{DLE}$. However, borrowing by individual firm-households may rise or fall relative to the first-best outcome since income and substitution effects offset one another. Similarly, the effects on aggregate borrowing are ambiguous. In the DLE, a RB equilibrium does not necessarily imply overborrowing. Financial market failure is reflected in financial prices – specifically, an excessive real interest rate – rather than in financial quantities.

In the pseudorational beliefs (PRB) equilibrium, the nonbank private sector is aware of the financial market failure. Nonbanks know that real interest rates are excessive. A number of equilibria are possible. For example, all domestic residents may wish to save rather than borrow from the banks to exploit the high returns on bank deposits. If all firm-households want to make deposits rather than borrow, the domestic capital market cannot operate because there are no external sources of funds. The banks will only be able to raise funds by offering a realistic interest rate, one that accurately reflects their privileged knowledge about macroeconomic developments. In this favorable – though perhaps unlikely – PRB equilibrium, market discipline can be relied upon to produce the optimal macroeconomic outcome.

Alternatively, the high real interest rate may merely encourage borrowers to engage in highly speculative activities. Only these will produce a payoff sufficient to service outstanding debt. In the event of an adverse outcome, borrowers know that they will be bailed out by the authorities' guarantee of bank debt and therefore they discount the lower tail of the probability distribution for α in the same way as the banks. In this unfavorable PRB equilibrium, the speculative, procyclical activities undertaken by the borrowers add to the systemic vulnerability and financial fragility of the banking system (as described in more detail in the subsequent section). Once firm-households understand that moral hazard exists in the banking system, they will begin undertaking projects that are "artificially" risky, knowing that banks will lend for such projects if their expected returns are as high as those associated with safer schemes. This extra risk can be generated by choosing projects in procyclical sectors. In the case of a bad macroeconomic outcome, bankrupted individual debtors are better protected against legal sanctions because they will all default together (as in Mexico in 1994–95). In the event of a good macroeconomic outcome, extra returns are available to those firms that had invested in procyclical sectors.

The choice between these two Pareto-rankable PRB equilibria is the solution to a coordination game among the private sector firm-households. The devolved, uncoordinated market interactions of the nonbank private sector may fail to replicate the Pareto-dominant, first-best equilibrium. There may be a role for government intervention to promote achievement of the optimal equilibrium. We will discuss this possibility in more detail in the context of the internationally liberalized economy.

11.2.3   The internationally liberalized economy

Once domestic residents are able to borrow freely from the international capital market, the equilibrium real interest rate must equal the exogenous world rate, r^*. Real interest rate equalization is a stringent definition of capital market integration. In assuming real rates are equalized, we implicitly require that both uncovered interest parity and purchasing power parity conditions hold. A large empirical literature rejects these conditions. Nevertheless, we maintain the assumption of real interest parity since, as emphasized in the introduction, we are abstracting from

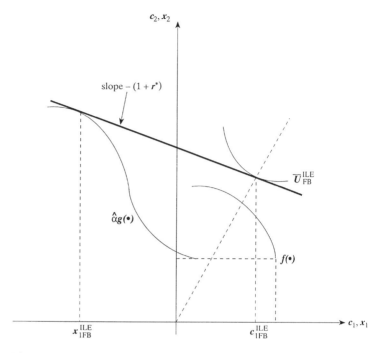

Figure 11.4. First-best solution in the internationally liberalized economy (ILE).

the issues raised by money and the foreign exchanges (which have been discussed widely in previous papers), and focus on the real aspects of overborrowing.

Using foreign savings intermediated through the domestic banking system, every firm-household will choose to borrow at the exogenous world rate and exploit the modern production process. Investment and consumption decisions in the first-best equilibrium are shown in Figure 11.4. Comparing the FB solutions, welfare in the ILE is greater than in the DLE. If the financial system is well behaved, it is unambiguously preferable to undertake structural economic reform with an open capital account.

With the real interest rate set exogenously in international markets, it can no longer rise in response to market failure in the financial system, as was the case in the DLE. Instead, moral hazard in the banking system becomes manifest through excessive capital inflows (as shown in the rational beliefs equilibrium, Figure 11.5). The overly optimistic macroeconomic signal implicit in credit conditions (based on the truncated conditional distribution of macroeconomic shocks with mean $\hat{\alpha}'$,

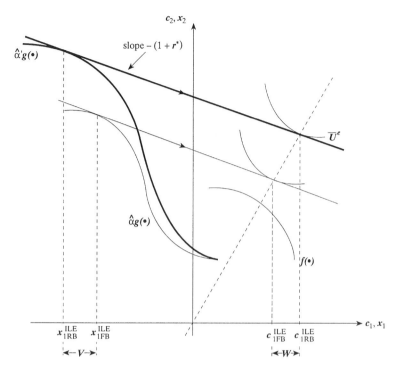

Figure 11.5. Rational beliefs equilibrium in the internationally liberalized economy (ILE): The overborrowing syndrome.

rather than the true distribution with mean $\hat{\alpha}$) prompts domestic residents to overinvest (at x_{1RB}^{ILE} in the first period, rather than x_{1FB}^{ILE}) and overconsume (at c_{1RB}^{ILE} rather than c_{1FB}^{ILE}) in the rational beliefs equilibrium relative to the first best outcome. Both overinvestment (V) and overconsumption (W) are financed by excessive borrowing from the rest of the world, beyond that which would occur in the absence of financial market failure. This is the essence of the overborrowing syndrome.

Ex ante, domestic firm-households believe economic reform is credible and the financial system is well behaved. This confidence in the success of the reform program is bolstered by the economic boom – high levels of consumption and investment – observed in the first period. Overborrowing occurs when the nonbank private sector becomes *euphoric* or *triumphalist* about the success of reform because of the overly optimistic implicit signal about macroeconomic developments contained in loose credit conditions. Triumphalism breeds even greater confidence in the liberalization process, creating a self-sustaining momentum of its own. Moreover, where the financial system was previously repressed, the transition to a liberalized regime allows consumers to increase their indebtedness toward higher equilibrium levels that were previously unattainable because of administrative controls. Even in the absence of triumphalism, consumer borrowing is likely to rise rapidly if liberalization is sudden.

Once the nonbank private sector becomes aware of the financial market failure, it may also begin to exploit the potential for moral hazard introduced by expectation of a bank bailout in the event of financial crisis. Interest rates are constrained to international levels by the open capital account. They cannot rise as in the DLE. All firms wish to borrow at world interest rates to invest in modern technology, even after financial market failure becomes apparent.

When a firm-household becomes aware of the financial market failure, it *may* choose to limit its borrowing to a level consistent with the FB equilibrium, $c_{1FB}^{ILE} - x_{1FB}^{ILE}$. If *all* firm-households were simultaneously to do likewise, the FB solution would be replicated. This is the socially optimal result – after all, it is the first-best equilibrium. The difficulty is ensuring that all firm-households make the switch from the unstable rational beliefs equilibrium to the optimal, FB equilibrium *simultaneously* – ensuring that the coordination problem is solved. Failure to ensure a coordinated, simultaneous move to FB levels may unleash highly destabilizing forces.

Consider the alternative. If all other firm-households are borrowing at a level consistent with the RB equilibrium, it remains possible that an adverse realization of the macroeconomic shock will result in financial crisis. If this eventuality occurred, a household that recognized the extent of financial market failure, and consequently limited borrowing to FB levels in anticipation of a productivity shock lower than that implied by the implicit signal in credit conditions, would not enjoy the benefits of so doing. The returns they enjoyed on their more conservative investment projects will be taxed away to finance the bailout of the financial system and those borrowers who had invested less conservatively. Naturally, in the event of a positive macroeconomic shock, these conservative firms will not reap the high returns obtained by those that invested more aggressively. Anticipation of the fiscal consequences of financial crisis truncates the payoff distribution for firms, just as deposit insurance truncates bank perceptions of macroeconomic shocks. In the PRB equilibrium, the moral hazard problem is extended to the nonbank private sector.

Because firms only enjoy the returns associated with above-average productivity shocks, it is individually rational for them to invest in

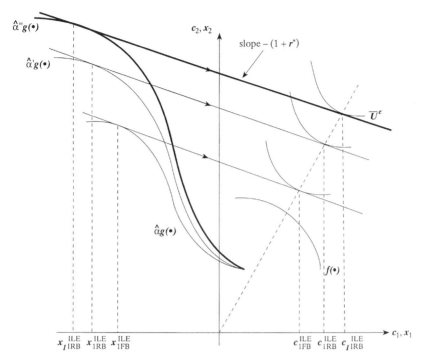

Figure 11.6. Pseudorational beliefs equilibrium in the internationally liberalized economy (ILE).

procyclical projects. Payoffs will be higher when macroeconomic shocks are positive and the returns are retained by the firm. Payoffs are lower in the event of an adverse macroeconomic shock, but losses on bankruptcy are transferred to the government, which finances a bailout. At the macroeconomic level, the results of such speculative behavior can be catastrophic. Borrowing will rise to even more excessive levels and the probability of a financial crisis will rise (see Figure 11.6). These effects increase the likelihood of a bank bailout and raise the costs should one occur. Both factors only serve to increase the individual incentive facing firms to invest in speculative sectors. A self-reinforcing cycle of increasing financial fragility is set in motion.

The challenge facing policy makers is to ensure that the nonbank private sector coordinates on the "good," rather than the "bad," equilibrium. The monetary authorities must carefully monitor the sectoral composition of aggregate bank lending. This will be the earliest indicator of a transition from rational to pseudorational beliefs equilibria and, by implication, from an economy merely vulnerable to adverse macroeconomic shocks into one exhibiting extreme financial fragility. Monitoring may prompt action. For example, the authorities could prevent excessive speculative lending by imposing guidelines or capping credit expansion to certain problem sectors. Indonesia has experimented with such an approach, labeled *"enhanced moral suasion,"* since 1994. Equivalently, the government may wish to carefully scrutinize the quality of investment projects in highly procyclical sectors, such as commercial property and construction. Rather than simply concluding that high investment is necessarily of economic benefit, our framework suggests policy makers should also be concerned about the quality of this investment. Overinvestment, especially overinvestment in speculative sectors financed by borrowing from abroad, is likely to have adverse consequences for financial and macroeconomic stability.

11.2.4   *Implications of financial crisis*

As we have seen, when financial crisis occurs, the government must raise funds to finance a bailout of the financial system, indebted domestic borrowers, and foreign creditors. In Mexico after December 1994, this postcrisis finance was accomplished by some increase in traditional taxation, but mainly by massive resort to the inflation tax, led by a deep nominal devaluation of the peso. In 1995, the inflation tax fell on money holders, wage earners (because money wages remained "sticky" while commodity prices rose dramatically), and borrowers with floating rate debt. The duration of this debt shrunk dramatically as nominal interest rates rose, compounding the financial problems of the nonbank private sector. In addition to raising funds for the various bailouts, these taxes will help to reduce domestic consumption to sustainable levels after the excesses of the overborrowing years.

Consequently, even where there is no external price competitiveness problem, the culmination of the overborrowing cycle in financial crisis may require a deep depreciation of the nominal exchange rate. Note that the direction of causality is the opposite of that suggested by Dornbusch and Werner (1994) for the recent Mexican crisis. In our formulation, the sharp nominal depreciation is a consequence of the financial crisis rather than its cause.

However, even when struck by a foreign exchange crisis along Mexican lines, Southeast Asian economies had the capacity – though not the will – to avoid deep devaluntions and inflation. Overconsumption in Malaysia, Thailand, and Indonesia has been much more modest than was the case in Mexico. Because liberalization has been more gradual, pent-up consumption demand from the years of financial repression has been released over a longer period, in contrast to the sudden boom seen in Mexico. Under Mexico's financial repression, a large number of households were liquidity constrained. Even if expectations of future income are unchanged, these households desire a one-time increase in consumer indebtedness once the capital market permits it. Liberalization – including the introduction of credit cards and other lines of consumer credit – facilitates this increased personal leverage.

Although borrowing to satisfy the pent-up consumption demand of liquidity constrained households would not proceed indefinitely – it merely requires a one-time rise in personal indebtedness – if all the borrowing occurs at once, it is likely to have serious macroeconomic consequences. Domestic savings will fall temporarily, but precipitately, creating higher interest rates (in the DLE) or greater dependence on foreign sources of capital and higher current account deficits (in the ILE). Either effect could exacerbate the problems of financial fragility associated with our overborrowing model. Mexico's economic crisis was exacerbated by the need to dramatically reduce personal consumption from clearly unsustainable levels. The aggressive use of the inflation tax and high nominal interest rates, while achieving this end, precipitated much wider economic problems than those caused by the collapse of the exchange rate, the initial, visible manifestation of the crisis.

Because liberalization has been more gradual in Southeast Asia, the one-time changes in personal indebtedness, and their effect on domestic saving, have been spread over a much greater period of time. Consequently, the effect on interest rates or current accounts in any one year has been much smaller. Consumption in Southeast Asia has not reached the level of excess seen in Mexico, nor has domestic saving fallen so low. Draconian measures to reduce consumption after a speculative attack on currencies would be unnecessary, and therefore the effects of a currency crisis on the wider economy would be smaller. Instead, reaction should focus on restraining Southeast Asian countries' overly aggressive investment programs. Retarding bank lending as described earlier is a possible instrument. Because real exchange rates had not appreciated to the same extent as in Mexico and other Latin American countries (see Table 11.1), the "surprise" devaluations in 1997 in Southeast Asia were not necessary to balance current accounts provided that "excess," low productivity investments were curtailed.

11.3   The dynamics of the overborrowing syndrome

The recent crises in Mexico and Southeast Asia are far from unique. Examples abound across geographic and temporal dimensions. Kindleberger (1989) and Galbraith (1990) offer economic histories of financial crisis that predate the most recent manifestations. Both chronicle the history of financial crises from the Dutch Tulipmania of 1636, through the South Sea Bubble (1720) and the various booms and busts of the nineteenth century, to the U.S. Savings and Loan crisis of the late 1980s. Other than Krugman (1995), few of the analyses of the Mexican–East Asian crises have drawn on this rich history.

Kindleberger uses historiographical methodology to describe a typical chronology of financial crisis. The various stages he describes correspond to different solutions to our model of the overborrowing syndrome. By mapping our simple framework into Kindleberger's description, we can use an evaluation of empirical data in the context of our model's results to evaluate how far certain economies have passed through the evolution of the overborrowing cycle. This permits an assessment of how close each economy is to the culmination of the cycle in financial crisis.

Drawing on the work of Minsky (1977, 1982), Kindleberger offers the following chronology. The overborrowing cycle begins with *displacement*, an initial macroeconomic shock. In our model, this corresponds to the introduction of the modern technology that had previously been unavailable to domestic firms. This was a shorthand description of a wide-ranging real-side reform, such as moving from extensive protectionism to free trade. A period of *euphoria* ensues, as, in expectation of the benefits from economic reform, consumption and investment increase, fueled by rapid credit growth and inflows of foreign capital. This corresponds to our rational beliefs equilibrium, maintained by the private sector's euphoric belief that economic growth arises out of the success of credible structural reform (as emphasized in McKinnon and Pill, 1996). Eventually, euphoria turns into *financial distress* as credit expansion becomes excessive and speculative, rather than productive and well directed. Clearly, this is the analogue to our pseudorational beliefs equilibrium in the ILE. Kindleberger's overborrowing cycle culminates in *panic* and *crisis* – in our model, these result from a sufficiently adverse realization of the macroeconomic shock to precipitate financial crisis.

We have demonstrated that overborrowing is characteristic of economies with open capital accounts. Overborrowing occurs in the ILE. History – at least as interpreted by Kindleberger and Galbraith – suggests the overborrowing cycle typically evolves through several stages. We interpret these as corresponding to different assessments of the extent of financial market failure. Following the initial structural reform, only the banks themselves are aware of the extent of moral hazard in the financial system. In the rational beliefs equilibrium that obtains, credit expansion is too rapid, but is well directed toward broadly based produc-

Table 11.3. *Chronology of the overborrowing cycle*

Stage	Kindleberger (1989)	McKinnon and Pill (1996)	Characteristics
1	"Displacement"	Allow possibility to adopt modern technology, $\alpha G(.)$.	Structural economic reform, possibly including financial liberalization.
2	"Euphoria"	Rational beliefs (RB) equilibrium in the internationally liberalized economy (ILE).	Broad-based credit driven consumption and investment boom, financed by borrowing from abroad. Large current account deficit.
3	"Financial distress"	Pseudorational beliefs (PRB) equilibrium in the internationally liberalized economy (ILE).	Credit growth rises further; credit expansion is increasingly directed toward "speculative" sectors.
4	"Panic"	Adverse realization of macroeconomic shock, a.	Collapse of real activity as "bubble" associated with speculative activity bursts.
5	"Crisis"	Inability of NBPS to service debts as payoff to investment in modern technology is less than outstanding debt liability. Financial system in crisis.	Financial crisis – widespread private debt default, failure of banks, and need for government intervention to bail out the financial system.

Note: NBPS = nonbank private sector.

tive activity across a range of sectors. Once the nonbank private sector becomes aware of financial market failure, credit expansion expands further and becomes increasingly concentrated in procyclical or speculative sectors.

Consequently, an investigation of the pace and direction of credit expansion offers an insight into the progress an economy has made through the overborrowing cycle. As the economy moves from displacement through euphoria to distress, borrowing from banks should grow more rapidly and be directed toward speculative sectors, such as real estate, construction, share purchase on margin, and personal consumption (see Table 11.3). Those countries that have this pattern of credit expansion are those which are most vulnerable to the financial crisis at the culmination of the overborrowing syndrome. Countries that have effective financial policies, especially bank supervision and prudential regulation of the financial system, should exhibit more broadly based lending growth.

11.4   The pace and direction of credit expansion

Mexico is a country that appears to follow the overborrowing chronology suggested by Kindleberger (1989) and formalized by our simple model. Structural economic reform and macroeconomic stabilization were pursued with new vigor in Mexico under the Salinas administration after 1988. This displacement resulted in rapid credit expansion – much of it financed by inflows of capital from abroad – during 1990–94. The sectoral composition of this bank lending offers a useful benchmark case with which to compare the Southeast Asian countries that are of interest here. While they exhibited somewhat similar macroeconomic conditions as Mexico, the composition of bank lending in Indonesia, Malaysia, and Thailand may offer different signals about the extent and perception of financial market failure in these economies. Before the 1997 crash, their problem was more one of overinvestment.

We have drawn data from a number of sources. There is little consistency in the reporting of sectoral credit flows across countries. The most detailed data are available for Mexico, where the Banco de Mexico[9] supplies a detailed disaggregation of credit to twenty-seven nonfinancial private sectors on a monthly basis. Bank Indonesia also makes monthly sectoral credit data available for the period since the introduction of structural and financial reform, albeit at a less disaggregated level than the Mexicans.[10] Date for Malaysia, Thailand, and Korea (included for comparison) are only available on an annual basis.[11] Summaries of the data are provided in Tables 11.4 through 11.8.

[9] These Mexican data were supplied directly by the Banco de Mexico. Special thanks are due to Mauricio Naranjo for his help in obtaining the data.
[10] The Indonesian data are from *Indonesian Financial Statistics*, a monthly publication of Bank Indonesia.
[11] The sources are for Malaysia, *Annual Report*, Bank Negara Malaysia; for Thailand, the Bank of Thailand; and, for Korea, *Monthly Statistical Bulletin* (March), Bank of Korea.

Table 11.4. *Mexico: Bank credit extended by commercial and development banks by economic sector of borrower (end-of-year stocks in millions of new pesos)*

Sector	1988	1989	1990	1991	1992	1993	1994
Agriculture	14,594.3	19,637.5	25,219.1	30,047.6	38,193.0	44,064.0	56,521.5
Energy	6,766.0	6,101.6	4,052.4	3,523.6	4,065.6	3,491.4	5,898.2
Manufacturing	21,134.4	31,258.3	43,733.8	57,769.2	72,513.9	84,270.2	122,069.5
Construction	1,487.3	3,342.4	8,834.1	18,299.8	34,571.8	32,511.1	52,330.6
Housing	6,127.6	8,523.0	12,452.6	15,484.0	18,568.6	77,114.1	104,321.2
Services	16,218.5	24,995.7	44,103.3	64,241.3	97,290.3	141,247.0	229,904.2
Consumption	5,534.0	8,295.5	18,257.1	35,343.2	55,771.1	41,627.6	44,468.7
Trade	8,633.8	20,331.8	31,910.9	49,430.7	78,983.6	86,682.7	128,902.9
Total	80,495.8	122,485.7	188,563.3	274,139.2	399,957.8	511,008.1	744,417.0

Source: Sistema Central de Informacion, Banco de Mexico, Mexico City.

Table 11.5. *Indonesia: Bank lending in domestic and foreign currency classified by economic sector (end-of-year stocks in rupiah billions)*

Sector	1986	1987	1988	1989	1990	1991	1992	1993	1994	1995
Agriculture	2.1	2.7	3.6	5.3	7.2	8.4	10.3	12.1	13.9	15.5
Mining	0.4	0.4	0.4	0.6	0.6	0.7	0.8	0.8	0.8	0.9
Manufacturing	9.0	10.9	15.0	20.3	30.5	30.5	37.3	51.4	60.2	72.1
Trade	8.4	10.2	13.9	20.1	29.7	31.8	32.9	37.8	44.4	54.2
Services	4.1	5.1	6.8	9.8	17.2	20.3	25.9	35.8	50.8	66.6
Other	1.3	2.2	2.7	6.8	11.7	16.7	15.8	12.4	18.8	25.3
Total	25.3	31.5	42.5	62.9	97.0	108.5	122.9	150.3	188.9	234.6

Source: Indonesian Financial Statistics, Bank Indonesia, Jakarta.

Table 11.6. *Malaysia: Direction of credit to nonfinancial private sector (end-of-year stocks in US$ billions, 1986–91, and ringgit billions, 1992–94)*

	1986	1987	1988	1989	1990	1991	1992	1993	1994
Loans and advances	73.9	74.2	83.0	98.7	128.1	155.1	178.1	201.5	233.9
Agriculture	5.1	5.1	5.4	6.2	7.0	7.4	7.1	7.0	6.2
Mining	0.6	0.7	1.1	1.1	1.1	1.2	1.2	0.8	0.7
Manufacturing	11.1	11.2	13.6	16.8	22.0	27.5	31.0	36.0	41.8
Construction	5.3	5.6	5.9	7.5	8.6	10.1	12.7	13.9	15.8
Real estate	11.3	11.8	12.3	12.4	12.9	14.3	15.3	15.2	14.8
Housing	12.1	12.4	14.2	15.6	18.8	22.2	25.3	30.2	35.0
Business services, financing	2.3	1.9	1.9	2.7	3.1	3.4	3.7	4.8	5.8
General commerce	11.6	10.5	11.3	12.9	14.1	15.7	15.2	15.7	17.1
Transport, storage	1.3	1.1	1.4	1.5	2.1	3.1	3.4	3.2	3.9
Purchase of shares				2.4	3.0	3.9	3.7	6.1	12.7
Consumption credit	2.8	2.8	3.8	6.6	11.7	15.8	17.1	19.5	22.6
Other	10.4	11.1	12.1	13.0	23.7	30.5	42.4	49.1	57.5
Investment in corporate securities	7.7	8.6	9.3	14.1	20.9	27.2	32.6	36.3	57.7
Total	81.6	82.8	92.3	112.8	149.0	182.3	210.7	237.8	291.6

Notes: Excludes credit to nonfinancial public enterprises.
Source: *Annual Report*, Bank Negara Malaysia, Kuala Lumpur, various years 1986–95.

Table 11.7. *Thailand: Bills, loans, and overdrafts of commercial banks classified by sector (end-of-year stocks in baht billions)*

Sector	1990	1991	1992	1993	1994
Agriculture	99.4	126.4	135.5	149.0	162.7
Mining	8.2	8.2	12.1	16.7	15.9
Manufacturing	375.1	457.6	517.9	635.6	797.2
Construction	59.3	72.1	88.4	103.1	138.9
Real Estate	177.7	207.1	251.1	303.2	368.8
Imports	68.6	71.5	87.0	89.2	109.2
Exports	91.4	95.3	116.7	134.9	170.3
Wholesale, retail trade	263.2	314.8	371.5	472.8	595.4
Services	91.4	123.2	159.1	208.7	264.6
Consumption	158.6	201.8	269.4	339.7	439.3
Subtotal	1,392.8	1,678.2	2,008.6	2,452.7	3,062.3
Public utilities	25.1	30.1	40.9	60.9	73.4
Banking, financial sector	76.2	99.3	132.8	157.5	172.0
Total	1,494.1	1,807.6	2,182.4	2,671.1	3,307.7

Notes: Banking, financial sector includes interbank loans.
Source: Bank of Thailand, Bangkok.

Unfortunately, lack of consistency in the data is a problem not only across countries but also through time. This renders systematic time series analysis extremely difficult.[12] What can we learn from Tables 11.4 through 11.8? Our model suggests the various stages of the overborrowing cycle can be distinguished by the pace and direction of bank credit expansion. Mexican nominal credit growth was strong throughout the 1988–94 period. However, inflation was also extremely variable over this time. Real credit growth was more volatile, showing two peaks: at the end of 1991 and at the start of 1993. This growth was relatively concentrated in construction, services, and trade, especially in the later years, at the expense of manufacturing. Unfortunately, the bias in lending measured by these statistics is not as strong as predicted by our model. In part, this may be due to the lax accounting and regulation procedures in

---

[12] For example, the Mexican data suggest a sharp fall in consumption debt between 1992 and 1993. This is a result of statistical reclassifications, the difference being absorbed into other sectors (mainly services and housing).

Table 11.8. *Korea: Flow of funds data on the sectoral composition of lending by deposit money banks* *(end-of-year stocks in won billions)*

Sector	1986	1987	1988	1989	1990	1991	1992	1993	1994
Government	666.5	592.8	911.6	580.5	1,209.7	1,203.8	1,392.6	1,592.6	1,713.9
Public enterprises	1,800.4	1.770.1	2,215.5	2,842.6	2,745.1	3,604.8	3,643.5	4,990.6	6,710.2
Private enterprises	24,145.2	28,704.3	33,051.4	39,012.3	46,591.2	58,568.7	66,807.5	73,976.8	90,346.7
IPFs	1.0	27.5	29.0	30.4	19.2	23.3	7.4	25.0	15.0
OFIs	763.8	704.6	2,289.5	6,815.2	6,880.1	5,803.8	7,973.4	8,365.7	6,535.1
Individuals	11,106.5	12,689.6	18,280.0	21,486.1	26,787.5	32,918.7	36,704.3	40,833.2	49,190.8
Total	38,483.4	44,488.9	56,777.0	70,767.1	84,232.8	102,123.1	116,528.7	129,783.9	154,511.7

Notes: IPFs are insurance and pension funds. OFIs are other financial institutions.
Source: *Monthly Statistical Bulletin* (March issue, various years), Bank of Korea, Seoul.

place in Mexico at this time (Desmet and Mann, 1996). Much of the speculative lending may have taken the form of credit being extended to bank insiders or affiliated firms, and used for consumption or speculation despite being statistically recorded as "productive" lending to manufacturing. If this is the case, it only serves to highlight the problems caused by the lack of financial infrastructure in economies vulnerable to the overborrowing syndrome.

How do the Asian countries compare? Malaysia, Thailand, and Korea all exhibited fairly stable credit growth during the early 1990s (inflation is less variable in these countries, so the nominal data are a more useful indicator than in Mexico). In Thailand, there was very little bias in lending growth to particular sectors (the sectoral breakdown in Korea is insufficient to make a sensible assessment in that case). In Malaysia, there was some evidence of the beginnings of speculative activity, because credit financing the "purchase of shares" jumped considerably, albeit from a low base. Nevertheless, little in the financial statistics of these Asian economies suggested that the crash of 1997 was in the offing.

Indonesia provided the most cause for concern. Since 1993 there was a surge of lending after the slowdown of 1991–92, although at nothing like the rates seen in the immediate aftermath of the 1987–88 financial liberalization. This lending was biased toward services and "other" sectors – those sectors which was include the problem "speculative" activities we described earlier. In combination with the high level of external debt and political uncertainty seen in Indonesia, this appears to be the combination of circumstances most similar to those seen in Mexico.

If the credit data gave mixed signals, the behavior of aggregate saving in Southeast Asia offered unambiguously benign signals in the context of our model. As shown in Figure 11.7, Mexican domestic saving fell precipitously following the introduction of economic reform in 1987–88. Capital inflows financed higher levels of consumption as expectations of permanent income were revised upward. A very similar pattern is evident from Chilean data from the late 1970s (see Figure 11.8). Yet none of the Southeast Asian nations exhibited the dramatic declines in national saving rates characteristic of Mexico and Chile (see Table 11.1). Their vulnerability to financial crisis at the culmination of the overborrowing syndrome was in the low quality of their huge investments.

11.5   Policy conclusions

Our model linking structural reform to financial liberalization has a number of important policy implications. It highlights the role financial

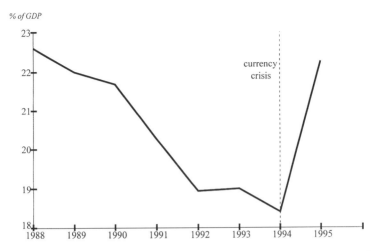

Figure 11.7. Mexico: Domestic savings rate 1988–95. *Source*: IMF, *International Financial Statistics*.

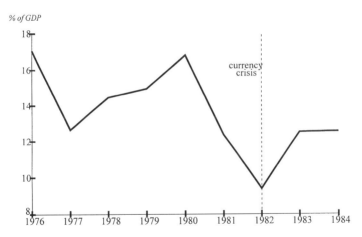

Figure 11.8. Chile: Domestic savings rate 1976–84. *Source*: IMF, *International Financial Statistics*.

supervision and control play in the achievement of successful macroeconomic stabilization and structural reform, including financial liberalization. Perversely, a deregulated financial system may be more in need of effective supervision than one that is subject to extensive administrative controls and government intervention. Since the problem of overborrowing is rooted in an institutional failure to manage the moral hazard problem introduced into the financial system by deposit insurance, a first-best solution would be to improve the institutional infrastructure of regulation and supervision. Attempts to liberalize the financial system in the absence of appropriately staffed and funded regulatory bodies and prudent and well-organized credit bureaus (as in Mexico) are likely to end in financial crisis. The "Washington consensus" in favor of structural reform and financial liberalization has tended to underemphasize the need to invest in this institutional infrastructure prior to the introduction of such reforms. This chapter suggests this failing requires urgent attention.

Nevertheless, prudent financial supervision is unlikely to be completely effective. Even the advanced industrial countries have failed to prevent financial crisis on occasion – recent episodes at BCCI, Barings, Continental Illinois, and Banesto and at British, U.S., and Japanese property lenders are all testament to this fact. Second-best remedies are also required. The chapter suggests that the monetary authorities would be well advised to monitor the composition of bank credit expansion, as well as its aggregate level. Specifically, the authorities should limit the ability of banks to lend for speculative activities, such as property, construction, and personal consumption. Such lending only serves to destabilize the financial system and increase the incentive for domestic firms and households to engage in excessive and speculative borrowing. Although "positive" directed credit schemes, where credit is channeled by administrative diktat to politically favored sectors, have long been discredited by the experience of the 1960s and 1970s (as recounted in McKinnon, 1973), "negative" directed credit programs – which would control excessive or speculative borrowing by limiting bank lending to problem sectors – may help stabilize the macroeconomy and improve individuals' welfare by helping them to coordinate on a Pareto-superior outcome in a multiple-equilibrium setting.

Third-best regulatory remedies may also be required. If the authorities are unsure of their ability to monitor the quantity and quality and bank credit, direct and indirect measures to restrain inflows of foreign financial capital may be necessary to control moral hazard in the banking system from deposit insurance or other ex post bailout provisions. During a major structural reform (such as a trade liberalization), we showed that leaving the capital account open (as in our ILE) sped the rate of transformation and increased future incomes *only if* the financial system was free of moral hazard.

If latent moral hazard exists, then a major structural reform that inevitably introduces new uncertainty may well activate and exacerbate it. Large inflows of foreign financial capital are often the manifestation of excessive risk taking by banks in their foreign exchange exposure and extension of domestic credit (see the chapter by Garber and Lall, this volume, for a dramatic description of the former). If the capital account is left unrestricted, the potential for overborrowing – leading to overconsumption and overinvestment – can be very high indeed, as the Mexican and Chilean experiences attest.

Direct controls on inflows of foreign financial capital may be difficult to implement and have undesirable side effects, such as the promotion of corruption. Often indirect methods will suffice. Reserve requirements (implicit taxes on intermediation) imposed on the banks' foreign borrowing, plus very tight rules governing the net foreign exchange exposure of banks and other financial institutions, can reduce risk taking directly while having the incidental effect of restricting capital inflows.

Clearly our model suggests that a policy of complete laissez-faire with regard to the financial system is extremely misguided. The Mexican and East Asian experiences provide compelling evidence to this effect. The Mexican authorities attribute the 1994–95 crisis to lack of institutional infrastructure to monitor and regulate the newly liberalized and privatized banking system after 1990. No doubt similar regulatory inadequacies will be found in the aftermath of the East Asian overborrowing debacle of 1997.

Does our model throw any light on the appropriate regulatory, monetary, and fiscal response of the authorities in the face of massive capital flight once a crisis does occur? The overborrowing crises in Chile 1978–81 and in Mexico 1990–94 were associated with unsustainable overconsumption, as indicated by the sharp falls in private saving in Figures 11.7 and 11.8. To curtail private consumption sufficiently to allow a trade surplus to develop in the aftermath of each of these crises, fiscal stringency was an appropriate macroeconomic response. However, because the fiscal capacity of each government to tax households by ordinary means was somewhat limited, the inflation tax also had to be employed. As a result, a deep nominal currency devaluation served in Chile and Mexico to reimpose the inflation tax on households for a year or two after each crisis. Since the real exchange rate had become overvalued prior to each crisis, the devaluation also worked to improve international competitiveness. So for both relative price and fiscal reasons, a policy of deep nominal devaluation cum inflation was warranted in these cases to generate a trade surplus and quick return to current account balance.

In contrast, as Table 11.1 shows, the Asian economies that came under stress in 1997 have been high savers, showed little evidence of overconsumption, and had little or no domestic inflation indicating real exchange overvaluation. Their problem was more one of massive overinvestment of poor quality. Thus, if one puts aside important questions of contagion and beggar-thy-neighbor exchange rate effects, the appropriate response of the Asian economies in this situation should be regulatory reform that curtails bank lending and other forms of finance for investment. Fiscal stringency per se – sharply increasing taxes, including the inflation tax, on households – is unwarranted. Hence, the policies of the Southeast Asian economies in 1997, of allowing their domestic banking problems to become currency crises and forcing deep exchange rate devaluations, seem inappropriate and unnecessary for restoring current account balance. The ensuing economic turmoil, including inflationary pressure and bankruptcies of domestic firms with large dollar debts, therefore may be worse than it needs to be as the crisis unwinds.

References

Agénor, Pierre-Richard, and Peter J. Montiel (1996). *Development Macroeconomics*. Princeton, N.J.: Princeton University Press.

Cho, Yoon (1986). "Inefficiencies from Financial Liberalization in the Absence of Well-functioning Capital Markets," *Journal of Money, Credit, and Banking* 17: 191–99.

Conley, John, and William F. Maloney (1995). "Optimum Sequencing of Credible Reforms with Uncertain Outcomes," *Journal of Development Economics* 48 (1): 107–19.

Desmet, Klaus, and Thomas Mann (1996). "Lessons from the Mexican Banking Crisis of 1995–96." Unpublished manuscript, Banco de Mexico, Mexico City.

Dornbusch, Rudiger, and Alejandro Werner (1994). "Mexico: Stabilization, Reform, and No Growth," *Brookings Papers on Economic Activity*, no. 1: 253–97.

Galbraith, John K. (1990). *A Short History of Financial Euphoria*. New York: Penguin Books.

Gavin, Michael, and Ricardo Hausman (1995). "The Macroeconomic Roots of Banking Crises." Paper presented at the IADB conference on Banking Crises in Latin America, Washington, D.C.: Inter-American Development Bank.

Goldstein, Morris (1996). "Presumptive Indicators / Early Warning Signals of Vulnerability to Financial Crises in Emerging Market Economies." Unpublished manuscript, Institute for International Economics, Washington, D.C.

Kaminsky, Graciela, and Carmen Reinhart (1996). "The Twin Crises: The Causes of Banking and Balance of Payments Crises," International Finance Discussion Paper No. 544. Washington, D.C.: Board of Governors of the Federal Reserve System.

Kindleberger, Charles (1989). *Manias, Panics and Crashes: A History of Financial Crises*. Rev. ed. New York: Basic Books.

Krugman, Paul (1979). "Interest Rates, Efficiency and Growth: A Theoretical Analysis." Unpublished manuscript, Massachusetts Institute of Technology, Cambridge, Mass.

(1995). "Dutch Tulips and Emerging Markets," *Foreign Affairs* 74 (4): 28–44.

Kurz, Mordecai (1994). "On the Structure and Diversity of Rational Beliefs," *Economic Theory* 4: 877–900.

(1997). "Asset Prices with Rational Beliefs." In Mordecai Kurz, *Endogenous Economic Fluctuations: Studies in the Theory of Rational Beliefs.* Berlin: Springer Verlag.

Kydland, Finn, and Edward Prescott (1977). "Rules versus Discretion: On the Consistency of Optimal Plans," *Journal of Political Economy* 85: 473–91.

McKinnon, Ronald I. (1973). *Money and Capital in Economic Development.* Washington, D.C.: Brookings Institution.

(1993). *The Order of Economic Liberalisation: Financial Control in the Transition to a Market Economy.* 2nd ed. Baltimore: Johns Hopkins University Press.

McKinnon, Ronald I., and Huw Pill (1996). "Credible Liberalizations and International Capital Flows: The Overborrowing Syndrome." In Takatoshi Ito and Anne O. Krueger, eds., *Financial Deregulation and Integration in East Asia*, pp. 7–42. Chicago: University of Chicago Press.

Minsky, Hyman (1977). "A Theory of Systemic Fragility." In Edward Altman and Arnold Sametz, eds., *Financial Crises: Institutions and Markets in a Fragile Environment*, pp. 138–52. New York: Wiley International.

(1982). "The Financial Instability Hypothesis: Capitalist Processes and the Behavior of the Economy." In Charles Kindleberger and Jean-Pierre Laffargue, eds., *Financial Crises: Theory, History, and Policy*, pp. 13–39. Cambridge: Cambridge University Press.

Pill, Huw (1996). "A Simple Model of the Overborrowing Syndrome," Harvard Business School Working Paper. Boston: HBS Division of Research.

Rojas-Suárez, Lilliana, and Steven Weisbrod (1995). "Financial Market Fragilities in Latin America: From Banking Crisis Resolution to Current Policy Challenges." IMF Working Paper No. 94/117. Washington, D.C.

CHAPTER 12

Capital inflows, financial intermediation, and aggregate demand: Empirical evidence from Mexico and other Pacific Basin countries

Steven B. Kamin and Paul R. Wood

12.1 Introduction

In recent years, a substantial literature has emerged to focus on the effects of capital inflows on macroeconomic performance in emerging-market countries. Clearly, capital inflows are necessary to finance the excess of investment over savings needed to build productive capacity and accelerate the process of growth in developing economies. However, recent experience has caused observers to take notice of a broad array of less desirable side effects associated with heavy inflows of foreign capital.

First, such inflows may lead to an appreciation – in both real and, perhaps, nominal terms – of the domestic currency, thereby inhibiting export growth and encouraging the widening of current account deficits. Second, to the extent that capital inflows lead to the accumulation of international reserves by the central bank, this may lead to undesirable increases in the money supply and in the balance sheets – on both the asset and liability sides – of domestic banks. The expansion of loanable funds available to domestic banks, in turn, may finance greater increases in consumption and/or investment than are sustainable over the longer run, leading to a further deterioration of external balance, increases in private net indebtedness, and the emergence of nonperforming loan problems. Observers acknowledge that the most obvious policy response to such developments – sterilization – may be too costly for governments to pursue on a sustained basis. Third, capital flows are volatile; economies that become too dependent on capital inflows to finance current

We are grateful to members of the International Finance Division Workshop for helpful comments and suggestions. David Carter provided excellent research assistance. This paper represents the views of the authors and should not be interpreted as reflecting those of the Board of Governors of the Federal Reserve System or other members of its staff.

account deficits and maturing debts may become significantly destabilized if some factor leads to a reversal of these flows.

However, notwithstanding considerable theoretical analysis and anecdotal evidence linking capital inflows to macroeconomic problems in emerging market economies, there has been little formal statistical analysis of the impact of capital inflows on monetary growth, banking activity, and aggregate demand. Such statistical analysis may be needed to distinguish the particular economic effects of capital inflows from the effects of other developments occurring simultaneously. Many of the emerging market economies experiencing heavy capital inflows during the early 1990s also were in the midst of macroeconomic stabilization, structural reform, and financial liberalization. It is possible that some undesirable economic developments that have been attributed to capital inflows may actually be the result of other changes taking place at the same time.

An example from Mexico's recent experience serves to highlight this problem. During the 1990–93 period, total net capital flows into Mexico rose to an average of $23 billion annually from $2 billion annually during the preceding 1982–89 period. At the same time, the growth of monetary aggregates, credit, and aggregate demand picked up markedly. It is natural to attribute the rapid monetary growth that took place in Mexico since the late 1980s to the surge in capital inflows. However, this surge in capital inflows took place concurrently with, and may to some degree have been caused by, a marked reduction in Mexican inflation. The Mexican government at that time was, to a first approximation, targeting the interest rate rather than the money supply, and reduced the nominal interest rate in line with the decline in inflation. This, in turn, may have induced an increase in the demand for real money that was accommodated by the monetary authority. In retrospect, therefore, it is not clear whether the growth in real balances that took place in the early 1990s was attributable more to capital inflows or to the decline in inflation. Put another way, it is possible that, even in the absence of heavy capital inflows, the authorities would have stepped up domestic credit creation so that monetary growth would still have picked up.

If the rapid monetary growth, banking expansion, and increases in domestic absorption observed in many emerging-market economies are being mistakenly attributed to capital inflows, this could lead governments to implement inappropriate policies in order to counter such inflows. The purpose of this chapter is to make a rough, initial stab at gauging empirically the extent to which capital inflows have altered macroeconomic performance in emerging market economies.

We start out with an econometric analysis of the impact of capital inflows on interest rates, the domestic money supply, consumption, and investment in Mexico. To analyze the impact of capital inflows on the supply of broad money (M2), we estimate a monetary "reaction function" that relates the domestic interest rate targeted by the authorities to its various determinants, including inflation, output, and different measures of capital inflows. We then estimate a model of the demand for M2, based on interest rates and output. These results allow us to assess the impact of capital inflows on interest rates, and hence the demand for money, once the evolution of domestic factors is held constant.

We then gauge the effects of capital inflows on Mexican consumption and investment rates, and the extent to which these effects were associated with the domestic financial intermediation of foreign capital inflows. We estimate separate econometric models relating consumption and investment to a standard set of determinants – output growth and interest rates as well as different measures of capital inflows. These regressions allow us to identify the impact of capital inflows on consumption and investment, controlling for their standard determinants. We also attempt to distinguish the effects on consumption and investment of different categories of capital inflows such as portfolio investment and foreign direct investment.

In the final part of the chapter, we seek to identify whether our broadest conclusions about the effects of capital inflows in Mexico apply to the experience of other Pacific Basin countries – Argentina, Brazil, Chile, Colombia, Indonesia, Korea, Malaysia, the Philippines, and Thailand – that experienced substantial capital inflows in the late 1980s and early 1990s. Using a pooled time series, cross-section set of annual data for the ten countries (including Mexico), we estimate econometric equations to gauge the effect of capital inflows on the money supply, consumption, and investment spending in a manner analogous to our analysis of Mexico. We determine whether there are significant differences in the response of economies in different regions to capital inflows, and also consider whether differences in the composition of capital inflows may help explain differences in macroeconomic performance between Latin America and East Asia.

12.1.1   Previous empirical work on capital inflows

Formal statistical research on capital flows to developing countries has, until very recently, focused primarily on the determinants of these capital flows. Calvo, Leiderman, and Reinhart (1993) applied vector-autoregression (VAR) analysis to the behavior of recent capital inflows – proxied by changes in international reserves – in several Latin

American countries, and determined that external factors such as declines in U.S. interest rates accounted for much, but not all, of the increases in capital inflows during the 1990s. Chuhan, Claessens, and Mamingi (1993) came to similar conclusions, but disagreement persists concerning the relative weight of external and domestic factors in the determination of capital flows to emerging-market countries.

A related issue has centered on the different time series properties of different types of capital inflows. According to the conventional wisdom that has developed on this subject, portfolio inflows are much more volatile than other types of capital inflows, particularly direct foreign investment (see Corbo and Hernández, 1994). Claessens, Dooley, and Warner (1995), however, showed that, based on comparisons of the statistical time series properties of the various categories of capital flows, foreign direct investment and other forms of long-term flows were as volatile and prone to reversal as short-term portfolio flows. These results have tended to qualify views that foreign direct investment should be regarded as more desirable than portfolio flows.

In contrast to the research into the determinants of capital inflows, empirical work on the macroeconomic effects of capital inflows in the recipient economy has been, until recently, based mainly on case studies and generalizations from country experiences. (See, among others, Corbo and Hernandez, 1994; Calvo, Leiderman, and Reinhart, 1994; Fernandez-Arias and Montiel, 1995; Khan and Reinhart, 1995; Spiegel, 1995; and Koenig, 1996.) These studies highlight various possible side effects of capital inflows that may occur, in addition to their expected effect of boosting investment and the importation of capital goods:

1 Capital inflows are likely to appreciate the real exchange rate, either by appreciating the nominal exchange rate in a floating exchange rate regime, or by boosting the money supply, aggregate demand, and hence nontradables prices in a fixed exchange rate regime.

2 In a fixed exchange rate regime, as noted earlier, unsterilized capital inflows may result in some loss of monetary control, resulting in higher monetary growth than otherwise would occur. This (perhaps) undesired monetary expansion may be the vehicle by which capital inflows lead to upward pressure on prices and aggregate demand, real appreciation, and hence a corresponding expansion of the current account deficit. Sterilization of capital inflows is likely to be costly and, if it keeps interest rates high and thereby encourages more capital inflows, ineffective.

3 The intermediation of capital inflows through the domestic banking system may be an important feature of the process by which capital inflows lead to demand expansion. Increases in the monetary base resulting from unsterilized intervention lead to an expansion of bank deposits and a corresponding expansion of bank loans. In an environment where the supervision and regulation of banks are imperfectly implemented, the expansion of bank balance sheets associated with capital inflows may enhance the prospects for financial fragility.

4 The effect of capital inflows on expanding the money supply, lowering interest rates, and expanding credit availability may well raise consumption (reduce savings) as well as increase investment. This is especially likely to occur if, prior to the resumption of capital inflows, consumption lending had been more tightly rationed than investment lending, so that in response to an easing of constraints, consumption spending rebounded to its unconstrained level.

5 It is possible that certain types of capital inflows may generate different macroeconomic effects than others. Foreign direct investment (FDI), for example, would appear, a priori, to be least likely to lead to expansions of the money supply, bank loans, and consumption, since FDI may be expected to lead immediately to corresponding imports of capital goods, thereby evading intermediation through the domestic financial system. Conversely, portfolio investment would seem more likely to lead to domestic monetary and bank loan expansion, and hence more likely to encourage consumption as well as investment.

Although all the effects of capital inflows described here have, to one degree or another, been observed in countries experiencing heavy inflows in recent years, relatively little work has been done so far to evaluate these effects econometrically. However, in the past year, a number of works have emerged to explore the impact of capital flows on macroeconomic outcomes using formal statistical methods.

Gunther, Moore, and Short (1996) focus on the case of Mexico and estimate a quarterly VAR model comprising the price level, output, foreign investment, international reserves, and the exchange rate. They find that shocks to foreign direct investment had little impact on Mexico's macroeconomic indicators, but that shocks to reserves and to portfolio investment significantly affected output and the exchange rate, thereby adding support to the view that different types of capital flows have different macroeconomic effects.

Gruben and McLeod (1996) analyze a multicountry set of annual data to evaluate the effects of different types of capital flows on macroeconomic performance, and vice versa. They find considerable evidence of two-way causation between capital flows and output growth, but this evidence weakens in some instances when subcategories of capital flows or countries are considered; for example, Asian growth is found to be less sensitive to capital inflows than Latin American growth. Capital inflows are found to affect savings rates *positively*, contradicting the conventional wisdom; interestingly, however, this result is significant only if Mexico is excluded from the sample.

Using instrumental variables estimation, Gruben and McLeod find stronger results for the effects of capital flows on growth, with foreign direct investment being somewhat more significant than equity portfolio flows in this regard. On the other hand, with instrumental variables estimation, the positive effect of capital inflows on savings becomes insignificant.

Antzoulatos (1996) takes an approach similar to Gruben and McLeod (1996), focusing on the impact of capital flows on the components of domestic demand in a multicountry panel of annual data. He finds that in Latin American countries, domestic demand, private consumption, government consumption, and investment all responded positively and significantly to the (scaled) levels of international reserves and of borrowings in international bond markets. Conversely, capital inflows were found not to affect measures of Asian domestic demand significantly in most specifications of the estimating equation, consistent with Gruben and McLeod, while only investment consistently showed a significant response to the level of international reserves.

On balance, the results of the empirical work surveyed here provide tentative evidence that capital inflows did have significant impacts on the macroeconomic performance of emerging-market economies in the 1990s. Further work in this area must address the following concerns, among others. First, the effects of structural reforms, stabilization programs, and other domestic developments need to be controlled for, so that the independent effect of the capital flows themselves can be identified more clearly. Second, further empirical work should address the channels through which capital flows influence the economy – exchange rates, bank loans, asset prices, and the like – not merely the reduced form linking capital flows to their final macroeconomic outcomes. Finally, it would be of interest to understand the magnitude of the impact of capital flows on the macroeconomic performance of emerging-market countries in recent years, not merely whether that impact was statistically significant or not.

12.2   The evolution of capital flows and economic performance in Mexico: 1988–1994

12.2.1   Capital flows

During the 1990s, Mexico experienced a nearly unprecedented inflow of foreign capital, coming after a period – coinciding with the debt crisis – when net inflows had all but dried up. As indicated in Figure 12.1, after averaging about $2 billion annually during 1982–88, net inflows rose to $8 billion in 1990 and $33 billion by 1993. The inflows, however, were distinctive in terms of the greatly increased importance of portfolio investment and the greatly decreased importance of bank borrowing.

Various factors explain the resurgence of capital inflows into Mexico during the 1990s. On the domestic side, the attractiveness of Mexican investments was raised by a series of reform and stabilization measures undertaken in the latter part of the 1980s and the early 1990s, including the lowering of trade barriers, the liberalization of the financial system and privatization of banks that had been nationalized in 1982, and the near elimination of the fiscal deficit. These reforms were coupled with a stabilization program, initiated in 1988, aimed at reducing the depreciation of the peso against the dollar and using agreements with labor and business to moderate wage and price increases. As evident in Figure 12.2, the peso stabilized dramatically and the rate of inflation declined from nearly 160 percent in 1987 to 7 percent by 1994, while GDP growth, which on balance had been nearly flat for the 1982–87 period, rose to relatively high levels by the early 1990s.

However, the surge in capital inflows did not begin in earnest until 1990, well after inflation had come down and output had begun to re-cover. A second important factor in stimulating capital inflows may well have been the Brady Plan for debt reduction, which Mexico signed with its commercial bank creditors in February 1990. An indication of the importance of the Brady Plan was the downtick in peso-denominated interest rates, shown at the top of Figure 12.3, in the months after the deal was signed.

Finally, the inflow of capital into Mexico undoubtedly was spurred by the decline in U.S. interest rates, as Calvo, Leiderman, and Reinhart (1993) have shown. The search for higher rates of return outside the United States, coupled with the discrediting of direct bank lending in the aftermath of the debt crisis, probably explains much of the shift from bank lending to portfolio investment in the composition of capital in-flows into Mexico and other emerging-market countries.

Capital Account and Change in Reserves

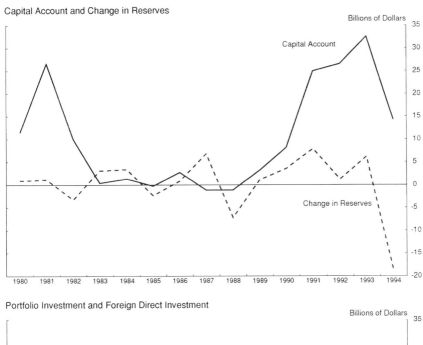

Portfolio Investment and Foreign Direct Investment

Figure 12.1. Mexican net capital inflows. *Source*: Banco de Mexico, unpublished data.

Exchange Rate

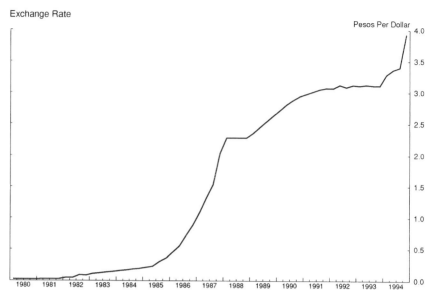

Inflation and Real GDP

Figure 12.2. Mexican economic indicators. *Source*: Banco de Mexico, *Indicadores Economicos* (various issues).

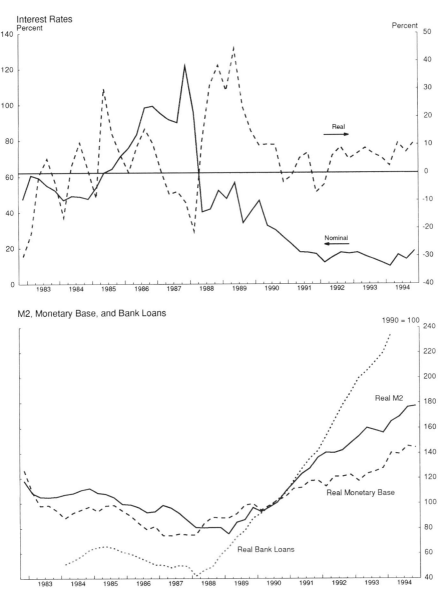

Figure 12.3. Mexican financial indicators. *Sources*: Banco de Mexico, *Indicadores Economicos* (various issues), except bank loan data from unpublished material.

12.2.2 *Monetary and banking conditions*

As shown in the bottom panel of Figure 12.3, monetary aggregates – M2 and the monetary base – expanded strongly during the 1990s. However, the extent to which monetary expansion can be attributed directly to capital inflows is not clear a priori. First, the Bank of Mexico actively sterilized reserve inflows so that, over the period, most increases in net foreign assets were offset by reductions of net domestic credit. Second, the real monetary base began to grow strongly in 1988 and slowed somewhat after 1990; conversely, real M2 did not pick up until 1989 and exhibited very strong growth after 1990. This suggests that much M2 growth resulted from increases in the money multiplier linking M2 to the monetary base, rather than balance-of-payments-induced expansions of the monetary base itself. Finally, and as a related point, the top panel of Figure 12.1 indicates that the surge in capital inflows led to the strongest rate of reserve accumulation only in the 1990–91 period, after which capital inflows primarily served to finance larger current account deficits. Nevertheless, real M2 growth remained strong throughout the period, suggesting, again, that if capital inflows tended to boost monetary growth, they must have done so through means other than reserve accumulation and monetary base expansion per se.

The top panel of Figure 12.3 indicates that along with an expansion of the monetary aggregates, the period of capital inflows was associated with sharp reductions in real interest rates as well as nominal interest rates. It is obvious that much of the reduction in nominal interest rates cannot be attributed to capital inflows, since the most marked decline occurred in 1988, prior to the recovery of capital inflows and coincident with the inflation stabilization program. On the other hand, ex post real interest rates were quite high in 1988 and 1989, perhaps serving to jump-start capital inflows, and declined in subsequent years as capital inflows reached their peak.

Finally, the reduction in inflation and interest rates, rise in the monetary aggregates, and recovery of access to international credit markets were accompanied by a recovery of bank lending to the nonfinancial private sector, shown in the bottom panel of Figure 12.3. As may be seen on that chart, however, the turnaround in bank lending actually preceded the recovery of M2. This may reflect the fact that the rise in bank lending reflected not only increases in the liabilities of the banking system – which increased loanable resources – but also the decline in the use of these resources to finance the public sector deficit, which declined from 15 percent of GDP in 1987 to approximate balance by the early 1990s.

Table 12.1. *Mexican investment, savings, and current account balance (percent of GDP)*

Year	Private fixed investment	Public fixed investment	Total fixed investment	Current account	Savings
1985	12.5	6.6	19.10	0.4	19.50
1986	12.9	6.5	19.40	−1.3	18.10
1987	12.9	5.6	18.50	2.8	21.30
1988	15.2	5.0	20.20	−1.7	18.50
1989	13.3	4.8	18.10	−2.9	15.20
1990	13.7	4.9	18.60	−3.6	15.00
1991	14.9	4.6	19.50	−5.2	14.30
1992	16.6	4.2	20.80	−7.4	13.40
1993	16.4	4.0	20.40	−6.4	14.00
1994	16.9	4.3	21.20	−7.7	13.50

Source: Banco de Mexico, *The Mexican Economy* (various issues).

12.2.3   Savings and investment

One of the most important criticisms of capital inflows is that, at least in some Latin American countries, they have encouraged – or at least, financed – an increase in consumption rather than in investment. Table 12.1 compares the evolution of savings, investment, and the current account as a share of GDP. In a comparison of 1994 with 1985, of the roughly 8 percent of GDP deterioration in the current account balance, a reduction in savings accounts for 6 percent of GDP and an increase in total investment spending for only 2 percent of GDP. On the face of it, therefore, capital inflows financed greater consumption more than greater investment. However, the relatively small increase in the total investment rate in part reflects a 2 percent of GDP drop in public investment resulting from government budget cutting. Private fixed investment rose about 4 percent of GDP, somewhat closer in magnitude to the rise in consumption.

Finally, it is worth noting that the sharpest reduction in the savings rate took place between 1987 and 1989, before capital inflows had begun to recover in earnest. Conversely, private investment did not begin to recover until after 1990, coincident with the largest increases in capital inflows. Hence, the prima facie evidence is at best mixed that capital flows encouraged consumption more than investment in Mexico.

12.3   The impact of capital flows on domestic money demand in Mexico

12.3.1   *Theory*

Capital flows conventionally are believed to affect directly the supply, rather than the demand, for money. Therefore, in principle, to assess the effect of capital flows on monetary growth in Mexico, we might focus on the transmission channel linking capital flows to international reserve changes, net foreign assets, the monetary base, and hence the broader monetary aggregates. However, as we will show, these linkages are not likely to remain constant over time.

Equation (1) establishes M2 as being linked through the money multiplier (mm) to the monetary base (MB):

$$M2 = mmMB. \tag{1}$$

(We omit time subscripts throughout.) Therefore, changes in M2 reflect changes in either the monetary base or the money multiplier:

$$\Delta M2 = MB\Delta mm + mm\Delta MB. \tag{2}$$

The change in the monetary base, in turn, depends on changes in net foreign assets (NFA) and net domestic assets (NDA) of the central bank:

$$\Delta MB = \Delta NFA + \Delta NDA. \tag{3}$$

The central bank determines the evolution of NDA directly. NFA is determined as the local currency equivalent of international reserve changes (we assume, for convenience, that the exchange rate, E, defined as pesos per dollar, is fixed):

$$\Delta NFA = E\Delta R. \tag{4}$$

Reserve changes, in turn, are the sum of the current account (CA) and the capital account (KA):

$$\Delta R = CA + KA. \tag{5}$$

Putting together equations (2) through (5):

$$\Delta M2 = \Delta mmMB + mm\left(\Delta NDA + E\left(CA\right) + E\left(KA\right)\right). \tag{6}$$

In principle, therefore, the impact of a change in capital flows on monetary growth can be calculated:

$$d(\Delta M2)/d(\Delta KA) = mmE. \tag{7}$$

Equation (7), however, presupposes that changes in capital flows affect neither the current account (CA) nor net domestic assets (NDA). (It also is assumed that the exchange rate, E, remains fixed.) In practice, both CA and NDA are likely to be affected by a change in capital flows. Hence, a more comprehensive description of the impact of capital flows on monetary growth can (after some manipulation) be derived:

$$d(\Delta M2)/d(\Delta KA) = mmE\left(1 + d(\Delta NDA)/d(\Delta NFA)\right)$$
$$(dCA/dKA + 1) + MB(d(\Delta mm)/dKA). \tag{8}$$

Equation (8) suggests that the impact of capital inflows on the supply of M2 will depend on the initial values of the money multiplier and the exchange rate, the extent to which changes in capital flows elicit changes in the current account balance, the extent to which the authorities sterilize changes in the monetary base resulting from reserve changes $(d(\Delta NDA)/d(\Delta NFA))$, and any impacts of capital inflows on the money multiplier.

In practice, the derivatives embedded in equation (8) are likely to vary over time. The extent to which the monetary authorities sterilize capital inflows will depend on the present state of the economy. The extent to which changes in the capital account lead to changes in the current account may depend on whether the economy is constrained in its access to international credit markets. Finally, the removal of reserve requirements in Mexico starting in 1988 means that the money multiplier subsequently has been determined very much by market conditions; it therefore is likely that capital inflows had a different (probably, much smaller) impact on the money multiplier before the removal of reserve requirements compared with afterward. The bottom panel of Figure 12.3 indicates that the money multiplier rose substantially in the 1990s.

In sum, explaining the surge in M2 growth that took place in Mexico in the early 1990s by decomposing the sources of the supply of M2 is likely to be fraught with difficulty. We therefore take an alternative approach in this chapter, and attempt to gauge the impact of capital inflows on the *demand* for M2. In this approach, we start with a conventional money demand function. A simple, static example of this function, in which M2 demand depends upon a domestic interest rate i and real income y, is shown here:

$$\log(M2/P) = \alpha - \beta i + \delta y + e_M. \tag{9}$$

If we assume that the demand curve for M2 remains stable, capital inflows can only affect M2 in the long run by affecting its demand – in the first instance, this means by affecting interest rates. As in Kamin and Rogers (1996), we posit an interest rate reaction function for the monetary authority, in which the authority sets the domestic interest rate in response to the prevailing level of inflation, output growth, and capital inflows. Increases in inflation lead the authorities to raise interest rates to keep the real interest rate from declining. Increases in output growth also should elicit a countercyclical rise in interest rates. Finally, increases in capital inflows induce the authorities to lower interest rates because (1) they bolster the monetary authorities' reserve position and hence reduce the need for additional inflows, and/or (2) capital inflows are costly to sterilize, and lowering interest rates both implies less sterilization and smaller future inflows. An illustrative static version of an interest rate reaction function is shown here (where a "hat" denotes log change):

$$i = v + \lambda \hat{P} + \phi \hat{y} - \theta KA + e_i. \tag{10}$$

The interest rate reaction function approach is supported by the fact that during most of the period prior to the December 1994 devaluation, the authorities appeared to be targeting the interest rate rather than a monetary aggregate. Kamin and Rogers estimated a dynamic version of an interest rate reaction function, which they found to be quite stable during the early 1990s in Mexico.

Based on equations (9) and (10), the impact of capital flows on money demand can be calculated as a function of the impact of KA on i, and then the impact of i on M2:

$$dM2/dKA = (dM2/di)(di/dKA) = (-\beta)(-\theta) > 0. \tag{11}$$

12.3.2 Estimation strategy

In this chapter, we take two related approaches toward calculating the impact of capital flows on money growth, as shown in equation (11). First, we estimate dynamic versions of equations (9) and (10) separately, and simulate a counterfactual path of interest rates and money balances that would have occurred, had capital inflows not surged as they did in the early 1990s.

Second, we add capital inflows as an explanatory variable in the money demand function (equation 9), and estimate it using two-stage least squares. Merely adding capital inflows (KA) to equation (9) and estimating OLS is problematic, since the interest rate in equation (9) already incorporates the effects of capital inflows. However, consider the result when we substitute equation (10) for the interest rate in equation (9) and slightly rearrange terms:

$$\log(M2/P) = \alpha - \beta\left(v + \lambda\hat{P} + \phi\hat{y} - \theta KA + e_i\right) + \delta y + e_M$$
$$= \alpha - \beta\left(v + \lambda\hat{P} + \phi\hat{y} + e_i\right) + \beta\theta KA + \delta y + e_M. \tag{12}$$

The terms within parentheses in the second line represent that part of interest rates which *is not* determined by capital flows, while the θKA term represents that part of interest rates that *is* a function of capital flows. We estimate (a dynamic version of) equation (12) through a two-stage procedure in which we first estimate a partial version of the interest rate reaction function equation:

$$i = v + \lambda\hat{P} + \phi\hat{y} + \sigma Z + e_i. \tag{13}$$

Z represents other potential instruments that are correlated with the interest rate (i) but not with KA. We then take the fitted values for i, denoted i', and use them as explanatory variables in the second stage regression:

$$\log(M2/P) = \alpha - \beta i' + \beta\theta KA + \delta y + e_M - \beta e_i. \tag{14}$$

Estimating equation (14) has an advantage over estimating equations (9) and (10), in that it is more general and imposes fewer restrictions on the data. First, it does not pin down the specific model linking capital flows to the interest rate. Second, it does not restrict KA to affect M2 demand exclusively by affecting interest rates. For example, KA may affect M2 directly by raising foreign currency (mainly dollar) deposits in Mexico, without requiring a reduction in peso-denominated interest rates to raise the demand for those deposits.

Finally, as in our first approach, we use the estimated version of equation (14) to determine how the money supply would have evolved, had capital flows not surged into Mexico in the early 1990s. These results can then be compared with those calculated using our first, explicitly two-equation strategy.

Data on Mexico's international reserves, capital flows, and bank loans were obtained from unpublished material provided by the Banco de Mexico. Data on monetary aggregates, interest rates, output, and prices were obtained from the Banco de Mexico, *Indicadores Economicos*.

12.3.3   *Equation specification and estimation results from the two-equation approach*

In implementing our first approach to gauging the effect of capital inflows on money demand in Mexico, we use quarterly data for 1982 to 1994 to separately estimate error–correction versions of the static money demand and interest-rate reaction functions shown in equations (9) and (10). We use two different measures of capital inflows: the capital account, which measures the net flow of capital into Mexico, and the change in international reserves, which measures the extent to which capital flows would increase the monetary base absent any sterilization. We scale the capital account variables, expressed in terms of nominal pesos, by dividing them by lagged nominal balances of M2. The interest rate used here is the rate on twenty-eight-day cetes (peso-denominated Mexican treasury bills). The inflation rate used is the log change in the consumer price index.

Focusing first on the specification of the interest rate reaction function, we start out with the most general specification of an error–correction function, where we regress the change in the interest rate on changes in the explanatory variables and lagged levels of the interest rate and the explanatory variables:

$$
\Delta i = \alpha + \lambda \hat{P}_{-1} + \phi \hat{y}_{-1} + \theta KA_{-1}
$$
$$
+ \sum_{n=1}^{4} \rho_n \Delta i_{-n} + \sum_{n=0}^{4} \lambda_n \Delta \hat{P}_{-n} + \sum_{n=0}^{4} \phi_n \Delta \hat{y}_{-n} + \sum_{n=0}^{4} \theta_n \Delta KA_{-n}. \tag{15}
$$

This is then reduced by progressively removing explanatory variables with nonsignificant coefficients, following Hendry's general-to-specific approach. We end up with a parsimonious equation similar to that in Kamin and Rogers (1996). As in Kamin and Rogers (1996), we were unable to estimate a coefficient on an output variable that was statistically significant and of the expected positive sign, and hence we dropped it from the equation.

The first column of Table 12.2 shows the results from estimating the basic interest rate equation without the capital flow variables. The lagged interest rate enters with the expected negative sign while lagged inflation and the change in inflation both enter with the expected positive sign. The second column shows that, when the lagged value of the capital account and the change in the capital account are included, they are estimated to have a significant negative effect on the change in the interest rate. The third column shows that the lagged value of the change in reserves and the change in the change in reserves also have significant

Table 12.2. *Results for Mexican interest rate reaction function (dependent variable: change in interest rate)*

	Basic equation	With capital account	With change in reserves	With both
Constant	2.03	6.76	−0.27	−1.25
	(0.66)	(1.86)	(−0.10)	(−0.30)
Interest rate (−1)	−0.25	−0.31	−0.27	−0.27
	(−2.28)	(−2.72)	(−2.67)	(−2.47)
Inflation (−1)	0.23	0.20	0.30	0.32
	(2.03)	(1.83)	(2.87)	(2.77)
Change in inflation	0.71	0.73	0.80	0.80
	(7.52)	(8.03)	(9.67)	(9.32)
Δ reserves (−1)			−0.23	−0.25
			(−3.86)	(−2.95)
Change in Δ reserves			−0.18	−0.19
			(−3.54)	(−2.61)
Capital account (−1)		−0.20		0.03
		(−2.35)		(0.31)
Change in capital account		−0.14		0.01
		(−2.27)		(0.16)
Seasonal Q1	−3.91	−2.46	−2.55	−2.68
	(−1.18)	(−0.77)	(−0.90)	(−0.91)
Seasonal Q2	6.90	9.43	9.08	8.86
	(1.79)	(2.48)	(2.75)	(2.55)
Seasonal Q3	2.11	3.10	3.35	3.23
	(0.63)	(0.97)	(1.19)	(1.11)
Adjusted R-squared	0.57	0.62	0.70	0.68
Durbin-Watson statistic	2.07	2.09	2.27	2.30

negative effects on the change in the interest rate. These results are consistent with the theoretical presumption that capital inflows can reduce the interest rate target of the central bank, either by lessening concerns over depleting international reserves or by reducing pressure for the exchange rate to depreciate.

The fourth column of Table 12.2 shows the results of including both the capital account and the change in reserves in the interest rate equation. The change in reserves continues to show a significant negative effect on the interest rate, but the effect of the capital account largely

Table 12.3. *Results for Mexican M2 demand function including capital account (dependent variable: change in log real M2)*

	OLS	OLS with capital account	IV for interest rate[a]	IV for interest and capital account[a]
Constant	−0.91	−0.85	−0.84	−0.84
	(−3.49)	(−3.27)	(−3.12)	(−3.09)
Interest rate	−0.15	−0.13	−0.12	−0.13
	(−5.88)	(−4.25)	(−4.08)	(−4.01)
Four-quarter interest rate change	0.10	0.09	0.08	0.08
	(3.07)	(2.51)	(2.05)	(1.92)
Log (real M2/GDP)(−1)	−0.15	−0.14	−0.14	−0.14
	(−3.68)	(−3.39)	(−3.23)	(−3.21)
Capital account		0.16	0.19	0.14
		(1.41)	(1.67)	(0.97)
Adjusted R-squared	0.42	0.44		
Durbin-Watson statistic	2.20	2.36	2.07	2.11

[a] IV = instrumental variable estimates.

disappears. This suggests that reserves may have a structural relationship with the interest rate while the capital account may affect the interest rate only indirectly, through its effect on reserves. That is consistent with the central bank caring about the reserve level but not caring about other effects of capital inflows.

The second stage of this two-stage approach to gauging the impact of capital inflows on M2 money growth is to examine the effect of interest rates on money demand. The first column of Table 12.3 shows the results from estimating a parsimonious model of money demand used in Kamin and Rogers (1996), where the log-change in real, seasonally adjusted M2 money demand depends negatively on the interest rate, positively on the four-quarter change in the interest rate, and negatively on the inverse of lagged velocity (real M2/GDP).

Simulation using the two-equation approach: We now attempt to gauge the impact of net capital flows on Mexican money demand during the 1988–94 period. Using the estimation results for the effect of capital flows on the interest rate from Table 12.2 and for the effect of the interest rate on the M2 money supply from the first column of Table 12.3, we simulate the path that interest rates and M2 would have taken if net capital inflows during 1988–94 had been zero. To do this, we first add-factor the estimated interest rate and M2 equations by adding the estimated residuals over the 1988–94 period back into them so that a dynamic simulation over that period yields the actual observations of the left-hand side variables. Next, we dynamically simulate the interest rate equation with the net capital flow variable set to zero over 1988–94. Finally, we substitute the simulation results for the interest rate into the M2 equation and then dynamically simulate it over the 1988–94 period. We do this exercise twice, once using the capital account as the net capital flow variable and once using the change in reserves as a proxy for net capital flows.

Figure 12.4 compares the actual path of Mexican interest rates with those simulated by the model, once the net capital flows variable is set to zero for the 1988–94 period. The top panel indicates that when the entire capital account is used as the net capital flows variable, setting that variable to zero results in a substantial increase in interest rates. This suggests that the capital inflows that took place in 1988–94 appreciably reduced Mexican interest rates. However, in the bottom panel, the change in international reserves is used as the capital flows variable, and setting this term to zero results in a much smaller rise in interest rates. In fact, since reserves actually declined in 1988 and early 1989, setting reserve changes to zero actually leads simulated interest rates to decline relative to actual in those years.

Based on the two simulated paths of interest rates, under the counterfactual hypothesis that net capital inflows were zero during 1988–94, Figure 12.5 compares the resultant simulated paths of real M2 in this period to their actual values. Regardless of whether the entire capital account or reserve changes are used as the proxy for net capital inflows, simulated real M2 (under the counterfactual hypothesis that net capital inflows are zero) rises strongly and persistently from its 1989 low point during the 1990s. This suggests that, even in the absence of strong capital inflows, other economic developments (perhaps, in particular, the reduction in inflation) would have induced declines in interest rates, substantial increases in money demand, and correspondingly substantial increases in money supply.

The counterfactual experiment using the entire capital account as a proxy for capital inflows (the top panel) suggests that capital inflows had a substantial effect in further boosting real M2, while the experiment using reserve changes (the bottom panel) indicates that capital inflows had a relatively minor effect on monetary growth. (These results mirror those for interest rates in Figure 12.4.) This inconsistency in the results largely reflects the divergence between decelerating reserve

Actual and Simulated Interest Rates

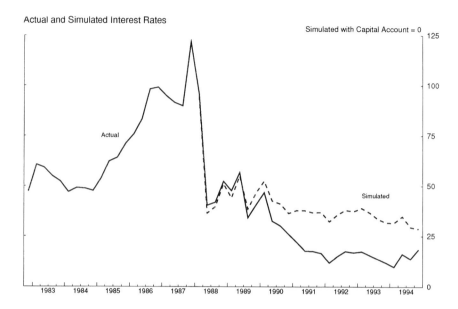

Actual and Simulated Interest Rates

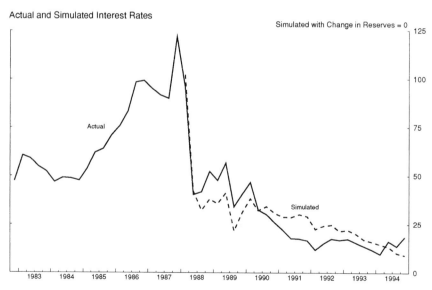

Figure 12.4. Mexican interest rate simulations.

Actual and Simulated Log of Real M2

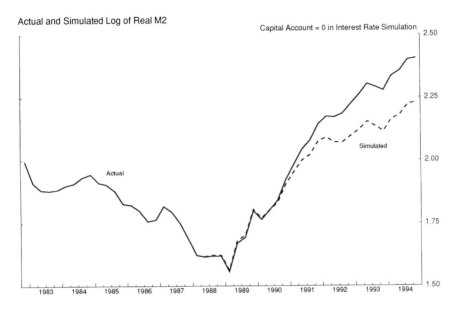

Actual and Simulated Log of Real M2

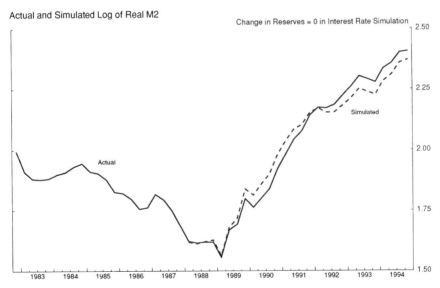

Figure 12.5. Mexican real M2 simulations.

accumulation and continued strong capital inflows after 1991. In attempting to reconcile the inconsistency, one possibility is that the results shown in the top panel are spurious. That is, as indicated in the estimation results in Table 12.2 (fourth column), capital inflows may affect monetary conditions only insofar as they affect reserves. In that case, the strong growth of real M2 in 1992–93, even as the capital account surplus surged relative to the pace of reserve accumulation, may have been merely a coincidence, not a causal outcome.

An alternative possibility is that the channels through which the capital account influenced monetary conditions changed during the 1990s. On balance over the entire 1982–94 estimation sample, it is possible that reserve changes (through their effect on the monetary base) were the proximate causes of monetary growth, and that the capital account affected monetary conditions mainly through its impact on reserve changes. However, during the 1990s, other determinants of monetary conditions may have become important, and these determinants may have been more directly influenced by the capital account. Figure 12.3 shows that the ratio of M2 to the monetary base started rising in mid-1990, about the same time as capital inflows began to come into Mexico. It is possible that the regaining of access to international financial markets, combined with financial liberalization and reductions in public sector borrowing, led to increases in the money multiplier that substantially raised monetary growth.

12.3.4   *Estimation and simulation results from the one-equation approach to estimating M2 demand*

Our second approach to estimating the demand for M2 is to directly include the capital flow variables in the M2 demand equation shown in equation (9). The second column of Table 12.3 shows the estimation results when the capital account is included in the parsimonious model of M2 money demand. Even with the interest rate and the four-quarter interest rate change in the equation, the capital account has some positive effect on the demand for M2 balances. As shown in the second column of Table 12.4, the same is true for the change in reserves.

However, these estimates of the effect of capital inflows on M2 may be biased if, as discussed in section 12.3.1, capital flows affect monetary conditions primarily by affecting the interest rate, since the interest rate already is included as an explanatory variable in the M2 equation. Therefore, as discussed in section 12.3.1, in order to measure the total effect of capital flows on M2 demand, we use instrumental variables estimation to constrain the interest rate from moving in response to contemporaneous

Table 12.4. *Results for Mexican M2 demand function including change in reserves (dependent variable: change in log real M2)*

	OLS	OLS with change in reserves	IV for interest rate[a]	IV for interest rate and change in reserves[a]
Constant	−0.91	−0.88	−0.84	−0.82
	(−3.49)	(−3.45)	(−3.25)	(−3.17)
Interest rate	−0.15	−0.15	−0.15	−0.16
	(−5.88)	(−6.06)	(−6.17)	(−6.25)
Annual interest rate	0.10	0.09	0.06	0.05
change	(3.07)	(2.74)	(1.73)	(1.41)
Log (real M2/GDP)(−1)	−0.15	−0.15	−0.14	−0.14
	(−3.68)	(−3.65)	(−3.45)	(−3.38)
Change in reserves		0.14	0.21	0.28
		(1.63)	(2.18)	(2.30)
Adjusted R-squared	0.42	0.45		
Durbin-Watson statistic	2.20	2.52	2.40	2.21

[a] IV = instrumental variable estimates.

capital flow indicators, while allowing it to move in response to contemporaneous domestic variables such as inflation as well as lagged external variables. This allows the coefficient on the capital flow variable to capture all of its effects on M2 demand, including those working through the interest rate. As indicated in the third column of Tables 12.3 and 12.4, the use of instrumental variables has the effect of raising somewhat the size and significance of the coefficients on both the capital account and reserve changes. Finally, the fourth columns of Tables 12.3 and 12.4 indicate the effects of instrumenting for the capital flow variable as well; this will be discussed further in the next subsection.

We now repeat the counterfactual simulation experiment shown in Figures 12.4 and 12.5, but using our one-equation approach to gauging the effect of capital flows on M2 demand. Figure 12.6 shows the simulation of what would have happened to real M2 if net capital flows had been zero during the 1988–94 period, using the results from the estimation of the M2 demand equation (we use the estimation results shown in the third column of Table 12.3 for the capital account and the fourth column of Table 12.4 for reserve changes). As in the two-equation approach, we find that even after setting the capital inflow variables (both

Actual and Simulated Log of Real M2

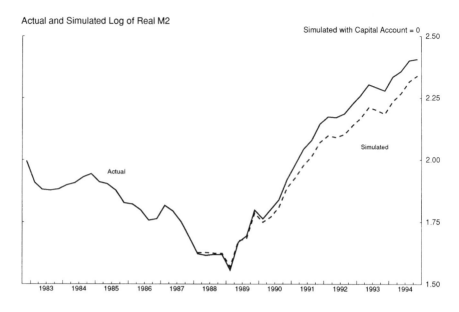

Actual and Simulated Log of Real M2

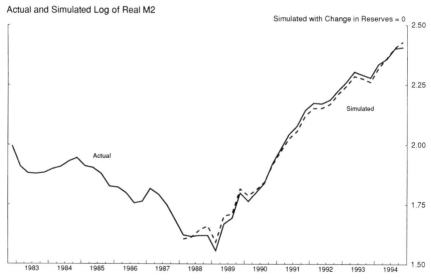

Figure 12.6. Mexican real M2 simulations: One-equation approach.

the capital account and reserve changes) to zero, the resultant simulated growth of real M2 still is quite substantial; in fact, the measured impact of capital flows on M2 is smaller under the one-equation approach than it is under the two-equation approach. Hence, these results reinforce our view that much of the rebound in the monetary aggregates after 1988 was not attributable to capital inflows. Additionally, the one-equation results indicate, as in the case of the two-equation results, that the capital account appears to have affected monetary growth more than reserve changes in the 1990s.

12.3.5 *Simultaneity issues*

We address three distinct simultaneity issues. First, in the conventional money demand function, the interest rate may be endogenous with respect to shocks to the supply of money, leading to simultaneity bias in the estimation of equation (9). In practice, however, simultaneity bias does not appear to be a problem here, as instrumental variables estimation of equation (9), shown in the third column of Tables 12.3 and 12.4, results in very little change to estimated coefficients on the interest rate and the four-quarter change in the interest rate. Using the fitted values does increase moderately the coefficient values of the capital flow variables (also shown in the third column of Tables 12.3 and 12.4), suggesting that at least some of the effect of capital flows on M2 demand is through the interest rate.

A second source of simultaneity bias stems from the endogeneity of capital flows with respect to the domestic interest rate. As indicated in equation (16), capital inflows probably respond to various factors, including deviations from uncovered interest parity, a country risk premium (RP), and other country-specific factors (X) that may influence the profitability of foreign investments. To the extent that movements in domestic interest rates (i) account for much of the variation of capital flows (KA), this raises two concerns. First, it may lead to significant bias in the estimation of equations (10) and (14) – in principle, it could even lead to estimation of a positive coefficient on KA in the interest rate equation (10) and a negative coefficient in the money demand equation (14). Second, the endogeneity of capital flows may undermine the relevance of seeking to determine the effects of capital flows, rather than their underlying determinants, on macroeconomic performance:

$$KA = \kappa + \xi\left(i - i^* - \hat{E}^e\right) - \vartheta RP + \rho X + e_{KA}. \tag{16}$$

The estimation results, however, suggest that the endogeneity of capital flows with respect to domestic interest rates probably is more apparent in theory than in practice. First, as was seen in Table 12.2, when dynamic specifications of equations (10) and (14) are estimated using OLS, coefficients on the capital flow variables are estimated with their expected signs. Second, the instrumental variables estimates of equation (14) (instrumenting for the capital flow variables as well as for interest rates) shown in the fourth column of Tables 12.3 and 12.4 do not result in large changes in estimated coefficients or their significance. Hence, to a first approximation, it appears that the variation in capital flows is sufficiently explained by nondomestic interest rate factors so as to make a focus on capital flows, rather than on their underlying determinants, intellectually defensible.

Finally, we should note that the results presented so far only address the *direct* effects of capital inflows on monetary conditions, and treat domestic conditions such as inflation and output (which was then dropped from the equation) as exogenous. However, inflation and output may have been, to a certain extent, endogenous with respect to capital inflows. To the extent that the reductions in inflation that boosted M2 demand were induced by the fixing of the exchange rate, which in turn was sustained by capital inflows, our estimates of the monetary effects of capital inflows ignore their *indirect* effect operating through the exchange rate regime. This serves to qualify our interpretation of Figures 12.5 and 12.6, to a certain extent, but does not alter our basic conclusion: capital inflows, operating through the standard interest rate and liquidity channels that are highlighted in the literature, did not significantly alter the evolution of real Mexican M2 during 1988–94.

12.4   The impact of capital flows on consumption and investment in Mexico

In this section, we attempt to gauge the impact of capital inflows on Mexican consumption and investment in the 1988–94 period. As in the case of Mexican money demand, we attempt to hold constant other factors that might be correlated with capital inflows in order to distinguish the independent impact of the capital flows themselves. Ideally, we would introduce proxies for various stabilization measures and structural reforms that were likely to affect consumption and investment decisions. These factors are difficult to quantify, however, and as a preliminary effort, we include only the more standard, quantifiable determinants of domestic demand: output, output growth, and the real interest rate. Our data on Mexican consumption and investment are obtained from Instituto Nacional de Estadistica Geografia en Informacion (INEGI), *Oferta y Demanda Final de Bienes y Servicios* (various issues).

12.4.1 Consumption

Theoretically, consumption demand will be negatively affected by the cost of funds (proxied by the real interest rate) and will be positively affected by income (real GDP). In addition, to the extent that consumption is constrained by the availability of credit (as distinct from the cost of credit), consumption may also depend positively on the size of bank balance sheets (proxied by M2 balances) and, indirectly, on capital inflows. Copelman and Werner (1995), in particular, find that the quantity of credit available in the Mexican economy does have real effects:

$$C = \beta_0 - \beta_1 GDP + \beta_2 rir + \beta_3 M2 + \beta_4 KA. \qquad (17)$$

We estimate an error–correction version of equation (17). The first column of Table 12.5 shows the estimation results when capital inflow variables are excluded. The lagged level and change of real GDP both show the expected significant positive effect on consumption. The long-run elasticity of consumption with respect to GDP (the coefficient on lagged real GDP divided by the coefficient on lagged real consumption) is close to unity. The real interest rate does not show the expected negative relationship with consumption, but that is not an uncommon result in this literature. As shown in the second column, the capital account has a nearly significant positive impact on consumption, even with the real interest rate being held constant.

As noted in section 12.1.1, different types of capital flows might have different effects on consumption. In the third and fourth columns of Table 12.5, we include separately in the consumption equation measures of two different types of capital inflow: net foreign direct investment and net foreign portfolio investment (scaled by lagged nominal M2). Neither foreign direct investment (column 3) nor portfolio investment (column 4) has significant impact on consumption, although their coefficients are quite different from each other. To gauge the significance of those differences, we rerun the consumption regression including both the capital account and a subcapital account variable (FDI or portfolio flows). Those results are shown in the last two columns of Table 12.5. The coefficient on a subcapital account variable measures the marginal effect of a movement in that variable, holding the capital account constant. Both FDI and portfolio flows have an insignificant additional effect when added along with the total capital account, so we cannot reject that their effects on consumption are the same.

The role of financial intermediation of capital inflows: If real M2 is taken as a proxy for bank deposits (and thus bank credit) it would be expected

Table 12.5. Results for Mexican consumption (dependent variable: log change in real consumption)

	Basic equation	With capital account	With FDI	With portfolio inflows	With capital account and FDI	Capital account and portfolio
Constant	1.17 (2.37)	2.02 (3.02)	1.26 (2.43)	1.93 (2.63)	1.99 (2.91)	2.26 (2.90)
Δ real interest rate	0.01 (0.51)	0.01 (0.51)	0.01 (0.43)	0.01 (0.42)	0.01 (0.48)	0.12 (0.46)
Δ log real GDP	0.88 (4.99)	0.85 (4.80)	0.85 (4.62)	0.83 (4.54)	0.84 (4.57)	0.83 (4.55)
Real interest rate (–1)	0.02 (0.85)	0.01 (0.69)	0.01 (0.64)	0.02 (0.85)	0.02 (0.70)	0.17 (0.78)
Log real GDP (–1)	0.42 (2.47)	0.51 (2.88)	0.42 (2.42)	0.41 (2.23)	0.50 (2.80)	0.48 (2.48)
Log real consumption (–1)	–0.35 (–2.61)	–0.47 (–3.17)	–0.36 (–2.59)	–0.40 (–2.81)	–0.46 (–3.07)	–0.47 (–3.06)
Δ log real consumption (–1)	0.07 (0.57)	0.12 (0.93)	0.08 (0.63)	0.11 (0.81)	0.12 (0.91)	0.13 (0.94)
Δ capital account		0.13 (1.73)			0.23 (1.45)	0.21 (1.22)
Capital account (–1)		0.39 (1.83)			0.36 (1.62)	0.32 (1.29)
Δ FDI			0.12 (0.16)		0.16 (0.22)	
FDI (–1)			–0.63 (–0.69)		–0.26 (–0.28)	
Δ portfolio investment				0.36 (1.03)		0.16 (0.41)
Portfolio investment (–1)				0.61 (1.32)		0.33 (0.64)
Adjusted R-squared	0.35	0.35	0.31	0.33	0.32	0.32
Durbin-Watson statistic	2.08	2.06	2.04	2.04	2.06	2.05

Table 12.6. *Results for Mexican consumption including real M2 (dependent variable: log change in real consumption)*

	Basic equation	With capital account	With FDI	With portfolio inflows
Constant	0.80	1.45	0.75	1.56
	(1.20)	(2.02)	(1.13)	(1.88)
Δ real interest rate	−0.00	0.00	−0.00	−0.00
	(−0.04)	(0.02)	(−0.10)	(−0.15)
Δ log in real GDP	0.91	0.90	0.92	0.86
	(5.25)	(5.22)	(5.12)	(4.83)
Real interest rate (−1)	−0.01	−0.00	−0.01	−0.00
	(−0.35)	(−0.39)	(−0.59)	(−0.22)
Log real GDP (−1)	0.60	0.70	0.66	0.57
	(3.18)	(3.64)	(3.35)	(2.88)
Log real consumption (−1)	−0.43	−0.54	−0.46	−0.46
	(−3.05)	(−3.63)	(−3.17)	(−3.13)
Δ log real consumption (−1)	0.02	0.06	0.03	0.04
	(0.19)	(0.50)	(0.26)	(0.32)
Δ capital account		0.27		
		(1.78)		
Capital account (−1)		0.48		
		(2.17)		
Δ FDI			−0.32	
			(−0.44)	
FDI (−1)			−1.37	
			(−1.47)	
Δ portfolio investment				0.23
				(0.67)
Portfolio investment (−1)				0.70
				(1.55)
Δ log real M2	0.05	−0.05	0.04	0.04
	(0.72)	(−2.17)	(0.55)	(0.59)
Log real M2 (−1)	−0.04	−0.01	−0.05	−0.04
	(−1.76)	(−0.15)	(−2.14)	(−1.80)

to have a positive effect on consumption, and the inclusion of real M2 in the regression might be expected to reduce the coefficient on the capital account and portfolio investment (because they may work indirectly through their effect on M2). Table 12.6 shows the same regressions as the first four columns of Table 12.5, but with the addition of lagged real M2 and the change in real M2. Surprisingly, real M2 has either an insignificant effect or a significant negative effect on consumption. Moreover, its inclusion slightly raises the significance of the capital account variable.

It is possible that M2 is not a good proxy for bank credit. As shown in Figure 12.3, real bank loans picked up in 1988, at least a year before the path of real M2 turned upward. Indeed, the path of real bank loans does appear to correspond more closely with that of consumption. When we included real bank loans, instead of real M2, in the consumption equation (not shown), we found a positive but insignificant effect of real bank loans on consumption.

Hence, while capital inflows appear to have been associated with increased Mexican consumption, even holding income and interest rates constant, our results do not support the existence of what we had expected to be the primary mechanism through which capital inflows encouraged consumption: increases in the money supply and hence bank lending.

A counterfactual simulation experiment: To gauge the impact of net capital flows on Mexican consumption during the 1988–94 period, we use the estimation results for the effect of the capital account on consumption from Table 12.5 (column 2) to simulate the path that consumption would have taken if the capital account during 1988–94 had been zero. This dynamic simulation uses the same basic approach as the M2 and interest rate simulations described in section 12.3.3. Figure 12.7 compares the actual path of Mexican consumption with that simulated by the model, once the capital account is set to zero for the 1988–94 period. The chart indicates that Mexican consumption would have been lower in the absence of capital inflows, but that the general pattern of substantial growth in consumption during 1988–94 would not have been altered. That implies that other factors such as the recovery of output, inflation stabilization, and financial liberalization may have been more important than capital flows in spurring the surge in consumption.

More simultaneity issues: The equations presented in Tables 12.5 and 12.6, and used to perform the counterfactual simulation in Figure 12.7, are subject to various forms of simultaneity bias, but these potential biases do not alter our final conclusion that capital inflows did not greatly change the path of Mexican consumption during 1988–94. First, capital inflows may well be caused by consumption, rather than vice versa, to the extent that additional consumption demand leads to additional international borrowing. If this were the case, however, then the coefficient on capital flows would be biased *upward*, meaning that our estimate of the

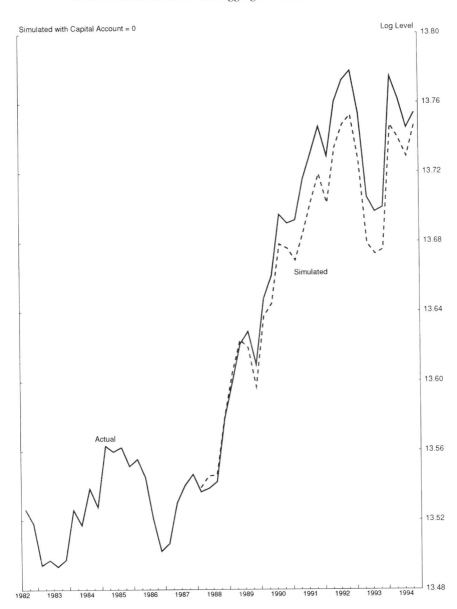

Figure 12.7. Mexican consumption simulation.

effect of capital flows on Mexican consumption shown in Figure 12.7 was *too high*. This possibility only reinforces our conclusion that even in the absence of strong capital inflows, Mexican consumption would likely have risen sharply after 1987.

As a second and related issue, the coefficient on the capital flows variable may be informative, even if the causality *does* run from consumption to capital flows. Presumably, in the event that access to international credit markets is cut off, consumption must be curtailed accordingly. Hence, the counterfactual experiment presented in Figure 12.7 may be interpreted as an estimate of the extent to which additional capital inflows permitted additional consumption.

Finally, it is possible that the output measures included in the consumption function are endogenous with respect to capital inflows, so that the counterfactual simulation presented in Figure 12.7 captures only the direct effect of capital inflows on consumption, not their indirect effect operating through income. However, private consumption and investment account for most of GDP. Therefore, it is unlikely that capital flows could affect GDP significantly except by affecting consumption and/or investment.

12.4.2   *Investment*

Table 12.7 shows the results of estimating an equation for private investment in Mexico. In the basic equation without capital inflow variables, we get the expected positive effects of real GDP and the change in real GDP on the change in investment. We also get the expected negative effect of lagged investment. The change in the real interest rate shows a near zero effect on the change in investment. None of the capital flow variables show any clear effect on investment, perhaps suggesting that capital inflows have not been an important determinant of investment in Mexico. These results, together with those presented in Tables 12.5 and 12.6, are consistent with a widespread view that capital inflows financed consumption rather than investment in Mexico. However, these results are too preliminary to confirm this view fully.

12.5   Tests of the impact of capital flows using a multicountry data set

Our results suggest that capital flows did not substantially alter the basic evolution of Mexican macroeconomic performance in 1988–94. We now consider whether the Mexican experience with capital inflows has been shared by other developing countries that recently experienced signifi-

Table 12.7. *Results for Mexican investment (dependent variable: log change in real investment)*

	Basic equation	With capital account	With FDI	With portfolio inflows
Constant	−15.62	−16.44	−15.39	−16.32
	(−4.11)	(−3.75)	(−3.95)	(−3.95)
Change in real interest rate	0.08	0.08	0.07	0.08
	(1.11)	(1.09)	(1.03)	(1.18)
Log change in real GDP	2.70	2.75	2.57	2.80
	(5.39)	(5.22)	(5.03)	(5.42)
Real interest rate (−1)	−0.00	0.00	0.00	−0.01
	(−0.05)	(0.03)	(0.11)	(−0.20)
Log real GDP (−1)	2.33	2.44	2.30	2.39
	(4.16)	(3.81)	(3.99)	(3.92)
Log real investment (−1)	−0.66	−0.68	−0.66	−0.62
	(−4.16)	(−3.90)	(−3.99)	(−3.45)
Log change in real investment (−1)	−0.09	−0.07	−0.04	−0.11
	(−0.91)	(−0.53)	(−0.33)	(−0.92)
Δ capital account		−0.09		
		(−0.23)		
Capital account (−1)		−0.31		
		(−0.52)		
Δ FDI			2.21	
			(1.09)	
FDI (−1)			−0.55	
			(−0.22)	
Δ portfolio investment				0.17
				(0.17)
Portfolio investment (−1)				−1.52
				(−1.11)
Adjusted R-squared	0.51	0.49	0.53	0.50
Durbin-Watson statistic	1.93	1.97	1.90	2.03

cant capital inflows, based on estimated econometric equations for a pooled time series–cross-section set of annual data from 1983 to 1994 for ten developing countries. Our data set includes Mexico, as well as Argentina, Brazil, Chile, Colombia, Indonesia, Korea, Malaysia, the Philippines, and Thailand. We exclude Argentina and Brazil from our interest rate and M2 regressions owing to difficulties introduced by their hyperinflations, but those two countries are included for the consumption and investment regressions. All data for countries other than Mexico were obtained from the International Monetary Fund, *International Financial Statistics*.

Looking first at Figures 12.8 and 12.9, we can see that overall capital flows, as measured by the capital account as a share of GDP, rose sharply for many of the Pacific Basin countries as they did for Mexico during the 1989–93 period. Mexico does appear to stand out, however, in terms of the rise in portfolio investment as a share of GDP. In addition, Mexico's experience with rising broad money balances as a share of GDP was shared by many of the Asian countries in our sample as was, to some extent, the decline in interest rates after 1990.

12.5.1   The impact of capital flows on money demand

First, we estimate an interest rate reaction function such as in equation (10) for the multicountry sample, based on the equation for Mexico described earlier. We include country dummies that allow a different constant for each country. The results are shown in Table 12.8. For the basic equation, without capital flow variables, the lagged interest rate (a short-term money market rate) has the expected negative effect on the change in the interest rate, while the change in inflation and the lagged level of inflation enter with the expected positive effects. In addition, the coefficients on the lagged interest rate and lagged inflation are of similar absolute magnitudes, suggesting that the real interest rate in this sample is stationary. As shown in columns 2 through 4, in contrast to our results for Mexico, the multicountry regressions do not show any significant effect of the capital account or the change in reserves on interest rates. This suggests either that many countries in the sample did not pursue an interest rate target, did not allow capital inflows to affect monetary conditions, or both.

Second, we estimate a demand equation for real M2 such as that in equation (9); it utilizes the conventional lagged-dependent-variable specification rather than the error–correction formulation used previously in this chapter. As shown in Table 12.9, the log of real GDP has the expected significant positive effect on real M2 while the nominal interest rate has the expected significant negative effect. Whether or not we use a fitted interest rate (using as instruments the inflation rate, the lagged interest rate, and the log of lagged real GDP) to address the endogeneity of the interest rate, we find that the change in reserves has a strongly significant positive effect on real balances while the capital account does not have a significant effect. Thus, as with the estimation results for

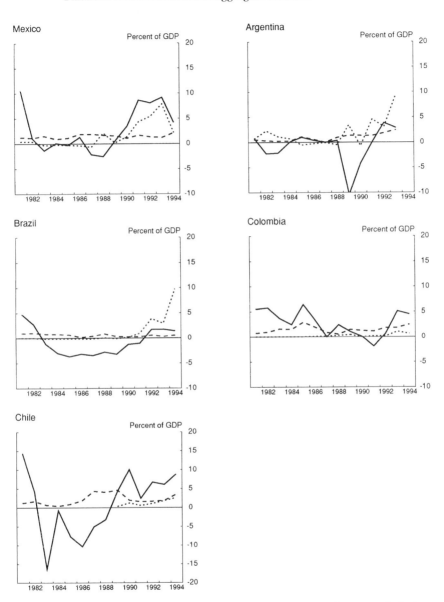

Figure 12.8. Capital flows: Latin America. Solid = capital account; dashed = FDI; dotted = portfolio investment.

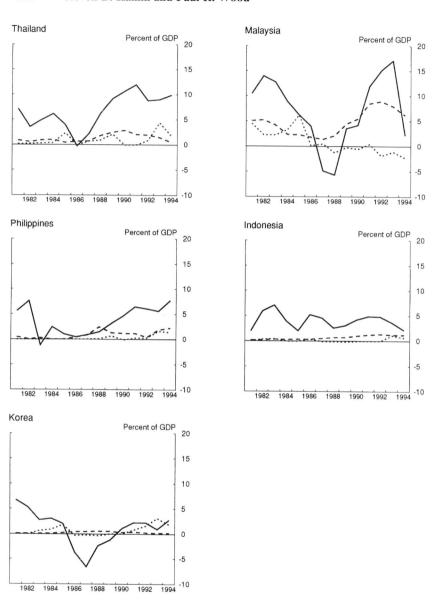

Figure 12.9. Capital flows: Asia. Solid = capital account; dashed = FDI; dotted = portfolio investment.

Table 12.8. *Multicountry results for interest rate reaction function (dependent variable: change in interest rate)*

	Basic equation	With capital account	With change in reserves	With both
Constant	3.28	3.47	3.36	3.43
	(2.27)	(2.17)	(2.51)	(2.35)
Interest rate (−1)	−0.50	−0.51	−0.51	−0.49
	(−5.36)	(−4.94)	(−5.55)	(−5.04)
Inflation (−1)	0.47	0.46	0.48	0.45
	(4.96)	(4.61)	(5.42)	(4.88)
Change in inflation	0.59	0.58	0.61	0.59
	(9.14)	(8.59)	(10.00)	(9.50)
Change in reserves (−1)			−9.26	−10.44
			(−1.29)	(−1.44)
Change in change in reserves			7.89	8.16
			(1.57)	(1.61)
Capital account (−1)		−1.78		−2.94
		(−0.35)		(−0.64)
Change in capital account		−4.06		−5.94
		(−0.74)		(−1.18)

Table 12.9. *Multicountry results for M2 demand function (dependent variable: log real M2)*

	OLS	OLS with capital account	IV for interest rate[a]	OLS with change in reserves	IV for interest rate[a]
Constant	−4.74	−4.73	−4.24	−3.25	−2.80
	(−4.28)	(−4.27)	(−4.02)	(−3.17)	(−3.07)
Interest rate	−0.43	−0.36	−0.69	−0.61	−0.84
	(−3.27)	(−2.48)	(−4.77)	(−4.96)	(−7.68)
Log real GDP	0.60	0.59	0.55	0.45	0.40
	(4.78)	(4.70)	(4.57)	(3.88)	(3.93)
Log real M2 (−1)	0.64	0.65	0.66	0.69	0.71
	(8.74)	(8.77)	(9.35)	(10.54)	(11.98)
Capital account		0.12	−0.07		
		(0.96)	(−0.01)		
Change in reserves				0.66	0.69
				(4.86)	(5.89)

[a] IV = instrumental variable estimates.

Mexico alone, we find that the change in reserves has a greater direct impact on the demand for M2 balances than does the capital account.

12.5.2   The impact of capital flows on consumption and investment

As we did for the case of Mexico, we estimate an equation for our multicountry sample where real consumption depends on real GDP and the real interest rate. As indicated in Table 12.10, we find real GDP, the change in real GDP, and lagged consumption to have a significant and positive effect on consumption (the long-run income elasticity of consumption is close to unity). However, in contrast to our results for Mexico, where the coefficient on the real interest rate was merely insignificant, here the real interest rate had an unexpected significant positive effect, and was dropped from the equation. In the remaining columns of Table 12.10, we add alternatively the capital account, foreign direct investment (FDI), and portfolio capital flows, each as a share of nominal GDP. We find the capital account to have a significant positive effect on consumption, but coefficients on its subcomponents – FDI and portfolio flows – are insignificant. Moreover, both FDI and portfolio flows have small and highly insignificant coefficients when added along with the capital account (the last two columns of Table 12.10), so we cannot reject that their effects on consumption are the same.

Table 12.11 indicates that, as in the Mexican case, we do not find any evidence that real M2 balances positively affect consumption. In fact, as for Mexico, we find that real M2 balances have a puzzling, highly significant negative effect on consumption.

Estimating an investment equation similar to that for Mexico (Table 12.12), we find that both the capital account and foreign direct investment have significant positive effects when entered separately and that portfolio investment has a positive but less than significant effect. That contrasts with what we found for Mexico, where none of the capital flow variables had any clear effect on investment. As shown in the last two columns of Table 12.12, the coefficients on the capital account subcomponents do not appear to be significantly different from the coefficient on the overall capital account, but, particularly in the case of FDI, this may reflect the low precision of our econometric estimates.

In order to explore whether Latin American countries in our sample have responded differently to capital flows than have the Asian countries, we reran the consumption and investment equations with regional interaction dummy variables. A summary of the results is shown in Table 12.13. While estimated coefficients of response differ somewhat between Latin America and Asia, these differences are not statistically significant, as reflected in the low t-statistics on the interaction dummies.

Table 12.10. *Multicountry results for consumption (dependent variable: log real consumption)*

	Basic equation	With capital account	With FDI	With portfolio inflows	With capital account and FDI	With capital account and portfolio inflows
Constant	0.03	0.08	0.06	0.04	0.08	0.07
	(0.24)	(0.76)	(0.51)	(0.34)	(0.67)	(0.60)
Log real consumption (−1)	0.75	0.73	0.74	0.73	0.73	0.70
	(12.25)	(12.07)	(11.74)	(10.92)	(11.85)	(10.39)
Log real GDP	0.23	0.24	0.23	0.24	0.24	0.27
	(4.37)	(4.68)	(4.40)	(4.08)	(4.63)	(4.50)
Δ log real GDP	0.55	0.55	0.54	0.58	0.55	0.56
	(7.83)	(7.97)	(7.45)	(7.78)	(7.79)	(7.59)
Capital account/GDP		0.20			0.21	0.21
		(2.83)			(2.72)	(2.27)
FDI/GDP			0.26		−0.04	
			(0.75)		(−0.13)	
Portfolio inflows/GDP				0.10		−0.02
				(0.56)		(−0.09)

Table 12.11. *Multicountry results for consumption including real M2 (dependent variable: log real consumption)*

	Basic equation	With capital account	With FDI	With portfolio inflows
Constant	−0.10	−0.03	−0.06	−0.10
	(−0.89)	(−0.30)	(−0.50)	(−0.90)
Log real	0.70	0.67	0.69	0.66
consumption(−1)	(11.87)	(11.78)	(11.39)	(10.01)
Log real GDP	0.33	0.35	0.34	0.37
	(5.97)	(6.50)	(6.03)	(5.80)
Δ log real GDP	0.51	0.51	0.50	0.53
	(7.52)	(7.80)	(7.20)	(7.38)
Capital account/GDP		0.22		
		(3.39)		
FDI/GDP			0.28	
			(0.89)	
Portfolio inflows/GDP				0.23
				(1.21)
Log real M2	−0.05	−0.05	−0.05	−0.05
	(−4.36)	(−4.65)	(−4.35)	(−4.37)

Counterfactual simulation experiments: To gauge the impact of the capital account on consumption and investment in the ten countries in our sample, we use the results from the multicountry panel regressions (second column of Tables 12.10 and 12.12) to simulate the path that consumption and investment would have taken in each of the ten countries if the capital account during 1988–94 had been zero. This counterfactual simulation uses the same basic approach described in section 12.3.3. Figures 12.10 and 12.11 compare the actual path of consumption in each of the ten countries to the path simulated by the multicountry model, once the capital account is set to zero for the 1988–94 period. Those charts indicate that, while the capital account had a statistically significant effect on consumption, setting the capital account to zero would not have altered substantially the basic trajectory of consumption in the ten countries. Recent capital inflows are estimated to have raised consumption by, at most, 1 percent of GDP, and usually by much less than that. As noted in reference to the Mexican consumption function (section 12.4.1), the coefficients on capital inflows in the multicountry equation may be biased upward due to reverse causation,

Table 12.12. *Multicountry results for investment (dependent variable: log real investment)*

	Basic equation	With capital account	With FDI	With portfolio inflows	With capital account and FDI	With capital account and portfolio inflows
Constant	-1.37	-1.59	-1.18	-1.27	-1.49	-1.53
	(-4.29)	(-5.32)	(-3.63)	(-4.11)	(-4.73)	(-5.17)
Log real investment (-1)	0.66	0.55	0.65	0.65	0.56	0.56
	(11.52)	(9.73)	(11.70)	(10.94)	(9.78)	(9.15)
Log real GDP	0.47	0.59	0.45	0.46	0.57	0.58
	(5.61)	(7.24)	(5.37)	(5.49)	(6.78)	(6.94)
Δ log real GDP	1.09	0.97	1.04	0.98	0.97	0.82
	(6.61)	(6.31)	(6.43)	(5.87)	(6.28)	(5.16)
Capital account/GDP		0.84			0.77	0.91
		(4.79)			(4.12)	(4.20)
FDI/GDP			1.98		0.82	
			(2.51)		(1.03)	
Portfolio inflows/GDP				0.55		0.01
				(1.32)		(0.02)

Table 12.13. *Multicountry results: Latin America versus Asia*

	Capital account	FDI	Portfolio inflows
Coefficients from consumption equation			
All countries	0.20	0.26	0.10
Asia	0.14	0.20	0.21
Latin America	0.24	0.90	0.06
t-statistic on interaction dummy	(0.73)	(0.53)	(−0.37)
Coefficients from investment equation			
All countries	0.84	1.98	0.55
Asia	0.87	2.19	0.37
Latin America	0.82	−0.18	0.63
t-statistic on interaction dummy	(−0.14)	(−0.75)	(0.27)

Notes: In equations with region-specific coefficients, the interaction dummy, D times the capital flow variable, was added to the equation along with the capital flow measure itself; D = 0 for Asian countries, D = 1 for Latin American countries. The coefficient for Asian countries is the coefficient on the capital flow measure alone. The coefficient for Latin American countries is the coefficient on the capital flow measure plus the coefficient on the interaction dummy.

but this only strengthens our conclusion that capital inflows had small effects on consumption.

Figures 12.12 and 12.13 compare the actual and simulated paths of investment in the ten countries. While the impact of capital inflows on investment does appear to have been somewhat greater than on consumption, the results suggest that recent capital inflows generally raised investment by less than 2 percent of GDP. The exceptions are Thailand and Malaysia, which experienced particularly large capital inflows during this period that appear to have raised investment by as much as 4 or 5 percent of GDP.

12.6   Conclusion

This chapter looks at the effect of capital flows on macroeconomic and financial variables in Mexico during the 1980s and 1990s and compares Mexico's experience with that of a cross section of Pacific Basin developing countries. Based on the admittedly very rudimentary analysis we have performed so far, we draw the following tentative conclusions:

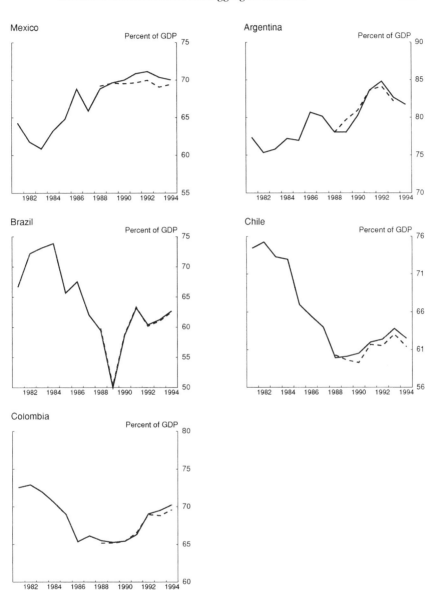

Figure 12.10. Consumption simulations: Latin America. Solid = actual; dashed = simulated with capital account = 0.

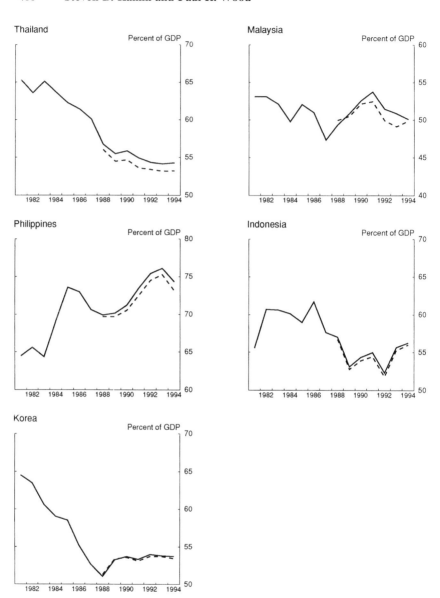

Figure 12.11. Consumption simulations: Asia. Solid = actual; dashed = simulated with capital account = 0.

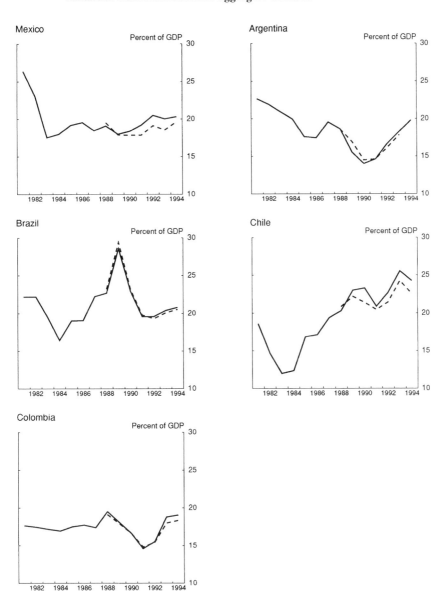

Figure 12.12. Investment simulations: Latin America. Solid = actual; dashed = simulated with capital account = 0.

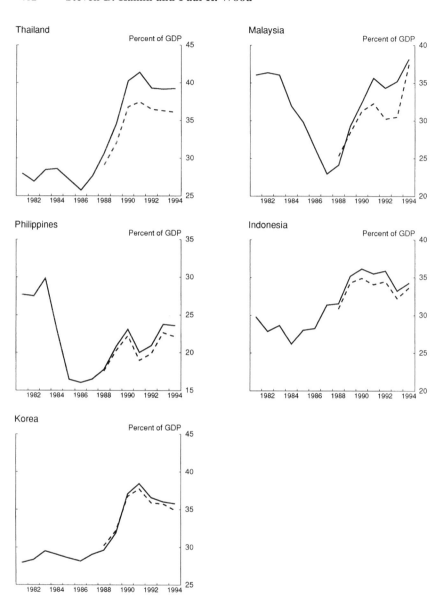

Figure 12.13. Investment simulations: Asia. Solid = actual; dashed = simulated with capital account = 0.

First, both for Mexico and for the multicountry data set, we *do* find evidence of an independent effect of capital flows on monetary conditions and domestic demand, once other domestic conditions such as inflation and output growth are controlled for. We found that in Mexico, both reserve changes and capital inflows tended to lower interest rates and raise M2, although the results were more limited for our multicountry sample. Consumption was found to respond positively to capital inflows both in Mexico and in the multicountry sample. Investment also responded positively to capital inflows, but only in our multicountry sample.

Second, notwithstanding the evidence in support of linkages between capital inflows and macroeconomic outcomes, there was, at best, mixed evidence in favor of the expected channels of transmission linking the two sets of variables. Regressions applied to our Mexico sample indicate that the capital account affected M2 mainly by affecting the level of international reserves, as might conventionally be expected. In our counterfactual simulations, however, setting the capital account to zero during 1988–94 had a larger effect on interest rates and M2 than setting reserves to zero, in part because the capital account rose more strongly than reserve accumulation over much of this period. This suggests that the capital account may have influenced monetary conditions by some means other than boosting reserves in these years, perhaps by raising the money multiplier linking M2 to the monetary base.

Additionally, the expected channel through which capital flows influence consumption – by raising bank deposits, bank credit, and hence spending – was rejected by our data. When measures of M2 were added to our consumption equations, both for Mexico and the multicountry data set, their coefficients were estimated to be negative, suggesting that capital inflows must influence consumption by some means other than the bank deposit and credit channel.

Third, we found mixed evidence in favor of the view that different types of capital inflows exert different effects on macroeconomic performance. Foreign direct investment and portfolio investment had quite different estimated effects on consumption and investment, but the standard errors on those estimates were sufficiently large so that those effects were not statistically significantly different.

Fourth, based on the multicountry data sat, we found mixed evidence that capital inflows affected investment and consumption differently in Latin American countries and in Asian countries. While estimated coefficients of response differed somewhat in the two sets of countries, these differences were not statistically significant, perhaps reflecting the imprecision of the estimates. Both results for Mexico and for the multicountry data set indicate positive effects of capital flows on consumption, but only the multicountry results support a positive effect of capital flows on investment. This is consistent with prior, impressionistic views that some, as yet unidentified, factors may have inhibited the response of Mexican investment to capital inflows.

Finally, and perhaps most importantly, notwithstanding our findings of statistically significant effects of capital inflows on macroeconomic performance, these inflows appear not to have altered substantially the basic trajectories of money, consumption, and investment in the recipient countries. Based on our Mexico data set, we find that even in the absence of capital inflows, the reduction in inflation and other factors would have led to strong growth in real M2 demand and in consumption in the 1988–94 period. Our results from the multicountry data set suggest that recent capital inflows raised consumption by, at most, 1 percent of GDP, and usually by much less than that. Finally, the results for investment indicate that, with the exception of Thailand and Malaysia, the effects of capital inflows were relatively modest as well.

In concluding, we should emphasize that our results, and particularly those based on the multicountry data set, are highly preliminary and represent no more than an initial exploration of correlations among the data. Should these results stand up to future investigation and testing, however, they will indicate that the role of capital inflows in laying the foundation for future macroeconomic imbalances and, perhaps, crises has been overemphasized. In particular, rapid expansion of the monetary aggregates and consumption might have taken place even in the absence of heightened capital inflows. Quite possibly, these developments have been mistakenly attributed to capital inflows when they actually reflect the effects of other developments – exchange rate–based stabilization, financial liberalization, privatization – occurring simultaneously.

References

Antzoulatos, Angelos A. (1996). "Capital Flows and Current Account Deficits in the 1990s: Why Did Latin American and East Asian Countries Respond Differently?" Research Paper No. 9610, May. Federal Reserve Bank of New York.

Calvo, Guillermo A., Leonardo Leiderman, and Carmen Reinhart (1993). "Capital Inflows and Real Exchange Rate Appreciation in Latin America: The Role of External Factors," *IMF Staff Papers* 40 (1): 108–51.

    (1994). "The Capital Inflows Problem: Concepts and Issues," *Contemporary Economic Policy* 12: 54–66.

Calvo, Guillermo A., and Enrique G. Mendoza (1996). "Mexico's Balance-of-Payments Crisis: A Chronicle of Death Foretold," International Finance

Discussion Paper No. 545, February. Washington, D.C.: Board of Governors of the Federal Reserve System.

Chuhan, Punam, Stijn Claessens, and Nlandu Mamingi (1993). "Equity and Bond Flows to Latin America and Asia: The Role of Global and Country Factors," World Bank Policy Research Working Paper No. 1160, July. Washington, D.C.

Claessens, Stijn, Michael P. Dooley, and Andrew Warner (1995). "Portfolio Capital Flows: Hot or Cold?" *World Bank Economic Review* 9 (1): 153–74.

Copelman, Martina, and Alejandro M. Werner (1995). "The Monetary Transmission Mechanism in Mexico," International Finance Discussion Paper No. 521, September. Washington, D.C.: Board of Governors of the Federal Reserve System.

Corbo, Vittorio, and Leonardo Hernández (1994). "Macroeconomic Adjustment to Capital Inflows," World Bank Policy Research Working Paper No. 1377, November. Washington, D.C.

Fernandez-Arias, Eduardo, and Peter J. Montiel (1995). "The Surge in Capital Inflows to Developing Countries: Prospects and Policy Response," World Bank Policy Research Working Paper No. 1473, June. Washington, D.C.

Gruben, William C., and Darryl McLeod (1996). "Capital Flows, Savings, and Growth in the 1990s." Unpublished manuscript, Federal Reserve Bank of Dallas.

Gunther, Jeffery W., Robert R. Moore, and Genie D. Short (1996). "Mexican Banks and the 1994 Peso Crisis: The Importance of Initial Conditions," *North American Journal of Economics and Finance* 7 (2): 125–33.

Kamin, Steven B., and John H. Rogers (1996). "Monetary Policy in the End-Game to Exchange-Rate Based Stabilizations: The Case of Mexico," International Finance Discussion Paper No. 540, February. Washington D.C.: Board of Governors of the Federal Reserve System.

Khan, Mohsin S., and Carmen M. Reinhart, eds. (1995). "Capital Inflows in the APEC Region," IMF Occasional Paper No. 122, March. Washington, D.C.

Koenig, Linda M. (1996). "Capital Inflows and Policy Responses in the ASEAN Region," IMF Working Paper 96/25, April. Washington, D.C.

Rojas-Suárez, Liliana, and Steven R. Weisbrod (1995). "Financial Fragilities in Latin America: The 1980s and 1990s," IMF Occasional Paper No. 132, October. Washington, D.C.

Spiegel, Mark (1995). "Sterilization of Capital Inflows through the Banking Sector: Evidence from Asia," *Federal Reserve Bank of San Francisco Economic Review*, No. 3: 17–34.

PART IV
POLICY RESPONSES TO CAPITAL INFLOWS

Speculative capital inflows and exchange rate targeting in the Pacific Basin: Theory and evidence

Kenneth Kletzer and Mark M. Spiegel

13.1   Introduction

While the large capital inflows experienced by developing countries from 1988 to 1993 provided welcome capital for investment, these inflows also raised challenges for monetary policy. Many of the nations experiencing surges in capital inflows, particularly those in the Pacific Basin, were committed to some level of exchange rate management. Maintaining their nominal exchange rate target levels required that the central banks of these nations acquire a sufficient magnitude of these capital inflows to finance their current account deficits.[1] In the absence of any response by monetary authorities, this increase in central bank holdings of foreign assets would imply an increase in the domestic monetary base, and hence an impetus for inflation.

Instead, many central banks attempted to "sterilize" the inflationary effect of capital inflows by selling domestic assets, such as government treasury obligations, in an effort to leave the monetary base unchanged. In a small open economy, such a sterilized capital inflow would leave the monetary base unaffected, by offsetting the increase in the level of foreign reserves held by the central bank by a decrease in the central bank's holdings of domestic assets.

A number of studies have emerged discussing the wisdom of sterilization policy. Calvo (1991) in particular has been associated with the idea

Warren Chiang and Laura Haworth provided excellent research assistance. Helpful comments were received from Peter Garber and Reuven Glick. The views expressed in this essay are those of the authors and do not necessarily represent the Board of Governors of the Federal Reserve System or the Federal Reserve Bank of San Francisco.
[1] To the extent that the foreign capital was used to finance a current account deficit, perhaps from the importation of capital equipment, the required accumulation of foreign reserves was diminished.

that sterilization programs designed to achieve low inflation levels may be self-defeating due to their budgetary implications. These studies argue that sterilized intervention has negative implications for the consolidated government balance sheet, which are sometimes referred to as "quasi-fiscal costs."

These quasi-fiscal costs stem from the reduction in the budget surplus of the central bank that results from sterilizing capital inflows. To maintain its nominal exchange rate target, the central bank must purchase the foreign assets entering the country. However, these assets yield a lower interest rate than the domestic assets that must be sold in order to leave the monetary base unchanged (Calvo, Leiderman, and Reinhart, 1993).[2] Estimates of the magnitudes of quasi-fiscal costs have indicated that they can become relatively large. Calvo, Leiderman, and Reinhart (1993) report estimates for quasi-fiscal costs for Colombia in 1991 of 0.5 percent of GDP, while Khan and Reinhart (1994) report estimates for Latin American countries between 0.25 and 0.5 percent per year.[3]

If these quasi-fiscal costs do represent a significant cost to government authorities, they may play a role in the timing of the abandonment of a sterilization program. Since the sterilization program represents an effort to maintain a downward peg on a nominal exchange rate while maintaining a monetary policy objective, a central bank that decides that these costs have become too high will rationally choose to abandon such a program, either by allowing its exchange rate to appreciate or its money supply to rise.

If one looks at this decision as a discrete one, the analogy with the literature on speculative attacks on nominal exchange rate pegs, beginning with Krugman (1979), is straightforward. The market will anticipate the decision to abandon the sterilization program and respond according to its expectations concerning the manner in which the program will be abandoned. Grilli (1986) has formulated a model that allows for such discrete "two-sided attacks" on nominal exchange rate pegs. He posits that in the case of a downward peg of the nominal exchange rate, there is an exogenous ceiling on the level of foreign reserves the central bank is willing to hold. When reserves reach this level, the central bank aban-

---

[2] In addition, Calvo (1991) demonstrates that sterilization programs mitigate the downward movements in interest rates which would be associated with capital inflows stemming from an external shock, such as a decrease in the world interest rate. This side effect tends to exacerbate the pressure for additional capital inflows, making sterilization programs somewhat self-defeating. Also see Frankel (1994).

[3] The original studies that yield the estimates reported by Calvo, Leiderman, and Reinhart (1993) and Kiguel and Leiderman (1993) are not currently being circulated for citation.

dons the sterilization program. Of course, speculators, anticipating the abandonment of the sterilization program, "attack" the program prior to the point at which the reserve limit would be reached in the absence of an attack and hasten the timing of its abandonment. The interesting distinction with a speculative attack on a downward nominal peg, however, is that speculators will attack the peg by purchasing assets denominated in the home country currency. Consequently, an attack on a downward nominal exchange rate peg will present itself as a surge in capital inflows. It therefore appears possible that the surges in capital inflows experienced by countries in Southeast Asia and Latin America represented beliefs by speculators that the downward pressure on nominal exchange rate pegs maintained by these nations would soon be eased.

In this paper, we investigate the role of quasi-fiscal costs in the monetary policies of a group of developing Asian and Latin American nations. We first derive a model of exchange rate determination for a small open economy. Our model is adapted from the large literature on speculative attacks on a managed exchange rate regime. Major theoretical contributions to that literature include Krugman (1979), Flood and Garber (1983, 1984a, 1984b), Obstfeld (1984, 1986a, 1986b), Connolly and Taylor (1984), and Buiter (1987). Initial empirical implementations of these models include Blanco and Garber (1986), Garber and Grilli (1986), and Grilli (1986). These papers can be distinguished between models, such as Krugman's original one, that derive the determinants and timing of speculative attacks on an exchange rate peg, taking the process of domestic credit creation by the central bank as exogenous and those, exemplified by the Obstfeld models,[4] which endogenize the policies of the central bank. Our model follows Obstfeld (1986b, 1994) and Buiter (1987) in both specifying the structure of the simple model economy and by endogenizing the policies chosen by rational central bankers who use the exchange rate as an instrument of optimal policy. The model is similar to Buiter's analysis of government borrowing to defend a fixed exchange rate in that the optimal policy for the central bank is chosen subject to an intertemporal budget constraint. The model implies a central bank reaction function which incorporates its intertemporal budget constraint and the quasi-fiscal costs of sterilization in its monetary policy decisions.

We then empirically examine the influence of these quasi-fiscal costs on monetary behavior in six capital-importing economies: Indonesia,

---

[4] See also Buiter (1987), Obstfeld (1994), and Buiter, Corsetti, and Pesenti (1995).

Korea, Mexico, the Philippines, Singapore, and Taiwan. The period estimated varies slightly by country according to data availability, but lies generally between 1980 and 1994. We were limited to this set of countries because of the relative lack of quarterly data available for the developing nations that experienced surges in capital inflows over the sample period.

We first construct upper-bound estimates of the quasi-fiscal costs borne by these nations from their sterilization activities. Our results indicate that our estimates of these upper bounds are typically too small to influence central bank behavior. However, these upper-bound estimates can increase dramatically during periods of surges in capital inflows. Our estimates reach as high as several percentage points of GDP for the Asian nations in our sample, while our peak upper-bound estimates for Mexico are implausibly even larger. Our estimates therefore leave open the possibility that the quasi-fiscal costs of sterilization may play a role in the abandonment of sterilization efforts during periods of capital inflow surges, such as those experienced by these nations between 1988 and 1993.

Our empirical analysis is in two forms. First, we use our entire sample of quarterly data from 1980 through 1994 to test predictions of the structural theoretical model. As mentioned earlier, because our estimated quasi-fiscal costs are quite small throughout the sample, it is unsurprising that they tend to fail to enter significantly as an argument in the reaction function of the central bank.

We also examine the impact of the surges on our quasi-fiscal cost estimates. Since these surges typically only occur once per nation in our sample, this exercise takes on more the nature of a "case study" rather than a formal test of the specification implied by our structural model. In particular, we use time series techniques to examine whether domestic credit responds to surges in these quasi-fiscal costs. We find that in fact they do for some countries in our sample, but not for others.

The remainder of this chapter is organized into five sections. In the next section, we derive our theoretical model of exchange rate determination and central bank behavior. In section 13.3, we estimate the level of current "quasi-fiscal costs" incurred for the countries in the study. In section 13.4, we test the predictions of the structural model. Section 13.5 concludes the chapter.

13.2   Exchange rate determination for a small open economy

We begin with a simple monetary model of exchange rate determination for a small open economy. Define aggregate supply as an increasing function of the relative price of output in terms of labor (inverse of the real wage) and a positive productivity shock, expressed in logarithms as

$$y_t = \alpha(p_t - w_t) + u_t \tag{1}$$

where p_t is the domestic price level, w_t is the nominal wage, and u_t is a productivity disturbance, assumed to be identically and independently distributed with zero mean. Output is measured relative to its equilibrium value. Nominal rigidities are introduced by assuming that nominal wages are set one period in advance of employment and production under rational expectations. Wage contracts last for only one period, and we assume that workers' objectives are quadratic in deviations of income from equilibrium income, so that

$$w_t = E_{t-1}p_t \tag{2}$$

where $E_{t-1}p_t$ is the expectation of the price level to prevail in period t conditional on information available in period $t - 1$.

The demand for domestic money is a function of income, the domestic nominal interest rate, i_t, and a velocity shock, v_t. All variables except interest rates are expressed in logarithms:

$$m_t^d - p_t = \varphi y_t - \delta i_t - v_t. \tag{3}$$

We assume that uncovered interest rate parity does not hold. In particular, we allow for systematic departures from interest parity expressed by

$$i_t = i_t^* + \left[E_t\left(s_{t+1}\right) - s_t\right] + \gamma_t \tag{4}$$

where s_t is the logarithm of the exchange rate expressed as units of domestic currency per unit of foreign currency, i_t^* is the (exogenous) foreign rate of interest, and γ_t represents the deviation from uncovered interest parity and is discussed later. Purchasing power parity is assumed to hold, so that

$$s_t = p_t. \tag{5}$$

The foreign interest rate is taken to be stationary and the foreign price level to be constant and equal to one. The exchange rate and domestic price level coincide.

The dynamics of the equilibrium exchange rate can be derived using equations (1), (3), (4), and (5) for a given domestic money supply process as governed by the difference equation

$$\left(1 + \delta + \alpha\varphi\right)s_t = \delta E_t\left(s_{t+1}\right) + m_t + \alpha\varphi w_t - \varphi u_t + \left[\delta\left(i_t^* + \gamma_t\right) - v_t\right]. \tag{6}$$

This can be solved forward using equation (2) by imposing the transversality condition

$$\lim\nolimits_{T \to \infty} E_t \left[\frac{\varphi}{1 + \varphi} \right]^{T-t-1} \varphi s_T \tag{7}$$

where $T \geq t$, to derive the current equilibrium exchange rate as a function of the current wage rate, the contemporaneous productivity shock, and a discounted sum of current and future money supplies and variables affecting money demand, obtaining

$$s_t = \frac{1}{1 + \delta + \alpha\varphi} \left[\alpha\varphi w_t - \varphi u_t + E_t \sum\nolimits_{j=0}^{\infty} \left(\frac{\delta}{1 + \delta} \right)^j \left[m_{t+j} + \delta \left(i_{t+j}^* + \gamma_{t+j} \right) - v_{t+j} \right] \right]. \tag{8}$$

The central bank is assumed to be inflation averse and interested in achieving a target level of output exceeding the equilibrium level of output. Because nominal wages are set before monetary policy decisions are made for each period, there is an inflationary bias in policy making in the tradition of Barro and Gordon (1983) and others. With rational expectations, agents in the private sector are cognizant of the ex post incentive for policy makers to create a surprise inflation (devaluation with a pegged exchange rate regime) to raise output and choose nominal wages to account for ex post depreciation or devaluation with positive probability. As in Obstfeld (1994), we can introduce the possibility that a preannounced exchange rate peg is used as a commitment device without explicitly modeling the game played between central bankers and private sector agents. This is done by simply adding a loss due to exchange realignment to the objective function. Our initial objective function is the quadratic loss function given by

$$L_t = E_t \sum\nolimits_{j=0}^{\infty} \beta^j \left[\theta \left(p_{t+j} - p_{t+j-1} \right)^2 + \left(y_{t+j} - y^* \right)^2 + c_{t+j} z_{t+j} \right] \tag{9}$$

where β is the discount factor applied by the policy maker, y^* is the target level of output (positive in logarithms representing output greater than equilibrium output), θ is a parameter indicating the degree of aversion toward inflation, c_t is a measure of the sunk welfare cost of reneging on the preannounced exchange rate peg, and z_t is a dummy variable equal to unity in a period of devaluation or revaluation from an exchange rate commitment and zero otherwise.

The optimization problem for the central bank includes the intertemporal constraints on the policy options that it can pursue in each period and beyond. One view that we pursue is that monetary policies are chosen by the central bank subject to the consolidated public sector solvency constraint. Another is that the central bank acts independently of fiscal authorities, treating the path for future primary budget surpluses as given, and takes into account the present value of the central bank's own portfolio in its decisions.

We first solve for the optimal monetary policy without imposing the budget constraint – this is equivalent to solving for the optimal policy when uncovered interest parity holds (γ_t equals zero for all t). The solution in that case is found by minimizing the single-period loss in every period since no intertemporal constraint restricts the optimal selection of monetary policies. The solution is simply given by the first-order condition

$$\left(\theta + \alpha^2\right)s_t = \left(\theta s_{t-1} + \alpha^2 w_t\right) + \alpha\left(y^* - u_t\right). \tag{10}$$

Imposing $w_t = E_{t-1}s_t$, we have that the equilibrium rate of depreciation equals

$$s_t - s_{t-1} = \frac{\alpha}{\theta}\left(y^* - \left[\frac{\theta}{\alpha^2 + \theta}\right]u_t\right). \tag{11}$$

According to (11), the depreciation rate should rise with the target output level and adverse supply shocks.

Equation (8) is then employed to calculate the current optimal supply of money. With a preannounced exchange rate peg, this is used, following Krugman (1979), to calculate the shadow exchange rate. This is the exchange rate that would prevail if the peg were abandoned at date t. The single-period loss can be calculated for both the flexible regime and for continuation of the peg for one more period. The difference is simply compared with the cost of abandoning the peg. If the gain from allowing the exchange rate to change exceeds c_t, then the exchange rate peg will be abandoned.

By going back a period, the probability of abandonment and determinants of speculative episodes can be calculated as functions of the parameters and distribution of the foreign interest rate and the shocks to real output and velocity. The equilibrium nominal wage rate set one period in advance equals the expected exchange rate using the derived distribution for the equilibrium ex post exchange rate. The equilibrium exchange rate in the event of abandonment of the peg is itself a function of the nominal wage. This implies the possibility of multiple equilibrium solutions for the wage rate and the probability of a regime switch as demonstrated in the example of Corsetti and Cavallari (1996).

We next consider how the equilibrium rate of depreciation and inflation chosen by the central bank is affected by its intertemporal constraints. The single-period budget identity for the consolidated public sector is given by

$$\left[B_{t+1} - B_t\right]S_t + \left[M_{t+1} - M_t\right] - \left[R_{t+1} - R_t\right]S_t = \Gamma_t + \left(i_t^* + \gamma_t\right)S_t B_t - i_t^* S_t R_t,$$

(12)

where Γ_t is the nominal primary (exclusive of interest) fiscal deficit for the government during period t and R_t is the stock of official foreign exchange reserves at date t. Public debt is denominated in foreign currency because we are not concerned with the possibility that unexpected devaluations might be useful for reducing the real value of public debt nominally indexed to the domestic currency. S_t is the spot exchange rate. Note that equation (12) is not written in logarithms.

The consolidated government budget identity can be solved forward to derive a solvency constraint for the government. Without writing out cumbersome algebra, we can describe this condition. The solvency condition states that the outstanding value of the government's net nonmonetary debt at time t,

$$S_t\left[B_t - R_t\right],$$

(13)

is no greater than the present value of current and future expected primary surpluses, Γ_{t+s} plus seigniorage revenue, $M_{t+s+1} - M_{t+s}$, minus the cost of holding official reserves, $\gamma_{t+s}S_{t+s}R_{t+s}$, $s \geq 0$.

The positive premium γ_t in the domestic real rate of interest over the foreign rate of interest in this economy implies that a successful open-market sale of government debt accompanied by an equal-size increase in official reserve holdings will tighten the solvency constraint. That is, for a given path of future primary surpluses and base money creation, the amount of outstanding net nonmonetary debt of the public sector compatible with solvency declines. With upper bounds on the future tax revenues net of transfers that fiscal authorities can be expected to generate and lower bounds on exhaustive public spending, the solvency constraint implies limits to the extent to which the government can borrow to defend a pegged exchange regime, as pointed out by Buiter (1987). This implies that sterilization of capital inflows cannot go on forever without jeopardizing the solvency of the public sector.

For the consolidated public sector problem, we minimize the loss function with respect to the exchange rate equation (8), the single-period budget identity, and the solvency constraint imposed with $\gamma_t > 0$. We obtain

$$\left(\theta + \alpha^2\right)s_t - \left(\theta s_{t-1} + \alpha^2 w_t\right) + \alpha\left(u_t - y^*\right) = \lambda_t\left(i_t^* + \gamma_t\right)M_t\left(1 + \delta + \alpha\varphi\right)$$

(14)

and

$$\lambda_t = E_t\left[\lambda_{t+1}\beta\left(1 + i_t^* + \gamma_t\right)\right]$$

(15)

and the transversality condition

$$E_t \lim_{T \to \infty} \left[\lambda_T \beta^T S_T B_T \right] = 0 \tag{16}$$

where λ_t is the multiplier on the single-period public sector budget identity. The solvency condition with upper bounds on the primary surpluses that can be sustained by fiscal authorities implies that λ_t is positive and increasing in $S_t B_t$.[5] Letting the equilibrium nominal wage rate equal the expected future nominal exchange rate, we obtain the equation for the ex post equilibrium rate of depreciation and inflation:

$$s_t - s_{t-1} = \frac{\alpha}{\theta} \left(y^* - \frac{\theta}{\theta + \alpha^2} u_t \right) + \frac{\left(i_t^* + \gamma_t \right) \left(1 + \delta + \alpha\varphi \right) M_t}{\theta} \left[\frac{\theta\lambda_t + \alpha^2 E_{t-1}\lambda_t}{\theta + \alpha^2} \right]. \tag{17}$$

These equations imply that reserve inflows will not be fully sterilized. That is, base money will increase by more in the presence of the interest differential γ_t and the offset will be less the larger is γ_t and the larger the outstanding stock of public debt, B_t. Moreover, a comparison of (17) and (11) demonstrates that the central bank allows the exchange rate to accommodate more of the adjustment when the intertemporal budget constraint is considered.

The second approach to modeling central bank behavior envisions a central bank that acts independently of a fiscal authority that pursues a fixed policy. In this case, we modify the model for the sake of illustrating our second approach for modeling endogenous policy. The central bank's value in real terms, V_t, is given by solving forward the difference equation:

$$V_{t+1} - V_t = i_t^* R_t + \left(i_t^* + \gamma_t \right) D_t \tag{18}$$

where D_t is the stock of domestic credit issued by the central bank at date t. Let the objective of the central bank be the minimization of the function

$$L_t = E_t \sum_{j=0}^{\infty} \beta^j \left[\theta \left(p_{t+j} - p_{t+j-1} \right)^2 + \left(y_{t+j} - y^* \right)^2 + c_{t+j} z_{t+j} \right] + k \left(V_t - V_t^* \right)^2 \tag{19}$$

where V^* is the maximum feasible value of the central bank given its current assets and liabilities. When the nation faces a positive domestic interest rate premium, the central bank achieves value V^* by holding

---

[5] In other words, the budget constraint is more binding the greater the amount of debt issued by the government.

only domestic credit and no official reserves. This quadratic loss function is minimized if one assumes $c = 0$ subject to the identity that the monetary base equals central bank domestic credit plus official reserves and equation (18). The necessary conditions for an interior optimum include

$$\left(\theta + \alpha^2\right)s_t - \left(\theta s_{t-1} + \alpha^2 w_t\right) + \alpha\left(u_t - y^*\right) = \psi_t\left(i_t^* + \gamma_t\right)M_t\left(1 + \delta + \alpha\varphi\right) \qquad (20)$$

and

$$k\left[V_t^* - V_t\right] = \beta E_t\left[\psi_{t+1}\right] - \psi_t \qquad (21)$$

where ψ_t is the multiplier for equation (18).

These imply that a smaller share of a given absolute reserve inflow will be sterilized as official reserves increase for a given stock of base money. That is, at a given exchange rate peg, the central bank will defend the parity with lower probability as official reserves increase. The increase in the probability of abandoning a preannounced exchange rate peg or the decrease in the portion of a reserve inflow that is sterilized can be measured by the opportunity cost of holding reserves, $\gamma_t S_t R_t$. The equilibrium rate of depreciation under a managed flexible exchange rate regime is given by equation (17) with the substitution of ψ_t for λ_t.

The domestic interest rate premium, γ_t, plays the crucial role of the quasi-fiscal costs of sterilized intervention, as identified by Calvo (1991). The model implies that the probability of realignments of pegged exchange rates or the extent to which reserve inflows are sterilized without an explicit peg depends on the opportunity cost of holding reserves instead of domestic credit by the central bank. We measure γ_t by taking the difference

$$\gamma_t = i_t - i_t^* - \left[E_t s_{t+1} - s_t\right]. \qquad (22)$$

For γ_t to represent an opportunity cost to the central bank, it must be assumed that this difference does not include any correctly priced risk premia such as a premium to compensate for political or sovereign default risk. If there is a perfect international financial market with risk-neutral speculators, then the measured premium would represent a payment by the government to its creditors equal to the expected value of the risk they assume. In that case, the reserve-holding costs estimated using equation (22) are just offset by a benefit equal to the present value of expected future defaults (or debasements if debt can be issued in domestic currency). If markets correctly price these risks in the presence of risk-neutral speculators, then the correct value of γ_t is not the estimated interest differential corrected for expected currency depreciation. It is zero. Quasi-fiscal costs require either barriers to financial capital mobility (capital controls) or informational asymmetries about the objectives and potential future behavior of policy makers that give rise to incorrectly priced risks on traded securities.

The empirical investigation of the sterilized net reserve inflows in the remainder of the chapter seeks to find out if there is any evidence for such quasi-fiscal costs influencing central bank reactions. Negative results may be interpreted as conforming with the hypothesis that correctly defined quasi-fiscal costs are not present and that financial markets work in pricing the relative riskiness of debt issued in different countries. We next turn toward constructing estimates of the magnitudes of these quasi-fiscal costs under the assumption that γ_t correctly identifies the interest differential. The following section then uses these estimates in an empirical implementation of our model of exchange rate intervention and the importance of official reserve holding costs.

13.3   Estimates of sterilization costs

In this section, we estimate the costs incurred from sterilization activities by the six economies in our study: Indonesia, Korea, Mexico, the Philippines, Singapore, and Taiwan. For the bulk of the economies in the sample, sterilization involved the sale of government securities in a standard open-market operation. For many Asian countries, however, sterilization may also take place in the form of the sale of other domestic assets, such as government pension funds. For example, Korea used central bank instruments to conduct its sterilization program during periods of rapid capital inflows, as did Taiwan and Indonesia. Since the Singapore government generally runs surpluses, it lacks treasury bills for conducting standard sterilization exercises. It was able to limit monetary growth through its ongoing fiscal surpluses and compulsory private saving in the Central Provident Fund (Glick and Moreno, 1994).

On the other hand, some countries also resisted increases in domestic credit through less standard means. The Philippines brought its monetary base into line by voluntarily retiring foreign debt, while some nations, such as Korea, eventually reduced private credit by increasing reserve requirements (Spiegel, 1995). Some nations also responded to the surge in capital inflows by increasing restrictions on capital movements. For example, in 1989 Mexico issued new restrictions on the foreign currency liabilities that could be issued by Mexican banks (Schadler, Carkovic, Bennett, and Khan, 1993). The opportunity costs associated with these "nonstandard" sterilization measures are difficult to quantify.

In the case of standard sterilization practices, regardless of the method used, the opportunity cost of replacing a domestic asset on the central bank's balance sheet with a foreign asset can be represented by the difference in the return on the two assets enjoyed by the central bank. Specifically, we define the interest rate differential in terms of γ_t in equation (4). As we discussed, however, γ_t will also contain any true default risk premia, resulting in an overestimate of the true interest rate differential.

We obtain an upper-bound estimate of the magnitude of quasi-fiscal costs of sterilization by proceeding as if γ_t represents the expected cost of sterilizing one dollar of foreign reserve accumulation by the central bank, that is, as if the default premium is zero. Our proxy then is equal to γ_t times the level of foreign reserves accumulated by the central bank at time t or:

$$QFC_t = \gamma_t S_t \Delta R_t. \qquad (23)$$

γ_t is a function of the expected future spot exchange rate, which is unobservable. Specification of the expected future spot rate is controversial.[6] In this study, we proxy exchange rate expectations in two ways. First, we invoke rational expectations using the realized future spot rate as our proxy for the ex ante expected spot rate.[7] There are obvious problems with this specification. The most interesting periods in the data are likely to be ones where realized rates are not close to expected rates, and therefore our proxy will perform poorly in these periods. Alternatively, we proxy expected rates as a random walk, so that the expected future spot rate is equal to its current level. While neither of these proxies is particularly satisfying, alternative measures all suffer their own difficulties. Moreover, we demonstrate here that the qualitative measures of quasi-fiscal costs are highly correlated across these expected spot rate specifications. This indicates that our results are not sensitive to our specification of exchange rate expectations.

Using the definition in equation (23), we estimated upper bounds for the quasi-fiscal costs of sterilization for the six nations in our sample for the period 1981 through 1994.[8] The annual quasi-fiscal costs as a percentage of nominal GDP are depicted in Figure 13.1 for both expected spot rate proxies. Our estimates are usually very small, indicating that the

---

[6] For example, Goldberg (1994) uses rolling ARMA regressions, while Frankel and Okongwu (1996) use survey data.

[7] Since default did not take place for any of the nations in the sample over the time periods included in the study (recall that the Mexican time series begins in 1985, after the period of default), the perfect foresight specification actually reflects the realized loss to the central bank from its acquisition of foreign assets in each period.

[8] Many countries only had data available for slightly shorter time periods. The exact sample periods for each country are displayed in Figure 13.1.

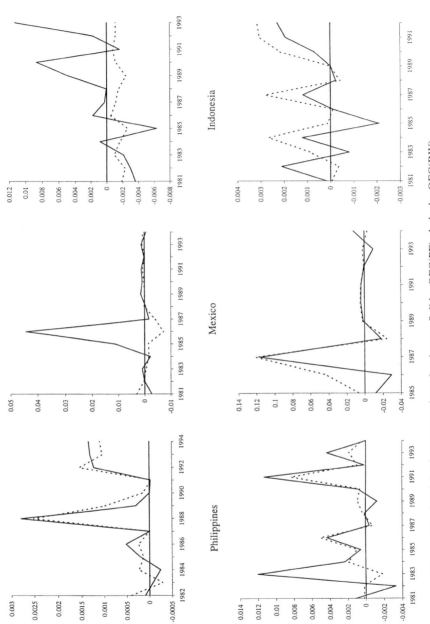

Figure 13.1. Quasi-fiscal cost upper-bound estimates. Solid = QFC(PF); dashed = QFC(RW).

actual values of quasi-fiscal costs are likely to be small as well. On occasion, however, our upper-bound estimates are quite large and comparable with those estimated in the earlier studies cited previously.

Both series of quasi-fiscal cost estimates for Indonesia are similar, indicating that our quasi-fiscal cost estimates are not sensitive to our specification of the expected future spot rate. Note that the magnitudes are very small. The mean levels of our upper-bound estimates of sterilization quasi-fiscal costs are only 0.05 and 0.12 percent of GDP if we use our perfect foresight specification and our random-walk specification, respectively. However, the data reveal larger levels for quasi-fiscal costs over brief periods of surges in capital inflows. Our perfect foresight estimate of quasi-fiscal costs reaches 0.12 percent of GDP in 1987 and 0.22 percent of GDP in 1992. The random-walk estimates reached 0.28 percent of nominal GDP and 0.31 percent of GDP respectively in the same years.

Our estimates of Korean quasi-fiscal costs are also very small. The mean levels of quasi-fiscal costs during periods of positive foreign asset accumulation are 0.06 percent of GDP for both the perfect foresight and random-walk specifications. Nevertheless, our data reveal a peak during 1988, a year in which Korea experienced a surge in capital inflows. The perfect foresight estimate of quasi-fiscal costs for that year was 0.28 percent of GDP while the random-walk estimate was 0.25 percent of GDP.

The Philippines sample exhibits a similar pattern. Quasi-fiscal costs are usually very small, but our measures rise to high levels during periods of surges in capital inflows. The 1983 estimate, which indicates quasi-fiscal costs of 1.2 percent using the perfect foresight specification is somewhat misleading, because the period actually exhibited a large capital outflow. Combined with a negative quasi-fiscal cost of sterilization per dollar of inflow, our specification yields a large positive value, but one we do not find representative. On the other hand, the peak in quasi-fiscal costs experienced by the Philippines in 1991 fits the typical pattern. In that year, which exhibited large capital inflows and a positive accumulation of foreign assets, our upper–bound estimates are 1.1 percent of GDP for the perfect foresight specification and 0.82 percent of GDP for the random-walk specification. Even including the unusual estimate for 1983, the mean of the sample for the Philippines using the perfect foresight specification is still a rather small 0.23 percent of GDP.

The data from Singapore exhibit marked differences in the magnitudes of the quasi-fiscal cost estimates depending upon the specification of the expected exchange rate. Using the random-walk specification, the quasi-fiscal costs estimates are slightly less than zero at –0.15 percent of

GDP throughout the sample. Under the perfect foresight specification, however, the quasi-fiscal costs have a small positive mean at 0.10 percent of GDP. If we use our preferred perfect foresight specification, the quasi-fiscal costs peak during the capital inflow surges of 1990 and 1993, reaching 0.86 percent of GDP in 1990 and 1.13 percent of GDP in 1993.

Our estimates of the quasi-fiscal costs for Taiwan are dominated by the surge in capital inflows experienced by that economy in 1986. The perfect foresight estimate of quasi-fiscal costs for that year are estimated to be 4.44 percent of GDP. Because of the large movements in exchange rates over this period, there is also a wide disparity this period in the two quasi-fiscal cost estimates. The random-walk estimate is −0.72 percent of GDP. Other than the peak at 4.4 percent, the Taiwan quasi-fiscal costs are also generally small over the sample. The perfect foresight estimate has a mean value of only 0.39 percent of GDP while the mean of the random-walk specification estimates is slightly negative.

The Mexican time series for quasi-fiscal costs demonstrates the potential for our proxy to overestimate the true costs of sterilization. The mean value of the perfect foresight upper-bound estimate for quasi-fiscal costs is a large-but-plausible 0.7 percent of GDP. However, this value masks an unbelievably large upper-bound estimate of 11.67 percent of GDP in 1987. The random-walk estimates are even larger, with a mean value of 1.56 percent of GDP over the sample and a peak value of 12.07 percent of GDP in 1987. The interest rate differential during this period clearly includes a large default premium that is not properly considered a cost to the central bank ex ante.

The results for Mexico illustrate the point that our proxies for quasi-fiscal costs will not always be close to their true values, particularly during periods where sovereign risk exposure is large. However, they can be considered upper bounds. Using our proxies as upper-bound estimates, they indicate that sterilization costs for these nations were small over the sample period. However, the upper-bound estimates can become large during periods of capital inflows. Since default risk is not likely to be a large factor for the assets of the Asian countries in our sample other than the Philippines, the results indicate that sterilization costs can be nontrivial during brief periods of surges in capital inflows.

13.4   Empirical evidence

13.4.1   Empirical specification

Our model suggests that the central bank will adjust the degree to which it partially sterilizes capital inflows to incorporate the costs of sterilization. In this section, we examine empirically whether the determinants of central bank behavior in our sample are consistent with the model.

Our specification is by no means a direct structural specification of the model. The model links the values of current variables, such as the exchange rate, with future expected values, such as the conduct of monetary policy necessary to satisfy the government budget constraint. Consequently, we attempt here to identify current state variables that proxy for these expectations, given the constraints on our specification by the quarterly data available for the nations in our sample.[9]

In particular, our empirical representation of the foregoing model will be in terms of the equilibrium change in domestic credit in each period, a representation referred to as the "standard sterilization equation" by Kearney and MacDonald (1986). As the model suggests, the equilibrium change in domestic credit in period t will depend positively on shocks to real income, y_t, and negatively on the world interest rate i_t^*.[10]

In addition, the change in the monetary base will reflect the central bank's reaction to the level of quasi-fiscal costs it associates with sterilization policy. The monetary base will respond positively to the current level of quasi-fiscal costs, QFC_t, associated with sterilization. These current costs are proxied by the change in the stock of foreign assets held by the central bank times the world interest rate plus the deviation from interest rate parity as defined in equation (4), or $(i_t^* + \gamma_t)\, S_t \Delta R_t$.

Moreover, since the decision made by the central bank is forward-looking, changes in the monetary base will also be positively related to expectations of future costs of sterilization. We introduce a number of potential proxies for state variables that should be correlated with these future costs. First, the future costs of sterilization will be increasing in the current share of domestic securities held by the central bank, which we term $BRAT$. We proxy this ratio by $B_t/(B_t + S_t R_t)$. This term reflects the fact that there is a limit to the amount of domestic assets the public is willing to hold so that current sterilization activity increases the costs of future sterilization. Second, the stock of domestic bonds held by the central bank times the deviation from uncovered interest rate parity, $\gamma_t B_t$, represents the opportunity cost to the central bank of carrying the current stock of sterilization into the future. Finally, the change in the value of central bank assets from sterilizing the current capital inflow, which

---

[9] In addition, our empirical specification is in terms of changes as a percentage of GDP rather than in log levels as in the theoretical model. The negative values of some proxies, such as our domestic credit measure, preclude taking logs.

[10] We assume a very simple specification for the shock to current income, specifying expected income as the product of a simple linear trend and four seasonal dummies. We also normalize the relevant variables by deseasonalized nominal GDP.

we term $ASSET$, can be represented as $(i_t^* + \gamma_t)\,\Delta B_t/i_t^* + S_t\Delta R_t$. All of these "forward-looking" variables are predicted to enter with a positive sign. The specification for the central bank reaction function equation then becomes:

$$\Delta DC_t = \alpha_0 + \alpha_1 S_t\Delta R_t + \alpha_2 i_t^* + \alpha_3 y_t + \alpha_4 QFC_t + \alpha_5 BRAT_t$$
$$+ \alpha_6 \gamma_t B_t + \alpha_7 ASSET_t + \epsilon_t \tag{24}$$

where ϵ_t is assumed to be an independently and identically distributed disturbance term distributed as normal.

Since the change in foreign assets held by the central bank is likely to be endogenous, a simultaneous equation specification is required. The change in foreign assets must equal the sum of the current and capital accounts of the nation as an identity. As we demonstrated in the model earlier, the capital account of the nation is likely to be dependent on domestic monetary policy. In particular, foreign investors are likely to "attack" a downward peg on the nominal exchange rate when they perceive that the monetary policy necessary for maintaining such a peg is unsustainable.

We therefore introduce a second equation, which we term the "offset equation," in which the change in foreign assets is allowed to be dependent on the current change in domestic credit. For other determinants of foreign asset changes, we look to the literature on the determinants of capital inflows. Many previous studies have identified both external and country-specific factors as determinants of capital inflows. As a proxy for "external" factors, we introduce the rate of interest on 3-month U.S. Treasury bills, i_t^*. This variable is expected to enter with a negative sign, as a decrease in the world rate of interest will increase the demand for domestic assets. As a proxy for country-specific factors, we introduce the country's external debt-to-export ratio, D_t. This variable is also predicted to enter with a negative sign as an increase in the debt–export ratio would be expected to reduce the demand for domestic assets, holding all else equal. The offset equation then satisfies:

$$S_t\Delta R_t = \beta_0 + \beta_1 \Delta DC_t + \beta_2 i_t^* + \beta_3 D_t + \beta_4 CA_t + u_t \tag{25}$$

where u_t is assumed to be an independent and identically distributed disturbance term distributed as normal and CA_t represents the current account, which should enter with a positive sign.

13.4.2 *Estimation results*

None of the quasi-fiscal cost proxies enter robustly throughout the economies in our sample. However, three of the economies in our sample, the

Philippines, Taiwan, and Mexico, each have some sterilization cost measure entering significantly. We therefore first discuss the results for these countries, for which some quasi-fiscal cost measure enters, and then the results for the remaining three countries in the sample that do not appear to incorporate sterilization costs in their reaction functions.

The results of independent country tests of the foregoing specification are shown in Table 13.1.[11] The strongest performance of the current quasi-fiscal cost proxy, QFC, was found for the Philippines (Table 13.1). QFC enters at a 5 percent significance level with the expected positive sign. In addition, although not reported, the ratio of domestic bonds held by the central bank to total central bank assets, $BRAT$, also entered significantly positively at a 10 percent significance level in isolation. The other quasi-fiscal costs proxies fail to enter with significance.

The endogenous variables also enter significantly. Both the sterilization measure, $S\Delta R$ in the reaction function equation, and the offset effect, ΔDC in the offset equation, enter with their expected negative signs at a 5 percent significance level. In addition, note that while the coefficient estimate for $S\Delta R$ is not measurably different from -1, which would imply complete sterilization, it consistently enters with a point estimate between -0.7 and -0.9. The negative values that are less than -1 in absolute value are consistent with the conjecture that partial sterilization is taking place.

Our results for Taiwan also exhibit some evidence that the quasi-fiscal costs of sterilization influenced the behavior of its central bank. γB and $ASSET$ enter with their expected positive signs at a 5 percent confidence level. The other quasi-fiscal costs measures fail to enter significantly. Moreover, the poor performance of these other proxies in the individual specification suggests that multicollinearity is not precluding them from entering into our standard specification. The sterilization and offset effects, $S\Delta R$ and ΔDC respectively, again all enter with significantly negative signs and magnitudes not measurably different than -1. We therefore cannot reject the hypotheses of either full sterilization or full offset.

The results for Mexico also indicate some limited influence of our sterilization cost proxies. The domestic bond ratio, $BRAT$, enters

---

[11] Since the quasi-fiscal cost measures are highly correlated, there is a potential that multicollinearity affects their performance. To explore the influence of the other variables, we also examined the performance of each individual measure of sterilization costs in isolation. By and large, the results of these regressions were very similar to the reported results. In addition, we tested the ordinary least-squares estimation of equation (24). The OLS results also were very similar to those in our base specification. All of these additional results are in an earlier version of this chapter, which is available from the authors upon request.

significantly positive at a 5 percent confidence level. However, none of the other quasi-fiscal costs proxies enter at any level of significance. Again, the significant negative coefficient on $S\Delta R$ whose point estimate is less than one indicates that Mexico engaged in partial sterilization of capital inflows over this period. However, we cannot reject full sterilization at a 5 percent confidence level. Finally, the offset effect, ΔDC, is significantly negative. Moreover, this value is measurably less than -1 in absolute value, which indicates less than full offset of domestic monetary policy. This would be expected for a relatively larger nation like Mexico.

For the remaining nations in the study, the proxies for quasi-fiscal costs fail to enter. Instead, the results indicate that these countries maintained an aggressive sterilization policy regardless of its cost. For example, in the Korean estimates both endogenous variables enter significantly negative with coefficient values that are not measurably different from -1. In addition, none of the proxies for sterilization costs enter in the reaction function equation. These results are consistent with both full sterilization and full offset for Korea.

Similarly, in our Indonesia sample the sterilization coefficient is negative, with a large point estimate of -2.78, but the large standard error measures preclude it from entering with statistical significance. However, the sterilization coefficient entered significantly negative with a point estimate not measurably different from -1 when we introduced the quasi-fiscal cost proxies individually. The offset coefficient also enters significantly negative with a point estimate not measurably different from -1, indicating full offset. As was the case for Korea, none of the sterilization cost variables enter significantly negative, which is consistent with the hypothesis that Indonesia maintained full sterilization over the sample.

Finally, since the Monetary Authority of Singapore did not hold government securities over this period, our specification for Singapore only includes two measures of quasi-fiscal costs. We measure the current costs of sterilization, QFC_t, with the same proxy as that of the other nations in our study. However, as a measure of the future benefits from abandoning the sterilization program we substitute foreign assets for central bank holding of domestic assets, so that our measure of $\gamma_t B_t$ is actually $\gamma_t R_t$. In addition, because quarterly data were unavailable, we were forced to substitute the trade balance for the current account in the offset equation. Our results are similar to those found for Korea and Indonesia. The sterilization and offset coefficients enter significantly negative, consistent with both full sterilization and full offset. Again, none of the sterilization cost proxies enters significantly at any standard significance level.

Overall, the results suggest that the nations in the sample acted

Table 13.1. *Regression results*

Reaction function equation: dependent variable = Δ domestic credit/GDP

	Philippines 1981:2–1993:2	Taiwan 1981:1–1992:2	Mexico 1985:1–1994:4	Korea 1982:3–1994:4	Indonesia 1983:2–1992:4	Singapore 1980:2–1993:1
Intercept	-0.0061	-0.1074**	0.0184	-0.0026	-0.0915	0.0451
	(0.0230)	(0.0424)	(0.0166)	(0.0171)	(0.2147)	(0.0539)
$S\Delta R$	-0.8552**	-0.7854**	-0.8207**	-1.8258*	-2.7817	-1.1958**
	(0.2677)	(0.2149)	(0.1050)	(1.0284)	(2.8031)	(0.4910)
i^*	-0.0011	0.0073**	-0.0063*	0.0008	0.0068	-0.0021
	(0.0017)	(0.0030)	(0.0036)	(0.0014)	(0.0140)	(0.0036)
y shock	0.1271	-0.1106	-0.1679	0.0079	0.0434	0.0710
	(0.0899)	(0.1712)	(0.1729)	(0.0775)	(0.1462)	(0.0809)
QFC	0.0038**	-0.0102	-0.0011	0.0333	0.1412	0.0056
	(0.0018)	(0.0094)	(0.0013)	(0.0461)	(0.2286)	(0.0262)
$BRAT$	0.0535	0.5236	0.0372**	-0.0262	-0.0235	
	(0.0405)	(0.8320)	(0.0157)	(0.0231)	(0.0746)	
γ^B	0.0007	0.1786**	-0.0043	-0.0033	-0.0455	
	(0.0019)	(0.0663)	(0.0028)	(0.0095)	(0.0825)	
$ASSET$	-0.0007	0.0413**	0.0304	0.0570	0.1618	-0.0004
	(0.0156)	(0.0137)	(0.0196)	(0.0579)	(0.3106)	(0.0011)
DW	2.8563	2.1122	2.8063	2.0621	2.1323	2.5246

Offset equation: dependent variable = Δ foreign assets/GDP

Intercept	0.0241	-0.0107	0.0991**	0.0106**	0.0303	0.0207*
	(0.0406)	(0.0233)	(0.0474)	(0.0042)	(0.0268)	(0.0115)
ΔDC	-0.7039**	-0.9075**	-0.5230**	-0.9165**	-0.9385**	-0.9528**
	(0.1051)	(0.0726)	(0.2261)	(0.0615)	(0.0637)	(0.0840)
D	-0.0034	-0.0628	0.0036	-0.0480**	-0.0058	-0.0931
	(0.0377)	(0.0384)	(0.0112)	(0.0144)	(0.0088)	(0.1381)
$i*$	-0.0008	0.0039	-0.0110**	0.0013	-0.0011	-0.0010
	(0.0023)	(0.0026)	(0.0045)	(0.0008)	(0.0019)	(0.0016)
CA	0.1064	0.2451**	0.7727**	0.1057**	0.1276	-0.0597
	(0.1297)	(0.1081)	(0.3522)	(0.0294)	(0.1701)	(0.0466)
DW	2.5168	2.2888	1.8638	1.8952	2.5317	2.5643

Notes: All models are run using 2SLS. Standard errors are in parentheses. ** = significance at the 5% level, * at the 10% level. See text for specification of γ^B variable for Singapore.

aggressively in sterilizing capital inflows, and that domestic monetary efforts were offset to some extent by external capital flows. The importance of sterilization costs in influencing monetary policy decisions, however, seems to be limited. While some form of sterilization costs entered into the reaction functions of the Philippines, Taiwan, and Mexico, no single proxy entered in all of these specifications. Moreover, none of the sterilization cost proxies entered significantly in the Korea, Indonesia, or Singapore samples.

13.4.3   Case studies of responses to surges in quasi-fiscal costs

As we demonstrated, our estimates of quasi-fiscal costs are usually quite small, only obtaining large magnitudes during brief surges in capital inflows. It may be the case then that the central banks of the nations in our sample ignore the quasi-fiscal costs over most of the period because they are unimportant. However, it may also be the case that during these brief periods of surges in quasi-fiscal costs they influence monetary policy. In this section, we investigate the possibility that the central banks in our study pursue their sterilization policies without regard to quasi-fiscal costs under normal situations, as the preceding results would indicate for most of the nations in our sample, but that they respond to the surges in quasi-fiscal costs by allowing domestic credit to increase.

Unfortunately, the series included in our sample provide us with only one (or in the case of Indonesia, two) true spikes in our quasi-fiscal cost estimates. Consequently we have too few observations of quasi-fiscal cost surges to evaluate parametrically whether this is the case. Instead, our time series provide us with evidence more akin to a "case study," where we can evaluate the behavior of the central bank before and after it experienced a surge in its quasi-fiscal costs.

As a loose examination of whether central banks responded to surges in capital inflows, we examine the behavior of domestic credit before and after their surge. We do this by estimating a simple ARIMA model for the behavior of domestic credit over the "pre-surge" period and then using our estimated model to forecast the behavior of domestic credit over the rest of the sample if it had followed its presample pattern. We then loosely evaluate whether a country loosened its monetary policy after the surge in quasi-fiscal costs by comparing the actual path of domestic credit with the forecast by the fitted ARIMA model.[12]

---

[12] We estimated AR(2) models for both Indonesia series, as well as for Korea and the Philippines. For both Singapore and Mexico, the data were differenced twice and an AR(4) model was required. For Taiwan, the data were differenced once and fit with an ARMA(1,1).

Identification of the timing of the initial surge in quasi-fiscal costs was relatively simple, given the time series depicted in Figure 13.1. For all nations except Indonesia we identified a single initial date corresponding to a large increase in our quasi-fiscal proxy. In the case of Indonesia, there were two distinct quasi-fiscal cost surge episodes and we evaluated both surges separately.

The results are depicted in Figures 13.2 and 13.3. Figure 13.2 depicts the countries in our sample who appear to have at least initially allowed domestic credit to increase in response to a surge in quasi-fiscal costs: the Philippines, Mexico, and Taiwan. In the case of Taiwan and Mexico, it can be seen that the presurge path of domestic credit was clearly unsustainable. While neither country allowed domestic credit to increase rapidly (prior to the Mexican peso crisis), they did not pursue the aggressive tightening of domestic credit that would have been necessary to offset fully the impact of capital inflows. In the case of the Philippines, we see that domestic credit was initially allowed to increase relative to its trend, but this was followed by sharp domestic credit reductions.

Figure 13.3 depicts the countries who appear to have maintained their sterilization programs in the face of quasi-fiscal costs surges – Indonesia, Korea, and Singapore. These countries all reduced domestic credit subsequent to spikes in quasi-fiscal costs. Unsurprisingly, these countries which did not even respond to large movements in quasi-fiscal costs are among those for which quasi-fiscal costs failed to enter into our earlier central bank reaction function estimates.

While this exercise is by no means a formal test of our model, the data analysis does indicate that some countries appear to respond to surges in quasi-fiscal costs even though they do not consider them on a day-to-day basis. In particular, the current level of quasi-fiscal costs failed to enter significantly in our parametric estimates for both Taiwan and Mexico when we looked at our entire time series. However, the times series of both countries indicate some upward movement in domestic credit subsequent to surges in our current quasi-fiscal cost proxy.

13.5   Conclusion

As we suggested in our discussion of the theoretical model, the relatively mixed results we obtained for the performance of our quasi-fiscal cost proxy may be interpreted as conforming with the hypothesis that correctly defined quasi-fiscal costs are not significant because financial markets work in pricing the relative riskiness of debt issued in different countries. For the bulk of the nations in our sample, it appears that this is largely the case. However, the mixed results of our parametric tests would not, in isolation, be sufficient to merit such a conclusion. The

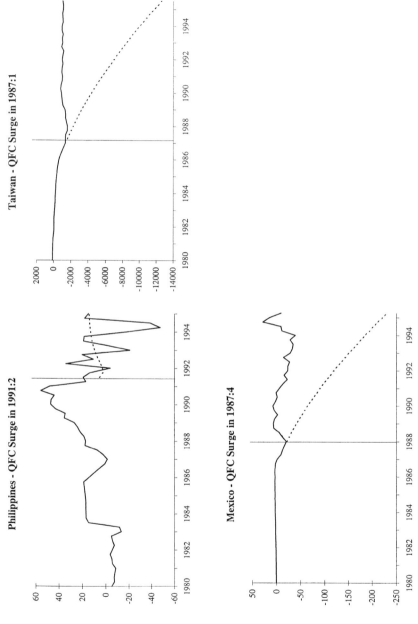

Figure 13.2. Domestic credit (in billions of national currency units). Solid = actual; dashed = trend.

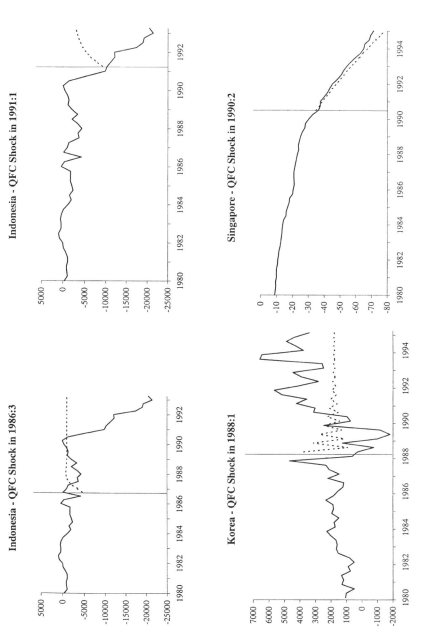

Figure 13.3. Domestic credit (in billions of national currency units). Solid = actual; dashed = trend.

specification we obtain from the model requires a number of highly unrealistic assumptions. For example, the assumption of a stable money demand function is likely to be problematic, due to financial liberalization which took place in all of these countries over the sample period. In addition, our proxies for the level of sterilization costs are by definition measured with error because they include any default premia contained in domestic assets. Combined with the severe shocks experienced by these countries over the sample period, there appears to be too much noise in our sample to form a strong negative conclusion concerning the role of sterilization costs based on our parametric results.

Nevertheless, our upper-bound estimates for the level of quasi-fiscal costs do indeed indicate that they are usually very small. This finding is particularly relevant for the Asian countries other than the Philippines. Debt issued by these other nations typically trades at or close to par, so that the default premia associated with these countries are likely to be relatively small. In addition, with the exception of Singapore, our quasi-fiscal cost estimates did not appear to be very sensitive to our proxy for the magnitude of expected future spot rates. These two factors indicate that our estimates of sterilization costs for Korea, Indonesia, and Taiwan are likely to represent the costs of sterilization to their central banks. If we restrict our attention to these economies, only Taiwan demonstrated some evidence that its monetary policy responded to the costs of sterilization. We found no such evidence for Indonesia and Korea.

References

Barro, R. J., and D. B. Gordon (1983). "A Positive Theory of Monetary Policy in a Natural Rate Model," *Journal of Political Economy* 91: 589–610.

Blanco, H., and P. M. Garber (1986). "Recurrent Devaluation and Speculative Attacks on the Mexican Peso," *Journal of Political Economy* 94: 148–66.

Buiter, W. H. (1987). "Borrowing to Defend the Exchange Rate and the Timing and Magnitude of Speculative Attacks," *Journal of International Economics* 23: 221–39.

Buiter, W. H., G. Corsetti, and P. Pesenti (1995). "A Center–Periphery Model of Monetary Coordination and Exchange Rate Crises," NBER Working Paper No. 5140, June. Cambridge, Mass.

Calvo, Guillermo A. (1991). "The Perils of Sterilization," *IFM Staff Papers* 38 (4): 921–26.

Calvo, Guillermo A., Leonardo Leiderman, and Carmen Reinhart (1993). "Capital Inflows and Real Exchange Rate Appreciation in Latin America: The Role of External Factors," *IMF Staff Papers* 40 (1): 108–51.

Connolly, M. B., and D. Taylor (1984). "The Exact Timing of the Collapse of an Exchange Rate Regime and Its Impact on the Relative Price of Traded Goods," *Journal of Money, Credit, and Banking* 16: 194–207.

Corsetti, G., and L. Cavallari (1996). "Policy Making and Speculative Attacks in

Models of Exchange Rate Crises: A Synthesis," Yale University, Economic Growth Center Discussion Paper No. 752. New Haven, Conn.

Flood R. P., and P. M. Garber (1983). "A Model of Stochastic Process Switching," *Econometrica* 51: 537–51.

(1984a). "Gold Monetization and Gold Discipline," *Journal of Political Economy* 92: 90–107.

(1984b). "Collapsing Exchange Rate Regimes: Some Linear Examples," *Journal of International Economics* 17: 1–13.

Frankel, Jeffrey A. (1994). "Sterilization of Money Inflows: Difficult (Calvo) or easy (Reisen)?" IMF Working Paper No. 94/159, December. Washington, D.C.

Frankel, Jeffrey A., and Chudozie Okongwu (1996). "Liberalized Portfolio Capital Inflows in Emerging Markets: Sterilization, Expectations, and the Incompleteness of Interest Rate Convergence," *International Journal of Finance and Economics* 1 (1): 1–24.

Garber, P. M., and V. Grilli (1986). "The Belmont-Morgan Syndicate As an Optimal Investment Banking Contract," *European Economic Review* 30: 649–77.

Glick, Reuven, and Ramon Moreno (1994). "Capital Flows and Monetary Policy in East Asia," Center for Pacific Basin Monetary and Economic Studies Working Paper No. 94-08. Federal Reserve Bank of San Francisco.

Goldberg, Linda (1994). "Predicting Exchange Rate Crises: Mexico Revisited," *Journal of International Economics* 36: 413–30.

Grilli, V. (1986). "Buying and Selling Attacks on Fixed Exchange Rate Systems," *Journal of International Economics* 17: 1–13.

Kearny, Colm, and Ronald MacDonald (1986). "Intervention and Sterilization under Floating Exchange Rates: The U.K., 1973–1983," *European Economic Review* 30: 345–64.

Khan, Mohsin S., and Carmen M. Reinhart (1994) "Macroeconomic Management in Maturing Economies: The Response to Capital Inflows," *IMF Issues Paper*, March. Washington, D.C.

Krugman, P. (1979). "A Model of Balance of Payments Crises," *Journal of Money, Credit and Banking* 11: 311–25.

Obstfeld, M. (1984). "Balance of Payments Crises and Devaluations," *Journal of Money, Credit and Banking* 16: 208–17.

(1986a). "Speculative Attacks and the External Constraint in a Maximizing Model of the Balance of Payments," *Canadian Journal of Economics* 19: 1–22.

(1986b). "Rational and Self-fulfilling Balance of Payments Crises," *American Economic Review* 76: 72–81.

(1994). "The Logic of Currency Crises," NBER Working Paper No. 4640. Cambridge, Mass.

Schadler, Susan, Maria Carkovic, Adam Bennett, and Robert Khan (1993). "Recent Experiences with Surges in Capital Inflows," IMF Occasional Paper No. 108. Washington, D.C.

Spiegel, Mark M. (1995). "Sterilization of Capital Inflows through the Banking Sector: Evidence from Asia," *Federal Reserve Bank of San Francisco Economic Review*, No. 3: 17–34.

CHAPTER 14

Too much of a good thing: The macroeconomic effects of taxing capital inflows

Carmen M. Reinhart and R. Todd Smith

14.1   Introduction

In addition to altering fiscal, monetary, and exchange rate policies in response to the surge in international capital inflows in the early 1990s, policy makers in many countries in Asia, Eastern Europe, and Latin America have resorted to measures to control capital inflows.[1] The types of measures used have varied widely across countries; in some cases the capital control took the form of a tax on capital inflows (Brazil, Chile, Colombia, and, more recently, Thailand), and in other instances quantitative restrictions were used (Czech Republic and Malaysia). In a number of countries (Indonesia, Philippines, and Thailand), the controls came in the form of "prudential measures" directed at the domestic financial sector; measures to curb banks' offshore borrowing or limit their foreign exchange exposure are examples of this type of policy response. Usually, these "sand-in-the-wheels" policies have targeted short-term capital flows, which are perceived to be relatively volatile and destabilizing. Not surprisingly, there is a renewed interest and considerable debate in academic and policy circles regarding the relative merits and effectiveness of such policies.

Recent policies aimed at curbing capital inflows have most often been thought of as "temporary" measures, either because they have been explicitly announced as such (Malaysia in early 1994), are used countercyclically – that is, restrictions and taxes are tightened in the heavy inflow phase of the cycle and relaxed as these subside or are reversed (Brazil and Colombia) – or simply are thought to become

The authors wish to thank Guillermo Calvo, Alberto Carrasquilla, Peter Montiel, and Vincent Reinhart for useful discussion, comments, and suggestions.
[1] Calvo, Leiderman, and Reinhart (1993, 1994).

ineffective after a while.[2] Hence, when analyzing the effects of these policies in a theoretical framework, two of their key features must be kept in mind – their temporariness (in the sense that controls are only in place or are binding during a finite horizon) and their asymmetry (in that, unlike a Tobin tax which is applied to *all* transactions, these policies target inflows).[3]

The aims of this chapter are twofold. First, we analyze the macroeconomic effects of a temporary tax on capital inflows in the context of a standard, representative-agent, intertemporal model. The temporariness of controls on inflows is by government design rather than eventual evasion. The emphasis of the analysis is on tracing the effects of this policy on key variables, such as consumption, the real exchange rate, the current account, and capital flows. Second, we review the stylized facts of the periods leading up to and following the imposition of capital controls in several countries in Asia, Eastern Europe, and Latin America, including Brazil, the Czech Republic, Chile, Colombia, and Malaysia. The aim is to assess to what extent these measures were able to achieve their intended goals of influencing the level and composition of capital flows – specifically, whether they were successful in reducing the volume of flows, lengthening their maturity, or both. We also examine the evolution of other key macroeconomic variables around these episodes. Along the way, we discuss the relative merits of such measures, document and chronicle the timing and highly varied nature of the measures that have been implemented, and review the recent literature on the topic, with particular emphasis on a variety of case studies. The main conclusions that emerge from the analytical exercise and from the review of the country experiences can be summarized as follows.

First, in the context of a theoretical model, we show that a temporary tax that increases the cost of borrowing abroad to domestic residents has the intended effect of reducing net cross-border capital flows. It enables the monetary authorities temporarily to keep domestic interest rates above world levels, thus raising the "effective price" of consuming today vis-à-vis consuming at a future date, when the controls are no longer in place. This induces households to postpone consumption; the temporary decline in consumption, in turn, depreciates the real exchange rate and reduces the current account deficit – fulfilling, at least in principle, the intentions of policy makers.

Second, we argue, as shown formally in Reinhart and Smith (1996),

---

[2] For instance, there is much debate within Chile and Colombia on the current usefulness of the controls. See Lefort and Budnevich (1996), and Valdés-Prieto and Soto (1995).
[3] See Reinhart (1996) for a comparison of the symmetric and asymmetric cases.

that the response to the policy change hinges importantly on the degree of intertemporal substitution and less so on the duration that the controls are in place. Formally, if the intertemporal elasticity of substitution is low, as has been found for a number of developing countries (see, for instance, Ostry and Reinhart, 1992, and Reinhart and Végh, 1995), then our results imply that the tax on inflows would have to be quite high to have the desired macroeconomic effect. Indeed, this observation concurs with the actual policies implemented by a number of countries; for instance, Colombia's reserve requirement rate on offshore borrowing of a maturity of thirty days or less is 140 percent.

Third, in light of the recent experiences of countries that have adopted measures designed to curb short-term capital inflows, it appears that, at least in the short run, such policies were effective in either reducing the volume of capital inflows, affecting their composition, or both, in a relatively brief period of time. Hence, it could be argued that if the capital inflows are perceived as temporary, such policies can be effective, especially because the reduction in the volume of net inflows reduces potential future outflows and thus the economic costs of such turbulence. This observation must be interpreted cautiously, in that often the controls were part of a larger policy package aimed at reducing capital inflows or lengthening their maturities. For example, the introduction of controls often coincided with increased exchange rate flexibility and the scaling back of sterilized intervention designed to encourage a reduction in domestic interest rates. Hence, it is difficult to isolate the effects of the controls per se.

Fourth, most of the empirical work on the effectiveness of capital controls has tended to conclude that controls lose their effectiveness relatively quickly. However, in most of this work no distinctions are made among the "types" of capital controls. Specifically, little distinction is made between measures to discourage inflows and controls on outflows. Indeed, there may be reasons to believe that their "lack of effectiveness" is not symmetric and that controls on inflows may be more effective than controls on outflows. One reason to believe this is that controls on outflows are usually resorted to during balance-of-payments or financial crises. (East Asia provides recent examples.) These episodes are characterized by large devaluations of the exchange rate, steep declines in the stock market, increased volatility in financial variables, a higher risk of default, and, in some cases, political instability. The imposition of controls, in and of itself, may send a "signal" that worse times are to come.[4] In such circumstances, spreads of domestic to foreign interest rates usu-

[4] See Bartolini and Drazen (1994) on this issue.

ally reach levels (particularly on a risk-adjusted basis) that provide a powerful incentive for outflows. In contrast, as the experiences of several countries in the early 1990s shows, controls on inflows tend to emerge under more "normal" economic circumstances. While rate-of-return spreads may still provide an incentive to evade the controls, the rate of return differentials tend to be smaller than those observed during crises and hence the desire to circumvent the controls may not be as strong. Further, from the viewpoint of an international investor, one can always redirect investments to countries where there are less impediments.[5]

The next section discusses the conditions under which controlling capital inflows may be desirable and chronicles the recent use of measures to curb capital inflows, while section 14.3 sketches the main features of a theoretical model and discusses the implications of the controls. Section 14.4 reviews for a range of countries the evolution and composition of capital flows and other macroeconomic variables around the periods when controls are introduced, while the last section discusses policy implications and areas for future research.

14.2   Controlling capital inflows in the 1990s

It is widely agreed that free cross-border movement of capital is a first-best solution in a world where markets function efficiently, prices are fully flexible, and there are no distortions. The rationale for controlling cross-border capital flows therefore usually stems from a variety of reasons that have to do with the presence of distortions, rigidities, and/or market failures (e.g., Tobin, 1978; see Dooley, 1996, for a recent review of the literature). The desire to maintain monetary policy independence in the face of a fixed exchange rate – a rigidity that is the result of an explicit policy – has also served as the motivation for introducing capital controls.[6] At present, the possibility of a sudden reversal of capital inflows is a key policy concern for the many developing countries that rely heavily on foreign capital to finance large current account deficits – and these concerns have intensified in the wake of the Mexican and Asian crises. Despite its policy relevance, however, there does not appear to be a consensus (either in academic or policy circles) on the usefulness or desirability of curbing international capital movements by imposing various forms of capital controls and/or prudential regulations. In the remainder of this section, we discuss what types of controls on inflows and on outflows may potentially mitigate the disruptive effects of sharp and

---

[5] This argument will, of course, not hold if everyone adopts uniform controls.
[6] A recent example is Thailand. See Glick, Hutchison, and Moreno (1995).

sudden reversals in international capital flows, reviews the various arguments made as to their relative merits, and chronicles their incidence during the 1990s.

14.2.1. Controlling capital inflows: The pros and cons

Although it is common to label certain types of controls or restrictions on cross-border capital flows as either controls on inflows or outflows, many types of controls are likely to influence *both* inflows and outflows. For example, a ban on the convertibility of the domestic currency, which is intended to curtail outflows, is also likely to make the country less attractive to foreign investors – thus reducing inflows. Similarly, Bartolini and Drazen (1994) and Labán and Larraín (1994) argue that a liberalization of outflows increases foreign investor confidence in that country and may result in higher net inflows. Keeping in mind this link between capital inflows and outflows, it is useful to approach the analysis of alternative capital controls according to whether they are targeted toward inflows or outflows.

Large-scale capital inflows could lead to an overheated economy, an appreciated real exchange rate, and an unsustainable current account deficit; large outflows could produce a recession and a decline in investment, which would tend to reduce the medium-term growth prospects. Large flows in either direction also tend to complicate the conduct of monetary policy and, if there are distortions in the financial sector, may increase the fragility of the domestic financial system. In the case of inflows, monetary and credit expansion may be greater than desired by the authorities, given their inflation objectives; massive outflows may require sustained and prohibitively high interest rates, placing additional strains on the banking sector. Further, as the recent Mexican and East Asian experiences vividly illustrate, the reversal of flows can be quite abrupt, threatening the stability of the financial system. Hence, one possible way of simultaneously avoiding some of the problems associated with large destabilizing inflows and even more problematic outflows might be to limit inflows to begin with.

In addition to this "precautionary" motive for restricting capital inflows, several arguments have been advanced in favor of controls, particularly when the inflows are perceived to be temporary (see Krugman, 1987). For instance, it has been argued that the temporary real exchange rate appreciation that often accompanies a rise in capital inflows may have adverse long-lived effects on exports – the so-called hysteresis argument. A second argument is that taxation of inflows may be warranted if the capital inflows are purely speculative.

One proposal (see e.g., Eichengreen, Tobin, and Wyplosz, 1995) that has recently gained some popularity is the worldwide implementation of a tax on foreign exchange trading or on short-term cross-border bank loans. Advocates contend that such a tax would give countries increased domestic monetary policy autonomy, raise the costs of speculative attacks on fixed exchange rate regimes, and encourage investors to focus on longer-term investments rather than short-term speculative opportunities. This proposal is a modern vintage of James Tobin's proposal to tax foreign exchange transactions in order to " throw sand in the wheels of international finance." Although there are a number of proposals of this sort that differ by the tax base or tax rate, they all aim to increase the cost of establishing short positions in currencies and thus to make speculators "pay" for their activities. As discussed later, some countries have in fact implemented variants of these types of policies.

There are, however, a number of practical problems with a "Tobin tax" that may significantly limit its appeal (see Garber and Taylor, 1995, and Dooley, 1996). First, to be effective, it would probably need to be adopted worldwide and uniformly; if it were adopted by just the major industrial countries, say, it would likely cause the taxed activities to shift to untaxed countries. Second, penalizing cross-border bank loans may not be very effective in restraining speculative activity if banks do not engage in large position taking.[7] Third, it is becoming increasingly easy to create synthetic positions through derivatives markets, complicating the effective taxation of "foreign exchange transactions."[8] Fourth, taxing foreign exchange trading is likely to remove significant liquidity from these markets. While the first of these may not be very relevant for developing countries where offshore foreign exchange trading may be limited or nonexistent, the remaining concerns are still a factor.

A more general criticism of any type of capital control is provided by the empirical finding that capital controls tend to lose their effectiveness relatively quickly as individuals find ways of dodging the controls.[9] Further, recent research suggests that countries that have capital controls in place often have higher inflation and lower real interest rates than other countries.[10]

---

[7] The experience of Spain during the 1992 exchange rate mechanism (ERM) crisis highlights the importance of this argument.

[8] See Garber and Lall (Chapter 7) in this volume.

[9] See Mathieson and Rojas-Suárez (1993) for a comprehensive review.

[10] See Grilli and Milesi-Ferretti (1995). One interpretation of this finding is that the controls are just another form of financial repression – the authorities can more effectively tax "captive" domestic currency deposits through higher inflation.

14.2.2. Short-term versus long-term: Is there a difference?

Several countries currently seek to promote long-term capital inflows but to discourage short-term inflows. The motivation for such a policy is presumably that long-term capital inflows take longer to withdraw from a country so that the lower the share of short-term capital in total flows, the lower the probability of a sudden reversal in capital inflows. Further, it is argued that long-term flows, such as foreign direct investment, tend to be more strongly guided by medium-term fundamentals and are less sensitive than short-term flows to cyclical fluctuations in domestic or international interest rates.[11]

In addition to the potential reversibility of inflows, there may be other reasons why the authorities may wish to limit short-term flows. Notably, a surge in short-term inflows often shows up as a rapid expansion in short-maturity bank deposits; if the domestic banking sector is inefficient or poorly supervised, the authorities may wish to minimize the role played by banks in intermediating capital flows. In this case, it may be preferable to have a larger share of flows routed through bond and equity markets.[12]

The current practices of several developing countries amount to restricting either the types of external financing of domestic entities or else the maturities of external financing. An example of the former approach is restricting the foreign issuance of securities by domestic entities, thereby encouraging direct investment instead. An example of the latter policy would be to restrict, say via a tax, short-maturity foreign bond issues or bank loans.

Just as there are practical problems associated with designing capital controls to target only inflows or only outflows, it is difficult to design capital controls that distinguish between short-term and long-term capital flows. Specifically, it is often not clear which capital flows are short-term and which are long-term. Standard balance-of-payments classifications – direct investment, portfolio flows, short-term flows, and the like – are in general not very informative as to the volatility, effective maturity, and liquidity of the flows. Indeed, as Claessens, Dooley, and Warner (1995) suggest, the distinctiveness of these flows may be significantly less clear than these categories suggest. Further, it seems likely that even if a set of controls is effective in limiting "short-term" foreign

---

[11] See Edwards (1991).
[12] This argument is reinforced by the fact that most countries view stability and solvency of the banking system as a much more important consideration than weakness in equity markets.

financing, if incentives are strong enough, even flows that are perceived by policy makers to be "long-term" flows may in fact be considerably more liquid. For example, selling direct investments may require time and significant transactions costs, but it is possible to create a "synthetic sale" by obtaining bank loans in the domestic currency that can be initiated rather quickly and with low transactions costs. In addition, to the extent that equity and long-term bonds – and, to a much lesser degree, term deposits and bank loans – have reasonably liquid secondary markets, asset sales by foreigners can be expected to require an adjustment in the secondary market, rather than an adjustment in the primary market as is the case when short-term flows dry up. Because large-scale liquidation of "long-term" securities (equity, long-term bonds) may well spill over to primary markets, it is not clear that this sort of policy would be effective precisely at those times when it would be beneficial. Indeed, the sell-off in late 1994 and early 1995 of emerging-markets securities not only reduced securities prices, but it also sharply contracted issuance activity in primary securities markets by most developing countries.

14.2.3   *Taxing short-term flows in the 1990s: The measures*

The preceding discussion suggests that one policy to reduce net inflows directly is the taxation of gross inflows, possibly in the form of a tax that falls more heavily on short-term inflows. The policies adopted by Chile in 1991, Colombia in 1993, and Thailand in 1995–96 (see Tables 14.1 and 14.2) are recent examples of this type of policy. In these cases, a nonremunerated reserve requirement is to be deposited at the central bank on liabilities in foreign currency associated with direct borrowing by firms. In the case of Colombia, the reserve requirement is to be maintained for the duration of the loan and applies to all loans with a maturity of five years or less, except for trade credit with a maturity of four months or less. The percentage of the requirement declines as the maturity lengthens; from 140 percent for funds that are thirty days or less to 42.8 percent for five-year funds. For Chile, the tax is of the form of a nonremunerated 30 percent reserve requirement to be deposited at the central bank for a period of one year on liabilities in foreign currency associated with direct borrowing by firms. The tax rate for various maturities is summarized in Table 14.3 and highlights how such a measure may act as a disincentive to borrow abroad, particularly at short maturities – that is, the tax is borne by the borrower. The table also highlights how high the tax rates are at short maturities, possibly suggesting that the authorities believed lower tax rates would not have been a

Table 14.1. *Restrictions on inflows and prudential requirements: Asia*

Indonesia (1990)
March 1991
 Central Bank adopts measures to discourage offshore borrowing. Bank
 Indonesia begins to scale down its swap operations by reducing individual
 banks' limits from 25 to 20 percent of capital. The three-month swap
 premium was raised by 5 percentage points.
October 1991
 All state-related offshore commercial borrowing was made subject to prior
 approval by the government and annual ceilings were set for new
 commitments over the next five years.
November 1991
 Further measures are taken to discourage offshore borrowing. The limits on
 banks' net open-market foreign-exchange positions were tightened by
 placing a separate limit on off-balance-sheet positions.
 Bank Indonesia also announced that future swap operations (except for
 "investment swaps" with maturities of more than two years) would be
 undertaken only at the initiative of Bank Indonesia.

Malaysia (1989)
June 1, 1992
 Limits on non-trade-related swap transactions were imposed on commercial
 banks.
January 17, 1994–August 1994
 Banks were subject to a ceiling on their non-trade- or non-investment-
 related external liabilities.
January 24, 1994–August 1994
 Residents were prohibited from selling short-term monetary instruments to
 nonresidents.
February 2, 1994–August 1994
 Commercial banks were required to place with Bank Negara the ringgit
 funds of foreign banking institutions (Vostro accounts) held in non-
 interest-bearing accounts. However, in the January–May period these
 accounts were considered part of the eligible liabilities base for the
 calculation of required reserves, resulting in a negative effective interest
 rate on Vostro balances.
February 23, 1994–August 1994
 Commercial banks are not allowed to undertake non-trade-related swap and
 outright forward transactions on the bid side with foreign customers.

Philippines (1992)
July 1994
 Bangko Central begins to discourage forward cover arrangements with
 nonresident financial institutions.

Table 14.1. *(cont.)*

Thailand (1988)

January 1990

Banks and finance companies net foreign exchange positions may not exceed 20 percent of capital.

Banks and finance companies net foreign liabilities may not exceed 20 percent of capital.

Residents are not allowed to hold foreign currency deposits except only for trade-related purposes.

April 1990

Banks and finance companies net foreign-exchange positions limit raised to 25 percent of capital.

August 8, 1995

Reserve requirements, to be held in the form of non-interest-bearing deposits at the Bank of Thailand, on short-term nonresident baht accounts were raised from 2 to 7 percent. While reserve requirements on domestic deposits are also 7 percent, up to 5 percent can be held in the form of interest-bearing public bonds.

December 1995

The 7 percent reserve requirement is extended to finance companies short-term (less than one year) promissory notes held by nonresidents.

A variety of measures aimed at reducing foreign-financed lending were introduced.

April 19, 1996

Offshore borrowing with maturities of less than 1 year by commercial banks, finance companies, and finance and security companies will be subject to a 7 percent minimum reserve requirement in the form of a nonremunerated deposit with the Bank of Thailand. Loans for trade purposes will be exempt.

Note: The date next to the country name denotes the first year of the surge in inflows.

Sources: Alfiler (1995), Bank Indonesia, *Annual Report*, various issues; Bank Negara, *Annual Report*, various issues; Bank of Thailand, *Annual Report*, various issues.

sufficient disincentive – an issue that will be taken up in the next section. In principle, because of their breadth, these measures affect the household sector, nonfinancial businesses, as well as the financial sector. In practice, it has mainly served as a deterrent for the banking system to borrow offshore.

More recently, Brazil has implemented a variety of taxes and mea-

Table 14.2. *Restrictions on inflows and prudential requirements: Eastern Europe and Latin America*

Brazil (1992)
October 1994
  A 1 percent tax on foreign investment in the stock market. Eliminated on March 10, 1995.
  The tax on Brazilian companies issuing bonds overseas was raised from 3 to 7 percent of the total. Eliminated on March 10, 1995.
  The tax paid by foreigners on fixed-interest investments in Brazil was raised from 5 to 9 percent. Reduced back to 5 percent on March 10, 1995.
  The Central Bank raised limits on the amount of dollars that can be bought on foreign exchange markets.

Chile (1990)
June 1991
  Nonremunerated 20 percent reserve requirement to be deposited at the Central Bank for a period of one year on liabilities in foreign currency for direct borrowing by firms.
  The stamp tax of 1.2 percent a year (previously paid by domestic currency credits only) was applied to foreign loans as well. This requirement applies to all credits during their first year, with the exception of trade loans.
May 1992
  The reserve requirement on liabilities in foreign currency for direct borrowing by firms is raised to 30 percent. Hence, all foreign currency liabilities have a common reserve requirement.

Colombia (1991)
June 1991
  A 3 percent withholding tax on foreign exchange receipts from personal services rendered abroad and other transfers, which could be claimed as credit against income tax liability.
February 1992
  Banco de la Republica increases its commission on its cash purchases of foreign exchange from 1.5 to 5 percent.
June 1992
  Regulation of the entry of foreign currency as payment for services.
September 1993
  A nonremunerated 47 percent reserve requirement to be deposited at the Central Bank on liabilities in foreign currency for direct borrowing by firms. The reserve requirement is to be maintained for the duration of the loan and applies to all loans with a maturity of 18 months or less, except for trade credit.

Table 14.2. *(cont.)*

August 1994

Nonremunerated reserve requirement to be deposited at the Central Bank on liabilities in foreign currency for direct borrowing by firms. The reserve requirement is to be maintained for the duration of the loan and applies to all loans with a maturity of five years or less, except for trade credit with a maturity of four months or less. The percentage of the requirement declines as the maturity lengthens, from 140 percent for funds that are 30 days or less to 42.8 percent for five-year funds.

Czech Republic (1992)

April 1995

The central bank introduced a fee of 0.25 percent on its foreign exchange transactions with banks, with the aim of discouraging short-term speculative flows.

August 1, 1995

A limit on net short-term (less than one year) foreign borrowing by banks is introduced.

Each bank is to ensure that its net short-term liabilities to nonresidents, in all currencies, do not exceed the smaller of 30 percent of claims on nonresidents or Kc 500 million.

Administrative approval procedures seek to slow down short-term borrowing by nonbanks.

Mexico (1990)

April 1992

A regulation that limited foreign currency liabilities of commercial banks to 10 percent of their total loan portfolio was passed. Banks had to place 15 percent of these liabilities in highly liquid instruments.

Note: The date next to the country name denotes the first year of the surge in inflows.

Sources: Annual reports of Banco Central de Chile (1991 and 1992), Banco de la Republica, Colombia (1993 and 1994), Banco de Mexico (1992), and Conselho Monetario Nacional, Brasil (1994 and 1995).

sures on inflows (Table 14.2), with greater variation across assets as well as across maturities.[13] As in the cases of Chile and Colombia, the tax on foreign issuance of bonds falls on the borrower. However, some other taxes are paid by foreign lenders. Notably, foreigners investing in the

---

[13] As capital inflows shrank in the wake of the Mexican crisis, Brazil eased or eliminated some restrictions on inflows in March 1995. For a detailed summary of all the measures taken since 1993, see Garcia and Barcinski (1996).

Table 14.3. *Tax rate on short-term capital inflows
according to maturity (in percent)*

Number of months	Chile	Colombia
1	95	140
2	90	137
3	74	135
4	67	132
5	61	129
6	55	127
7	50	123
8	45	122
9	41	119
10	37	117
11	33	115
12	30	112
13	27	110
14	25	108
15	22	106
16	20	104
17	18	102
18	16	100
19	15	98
20	13	96
21	12	94
22	11	92
23	10	90
24	9	88
25	8	86
26	7	85
27	7	83
28	6	80
29	5	78
30	5	77
31	4	75
32	4	73
33	4	74
34	3	72
35	3	71
36	3	69
48	1	56
60	0	43

Sources: Banco de Chile, *Annual Report* (1992) and
Banco de la República, *Annual Report*, Colombia
(1994).

stock market have to pay a 1 percent tax *up front*.[14] Hence the tax falls more heavily on active investors who trade more often and hold equity for only relatively short periods of time, but falls less heavily on more passive "buy and hold" investors. Hence, these measures are designed to target the speculative, "hot money" variety of capital inflows. The tax to be paid by foreigners on fixed-income investments has similar characteristics.

The main disadvantage with these measures is that flows are likely to be rerouted through other channels – for example, the over- or underinvoicing of imports and exports so long as trade credits are exempt from the tax (see Mathieson and Rojas-Suárez, 1993). Labán and Larraín (1994) have argued that, in the case of Chile, overinvoicing of imports is not likely to be an attractive alternative since imports are taxed at a comparable rate.[15] Indeed, as discussed in detail later, inflows to Chile in 1991 were below those observed in 1990, possibly attesting to the success of this policy. While net inflows increased, once again, in 1992 and subsequently, the increases came primarily in foreign direct investment and other long-term flows. A similar pattern emerges in Colombia during 1994, with short-term flows accounting for a declining share of total flows.[16]

In other instances, capital controls have been quantitative in nature (Tables 14.1 and 14.2). Measures implemented have included prudential limits, or prohibition, on non-trade-related swap activities, offshore borrowing, banks' net foreign exchange positions (Czech Republic, Indonesia, Malaysia, Philippines, Thailand), caps on banks' foreign currency liabilities (Mexico), and even blanket measures that prohibited domestic residents from selling short-term money market instruments to foreigners (Malaysia).

In the case of Malaysia, wide domestic–foreign interest rate differentials in tandem with widespread expectation of an appreciation of the ringgit during the late 1993 led to a surge in short-term capital inflows, which culminated with the imposition of six measures to restrict inflows in January 1994 (Table 14.1). The inflows came in the form of a marked rise in short-term bank deposits, which were seen by policy makers as speculative in nature.[17] Consequently, most of the measures were

---

[14] This was eliminated on March 10, 1995, in order to encourage inflows in the wake of the Mexican crisis.
[15] However, some circumvention of the tax is effected by reclassifying loans as trade-related.
[16] However, *total* inflows to Colombia continued to increase in 1994.
[17] See Aziz (1995).

directed toward the control of the activities of financial sector participants and most were announced to be temporary.[18] The most successful
measure in reducing short-term inflows was apparently the measure that
prohibited domestic residents from selling short-term money market
instruments to foreigners; as the certificates of deposits (CDs) matured
and could not be rolled over, short-term inflows (and the monetary
aggregates) began to shrink. However, if such policies are maintained
indefinitely they will likely reduce the competitiveness and retard the
development of the financial sector.[19] As far as a foreign investor is
concerned, the cost of this particular measure would be the forgone
return from not being able to roll over CDs. In practice, this opportunity
cost does not appear substantial since in 1994 Malaysian short-term
interest rates were close to world levels.

In April 1992, Mexico passed a regulation that limited foreign currency liabilities of commercial banks to 10 percent of their total loan
portfolio. However, it is not clear to what extent this measure acted to
reduce the size of the capital inflows, since banks' total loan portfolios
had been expanding rapidly throughout that period and the initial share
of loans in foreign currency was below the 10 percent limit. For example,
during 1992 bank assets grew by 41 percent while foreign currency loans
grew by 88 percent; a similar pattern emerges in 1993, with foreign
currency loans increasing by 50 percent while total loans rose by 25
percent. Indeed, the constraint only appears to have become binding in
1994 when total and foreign currency loans both rose by 27 percent.

14.3   The model

The model we study is a standard, infinite horizon, representative agent
cash-in-advance model with two goods – a traded good and a nontraded
good. Reinhart and Smith (1996) study this model in detail, and thus
in what follows we only briefly review the model and illustrate a few of
its key qualitative predictions. The "home country" is a small open
economy facing a constant world real interest rate of $r > 0$ each period.
The representative agent in the home country has preferences:

$$\int_0^\infty e^{-\beta t} U\left(C_t, \ C_t^*\right) dt,$$ (1)

where C_t and C_t^* denote consumption of the nontraded and traded goods
respectively, $\beta = r$ is the subjective discount rate, and $U(C_t, C_t^*)$ is strictly

---

[18] Only two measures (of the original six) remained in place.
[19] Malaysia removed most capital controls during the second half of 1994.

concave, increasing in each of its arguments, and is twice continuously differentiable.

There is free trade in goods, and the world price of the traded good in units of foreign currency is constant and is denoted P^*. The home country currency price of the nontraded good is denoted P_t, and the home country currency price of a unit of foreign currency is denoted E_t. The real exchange rate is therefore $e_t = E_t P^*/P_t$. We assume that the nominal exchange rate depreciates at rate $\epsilon \geq 0$.

There are three assets available to home country residents: the domestic currency (which is not held by foreigners); foreign bonds, which yield an instantaneous return of $1 + r$ per unit invested, expressed in units of the traded good; and one-period bonds issued by home country entities, which yield an instantaneous return of $1 + \rho_t$ per unit invested (also in terms of the traded good).

The representative agent in the home country receives an endowment of nontraded and traded goods each period equal to y and y^* respectively. Let $a_t \equiv m_t - b_t$ denote the representative agent's real wealth at t, where m_t is real cash balances and b_t is the level of indebtedness. The budget constraint is therefore:

$$\dot{a}_t = \frac{y}{e_t} + y^* - \frac{C_t}{e_t} - C_t^* - \rho_t b_t - \epsilon m_t + \tau_t. \tag{2}$$

Here, τ_t is lump-sum transfers from the government. The appropriate interest rate in formulating this budget constraint is the domestic real rate ρ_t because we are interested only in restrictions on capital *inflows*, and thus $\rho_t \geq r$.

Money is valued in this economy because it is useful for making transactions. Formally, the representative agent's consumption purchases must satisfy a cash-in-advance constraint:

$$m_t \geq \alpha\left(C_t^* + C_t/e_t\right), \tag{3}$$

where α is a positive constant. It is well known that expression (3) holds as an equality if the nominal interest rate is positive; our assumptions on the rate of depreciation of the nominal exchange rate ($\epsilon \geq 0$) and the positive world real interest rate will ensure this is always true.

To motivate our study of taxes on capital inflows, it is convenient to assume that the representative agent has an initial level of indebtedness: $b_0 > 0$. For simplicity, let $b_0 = m_0$ so that $a_0 = 0$. With these assumptions, the budget constraint can be written:

$$\int_0^\infty D_t \left(\frac{C_t}{e_t} + C_t^* \right)(1 + \alpha i_t)dt = \int_0^\infty D_t \left(\frac{y}{e_t} + y^* + \tau_t \right)dt, \tag{4}$$

where

$$D_t = \exp\left(-\int_0^t \rho_s ds \right). \tag{5}$$

Home country residents therefore seek to maximize (1) subject to (4).

The consolidated budget constraint of the government–central bank in the home country is:

$$\dot{f}_t = rf_t + \epsilon m_t + \dot{m}_t - \tau_t + \gamma_t \rho_t I_t. \tag{6}$$

Here, f_t is foreign exchange reserves (foreign bonds), and the final term on the right side is the revenues from taxing capital inflows, I_t. If there are outflows of capital, then $I_t = 0$. It simplifies the exposition to assume that the tax base is the net interest payments: an interest payment to a foreigner of $\rho_t I_t$ causes the foreigner to incur a tax liability of $\gamma_t \rho_t I_t$, where $\gamma_t \in [0, 1]$. The choice of tax base is of no material consequence for the results. Our focus is on situations in which these taxes are only tempo- rary – they are levied during the interval of time $[0, T)$ for $T \geq 0$. We assume that $f_t = 0 \ \forall \ t$, and thus net revenue from seigniorage and from taxing capital inflows is rebated lump-sum to residents in the home country.

Note that in equilibrium $\rho_t = r/(1 - \gamma)$ so long as inflows are positive, $I_t = b_t > 0$. This is true because a foreign investor receives a net return of $(1 - \gamma_t)\rho_t$ per unit invested in home country bonds, and thus if foreign investors are going to want to purchase home country bonds, these bonds would have to offer a rate of return that is at least as attractive as the return on foreign bonds: $\rho_t = r/(1 - \gamma_t)$ so long as $b_t > 0$. It is possible that, at some date, $b_t < 0$, and thus there are capital outflows. In that case, taxes on inflows have no effect on domestic interest rates, and $\rho_t = r$.

The equilibrium conditions for the nontraded goods market, the money market, and the traded goods sector respectively are:

$$C_t = y, \tag{7}$$

$$m_t = m_t^s, \tag{8}$$

$$\int_0^\infty e^{-rt} C_t^* dt = \frac{y^*}{r} - b_0. \tag{9}$$

In the case of free capital mobility and no taxes on inflows we have $\rho_t = r$, $\forall\, t$. Thus, if φ denotes the Lagrange multiplier on the constraint, the first-order conditions associated with optimal consumption of traded and nontraded goods respectively are:

$$U_{C_t}\!\left(C_t, C_t^*\right) = \varphi\left(1 + \alpha i_t\right), \tag{10}$$

$$U_{C_t^*}\!\left(C_t, C_t^*\right) = \frac{\varphi\left(1 + \alpha i_t\right)}{e_t}. \tag{11}$$

Equilibrium consumption of nontraded and traded goods are therefore $C_t = y$ and $C_t^* = y^* - rb_0$. Finally, the equilibrium real exchange rate is constant and equal to:

$$e_t = \frac{U_{C_t^*}\!\left(y, y^* - rb_0\right)}{U_{C_t}\!\left(y, y^* - rb_0\right)}. \tag{12}$$

14.3.1 *Taxing capital inflows*

The first-order conditions for the representative agent in the home country when there are controls on capital inflows are:

$$U_{C_t^*}\!\left(C_t, C_t^*\right) = \exp\!\left(-\int_0^t (\rho_s - \beta)ds\right)\varphi\left(1 + \alpha i_t\right), \tag{13}$$

$$U_{C_t}\!\left(C_t, C_t^*\right) = \exp\!\left(-\int_0^t (\rho_s - \beta)ds\right)\varphi\left(1 + \alpha i_t\right)\big/e_t, \tag{14}$$

where φ is the Lagrange multiplier on the constraint. For exposition purposes we assume that $\gamma_t = \gamma$ for all $t \in [0, T)$. Suppose that the domestic interest rate is bid up to its maximum possible equilibrium value at $t = 0$, $\rho_0 = r/(1 - \gamma)$, and that at this interest rate $b_0 > 0$.[20] It follows that the domestic interest rate will also be bid up to this level at all future dates prior to the removal of capital controls so long as $b_t > 0$ at each date. Let $t^* > T$ denote a future date for which $b_t > 0$ for all $t < t^*$. Thus, $\rho_t = r/(1 - \gamma)$ for all $t < t^*$. It follows that, for all $0 \le t < t^*$, we can write:

$$U_{C_t^*}\!\left(y, C_t^*\right) = \varphi\left(1 + \alpha\left(\frac{r}{1 - \gamma} + \epsilon\right)\right)\exp\!\left(-\frac{\gamma r}{1 - \gamma}t\right). \tag{15}$$

---

[20] Reinhart and Smith (1996) discuss the general case.

Hence, the marginal utility of consumption of traded goods is declining over the interval $(0, t^*)$, and thus the consumption of traded goods is increasing over this time interval. But note that at date $t = 0$, the level of consumption jumps downward to accommodate a jump in saving, so this increasing rate of consumption over the time interval $(0, t^*)$ begins from a lower initial level of consumption. The real exchange rate, $e_t = U_{C_t^*}(y, C_t^*)/U_{C_t}(y, C_t^*)$, must also depreciate initially and then subsequently appreciate over the interval $(0, t^*)$.

At $t = 0$, the imposition of controls on capital inflows causes the real and the nominal interest rate to jump immediately upward in order to either attract foreign capital or to entice residents to substitute out of current consumption and therefore finance domestic credit needs. After this initial impact effect, the real interest rate remains higher than the world interest rate because the home country still must attract foreign capital, but the higher interest rate continues to encourage saving in the home country. The higher real interest rate is therefore encouraging residents to substitute consumption intertemporally, which explains the upward slowing consumption path. However, if at some date t^* domestic savings satisfy $b_t = 0$, then foreign capital is not required to finance domestic consumption and thus the real interest rate would fall to $\rho_t = r$ after this point is reached. Of course, if capital controls are removed before b_t is reduced to zero, then the real interest rate would fall to r at date T as foreign capital could finance the amount $b_T > 0$ at the world real interest rate. In either case, the level of consumption after t^* or T (whichever comes first) is permanently higher than before the capital controls were imposed because the tax liability associated with the public debt is lower. Consequently, the imposition of a tax on capital inflows initially causes a real exchange rate depreciation, and then the real exchange rate appreciates to a level above its level before the tax was imposed.

Taxes on capital inflows are often implemented with the aim of changing the maturity of composition of capital inflows. In particular, levying taxes on short-term capital inflows are often implemented with the intention of lengthening the maturity composition of inflows. In our simple model without capital flow restrictions, different maturities are perfect substitutes to investors because there is a perfectly liquid secondary market and there is no uncertainty. Thus, if we assumed that outstanding debt could be refinanced costlessly in different maturities, then any tax on short-term capital inflows would have no important effect in this model other than to shift the maturity composition of debt, as foreigners would undercut higher short-term interest rates by offering to lend funds long-term at lower per-period rates.

14.4   Some stylized facts

Many case studies have recently examined the role played by capital controls in managing the surge in capital inflows during the early 1990s.[21] However, there has been little effort to systematically examine the "stylized facts" before and after the controls are introduced for those countries implementing these measures. In this section we consider five episodes in which capital controls on inflows were introduced during the 1990s: Chile (June 1991), Colombia (September 1993), Malaysia (January 1994), Brazil (October 1994), and the Czech Republic (August 1995). Although, as shown in Tables 14.1 and 14.2, other countries have adopted numerous "prudential" measures, these five constitute the major and most unambiguous cases of the use of capital controls to curb short-term inflows. Thailand's measures in late 1995 and early 1996 are another important case, but the recentness of many of the stiffer measures makes it difficult to obtain sufficient data to analyze the consequences of the controls. However, events in 1997 in Thailand highlight that the controls were not successful in preventing a Mexico-style currency and banking crisis.

In what follows, we examine the evolution of the capital account and its composition as well as the behavior of key macroeconomic variables, which, as shown in the previous section, should be influenced by the controls. Of course, any assessment of the impact of the capital account measures has to be tempered by the fact that we do not observe the counterfactual – that is, what capital flows and the macroeconomic environment would have been in the absence of the controls.

14.4.1   *The volume and composition of capital flows*

Table 14.4 summarizes capital account developments around the time capital controls are introduced (denoted in the table by *t*). We can make the following observations based on these recent experiences with policies directed toward curbing short-term capital inflows.

First, reviewing the Chilean and Malaysian experiences (and, to a lesser extent, the Czech case) at least in the short run, these distinctly different policies were successful in reducing the *volume* of inflows in a relatively brief period of time. Indeed, in the case of Chile and Malaysia the capital account surpluses (as a percent of GDP) shrank by 7.6 and

---

[21] For a comparison of Chile and Colombia, see Lefort and Budnevich (1996); Labán and Larraín (1994) examine the Chilean experience; and Garcia and Barcinski (1996) describe the Brazilian experience.

Table 14.4. *Capital account developments*

	$t-1$	t	$t+1$	$t+2$
Capital account balance (as % of GDP)				
Brazil (August 1994)	2.4	2.5	4.7	n.a.
Chile (June 1991)	10.0	2.4	6.8	6.1
Colombia (September 1993)	0.3	4.7	4.4	5.5
Czech Republic (August 1995)	6.6	16.7	14.2	n.a.
Malaysia (January 1994)	17.2	2.1	7.9	n.a.
Direct investment (as % of GDP)				
Brazil	−0.1	0.2	0.4	n.a.
Chile	0.8	1.3	0.8	0.8
Colombia	1.4	1.3	2.2	2.7
Czech Republic	2.1	5.3	2.9	n.a.
Malaysia	5.2	3.5	4.7	n.a.
Short-term capital flows (as % of GDP)				
Brazil	0.2	−0.1	1.3	n.a.
Chile	3.2	−0.7	3.8	1.6
Colombia	0.6	1.1	0.7	0.3
Czech Republic	0.1	0.7	1.7	n.a.
Malaysia	8.6	−4.6	−0.7	n.a.
Change in international reserves (in billions of US$)				
Brazil	8.1	6.5	12.6	n.a.
Chile	2.4	1.0	2.1	0.5
Colombia	1.4	0.7	0.2	0.4
Czech Republic	2.4	7.7	−1.3	n.a.
Malaysia	10.0	−1.8	−1.6	n.a.
Portfolio flows (as % of GDP)				
Brazil	1.6	1.3	2.1	n.a.
Chile	1.2	0.1	0.8	1.8

Notes: $t-1$ refers to the year before the capital controls are introduced. The dates in parentheses indicate when the controls were introduced. See Tables 14.1 and 14.2 for details on the measures. An n.a. denotes the pertinent data were not yet available.

Sources: International Monetary Fund, *World Economic Outlook*, various issues.

15.1 percentage points, respectively, in the year the controls were intro-duced. In the case of the Czech Republic, the decline in inflows was more modest (3.5 percent) and was not apparent until 1996 ($t + 1$), as the inflows were introduced in the latter half of 1995. No decline in the volume of flows is apparent in the Colombian and Brazilian cases.

Second, it could be argued that the effect these policies had on the *composition* of flows was the "desired" effect of lengthening maturities in the cases of Chile, Colombia, and Malaysia, where a marked decline in capital inflows occurred at the short maturities. As the third panel of Table 14.4 highlights, in these three cases the decline in inflows was concentrated in the short-term maturities that were targeted by the measures. Brazilian measures, on the other hand, primarily targeted portfolio flows – and, as Garcia and Barcinski (1996) argue, these do not appear to have much success in reducing these inflows (see bottom panel of Table 14.4).

Third, in four of the five cases (Brazil is the exception) reserve accu-mulation slowed following the introduction of the measures, suggesting that either the pressures to intervene in the foreign exchange market had diminished (as inflows eased); the central banks had opted to allow the exchange rate to adjust more freely, so as to reduce the scope of costly sterilized intervention policies (an issue that will be discussed later); or a combination of these developments.

Fourth, if the inflows are largely seen as a temporary phenomenon, such policies appear to be quite effective (as least when complemented by a reenforcing monetary policy stance, an issue to be discussed). However, it is not possible from these experiences to draw any infer-ence about the usefulness of the controls if the inflows persist over longer periods of time or if the policies remain in place indefinitely. In Malaysia the controls were subsequently removed, while in the case of Colombia these measures have been eased; in the case of Chile there is much debate over whether the reserve requirement and other measures have become less binding; and in the cases of the Czech Republic and Thailand the measures are recent. Lastly, in the Brazilian case it appears that the measures were not particularly effective, even in the short run.

14.4.2   *Monetary policy and capital controls*

Besides a desire to affect capital flows, a motivation for introducing controls is that it permits the central bank (at least in the short run) a greater degree of monetary policy independence, even with a relatively rigid exchange rate regime (see Labán and Larraín, 1994). Hence, in

Table 14.5. *Monetary and exchange rate policy indicators*

	$t-1$	t	$t+1$	$t+2$
Real ex-post lending interest rates (% per annum)				
Brazil (August 1994)	7.1	21.1	26.0	10.6
Chile (June 1991)	22.0	11.2	10.6	11.0
Colombia (September 1993)	8.1	10.7	13.5	17.9
Czech Republic (August 1995)	3.0	3.7	4.4	n.a.
Malaysia (January 1994)	8.0	2.6	2.0	n.a.
Money and quasi money (% change, period end)				
Brazil	2,652.0	1,081.8	43.4	n.a.
Chile	23.6	28.1	23.3	23.4
Colombia	37.4	30.8	33.3	27.6
Czech Republic	20.4	29.3	6.2	n.a.
Malaysia	26.6	12.7	19.9	n.a.
Nominal exchange rate (% change, period end)				
Brazil				n.a.
Chile	13.4	11.1	2.0	12.1
Colombia	14.8	13.0	−11.3	21.4
Czech Republic	−6.5	−5.2	3.8	n.a.
Malaysia	3.4	−5.3	−0.7	n.a.

Notes: $t-1$ refers to the year before the capital controls are introduced. The dates in parentheses indicate when the controls were introduced. See Tables 14.1 and 14.2 for details on the measures. An n.a. denotes the pertinent data were not yet available.

Sources: International Monetary Fund, *World Economic Outlook*, various issues.

examining the effectiveness of the capital controls it is important to assess what the course of monetary policy was during that period.

As the top panel of Table 14.5 highlights, an important determinant of the relative success of the capital account measures appears to be the stance adopted by monetary policy at the time of the introduction of controls, and in the period immediately following their introduction. Specifically, in the most "successful" cases (Chile and Malaysia), aggressive sterilized intervention policies were abandoned when the controls were introduced, allowing domestic nominal and real interest rates to fall sharply (see Reinhart and Dunaway, 1995). The decline in domestic rates of return further reduced the attractiveness of domestic financial assets and reinforced the aims of the capital controls. In the two intermediate cases (Colombia and the Czech Republic), where the decline in inflows were either more modest, or the only effects were to alter the composition of flows, monetary policy remained relatively neutral and real interest rates rose modestly (as suggested by the theoretical model outlined in the previous section). Note also that the slowing of reserve accumulation in these countries may also have tempered the rise in interest rates by reducing the impact of the controls on capital flows. However, in the case of Brazil – where capital account measures appear to be least successful in either discouraging inflows or altering their composition – a dramatic tightening in monetary policy accompanied the controls. Aggressive sterilization through open-market operations led to a substantial build-up of domestic debt (see Garcia and Barcinski, 1996), and marked increases in reserve requirements (see Reinhart and Reinhart, 1995) drove the lending rate substantially higher. The outcome of these policies was reflected in a sharp increase in real interest rates, which still remain above 20 percent (see Table 14.5). In turn, the high real interest rates have fostered capital inflows, as rates of return remain quite attractive by international standards, even on an after-tax basis. In effect, as shown in Table 14.4, the surge in inflows was led by portfolio investments – a large share of which was funneled into the domestic fixed-income market.

With regard to monetary growth, despite an easing in monetary policy in Chile and Malaysia and neutral policies in Colombia and the Czech Republic, the tendency in the growth rates of the monetary aggregates following the introduction of controls appears to be toward a deceleration (Table 14.5). The tendency toward slower monetary growth does not, however, appear to be a product of a weaker demand for money due to lower economic activity (discussed later). Instead, it appears to reflect either a slowdown in nonresident banking sector deposits (most notably in Malaysia), less offshore borrowing by domestic banks (Chile and Colombia), or a slowing in foreign exchange reserve accumulation by the central bank. In any case, it has usually been part of the objective of the central banks for either prudential reasons (i.e., concerns about an unstable deposit base fueling a boom in bank lending) or for macroeconomic reasons (e.g., limiting inflationary pressures).

14.4.3 *Capital controls and selected macroeconomic indicators*

As noted earlier, examining the links between capital controls and macroeconomic developments is complicated by the lack of information on how the economy would have fared in the absence of controls. However, a perusal of the indicators presented in Table 14.6 does not high-

Table 14.6. *Selected macroeconomic indicators*

	$t-1$	t	$t+1$	$t+2$
Current account balance (as % of GDP)				
Brazil (August 1994)	−0.2	−0.3	−2.7	n.a.
Chile (June 1991)	−1.8	0.3	−1.6	−4.6
Colombia (September 1993)	1.8	−3.8	−4.5	−5.3
Czech Republic (August 1995)	−0.1	−4.2	−4.5	n.a.
Malaysia (January 1994)	−4.6	−5.9	−8.5	n.a.
Real GDP (% change)				
Brazil	4.2	5.8	4.2	n.a.
Chile	3.3	7.3	11.0	6.3
Colombia	4.0	5.2	5.7	5.3
Czech Republic	2.6	4.8	5.2	n.a.
Malaysia	8.3	9.2	9.6	n.a.
Real consumer spending (% change)				
Brazil	5.9	8.2	8.6	n.a.
Chile	0.4	8.9	11.6	8.1
Colombia	−0.1	5.2	5.6	3.0
Czech Republic	5.4	6.0	6.6	n.a.
Malaysia	5.3	7.0	13.7	n.a.
Real exchange rate (% change)				
Brazil	11.9	34.1	n.a.	n.a.
Chile	−2.6	5.4	10.7	−2.1
Colombia	9.1	5.1	11.9	1.1
Czech Republic	n.a.	n.a.	n.a.	n.a.
Malaysia	−0.4	−3.2	0.4	n.a.

Notes: $t-1$ refers to the year before the capital controls are introduced. The dates in parentheses denote when the major controls were introduced. See Tables 14.1 and 14.2 for details on the measures. An n.a. denotes the pertinent data were not yet available.

Sources: International Monetary Fund, *World Economic Outlook*, various issues.

light any substantive countercyclical effects of the capital controls on many key macroeconomic indicators. Indeed, it is hard to detect in the data the temporary contraction in consumption, the real exchange rate depreciation, and the narrowing current account deficit postulated by the theoretical model of the previous section. The current account usually continued to deteriorate, as consumption and real GDP growth continued to expand briskly. This observation confirms that the reduced capital account surplus is, at least initially, associated with a slowing in central bank reserve accumulation and not a swift shift in trade in goods and services. As to the real exchange rate, the picture is mixed. In some countries the introduction of controls was followed by a period of moderating real exchange rate appreciations (or a depreciation) while in others the tendency to appreciate remained unabated.

The insensitivity of consumption, the real exchange rate, and the current account surplus in the face of controls on capital inflows should not be particularly surprising for the following reason. Specifically, the weak response of these variables is precisely the prediction of the theoretical model already studied when the intertemporal elasticity of substitution in consumption is small. Ostry and Reinhart (1992) and Reinhart and Végh (1995) find that these elasticities are indeed very low for developing countries. Reinhart and Smith (1996) use the model sketched previously to show that for reasonable elasticities of substitution, significant responses in consumption, the current account, and the real exchange rate would require enormous changes in real interest rates induced by very high tax rates on capital inflows. Moreover, many countries appear to have used official reserves to buffer the impact of the controls and this would further weaken the link between controls and these macroeconomic variables.

14.5   Conclusion

In light of the recent experiences of countries that have adopted measures designed to curb short-term capital inflows, it appears that, at least in the short run, such policies are effective in either reducing the volume of capital inflows, affecting their composition, or both, in a relatively brief period of time. Hence, it could be argued that if the capital inflows are perceived as temporary, such policies could be effective, although the evidence reviewed here suggests those measures may be more effective in shaping the composition of flows than in reducing their overall volume. This is especially true insofar as by reducing the volume of net inflows they reduce potential future outflows and the economic costs of such turbulence. Of course, the longer the inflows persist or the longer the policies remain in place, the greater the chances that the controls become ineffective.

Most of the empirical work on the effectiveness of capital controls has tended to conclude that controls lose their effectiveness relatively quickly. However, in most of this work no distinctions are made among the "types" of capital controls. Specifically, little distinction is made between measures to discourage inflows and controls on outflows. Indeed, there may be reasons to believe that their "lack of effectiveness" is not symmetric and that controls on inflows may be more effective than controls on outflows. Such differences may have little to do with the design of the measures per se and have more to do with incentives to circumvent the controls.

Controls on outflows are usually resorted to during balance-of-payments or financial crises. These episodes are characterized by large devaluations of the exchange rate, steep declines in the stock market, increased volatility in financial variables, a higher risk of default, and, in some cases, political instability. The imposition of controls, in and of itself, may send a "signal" that worse times are to come. In such circumstances, domestic–foreign interest rate spreads usually reach levels (particularly on a risk-adjusted basis) that provide a powerful incentive to evade the controls. In contrast, as the experiences of several countries in the early 1990s show, controls on inflows tend to emerge under more "normal" economic circumstances. While rate-of-return spreads may still provide an incentive to evade the controls, the rate-of-return differentials tend to be smaller than those observed during crises, and hence the desire to circumvent them may not be as great. Moreover, from the viewpoint of an international investor, one can always redirect investments to countries where there are fewer impediments.

References

Alfiler, F. Enrico (1995). "Monetary and Exchange Rate Policy Responses to Surges in Capital Flows: The Case of the Philippines." In *Monetary and Exchange Rate Management with International Capital Mobility: Experiences of Countries and Regions along the Pacific Rim*, Hong Kong Monetary Authority, pp. 226–45.

Aziz, Zeti Akhtar (1995). "Capital Flows and Monetary Management: The Malaysian Experience." In *Monetary and Exchange Rate Management with International Capital Mobility: Experiences of Countries and Regions along the Pacific Rim*, Hong Kong Monetary Authority, pp. 175–85.

Bartolini, Leonardo, and Allan Drazen (1994). "Capital Account Liberalization As a Signal," November. Unpublished manuscript, University of Maryland at College Park.

Calvo, Guillermo, Leonardo Leiderman, and Carmen M. Reinhart (1993). "Capital Inflows to Latin America: The Role of External Factors," *IMF Staff Papers* 40 (1): 108–51.

(1994). "The Capital Inflows Problem: Concepts and Issues," *Contemporary Economic Policy* 12 (July): 54–66.

Claessens, Stijn, Michael P. Dooley, and Andrew Warner (1995). "Portfolio Capital Flows: Hot or Cool?" *World Bank Economic Review* 9 (1): 153–74.

Dooley, Michael P. (1996). "A Survey of Academic Literature on Controls over International Capital Transactions," *IMF Staff Papers* 43 (4): 639–87.

Edwards, Sebastian (1991). "Capital Flows, Foreign Direct Investment, and Debt-Equity Swaps in Developing Countries." In Horst Siebert, ed., *Capital Flows in the World Economy*, pp. 255–81. Tübingen: Mohr.

Eichengreen, Barry, James Tobin, and Charles Wyplosz (1995). "Two Cases for Sand in the Wheels of International Finance," *Economic Journal* 105: 162–72.

Garber, Peter, and Mark P. Taylor (1995). "Sand in the Wheels of Foreign Exchange Markets: A Sceptical Note," *Economic Journal* 105: 173–180.

Garcia, Marcio G., and Alexandre Barcinski (1996). "Capital Flows to Brazil in the Nineties: Macroeconomic Aspects and the Effectiveness of Capital Controls." Unpublished manuscript, Pontifical Catholic University, Rio de Janeiro.

Glick, Reuven, Michael Hutchison, and Ramon Moreno (1995). "Is Pegging the Exchange Rate a Cure for Inflation? East Asian Experiences," Center for Pacific Basin Studies Working Paper PB95-08. Federal Reserve Bank of San Francisco. Forthcoming in Richard Sweeney, Clas Wihlborg, and Thomas Willett, eds., *Exchange Rate Policies for Emerging Market Economies*. Boulder, Colo: Westview Press, 1998.

Goldstein, Morris, David Folkerts-Landau, Peter Garber, Liliana Rojas-Suárez, and Michael Spencer (1993). *International Capital Markets: Exchange Rate Management and International Capital Flows*. Washington, D.C.: International Monetary Fund.

Grilli, Vittorio, and Gian Maria Milesi-Ferreti (1995). "Effect Effects and Structural Determinants of Capital Controls," *IMF Staff Papers* 42 (3): 517–51.

Krugman, Paul (1987). "The Narrow Moving Band, the Dutch Disease, and the Competitive Consequences of Mrs. Thatcher: Notes on Trade in the Presence of Scale Economies," *Journal of Development Economics* 7: 41–55.

Labán, Raúl, and Felipe Larraín (1994). "Can a Liberalization of Capital Outflows Increase Net Capital Inflows?" Unpublished manuscript, Pontificia Universidad Católica de Chile, Santiago.

Lefort, Guillermo, and Carlos Budnevich (1996). "Capital Account Regulation and Macroeconomic Policy: Two Latin American Experiences." Unpublished manuscript, Banco Central de Chile, Santiago.

Mathieson, Donald J., and Liliana Rojas-Suárez (1993). "Liberalization of the Capital Account: Experiences and Issues," IMF Occasional Paper No. 103. Washington, D.C.

Ostry, Jonathan, and Carmen M. Reinhart (1992). "Private Saving and Terms of Trade Shocks," *IMF Staff Papers* 39 (3): 495–517.

Reinhart, Carmen M., and Steve Dunaway (1995). "Dealing with Capital Inflows: Are There Any Lessons?" United Nations University WIDER, Research for Action No. 28. Helsinki, Finland.

Reinhart, Carmen M., and Vincent Reinhart (1995). "On the Use of Reserve Requirements to Deal with Capital Flow Problems," Center for International Economics Working Paper No. 16. University of Maryland at College Park.

Reinhart, Carmen M., and R. Todd Smith (1996). "Temporary Capital Controls." Unpublished manuscript, University of Maryland at College Park.

Reinhart, Carmen M., and Carlos A. Végh (1995). "Intertemporal Consumption

Substitution and Inflation Stabilization: An Empirical Investigation," Center for International Economics Working Paper No. 3. University of Maryland at College Park.

Reinhart, Vincent (1996). "How the Machine of International Finance Runs with Sand in Its Wheels," Unpublished manuscript, Board of Governors of the Federal Reserve System, Washington, D.C.

Tobin, James (1978). "A Proposal for International Monetary Reform," *Eastern Economic Journal* 4 (July–October): 53–59.

Valdés-Prieto, Salvador, and Marcelo Soto (1995). "New Selective Capital Controls in Chile: Are They Effective?" Unpublished manuscript, World Bank, Washington, D.C.

CHAPTER 15

Exchange rate policies and capital account management: Chile in the 1990s

Kevin Cowan and José De Gregorio

15.1   Introduction

Chile, an early reformer in Latin America, has enjoyed strong economic performance during the past decade. Real growth has averaged 7 percent per year and inflation, which averaged more than 20 percent in the 1980s, has gradually fallen to less than 10 percent. Chile's ability to maintain strong growth and low inflation through the period of capital inflows of the early 1990s and outflows during the "tequila" period after Mexico's crisis in 1994 is notable. This success has been attributed to a combination of conservative fiscal and monetary policies, flexible exchange rate management, and capital inflow restrictions.

The purpose of this chapter is to examine Chile's experience both with exchange rate management and the policies implemented to deal with capital inflows during the 1990s. In particular, we evaluate the extent to which these policies have complemented Chile's overall strategy of stabilization and contributed to its successful economic performance in this period.

Policy makers in Chile, as in other emerging markets, faced several options for responding to the capital that flowed into the economy in the early 1990s. One option was to allow the exchange rate to appreciate; another was to limit appreciation through sterilized intervention accompanied by tight fiscal policy to offset the inflationary effects of sterilization and reserve accumulation. A third option involved placing controls on capital inflows and at the same time liberalizing restrictions on outflows. Chile's strategy has been a combination of all of these options. It has sterilized and maintained fiscal surpluses while permitting some

The authors are very grateful to Reuven Glick, Rodrigo Valdés, and conference participants for useful comments and suggestions. The views expressed in this chapter are exclusively those of the authors.

appreciation, employing controls on inflows, and liberalizing restrictions on outflows. Capital controls allowed Chilean policy makers to rely on the domestic interest rate as the main instrument for reducing inflation. Flexible management of the exchange rate reflected the desire to avoid the traumatic changes in the exchange rate that had marked earlier periods, while still maintaining export competitiveness. Perhaps this combination of policies has led Calvo, Leiderman, and Reinhart (1996) to conclude that "Gauging for their economic performance and their ability to withstand the adverse effects of the Mexican crisis, the countries that have been most successful in managing capital flows (for example, Chile and Malaysia) have implemented a comprehensive policy package and not relied on a single instrument" (p. 137).

The chapter is organized as follows: section 15.2 discusses the policies that have been implemented to control capital flows, section 15.3 discusses exchange rate management in Chile focusing on its effects on the volatility of exchange rates and the crediblity of the exchange rate band, and section 15.4 concludes.

15.2   Management of capital flows

When the surge in capital inflows to emerging markets began in 1990, Chile was able to return to private international financial markets for funds. Since then, a number of measures aimed at increasing integration have been adopted.[1] For example, the minimum 120-day term for import credits was eliminated in 1990. That same year Chilean companies were allowed to sell equity in international markets in the form of American depositary receipts (ADRs). In 1992, companies with low-risk classification were allowed to issue bonds in foreign markets. Then, in early 1993, the tax rate on repatriated profits of foreign investors[2] was reduced from 50 to 42 percent, and the restriction that precluded repatriation before three years was reduced to one year.

As capital inflows increased and the need to secure foreign saving declined, other policies were implemented to allow domestic residents to

---

[1] There are several papers that have analyzed the liberalization of the capital account in recent years and the effects of controls on capital inflows. See, for example, Labán and Larraín (1994), Ffench-Davis, Agosín, and Uthoff (1995), Budnevich and Lefort (1996), Chumacero, Labán, and Larraín (1996), Eyzaguirre and Rojas (1996), and Soto and Valdés-Prieto (1996). See also Williamson (1996) for a recent discussion on exchange rate bands and capital inflows in Chile, Colombia, and Israel.

[2] This applies to foreign investment entering through Decree Law 600, which involves a contract between the Chilean national government and the foreign investor and that provides guarantees in terms of tax treatment and nonexpropriation.

increase investments abroad. For example, restrictions on international investment by pension funds, mutual funds, and other institutional investors were eased.[3]

However, while the overall drive in Chile has been toward opening the capital account, growing concerns about inflation and the exchange rate pressure of rising capital inflows have led policy makers to introduce specific capital controls. The most important restriction on capital inflows imposed in this period was an unremunerated reserve requirement (URR) to be held at the central bank that was introduced in June 1991. Initially this reserve requirement was set at 20 percent for nearly all external credits, with a holding period of from 90 to 365 days. For all credits with terms less than 90 days the holding period was set at 90 days, while for periods between 90 days and one year the holding period was set equal to the length of the term. For longer-term credits the holding period was limited to one year. In May 1992, the reserve requirement was raised to 30 percent, the holding period set at one year regardless of the term of the credit, and its coverage extended to credits associated with foreign investment. Finally in July 1995 the reserve requirement was extended to cover the issue of secondary ADRs[4] and other investment flows.[5]

Because the reserve requirement is fixed regardless of the term of the credit, its cost decreases with the length of the term, as can be seen in Table 15.1. With the reserve requirement at 30 percent and an international interest rate (LIBOR) of 5 percent, the cost of borrowing abroad to invest in Chile for a one-month period is 29 percent; for a two-month period the cost falls to 13.5 percent. Consequently, the impact of the URR should be to discourage short-term inflows and therefore lengthen the maturity of foreign debt and other capital inflows. The table also illustrates how the cost of the URR depends on the international interest forgone while the reserve requirement is tied up in the central bank. Higher international interest rates increase the wedge between domestic interest rates and international interest rates due to the URR. As Table 15.2 confirms, there indeed has been an increasing share of long-term flows in recent years. For example, comparing 1992 and 1994, two years

---

[3] Pension funds are currently allowed to invest up to 9% of their portfolio abroad.
[4] These are ADRs that are not part of the initial placement, but stocks traded in Chile that are converted into ADRs by foreign investors.
[5] In order to avoid liquidity problems arising from the requirement to hold a non-interest-bearing deposit at the central bank for a period of one year, foreign creditors are given the option to pay the interest cost of the required deposit up front. This is done through a promissory note with a repurchase obligation at an interest rate currently set equal to LIBOR + 4% applied to 30% of the credit.

Table 15.1. *Annual percentage cost of the unremunerated reserve requirement (URR)*

Investment term in months	URR = 20%		URR = 30%	
	LIBOR = 5.0%	LIBOR = 7.5%	LIBOR = 5.0%	LIBOR = 7.5%
1	16.0	24.8	28.8	45.6
2	7.7	11.8	13.5	20.8
3	5.1	7.7	8.8	13.4
6	2.5	3.8	4.3	6.5
12	1.2	1.9	2.1	3.2
24	0.6	0.9	1.1	1.6
36	0.4	0.6	0.7	1.1
60	0.2	0.4	0.4	0.6
120	0.1	0.2	0.2	0.3

Note: The annual cost of the URR (r) is calculated as follows:

$$(1+R) = \frac{(1+i^*) - u(1+i^*)^{t-1}}{(1-u-T)} = (1+i^*+r)$$

where i^* is the dollar LIBOR for the corresponding investment term; u, the URR as a percentage of the credit; t, the term of the credit in years; T, an additional tax levied on credits equal to 0.1% of the credit per month, with a maximum rate of 1.2% for credits over one year; and R is the effective cost of borrowing abroad when investing in Chile.

Table 15.2. *Balance of payments, 1990–1995 (as a percent of GDP)*

	1990	1991	1992	1993	1994	1995
Current account	−1.8	0.3	−1.6	−4.5	−1.2	0.2
Capital account	9.6	3.2	7.5	5.9	7.2	1.4
Direct investment	1.9	1.1	0.7	0.9	1.6	1.5
Inflow	1.9	1.5	1.6	1.8	3.4	2.5
Outflow	0.0	−0.4	−0.9	−0.9	−1.8	−1.0
Portfolio investment	1.2	0.5	1.1	1.6	1.7	0.1
Inflow	1.2	0.5	1.1	1.8	2.4	0.1
Outflow	0.0	0.0	0.0	−0.2	−0.7	0.0
Medium- & long-term capital	2.3	−0.7	0.4	1.1	2.5	2.4
Prepayments	0.0	0.0	0.0	0.0	0.0	−2.7
Short-term capital	4.2	2.3	5.3	2.3	1.4	0.1
Balance of payments	7.8	3.5	5.9	1.4	6.0	1.6

Note: Short-term capital includes errors and omissions.
Sources: Central Bank of Chile, *Boletín Mensual*, various issues.

with surpluses in the capital account of similar magnitude, short-term capital declined from more than 5 percent of GDP to 1.4 percent. Chumacero, Labán, and Larraín (1996) confirm econometrically that this decline has been at least partically the result of the URR, although Soto and Valdés-Prieto (1996) argue that this effect is small, but without offering any explanation.

By raising the cost of short-term credit and discouraging short-term arbitrage, the URR also worked to lessen fluctuations in the exchange rate. In the next section we show that after the URR was introduced the volatility of the nominal exchange rate remained constant, despite the fact that the central parity became more volatile. In addition, we show that volatility of the real exchange rate actually declined.

The most important effect of the URR has been to create a wedge between domestic and international interest rates.[6] The no-arbitrage condition for capital inflows is:

---

[6] There is an additional cost for domestic and foreign credit (0.1% monthly up to twelve months), which should be added to the cost of domestic (foreign) credit when comparing incentives for outflows (inflows). We ignore this cost term in the exposition in the text, but it is incorporated in the interest rate calculations underlying all figures and tables.

$$i < i^* + E\Delta e + r, \tag{1}$$

where i and i^* are the domestic and foreign interest rates, respectively, e the log of the exchange rate, Δ the first difference operator, E the expectations operator, and r the percentage cost of the reserve requirement (assuming r is actually paid).[7] If the inequality in (1) is reversed, there will be incentives for infinite capital inflows.[8] However, since there are no additional exit costs on capital outflows, the no-arbitrage condition for outflows is:

$$i > i^* + E\Delta e. \tag{2}$$

If the inequality in (2) is reversed, there will be incentives for infinite capital outflows. These no-arbitrage conditions imply that as long as the interest rate differential lies within the band

$$E\Delta e < i - i^* < E\Delta e + r, \tag{3}$$

there are no arbitrage possibilities, and hence, no incentive for capital flows.[9]

Figure 15.1 compares the evolution of the domestic interest rate, measured by the return on ninety-day Central Bank bonds,[10] and foreign interest rates, adjusted and not adjusted for the cost of the URR. As can be seen from the figure, when the URR was introduced in 1991, it caused the adjusted LIBOR rate to rise sharply above the domestic rate, discouraging the appreciation of the peso. However, as foreign interest rates declined, and domestic monetary policy tightened to dampen an overheating of the economy in 1992 (output grew 11 percent in 1992), the adjusted interest rate differential narrowed significantly. This period coincides with continuing capital inflows and a strengthening of the currency. After mid-1994, the adjusted LIBOR rate rose sharply and the incentives for one-year inflows or less declined.

---

[7] The variable r is the cost of the URR for a given maturity investment. However, as Herrera and Valdés (1996) have argued, the existence of a fixed cost of entry generates an option value for investing and liquidating an investment in Chile. Depending on the stochastic processes of interest rates and the specifics of the financial operations involved, it is possible to determine the expected optimal length of time that an investor will stay in Chile, and r should be calculated for that horizon.

[8] We do not consider the role of any risk premium.

[9] When r is computed for optimal investment horizon, it represents the maximum interest rate differential that can be supported by a given URR. Herrera and Valdés (1996) find that for ninety-day bonds the maximum interest rate differential that the URR can support is 2.3 percentage points, which implies that an investor in ninety-day bonds will stay about one year. In the discussion that follows we assume the term of investment is one year.

[10] Central Bank bonds are denominated in UF (Unidad de Fomento), which is a daily unit of account, expressed in terms of pesos, indexed to the previous month's inflation.

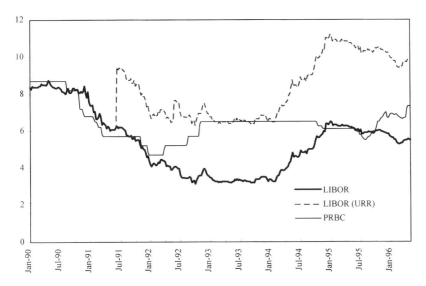

Figure 15.1. Weekly average of domestic and international interest rates, annual percent. PRBC, ninety-day Central Bank bonds in UF; LIBOR, ninety-day dollar LIBOR with and without the cost of the URR and the specific tax. *Sources*: Interest rate on central bank bonds: Central Bank of Chile, Santiago. U.S. dollar LIBOR: Reuter's data base.

Many effects of the URR still remain controversial. For example, it has not been proved that the URR has been effective in slowing the gradual long-term appreciation of the peso. Furthermore, there is no clear assessment of the microeconomic costs of the URR through its impact on economic efficiency. Nevertheless, one would tend to believe that in its absence it would have been extremely difficult for Chile to raise interest rates in 1992 without an additional appreciation of the peso (Figure 15.1), thus rendering the combined objectives of exchange rate stability and reduction of inflation infeasible. It has been in this way that the reserve requirements have complemented the overall strategy of macroeconomic stability, supported by an independent central bank and a fiscal policy that has generated an average surplus of 1.8 percent of GDP during the 1990s.

15.3   Exchange rate policies

15.3.1   Changes in exchange rate policies

Chile's real exchange rate has displayed dramatic fluctuations during the past thirty years (Figure 15.2). This variability, together with bad

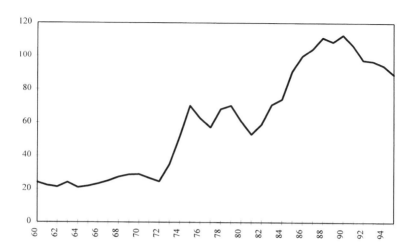

Figure 15.2. Yearly average of the real exchange rate, 1960–95 (1986 = 100).
Source: Central Bank of Chile, Santiago.

previous experiences with fixed exchange rates and the successful experience of a depreciated real exchange rate in the second half of the 1980s, have led to a deliberate effort to produce a stable exchange rate path.

After the 1982 debt crisis, Chile abandoned the fixed exchange rate regime in effect since June 1979 and devalued by 70 percent between June and September 1982. Subsequently, a crawling peg regime with an exchange rate band was adopted. This system has been operated flexibly with discrete changes in the central parity and the band's width implemented as deemed appropriate over time. The crawling rate is set by a purchasing power parity (PPP) rule according to which the peso is devalued daily by the difference between domestic inflation and foreign inflation. The central parity was devalued several times in the 1980s, and revalued three times in the 1990s – by 2 percent in June 1991, 5 percent in January 1992, and by 10 percent in December 1994. In late 1995 a drift appreciation of 2 percent was incorporated into the PPP rule which allowed for an "equilibrium" 2 percent real appreciation in the central parity rate. When the band was first implemented in September 1982 its width was set at ±2 percent around central parity. The band was widened to ±5 percent in mid-1989, and then to ±10 percent in January 1992.

Before going into the analysis of the performance of the exchange rate regime during the 1990s, it is illustrative to provide some further background on exchange rate developments in the 1980s. As can be seen in

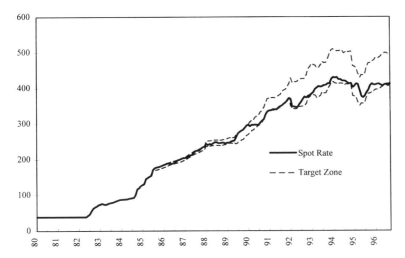

Figure 15.3. Monthly average of the nominal exchange rate, 1980–96. Chilean pesos per U.S. dollar. *Source*: Central Bank of Chile, Santiago.

Figures 15.2 and 15.3, from the debt crisis in 1982 up until 1990 the continuous devaluations of the nominal exchange rate were accompanied by a real depreciation, rather than offsetting domestic price inflation.

Devaluation was achieved without inflation for two main reasons. First, the devaluations helped to correct a large currency overvaluation in the early 1980s, reflected in an unprecedented current account deficit of 15 percent of GDP and poor export performance, with annual growth of 4.8 percent in 1981–82 even after completing widespread trade reform in 1979. Second, after the debt crisis, Chile experienced a large negative terms-of-trade shock in 1980–82; the devaluations helped restore competitiveness without stimulating inflation.[11]

Beginning in 1990, the real exchange rate began to appreciate (see Figures 15.2 and 15.3) as the economy reached full employment, the external accounts appeared in balance, and productivity growth was strong. During this period Chile also returned to borrowing in private international capital markets. Between 1990–95 the real exchange rate appreciated at an average annual rate of 4.6 percent. This appreciation, in view of the trend depreciation of the peso since the 1970s, made the conduct of exchange rate policy considerably more complex.

---

[11] Between 1981 and 1988, a period of persistent depreciation, the average devaluation rate was 30% per year, while average inflation was only 20% per year.

15.3.2   *Exchange rate volatility*

As we stated, one of the main objectives of Chile's macroeconomic policy in the 1990s has been economic stability. This being true, one would like to know whether exchange rate policy has actually had the desired stabilizing effects on the nominal and real exchange rates. We answer this directly by analyzing the volatility of exchange rates in the 1990s. In subsection 15.3.3 we examine the credibility of the exchange rate band during this same period.

As we explained earlier, the exchange rate regime underwent major changes during 1992. First, the band was widened to 10 percent (January 1992) and, second, the central parity, which originally was defined with respect to the dollar, was set according to a basket of currencies (July 1992). In addition, the URR, introduced at 20 percent in June 1991, was raised to 30 percent in January 1992. To shed some light on the stabilizing effects of the exchange rate and capital control policies, we compare volatility of the exchange rate for the periods before and after these changes, using three different split dates – January 1992, when the band was widened; June 1991, when the reserve requirement was introduced; and July 1992, when the currency basket parity rate was introduced. For each of these periods we compute the variability of the nominal exchange rate, the central parity of the bank, and the real exchange rate, using both daily and monthly data (although the real exchange rate can only be calculated at a monthly frequency).

Tests of unit roots for all the variables did not reject the hypothesis of unit roots at conventional significance levels. Volatility was measured as the standard deviation of the first differences of each variable and, alternatively, as the standard deviation of the forecast error of an AR(1) process for the first differences of the monthly series and an AR(5) process for the daily series.

The main findings, presented in Table 15.3, are:[12]

1   The nominal exchange rate experienced similar variability across periods at daily frequencies, while at monthly frequencies the variability appears constant across periods only when the rebasing of the central parity to a basket of currencies is used as the split date (July 1992).
2   The central parity was more volatile in the second period.
3   The real exchange rate was less volatile in the second period.

---

[12] Similar results are obtained if first differences of the log of the exchange rate instead of the level are used.

Table 15.3. *Volatility of the exchange rate*

	Nominal	Central parity	Real	Nominal	Central parity	Real
Monthly data	January 1990–June 1991			June 1991–May 1996		
STD Δe	4.3	3.5	2.4	6.4	7.5	1.7
STD ε	13.6	7.4	5.5	33.8	50.1	2.6
	January 1990–January 1992			February 1992–May 1996		
STD Δe	3.9	3.4	2.2	6.7	7.9	1.8
STD ε	12.3	9.3	4.5	37.8	55.9	2.7
	January 1990–June 1992			July 1992–May 1996		
STD Δe	6.0	4.2	2.3	6.1	8.2	1.6
STD ε	32.5	13.7	5.2	28.9	57.6	2.1
Daily data	January 1, 1990–June 14, 1991			June 15, 1991–May 31, 1996		
STD Δe	1.1	0.3	—	1.4	1.9	—
STD ε	1.1	0.1	—	1.8	3.5	—
	January 1, 1990–January 23, 1992			January 24, 1992–May 31, 1996		
STD Δe	1.3	1.0	—	1.3	1.9	—
STD ε	1.6	0.9	—	1.7	3.6	—
	January 1, 1990–July 3, 1992			July 4, 1992–May 31, 1996		
STD Δe	1.3	0.9	—	1.3	2.0	—
STD ε	1.6	0.8	—	1.7	4.0	—

Note: STD Δe is the standard deviation of the first difference of the level of the exchange rate. STD ε is the standard deviation of the residual from an AR(1) process for monthly data and an AR(5) process for daily data. The sample splits are as follows: June 14, 1991, when the unremunerated reserve requirement (URR) is imposed on most external credits; January 13, 1992, when the exchange rate band is widened from 5% to 10%; and July 3, 1992, when the central parity is rebased to a basket of currencies.
Source: Central Bank of Chile, Santiago.

These results are interesting. The fact that the central parity rate became more volatile in the later period when it was defined in terms of a basket of currencies (the U.S. dollar, yen, and deutschemark) instead of a single currency (the U.S. dollar) is due to the fact that the center of the band not only fluctuated with changes in the difference between domestic and foreign inflation, but with changes in the parities with respect to the dollar of the other currencies that make up the basket.

Nevertheless, the variability of the nominal exchange rate was similar across periods, indicating that the added variability in the center of the band did not translate directly into increased volatility in the nominal exchange rate. A decline across subperiods in the cross-correlation between the central parity and the actual exchange rate confirms that the added variability of the central parity did not necessarily translate into added variability of the actual exchange rate.

One reason usually given for allowing variability in the central parity is that it prevents the market from betting against a sure exchange rate. Thus, a more volatile central parity may reduce volatility of the actual exchange rate by reducing the incentive for capital inflows or outflows. The results reported here at least partially support this view.

Since the band in the second period was wider, the results also indicate that increasing the width of the band does not necessarily increase the volatility of the exchange rate. This confirms target zone models that show that there is no monotonic relationship between the width of the band and the variability of the exchange rate (e.g., Bertola and Caballero, 1992; Werner, 1995), because although the variability within the band may fall for narrow bands, expectations of realignment may be greater.

Another interesting result is that even though the variability of nominal exchange rates was relatively constant across periods, real exchange rate volatility was lower in the second period, despite the adoption of a wider band and a currency basket for the central parity. This last feature may have been particularly important since, given the correlation of the nominal exchange rate and the central parity, pegging the exchange rate against a basket of currencies of the country's main trade partners provides a way of offsetting the effects of foreign price changes.[13] Thus, the use of a basket of currencies can help keep the exchange rate closer to its PPP level than simply using the dollar to determine the center of the band.

Examining volatility just by looking at the evolution of exchange rates may be misleading because the variability of exchange rate fundamentals may have changed across periods. In this case the reduced volatility in the real exchange rate may have been the result of greater stability of

---

[13] The variability of the real exchange rate as traditionally defined ($ep*/p$ with the usual notation) may decline when the central parity is defined in terms of a basket of currencies rather than a single currency. This may occur even when the volatility of the nominal exchange rate is constant. The reason is that movements in $p*$ caused by changes in bilateral exchange rates for major trade partners would be partially offset by movements in e.

Table 15.4. *Monthly volatility of exchange rate fundamentals*

Variable	STD of first differences	
	January 1990–June 1992	July 1992–May 1996
Monthly GDP indicator (IMACEC)	10.04	10.19
Annual interest rate on 90-day Central Bank bonds[a]	0.26	0.19
Average interest rate of banking system (ask rate)[a]	0.70	0.19
Terms of trade	0.06	0.06
LIBOR (90-day U.S. dollar)	0.21	0.20

Note: Monthly terms of trade are authors' estimates based on the prices of major exports and imports.
[a] These interest rates are expressed in terms of the "unidad de fomento" (UF), a unit of measurement that varies daily according to the previous month's inflation rate.
Sources: For GDP indicator, annual interest rates on Central Bank bonds, and average interest rate of the banking system: Central Bank of Chile, Santiago. For 90-day U.S. LIBOR: Reuters data base.

fundamentals rather than the stabilizing effects of exchange rate policy. To explore this possibility, in Table 15.4 we report the volatility of various fundamentals such as the terms of trade, domestic and foreign interest rates, and the level of economic activity. The table shows that the variability (of the first differences) of the terms of trade, level of activity, and foreign interest rates were similar across periods. Only the domestic interest rate appears to have been more stable during the second period. We think that this may have been the result of imposition of the reserve requirement, which weakened the link between foreign and domestic interest rates. Overall, the reduced volatility of the real exchange rate in the second period cannot be attributed to reduced volatility in fundamentals and, hence, it is more likely that it was due to the changes in exchange rate policy we mentioned earlier.

15.3.3   Credibility of the exchange rate band

A key issue in the functioning (and therefore the stabilizing effects) of an exchange rate band is its credibility. The simplest way of testing the credibility of the band (see, e.g., Rose and Svensson, 1994) is to look at the expected changes of the exchange rate implied by the interest rate differential and infer whether it is consistent with the exchange rate staying within the band. However, the existence of a reserve requirement for capital inflows, and the absence of any cost for outflows, imply that in the Chilean case interest differentials do not exactly reflect expectations of exchange rate depreciation.

An alternative approach is to use the forward dollar–peso discount rate. Under the assumption of free capital mobility, which insures covered interest rate parity, the forward discount rate equals the interest rate differential. However, in the Chilean case, where reserve requirements on capital inflows have created a wedge between domestic and foreign interest returns (see equation (3)), forward rates may provide a better measure of expected depreciation. To see this, note that covered interest rate parity implies

$$i - i^* - r < f_{t+k} - e_t < i - i^* \tag{4}$$

where f_{t+k} is the log of the time t forward exchange rate for k periods ahead. This equation shows that given the interest rate differential, current exchange rate, and the reserve requirement, the forward exchange rate must lie within a specific range in order to be consistent with covered interest rate parity. Figure 15.4 plots the forward market discount rate and the rates implied ("estimated") by the interest differential adjusted and unadjusted by the URR. It shows that six-month forward rates were effectively within the range given by equation (4). This suggests that fluctuations in the forward rate within this range can be attributed to changes in expected currency depreciation.

In order to test credibility we use two traditional methods. The first one is based on the *simplest test* of Svensson (1991) and Lindberg, Svensson, and Soderlind (1991), but, for the reasons explained earlier, instead of looking at interest rate differentials we look directly at forward rates. The second method is the *drift adjustment method*, described in Svensson (1993) and Rose and Svensson (1994).

In the simplest test, we use three-month forwards. Denote the expected value for the upper bound of the band by $E\bar{e}_{t+k}$, and for the lower bound by $E\underline{e}_{t+k}$. To construct an expected central parity, which is then used to compute the bounds of the expected band, we assume uncovered interest rate parity between the currencies that make up the basket, and

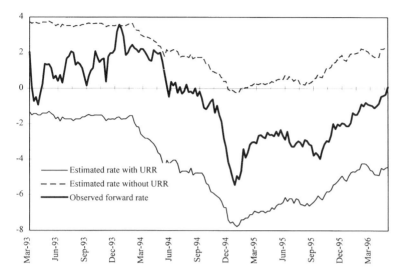

Figure 15.4. Estimated and market forward discount rate for the UF–U.S. dollar exchange rate. The estimated rate of depreciation is calculated from an arbitrage equation between the interest rate in UF on Central Bank bonds in Chile and the 180-day U.S. dollar LIBOR. A 180-day term is used in calculating the effect of the URR and specific tax. *Sources*: Forward market rate, interest rate on Central Bank bonds: Central Bank of Chile, Santiago. LIBOR: Reuter's data base.

calculate expected future values for the deutschemark–dollar and yen–dollar exchange rates.[14] Assume that the market believes at period t that, with a positive probability, the band will be realigned before period $t + k$ when f_{t+k}, the period t forward exchange rate for period $t + k$, is outside the band, thus the simplest test presumes the band is credible if:

$$E\underline{e}_{t+k} < f_{t+k} < E\bar{e}_{t+k}. \tag{5}$$

The value of the expected exchange rate with respect to the band is plotted in Figure 15.5. The figure shows that the forward rate was above the expected floor of the band for the entire period, suggesting that the credibility of the exchange rate band was never in question.

[14] An additional complication is that the band's central parity crawls with domestic inflation minus foreign inflation (set at 2.4%). However, forward rates are set in UF, and therefore, for a given band, the central parity expressed in UF is known three months ahead. For this reason we compute the UF–U.S. dollar exchange rate rather than the peso–U.S. dollar rate.

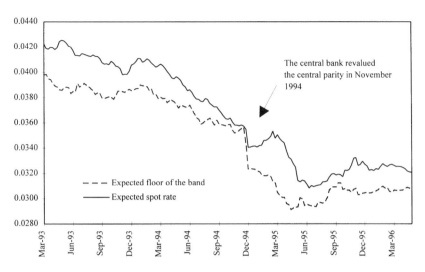

Figure 15.5. Simplest test of target zone credibility. Expected spot rate is the UF–U.S. dollar 180-day forward exchange rate, calculated from the forward market discount rate. The expected floor of the band for a 180-day period is calculated assuming uncovered interest rate parity among the currencies that make up the basket to calculate the expected value of the basket and then adding the preannounced rate of crawl. All figures are weekly averages and are expressed in UF. *Sources*: Forward market discount rate, UF–U.S. dollar exchange rate and central parity: Central Bank of Chile, Santiago. International interest rates: Reuter's data base.

Svensson (1992), however, has argued that the simplest test is usually inconclusive for short horizons because expected rates of realignments vary more than interest rate differentials. In addition, although the simplest test can identify when the band is not credible it cannot identify when it is credible, because forward rates may be inside the band regardless of its credibility. For these reasons we turn now to the drift adjustment method of testing credibility. To apply this method we express the log of the peso–dollar exchange rate (e_t) as the sum of two components: the log of the central parity (c_t) and the deviation of the spot rate from the center of the band (x_t):

$$e_t = c_t + x_t. \tag{6}$$

Incorporating the central parity rule (adjustment by PPP for a basket of currencies), and taking expectations conditional on information at time t we get:

$$E_t \Delta c_{t+1} = E_t \Delta INF_{t+1} + E_t \Delta PAR_{t+1} + E_t \Delta z_{t+1}, \tag{7}$$

where INF denotes preannounced changes in central parity based on the difference between domestic inflation and estimated foreign inflation,[15] PAR is the expected change in the central parity due to fluctuations among foreign currencies to which the central parity is tied, and z is the expectation of a realignment of the central parity.

Writing (6) in first differences, taking expectations, and combining it with (7), we get the following expression for the expected depreciation of the central parity ($E_t\Delta z_{t+1} > 0$ means an expected depreciation of the central parity for the peso):

$$E_t\Delta z_{t+1} = E_t\Delta e_{t+1} - E_t\Delta x_{t+1} - E_t\Delta INF_{t+1} - E_t\Delta PAR_{t+1}. \tag{8}$$

Other studies of the Chilean economy (Helpman, Leiderman, and Bufman, 1994; and Magendzo, Rojas, and Vergara, 1996) have used interest rate differentials as a proxy for $E_t\Delta e_t$, but, because the unremunerated reserve requirement renders any assumption of uncovered interest rate parity inappropriate after 1991, we use forward discounts instead.

Using forward rates as a proxy for $E_t\Delta e_{t+1}$, the explicit preannounced rules for INF, and inferences for PAR,[16] only $E_t\Delta x_{t+1}$ – the expected change in the position of e_t within the band – is unknown on the right-hand side of equation (8). To estimate $E_t\Delta x_{t+1}$ we use a linear model, where future changes in x_t depend on the current level of x_t, the domestic interest rate i, and international interest rates, $i*$,[17] as well as the reserve requirement, URR. Specifically, we estimate the following equation for the period January 1990 to May 1996 using ordinary least square:

$$x_{t+1} - x_t = \sum_j \beta_{0j} d_j + \beta_1 x_t + \beta_2 i_t + \beta_3 i^*_t + \beta_4 URR_t + \mu_{t+1}, \tag{9}$$

where the d_j's are dummy variables for the various changes in the exchange rate regime during the period.

The results are shown in the first column of Table 15.5, where it can be seen that the coefficients are significant and all signs are as expected except for β_2. Column 2 shows the results of estimating (9) with international interest rates adjusted to reflect the cost of the URR. All coefficients are significant, with the expected signs, except for β_2, which once

---

[15] All variables are expressed in UF since future inflation is unknown.
[16] We use LIBOR rates in U.S. dollar, deutschemark, and yen terms to infer the corresponding forward rates and to calculate the value of *PAR*.
[17] Rigorously, we should estimate expectations of x_t conditional on no realignment. However, this would require the elimination of thirteen observations before each realignment, substantially reducing the sample size. We use weekly data for three-month rates, implying period $t + 1$ is thirteen weeks after t.

Table 15.5. *Determinants of change in the exchange rate band position,* $x_{t+1} - x_t$, *January 1990 to May 1996 (weekly date)*

Explanatory variables	Coefficient estimates				
	(1)	(2)	(3)	(4)	(5)
C			−0.12		
			(−8.92)		
$d1$	−0.125	−0.119		−0.097	−0.093
	(−9.16)	(−8.62)		(−6.66)	(−6.40)
$d2$	−0.135	−0.119		−0.111	−0.10
	(−10.11)	(−7.73)		(−7.96)	(−6.30)
$d3$	−0.162	−0.145		−0.130	−0.118
	(−19.11)	(−7.85)		(7.49)	(−6.3)
x	−0.989	−0.994	−0.910	−0.771	−0.799
	(−19.11)	(−19.29)	(−17.98)	(7.48)	(−7.60)
x^2				−5.934	−5.854
				(−1.90)	(−1.88)
x^3				−84.08	−81.84
				(−3.25)	(−3.16)
i^*	0.538			0.470	
	(5.71)			(5.21)	
i^{**}		0.729	0.379		0.623
		(5.54)	(4.09)		(4.79)
TAX		0.264			0.278
		(1.21)			(1.76)
i^a	0.472	0.229	0.542	0.304	0.132
	(3.16)	(1.21)	(3.68)	(2.05)	(0.71)
R^2	0.56	0.56	0.52	0.59	0.59

Note: t-statistics are shown in parentheses. Variable definitions are: x, the position of the exchange rate within the band; i, the interest rate on 90-day Central Bank bonds; i^*, 90-day dollar LIBOR; i^{**}, 90-day dollar LIBOR adjusted to include the cost of the URR and a specific tax levied on foreign credits (impuesto de timbres y estampillas); TAX, the annual cost of the URR and the specific tax; $d1$, dummy for January 1990 to January 1992; $d2$, dummy for January 1992 to November 1994; $d3$, dummy for November 1994 to May 1996; and C, a constant.
[a] These interest rates are expressed in terms of the "unidad de fomento" (UF), a unit of measurement that varies daily according to the previous month's inflation rate.

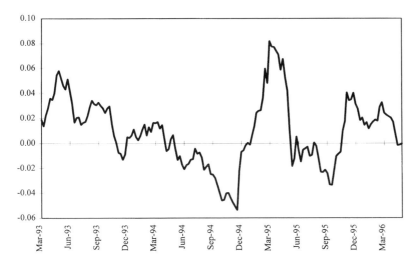

Figure 15.6. Weekly expectations of realignments in the central parity expressed in UF–U.S. dollar. Negative values indicate expectations of an appreciation of the UF with respect to the dollar.

again has the wrong sign, but it is not significantly different from zero at conventional significance levels. Finally, columns 4 and 5 show the results of estimating equations that include a nonlinear relationship between the expected future value and current value of x_t.

Figure 15.6 shows the expectations of realignment obtained from (8) using the fitted values of (9), which correspond to the first column of Table 15.5.[18] As can be seen from this figure the band was clearly not credible in the months before the 10 percent revaluation realignment of November 30, 1994. The market started expecting an appreciation of the central parity by May 1994, and the expectations of realignment grew systematically afterward. In the days prior to the revaluation the market expected a 6 percent change in the central parity. There have been other periods with expectations of revaluation, but they were not long or large enough to have seriously threatened the sustainability of the exchange rate.

We think that the drift adjustment method provides a useful policy guide for ascertaining the sustainability of the exchange rate target zone. On the other hand, when not credible, the target zone may lose its

[18] There is no significant change when other regressions are used to generate realignment expectations.

stabilizing capacity and therefore fail to fulfill its policy objective. In the case of Chile, it shows clearly that the band prevailing in 1994 was not credible and therefore would have had to be abandoned at some point or, as in practice occurred, modified to accommodate the appreciation expectations, caused by a clearly misaligned central parity. By comparison, the simplest test never indicated that the exchange rate regime was not credible. Although before December 1994 the forward rate was at the edge of a band, it was never outside the band.[19] Additional evidence for a lack of credibility by late 1994 is provided by the significant accumulation of foreign reserves in this period. Reserves increased by 17 percent between September and December 1994.

In Figure 15.7 we examine whether credibility diminishes as the exchange rate moves closer to an edge of the band. In the case of a fully credible band, credibility should not change as the exchange rate moves closer to the band's bottom or top. Figure 15.7 shows that the closer the exchange rate is to the bottom of the band the more likely it is that the market believes that the band will not be kept. This supports models of target zones where the probability of realignment is increasing as the exchange rate gets closer to the bounds of the band (see Chen and Giovannini, 1992, and Werner, 1995). In this case, as shown by Werner (1995), the stabilization effects of target zones can be reversed. However, as long as the exchange rate is kept within the band, commitment to the band may increase variability within the band but decrease overall variability.

Recent literature on exchange rate regimes has attempted to distinguish realignments and exchange rate crises, between those caused by fundamentals and those that result from pure speculation. In the Chilean case, the realignment of 1994, similarly to that of 1992, was the result of a policy that set the central parity following a PPP rule in a way that was inconsistent with the appreciation of the real exchange rate. Indeed, in a fixed exchange rate regime an appreciation can be achieved through an increase in domestic inflation relative to foreign inflation. This cannot be the case when the exchange rate is very close to the bottom of the band and the band depreciates faster as domestic inflation rises. In this case, a nominal appreciation is necessary. This has been the main cause of Chile's misalignments, as the real exchange rate appreciated at a yearly rate of 3 percent between 1992 and 1995.

Since late 1995 the center of the band has been allowed to appreciate at a rate of 2 percent a year with respect to PPP to allow for a short-term

---

[19] Daily forward rates may have been outside the band at some points in time, but this movement does not appear in weekly data.

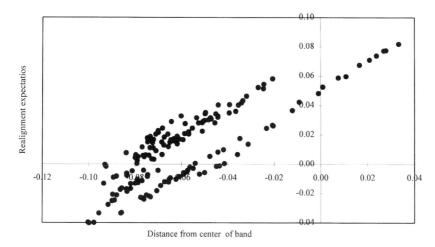

Figure 15.7 Expected realignment and distance from center of band. Realignment expectations, which correspond to the estimated value of changes in the central parity, are plotted against the distance of the spot rate from the center of the band.

trend appreciation. An alternative policy is to allow the central parity to crawl according to some inflation target. In this way, an appreciation could be achieved by an increase in inflation. However, this has the possible cost of causing a deviation from a disinflation policy target.

15.4   Conclusion

Open economies like Chile are extremely vulnerable to the volatility of international financial markets. Of course, the potential benefits of financial openness are large, especially when capital has been historically scarce. However, for small economies like Chile, the inflows may be larger than what the economy can absorb in a short period of time without major economic consequences. Analogously, when capital reverses direction and flows out, the domestic effects may also be sizable. Much of the large volumes of capital inflows to emerging markets in the 1990s can be interpreted as a stock adjustment phenomenon, by which foreign investors adjusted their portfolios in response to opportunities in emerging markets. Thus, even if we presume that these capital movements reflect rational decisions by international investors and that overall financial openness is desirable, the sheer magnitude of the flows can pose considerable problems for policy makers.

Chile has chosen to dampen its share of these capital inflows through the use of a reserve requirement and to stabilize the exchange rate through a target zone mechanism. The reserve requirement has achieved two main results. First, because the reserve requirement applies for one year regardless of the loan's maturity, it imposed a relatively higher cost on short-term inflows. As the evidence partially shows, this has tilted the composition of capital flows toward longer maturities. Second, the reserve requirement has permitted maintaining domestic interest rates above international interest rates, without imposing excessive pressures on the exchange rate. However, it is necessary to note that despite use of this specific control, Chile now has the most open capital account in its history and the least constraints on foreign exchange transactions.

In theory, a perfectly credible target zone should have stabilizing effects on the evolution of exchange rate. Imperfect credibility, in contrast, may in some circumstances induce the exchange rate to be closer to the edges of the band. However, the target zone mechanism may still have stabilizing effects as long as the band is maintained at its edges through explicit intervention to keep the exchange rate within the band.

Perhaps the most important lesson from the Chilean experience is the desirability of managing exchange rates in a flexible manner. Pegging the central parity to a basket of currencies may induce more short-term volatility, reducing incentives for speculation. Furthermore, pegging the exchange rate to a basket of currencies may provide a better approximation of international prices if one wants to follow a PPP rule and, hence, stabilize the real exchange rate. As shown in this chapter, despite the higher variability of the central parity when the currency basket was adopted, the URR was introduced, and the band was widened, the volatility of the real exchange rate actually declined. Attempting to guide the exchange rate according to a PPP rule when fundamentals require an appreciation generates a misalignment of the central parity over time. The recent adjustment, allowing a 2 percent appreciation with respect to the PPP rule, is intended to increase the credibility and sustainability of the exchange rate band.

Overall, Chile's exchange rate and capital account policies have been part of a broader macroeconomic policy program involving prudent fiscal and monetary management, systematically lower inflation, high output and export growth, and external balance. The successful coordination of these policies has allowed Chile to cope with the capital inflows of the 1990s, while also maintaining some degree of monetary policy independence.

References

Bertola, Giuseppe, and Ricardo J. Caballero (1992). "Target Zones and Realignments," *American Economic Review* 3: 520–36.

Budnevich, Carlos, and Guillermo Lefort (1996). "Capital Account Regulation and Macroeconomic Policy: Two Latin American Experiences." Unpublished manuscript, Central Bank of Chile, Santiago.

Calvo, Guillermo, Leonardo Leiderman, and Carmen M. Reinhart (1996). "Inflows to Developing Countries in the 1990s: Causes and Effects," *Journal of Economic Perspectives* 2: 123–39.

Chen, Zhaohui, and Alberto Giovannini (1992). "Estimated Expected Exchange Rates under Target Zones," NBER Working Paper No. 4291. Cambridge, Mass.

Chumacero, Rómulo, Raúl Labán, and Felipe Larraín (1996). "What Determines Capital Inflows? An Empirical Analysis for Chile." Paper presented at the Conference on Capital Flows organized by the Universidad Católica de Chile, July 30–31, Santiago.

Eyzaguirre, Nicolás, and Patricio Rojas (1996). "Restricciones al Flujo de Capitales y Política Macroeconómica: El Caso Chileno." Paper presented at the Conference on Capital Flows organized by the Universidad Católica de Chile, July 30–31, Santiago.

Ffrench-Davis, Ricardo, Manuel Agosín, and Andras Uthoff (1995). "Movimientos de Capitales, Estrategia Exportadora y Estabilidad Macroeconómica en Chile." In R. Ffrench-Davis and S. Jones, eds., *Las Nuevas Corrientes Financieras Hacia la América Latina: Fuentes, Effectos y Políticas*, pp. 197–252. Santiago: Fondo de Cultura Económica.

Helpman, Elhanan, Leonardo Leiderman, and Gil Bufman (1994). "New Exchange Rate Bands," *Economic Policy* 19 (October): 260–306.

Herrera, Luis Oscar, and Rodrigo Valdés (1996). "Encaje a Flujos de Capital y Diferencial de Tasas de Interés en Chile," November. Unpublished manuscript, Central Bank of Chile, Santiago.

Labán, Raúl, and Felipe Larraín (1994). "The Chilean Experience with Capital Mobility." In B. Bosworth, R. Dornbusch, and R. Labán, eds., *The Chilean Economy: Policy Lessons and Challenges*, pp. 117–63. Washington, D.C.: Brookings Institution.

Lindberg, Hans, Lars E. O. Svensson, and Paul Soderlind (1991). "Devaluation Expectations: The Swedish Krona, 1982–1991," Institute for International Economic Studies Seminar Paper No. 495. Stockholm, Sweden.

Magendzo Igal, Patricio Rojas, and Rodrigo Vergara (1996). "Bandas Cambiarias: Experiencia Chilena, 1990–1994." In F. Morandé and R. Vergara, eds., *Análisis Empírico del Tipo de Cambio en Chile*, pp. 169–203. Santiago: Centro de Estudios Públicos and Georgetown University, Institute for Latin American Developing Economy Studies.

Rose, Andrew K., and Lars E. O. Svensson (1994). "European Exchange Rate Credibility before the Fall," *European Economic Review* 38: 1185–1216.

Soto, Marcelo, and Salvador Valdés-Prieto (1996). "New Selective Capital Controls in Chile: Are They Effective?" Paper presented at the Conference on Capital Flows organized by the Universidad Católica de Chile, July 30–31, Santiago.

Svensson, Lars E. O. (1991). "The Simplest Test of Target Zone Credibility," *IMF Staff Papers*, 38: 655–65.

(1992). "An Interpretation of Recent Research on Exchange Rate Target Zones," *Journal of Economic Perspectives* 4: 119–44.

(1993). "Assessing Target Zone Credibility. Mean Reversion and Devaluation Expectations in the ERM, 1979–1992," *European Economic Review* 37: 763–802.

Werner, Andrés (1995). "Exchange Rate Target Zones, Realignments and the Interest Rate Differential: Theory and Evidence," *Journal of International Economics* 39: 353–67.

Williamson, John (1996). *The Crawling Band as an Exchange Rate Regime: Lessons from Israel, Chile and Colombia*. Washington, D.C.: Institute for International Economics.

Index